Praise for *Ab*

You can hear the passion, the decenc⸱ ⸱⸱⸱ ⸱⸱⸱ pe in this insider–outsider story about England's education pu⸱⸱ᵧ ⸱ ⸱ears. *About Our Schools* documents the storms, showers, glimpses of sunshine, the fronts, doldrums, cloudy times, and ends with brighter spells ahead. It shows the silencing of the profession and the cacophony of experts, the motives, hopes and honesty from many of the key political players, documents a cocktail of unfairness, and is the most exciting and exacting book I have read in a long time.

John Hattie, Emeritus Laureate Professor, Melbourne Graduate School of Education

It seems odd to refer to a book on education as a page-turner, but *About Our Schools* really is just that. Hardly surprising though, as it has been written by two of the greatest storytellers in the field, whose careers at the heart of the action mean that they know everyone and have a view on pretty much everything. They survey the past and critique current initiatives, always through the lens of the teacher and the child in the classroom. It's full of anecdotes, balanced critiques and a surprisingly compassionate appraisal of politicians. *About Our Schools* is a masterpiece, and I shall be returning to it again and again.

Mary Myatt, education writer, speaker and curator of Myatt & Co

More than two men's memoirs, less than a treatise in political science, this fascinating book opens up its readers to 45 years inside the corridors of power in UK education, like no book has ever done before. This work, from two living legends of British education, brings forward extraordinary levels of candour and insight from political figures as ideologically disparate and strategically different as Estelle Morris and Michael Gove. How did academies evolve? What was the purpose of chains and trusts? How has England's education system become so chaotically marketised and incredibly centralised all at the same time? And how should we judge what's happened to the training of teachers and leaders? It's all here, unexpurgated and unplugged, from the mouths of government ministers, civil servants and education professionals. Dip in, breathe deep, keep an open mind, and enjoy!

Andy Hargreaves, Director, CHENINE (Change, Engagement and Innovation in Education), University of Ottawa, and Honorary Professor, Swansea University

Education in England is in a mess – more so than in the rest of the United Kingdom and in many other countries around the world. Buffeted by pundits and politicians who mostly know much less than they think, we are in desperate need of cool, wise, experienced thinkers who can share their good, deep, well-informed common sense. Hoorah, then, for Tim Brighouse and Mick Waters, two battle-scarred warriors of educational reform who can rise above the fray, remind us of the long view, and talk truth to power. Let us pray the powerful are listening.

Guy Claxton, author of *The Future of Teaching: And the Myths That Hold It Back*

Did you ever miss someone like crazy, thinking that you would never see them again, only to have them show up out of the blue better than ever? That's how I feel about Tim Brighouse and Mick Waters and their new stupendous magnum opus *About Our Schools*.

Based on much original material from interviews with central players including nearly all secretaries of state for education since 1975, and scores of key officials in positions at all levels of the education system in England, *About Our Schools* is a goldmine of inside thinking and action. It is as if the authors were standing over the shoulders of people when they made significant decisions, asking: 'What were they thinking when they did X and Y?' And Tim and Mick *were there* much of the time as they worked at all levels of the government, but most of all immersed themselves in the daily lives of the pupils and communities that they served.

I can say that I was never bored with a single page. Every chapter was interesting and insightful, and I felt the authors were speaking to me as a reader throughout. The authors' cumulative critique of the worsening of the policies that have been presented over the years is so damning that their solutions bear careful scrutiny. It is time for a new approach to system change, and in the final section Brighouse and Waters serve up six foundational stones to get us started.

About Our Schools is a treasure trove of the past, and a treasure map for the future – compiled by two human explorers who combine more than 100 years of caring and action in tackling the most vexing problems of the day. Now I know in detail why I am glad they are back on centre stage.

Michael Fullan, Professor Emeritus, OISE/University of Toronto

In *About Our Schools*, Tim Brighouse and Mick Waters use their considerable experience to reflect on how we got to where we are in education, and what should happen now. Through sensitive and revealing interviews with a range of politicians, policy-makers and practitioners, they argue for a new era in our education system – moving away from the past 30 years of centralisation, marketisation and managerialism.

Lucid, accessible and attractively exploratory in tone, the book concludes with some important proposals for reform, including a change in our outmoded accountability system, acceleration of the productive blending of place-based and online schooling, new limits on centralised power and a broader curriculum fit for the education – and diverse experiences and talents – of children and adolescents living in the 21st century.

Melissa Benn, writer and campaigner

Publications like this are few and far between. I cannot remember the last time I read a book that so skilfully sets out its historical context in an analysis of our current educational landscape and its optimistic vision for the future. Tim Brighouse and Mick Waters have brought their trademark humanity, pragmatism and insight to a fascinating book that has the importance of teachers and teaching at its heart. Drawing on their unrivalled perspectives of our education system over the last 40 years, the authors have created a book that is full of fascinating anecdotes, illustrations and personal accounts that enrich the overall narrative beautifully.

The panel of witnesses is a veritable 'who's who' in education over the last several decades, which is testament to the regard in which the authors are held. This has enabled a fascinating set of perspectives on the inner workings of government, with all its challenges, political machinations and surprises.

About Our Schools is a must-read for anyone working in education. You may not agree with everything, but it will certainly get you thinking.

Andy Buck, founder, Leadership Matters, creator of the BASIC coaching method, and former teacher and head teacher

Over the past six decades and in a wide variety of roles in education, Tim Brighouse and Mick Waters have inspired, challenged and supported teachers and head teachers across the country. Their status as education heavyweights is shown by the truly impressive cast of A-listers interviewed by them in their research for this important new book.

About Our Schools is packed with fascinating insights into the motivations of and influences on the secretaries of state for education in England since 1976. It charts the key features of and changes in the education system over the last 45 years, giving the perspectives of key players and sharing amusing and moving tales from the authors' careers. The final chapter also offers a powerful and compelling rallying cry – a manifesto for 'building forward together'.

Younger readers will find this a fascinating history lesson, and those who have lived and taught through the years described will find it brings back a host of memories – but all who read it will gain an enhanced contextual understanding of how our education system has evolved.

Rachel Macfarlane, Director of Education, Herts for Learning, and author of *Obstetrics for Schools*

With sweeping ambition, Brighouse and Waters' *About Our Schools* provides a compelling narrative of how markets came to dominate education policy-making since the 1970s – and how we can change course. Throughout the bulk of the book is a detailed review of educational policy in England and its trend towards centralisation, their insights, drawing upon personal interviews with dozens of policy-makers, also ring true for those of us on the other side of the Atlantic. They provide a compelling account of what happened to the hope and optimism of the post Second World War era, avoiding nostalgia, and acknowledging where trust in the system of public education went awry. And by proposing 39 policy solutions ranging from smarter accountability to fairer admissions, the authors deliver a sweeping road map to transform English schools from islands of autonomous competition towards a cohesive, collaborative whole.

Dr Adam Kirk Edgerton, Senior Researcher, Learning Policy Institute

I had to smile when I got to the 39 steps. I read John Buchan's novel at secondary school and the hero, Richard Hannay, sets an example to his readers of an ordinary man who puts his country's interests before his own safety. Mick Waters and Tim Brighouse are extraordinary men who have always put the interests of children first.

As the authors tell us, *About Our Schools* is not meant to be read from cover to cover. Instead, it will become the go-to guide to education in England. A guided tour – with expert guides – through education policy and practice. I hope, and expect, it will be on every student's reading list when they start teacher training and will be kept as an essential reference book.

Chris Waterman, commentator, satirist and co-author of *Animals' Tails*

I was hooked from the start in this epic educational journey. Tim Brighouse and Mick Waters are honest, passionate and crystal clear on the values and beliefs that under-pin their mission. Blending evidence, including fascinating perspectives from highly influential witnesses, with story-like reflections on their own wealth of experiences, they delve into key themes that have shaped education in England as we know it. Tim and Mick fill their exploration of the history, complexities, challenges and potential of the current system with rich insights, while their bold suggestions to reimagine schooling for a more equitable system make for a rousing conclusion. And, of course, as many expect and admire from these two champions of education, the authors' hope, ambition and collaborative partnership shine through. *About Our Schools* is just the book to provoke powerful reflection, courageous conversations and con-certed action.

Louise Stoll, Professor of Professional Learning, UCL Institute of Education

In *About Our Schools* Tim and Mick bring to life, with passion and purpose, the les-sons of history and the potential and promise of tomorrow. This book is a masterclass in how our education system shapes and reshapes itself over time, and who better to learn it from than these two giants of the education world.

Eavesdrop on their personal memories and recent conversations with a stellar cast of educators and politicians, where nothing escapes their scrutiny – equally warm in their praise and excoriating in their criticism. I cheered mightily at many sections.

Tim and Mick love our schools and those who work to improve them, and this heart-felt hope and optimism is imprinted on every page. For those who see these times as a 'hinge of history' and seek a COVID legacy that leads to the transformation of our schools, I urge you to read it. This is an education manifesto like no other.

The authors say this is a book to be dipped into. I say it is much more than that. *About Our Schools* is a book that will keep our 'reservoirs of hope' full at times when we most need it. Buy it, read it, act on it, and keep it close.

**Maggie Farrar, education consultant and former director
of the National College for School Leadership**

In *About Our Schools* Tim Brighouse and Mick Waters have brought together their own unparalleled depth and breadth of knowledge about the schooling system, along with invaluable further testimony from movers and shakers at every level in education. Read on!

Professor Margaret Maden, former head teacher and county education officer

This book of historical context, present vexations and plans for a brighter future throws a light on the range of deep-seated barriers that need pulling down if children are to have a productive and enjoyable schooling. Brighouse and Waters offer both national decision-makers and school leaders a nuanced and insightful vantage point to look at the challenge of providing education in a post-pandemic world, and provide suggestions for planning ways forward.

About Our Schools is a must-read if you want change in our educational landscape.

Martin Illingworth, Senior Lecturer in Education, Sheffield Hallam University, education consultant and author of *Forget School*

What has happened to English schools over the past 40 years? Are they stronger after decades of rapid and often bewildering change? Tim Brighouse and Mick Waters, with their extensive knowledge and experience of all levels of schooling, are uniquely qualified to give us the answers.

Drawing on lengthy interviews with dozens of leading educational figures – ministers and former ministers, civil servants, directors of academy trusts, school inspectors, local authority officers and more – as well as their own personal recollections, Tim and Mick share new and sometimes shocking discoveries about how decisions that affected millions of children were reached.

Through sometimes hilarious anecdotes as well as unfailingly perceptive analysis, this book reveals the truth about what was happening behind the scenes as almost everything in the world of education changed – from the school curriculum to marking schemes, from teaching methods to pupil exclusions, and from the rise of academy trusts to the role of head teachers.

Peter Wilby, former education editor of *The Independent*

Tim Brighouse and Mick Waters are two sages of the educational world that are resisting the call to 'retire to the woods'. We are the richer for their delayed departure.

About Our Schools has been crafted to provide information, inspiration and direction for anyone interested in education and social change. These stimulating and informative interviews are testimony to the power of dialogue to connect and transform individuals and communities. These two wise men provide us, in the final chapter, with the foundation stones and steps we need to take in order to continue our shared journey of school improvement. It would be fitting testimony to their efforts over the past 45 years if we followed their advice and good counsel.

About Our Schools is essential reading for those interested in understanding our educational past and shaping our educational, social and economic future. The fact that the royalties will go to support the work of Barnardo's and the Compassionate Education Foundation is another good reason to buy the book.

Roy Leighton, Co-chair of the Cambridge Peace and Education Research Group (CPERG) and co-author of *101 Days to Make a Change*

About Our Schools takes the reader on a thought-provoking and insightful journey through education policy, positioning and practice in examining the interdependencies, levers and drivers within the school system and the classroom. Most of all, however, the book focuses on the prize of ensuring we have an equitable, engaging and outcome-led approach to equipping our young people to positively impact upon their and our future society. In doing so, the authors reinforce the importance (and difficulties) of working beyond short-term political gains and boundaries, and towards deploying a multi-partner and holistic view of the purpose of benefits of education.

Whether you are a practitioner, student teacher, civil servant, community worker, policy-maker or education leader, *About Our Schools* will both challenge and inform you.

Professor Julie Mennell, Vice Chancellor, University of Cumbria

About Our
Schools

Improving on Previous Best

Tim Brighouse and **Mick Waters**

Crown House Publishing Limited
www.crownhouse.co.uk

First published by

Crown House Publishing
Crown Buildings, Bancyfelin, Carmarthen, Wales, SA33 5ND, UK
www.crownhouse.co.uk

and

Crown House Publishing Company LLC
PO Box 2223, Williston, VT 05495, USA
www.crownhousepublishing.com

British Library Cataloguing-in-Publication Data

A catalogue entry for this book is available from the British Library.

Print ISBN: 978-178583586-5
Mobi ISBN 978-178583602-2
ePub ISBN 978-178583603-9
ePDF ISBN 978-178583604-6

LCCN 2021948530

Printed and bound in the UK by
CPi Anthony Rowe, Melksham, Wiltshire

The authors are donating all royalties from the sale of this book to be shared between two charities: Barnardo's and the Compassionate Education Foundation.

For over 150 years, Barnardo's has worked to protect and support children and young people facing a range of issues from homelessness, drug misuse and disability to sexual abuse and domestic violence. In 2020, Barnardo's supported over 350,000 young people across the UK.

The Compassionate Education Foundation exists to bring compassion into everything we do in education by engineering innovative collaborative projects designed to enhance the processes, practices and products of individuals, schools, colleges and universities as well as the varied organisations that support them.

Tim Brighouse and Mick Waters thank you for buying this book and, in doing so, supporting two very worthwhile causes.

To those of our grandchildren still within the school system: Poppy, Oliver, Alfie, Charlotte and Arthur. In the writing of this book we have talked often about our hopes for their futures.

Foreword by Danny Dorling

We often don't truly value something until we have lost it. In the short term, children losing access to schools in the UK in 2020 suddenly brought home not just what schools do for most children physically but also what they do in the round. Schools are about far more than education. They are places where we become socialised into our society, where we learn to respect others and, in some cases, to look up to or down on others. They don't just teach skills. Schools help us to form our attitudes, beliefs and prejudices.

At some times and in some schools, we are told that other people are our betters, often others not at our school. We learn to behave and to be disciplined, so that later in our lives our apparent superiors will find that we have been well trained; that we are respectful; compliant; that we know our place. This still occurs in England today. Not everywhere, of course, but the idea that different children are of different rank and worth is still endlessly stamped into young minds in ways that do not often occur so forcefully elsewhere in Europe.

When classrooms emptied during the COVID-19 crisis of 2020 and 2021, it quickly became clear which schools were equipped and had the resources to teach online and which schools could not cope and handed out paper worksheets instead. The huge advantage of very low pupil–teacher ratios in private schools suddenly became glaringly obvious, not just normally but especially during a crisis. At the other end of the scale – for those for whom school was a sanctuary from harm and indifference at home – no longer being able to go to school was devastating. In a very small number of cases it will have been deadly. Schools do far more than teach. If we have learned anything from the pandemic, we now know that schools should be the last public institutions to close and the first to reopen.

The authors of this excellent book began writing in earnest in early 2021 in the weeks when it became clear that, yet again, schools would be closed for many months. State schools were only kept open physically for the children of 'key workers' and those identified as being in special need. It turned out that everyone who worked in a school was a key worker – something that had barely been acknowledged before. It also turned out that the politics of education was not quite as clearly divided between good and bad as we might have thought. You are probably reading these words many months after it has been accepted that the new coronavirus is endemic and a zero-COVID strategy is impossible. However, it was a right-wing government that tried to keep the schools open and left-wing unions (championing zero COVID) that demanded they close.

In hindsight, it is much easier to see what the right course of action would have been. This book has been written in contemplation of a much longer period when we could all take stock of what we were losing without our schools even being closed – the decades during which funding per head was cut for 13 out of 14 children; that is, all those who attended a state school in England. Note: it is a much higher proportion than 93% in most parts of the UK and a much lower proportion among those people who get to determine education policy. Furthermore, division had been sown within the state system, with schools forced to compete against each other for pupils, to attract and retain staff (not least teachers) and to be able to afford the upkeep of their buildings.

This book begins in 1976, which was the year that marked the end of optimism and trust in teaching and saw the dial adjusted to a new belief in the power of markets, centralisation and managerialism. The authors confess the hope that the previous system would have thrived was 'probably misplaced', which illustrates their freedom from conventional dogma. However, it is worth noting that in 1976, the UK was one of the most economically equitable large countries in Europe, second only to Sweden in terms of income equality. By that measure, Germany, Italy, Spain and France all had more socially fractured societies in that year. In contrast, in the decades that followed – when markets, centralisation and managerialism were allowed to take over much of life in Britain, not just in education – the UK saw its levels of economic inequality grow to become by far the largest of any Western European country. It was not just education that fractured after 1976. Health, housing, employment and the distribution of material assets, including wealth, and other life chances all also saw developments that worsened lives and increased division.

Economic inequality matters in education. In the 1980s, a large number of places in private schools were sponsored by the government under the Assisted Places Scheme for the academically able children (or those deemed to be) of parents who would not otherwise be able to afford the fees. Furthermore, incomes were more equal at the start of the 1980s, and therefore not enough adults were paid so much more than other individuals that they could meet the cost of educating their children privately. This meant that the commercial future of private schooling was at stake. Private education only prospers in places where there is high income inequality.

However, by the time Tony Blair abolished the Assisted Places Scheme in 1997, the gap in incomes in England had grown to such an extent that there were now enough pupils with very well-paid parents to fill the private school quotas without the need for a direct government subsidy. (The indirect subsidies that enabled tax avoidance were maintained.) But it is important to note that in no single year during the period since 1997 (which included all the New Labour years as well as the decade of austerity) did income inequality fall by any measurable amount.

It is perhaps unsurprising that during the same period there have been many changes in education but few progressive movements. In fact, there has been no progressive government in the UK since the early and mid-1970s. Most recently, under New Labour and then the coalition, we have witnessed the almost wholesale privatisation of universities.

One of the ways we hold on to hope is in the belief, at times not entirely unfounded, that after many decades of banging your head against a wall and going in the wrong direction, a group of people – in this case, those interested in education in Britain – realise that a change of tack is required. At this point we need to know what to do next. The solutions offered in this excellent book are based on learning from what did and did not work in England between 1976 and today. Although the overriding ethos of markets and competition was not conducive to progress, many individuals and some organisations, most schools and millions of children and their parents struggled over those long years to improve many things. For example, we should not forget that these were the years in which schools became dramatically less violent places, a significant part of which was banning teachers from beating pupils. Not everything was rosy before 1976.

There are so many wonderful suggestions in this book that you will have to read it to discover them; they cannot be summarised in a short foreword. One I particularly like is that 'we should treat pupils not as they (sometimes infuriatingly) are but as they might become'. Recently, I met a teacher who is teaching in a school that I attended almost four decades ago. She told me she thought that none of her pupils would ever write a book. It was an 'average school': avoided by most of the wealthiest parents in the city and aspired to by many of the parents who lived just outside its catchment area. I had some sympathy with her exasperation, but I had also been a child who failed at English at age 16. I knew that did not mark me for life. I read my first word in 1976 – very late at age 8. I had good teachers but I found reading hard. In the end, my mum taught me to read; my school barely improved on that, although they tried, but they taught me enough of maths, geography and science that I ended up writing many books. No one would have believed it if they had seen how I wrote when I was at school.

We have all followed our own individual educational paths and each of them will have shaped us and, in turn, our views on education. Very probably, Margaret Thatcher, the education secretary from 1970 to 1974, would not have believed so strongly in her own personal superiority had she not been sent to a grammar school by her father or been awarded a place at an elitist university. Tony Blair, who came to power with the mantra 'education, education, education', and his one-time education adviser Andrew Adonis might have had very different views on what a good education consisted of had they been differently educated too. In contrast, the authors of this book explain how every 'young person can walk more than a few steps with genius'. They could have added that the geniuses among us tend not to seem quite so clever when you spend long enough hanging around them.

So many people who have steered the course of English education in recent decades, from prime ministers through to policy wonks, appear to have held the belief that they have truly realised their own personal potential and that it was because they held within themselves such great potential, which had somehow been allowed to burst forth and be realised, that their amazing ideas should be implemented. Such pomposity is pricked at many points in the pages that follow, including examples such as how, for all the hours of senior management teams brainstorming risk assessments, no one foresaw what might happen during a pandemic, through to how ridiculous it is that so many children are excluded from schools in England. Some 1,579 pupils are permanently excluded from English schools each year for each one of the five children excluded a year in Scotland – almost 8,000 a year in England in total. Try to imagine how that feels for each and every one of those children, that year and for the rest of their lives.

Education, at its best, frees you from being told to believe that you are the natural inferior of others. At its worst, it leaves you with the impression that you are the natural superior of others. Education in England is in a terrible mess. If you don't believe me, try describing what happens in your town, city or village to someone from elsewhere in Western Europe. Tell them how different children are selected to go to different schools. Tell them about the languages and arts that we no longer even try to teach. Tell them what ensues when our children are asked a maths or science question that is not directly connected to one of the answers they and their teachers have guessed would be on the exam paper. And then ask them what happens where they live in other Western European countries that did not travel the post-1976 road we took in England.

Preface

Why did we write this book?

We decided to write this book in December 2020 as we entered the third restrictions of the COVID-19 pandemic. We thought it might just be the right time to find what we call in Chapter 7 on school improvement and leadership a 'gap in the hedge'. That is, an unexpected opportunity for schools and the schooling system to create a new age of renewed hope and ambition through collaborative partnerships where schools are encouraged to meet the challenges of today and tomorrow rather than being locked in a relentless grind of yesterday. We wanted to think about the future for our schools in terms of the steps that can be taken as we move forward from the pandemic.

We believe that the school system was already at the point of moving into a new age of hope, ambition and collaborative partnerships, and that extraordinary circumstances provide us with an opportunity not just to build back better but to be more adventurous still.

Nobody can deny that we live in a world of accelerating change, and we therefore thought we should remind ourselves that in such a world it is the learners who inherit the world, while the learned are beautifully equipped for a world that no longer exists. We have spent a long time in and around schools and those who influence them, and we thought – correctly, as it turned out – that we could persuade these key influencers to help us by volunteering to be interviewed.

Who do we hope will read this book?

Different chapters will seem worthwhile to different audiences and all of them to some. Politicians ought to be considering all the issues in the later chapters and should be fascinated by the words of their colleagues past and present which dominate the first half of the book. Teachers in training will find Chapter 5 on curriculum, pedagogy and assessment illuminating and informative, as will all those existing teachers still full of the intellectual curiosity which is their vital stock in trade. Head teachers and would-be school leaders will prefer to glean what they can from Chapter 7 on school improvement and leadership. Parents, governors, chief executive officers (CEOs) of multi-academy trusts (MATs), directors of children's services and those in local government should all be considering the issues we raise in various parts of the book.

It is not to be read at one sitting but can be dipped into when grappling with a particular theme. We hope everyone will read our opening chapter which provides an overview and consider the suggestions we make for change in the final chapter. There are some recurring issues that emerge in several chapters which, although similar, are addressed within different contexts.

What was our methodology?

Methodology sounds rather grander, more rigorous and organised than is usual for us! We read a lot and spent around 150 hours interviewing our witnesses. Along with the invitation to take part, we sent them a brief guide to the questions we intended to use in our Zoom-enabled interviews. (At the request of our witnesses, two of the interviews were conducted by phone.) But we allowed our interview conversations to flow – and flow they certainly did – before carefully transcribing what was said. We drew on the bank of witness statements as we put together the chapters.

We would not say that our research methods would pass muster if the most rigorous academic standards were applied, but we have stuck to the evidence for the most part – and where we haven't, we have made that clear.

What are our underlying values or prejudices?

Anybody reading a book of this sort will seek to work out the values or prejudices that are driving the authors – in this case, about those that underpin the schooling system. We cover these in our first chapter. We focus on what has worked well and argue that now is the time to improve on that. Hence our title: we look at and question development over time and propose next steps for our school system, always with the intent of improving on previous best.

Who were our witnesses?

We started out thinking that we wanted to interview all the available secretaries of state since 1976. There followed some mission creep. At one point we thought of calling the book, 'You Ought To Talk To ... ' as so many of our witnesses pointed us to another source of insight.

Having talked with some of our secretaries of state, we realised there were other players whose views would help us with our enquiries. In the end, we have interviewed fourteen secretaries of state, four heads of Ofsted and Her Majesty's Chief Inspectors of Schools (HMCIs), two permanent secretaries at the Department for Education (DfE), three other senior civil servants at the DfE, five ministers for schools, one national schools commissioner, three regional schools commissioners, sixteen CEOs of MATs and free schools, four directors of children's services, four leaders of the teacher and head teacher unions, one children's commissioner, governors and trustees of schools and MATs and the CEO of their national organisation, several representatives of educational organisations, charitable causes and interest groups, and many head teachers and teachers. All have been generous with their time, their forthright opinions about their term in post and where they think the schooling system should go now. We have set out in the list of contributors the names of all those individuals we have spoken to and either quoted in their own words or recounted their views. Occasionally, our witnesses asked that their observations were not directly attributed to them and we have respected that wish.

We are grateful to all who have spent time with us, many of whom sent us further thoughts, recollections or documents that were enormously helpful. We have also read extensively relevant autobiographies, books about schooling and politics as well as many of the education acts, reports and reviews of the last 45 years. To point us in the right direction, we have turned regularly to Derek Gillard's comprehensive web-based History of Education in England, which has provided a valuable reminder of the events we ourselves witnessed.[1]

The royalties from this book are being donated to Barnardo's and the Compassionate Education Foundation. Our witnesses and the readers of our book will have each contributed to these worthwhile causes.

We thank all our witnesses for their involvement: they have clarified events, enlightened our thinking and stimulated ideas.

---

1   See http://www.educationengland.org.uk/history.

Acknowledgements

Both of us owe a huge debt to those who have helped us over the six months we spent interviewing, writing and rewriting drafts. Their comments have helped us consider and reconsider many of the issues covered. So, thank you to our many friends who have offered advice on how we might improve the schooling system, including: Sebastian Benney, Jim Briden, Nigel Chapman, Jonathan Crossley-Holland, Iain Erskine, Graham Fraser, Andrew Freeland, John Harrop, Lisa Hinton, John Lloyd, Ron Lloyd, Doug Lowes, Giti Paulin, Vikki Pendry, Graham Phillips, Aimée Tinkler, Trevor Walker, David Winkley, Tom Wylie and David Young. Special thanks are due to (The Real) David Cameron, Mike Davies, John Fowler, John Jones, Phil Marshall, Bob Moon, Wendy Rawlinson and Les Walton who joined the many who have taken to Zoom for long, focused conversations, and to Julie Bloor, David Boyle, Andrea Curran, Peter Hall Jones, Paul Keane, Vanessa Ogden, Gary Phillips, Terry Wrigley and others who commented on drafts.

We are also grateful to Nancy Cartwright, professor of philosophy at Durham University, who invited us to join a very fruitful seminar at the Centre for Humanities Engaging Science and Society. We were fortunate to be able to share our thinking with the New Visions for Education Group and gained valuable advice from their collective wisdom and experience. The Charter for Compassion was also a source of insight.

We would like to thank Danny Dorling for his foreword. He is a social geographer and the Halford Mackinder Professor at the University of Oxford. He has researched widely on inequalities in Britain and has written extensively on housing, health, employment, education and poverty. His writing is accessible and brings alive the essence of official reports and statistics to offer thought-provoking and often challenging arguments about social trends and patterns. The insights that Danny offers have proved increasingly interesting to educationalists who believe that schooling should be life-affirming and develop society for the common good.

We have been especially fortunate to be assisted in our fallible organisational capabilities by Amarjot Butcher and Linda Kilmurry, who managed the transcriptions and filing of drafts. We have also been ably supported by the team at Crown House Publishing. Our last word goes, as it always has, to our editors, Louise Penny and Emma Tuck; we are enormously grateful to them both.

Contents

List of abbreviations

AAA	area admissions authority
AAE	adverse adolescent experience
ACC	Association of County Councils
ACE	adverse childhood experience
ACSET	Advisory Committee for the Supply and Education of Teachers
ADHD	attention deficit hyperactivity disorder
AEC	Association of Education Committees
AI	artificial intelligence
ASBO	anti-social behaviour order
AMA	Association of Metropolitan Authorities
ASD	autism spectrum disorder
AST	advanced skills teacher
ATO	area training organisation
AWPU	age-weighted pupil unit
Becta	British Educational Communications and Technology Agency
BEd	Bachelor of Education
BELMAS	British Educational Leadership, Management and Administration Society
CAG	centre assessment grade
CAMHS	child and adolescent mental health services
CATE	Council for the Accreditation of Teacher Education
CBI	Confederation of British Industry
CEO	chief executive officer
CIEA	Chartered Institute of Educational Assessors
CNAA	Council for National Academic Awards
CPD	continuing professional development
CQC	Care Quality Commission
DBS	Disclosure and Barring Service
DCS	director of children's services

DfE	Department for Education
	The Department for Education has had various names from the 1960s until the present day. Unless relevant to the period under discussion, we have used the catch-all term DfE.

- 1964–1992: Department of Education and Science (DES)
- 1992–1995: Department for Education (DfE)
- 1995–2001: Department for Education and Employment (DFEE)
- 2001–2007: Department for Education and Skills (DfES)
- 2007–2010: Department for Children, Schools and Families (DCSF)
- 2010–present day: Department for Education (DfE)

DIRT	directed improvement and reflection time
DR ICE	deepening thinking, role modelling learning, impact on learning, challenging expectations, engaging in learning
DT	design and technology
EAL	English as an additional language
EAZ	Education Action Zone
EBacc	English Baccalaureate
EBD	emotional and behavioural disorder
EBI	even better if
ECF	early career framework
ECT	early career teacher (2021 onwards; see also NQT)
EDP	education development plan
EEF	Education Endowment Foundation
EFSA	Education Funding and Skills Agency
EHCP	education, health and care plan
EiC	Excellence in Cities
ELECT	Extraordinary Learners with Exceptional Creative Talent

EMA	Education Maintenance Allowance
EPA	education priority area
EPQ	Extended Project Qualification
ESFA	Education and Skills Funding Agency
ESG(E)	expenditure steering group (education)
ESN(M) or (S)	educationally subnormal (moderate/mild) or (severe)
FE	further education
FED	Foundation for Education Development
FFT	Fischer Family Trust
FSM	free school meals
FTSE	Financial Times Stock Exchange
GDPR	General Data Protection Regulation
HeadLAMP	Headteacher Leadership and Management Programme
HEI	higher education institution
HMI	Her Majesty's Inspectorate or Her Majesty's Inspectors
HMRC	Her Majesty's Revenue and Customs
IEB	interim executive board
ILEA	Inner London Education Authority
INSET	in-service education and training
ITE	initial teacher education
ITT	initial teacher training
JTC	junior training centre
KPI	key performance indicator
LAP	Low Attainers Project
LEA	local education authority
LFM	local financial management
LMS	local management of schools
LO	learning objective
MAC	multi-academy company
MAT	multi-academy trust
MLD	moderate learning difficulties

MRHA	Medicines and Healthcare Products Regulatory Agency
MSC	Manpower Service Commission
NASUWT	National Association of Schoolmasters/Union of Women Teachers
NCC	National Curriculum Council
NCS	National Citizen Service
NCSL	National College for School Leadership
NDPB	non-departmental public body
Nesta	National Endowment for Science, Technology and the Arts
NEU	National Education Union
NFER	National Foundation for Educational Research
NGA	National Governance Association
NICE	National Institute for Health and Care Excellence
NLE	national leader of education
NPQ	national professional qualification
NPQH	National Professional Qualification in Headship
NQT	newly qualified teacher (pre 2021; see also ECT)
NS	national strategies
NUT	National Union of Teachers
OECD	Organisation for Economic Co-operation and Development
Ofqual	Office of Qualifications and Examinations Regulation
Ofsted	Office for Standards in Education, Children's Services and Skills
OSA	Office of the Schools Adjudicator
P4C	Philosophy for Children
PACE	Pedagogy, Assessment and Curriculum in Education
PAN	published admission number
PFI	private finance initiative
PGCE	Postgraduate Certificate in Education
PIRLS	Progress in Reading Literacy Study
PISA	Programme for International Student Assessment

PPA	planning, preparation and administration
PRU	pupil referral unit
PSHE	personal, social, health and economic (education)
PTA	parent–teacher association
QCA	Qualifications and Curriculum Authority
QCDA	Qualifications and Curriculum Development Agency
QTS	qualified teacher status
RADY	Raising Attainment for Disadvantaged Youngsters
RAG	red, amber, green
REF	Research Excellence Framework
RI	requires improvement
RPI	retail price index
RQT	recently qualified teacher
RSC	regional schools commissioner
RUCSAC	read, understand, choose, solve, answer, check
SAT	Standard Assessment Task/Test
SCAA	School Curriculum and Assessment Authority
SCC	Schools' Curriculum Council
SCITT	school-centred initial teacher training
SEAL	social and emotional aspects of learning
SEN/SEND	special educational needs (and disabilities)
SENCO/SENDCO	special educational needs (and disabilities) coordinator
SIP	school improvement partner
SpAd	special adviser
STEPS	Seeking Talent and Extending Participation Scheme
TGAT	Task Group on Assessment and Testing
TIMSS	Trends in International Mathematics and Science Study
TTA	Teacher Training Agency
TVEI	Technical and Vocational Education Initiative
UCET	Universities Council for the Education of Teachers
UNICEF	United Nations Children's Fund
UTC	university technical college

WAGOLL	what a good one looks like
WALT	we are learning to
WCF	Worcestershire Children First
WILF	what I'm looking for
WWW	what went well

List of contributors

Andrew Adonis, Baron Adonis of Camden Town	Parliamentary Under Secretary of State for Schools and Learners (2005–2008) and adviser to the Prime Minister's Delivery Unit (1998–2005)
Professor Melvin Ainscow, CBE	Emeritus Professor of Education, University of Manchester, and Visiting Professor, University of Glasgow
Professor Robin Alexander	Fellow of Wolfson College, University of Cambridge. Former Director, Cambridge Primary Review and Chair, Cambridge Primary Review Trust
Janice Allen	Head Teacher, Falinge Park High School, Rochdale
Gwyn ap Harri	CEO, XP School Trust
Vincent Ashworth	Ofsted inspector for initial teacher education (2005–2020) and independent education consultant
Jill Attenborough	CEO, The Country Trust
Dave Baker	CEO, Olympus Academy Trust
Kenneth Baker, Baron Baker of Dorking	Secretary of State for Education and Science (1986–1989) and co-founder of the Baker Dearing Educational Trust
Ed Balls	Secretary of State for Children, Schools and Families (2007–2010)
Claire Banks	Director of Education, Olympus Academy Trust
Sir Michael Barber	Chief adviser to the Secretary of State for Education on School Standards (1997–2001) and Head of the Prime Minister's Delivery Unit (2001–2005)
Geoff Barton	General Secretary, Association of School and College Leaders (since 2017)

Sir David Bell	Vice-Chancellor and Chief Executive, University of Sunderland. Former HMCI (2002–2005), Permanent Secretary at the DfE (2006–2011) and Vice-Chancellor, University of Reading (2012–2018)
Nikkie Beniams	Executive Head Teacher, Keeble Gateway Academy and Thornton Dale Primary Academy (both part of Elevate Multi Academy Trust)
Tom Bennett	Director, researchED, and school behaviour adviser to the DfE (since 2016)
Katharine Birbalsingh, CBE	Joint founder and Head Teacher, Michaela Community School, London
Louise Blackburn	Director of Challenging Education, RADY
Simon Blackburn	Director of Challenging Education, RADY
Julie Bloor	Principal, Shirebrook Academy and other schools and School Improvement Director/adviser for two MATs
David Blunkett, Baron Blunkett of Brightside and Hillsborough	Secretary of State for Education and Employment (1997–2001)
Dr Mary Bousted	Joint General Secretary, National Education Union (since 2017)
Nick Brook	Deputy General Secretary, National Association of Head Teachers (since 2016)
Reverend Gilroy Brown	Former Principal and Governor, King Solomon International Business School, Birmingham
Kate Brunt	CEO/Executive Principal, The Rivers Church of England Academy Trust
Kevin Butlin	Director of Education, Plymouth CAST
Rob Carpenter	CEO, Inspire Partnership
Sir David Carter	National Schools Commissioner (2016–2018), Regional Schools Commissioner for South-West England (2014–2016) and CEO, Cabot Learning Federation (2007–2014)

Dave Claricoates	Senior Assistant Principal, Bosworth Academy (LiFE Multi-Academy Trust), Desford
Rt Hon. Charles Clarke	Secretary of State for Education and Skills (2002–2004)
Kenneth Clarke, Baron Clarke of Nottingham	Secretary of State for Education and Science (1990–1992)
Dame Julia Cleverdon, DCVO CBE	Director of Education, Industrial Society. Former CEO, Business in the Community, speaker, campaigner and charity worker
Sir Jon Coles	CEO, United Learning. Former Director General for Schools and for Education Standards
Sir Kevan Collins	Education Recovery Commissioner. Former CEO, Education Endowment Foundation; CEO, Tower Hamlets; and Director of Children's Services, Tower Hamlets
Andy Couldrick	CEO, Birmingham Children's Trust
Stephen Cox	CEO, Osiris Educational
Lucy Crehan	Teacher, education explorer, author and international education consultant
Claire Delaney	Managing Director, Schools' Buying Club. Former Managing Director, Place Group, and Chair, Bellevue Place Education Trust
Susan Douglas	CEO, Eden Academy Trust
Sir John Dunford	General Secretary of Association of School and College Leaders (1998–2013) and Pupil Premium Champion (2013–2015)
Ben Erskine	Principal, Fulbridge Academy, Peterborough
Sarah Finch	CEO, Marches Academy Trust
Clare Flintoff	CEO, ASSET Education Trust
Sam Freedman	CEO, Ark, Education Partnerships Group. Former special adviser at the DfE (2010–2013); Head of Education Unit, Policy Exchange; and Executive Director of Impact and Delivery, Teach First
Christine Gilbert, CBE	Her Majesty's Chief Inspector (2006–2011)

Narinder Gill	School Improvement Director, Elevate Multi Academy Trust. Former Head Teacher, Hunslet Moor Primary School, Leeds
Richard Gill, CBE	CEO, Arthur Terry Learning Partnership, and Chair, Teaching Schools Council
Rt Hon. Michael Gove, MP	Secretary of State for Education (2010–2014)
Rt Hon. Justine Greening	Secretary of State for Education (2016–2018)
Sir Mark Grundy	CEO, Shireland Collegiate Academy Trust
David Gumbrell	Senior lecturer at Kingston University, education consultant and founder of the Resilience Project
Lucy Heller	CEO, Ark Schools
Robert Hill	Special adviser at the DfE and Prime Minister's Policy Unit (1997–2002)
Rt Hon. Damian Hinds, MP	Secretary of State for Education (2018–2019)
Alex Hope	Head Teacher, Knaresborough St John's C of E Primary School (Elevate Multi Academy Trust)
Sir Peter Housden	Director General for Schools (2001–2005), Permanent Secretary of the Office of the Deputy Prime Minister (2005–2010) and Permanent Secretary of the Scottish Government (2010–2015)
Peter Hyman	Co-founder and Director, Big Education, and founder and Executive Head Teacher, School 21. Strategist and speechwriter to Tony Blair (1994–2003)
Rt Hon. Alan Johnson	Secretary of State for Education and Skills (2006–2007)
Jonathan Johnson	CEO, West Lakes Multi Academy Trust/One Cumbria Teaching School Hub
Christine Keates	General Secretary, National Association of Schoolmasters/Union of Women Teachers (2004–2020)

Rt Hon. Ruth Kelly	Secretary of State for Education and Skills (2004–2006)
Javed Khan	Former CEO, Barnardo's, and Director of Education, London Borough of Harrow
Debra Kidd	Teacher and author
Richard Kieran	Head Teacher, Woodrow First School, Redditch
James Knight, Baron Knight of Weymouth	Minister of State for Schools and Learners (2006–2009)
Emma Knights, OBE	CEO, National Governance Association (since 2010)
Rt Hon. David Laws	Minister of State for Schools (2012–2015)
Rt Hon. Dame Andrea Leadsom, MP	Early Years Healthy Development Adviser for the Government (since 2020)
Anne Longfield, CBE	Children's Commissioner for England (2015–2021)
Sir Alasdair Macdonald, CBE	Educationalist and former Head Teacher, Morpeth School, Tower Hamlets
Rebecca Maiden	Head Teacher, Meadowside Primary Academy (Elevate Multi Academy Trust), Knaresborough
Nicola Morgan, Baroness Morgan of Cotes	Secretary of State for Education (2014–2016)
Estelle Morris, Baroness Morris of Yardley	Secretary of State for Education and Skills (2001–2002)
Sir Dan Moynihan	CEO, Harris Federation. Former Head Teacher of Valentines High School, Ilford
Dr Steve Munby	CEO, National College for School Leadership (2005–2012), consultant and speaker
James Noble-Rogers	Executive Director, Universities Council for the Education of Teachers (since 2004)
Georgina Nutton	Head Teacher, Preston Park Primary School, Wembley
Helen O'Donnell	CEO and Director of Partnerships, Children's University
Tim Oates, CBE	Group Director of Assessment, Research and Development, Cambridge Assessment

Alan Parker	Former Education Officer, Association of Metropolitan Authorities, and Director of Education, London Borough of Enfield
Pank Patel	Former Regional Schools Commissioner, West Midlands, and Head Teacher, Wood Green Academy, Wednesbury
Dame Alison Peacock, DBE DL	CEO, Chartered College of Teaching
Robert Peston	Founder of Speakers for Schools, journalist and broadcaster
Colin Pettigrew	Corporate Director for Children and Families, Nottinghamshire
Jemima Reilly	Head Teacher, Morpeth School, Tower Hamlets
Nigel Richardson	Former Director of Children's Services in Hull and Leeds, writer and consultant
Hywel Roberts	Teacher, author and speaker
Sharon Robertson	Executive Head Teacher, Aspin Park Academy (Elevate Multi Academy Trust), Knaresborough
Andreas Schleicher	Director for Education and Skills, and Special Advisor on Education Policy to the Secretary-General, Organisation for Economic Co-operation and Development
Sir Anthony Seldon	Former Master of Wellington College, academic and author
Sarah Sewell	Founder and CEO, Yes Futures
Gillian Shephard, Baroness Shephard of Northwold	Secretary of State for Education and Employment (1995–1997)
Tracy Smith	Executive Director, Tower Hamlets Education Partnership
Nick Stuart, CB	Director General for Lifelong Learning, DfES (2000-2001), Deputy Secretary for Schools (1987–1992), career civil servant and Chair of the Specialist Schools and Academies Trust and other charities

Trevor Sutcliffe	Director of Challenging Education, RADY
Sir Michael Tomlinson	Her Majesty's Chief Inspector (2000–2002) and Chair of the Working Group for 14–19 Reform
Rachel Tomlinson	Head Teacher, Barrowford Primary School, Nelson
Professor Samantha Twiselton, OBE	Director of Sheffield Institute of Education at Sheffield Hallam University and member of DfE review panels
John Vickers	Chair of Trustees, Arthur Terry Learning Partnership, and former Head Teacher
Dr Mick Walker	Vice Chair, Chartered Institute of Educational Assessors and Chair, Evidence Based Education Advisory Board
Rt Hon. Robin Walker, MP	Minister of State for School Standards (since 2021)
Carl Ward	Executive Chair, Foundation for Education Development and CEO, City Learning Trust
Rachael Wardell	Executive Director of Children's Services, Surrey
Chris Waterman	Secretary of the All-Party Parliamentary Group for the Teaching Profession, political adviser in the House of Lords and commentator on public policy issues
Professor John West-Burnham	Independent writer, teacher and consultant in education leadership
Lisa Williams	Head Teacher, Rushey Green Primary School, London. Former education adviser in Hackney
Rt Hon. Gavin Williamson, MP	Secretary of State for Education (2019–2021)
Sir Michael Wilshaw	Her Majesty's Chief Inspector (2012–2016)
Hannah Woodhouse	Regional Schools Commissioner, South-West England, and previously DfE civil servant

Note: Formal titles and honours have been checked with *Who's Who* for accuracy; we apologise for any errors or omissions. We have taken the decision, as a matter of editorial style and chronology (for example, some contributors had not received their honour or award at the time of the events described in this book), not to include honorific titles in the main text. We have used the names by which our contributors are commonly known in the world of education. We hope they and readers will understand.

Part One

Political influence – storms, showers and sunny periods … and the realities of a changing climate in schooling

Chapter 1
School climate changes over the years

The state's involvement in schooling and how 1976 was a turning point from one educational age to another – a brief synopsis

What sort of climate should we want?

The teacher is the most important influence in the schooling system.

We have each spent a lifetime in state-provided education, first as pupils, then as teachers and finally in various leadership positions both in and out of schools. We have never stopped learning or making mistakes from which we like to think we have sometimes learned. We know that the best teachers use pupil mistakes as a positive opportunity to learn, and we believe that the same is true of ourselves and the other professionals with whom we have worked and to whom we owe so much. Our endeavour has always been to improve on previous best.

This book has been born out of a shared passion for education as it occurs in schools, where it can so often be transformative of children and young people's lives. Teachers at their best – and we have witnessed myriad examples of this – change for the better the attitudes and future trajectory of young lives. We agree with the wisdom and judgement of Haim Ginott when he famously said: 'I have come to a frightening conclusion. I am the decisive element in the classroom. It is my personal approach that creates the climate. It is my daily mood that makes the weather. As a teacher I possess tremendous power to make a child's life miserable or joyous.'[1]

---

1 H. G. Ginott, *Teacher and Child: A Book for Parents and Teachers* (New York: Macmillan, 1972), pp. 15–16.

Nor do we disagree with Robert Fried's judgement:

> Of some of our teachers, we remember their foibles and manner-
> isms, of others, their kindness and encouragement, or their fierce
> devotion to standards of work that we probably did not share at
> the time. And of those who inspired us most, we remember what
> they cared about, and that they cared about us, and the person
> we might become. It is the quality of caring about ideas and val-
> ues, this fascination with the potential for growth within people,
> this depth and fervour about doing things well and striving for
> excellence, that comes closest to what I mean in describing a 'pas-
> sionate teacher'.[2]

In our experience as pupils, we were each fortunate when we met such teachers and the ones who, as Fried says, 'inspired us most', and know of their effect on us. In our adult lives, in and around schools, we have witnessed the sometimes profound impact of a teacher on pupils and sought to spread it and improve the chances of it occurring more often and more widely. Dylan Wiliam is surely right when he reminds teachers in workshops that their individual effectiveness is the most significant influence on pupil success and that this can explain why variations in quality and outcome within a school are greater than that between schools.

But we also think that the school is powerfully influential too. It creates the 'climate' within which the teacher has a better or worse chance of making the best 'weather'. That is why consideration of school improvement, which only surfaced as a concept with research by Michael Rutter at the very start of the period we have chosen to examine, is so important in the improvement of pupil experiences and outcomes that has occurred in our lifetimes.

To extend the search for improved schooling and pupil outcomes, we must also look beyond the school itself. The climate and the weather are affected deliberately (and indirectly by many other factors, such as the community and the socio-economic background of the individual families that the school serves) by two further agents: first, by the MAT and/ or the local authority within which the school operates and, second, and most insistently, by central government through the secretary of state for education, the DfE and other central agencies such as the Office for

---

2   R. L. Fried, *The Passionate Teacher: A Practical Guide* (Boston, MA: Beacon Press, 2001), p. 17.

Standards in Education, Children's Services and Skills (Ofsted) and the Office of Qualifications and Examinations Regulation (Ofqual).

That is why we sought to interview some of the key civil servants and special advisers (SpAds), as well as the former secretaries of state who were available, since the Ruskin College speech by Prime Minister Jim Callaghan in October 1976, which launched what was described as the 'Great Debate' about education and the schooling system.[3] We chose 1976 as the starting point for our story because it punctuates the period from 1945 to the present day. Before 1976 was an age which might be dubbed one of optimism and trust (probably misplaced), and afterwards one of markets, centralisation and managerialism, while the speech itself was given during a period of doubt and disillusion when the developments in schooling set up at the end of the Second World War were called into question.

We have focused on what we might learn from this second period – as well as acknowledging what the early phase taught us – because we feel that the time is ripe. We also want to take the best of 'what is' and speculate about 'what might be' to improve on our 'previous best' – always the quest of successful teachers, whether in respect of their own practice or that of their pupils. In short, it is time to move towards a new age, just as happened in the 1970s as we transitioned from optimism and trust to markets, centralisation and managerialism.

Despite its undoubted successes, there are similar doubts gathering now about the effectiveness of this present age in meeting present and future needs in what is a world of accelerating change. That change comes in many forms – social, technological and natural – and it will be confronted and solved or harnessed by the present and future generations of educated citizens. Our schools and schooling system need to be sure they are preparing all our present and future pupils to live confidently as fulfilled citizens in a world affected by climate change, the global shift of populations, the application of artificial intelligence and robotics refined by nanotechnology, as well as the changes ushered in by the creation and expansion of the World Wide Web, meaning that use of the internet and its associated technologies will have profound implications for curriculum, pedagogy and assessment and how to handle the revolution in human communications. All our practitioner witnesses were profoundly

---

3   J. Callaghan, A Rational Debate Based on the Facts. Speech delivered at Ruskin College, Oxford (18 October 1976). Available at: http://www.educationengland.org.uk/documents/speeches/1976ruskin.html.

worried about the impact of social media on children, adolescents and parents.

We will therefore explore the elements external to the school which influence how successful teachers and schools can be in raising the competence, learning and horizons of all their students, whatever their talents, challenges, advantages or problems. In doing so, we try to be led by the evidence, although we are aware of the pitfalls of 'evidence-based policy', even though it is now a phrase widely used by decision-makers at all levels of the schooling system.

What should we expect schools to be achieving, and what are the values that underpin those purposes?

Hovering in the background, however, is another powerful influence on policy-makers and those in leadership positions – namely, the values and beliefs we all hold, together with what we think the aims of schools and the schooling system should be. Let us therefore be explicit: if we had to create agreed aims for our schooling system, which surprisingly are not set out for England or the United Kingdom as a whole, we might start with the list below.

We want our children to understand through their schooling that:

- It will be their duty as adults to guard and participate in a representative democracy that values national and local government. To that end, schools will progressively involve students in many aspects of school life and the community in which the school and the families are located.

- Their religious faith and beliefs will be respected and they will be encouraged through their schooling to respect all faiths and the humanist position.

- The many differently rewarded jobs and careers, which are vital to the well-being and practical operation of our society and others elsewhere in the world, are open to them. These include producing our food, construction and manufacturing, providing energy, medicine and care, logistics, information and entertainment, defending us, making and upholding our laws, cleaning up our mess and doing the tasks that only few can face, caring for our world and working to support less fortunate people and causes, offering solace and helping others to learn, perhaps in classrooms, libraries, galleries or museums. This kaleidoscope of employed and self-employed opportunities, available in the private, public and voluntary sectors, is ever changing and expanding under the influence of accelerating political, economic, social and technological developments.

- These careers require differing talents and schooling experiences will be based on valuing them as individuals and equipping them with the values, attitudes, knowledge and skills to make a successful and rewarding contribution to society as adults, in and out of work.

- They will be encouraged and expected to think for themselves and act for others through their life at school and in the community. They will be aware of how decisions are reached and how actions can work to solve or create problems. In doing so, they will explore and understand the range of obligations, contributions, rights and choices open to them in our own and other societies.

- They will build a desire to learn and a love of learning by being offered a range of learning opportunities that will reap more benefit if they commit to learning and seek further learning experiences in other positive contexts.

- They will encounter through their schooling experiences expert help in acquiring a foundation of skills and knowledge which will allow them to survive and flourish in our own and other societies.

- They will be thirsty to learn about the way civilisation has sought to solve its problems and made incredible discoveries and achievements, while also, at times, making mistakes.

- They will have the ability to navigate media, including social media, and become critical and discerning users of developments in this field.

- They will be equipped to make good arguments for a just cause by understanding the views of others and thereby influencing their social and political environment.

- They will understand and appreciate that our world is comprised of people from different cultures, races and orientations and be aware of the ways that power can be exercised with care or can be abused and that people can be respected and valued or exploited and persecuted. Their actions in the present and the future will reflect an understanding of our civilisation's past accomplishments as well as acknowledging that some of those achievements have come at the cost of prejudiced and flawed thinking.

- They will recognise their responsibility to protect the planet and contribute by living sustainably with the aim of preserving biodiversity and limiting global warming.

Our experience tells us that there would be a broad consensus of agreement about these purposes. Some might wish to question specific wording or terminology, to add or amend, but what we want from our school system will be largely acceptable albeit with different emphases. It is when we come to values that the tensions seem to arise. Some of our values are implicit in this list but not all. Some will be contested but it is important to be explicit, so here they are.

We believe that:

- Pupils need different approaches and experiences at different times, and teachers are in the best position to judge the approach and, with support from the school, secure those experiences.

- Teachers are at their best when pupils are persuaded to be striving always to see their previous best work as a marker against which to improve, develop or extend, while giving due consideration to making sure their recent learning is secure.

- We therefore need to make it a top priority to secure and then continuously support high-quality teachers and support staff.

- What works for one teacher may not work for another, be they equally good, but some practices are better than others and research should provide the evidence.

- The context in which teachers work will vary their approach to teaching.

- The best teachers treat children as they might become rather than as they (sometimes infuriatingly) are.

- Schools should be seen by pupils and their families as inclusive places where they are keen to spend their time.

And of the system (beyond the school) we think that:

- Admission of pupils to school should be managed to ensure that the entitlements of all children are preserved.

- Schools should not be selective, at least not until the later teenage years when the practical reality of existing resources and buildings may require some separation for differing pupil paths and destinations.

- Accountability arrangements for schools are essential but need to be intelligent. (We will explain what we mean by this in Chapter 11.)

- We should judge and recognise achievements in young people in ways that are helpful first to the pupil and second to enable their achievement to be helpful in the future, with this being separate from the accountability arrangements for our schools.

This list of beliefs (or prejudices) is not meant to be exhaustive, but they are central; others will be detected as we proceed with this book.

We elaborate on one of the beliefs set out above – namely, that we should treat pupils not as they (sometimes infuriatingly) are but as they might become. Skilled teachers in inclusive schools know how to do this. It is not achieved easily, however, and the dilemma lies at the heart of one of the issues we expose later in this book – that is, the frequent and, in our view, unhelpful use of fixed-term and sometimes permanent exclusion.

We only have to think of the need of some distressed children – for example, with Asperger's syndrome or disassociation disorder – for the space and time to go somewhere and cool down as they wrestle with impulses for fight or flight to realise just how complex is the teacher's task. Yet, the justification for their approach is the teacher's knowledge that children grow and change. The justification for their approach lies in one aspect of the first age that inspired Rab Butler, and was arguably only partially realised, but now deserves a more prominent place in the schooling firmament after the coronavirus pandemic and as a guiding principle in what we argue should be the new age of hope, ambition and collaborative partnerships.

William Temple – who, as well as being a writer on matters theological and social, was at different times the head of a leading public school, president of the Workers' Education Association (WEA) and Archbishop of Canterbury – wrote a passage on the purposes of education which appealed to Butler (we know because he quoted from it in his autobiography) as follows:

> Until Education has done more work than it has had an opportunity of doing, you cannot have a society organised on the basis of justice, for this reason ... that there will always be a strain between what is due to a man, in view of his humanity with all his powers and capabilities and what is due to him at the moment of time as a member of society with all his faculties still undeveloped, with many of his tastes warped, with his powers largely crushed.

> Are you going to treat a man as what he is or what he might be? *Morality, I think, requires that you should treat him as what he might be, as what he might become ... and business requires that you should treat him as he is.*

> *You cannot get rid of that strain except by raising what he is to the level of what he might be. That is the whole work of education.* Give him the full development of his powers and there will no longer be that

conflict between the claim of the man as he is and the man as he might become.

And so you can have no justice as the basis of your social life until education has done its full work … And you cannot have political freedom any more than you can have moral freedom until people's powers are developed, for the simple reason that over and over again we find men with a cause which is just … are unable to state it in a way which might enable it to prevail … there exists a form of mental slavery which is as real as any economic form … We are pledged to destroy it … if you want human liberty, you must have educated people.

We are writing this book during a pandemic when most of our schools have performed heroics, often going well beyond their normal remit, and when some of our best school staff have been lost, not to mention the losses that pupils and their families will have experienced. Much has been said of the disadvantages being suffered by already disadvantaged youngsters – even of a 'lost generation'. While not denying or minimising the significant, if variable impact, we think the latter risks being overstated. Most schools and teachers will find a way to unlock the minds and open the hearts of their pupils and inspire them to realise enough of their limitless potential to live fulfilled lives and help our society solve the many issues that COVID-19 and other developments have thrown in our path. We think we can increase the number comprising 'most schools' if we can persuade enough people that the time is ripe to establish this new age of hope, ambition and collaborative partnerships and to adopt some of the changes we have outlined in Chapter 13, which focuses on some improvements which, if adopted, we think will make a huge difference to the number of youngsters whose school experience creates a quest for learning and leads to a fulfilling life.

The Temple quotation, never realised for more than a few in the first age and many more in the second, deserves to be the guiding principle in the period following on from the disaster of COVID-19.

First, we focus on the ambition we have for children to express their talents, drive, individuality and skills. We make proposals for six foundation stones which will reveal genius and unleash commitment in children to make a difference to their society and their world.

Second, we make no apology for suggesting a range of changes, with the twin and related objectives of reducing the suffocating over-centralisation of decision-making in schooling and ensuring at the same time that schools are both more effective and fairer in their goal of unlocking the potential of not the few or even the many, but *all* pupils, which has always been the sometimes tantalisingly elusive but nevertheless real aim of all successful teachers and schools.

Before we embark on this journey for the future of our schooling system, it is important to describe briefly in this introductory chapter the two educational ages since the Second World War, which were punctuated by Callaghan's Ruskin College speech. We end the chapter with the words of some of our ministerial witnesses as we attempt to draw up a balance sheet of the pluses and minuses.

Influences on the classroom weather

The English have shown an ambivalent attitude to state-funded education and came to it rather reluctantly. As long ago as 1803, the Bishop of London declared that 'Men of considerable ability say that it is safest for both the Government and the religion of the country to let the lower classes remain in that state of ignorance in which nature has originally placed them.' He put himself outside such company by adding: 'It is not proposed that the children of the poor be educated in an expensive manner, or even taught to write or cypher ... There is a risk of elevating by indiscriminate education, the minds of those doomed to the drudgery of daily labour above their condition and thereby render them discontented with their lot.'[4]

It was the Church that preceded the state in providing education for the poor, while the rich and the upper classes relied on governors, governesses and independent public schools for the education of their offspring. In short, the ruling classes regarded state education as something that did not concern them directly. It is important to remember that these views, intertwined as they were with the philosophies of the Whig and Conservative political parties of the Victorian era, assumed that it was for the individual to survive through their own best efforts and that the

---

4   J. Leese, *Personalities and Power in English Education* (Leeds: E.J. Arnold & Son, 1950), p. 28.

state should intervene only as the provider of last resort. These views still linger within the unspoken assumptions of many, despite the very recent cross-party agreement about the desirability of equal opportunity, equity and social mobility to which all our witnesses testified their commitment.

Just as there is now an understanding that negative attitudes to race and gender can remain deep-seated, even when behaviour and language are appropriate and acceptable, so, we fear, there lies in many of our educational decision-makers what is now called 'unconscious bias' or 'institutional prejudice' which allows an unnecessary waste of human talent to persist and which bears heavily on certain already disadvantaged groups with a common thread of either poverty, gender, religion or race.

The first age of optimism and trust: 1945–1976

We both first heard about the importance of Butler's Education Act 1944 at secondary school. It clearly stirred the imagination of our teachers, many of whom had fought in the Second World War and were determined to build a better society than the one that had existed in their own childhoods. They, along with others in what would become the 'public services', were the architects of a Beveridge-inspired world and were the front-line troops in a war on 'ignorance' which – along with 'idleness', 'disease', 'want' and 'squalor' – were seen by Beveridge as stains on a society's right to be called civilised and therefore a template for post-Second World War government programmes.[5] It enjoyed the support of all three political parties.

How was the war on ignorance to be won through our education system? Unlike health, which was run centrally, in that age of optimism and trust, education was described as a 'national education service locally administered'. The nature of this arrangement involved the secretary of state for education suggesting a few strictly limited general policies within the purposes outlined in the Education Act 1944. It was then up to each local

---

5   William Beveridge produced a hugely influential report in 1942 called *Social Insurance and Allied Services* (London: HMSO), which became known as the Beveridge Report, and was the blueprint used by the 1945–1951 Labour government to found the welfare state.

education authority (LEA) to decide whether to accept the minister's suggestions.

When Anthony Crosland, the secretary of state for education during the Swinging Sixties, wanted England and Wales to reorganise their secondary schools along comprehensive lines, he issued Circular 10/65 which did not 'require' but merely 'requested' LEAs to submit plans.[6] Some politely declined to do so. In the end, even after Margaret Thatcher as secretary of state for education in Edward Heath's government 10 years later had approved more movements to comprehensive schools than any other minister before or since, the Callaghan government passed an Education Act in 1976 requiring the few remaining backsliders to go comprehensive, reflecting his doubt and mistrust as well as disillusion – only for the incoming Thatcher government to repeal the Act in its first months.

The extent of the minister's powers over schools in the first age was confined to discharging three main duties and responsibilities: securing a sufficient supply of suitably qualified teachers, approving (or not) any proposal from an LEA or the governors of a voluntary-aided school to remove an air-raid shelter; and approving LEA proposals for the opening or closure of schools and any loan consents required to pay for new or extended school buildings.

The main engine of action lay in the LEAs, all of which were part of democratically elected local government in county councils, county boroughs or city councils. LEAs were therefore busy in the 30 years that followed, not simply in supporting schools directly but also in setting a generally positive educational climate in the communities they and their schools served.

In discharging the first set of these responsibilities, LEAs built new schools for the growing post-war population and to accommodate more pupils as the school leaving age was raised on two occasions (to 15 in 1947 and 16 in 1972). They also created and expanded advisory and inspection services to support schools and their teachers and established a set of support services for schools such as education welfare officers, education psychologists and youth employment officer (careers) teams. In interpreting their wider role, LEAs created youth services, extended their pre-war network of adult education courses, bought outdoor pursuit and

---

6   Department of Education and Science, Circular 10/65: The Organisation of Secondary Education (1965). Available at: http://www.educationengland.org.uk/documents/des/circular10-65.html.

other residential centres, built new (and extended existing) colleges of further education, and were trusted to oversee the governance and management of a new network of teacher training colleges and colleges of advanced technology, some of which subsequently became polytechnics and then universities.

The received and largely uncontested wisdom was that intelligence was generally inherited and fixed, so that all-age elementary schools were replaced by grammar schools and secondary moderns, with LEAs administering selection via the 11+. In this first age, there were three main players: central government through the secretary of state and civil servants in the Ministry of (later Department for) Education, local government through LEAs and their councillors and officers, and schools through their teachers and head teachers.

The churches (mainly but not exclusively Church of England or Roman Catholic) also had a role as part of the 1944 settlement. Church schools were either voluntary aided with significant greater control[7] or, only in the case of the Anglican Faith, voluntary controlled, which involved some privileges, such as the right of the vicar to be on the governing or managing body and ownership of the buildings themselves, the value of which reverted to the church in the event of closure.

The main power lay with the middle tier of local government, although the curriculum and how it was taught was left very much to the schools and individual teachers. National pay scales for teachers and head teachers were determined by the Burnham Committee, where the most notable protagonists were teachers led by Ronald Gould, general secretary of the National Union of Teachers (NUT), and William Alexander of the Association of Education Committees (AEC). The Ministry of Education simply had an observer status – albeit a strong one, since convention demanded that the overall envelope of teachers' salaries should be contained within what the Treasury determined the nation could afford.

At first, in the period of shortages after the war, the whole local education budget was settled through a percentage block grant from central government. However, in 1958, the central control of revenue spending was abandoned. How much was spent each year on schools became an LEA matter. The chief education officer and education committee had to

---

7   Voluntary-aided school governing or managing bodies were the employers of the staff, although the LEA bore the salary bill. The governors/managers retained the right to make appointments and shouldered the costs of building maintenance and a percentage of the costs of new schools.

fight their corner with other services about budgets, and therefore how much local rates should be raised and spent on schools. Spending on schools therefore began to diverge: some chief education officers were more persuasive than others, and some councils, especially county councils, placed less importance on state schooling because county councillors often had no stake in it, sending their own children to the independent schools that they themselves had attended.[8]

Prime Minister Clement Attlee described the process as 'building a new Jerusalem' during the years in which there was a general acceptance that education was an unquestioned and unquestionable 'good thing'.[9] However, as the years went by and the post-war consensus faded, doubt and disillusion crept in for a variety of reasons.

In 1968, Prime Minister Harold Wilson had summoned university vice chancellors to a meeting in Downing Street to demand an explanation for the causes of student campus unrest, which in fairness to them was a phenomenon not confined to the UK in that year. In London, two schools, one primary (William Tyndale) and the other secondary (Risinghill) had attracted unwelcome headlines as the press represented them as out of control. The first led to a long-running inquiry (the Auld Report) commissioned by the Inner London Education Authority (ILEA), which completed with considerable criticism of both the school and the educational infrastructure.[10] However, more influential and popularised by the media were a stream of 'Black Papers' which suggested that the basics were not being given sufficient attention by the schools.[11]

Doubt and disillusion were epitomised in Callaghan's Ruskin College speech of 1976.[12] In it, he referred to an earlier Conservative minister's description of the 'secret garden' of the curriculum, which Callaghan

---

8   When Tim Brighouse joined Oxfordshire in 1978 as its chief education officer, the chair of the education committee asked why he wasn't going to send his children to one of the many famous independent day schools in Oxford.

9   J. Bew, *Citizen Clem: A Biography of Attlee* (London: Riverrun, 2016), pp. 307 and 409.

10   R. Auld, *The William Tyndale Junior and Infants Schools. Report of the Public Inquiry* [Auld Report] (London: Inner London Education Authority, 1976).

11   The Black Papers (1969–1977) were a series of articles first published by the Critical Quarterly Society attacking so-called 'progressive methods' in English schools. Their authors included Kingsley Amis and Philip Larkin as well as Rhodes Boyson, who subsequently became a minister in Margaret Thatcher's government. The first Black Paper, *Fight for Education* by Brian Cox and Anthony Dyson, was published in 1969 and arguably had the most influence in drawing attention to the shortcomings of the first age we have described.

12   Callaghan, A Rational Debate Based on the Facts. The three quotes below are from this speech.

implied should no longer be secret and that the state had a right and a duty to be more involved in the outcomes of schooling.

Callaghan's secretary of state was Shirley Williams. She recounted the prelude to the speech in *Climbing the Bookshelves*, which involved the production of a 'Yellow Book' within the DfE and brought to a head some of the festering arguments in the education sector.[13] Doubtless, Williams also had a hand in the speech itself.

Callaghan was always a mediator and his speech set out the challenge as he saw it without siding with any group:

> I do not join those who paint a lurid picture of educational decline because I do not believe it is generally true, although there are examples which give cause for concern. I am raising a further question. It is this. In today's world, higher standards are demanded than were required yesterday and there are simply fewer jobs for those without skill. Therefore we demand more from our schools than did our grandparents.

Callaghan was also keen to dissociate himself from the rantings of the Black Paper writers:

> These are proper subjects for discussion and debate. And it should be a rational debate based on the facts. My remarks are not a clarion call to Black Paper prejudices. We all know those who claim to defend standards but who in reality are simply seeking to defend old privileges and inequalities.

Nonetheless, he argued, there was now a good case to be made for 'a basic curriculum with universal standards', and he concluded:

> I have outlined concerns and asked questions about them today. The debate that I was seeking has got off to a flying start even before I was able to say anything. Now I ask all those who are concerned to respond positively and not defensively. It will be an advantage to the teaching profession to have a wide public understanding and support for what they are doing. And there is room for greater understanding among those not directly concerned of the nature of the job that is being done already.

---

13 S. Williams, *Climbing the Bookshelves: The Autobiography of Shirley Williams* (London: Virago, 2009). The Department of Education and Science's *School Education in England: Problems and Initiatives* (London: HMSO, 1976) is often referred to as 'The Yellow Book'.

It was a watershed speech for the schooling system, with some seeing the need to defend their position and others believing that their criticisms of the system had been recognised, validated and supported.

During these years, the reliable middle-tier engine room of change and development, the LEA, also lost its apparently trusted status. Local government reorganisation in 1974 led to the sidelining and eventual demise of the AEC's new 'corporate management' took hold, both locally and in its representative bodies – the Association of Metropolitan Authorities and County Councils (AMAs and ACCs), matching the reorganisation of councils.[14]

This meant that education, long regarded as the cuckoo in local government's nest, was more exposed and vulnerable in budget discussions locally. As a consequence, the civil service and ministers began to believe that they could no longer rely on local government to reflect national government's general wishes through its actions. As Nick Stuart, a distinguished career civil servant who was with DfE at the time, confirmed: 'We felt that we could no longer rely on local education authorities. It was a long, slow breakdown in trust as local government became more corporate and the position of education within it less independent in the years after the introduction of general grant.'

This was a far cry from the days of Edward Boyle who, as secretary of state (1962–1964), told his civil servants that whenever they were making decisions on a tricky issue they should ask what Mr Clegg would advise 'as the conscience of the education service'.[15] Alec Clegg was chief education officer of West Riding LEA and the pre-eminent figure among a group of chief education officers who led thinking in that first age.

Just how far the pendulum of trust eventually swung to a diametrically opposite position is revealed by Kenneth Clarke, who told us that when he was secretary of state (1992–1994), 'Some of the LEAs in my time were awful; of course, some were reasonably good but others were run by people who were little short of political bandits. One of my great

---

14 The Redcliffe-Maud Commission in 1969 saw the creation of new councils, such as Cleveland, Avon and Cumbria, and the bringing together of councils such as Nottingham and Nottinghamshire. Over time, many of these arrangements have dissolved and unitary authorities created.

15 Sir Alec Clegg was a renowned director of education in the West Riding of Yorkshire. He was known for his views on using aesthetic aspects of learning to inspire children. For more on Clegg and Bretton Hall College of Education, which he founded, see: C. Burke, P. Cunningham and L. Hoare, *Education Through the Arts for Well-Being and Community: The Vision and Legacy of Sir Alec Clegg* (Abingdon and New York: Routledge, 2021).

achievements was to free the colleges from LEA control … there wasn't much objection as they hadn't been much interested in them.'

The second age of markets, centralisation and managerialism: 1976–2021

The full implications of the second age took some years to be clearly defined. It became abundantly clear with the appointment of Kenneth Baker and the passage of the 1986 and 1988 Education Acts, but those with the eyes to see would point to increased emphasis on accountability and the use of the same mantra words (choice,[16] autonomy, diversity and accountability) in the educational White Papers that preceded those Acts.

Although the 1980 Act introduced parental *choice* of school, perhaps the lack of impetus was because the government had its hands full applying economic theory to British industry, or maybe it was the unpreparedness of the first secretary of state, Mark Carlisle. Whatever the reason, apart from establishing parental choice of schools, the full extent of applying neo-liberal economic theory to schools and the beginning of the age of markets, centralisation and managerialism became apparent with the Education Act of 1988.

Markets, centralisation and managerialism were gradually promoted by measures enshrined in legislation. However, in those early days, choice did not extend to pupils or schools having significant control over the curriculum – which, for the first time, was prescribed nationally and described as broad and balanced. As our witnesses confirmed, this was really against the wishes of Margaret Thatcher herself, who favoured the idea of laying down what the core subjects (English, maths and science) should encompass, while leaving the rest open to each school to decide. Her education minister's views prevailed, however.

---

16 Choice implied that parents needed a choice of school, although they were arguably misled since clearly absolute choice could not be guaranteed because school size is not without a limit. In reality, the most that successive Education Acts have given parents is the ability to express a *preference* for the school their child might attend.

The curriculum, prescribed in detail after the 1988 Education Act, was assessed nationally through the Standard Assessment Tests (SATs) and General Certificate of Secondary Education (GCSE), initially at 7, 11, 14 and 16, to enable comparisons to be made of different schools' performance. The collective performance of individual schools (GCSEs and (Advanced) A levels) were first published in league table format in 1993. The publication of SATs results from primary schools soon followed.

Autonomy referred to the self-sufficiency of individual schools, which was encouraged by legally established imperatives such as the delegation of decision-making over budgets, initially called local management of schools (LMS). A recurring theme has been the wish to discourage schools from being overly dependent on their maintaining LEAs. Over the years, diversity has therefore been encouraged through establishing different sorts of school.

To reflect the need for more *diversity*, new types of schools were devised. Just over a dozen city technology colleges, directly run from the DfE and funded with substantial private sponsorship, were created between 1986 and 1990. The 1988 Act also made provision for secondary schools to 'opt out' of LEA control and enjoy what was called grant-maintained status. Later there were specialist, foundation and trust schools. More recently, academies and free schools have emerged, both in effect revivals of the grant-maintained model, which the incoming Blair government had initially abolished.

By means of greater diversity in schooling, backed by each school's autonomy and coupled with increased parental choice and the publication of school outcomes, a quasi-market in schooling was created and continued throughout the whole period, whichever party has been in power. Charles Clarke epitomised this acceptance of bipartisan agreement in the following way: 'We have to accept the private sector has a role and has always done; textbooks and publishing are an example and we would never have achieved Building Schools for the Future without PFI [private finance initiative], even though there were many issues about the exact PFI terms.'[17] Competition among and between schools was encouraged as their results are published – and parents, as consumers, could make choices among an array of schools following roughly the same curriculum.

---

17   See Chapter 4 for more on Building Schools for the Future.

Accountability was also encouraged. However, accountability for schools manifested itself most sharply in school inspection, which changed from oversight by a body with a relatively imprecise and professionally trusting approach – schools might not be visited by Her Majesty's Inspectors (HMI) in 40 years – to one that was more systematic and public. In 1983, Keith Joseph approved the first publication of HMI reports on schools, while one of Kenneth Clarke's achievements was to set up the Office for Standards in Education (Ofsted) in 1993.

Schools were now inspected on a regular four-year cycle and their Ofsted school inspection reports were published and made available to the local and national press, with a letter sent to parents summarising the main findings. At first it introduced a seven-point school ranking system, which was later reduced to four: outstanding, good, requires improvement and, with drastic consequences, special measures. The bottom category, synonymous with failure and inadequacy, has often led to the departure of head teachers and other senior staff or governors in the school concerned. Ofsted therefore became a feared entity for many schools – especially those serving socially disadvantaged communities, which seemed to fail disproportionately.

The case for adding 'centralisation and managerialism' to 'markets' as an apt descriptor of this age rests on two factors. First, as happens in all markets, schools fail as well as succeed and so must either be made viable or close. This task fell to LEAs, which were used to wrestling with school closures during the decade of declining pupil population between 1977 and 1987, but they were initially unused to the role of school improver. (Eventually LEAs were themselves inspected by Ofsted and some found to be so poor that their powers were removed in favour of either a private or not-for-profit third-party time-limited replacement.) The emergence of academies, at first a device to give a boost to schools that had underperformed for long periods, has increasingly involved central government through a set of regional commissioners taking over the LEA's role in clearing up the mess involved in failing individual schools and eventually brokering entry into MATs or reconfiguring those trusts when they themselves fail.

Second – and this is where managerialism comes in – as soon as there was a national curriculum that went beyond broad aims, there would be the need from time to time to update it, and therefore the temptation to promote, induce or, eventually, enforce changed practice in schools would, and did, become irresistible. Ironically, it was Sir Keith Joseph, the politician credited with being the instigator of neo-liberal ideas and who supported a social market economy as well as believing that the 'market itself will find the solution', who first introduced the idea that central government should directly fund what he deemed to be desirable changes in schools through financial inducements.

Joseph announced his intention to do so at the Council of Local Education Authorities Conference in 1982 where, to a surprised audience, he stipulated that central government would promote projects through specific grants to enable schools and their local authorities to address certain issues. Joseph's first two priorities in this form of specific as opposed to general grant were the Low Attainers Project (LAP) and the Technical and Vocational Education Initiative (TVEI), controversially managed through the Manpower Service Commission (MSC) as part of the Department of Business which, run by Kenneth Baker, simultaneously introduced the first computers into schools.

Joseph's decision paved the way for national interventions such as the literacy and numeracy strategies in primary schools, followed closely by a growing set of wider national strategies, Education Action Zones (EAZs), Excellence in Cities (EiC), the London Challenge and the consequential Greater Manchester and Black Country Challenges. In turn, central government evolved local solutions to target help for needy communities – for example, the opportunity areas established by Education Secretary Justine Greening. In the years before and after this range of substantial focused initiatives, there had been a multitude of smaller and annually varied targeted interventions for which LEAs could bid for (or not) as specific grants to use with their schools.

None of our ministerial witnesses, with the possible exception of Gillian Shephard, thought they had too much power. Over the years, however, the product of so much legislation – there were just a handful of Education Acts of Parliament between 1944 and 1980 and there have been almost 50 since – has been to centralise power at the expense of local government and, in some important respects, the schools. As a consequence, successive secretaries of state, empowered by so many Education Acts, have not been able to resist meddling in what schools do. They have pronounced not just on the curriculum and what is taught, but also on how it is taught. Nick Gibb, for example, is credited not just with giving priority to the basic skill of reading but also prescribing a particular form of phonics. He also determined the approach to be used to teach subtraction in the revised national curriculum. He and all other ministers were enabled to do this by Joseph's trail-blazing initiatives with LAP and TVEI.

It is tempting for a secretary of state to want to make a mark not just for reasons of legacy but also as a means of political advancement and occasionally as a personal whim. Michael Gove's sending of a King James Bible to every school in 2010 was the most public and well-known example of this tendency. Almost all incumbents of the post since the Education Act 1988 have been tempted to extend their range of interference in matters formerly left to local decision-makers, whether by the schools themselves or local authorities. Hence the increased legislation.

Local authorities have been progressively stripped of their educational powers and responsibilities during the period of markets, centralisation and managerialism. Successive iterations of the rules of local financial management (LFM) in schools, as a means of distributing money for schools' budgets, removed from LEAs the capacity to set their own educational priorities. From 2006, LEAs began to be called local authorities and hence, almost symbolically, lost their clear responsibility. Since 2010 and the imposition of austerity measures, and the simultaneous encouragement of schools to seek academy status, local democratic influence has diminished precipitously as shrinking local authorities have been stripped of powers and cash through cuts in government grants and centrally imposed limits on their ability to increase revenue via household council tax and business rates.

For schools that have become academies, however, the perverse outcome has been that, having acted on central government's encouragement to become academies to avoid being dependent on (and controlled by) local authorities, they have often ended up being more dependent on (and controlled by) a distant but nevertheless interfering national government in the form of the DfE and the Education Funding and Skills Agency (EFSA), through whom they have a contract directly with the secretary of state. For those schools that have joined a MAT, life has become even more controlled. As David Bell told us: '[Some schools] have far less autonomy than they would have had in the most interfering LEA of old. Some are told exactly what to do and have no governing body to support or challenge them. It is bizarre, and I often wonder if this is really what Michael Gove intended.' In effect, this group of academies – about a third of state-maintained schools by 2020 – are obliged to become a hybrid of private limited company and charitable body.

Meanwhile, the schools themselves have exchanged power over the curriculum, which in the first post-war age was left almost entirely to them, for almost complete power over how they spend their budgets. (Although, ironically, some schools that have joined a MAT very recently have found that the process of delegation has been reversed, as the chief executive of the MAT and the trust board decide what policies and practices they must adopt and, in some cases, how they should spend their budget.)

If that broadly describes what has happened in the two educational ages that sandwiched the last period of doubt and disillusion, it is perhaps appropriate to draw up a balance sheet of successful and less successful interventions and characteristics of the two periods, as well as considering why efforts to effect change were more or less successful. We will do that in each of the following chapters.

In concluding this chapter, however, it may be helpful to attempt both to clarify the different emphases, values and beliefs that drove the two ages and to sketch out briefly what it has been like in schools. In short, what was the climate like which influenced the weather as teachers worked in their classrooms and schools?

The different emphases and values that drove the two ages

As we have noted, the experience of the Second World War heavily influenced the schooling system, but the Beveridge-inspired belief that the state had a role and duty to defeat ignorance played an even larger role. Teachers felt part of that noble cause and many men – and it was men – returned from the war to undergo 'emergency training' to become teachers in primary schools.

Temple's quotation earlier in this chapter perhaps helps to explain our concern about the application of *unbridled* competitive principles to schooling when the pupils are not yet adults. For an individual pupil or student to compete against their own previous best should be – and often is – the starting point for the teacher's intervention to encourage learning. It will be the governing principle of the teacher's feedback to the student. However, a good teacher would not allow a vulnerable pupil, or one who is in the foothills of learning, to compete with another who is far ahead in a test of skill, proficiency or knowledge learned. It would be pointless, even damaging, for both, although the more expert pupil helping the other is, of course, to be encouraged.

This raises another question, namely: how to secure collaboration while not sacrificing the vital goal of personal improvement? They are not mutually incompatible, as team games show, but they are elusive among schools if they are in public competition with one another for pupils. Applying competitive principles among schools is less dangerous, but in our experience it can militate against schools learning from each other or cooperating wholeheartedly in pooling resources to handle the learning of those pupils presenting the most opposition or potential detriment to the efforts of the school.

However, the Temple quotation embodies an approach markedly different from that which has prevailed in either age, especially the second, which is often represented as one where the actions of the individual are dominant in shaping prosperity. We were not able to talk to Keith Joseph among our secretaries of state for education since 1976, for obvious reasons. He is widely credited with being the decisive influence on Mrs Thatcher's thinking; she once famously said: 'there is no such thing [as society]! There are individual men and women … and no government can do anything except through people and people look to themselves first.'[18] Joseph's views – which, in fairness, are not typical of any of our witnesses – were reminiscent of his Victorian predecessors:

> We have a bloody state system, I wish we hadn't got. I wish we'd taken a different route in 1870. We got the *ruddy* state involved. I don't want it. I don't think we know how to do it. I certainly don't think Secretaries of State know anything about it. But we're landed with it. If we could move back to 1870 I would take a different route. We've got compulsory education, which is a responsibility of

---

18   D. Keay, Aids, Education and the Year 2000! [interview with M. Thatcher], *Woman's Own* (31 October 1987). Available at: https://www.margaretthatcher.org/document/106689.

hideous importance, and we tyrannise children to do that which they don't want, and we don't produce results.[19]

Joseph was full of commendable self-doubt, so he didn't introduce any legislation to give reality to the ideas of choice, autonomy, diversity and accountability which ministers in this second age hoped would lead to excellence. That was left to his successor, Kenneth Baker, to start and for every one of his successors, including those of New Labour (1997–2010), to continue.

What was it like to be in schools in the two ages?

In the primary sector in the first 20 years after the war, the only national advice about practice came in the form of a booklet, *Story of a School*, published in 1949 and reissued twice in the 1950s, with a ministerial fore-word explaining that it was written by a practising head of what Ofsted would now call an 'outstanding school' and encouraging other schools to use their professional judgement to do similarly creative things with their school.[20] Until the Plowden Report in 1967, it was all that primary heads had to guide them.[21]

Only a handful of LEAs had primary school advisers, so schools were left to their own devices professionally, even if they were dependent on the LEA to fix their buildings, install a telephone when that invention became ubiquitous and supply all manner of things, from light bulbs to exercise books to toilet rolls. If they were in a rural county setting, they reported to a set of 'managers', mainly local worthies; in an urban authority, it could and often did take the form of the LEA's school subcommittee, which ran through all the head teachers' termly school reports, which focused mainly on resources and staff changes. The LEA also allocated and deployed newly qualified teachers (NQTs) to schools from a 'pool'.

---

19   K. Joseph quoted in S. Ball, *Politics and Policy Making in Education: Explorations in Policy Sociology* (Abingdon and New York: Routledge, 1990), p. 62; original emphasis.
20   Ministry of Education, *Story of a School*. Pamphlet No. 14 (London: HMSO, 1949).
21   B. Plowden, *Children and their Primary Schools: A Report of the Central Advisory Council for Education (England)* [Plowden Report] (London: HMSO, 1967). Available at: http://www.educationengland.org.uk/documents/plowden.

The main public relations concern of the LEAs, but only in a few better-off neighbourhoods, was how many pupils passed the 11+, which sorted the sheep from the goats – that is, who would go on to a grammar or a secondary modern school. Girls did rather better than boys in the exam, so their marks were lowered, consequently making it harder for them to 'pass'. In all local areas, the proportion of pupils that passed was limited by the number of places available in the grammar schools. This was the beginning of the use of unfair 'norm-referencing' exam and assessment models which still prevail today. Teachers believed that intelligence was general, inherited and predictable; hence, the 11+ was theoretically underpinned by the research (subsequently exposed as partly invented) of educational psychologist Cyril Burt.[22]

If they were lucky, teachers in urban areas had access to Teachers' Centres where courses ran in twilight hours and on Saturdays for keen practitioners. In most schools, someone might acquire a reputation for being good with top juniors (Year 6), while another colleague might be a wizard in getting children to read. However, about 20% of children were still reportedly emerging from school illiterate. To capture a graphic picture of what was happening in primary schools, we recommend *The Harpole Report* by J. L. Carr, which, while a work of fiction, gives a recognisably truthful and amusing impression of that world by an author who was both a respected head teacher and a remarkable writer.[23]

To be in a primary school or academy today is vastly different, and not just as a result of Ofsted inspections, SATs, phonic and baseline tests, and a prescribed curriculum with frequent nationally imposed changes of emphasis and content, together with fierce accountability. The theoretical class size limit in primary schools has been reduced from 40 to 30, but the substantial extra resources made available during the New Labour years were stripped away again under the coalition and Conservative governments from 2010.

The world of secondary schools changed in the second period too – and not just, like their primary colleagues, in providing for more pupils

---

22   Sir Cyril Burt was a psychologist for London County Council (1913–1931) and later appointed as a professor of psychology at University College London, where he remained until his retirement in 1951. He was a eugenicist, a supporter of the view of general and inherited intelligence, and a creator of the IQ tests used in the 11+. His research to support these theories was discredited after his retirement when it was found that he had falsified the evidence about identical sets of twins allegedly brought up in different circumstances on which his theory of intelligence depended.

23   J. L. Carr, *The Harpole Report* (London: Secker and Warburg, 1972).

presenting with more challenges, for one reason or another, and trying to unlock their talents. Results days for external exams at GCSE and A level are now occasions when staff are present and where pupils' futures (as well as some of their own) are an occasion for acute anxiety, celebration and/or disappointment. Before the publication of results in the early 1990s, pupils' exam results were sent to their homes by pre-written self-addressed letter cards: all very low-key.

Most of the attempts to bring about change have been focused on the secondary sector, whether it was, as at the start of our story, still coming to grips with an unexpected rise in the school leaving age for which many were unprepared, or living through the move to comprehensive reorganisation for which many were also unprepared, or the huge shift in approach in urban areas as a result of EiC, which was introduced by the New Labour government. EiC involved identifying and then making provision for 'gifted and talented' children or the deployment of learning mentors. It also signalled an end to the attitude of 'What more can you expect from children from this sort of background?' Records of achievement have come and gone; exams have been changed time and time again.

As we will show in Chapter 12, what made the New Labour period different was that, in general, it was accompanied by significantly more cash, albeit with accountability targets for pupil outcomes that were rigorously enforced. What has followed since is austerity coupled with further changes, such as the introduction of the English Baccalaureate (EBacc) and modifications to the assessment arrangements to remove coursework and therefore teacher assessment.[24]

Society has changed too. For example, medical advances mean that more babies survive childbirth and infancy, and in some cases this means more children in mainstream classes with special educational needs and disabilities (SEND), for whom provision has changed enormously over the years. LEAs first began providing for children who previously had been deemed 'ineducable' in 1971, following an Act in the previous year, which transferred responsibility from health to education and renamed junior training centres (JTCs) as special schools for the educationally sub-normal

---

24 One of the surprising effects of the COVID-19 pandemic on schools has been the realisation, commented on by many of our witnesses, that teachers whose careers span just the last 10–15 years have no experience of externally moderated teacher assessment. This is a feature of teachers in England rather than their counterparts in Wales and Scotland who have retained teacher assessment as part of their system.

(severe) (ESN(S)). The whole special school sector received the first of its many attentions from government following the Warnock Report of 1978, which changed our thinking on how to educate children with what turns out to be an ever-growing list of definable and different disabilities.[25] It launched a movement, still strong and certainly unresolved, focused on the desirability of what we have called 'inclusion'. We will return to this issue in Chapter 9.

The concept of inclusion gradually widened, moving out from SEND to consider the needs of children from disadvantaged backgrounds. The Every Child Matters agenda grew from some examples of terrible cruelty to children, and its principles were enthusiastically embraced by schools. While data gradually exposed poorer school achievement related to poverty, the government has supported schools with resources or initiatives, while at the same time expressing frustration or exasperation if improvement (as measured by data) was not swift enough. But, as the accountability system tightened and stakes heightened, schooling began to game the system, with the casualties being pupils excluded or lost to schooling. As the proportion of schools judged good grew, the tail of despair grew longer.

For all teachers since the 1988 Education Act, there are at least five in-service education and training (INSET)/continuing professional development (CPD) days – still called 'Baker days' by some schools after the minister who introduced them. Before that it was unusual for staff to be in school when the pupils were on holiday.

The way teachers exercise their professional development has changed too. Teachers' Centres have closed to be replaced by TeachMeets and online groups which exchange useful ideas. Planning, preparation and administration (PPA) time for classroom teachers has been introduced. The way we introduce teachers to the profession has also been transformed with a comparatively vast range of routes to qualification.

Perhaps the biggest change between the age of trust and optimism and that of markets, centralisation and managerialism has its roots in two pieces of research in London. The first, Michael Rutter's *Fifteen Thousand Hours* in 1979, illustrated what seemed to be the features that influenced comparative success in secondary schools, and the second, Peter

---

25 H. M. Warnock, *Special Educational Needs: Report of the Committee of Enquiry into the Education of Handicapped Children and Young People* [Warnock Report] (London: HMSO, 1978).

Mortimore's *School Matters*, did the same for primary schools.[26] Apart from a few LEAs, it took more than a dozen years for national policy-makers to catch up with the significance of this research in drawing attention to what came to be seen as a consideration of 'school effectiveness' and, eventually, as the need for 'school improvement'.

Certainly, until Gillian Shephard became secretary of state, education was not a dominant feature of national policy. In a way not generally recognised, she paved the way for David Blunkett to fulfil Blair's clarion call of 'education, education, education' as his priority for the 1997 general election campaign. She recalled to us:

> I have just been looking at John Major's autobiography, in which he includes a long passage on how he thinks that education is the most important policy area for any government. He lays out a series of priorities, such as keeping assisted places and having more grant-maintained schools, publication of school test results and an independent inspectorate. He also mentions his enthusiasm for early years, specifically nursery places, and that his preferred solution is for a voucher scheme, and for more technical education and expansion of the university sector.
>
> I must say, I never heard all this articulated in one go when I was in government, but it is certainly the case that quite a lot of it was achieved with more or less success, and there is no doubt about his sincerity. He also certainly did say, when appointing me to the department, that it was because 'I knew about education'. And it would be fair to say that he had a clear picture of where he wanted to go with education policy – quite as clear as Blair's. It is also the case that because he had such a slender majority, a lot of his clarity on these policies was crowded out by events, the ERM [exchange rate mechanism] crisis, rebellions and so on.
>
> Looking back, therefore, it was a compliment to be asked by him to achieve all this! ... But it was still a real disappointment not to be supported by him in the spending round before the 1997

---

26   M. Rutter, B. Maughan, P. Mortimore and J. Ouston, *Fifteen Thousand Hours: Secondary Schools and Their Effects on Children* (Cambridge, MA: Harvard University Press, 1979) and P. Mortimore, P. Sammons, L. Stoll, D. Lewis and R. Ecob, *School Matters: The Junior Years* (Somerset: Open Books, 1988) revolutionised thinking on school effectiveness and school improvement. Before their work, the conventional wisdom, backed by research, was that social factors explained differing outcomes between schools.

election, and even more of a disappointment that people like Brian Mawhinney and John Redwood insisted that we included promises on increasing the number of grammar schools in the manifesto for that election – something I opposed and knew absolutely that it would make no difference to the result. During the election itself, I crossed paths with John Major … and he said in passing that the grammar schools pledge did not seem to be having the reception he had expected.

Shephard also recalled that she'd had successful meetings involving Blair, Major and Blunkett to pave the way for policy continuity with regard to higher education and getting rid of the binary line between universities and the rest of the provision for students over 18 years of age.[27] Her small interventions, with specific grants to LEAs for primary English and maths, were forerunners of the literacy and numeracy hours presented by Michael Barber during the early years of the Blair government in his role as head of the DfE's newly established Standards and Effectiveness Unit. Shephard also established the pilot leadership programmes – the National Professional Qualification in Headship (NPQH) and Headteacher Leadership and Management Programme (HeadLAMP) – thus paving the way for the establishment of the National College for School Leadership (NCSL). The catalogue of acronyms was growing.

Our point is that these were the years when schools were receiving a combination of much more money, attention and, consequently, accountability, and in turn became much more managerial in outlook. Managerial is more subtle than 'managed' or 'organised'. It occurs when the management of a school or community of schools is subject to detailed processes and procedures which reduce the wider influence of participants who thereby become intent on meeting accountability requirements, providing evidence of efficiency rather than effectiveness, and are scrutinised rather than provided with support.

One further change was taking place which aided managerialism and led to a shift in emphasis in the aims of schooling. The use of data, which the DfE had ignored in its dealings with schools and LEAs until the mid-1990s, enabled policy-makers at a national level to observe inequalities

---

27   David Blunkett confirmed in our interview his high regard for Gillian Shephard and seemed to know in impressive detail the salient points of her memoir, *Shephard's Watch: Illusions of Power in British Politics* (London: Politico's Publishing, 2000). Polytechnics and other higher education institutions (e.g. colleges) would all be called universities and funded from the same body.

in outcome. That data was made possible and more manageable and easier to categorise and interrogate through the introduction and rapid development of computer technology. Equality of opportunity, differential outcomes and now social mobility have gradually become accepted priorities across all political parties. They may differ in respect of their preferred methods of achieving these three ambitions, but there is common ground – in a way there was not in the 1980s and 1990s – that they are important aims of schooling generally.

All those we interviewed, especially the politicians, agreed on the desirability of using schooling as a vehicle for greater equity, equality and social mobility in society. We hadn't expected politicians from both right and left to agree on this, but then it dawned on us that they – and many other of our witnesses – meant different things when using the same words. For example, did they mean equality of opportunity, of input or of outcome? Did they mean by social mobility that it was relative – that is, in a meritocratic society, that everyone, not just the privileged, has the chance to get the top jobs but that for every person going up the mobility ladder someone also has to come down? Or was it absolute, and that there should be a review, for instance, of the relative salaries of those whom we have all come to call and appreciate as 'key workers' during the pandemic?

We were reminded, therefore, of the need to clarify what we mean by these terms. Many in education have come to realise the distinction through the well-known image of three children of varying heights watching a baseball game over a fence, which was originally created by Craig Froehle.[28]

Adapted by Dave Bull from the original image by Craig Froehle

---

28   See C. Froehle, The Evolution of an Accidental Meme, *Medium* (14 April 2016). Available at: https://medium.com/@CRA1G/the-evolution-of-an-accidental-meme-ddc4e139e0e4#.pqiclk8pl.

Equality sees all the children standing on a box of the same height, while equity sees the boxes adjusted in height so that all the children have the same opportunity to see. The final scene shows an adjustment to the fence itself to ensure equity for everyone. The image is unidimensional in the sense that it deals only with the issue of height: giving everybody what they need to make them sufficiently tall to have a fair view of the game. It begs lots of questions for those of us in education because achieving equity via schooling is multidimensional. (What if one of the spectators has poor eyesight, for example?) We need different solutions for different purposes. In schools, as well as eyesight problems, there are pupils with hearing loss, with neurodiverse conditions and with cognitive, emotional and socio-economic difficulties, and they lead us to ask how all pupils, whatever their talents and differences, receive what they need in order to succeed. But succeed in what way?

That is why we need to be clear about the purpose of schooling. Michael Gove told us: 'Every child should have access to the best that has been thought and written. Every child should leave school fully literate and numerate.' Is that *all* we want from schooling?

We set out in this book what we think the purpose of schooling should be, and if our hope is that all pupils grow up to lead fulfilled lives as citizens who contribute to the fulfilment of others, then that is where equality is relevant. It will demand responsive provision for young people, not just the same for all or equal for all, and it will involve not prejudging a pupil's potential or categorising them based on spurious criteria. To promote true equity, some individuals will need more resources and more time; pupils who live with disadvantage and those with SEND are obvious examples. On the other hand, spending four times as much on already privileged children in private schools seems inequitable. These are vital issues that we will explore.

The age of markets, centralisation and managerialism has been on the brink of decline for a few years; a mood of intolerance and the search for hope and ambition was stirring with positive collaboration acting as a stimulus. Whether that is because of, or despite, Michael Gove and Nick Gibb's assault on the status quo from 2010 is not really at issue. It was in the air as the unexpected and tumultuous coronavirus pandemic threw the world, our country and our schools back on their own initiative. All of the managerial hours spent on risk assessments over the last 20 years, all of the hours spent by strategic leaders on developing mitigation measures to put on charts and colour red, amber or green counted for nothing. It seemed that virtually nobody turned to their plans, but rather fell back on goodwill, initiative, decent human kindness and commitment to their school, community and cause.

As COVID-19 subsides, for now, there is a widespread belief that we should look to 'build back better'. We suggest that we should not think back but forward. We should build forward together and resist seeking simply to be better than we were back in 2020, but instead strive to establish, with 2050 in mind, a school system working to achieve agreed purposes in a series of collaborative partnerships, with clear and shared ambitions and fuelled by hope. Some would argue that hope will only take us so far; but it will take us a lot further than we realise when we acknowledge that hope is continuously recharged by the success of our schools and the pupils within them.

The aims, values and purposes outlined at the beginning of this chapter are touchstones for the recommendations we will make in each of the following chapters. First, we will explore the role of the secretary of state and how their work is perceived by themselves and others. What we find is that most have a hand on the tiller for a brief period, but a few have created the agenda for change that we have outlined in this chapter. What we see now is a school system that has much to commend it and could achieve yet more if certain barriers were removed and new steps forward were made possible. Each of those barriers is addressed in subsequent chapters.

We believe that after the pandemic there should not be a wish to get back to the schooling world before COVID, just as there was no wish to return to the 1930s after 1945. Instead, we need a determination to create a new educational age – a time of hope, ambition and collaborative partnerships. We signpost the changes that will lead us to that world in what follows as we seek to improve on previous best.

Chapter 2
Do politicians make a difference?

Do they help or hinder? Who creates the climate in which teachers work?

In this chapter, we explore the various influences in the school system since 1976 as we moved from the age of optimism and trust into doubt and disillusion and then onwards into markets, centralisation and managerialism. We examine the world that many in schools do not experience or even appreciate exists; they know that something is changing in their working life but often wonder how and why.

We begin by looking at the function of the secretary of state, explore the influences on them and the way the system has changed – for good or ill. We consider the work of our secretaries of state as they reveal their style, doubts, hopes, fears and humanity; after all, they are only human in a political world.

When Nadhim Zahawi took up his new role in September 2021, he became the twentieth secretary of state for education in the 45-year period that our book covers. The average length of tenure was just over two years and three months. The longest incumbent was Keith Joseph at four years and eight months. Only 11 were in post for more than two years. The shortest tenure was that of Alan Johnson at one year and one month. Five went on to one of the three great offices of state (Kenneth Baker, Kenneth Clarke, David Blunkett, Charles Clarke and Alan Johnson). It is hardly a job that offers the chance to embed policy, practice or belief. Given this musical chairs approach to the role, it is surprising that policy or practice shifts at all.

Broadly, the approach to the role taken by secretaries of state has matched the stages we outline in our analysis of the climate over time. In the period following the end of the war – that time of sometimes misplaced optimism and trust in the schooling system – the outlook from central government seemed to be, 'What can we do *for* our school system?' With limited but increasing resources, an effort was made to support the school system and other public services.

Callaghan's Ruskin College speech acknowledged that there had been a period of growth, but the doubt and distrust he expressed initiated a phase when the government outlook became, 'What can we do *about* our school system?' This concern about how to make progress continued for the next 12 years and through the tenure of three secretaries of state.

Baker's Education Reform Act of 1988, some 12 years later, set central government on the path of asking, 'What can we do *to* our school system?' How can we manipulate the system to make our schooling better? This is the era of markets, centralisation and managerialism.

After 30 years of increased central control, we would suggest that the time is right for a new phase when central government asks, 'What can we do *alongside* our school system?' – a period of ambition, purpose and collaborative partnership.

Four secretaries of state seem to us to have made a significant impact in moving policy and practice. Kenneth Baker, David Blunkett, Ed Balls and Michael Gove each brought new emphasis, urgency and drive for new expectations; they changed gear. Each was met by questions from the profession and beyond about their strategy. Each grappled with the complexity of the educational hinterland and the tangle of what went before in trying to create a new order. Each centralised the agenda yet further, but whether this was intentional and by design is unclear.

Andreas Schleicher of the Organisation for Economic Co-operation and Development (OECD) reflected:

> About centralisation ... I'm not even sure that this is something the Department for Education ever wanted to do but it's the inevitable consequence of a weak profession. If you eliminate the kind of middle layers of the administration, and then you don't have teachers who are well organised professionally, you end up doing the work yourself. I think it has been not intentionally driven as a centralisation of effort. It is more that nobody else took care of the issues.

He talked about other nations and jurisdictions where school leadership is instrumental in co-constructing the school improvement agenda: 'If you are a school leader in Finland, you spend two-thirds of your time at your school and one-third of your time in the local authority to manage your schools, to design the policies that you have to implement with your colleagues or other schools.' Our system increasingly sees school leadership in a branch manager capacity, carrying out the policies and practices determined by the centre. Today's talk of a 'self-improving school system' is seen by many as a smokescreen; the system will improve as long as schools improve themselves, rather than the system itself seeking to be self-improving.

We can trace the move towards centralisation in the chronology of development. Our account begins as Shirley Williams sought to bring people together in an increasingly criticised system by building on Callaghan's call for a Great Debate. She failed to reach a consensus before the general election three years later, which left her two conservative successors, Mark Carlisle and Keith Joseph, trying to work out what to do *about* schooling.

Kenneth Baker grabbed the agenda in 1988 with his Education Reform Act, which wrestled the school system into the grip of central government. He set in train the extended period of central government doing things *to* schooling. David Blunkett drove this central agenda into classrooms and teachers' daily lives with his national strategies for literacy and numeracy. Ed Balls brought social care and education together within a multi-agency approach under the banner of Every Child Matters which had five outcomes for children. Michael Gove carried out wholesale reform of every aspect of schooling. The two conservatives, Baker and Gove, were open about their perceived need for major system reform and the need for increased momentum. The two labour secretaries, Blunkett and Balls, expressed their mission as seeking to accelerate the reach and benefit of the school system.

After three secretaries of state whose tenures were marked by abundant energy and pressure on the system to shift, there came a period of relative calm, sometimes leading to drift; the momentum developed by Balls was stalled by a general election defeat. However, his successor, Gove, instigated a controversial period of turbulence and a rapid change of direction, which was perceived by many as a reversal and by others as a welcome return to tradition.

Our conversations with the secretaries of state were revealing in terms of what they tried to achieve, where they felt they had succeeded, what problems they faced and how they had addressed them. Their perception of the relationships they had with other parts of the system, including schools themselves, was also illuminating.

All were committed to doing a good job. At the end of each interview we were left feeling we had learned something subtly different about the role and had spent time with a decent human being. They all cared. Each of the prime ministers for whom they served was mentioned at various times as being interested in education and seeing it as a priority, although the Blair/Brown years pick themselves out as an exceptional time when education was *the* national priority. Each secretary of state had enjoyed their time at education to an extent, some clearly more than others. They all talked with purpose and commitment about the progress they made and the solutions they found, while at the same time recognising some of the failings and shortcomings both in the schooling system and in the policies they pursued.

How is it that genuinely decent, competent and thoughtful people often find it so difficult to make progress, to take many people, including teachers, with them and to secure the sort of school system of which the nation can be consistently proud? They have had experiences that help them to learn how to run things, they have values and beliefs that they bring to bear, they have feelings and foibles, and they react to circumstances. However, when they are appointed as secretary of state for education, they are taking on one of the most complex public services – a service that is a universal provider for every child, with schooling just part of their remit. The education brief includes early years, further education, universities, apprenticeships, adoption and fostering, prison education and more. It is a daunting task. We teased out from our conversations some of the themes that determine the extent to which their period in office had been a success.[1]

---

1   Estelle Morris cited her lack of experience and understanding of higher education as her reason for resigning, unusually declaring she was 'not up to the job' – ironically prompting the comment from so many teachers in schools that she was the only one who was 'up to the job'.

Most have no notice that they will be doing the job

Nearly all our secretaries of state told us that they had no notice of their appointment. There were a few exceptions that prove the rule. Michael Gove had been shadow education secretary for three years before the coalition government replaced Labour in 2010, while David Blunkett told us: 'I remember in 1994 that Tony [Blair] and I had dinner in the kitchen at his place one evening. It was a tester to see whether his ideas on educational reform and mine could be compatible, given our very different backgrounds. We knew the focus had to be on standards.'

Generally, though, we heard stories of people being unaware that they would be appointed to cabinet or to which department. Estelle Morris, who had served with Blunkett for four years, told us that she had been so consumed by retaining her marginal constituency in the 2001 general election that she had barely given any thought to her role in the new parliament if elected. She had been miles away on a prearranged visit to a school when she was asked to make the walk along Downing Street for the benefit of the cameras and be appointed by the prime minister.

Some had a blank sheet. Kenneth Baker told us: 'When I was appointed by Margaret [Thatcher], I went in and I thought I would get a list from her, but she didn't tell me to do anything in education. Margaret said, "Go away, work up your ideas and come back to me in three weeks' time." I was amazed.'

In her autobiography, Shirley Williams tells the story of being approached by James Callaghan and having concerns because of a possible compromise between her own daughter's schooling and Labour policy: 'I told Jim it would be very difficult. He was getting understandably irritated. "You are hard to please," he said. I knew I couldn't expect him to leaf his way through every cabinet post, like someone trying to sell a suit, so I agreed to do it.'[2]

Ruth Kelly arrived as a result of a reshuffle:

> I had spent three months at Number 10 in the Cabinet Office, where I was effectively running the policy unit and then David

---

2   Williams, *Climbing the Bookshelves*, p. 226.

Blunkett resigned on 14 December 2004. I was called into Number 10 and was given a minute or so to reflect (as most people are) and I accepted the role. I had no sense that this was going to happen. I had just changed jobs – I was just getting used to the environment. It was a huge shock to the system, but I usually take the view with regard to myself that if someone else thinks it's a good idea then it probably is, because we are very bad judges of our own capacities.

These sorts of accounts indicate the ad hoc nature of appointment and the almost hand-to-mouth behaviour of government at times, where manifestos take second place to pragmatism in the light of what Harold Macmillan allegedly called, 'Events, dear boy, events.'[3]

Limited experience and poor handover with a lack of preparation and knowledge

Many of those appointed to secretary of state have limited experience, either of education and schooling or of running a government department. Half of our secretaries of state had not served in the cabinet before their appointment. In the case of Michael Gove and David Blunkett, they had neither been a minister nor led a department – and neither had the prime minister they each served.

When Alan Johnson was asked to be universities minister by Tony Blair, who rang him during a car journey, he said, 'You do realise that I left school at 15 with no qualifications.' Blair replied: 'Precisely.'

For some, their arrival is as part of a new prime minister's team, sweeping in as the new government's representative. For others, it is a case of picking up the baton that a colleague has thrown or left hanging in the air on their way out. They don't need new policies; there is plenty of unfinished business from the turbulence of the system reformers to keep them going.

---

3   Macmillan reputedly said this in reply to a question about the most troubling problem of his prime ministership.

Damian Hinds observed: 'You inherit your predecessor's unfinished work and you leave a bundle of things for your successor. There is a bundle of things that inevitably don't get finished in your time in post.' Julia Cleverdon also noted this transitional outlook when she remarked: 'The things I've ever been involved with, which have been led by government, are nearly always a lunch, a launch and a logo ... and then they disappear with the next minister that comes through the door.'

The job involves establishing a remit for themselves without much more than a briefing from the permanent secretary at the department, a pointer in a general direction from the prime minister and a variable dose of understanding of the agenda gained from their previous links to education, which are sometimes slight.

Kenneth Baker summarised the handover to him in 1983:

> Keith Joseph gave me a little list of problems he was dealing with. One was whether the Japanese way of teaching the violin was appropriate or not. Another was how could you use visiting teachers in rural areas to increase the teaching of the minority subjects. But they weren't central issues in the department. I remember there was one physics professor who tried to think about curriculum change and that was about it! There was no real prospect of change.

Few could match the comment made by Mark Carlisle, Thatcher's first secretary of state for education in 1979: 'I never expected to be made secretary of state for education ... I had no direct personal knowledge of the state sector, either as a politician, pupil or parent.'[4]

For Ruth Kelly, though, it was sink or swim: 'I went in straight at the deep end with the first big speech being the North of England Conference, which I wrote over that Christmas holiday. I had four small children of 6 and under – the youngest was 1 – and in retrospect it was probably too much to ask anybody to do: bringing up four very small children as well as holding a very high-profile cabinet job. But I did enjoy it enormously.'

Damian Hinds explained how the agenda falls into place: 'When you are appointed, you turn up with 10 priorities and the civil servants give you another 10, so that is 20 that are really important. Everyone tells you that

---

4   P. Ribbins and B. Sherratt, *Radical Educational Policies and Conservative Secretaries of State* (London and New York: Network Continuum, 1997), p. 55.

you should focus on three top priorities, but with the breadth of what the department covers, I don't see how, realistically, you could be that narrow in your top priority list.'

Nicky Morgan picked up more than just Michael Gove's agenda: 'I inherited the "Trojan Horse" issue in Birmingham. People in the DfE wanted to lodge that with the Home Office but I believed that schools should be helped by the DfE.'

While also adjusting to a set of competing demands, for a good proportion of our secretaries of state the agenda they were managing had been set some years previously. Damian Hinds explained: 'It is never completely up to you in politics. There's always Number 10, the Cabinet Office, the matter of finance, the parliamentary party and so on.'

For Gavin Williamson, much of the agenda was defined for him in a way that nobody could have expected. The 'urgent' policy issues of two years previously seemed almost trivial in comparison with the organisational difficulties he had to manage during the pandemic, which were probably more complex than any since the logistical practicalities of schooling during the mass evacuation of children from cities during the Second World War. Williamson seemed to believe that, contrary to the popular image, he had pursued a productive policy agenda after his appointment following the 2019 general election. He told us:

> When I got to the department, the cupboard was actually quite bare in terms of policies and initiatives. I think we've actually driven so much change, in spite of the turmoil. I'm incredibly proud of that. All the way through the pandemic we really drove the legislation, and despite the pandemic and all the stuff that was going on, we were able to bring the White Paper forward which led to the Skills [and Post-16 Education] Bill being introduced into Parliament. I genuinely believe that the things we have put in place are going to matter.

Nadhim Zahawi, moving to education from the role of minister for COVID vaccine deployment, has taken up responsibility for a range of contentious issues including exams and initial teacher education (ITE). He will also be grappling with the repercussions of the policy direction set by Michael Gove and pursued by Nick Gibb, while at the same time shaping schooling to address more recent government imperatives, such as 'levelling up'. How will any eye-catching initiatives be received? His school standards minister, Robin Walker, told us: 'There's a huge focus on catch-up and we've inherited the National Tutoring Programme. But there's an opportunity to set a new agenda and to move things forward. What Nadhim is certain of is that we want to make sure that we are taking an evidence-based approach.' He appeared to be open when considering policy areas while holding to some established mantras: 'It's very easy to get fixated on literacy and numeracy but we need to do that, while also maintaining the breadth of the curriculum.'

The few who had significant time to make preparations hit the ground running. David Blunkett used the three years' notice of possible appointment to prepare:

> I had the advantage of being steeped in the issues as shadow minister. I had time to do my homework. I had decided to get advice from working groups. There was Ted Wragg, Michael Barber and Tim Brighouse. I wanted to build on the example of what had been done in Birmingham, particularly in early years and primary. Labour had a history of campaigning for early years, so I was standing on the shoulders of those who had battled before and I wanted to be ready.

Michael Gove not only mapped out the agenda prior to his arrival but also had a campaign plan. Indeed, he seemed to be in campaign mode for much of his tenure.

While he had no notice of his appointment, Ed Balls was probably one of the best prepared. He had served in a range of significant roles in the Treasury for the eight years of the Labour government before he assumed the role as secretary of state for the new Department for Children, Schools and Families (DCSF). He had experience of working for the new prime minister, Gordon Brown, and of his commitment to early years provision, and he had also been close to the standards agenda that Labour had pursued from the outset. He brought a principled commitment and was desperate to make a success of his new role, being ideally placed to bring together the two agendas in the next phase of government.

But handovers can be anything but smooth. The jolt that our secretaries of state reported as they enter their role compares well with the experience of youngsters and their families as they make the transition from primary to secondary school. Estelle Morris took over from David Blunkett, having been a minister for the previous four years, but her core team, chief of staff, press secretary and SpAds all had to be assembled: 'In effect, I reckon we lost a good three months getting sorted out and I was disappointed about that.'

Evidence for decisions and policy direction

Politicians make decisions about the direction of policy. They make those decisions based on a combination of secure evidence, personal outlook (emerging from a whole gamut of experiences) and an anticipation of the impact of their decision. Politicians are no different from the rest of us in making judgements about courses of action on the basis of a range of considerations, the emphasis of which will change in different circum-stances and often appear illogical to others.

Nearly all of our secretaries of state mentioned basing their policies on evidence, but it is where they get that evidence and the importance they place on certain elements that create the policy. One of the decisions they often need to make is whether to continue the policy direction of their predecessors; given the short tenure of many, the policy in question could have been inherited and bequeathed several times. Many policies are enshrined in law, so the question then is whether to let it continue unheeded, to give it added momentum, to slow its pace or to water it down.

Sometimes a secretary of state can reverse a policy direction, as Michael Gove did with the national curriculum in 2010. They can reframe policy, such as the way that David Blunkett managed the issue of grant-maintained schools when Labour took office in 1997. They can also reinvigorate policy, as Kenneth Clarke did when he picked aspects of Kenneth Baker's reforms that he judged were being diluted. When government changes, policies can stop almost overnight; Michael Gove ended the Building Schools for the Future programme within days of taking office on the grounds that it could not be afforded in a climate of austerity. Some policies are pushed through at speed, such as the requirements for Criminal Records Bureau checks,[5] as Ruth Kelly and then Alan Johnson tried to respond to growing public and media concerns.

Nick Stuart, a senior civil servant at the Department of Education and Science in the 1980s, told us about Keith Joseph's views on decisions:

> Keith Joseph didn't really have the courage to do very much. He used to say to me that most government actions end in failure. He gave the ILEA and tower blocks as examples. He used to say, 'Most of the government policies I recall have not been as successful as people anticipated.' He liked to galvanise discussion and thought that things would improve through a shared understanding of the problem.

Kenneth Baker offered a charming reflection on Keith Joseph's tenure when he told us:

> The main reason why I think Keith produced so few policies was that Walter Ulrich [deputy permanent secretary at the Department of Education and Science] seduced him into discussing the philosophy of education on so many occasions, and diverted him. Keith really wasn't an executive. He was far cleverer than I am and more intellectually distinguished than I am. I loved him dearly, but he really didn't have the executive skills to settle matters like the strike which had lasted for 18 months.

So, what leads a secretary of state to a decision or policy direction? It has become the fashion to 'follow the evidence', but how is the evidence assembled? In 1976, and for some time afterwards, the government used the insights of advisory bodies, usually referred to by their initials. The Council for the Accreditation of Teacher Education (CATE),[6] the Schools' Curriculum Council (SCC) and the Council for National Academic Awards (CNAA) came and went as different ministers sought the advice that would suit their purpose. Baker's reforms needed delivery organisations such as the National Curriculum Council (NCC), which were expected to implement rather than advise the system in general.

Throughout the mid-1980s, central government established significant commissions to recommend a course of action on key topics affecting

---

5   The Disclosure and Barring Service (DBS) replaced the Criminal Records Bureau and Independent Safeguarding Authority in December 2012.
6   CATE was responsible for determining the supply of teachers and which colleges of education and universities would provide courses.

schools, which would result in major reports, much awaited and much debated at every level of the system. Examples in our period would be the Bullock Report on English (1975), the Warnock Report on special educational needs (1978), the Cockcroft Report on mathematics (1982), the Elton Report on behaviour (1984) and the Swann Report on equality (1985). These reports were detailed and complex, and the commissions that generated them had members with wide-ranging experience and demanded considerable evidence to support their considerations. What has happened over time, however, is that, as centralisation has grown, central government has tended to build an evidence base for policy more quickly and simply. The analysis of school performance data and Ofsted inspections generate the trends that need to be addressed. Where action was prescribed, secretaries of state would sometimes be expected to ask their own units to produce the evidence in justification.

Another source of evidence comes from reviews as opposed to commissions. Secretaries of state appoint a trusted and respected individual to set out a policy direction. Examples would be the Ajegbo Review on diversity and citizenship (2007), the Macdonald Review on PSHE (2008), the Wolf Review on vocational education (2011) and the Henley Review on music education (2011). All of these reviews, for both Labour and Conservative governments, were carried out relatively rapidly and contain serious proposals based on insights gathered through detailed enquiry. However, they often lack the detailed evidence bases of the major commissions of previous times.

One example of a hybrid was the Crick Review of the teaching of citizenship (1998). As David Blunkett explained: 'We needed an independent panel to dampen down the idea that we were trying to teach party politics. I got Bernard Crick to lead that.'

In December 1991, Kenneth Clarke wanted to push Baker's original agenda forward, so he set up a commission to produce a discussion paper on the organisation and practice of the curriculum in primary education.[7] Its findings led, among other things, to the establishment of Ofsted. This development was an example of a team being established to review an area of schooling at speed, without the usual consideration of extensive evidence and alternative interpretations. This was a turning point in the

---

7   R. Alexander, J. Rose and C. Woodhead, *Curriculum Organisation and Classroom Practice in Primary Schools: A Discussion Paper* [Three Wise Men Report] (London: Department of Education and Science, 1992).

way secretaries of state would gain some justification for policy. From thereon, the tactic has been to engage someone who is known to be 'reliable' to produce a report in support of the policy that has already been determined.

Probably, the last reporting commission was established by Labour soon after the 1997 election and reported two years later under the title, *All Our Futures: Creativity, Culture and Education*, chaired by the fondly remembered Sir Ken Robinson.[8] The expertise that contributed to the report was immense, and so was the disappointment when their recommendations seemed to be shelved. As Labour pushed forward with the standards agenda and its focus on literacy and numeracy, there was considerable resentment from those on the commission – many in influential circles and some of them with celebrity status – about the way the report was received. Two years into the Blair government, the quest for 'education, education, education' was alleged by some to be 'results, results, results' or 'targets, targets, targets'. Those who had thought that the arrival of a Labour government would provide an opportunity to right what they saw as the wrongs in Baker's original national curriculum were frustrated.

As we have observed, each secretary of state had policy priorities, some of their own and some rolling on from a previous incumbent, but as Estelle Morris told us: 'The problem when you say something is a "priority" is that people think that nothing else matters.' This was certainly the case in the Blunkett and Morris years when the national strategies seemed to trump everything else under discussion. Many of our secretaries of state were quick to tell us that they tried to support the world of creativity but, in reality, it was comparatively minimal support and against a backdrop of a massive emphasis on literacy and numeracy.

In the last 20 years, the OECD has furnished politicians with considerable evidence through its triennial testing regime across a growing group of nations and jurisdictions. The Programme for International Student Assessment (PISA), Trends in International Mathematics and Science Study (TIMMS) and Progress in Reading Literacy Study (PIRLS) tests provide streams of comparative data with accompanying analysis that points

---

8   K. Robinson, *All Our Futures: Creativity, Culture and Education. Report of the National Advisory Committee on Creative and Cultural Education* (London: Department for Education and Employment/ Department for Digital, Culture, Media and Sport, 1999). Available at: http://sirkenrobinson.com/pdf/ allourfutures.pdf. Ken Robinson was much-loved figure on the education scene until his untimely death in 2020.

to influences on performance – and, vitally, performance that can be measured. Politicians and the media have been quick to seize on the headlines, comparing the performance of pupils in England against those in other parts of the globe. The data has been used often by secretaries of state to justify their policy direction, although few mentioned international comparisons without prompting in our discussions.

There were examples of policies brought in from elsewhere, often on the basis of a ministerial visit. The charter schools initiative and Knowledge is Power Programme (KIPP) in the United States were adopted and adapted by Labour during Blunkett's years,[9] and more recently some primary schools in England piloted Singapore Maths following ministerial visits to the city-state by Nick Gibb which were linked to exceptional OECD test results.

Andreas Schleicher of the OECD, an organisation which has attempted to spread international understanding and collaboration about policy in schooling, told us:

> I think that many policy mistakes are made because we think we can just buy and plug a fixed set of parameters into a new system, and that rarely works. What the Singaporeans do really well is to go through a thing deeply. They would go to Japan, they would go to China, they would go to the United States. They look at everything, and they asked themselves questions; not just what is the system like but what drives the success of each system? When they have understood that, they try to configure those drivers in their own context to make it work better than in the original place. People from Shanghai went to Atlanta and studied how the pairing of schools operated, but they made it work better in a way. They embedded it more deeply into the education system and it is still operating. It has become part of the philosophy of schools and it has dramatically reduced between-school variation. I think that is the approach: don't copy the solution. They understand the drivers of the success of that solution.

The perception too often in England is that an off-the-shelf solution is being imported from elsewhere and, apart from the selected early

---

9   KIPP began in 1994 after co-founders Dave Levin and Mike Feinberg completed their two-year commitment to Teach for America. A year later, they launched a programme for fifth graders in a public school in inner-city Houston, Texas. Feinberg developed KIPP Academy Houston into a charter school, while Levin went on to establish KIPP Academy New York in the South Bronx.

adopters, the potentially transformative innovation is viewed with suspicion.

For policies less vital than these central ones, prominence is difficult to gain and without momentum is likely to fade. Indeed, the back burner, shelf and long grass are classic places for secretaries of state and/or their advisers to allow policies to rest, whether to avoid negative publicity or to allow other policies deemed more important to take priority. Some issues are simply fit for Charles Clarke's 'too difficult box', which is probably used more than many would care to admit.[10]

The politics of it: balancing what is 'right' with what the party will stomach and the prime minister will support

For all politicians, there is a constant tension between the needs of schools and pupils and the needs of their party in government. For some, understandably, their personal political future means that education policies are influenced by doing what receives credit, sometimes with a landmark or legacy policy.

The influence of Number 10 and the prime minister is always present. Most report a limited level of direction from the prime minister. Nicky Morgan described David Cameron as 'important': 'David Cameron was really interested in education. He had been a shadow minister for a while and I think he would have enjoyed it as a department. He cared.'

Cameron's interest was highlighted when, in 2007, David Willetts, the then shadow minister for education and skills (whose intellect earned him the epithet of 'two brains'), had misjudged the mood and made a conference speech supporting the party's then policy on grammar schools and exposing the unfairness of selection processes. At first Cameron backed Willetts, but later, in what was seen by many as the Tories' 'Clause 4 moment', he described critics as 'clinging on to mantras that bear no

---

10   C. Clarke, *The Too Difficult Box: The Big Issues Politicians Can't Crack* (Hull: Biteback Publishing, 2014). Clarke's book is not about education as such, but pinpoints the difficulty that politicians face when making decisions about long-term controversial issues of great importance to the country.

relation to the reality of life' and 'splashing around in the shallow end of the educational debate'.[11] In the next reshuffle, Willetts was gone and Gove, a close personal friend of Cameron at the time, was installed.

When Cameron became prime minister in 2010, it was as the leader of a coalition. David Laws reflected that:

> Michael Gove was secretary of state, and the prime minister [Cameron] and the deputy prime minister [Nick Clegg] had a very strong interest in education. On the Tory side of the coalition, Cameron's view was to get on with it. He didn't really like interfering in what Michael did and Michael did his best to keep him out of education matters and not involve him on policy until it was pretty much over the wire. That is until he finally demoted Michael.

David Blunkett had a clear brief when Labour entered government: 'In 1994, Tony had insisted on putting education alongside the economy at the top of the agenda so there was no doubt about the direction in which we were heading.'

Estelle Morris, who took over from Blunkett, told us more about prime ministerial policy: 'Tony was never over directive. He was very good at his "tell me what you want to do" approach.' He had three priorities: he wanted to focus on higher education, push autonomy for schools and get a better working relationship with the profession, and be careful with the 16–18 curriculum and qualifications agenda. These were the issues that were now to the fore for the government after their first term in office. Charles Clarke had been asked to keep the policy on track and smooth things over after Estelle Morris' resignation. A few years later, Alan Johnson had been moved into post to settle things down after Clarke's successor, Ruth Kelly, had found herself in controversy.

Some are appointed to calm things down after turbulence. Gillian Shephard, who took over following the abrupt departure of John Patten, revealed: 'The prime minister told me when he offered me the job that he wanted me to bring peace to the education sector' and 'education and

---

11   *BBC News*, Cameron Steps Up Grammars Attack (22 May 2007). Available at: http://news.bbc.co.uk/1/hi/ uk_politics/6679005.stm. David Willetts is generally acknowledged to be one of the most knowledgeable and well-researched politicians.

teachers were of such vital importance to the nation that they could not be put to one side'.[12]

In the same vein, Margaret Thatcher had appointed John MacGregor to follow Kenneth Baker's controversial tenure and with the job of making his reforms work. He described his task as 'not to achieve one of those great creative drives forward in policy change, but rather to make a big change in policy actually work'.[13] MacGregor was portrayed as a more popular secretary of state, although his prime minister became irritated that he was too accommodating to the teaching profession and to the bureaucracy that she believed was complicating and slowing reform.[14]

On appointment, Nicky Morgan reflected: 'The education brief and Michael [Gove] himself had become political hot potatoes. I was asked to ensure the agenda continued, but to try to be less confrontational in style and to talk with parents as much as teachers.' Gove had always anticipated a less than easy ride, though. In a major speech a year into office, he said: 'There will be glitches and hurdles along the way. Reform is untidy business; sweeping reform even more so. There are no smooth revolutions.'[15]

Sometimes, secretaries of state are overtaken by events, a sort of 'sliding doors' moment where schooling could have been different but for certain circumstances. An example occurred at the beginning of John Patten's tenure when he inherited the bill on inspection from Kenneth Clarke. In the rush to get the bill through the Commons before the general election, the government was forced to compromise with the House of Lords over the bill's form and provision. Persuaded by the bishops, the Lords made changes to include the social, moral, cultural and spiritual aspects of the school within the inspection framework. The government acquiesced to ensure that the Education and Inspections Act was passed to make

---

12 Shephard, *Shephard's Watch*, p. 109.
13 Quoted in Ribbins and Sherratt, *Radical Educational Policies and Conservative Secretaries of State*, p. 127.
14 Thatcher believed that Baker's reforms were becoming too complicated and were at risk of losing momentum. Her autobiography (and that of her chancellor, Nigel Lawson) shows that she believed particularly that the proposals for the national curriculum were watering down intentions. For example, she thought more weight should be given to British history and less to interpretation and enquiry – an outlook that continues in a Conservative Party which does not seem to appreciate the link with the Black Lives Matter agenda for which they declare support. See M. Thatcher, *Margaret Thatcher: The Autobiography* (London: Harper Perennial, 2013).
15 Department for Education and M. Gove, Michael Gove's Speech to the Policy Exchange on Free Schools (20 June 2011). Available at: https://www.gov.uk/government/speeches/michael-goves-speech-to-the-policy-exchange-on-free-schools.

sure Labour would not pull back from mass inspection. In the event, the Conservatives were re-elected so it was unnecessary haste. Another change in the same negotiation was to alter the proposed system from one where schools were allocated funding to purchase their own inspection to insist on a centrally managed system – the one we have today.

A further example occurred at the end of the Labour government in 2010 in the 'wash-up' at the end of the parliament. Ed Balls told us how disappointed and upset he was that the Conservatives would not agree to the passing of proposals for sex and relationships education and dramatically stopped the proposed new primary national curriculum in its tracks. In terms of proposals for sex education, Balls said:

> It was all done. We had worked out legally the right way to allow parental engagement and got a piece of legislation. How it works is, when you go into the final wash-up you can only get stuff through that was consensual, and Gove decided to ditch it. Just for the narrowest of rubbish politics. The frustration you have when Conservative ministers start the same discussion again two years later. And that was a really good example of schools, wider agencies, parents and the best interests of the child being frustrated. We built the coalition; the only person we didn't get into it was Gove. David Cameron was happy with it but Gove just blocked it.

A similar moment occurred in respect of developing diplomas and the proposed reforms to 14–19 education. In 2005, with an election approaching and media interest growing, Tony Blair announced that A levels would be strengthened and remain the 'gold standard'.[16] On such moments does our school system turn, and secretaries of state must sometimes despair at the futility and waste of resources as so much work bites the dust.

---

16   See R. Smithers, M. White and L. Ward, Blair Insists A-Levels Will Stay in Shakeup, *The Guardian* (19 October 2004). Available at: https://www.theguardian.com/uk/2004/oct/19/politics.schools.

Whom do they trust and listen to, and how do they use contacts?

The DfE came out of our interviews with many of our secretaries of state in a poor light. From 1976 onwards, there seemed to be a sense of seeing the department as unable to make the necessary difference. At the same time, most believed that local authorities were not fit for purpose. While most secretaries of state talked about schools positively, they also criticised their level of effectiveness. Given the volume of policy change over the years, it is obvious that all felt the need for improvement.

One consistent theme in our conversations was the lack of trust in major parts of the system to get things done. Different ministers tried various approaches, but they felt that they were often met with inefficiency, ineptitude, disloyalty, a lack of commitment, benign opposition or prevarication. Perhaps, given their general lack (in most cases) of experience and expertise in education and (in some) of ministerial office, coupled with poor briefing and the scale of the department's responsibility, it is entirely predictable that an agenda of constant change would be difficult to implement when overlaid on to the routine servicing of the school system.

More than one witness pointed out that until David Blunkett's tenure, the DfE wasn't used to managing things in the same way as other departments. Nick Stuart, whose experience of the DfE stretches from the 1960s to the 2000s, said that the department was at its best when producing policies. 'Other agencies ... LEAs and so on were expected to run things,' said Kenneth Clarke, remembering Stuart fondly 'as a wonderful man to argue with', before reminding us that *Yes Minister* was remarkably accurate and that you needed 'someone to keep records of meetings with top civil servants and remind them frequently what had been agreed so that progress could be made'.[17]

This dissatisfaction, uncertainty and lack of confidence in their own department's capacity to drive the various levels of reform and policy development meant that our secretaries of state were minded to use a range of approaches, techniques and strategies. As most seemed to be of the belief that significant parts of the infrastructure would not work, it is

---

17 *Yes Minister* was political satire which aired on BBC Two in the early 1980s. It consisted of a skit on life at the top of a fictitious government department.

perhaps unsurprising that they turned to other players for advice on how to make it do so or sidestepped it altogether.

The risk, of course, is that these key players – from delivery agencies to influential friends or allies – begin to vie for position, influence, resource or authority, driven by their own particular brand of altruism or ambition. Secretaries of state can find themselves at the centre of a web of organisational intrigue and their political instinct may come to the fore – or not, as the case may be.

With varying degrees of mistrust in the machinery of the system, it is perhaps predictable that the role of ministers of state and SpAds has become increasingly significant in enabling the presentation and progress-chasing necessary to drive the agenda. In the next section of this chapter, we unpick our conversations with a range of key players and tease out some of the issues in policy communication, progress and effectiveness in the school system. We will look in detail at:

- Our secretaries of state and the DfE itself.

- Other angles: the value and use of advice from policy advisers, SpAds, ministers and Downing Street.

- Other voices: the evidence they use, the people they listen to, their contacts, think tanks and unions.

- The deterioration in the relationship between the secretary of state and local authorities.

- The secretary of state and the rise of MATs.

It seems accepted as an unwritten rule that the political system is appropriate because politicians are elected, ministers are selected and they are in a time-limited role until they 'get it wrong', or until they are needed elsewhere because a colleague has 'got it wrong', or until, of course, at an election they are all rejected.

Few of our secretaries of state admitted to failings in themselves, either in their approach or in the wrong steps they may have taken. Ed Balls talked of 'some very difficult times' and had some regrets about the situation that arose around the awful Baby P tragedy when he was children's secretary[18] and the delayed Key Stage 2 test results. Estelle Morris seemed to gain a level of lasting credibility, even affection, through her admission on leaving office in October 2002 that she felt the job was too complex and, 'I have not done the job as well as I should have done.'[19]

While secretaries of state are prey to lobby groups, they seem to be very circumspect about whom they trust. Jim Knight, schools minister for three years from 2006, told us: 'When the pandemic started, I sent a message to one of Williamson's SpAds and said, "I did all this work on home access and I am happy to help if you want to get in touch." I never heard a word.'

Most accept that their policies will be only partially successful and, even then, subject to amendment at a later date. Some are putting right the problems created by previous policies; some are overseeing policies that have no prospect of becoming a reality. As Ed Balls recalled:

> I spent a lot of time on things which, in the end, didn't work. I inherited the diploma programme. You spend hours trying to think about post-16 curriculum reform and trying to build a coalition; the truth was that that had been sold the moment Tony Blair dumped the Tomlinson Report. And there may have been no way back, so we should have done less and should have not tried to rescue these kinds of things.

Some secretaries of state seek to put in place irreversible policies. The prime example of this is Michael Gove with his policy of academies and the parallel fracturing of the local democratic role in schooling: 'Change is coming. And to those who want to get in the way, I have just two words: hands off.'[20]

---

18 Seventeen-month-old Peter Connelly died after suffering a series of horrific injuries inflicted by his mother and her boyfriend over a period of eight months. The London borough of Haringey children's services and other agencies were criticised following his death, particularly as Haringey Council had been involved in the Victoria Climbié case some years previously. The tragedy led to a public inquiry and the dismissal of Sharon Shoesmith as head of children's services at Haringey, although the Supreme Court later ruled that she had been unfairly dismissed. In 2013, Balls told the BBC that he had no misgivings about removing Shoesmith from her post and would do the same thing again: P. Butler, Ed Balls: No Regrets About Sacking Sharon Shoesmith Over Baby P Affair, *The Guardian* (29 October 2013). Available at: https://www.theguardian.com/society/2013/oct/29/ed-balls-sharon-shoesmith-baby-p-sacking-payout.

19 Quoted in P. Curtis, Estelle Morris's Road to Resignation, *The Guardian* (9 January 2003). Available at: https://www.theguardian.com/education/2003/jan/09/schools.uk.

20 Department for Education and M. Gove, The Education Secretary's Speech on Academies at Haberdashers' Aske's Hatcham College (11 January 2012). Available at: https://www.gov.uk/government/speeches/michael-gove-speech-on-academies.

Kenneth Baker is in the position, over 30 years on from his policy reforms, of arguing against certain aspects of them. He chairs and takes a very active role in the Baker Dearing Educational Trust, which promotes a range of university technical colleges (UTCs) for youngsters from the age of 14. His mission is to provide a more balanced experience that brings practical application interwoven with knowledge and abstract concepts in an effort to address the assumptions he acted on in establishing the national curriculum. He bemoans the exam system at 16 and proposed new models of purposeful assessment – in effect, having second thoughts and pulling up his own plants.

Few of our secretaries of state questioned the way in which policy is formed. It is easy for those in classrooms and schools to get the impression that schooling is a plaything and that each secretary of state does different things with it. Some bounce it up and down, some shake it, some roll it and some hit it. Few ignore their toy. Those in the classroom are mostly at the far end of a policy decision. If the partners in the schooling system were figures suspended on a mobile above a baby's cot, they would hang in various layers. The first tier would be the department and below that the local authorities and MATs in an uncertain configuration. There would be other circles of influence too, with characters representing government agencies and related services. Down at the bottom would be the thousands of schools all connected to their various MATs or local authorities.

On rare occasions, usually during school holidays, the mobile is serene; each section is in harmony with the others and the whole mechanism moves gently, touched only by the faintest breeze. When the secretary of state makes a decision, the first layer moves to accommodate it and create turbulence right down to the bottom of the mobile. At other times, decisions made at the top send certain parts of the mobile spinning and, as a result, other parts become unsettled. Some decisions cause the entire system to go into a whirl, although down at the bottom, schools often remain oblivious to it on a daily basis. However, some decisions shake the whole structure, and those at the bottom – the people who work in classrooms – find themselves, sometimes reluctantly, occasionally with grudging acknowledgement, conceding that 'Something needed to be done.'

Occasionally, the mobile is battered by a gale from outside and it needs the top layer to calm things down with a strong and steady hand. The COVID crisis is an example of a situation where the whole system is spinning, with every level trying hard to manage something that is at the limit of their control. What is needed is an authoritative and soothing response, but sadly the hand seemed to delight in flicking at different parts of the mobile and sending them in opposite directions.

Ministers must avoid causing trouble for colleagues or their government

Upheaval is bearable as long as it is planned. What most prime ministers seem not to like is trouble with the media, as that looks as though the agenda is getting away from them. Sometimes, it can be a signal that it is time to move on. Ruth Kelly became secretary of state because of a reshuffle triggered elsewhere in government and left when a fuss over List 99 got stuck in the headlines.[21] Alan Johnson told us: 'Tony wanted me to try to calm things down around the List 99 problem that had bedevilled Ruth Kelly and also to make sure the Education and Inspection Bill made progress. Both were causing problems – the first with the media and the other within our own party.'

Estelle Morris stood down over a problem with A levels; one of our national treasures, departing because of a problem with another of our national treasures. Conversely, with the exam fiasco of 2020, Gavin Williamson was able to cope with the backwash of the 'mutant algorithm' and again with the closure of schools in the following January, presumably because he was serving a prime minister who was more tolerant of such things at a time of national emergency. In the end, though, his more minor errors in media interviews created an image of a hapless incumbent and his departure in the cabinet reshuffle of September 2021 was predictable.[22] When asked about his treatment by the media, Williamson told us it is something that politicians get used to and that complaining would be 'like a fisherman complaining about the rough sea'.

---

21 List 99 was a confidential register of people who were prohibited from working with children in schools and other settings by the Department for Education and Skills. Following various mergers and name changes it became the DBS.
22 Williamson claimed not to remember his A level results in an interview with Nick Ferrari on LBC radio on 10 August 2021 (see https://www.youtube.com/watch?v=aefgFcxMc6M) and then confused rugby player Maro Itoje with soccer player Marcus Rashford in an interview with the *Evening Standard*: S. Butler, Gavin Williamson Interview: 'I've Got the Hide of a Rhino – You Need to in This Job' (8 September 2021). Available at: https://www.standard.co.uk/news/politics/gavin-williamson-interview-education-b954132.html.

On occasion, the secretary of state is moved on because things seem to have reached a stalemate or the splash caused by big boulders is creating too much turbulence. Kenneth Baker's and Michael Gove's reform agendas both eventually reached a point where even the onlookers were tired of the constant strife. John MacGregor succeeded Baker and Nicky Morgan succeeded Gove with similar briefs: quieten it down.

Sometimes problems are of their own making, but often the media question of 'Will they survive?' in respect of a crisis that will not go away is about a matter that the secretary of state has not directly affected. Problems with exams and test results have seen the departure of three chief executives of the Qualifications and Curriculum Authority (QCA) and Ofqual, yet each time questions are asked about the competence of the secretary of state.

When child protection issues make the headlines, especially when a failing in the system can be identified, the media calls for their resignation. Ruth Kelly experienced this when she hit choppy waters: 'I had the whole sex offenders thing to deal with. We were totally reforming the whole system with List 99 and how the whole thing worked for vulnerable adults as well as children. I was in the news for weeks. Alistair Campbell had a saying – if a government minister was in the top three news items for more than 10 days that was it, they were out! I was there for two weeks!'

Riding out the storm is a political imperative for office; no wonder there is a belief that spin is important and working with a closed group of confidantes is vital.

Robin Alexander explained how the Cambridge Primary Review that he led, issuing interim reports regularly over two years from 2007 prior to the final composite report, had been treated:

> It was very sad. The publication of every one of those 31 interim reports, and of course the final report itself, was preceded by discussion of the final drafts with a team headed by the DfE standards adviser, and from time to time we also met ministers. These were amiable discussions in which we discussed the findings in a constructive way. But then much of the press spun them towards the negative and critical and the government found itself on the back foot, responding not to what we had reported but to the media headlines.

I think that's a fairly familiar situation, although I hadn't personally encountered it to that extent before. It was an inevitable consequence of centralisation, for when a government pulls so much control to the centre and things at the periphery go wrong, nobody else can be blamed. But it did tremendous damage to the whole enterprise. Having said that, Labour lost power a few months later and the new government was better disposed towards the review and, indeed, acted on some of its recommendations. And, of course, we built on it with schools over the next seven years through the review network and trust, and that's the legacy that matters.

An exception to the rule in terms of avoiding negative reactions and headlines was Michael Gove, who seemed to positively relish upset and conflict in pushing his agenda. He was gracious enough to tell us openly about his errors. He confided, 'My handling of the closure of Building Schools for the Future was maladroit and insensitive. And there are a number of other examples of clumsy or insensitive announcements I blush to recall. But I think our fundamental reform programme was right and now commands broad support.'

In her book about our political system, Isabel Hardman lists a number of reasons why politicians struggle to do their jobs well. They try to be all things to all men; they only partially understand the agenda and the legislation and fail to see the pitfalls; they become, as she calls it, 'Yes men' and eventually become trapped in the lair of political intrigue within and beyond their own party.[23] When asked to become secretary of state for education, they carry a brief that they must protect, while at the same time playing an active part in other agendas, each supported by a range of factions inside their party.

Their view of reality

Secretaries of state gain a partial view of reality and can easily become stuck in an echo chamber of beliefs and opinions. They hardly ever see real life on the ground. They do visit schools, too often in London, although obviously they see some in their own constituencies. They

---

23   I. Hardman, *Why We Get the Wrong Politicians* (London: Atlantic, 2019).

regularly contribute to conferences, but usually arrive just before and leave just after their platform address, hearing none of the other – sometimes critical – presentations.

Ed Balls talked about trying to get a better understanding of reality:

> We go out and meet people who are doing it. I spoke to John Dunford [from the Association of School and College Leaders] on my first day, actually, and said, 'I want to spend a day with a head teacher in a school which is really challenged but doing well, so I can see from a head teacher that you recommend what works and what doesn't.' The following week, I went and spent a whole day in a school in Banbury. I had never realised Banbury was such a deprived town – it is really, really tough. And so you learn lots of things, and I did that a number of times.[24]

However, when they get to schools, secretaries of state are often treated as a form of royalty, with schools keen to show themselves in their best light. They also tend to be taken by advisers to 'tame' schools – those that are going to say the right thing about their MAT or local authority or about the latest government policy. Heads might make the case for more resources or express their concern about staff workload, but because of the way the visit is managed, they rarely tell it as it is. This is probably due to a mixture of respect for office and fear of the consequences.

Equally, secretaries of state are often restrained with professionals. Most of us have been taught to be polite guests and not to criticise our host. Few secretaries of state would leave a school having made clear their dissatisfaction or discomfort with what they have seen. Yet, given the almost constant implied criticism of what goes on in schools, their visits are likely to produce a significant degree of unease.

These schools have been selected for them because they 'fit', and seldom does the secretary of state see schools at the other end of the spectrum of practice or effectiveness. There are exceptions, though. One secondary head teacher told us: 'Ed Balls visited my school and was very complimentary, but he left me in no doubt that results needed to improve. He said the

---

24 Mick's sister lives in Banbury and doesn't think of it as a 'deprived' town. Parts of most towns and cities, even villages, are deprived. A problem for politicians – indeed, for all of us – is the granular understanding of context. Tim, who lives close by and ran Oxfordshire's education system for 10 years, agrees. He also confirms that Ed Balls had visited the secondary school in Drayton which served the social housing area of Hardwick and Brecht Hill.

school would close if we didn't hit the floor. I knew he meant floor targets, but at the time I thought it a strange ambition to try to aim for the floor.'

One primary head teacher told us about his local MP, who had suggested that she would 'send the minister' to see what the school was doing to help young children in an area of deprivation. He told us: 'I went cold. I wondered how I could explain to staff that Michael Gove was coming. We had always got on so well as a staff, but how would I explain this? I breathed an audible sigh of relief when she said it was David Laws. It was a really positive visit.'

School visits are often accompanied by cameras from the national and local media, so what is seen needs to be acceptable to host and visitor. Both the school and the politician gain a bit of useful publicity and most visitors leave schools feeling better for their presence. But they are not gaining evidence beyond how things can be when a government minister is passing through. They rarely see a 'normal' day in school, if there is such a thing. Equally, they rarely visit a school that is in special measures with an ineffective head teacher who is denying the failings. They seldom see the lunchtime arrangements because they are either travelling between schools or taking the opportunity for a conversation with key people over a lunch elsewhere.

The complexity of the recollections, outlooks, views and opinions of our not exhaustive list of key players tells us that the chances of everyone being in harmony are slim, and that perhaps we expect too much if we imagine that a secretary of state could achieve complete success in educational terms while also grappling with the competing agendas of the communities of interest involved.

Those secretaries of state with a reform agenda, like Baker, Blunkett and Balls (but strangely not Gove), take the opportunity to galvanise significant parts of the community in support of their grand plans. They do so in the knowledge that their party's majority in Parliament gives them significant confidence in their own tenure – a confidence that can override opposition.

Most, though, grapple with the challenge of a hungry media, increasingly quick to attack and maul any inconsistency and skilful at shining the spotlight on any isolated example of failure. To manage the media, politicians turn to spin themselves, but then find that they get tangled in a web of relationships and let down by the very parts of their world that they were uncertain about in the first place.

It must be a very lonely job. Most people who have been in any leadership role will identify with the feelings of being isolated, doubted, embarrassed by mistakes, burdened by the weight of responsibility – and, occasionally, appreciated, thanked and even feted. But the role is unforgiving. Our politicians are increasingly scrutinised, criticised, questioned, challenged, faulted. To admit to a lack of detail, a mistake or a change of direction is to run the risk of being mocked or castigated. An apology for an error somewhere in the system can lead to vilification on so-called social media and calls for resignation. Carl Ward of Foundation for Education Development (FED) observed:

> The use of social media over recent years has created an illusion – one that the FED's national consultation has found does not exist at scale – that there is great division in our education system. The importance of social media as a mechanism to provide real-time feedback to politicians has created a myopia in our system.
>
> People on social media have an immediate presence and opinion, they are in the here and now, and our politicians tend to find that useful in a speedy society. The FED is helping to redress this imbalance and provide an environment that can bring stakeholders together to hold qualitative, serious and timely debate. It is also showing that there is a lot more agreement in the centre ground than we think and that the tone of any debate is important for our profession.

This public discourse is one with which politicians have to live and in which many thrive. Nevertheless, the leaders of local authorities, MATs, schools and classrooms experience an interest in their effectiveness which was unimagined in 1976.

The Australian researcher Jennifer Lees-Marshment has drawn attention to the way politics has changed over the time period of our book and the way politicians have adapted their approaches without ever truly understanding how they can help their policies succeed.[25] She suggests that politicians need to be good at the 'dance of politics and government'. On a floor that is crowded with other dancers, they need to dance through the complex web of opinion to construct and deliver a policy agenda.

---

25   J. Lees-Marshment, *Political Management: The Dance of Government and Politics* (Abingdon and New York: Routledge, 2021).

So, how well have our 20 secretaries of state danced with the schooling system to the tune of education? Some were plainly good at being in step with their partners, some trod on toes and some tripped over their own feet. Their various dances – with their spins, leaps of faith, aggressive paso dobles, gracious waltzes and hokey-cokeys, with its 'in, out, shake it all about' energy – have somehow helped schooling in this country to reach a place that is better than ever, and certainly much improved from the place where they started their dance and we started our story in 1976.

Ministers have their personal beliefs and motivations too

Most of our ministerial witnesses were driven by a deep commitment to positively affect the schooling experience of children and young people based on their social beliefs and sometimes on their personal experience of education. Very few seemed to be guided in their policy agenda by their political outlook, political opportunism or political survival. Those driven by a sense of social or personal responsibility were eager to see their policies make the sorts of impact and difference that they envisaged. They wanted to see policy through to practice and leave a lasting legacy of change. They would build a plan for implementation that was coherent with their objectives and would stop at nothing to push their policies over, around and through obstacles. They made the machine of government work for them, and if there was doubt about capacity, they increased it.

All realised, though, that however strongly they believed in something, it might be out of reach – whether it was David Blunkett over ending selection or Alan Johnson telling us that altering the admission policies of faith school was impossible because of what he called 'realpolitik'. Politically astute Charles Clarke talked about the reality and the implications of the 'too difficult box'. He explained: 'You set off and the difficulty you have in trying to make change is significant. There are various obstacles that occur and eventually it becomes simpler to leave it to the next secretary of state. The risk is that this gives rise to the idea that politics is irrelevant to the idea of solving problems of society. If you can't convince people, they will drift to the margins. What I think is important is trying to find common ground which locks change in.'

Kenneth Baker's starting point for aspects of policy and his justification for structural change was his own constituency: 'I wanted to make some schools independent of local education authorities because Marylebone had suffered from the ILEA long enough. The schools in my constituency in Marylebone were in a shocking state, a really shocking state. Shirley Williams had closed the last remaining excellent grammar school.'

David Blunkett echoed the importance of the influence of local and personal circumstances on his imperative for standards. His ambitions were clear and rooted in his experiences both in childhood and as a member of Parliament in tune with his constituency: 'My own constituency was a driving force. I was determined that others shouldn't have to struggle to catch up as I did from childhood. We had 17 primary schools and there were only four where 50% of pupils reached Level 4. I had a personal determination as well as an imperative from the leader of the party.'

Ed Balls, several secretaries of state later, had a similar clarity of educational objective in his reforms as he addressed the wider children's agenda: 'We had certain strands of work we were looking at in preparation for the transition in 2007 from Tony Blair to Gordon Brown. One of those was changing and broadening the approach to children's education policy and trying to take forward the Every Child Matters philosophy, which took the Children Act legislation to a local level, with the bringing together of children's services and education under one person – the director of children's services.'

Justine Greening was so committed to the concept of social campaigning that she left Parliament and set up the Social Mobility Pledge, cementing the beliefs she had carried through her parliamentary career: 'I always said education secretary was the best job I will ever have and the one I really wanted to do. The rationale was that I knew what a state education had done for me in transforming my own future and I wanted to do that for children everywhere.'

Gillian Shephard brought to bear her insight on schooling, particularly from her husband's perspective as the head of a state secondary school, to quietly implement pilot schemes to address the evidence she was building about the school system: 'I felt I knew a fair amount already, and therefore if I wanted to test out ideas or gauge opinion, I would talk to people I had known for a long time in the field.' Shephard's controversial predecessor, John Patten, who had presided over periods of turmoil which many saw as manipulated for political ends, had 'wanted to make education more interesting, more debated nationally ... although not always in ways I have found comfortable'.[26]

Michael Gove received plaudits, especially from within his own party and from much of the media, for getting things done. With him, though, there was always the nagging doubt that, while he talked eloquently about a better future for young people, the thing he most wanted to get done was to establish his image as a politician able to get things done. What he could get done would be summarised by many in his party as 'sorting out education', but the way to create that image would be the fragmentation of the state system for education along with engaging in battle with what he saw as the education establishment. As one of our primary head teacher interviewees remarked: 'Michael Gove seemed to delight in the limelight. He seemed to want to be noticed. He had a sort of Cruella de Vil image about him.'

The future beckoned for a politician appreciated for his uncompromising principles, tenacity and radical solutions, along with the nerve to take on the big challenge. This was to serve him well when, shortly after leaving education, he announced that he was to join the campaign to leave the European Union.

Gove's tenure at the DfE was one of the most personalised in terms of his willingness to put himself at the forefront and to touch nerves that few had dared. The pace of change was enormous, often reversing previous policy, while at the same time driving innovation. Michael Barber offered an explanation for the tumultuous nature of Gove's tenure:

> I think he misjudged things. Tony Blair wrote in his autobiography that he wished he had acted more quickly and decisively, and I think Cameron and Gove read that in their time in opposition and then took on too much when in power. My advice to them was to prioritise education and move with urgency, and they should get on top of funding issues in health. But they chose to go with all the Lansley reforms which had to be abandoned before they brought in Jeremy Hunt to calm things down, just as they did with Nicky Morgan in education.

Gove was intolerant of lack of progress, a trait that was admired by his supporters. At the same time, he unsettled those who were trying

---

26   Quoted in Ribbins and Sherratt, *Radical Educational Policies and Conservative Secretaries of State*, p. 195.

to enact his policies because, while the direction disrupted the status quo, there was little sense of destination. David Bell tells the story of a conversation in which he asked Michael Gove to describe how the new academies movement would be managed on a potentially large scale. 'That's exactly the sort of question I would expect someone in Whitehall to ask,' was Gove's response, implying intolerance of the need for clarity about the future while changing the present.

Nicky Morgan's beliefs saw her at odds with her prime minister, Theresa May, who announced the expansion of grammar school provision in places where they already existed by finding a way around the legislation.

Almost all held deep convictions and made attempts to influence policy, but they always seemed to be rowing against a tide of political urgency taking them elsewhere. Alan Johnson, who was in post for the shortest period, had a similar policy commitment to David Blunkett as a result of his own childhood experiences, but he could never really promote his own agenda in the time available, especially when other matters seemed to dominate.

Other secretaries of state acted as custodians of the system, trying to steer a course through the issues as they came towards them and manage the agenda. They implemented policy at the prompting of others, often as a hangover from previous legislation. An example would be Damian Hinds, perfectly pleasant and energetic, but clearly caught up in the cauldron of a parliamentary period consumed by Brexit. Another is Gavin Williamson, who found it hard to articulate clearly his vision for the system against the constant turmoil of the COVID crisis. He could offer a few sound bites about the importance of education, even try to shift the focus on to new national imperatives – such as T levels or the proposed introduction of an institute for teaching – but inevitably the conversation turns to the urgent and immediate.

Some observers suspect that policy announcements about new developments are in fact intended to create a smokescreen – a distraction from less palatable news and events. This is when it becomes difficult to discern whether the politician is genuine in their pronouncements about our young people.

And what of Kenneth Baker, so often mentioned by commentators as the most influential secretary of state for education of the 20th century? Were his reforms driven by a deeply personal set of beliefs, by political agenda or by political opportunism? We were perplexed by this. Our conversation with him drew on his over 30 years of involvement in education policy. He remains extremely active, negotiating for young people to experience the sort of balanced practical and academic learning and qualifications that will fit the modern age. Surely, he would not do that without a deep commitment to education?

Yet some of the reforms he generated following the 1988 Education Act seemed to have a political imperative. There was a willingness to take on the unions (and for the unions to take on him), not simply to secure a better future for the young but almost as a hangover from the miners' strike of three years earlier. In the same way that there was with Michael Gove, there was often the suspicion that Baker had his eyes on a bigger prize. In their different ways, Kenneth Clarke and John Patten seemed to bring that same drive to the post. While they were energetically stirring the pot and pronouncing, much of what they did or said seemed to be capitalising on a more politicised agenda.

What our conversations with the secretaries of state showed us was that they felt far less powerful than we might imagine. Indeed, almost all held the view that they were constrained in what they could achieve. Most saw themselves as trying to push things forward in an environment where almost everyone has a view on what should happen and success can only be achieved through working successfully with very complex communities of interest. Nicky Morgan reflected: 'I have got three departments to compare. Education was the toughest in terms of stakeholders feeling that they have personal stake in what you were doing.'

So, what were our impressions of the impact of our secretaries of state?

We enjoyed our conversations with each of our secretaries of state and ended each one thinking we had learned from individuals who were generous with their time and insight. Many were impressive and for different reasons.

David Blunkett impressed us for his ongoing understanding of a complex agenda and his sometimes astonishing grasp of detail and its connection with the bigger picture, as well as his relentless commitment to improving the life chances of children and communities previously poorly served.

Estelle Morris, as did many, impressed us with her belief in public service, and especially teaching, as well as with her realism about politics and politicians and her uncanny ability to get on with people, sometimes of totally different outlook.

Charles Clarke impressed us with his commitment to engaging people in democratic processes and his wisdom about societal and global challenges, with education being a lever for good.

Michael Gove is known for his impressive and engaging debating style and his willingness to challenge the status quo, although less so for his appreciation of the consequences.

Justine Greening was striking in her commitment to what she describes as the social mobility agenda, aligning with David Blunkett, Ed Balls and others on issues of equity and social justice.

Nicky Morgan was open-minded and showed a genuine cheerful willingness and business-like attitude in trying to clear up some of the difficulties she inherited.

Gillian Shephard impressed with her commitment to identifying and addressing some of the challenges in the schooling system. She seemed to be the first to identify that variability in schools is related to leadership and to the classroom effectiveness of teachers. She put this down to her previous career in education where she had been a teacher, school inspector, LEA officer and county councillor. She told us: 'My husband was a head teacher and he and I used to disagree when I said you could tell very quickly what a school was like, but when he then helped Norfolk with the introduction of LFM and had to visit lots of schools, he agreed that I had been right and was disappointed by the enormous variability in the quality of what went on.' She initiated strategies to help local authorities address issues of literacy and numeracy and build a training and qualification structure for school leadership, which had long-term impact through her willingness to work with the incoming Labour government to ensure continuity of ambition.

Kenneth Baker would have impressed anyone with his continuing analysis of the priorities for the country's schools and children's learning. His capacity to identify with the views of teenagers 70 years younger than himself and see the need for change in the school system was sharp. He was able to relate incisively to the changing world and the need for relevance in learning, to the place of technology in learning, to look across the globe at innovation and to see potential in our own system. He told us of the 'silver bullets' he would use today and was not unwilling to reject the spent carcasses of those he had used in 1988. In the last 30 years, he has adapted and modified his thinking to match circumstances based on the evidence before him, while holding to his principles.

Ed Balls impressed us as the secretary of state with the clearest and most coherent commitment to the life chances of all children and young people, set alongside the most coherent approach to seeing schooling as part of society. Other secretaries of state had shown commitment to the life chances of children and to better schooling. Others had shown determination to improve schooling and particularly the poorest schools. However, his effort to bring together social care, health, housing, policing and leisure around childhood – and at the same time begin to explore the way the employment agenda should contribute as well as comment on the effectiveness of schooling – left us regretting that such a worthwhile agenda had been lost.

His insistence on identifying underperformance and expecting it to be addressed locally, along with the balance between challenge and support to the system, probably emerged from the policies he inherited. We were left wondering what might have happened if Gordon Brown had called and won the 'election that never was' in late 2007. With five more years to shape schooling within the landscape of society and to drive forward improvements in schooling beyond the cities, with the Building Schools for the Future programme seen to completion and integrated services in place, would Balls have secured what James Callaghan had asked Shirley Williams to do as his secretary of state for education in 1976? Might he have built consensus, a unity of purpose and collective pride in our schools? Then again, Balls would probably have been moved to the post of home secretary in a cabinet reshuffle immediately after an election victory. One thing we have learned is that nothing in politics is guaranteed.

What do others think of them?

How are secretaries of state viewed by the people who work in the system? Does it matter whether they are liked, respected, admired, appreciated or despised, as long as the system is getting better and improving on its previous best?

It became clear to us that few ministers make any significant impact. Anthony Seldon, an experienced educationalist and author, summed up the sentiments and comments of many when he remarked: 'Vision for education and education secretaries tend to be in different rooms in the hotel. Indeed, I don't even think they're in the same hotel.' He reflected, 'In the last 80 years, it's hard to point to many education secretaries who made a difference. Major changes have tended to come from other places. Nick Gibb had more influence than most education secretaries, although I don't agree with him. Andrew Adonis has also had more influence than many education secretaries.'

For most teachers and heads in schools, the world of politics is largely an unknown. They might be interested in their local political scene and they will know who is the sitting secretary of state, but they will have little direct knowledge of how the DfE works or the impact of policy advisers and SpAds. The interwoven world of government-sponsored organisations that support schooling is just too complicated. For people doing the day job, it is often lumped together as 'the system', which for them starts with their classroom and school and extends to their MAT or local authority and beyond. They all know what Ofsted is, however, and so who is the current HMCI often matters more to them than who is the secretary of state.

When talking with teachers and heads, we realised that our recent memories are their histories. A head teacher aged 40 today will have no career memory of David Blunkett and the Labour government's radical national strategies to influence pedagogy in the classroom; for them, significant national influence is a given. We talked with some head teachers whose teaching careers extended back only as far as the time of Ruth Kelly and Alan Johnson. They told us that they 'woke up to the wider world of professional determination' when Michael Gove arrived on the scene with a dynamic agenda. One head teacher laughed as she told us kindly that she had 'never talked with anyone with such long memories of how schools used to be'.

One of the problems is that, in order to improve on the previous best, our secretaries of state seem to feel the need to criticise the previous best and, in doing so, they upset hard-working people in schools and provoke doubt in the public, especially parents. Politicians offer gentle 'Ratner moments',[27] but they are always accompanied by comments on the positive aspects of schooling, especially teachers, and the promise to put things right. In order to make the case for fresh policies, the doubt and mistrust of 1976 is stirred up again to vindicate central direction, market forces or a managerial approach. New policies are too often justified by diminishing what exists and what has gone before, and in doing so, diminishes the service being offered and received.

Lisa Williams, a primary head teacher in London, reflected on the influence of politicians:

> I think as a school leader it's so frustrating. With the next change in minister, it always makes you think, 'What are they going to change now? What system have I got to try and unpick or shoehorn in to fit the criteria they think will work within schools, while also keeping my own reality?' I think that is what lots of us do as leaders. We'll carry on doing what we're doing, but we'll make it look as if we've met your criteria somehow without changing too much.

At the heart of many concerns we heard expressed was the need for a focus on the purpose of schooling and clarity about shared ambitions. Our primary head teacher described the tensions between central policy and the needs of the pupils in her school:

> How much difference did [the secretary of state] make? Well, I can tell you about the time of my first headship from 2010 to 2016, when we moved from a notice to improve to outstanding. It was absolutely not a success because of the influence from Michael Gove. In fact, it just made us really think about how we work within this system that he's trying to impose on us. The curriculum that we're trying to build, focused on the holistic education that really develops the children's character, was restrained by his policies.

---

27 Gerald Ratner made a throwaway humorous comment about the products sold in his chain of high street jewellery shops in a speech at a dinner in 1991 for the Institute of Directors: 'We also do cut-glass sherry decanters complete with six glasses on a silver-plated tray that your butler can serve you drinks on, all for £4.95. People say to me, "How can you sell this for such a low price?" I say, "Because it's total crap."' See https://www.youtube.com/watch?v=sKtBkVrqYYk.

Anthony Seldon summed up the underlying objective: 'Education is more important than anything. It is more important than health, it is more important than welfare, it is more important than defence. It is the most important of all aspects of government policy because, if properly done, it will be freeing up young people to lead a life that is meaningful, enjoyable, helpful, responsible and ever deepening in meaning.'

The vast majority of the teaching profession would subscribe to Seldon's sentiments. Yet few of the secretaries of state who impressed us with their diligence and concern for a better education system had registered with the teaching profession as being committed to a shared purpose. With few exceptions, the general image that was painted is summed up in this observation from Seldon: 'They are not appointed to their place because they have an education philosophy. They are often appointed to the post as a stepping-stone or as a way of keeping the lid on spending or keeping teachers on side ahead of general elections.'

Rachel Tomlinson, a primary head teacher from the North of England, when asked the same question, spoke with disappointment about criticisms by politicians in order to promote policy direction:

> I would just like the teaching profession to be respected, and our politicians seem to do so much to undermine that. Of all the public services, teaching seems to be the one that is so easily criticised for political gain. I wish we could be trusted. With health, we can have a bad experience but we know inside ourselves that generally the health service is a good thing, that the people in it are special and we know it's doing the best it can. I just wish we had the same outlook on our national education service.

We need our politicians to take on a harmonising role, to allow our national education service to grow and to enable the communities around schools to build a better future. We need the teaching profession to believe it can influence the way schooling works and is received. We believe that we are on the cusp of the next era – one of hope, ambition and collaborative partnerships. Let's enjoy it together.

Chapter 3

How policies are made

What helps and what gets in the way

For a good proportion of those who work in schools, the DfE is the centre of the schooling universe. A common view is that the secretary of state determines a policy, the DfE takes the legislation through Parliament and then makes it happen by liaising with each school, either directly or via MATs, local authorities and other agencies. In the past year, schools have been inundated with communiqués from the DfE about issues such as closures during lockdown, arrangements for vulnerable and key worker children, home learning, the distribution of laptops, cancelled examinations and managing the safe return of children to schools. Much of this advice has been reinterpreted by local authorities to ensure that they meet their responsibilities for the children in their care. For academies, there has been a flood of third-hand communications from their MAT referencing DfE expectations.

Many in schools believe that the DfE calls the tune, although many also believe that the DfE doesn't know the music for the tune it is calling. As the system has centralised over the last 30 years, so the Big Brother image has grown. Nowadays, there is more straight-through communication between the DfE and schools than was ever the case previously, and ministers are more likely than ever to intervene with an individual school over policy, either directly or indirectly.

Several of our head teachers told us that their local authority had contacted them implying that 'The DfE isn't happy with what you are doing'. Of course, this could simply be about shifting the blame elsewhere, rather like a teacher admonishing a child with, 'Would you do that at home?' Sometimes, though, head teachers told us of direct contact from a minister, such as a northern secondary school head teacher who showed us a letter from Nick Gibb, the long-serving schools minister, complaining about the arrangements for the teaching of modern foreign languages in their school. Many heads would view the receipt of such a letter as career threatening or at least a slap on the wrist, but she also showed us her uncompromising reply. But it makes one wonder if doctors receive similar letters from the minister of health criticising their personal prescription practices or surgical procedures.

The truth is that the DfE *is* the centre of a complex and intriguing web of policy relationships around the secretary of state. These groups and individuals are responsible for building policy through legislation and enacting it through what most call 'delivery'. Secretaries of state need to feel that the advice they are receiving is good enough to inform the legislation they are promoting and that the delivery is secure and efficient. This is what affects the weather in the classroom. The red sky at night or the morning, the dark clouds massing, the sunshine in which to bask, the downpours, frosts and heat waves of schooling mostly emanate from the DfE. How far they travel on the equivalent of the gulf stream towards classrooms is the result of the complex ecosystem that exists between the DfE and schools.

Many of our secretaries of state admitted to a lack of confidence in the work of their own department. Most sought intelligence from a range of sources: their own ministerial team and SpAds, policy advisers based in the DfE, agencies established by government (quangos or delivery arms to enable its work), people from outside government with expertise or insight on particular matters, and trusted individuals from the world of schools, MATs or local authorities.

If this is the catchment area of their advice, they are also guided – to a greater or lesser extent – by the prime minister's office, which is pushing government objectives, as well as the unions (of which there are several representing teachers and others representing all manner of workers within the system, both in schools and the civil service) and lobby groups (formal and informal), who are all trying to ensure that their key issues are addressed. One of our witnesses described herself as 'a dame with a campaign' when talking about how to bring influence to bear on the cause she wanted ministers to address. Secretaries of state may also have MPs raising matters on behalf of constituents and members of the House of Lords offering their twopenn'orth about the latest bee in their bonnet. And all this against a backdrop of potential opposition from other parties and often critical commentary in the media.

With all this advice, and varying levels of support, it is a wonder that the secretary of state achieves anything very much at all.

Secretaries of state and the DfE

The lack of confidence in the contribution of the DfE seems to have been humoured, tolerated or sidestepped by many secretaries of state. It is also regarded as one of the anchors on progress within the school system. Whether their input is as poor as it was described to us is uncertain. However, it did occur to us that someone appointed to lead an organisation that they find to be disorganised or dysfunctional would try to address its shortcomings directly. Until relatively recently, few seem to have tried. Perhaps it is the knowledge that they will be in post for only a short period of time that makes reform of the DfE a time and energy trap – another thing to put in Charles Clarke's 'too difficult box' (it gets very full). Of course, each secretary of state meets the permanent secretary and chief of staff (the clue being in the name), which implies the stewardship of an organisation to carry out the bidding of government.

Kenneth Baker described his move from the Department of the Environment to Education (which was then based at Waterloo) as 'at the time, like moving from the manager's job at Arsenal to Charlton. You crossed the River Thames and dropped down two divisions.' Baker went on to articulate the way in which secretaries of state were bullied, ignored, railroaded or undermined by the Department for Education and Skills (as it was then). Baker's criticism is backed up by reference to the Labour government of James Callaghan and the Green Paper that followed the Ruskin College speech being 'sparse in content and complacent in tone'.[1] It was, as he quotes from a senior official in the then prime minister's team, 'Whitehall at its self-satisfied, condescending and unimaginative worst', and evidence of the problems of the DfE as the voice of 'resistance of vested professional interests to radical change'.

Gillian Shephard pinpoints the difficulties that secretaries of state experience in their own department: 'One of the problems experienced by John Patten was that the Conservative reforms conceived by Sir Keith Joseph and introduced by Kenneth Baker and Kenneth Clarke, presupposed an administrative function in the department that was not there.' She adds: 'If a minister is not aware of how things are made to happen, he may push the levers of power but no action will follow.'[2] These sorts of sentiments

---

1   Department of Education and Science, *Education in Schools: A Consultative Document* [Green Paper] (London: HMSO, 1977). Available at: http://www.educationengland.org.uk/documents/gp1977/educinschools.html.
2   Shephard, *Shephard's Watch*, pp. vi, 114.

seem to parallel the period of doubt and mistrust that had begun in the school system some 10 years earlier. Now a secretary of state was having similar misgivings about schooling closer to home.

This inability to convince the DfE (or at least senior officials) seems to have dogged several secretaries of state, who have adopted various strategies to beat what they see as the problem. For many, the department was ideologically opposed to what they wanted to achieve and for others it was inefficient, yet they seemed to have few solutions other than to appoint people they trusted to work around the blockage.

Perhaps it is size and complexity. The DfE employs a little over 2,000 people. Some are located in Darlington, Sheffield and Runcorn but most are based in Sanctuary Buildings in Westminster, within easy walking distance of Parliament. It is such an apt address for a department so often under pressure. For anyone who has never visited, Sanctuary Buildings is an eight-floor office block designed with an inner atrium surrounded by glass balconies and marble-clad walls. The atrium is filled with beautiful greenery and water features. Whether this is the nerve centre or mission control or simply the service point for schooling in England is never clear. It is a lovely place to work, but it proves the adage that culture and ethos need more than a good environment to be productive. And it is a far cry from 1976 and Curzon Street, with its air-raid bunkers, where the DfE started its life post-war.

While the number of employees may sound sizable, it is less than one employee per 1,000 schools (and don't forget that the DfE services far more than schooling), so the claim of centralism might seem questionable. However, the DfE's capacity to influence the system relies more on regulation and other agencies like Ofsted than the size of its workforce.

One of the aspects of society that has changed dramatically since 1976 has been the speed and ease of communication. At that time, in so far as it had the power (which, as Chapter 1 has shown, was minimal), the DfE would send 'circulars' to local authority directors about new policy developments or arrangements, which would be either interpreted locally and distributed to schools if it was seen as urgent or, more likely, discussed with head teachers at a termly meeting. This discussion would usually involve a consideration of the merits of the DfE's pronouncement and often a response for the local authority director to propose to the DfE. Schools would receive a weekly mail drop from the local authority, with all the communications from a whole range of sources channelled through a 'schools post' team.

As personal computers arrived in abundance in the 1990s, communication became looser and more spontaneous. This meant that DfE policy could be posted on a website and used as reference when necessary. It also meant that, at the touch of a key, every one of the 20,000-plus schools in the country could receive the same letter at the same moment via email. The DfE could now contact schools quickly and directly, individually, en masse or in groups depending on the data sets they were building. Local authorities could be sidestepped.

In 1986, Kenneth Baker, in an attempt to settle a protracted pay dispute by appealing to their professionalism, had communicated directly with teachers: 'To keep the initiative, I set out the terms of my offer in a letter to all head teachers. This was the first time that a secretary of state for education had attempted to communicate directly with the profession. I also wanted to ensure that every teacher knew … and the only way to communicate this was to take full page press advertisements consisting of a "Dear Teacher" letter.'

This still happens from time to time, and certainly 'Dear Head Teacher' letters are common, although nowadays personalised. The teaching profession is generally fairly compliant and, in the main, head teachers do not reply individually, each asking a different question in respect of their own situation, which the department is duty-bound to answer. If they did so, the machinery of government might grind to a policy-making halt. It always seems odd to us that unions don't encourage this tactic.

In communicating directly with the profession, Baker had taken a big step towards a centralised approach. Driven by the wish to break through a crisis, he was also determined to ensure the message got through the layers in the system that might distort or dilute the policy intention. By leapfrogging his own department and local authorities, he displayed both impatience and a lack of confidence in those around him.

A head teacher from 1976 could only have imagined the ease of communication today. Heads now carry a mobile phone to keep them in touch with the school, although in reality it keeps the school in touch with them. Imagine being a head teacher where the only interruption is an occasional call from the office of the local authority and a once-a-week bag of mail.[3]

Tim recalls:

In my first administrative post in Monmouthshire in the 1960s, one of my tasks was to complete the process of all primary schools having at least one phone installed. One head teacher refused the offer, so I drove on from another meeting in Abergavenny about new buildings to visit her remote village primary school set high in the hills near Offa's Dyke. She was nothing if not frank in her determination to avoid the unwanted telephonic revolution: 'I don't want Mr Jones (the assistant education officer for primary education) ringing me to tell me what to do next, thank you very much. It's bad enough now. I have enough of his nonsense already through his letters. He sends me one every half-term.' Another head was thought to use the phone for his own use, so it was moved to the school kitchens.

Secretaries of state today, like those working in schools, are operating in a world of constant communication, both directly and against the background of traditional and recent social media, all of which influence their decisions. They need to make sure they are on message. At the same time, the secretary of state also has access to the policies of individual schools via their websites, which must meet statutory requirements regarding content.

The centralising of information and communication has elevated the DfE to the position of prime influencer in the eyes of many in schools. Our secretaries of state seemed to think they were on top of communication; most of the more recent ones talked about their 'comms people'. However, so often this is about getting the message to the media rather than to schools. Hence, much of the discussion, debate and decisions about the response to the coronavirus pandemic has been played out through the media. The impression given was that during the first lockdown Gavin Williamson and the various unions, individually or collectively, used the media to make their points rather than speaking directly to each other. Those in schools may receive official information after it has been in the

---

3   Many telephone exchanges were not automated until the late 1960s and subscriber trunk dialling (an earlier use of the initials STD) did not reach the whole of the country until 1979.

news media and often after parents and others, including pupils, have interpreted what they have heard and begun to ask specific questions.

The other angles: the influence of government beyond the DfE

Michael Barber told us: 'Before the general election, David Miliband, David Blunkett, Conor Ryan and I had talked and asked ourselves the question, "Is the DfE up to the job?" The answer was, "No, it isn't." So, setting up the Standards and Effectiveness Unit was central to addressing this. The idea was that we would bring not just competence but also be in touch with the system.'

This was a watershed moment: Labour had decided that, for their policies to work, they would have to manage them, as opposed to hoping the DfE would do so. The Standards and Effectiveness Unit was set up within the DfE, but to the outsider, and certainly to schools, it appeared to be a ministerial unit. Barber became communicator-in-chief; he was seen constantly with David Blunkett and delivered strategic talks to large regional conferences. In effect, a new quasi-national education authority was explaining to each local authority how policy would affect them.

Barber was Blunkett's 'fixer' and he was driven hard: 'We published the White Paper on 3 July 1997, the fastest ever after an election. I was quite pleased with myself and David Blunkett's reaction was, "You haven't touched the education of a single child yet."'

Here it was writ large. The DfE was there to connect with children, every single one of them. But, of course, for all the leadership theory emerging and being pushed towards school leaders, the concept of 'Team DfE' was sadly lacking. The Standards and Effectiveness Unit was working in front of the DfE on the big agenda and in parallel on others.

Jon Coles, who worked as a career civil servant in the DfE, told us: 'David Blunkett galvanised the department by starting with mission and purpose. The measure of success was to be the extent to which schools were getting better or not (especially in poor communities) and there was nothing else. The clarity of mission brought the system together. Exam results became the key measure of the success of the department along-side some other outcome measures. That hadn't been the case in the past.'

Coles' image of the department prior to Blunkett's arrival mirrored that of Kenneth Baker's description of a decade earlier: 'The DfE had an intellectual approach. They would think through the different issues and offer wise words of guidance. The admin systems were good but the department seemed focused upon preserving the status quo. Thatcher had gone with the notion of "next steps" agencies so that we could separate policy and delivery. It wasn't really considered the job of the DfE to worry about whether policy worked.'

Coles found a similar clarity of purpose with the incoming coalition government of 2010. He told us: 'Michael Gove had a clear agenda for schools. That was a motivating time too. He had a big agenda for the department.'

Some of the more recent secretaries of state were extremely complimentary about the department and the people working within it. Charles Clarke did not see this as one of his 'too difficult box' issues: 'I don't go along with the thesis that the civil service is useless. Some successors of mine seemed to have completely disregarded civil servants.'

Damian Hinds remarked: 'I think the civil servants that I worked with at the DfE were among the most impressive people I have worked with in my life. In this department I met amazing professionals. Of course, all big organisations are difficult to turn around and people always have personal objectives, but we were not talking about trying to effect a wholesale change in direction.'

Hinds puts his finger on a key issue in that final point. Perhaps, since Baker's time, the work of the DfE has moved towards a different purpose. Was Baker an early example of a minister who was impatient to see reforms making a difference to the lives of children and young people, as opposed to others who had assumed their policies would have an impact eventually? Blunkett, aided by Barber, had clearly articulated the purpose, and successive secretaries of state have, to a greater or lesser extent, built on the sense of mission.

As Blunkett moved on after the 2001 election and Barber went to the Number 10 Policy Unit, the prime minister's office increasingly held sway in what was Blair and Brown's key policy area. As they did so, power moved away from the DfE – but some resisted. Charles Clarke told us: 'I was at an advantage in that I had been at the DfE before. What I always rejected was the idea that Number 10 would set the agenda without reference to the department.'

Naturally, government policy is a driver and Downing Street would exercise its interests over education and sometimes create distraction. Justine Greening, who was promoting a social mobility agenda, was wrong-footed when Prime Minister Theresa May proposed an expansion of grammar school provision dependent on parental interest. She said: 'It didn't hold us back, though time was spent dealing with it. In many ways it was helpful that Number 10 was so myopically focused at the time.'

From time to time, the prime minister intervenes directly, such as when Boris Johnson appointed Kevan Collins as the education recovery commissioner in February 2021. Collins resigned from the post just four months later saying: 'I do not believe it will be possible to deliver a successful recovery without significantly greater support than the government has to date indicated it intends to provide.'[4] As a result, Gavin Williamson faced calls for his own resignation. It is a cruel world.

As well as the influence of DfE officials and SpAds, secretaries of state are supported by a team of ministers. Some of these are able lieutenants, even understudies, and some create their own role and image centred around their own agenda. There have been many prominent schools ministers in recent years, including David Miliband, who was particularly well regarded; Jim Knight, whose influence on the development of IT was considerable; and Estelle Morris, who went on to become secretary of state.

Peter Hyman was an adviser in Blair's Policy Unit and later decided to work in schools, first as a teaching assistant, then as teacher and now as founder of School 21 in London. He reflected on ministers who had supported secretaries of state.

> David Miliband's work on personalised learning had a very good intent behind it. David really majored on it and I think he was very thoughtful. Andrew Adonis was very influential. He had a

---

4   S. Coughlan and K. Sellgren, School Catch-Up Tsar Resigns Over Lack of Funding, *BBC News* (2 June 2021). Available at: https://www.bbc.co.uk/news/education-57335558. Collins had estimated a cost of £15 billion, far in excess of what the Treasury would approve.

single-minded focus on getting things done; that focus on fresh starts for areas where there had been generations of disadvantage. Nick Gibb is a figure of influence because of sheer length of time and maniacal focus on the knowledge-rich curriculum to the exclusion of all else. But you have to say, even if you don't agree with his policies, he was enormously influential.

We had conversations with four people who had served as ministers, two of whom have had a major and direct influence on the weather in schools. One was Andrew Adonis, who served for five years as minister after his four years at Number 10. The other, Nick Gibb, became a minister in 2010 and had worked with five secretaries of state (until he left in 2021), with a break of just under two years during Gove's tenure.

Both Adonis and Gibb have sometimes been perceived as ploughing a separate furrow rather than being part of the team – a bit like a secondary school art department that does its own thing or the quirky teacher in Year 3 who is way off school policy but still gets results.

Of Adonis, David Blunkett remarked: 'Andrew Adonis joined us after about 18 months. He spent most of his time going around listening to people telling him what they thought he wanted to hear.' Adonis' position is fascinating. He was very much Blair's and Barber's man in the department and had his own very important agenda, which was supported by the prime minister. Jim Knight told us: 'The prime minister asked me if I would take a ministerial role in education and I was delighted. He told me that I would be working to Andrew Adonis. He didn't mention Alan Johnson, the lovely man who was secretary of state at the time.'

David Bell, who served as a permanent secretary at the DfE, observed:

> Andrew Adonis was a very significant figure in Downing Street, and his role in education policy formulation and his wider influence are often underestimated. To put it more simply, post-2001 he was a pivotal figure. When he went to the DfE, he was suspected of being Blair's man in the department and, at times, it was clear that there was a tension between him and Ruth Kelly, the secretary of state. I don't think he ever took advantage of his position, but Andrew Adonis was more influential on the prime minister than on the secretary of state.

Robert Hill, one of the SpAds in the DfE at the time, and who had himself worked in the Number 10 delivery unit on health reforms, told us:

> One of the issues was some of the problems and tension between Number 10 and the Department for Education. Andrew Adonis, the education adviser in Number 10, was a strong character with lots of ideas and was pushing the prime's minister's reform agenda.
>
> There was mutual respect between Andrew and Estelle, but they had sort of agreed that they were ships that passed in the night in terms of their worldview and approach to education improvement. I said to Tony Blair, 'Look, let me go to the DfE and I will help to be the link between the department and Number 10.' I knew and had worked with Andrew and that was what was agreed.

Adonis served as minister through the course of six Labour secretaries of state. What was interesting was the amount of influence he had on national policy from the position of not being a secretary of state. Most significant was his work on the development of city academies and later his work on the London Challenge. Adonis was an 'active' minister, known for getting things done, and he gave us some frank insights into the frustrations of government:

> The whole of the central machinery loves Acts of Parliament because they love this business of preparing bills, passing them and all of that, which is all a massive displacement activity for actually getting on with the job of improving the schools.
>
> I had a personal experience of this which made me dead set against further big legislative changes, which is: when I became a minister in 2005, there was me wanting to do the London Challenge and get back to the actual nuts-and-bolts job of transforming schools. Instead, I'm stuck in the House of Lords for literally whole days at a time in the fifteenth, sixteenth and seventeenth days of the committee stage of the School Standards and Inspection Bill, with amendments, most of which were seeking to undermine the central purpose of the bill. We had to make all kinds of compromises to get the bill through, so by the end of that whole process of legislating the framework, I thought that the position was worse than before. A whole chunk of my life had been taken out, literally (I calculate something like 160 hours that I spent

personally just chained to the front bench in the House of Lords), steering this legislation through.

And the reason why we never got the London Challenge established in the Midlands and the North was because I had to spend the equivalent amount of time in Parliament handling the passage of legislation that actually made the education system worse than it had been before. By the way, a large chunk of that bill was all about reforming the inspection system, which was totally pointless and was Treasury driven. There had been four education inspectorates before they were all turned into one. Ofsted became the school, children's and social work inspectorate under this big reform, whereas before they had been separate inspectorates. I said to Tony Blair, "This is a total waste of time." The idea that inspection of early years settings or FE [further education] colleges is going to be improved by simply having them in an institution called Ofsted is for the birds. What matters is who the inspectors are who actually do an inspection in those areas. I spent about 30 hours in committee in the House of Lords, because we had several former chief inspectors in the Lords, on the minutiae of arrangements for the creation of a new inspectorate, which, to my mind as the minister responsible, was totally pointless.

Unfortunately, as a minister, I was constantly stuck in time and energy traps which I couldn't avoid. The biggest of them was legislating for things that sounded good and appeared to be big education, but in fact actually made the system worse or didn't really change it or improve it in any way.

Nick Gibb had a similar role to Adonis within the Conservative government (although he was a member of the House of Commons rather than the Lords). Apart from two years under Gove, when he was shuffled out of office, he was an ever-present in the education team since 2010 and influenced at close hand the work of all five of the secretaries of state until 2021. He had also shaped their work and the work of schools considerably by leading a personal crusade for traditional approaches to teaching, including the use of synthetic phonics in early reading, the memorising of multiplication tables, determining a curriculum built on knowledge accumulation, the restructuring of qualifications and reform of the profession through different routes into teaching.

A number of these campaigns have been promoted by secretaries of state, and Gibb is talked of by many as a hard-working and loyal minister. Others refer to him in derogatory terms, believing he had disproportionate influence and criticising his narrow pedantic views, unwillingness to engage in discussion and debate, and his inability to accept challenge in a mature way.

Gibb declined to be interviewed by us, citing pressure of work, but his speeches show a commitment to the government agenda, as in 2016 when he spoke to his old college: 'Since 2010, we have put teachers in the driving seat of our reforms to improve state education in England. We have given schools, and teachers, unprecedented freedom to teach as they see fit, without an overbearing education bureaucracy driving their actions.'[5] The perceived reality for many in schools was very different. Gibb became an increasingly divisive figure and his departure probably came just in time to avoid growing strife with various parts of the professional schooling community.

In the reshuffle of 2021, Nadhim Zahawi found himself in the relatively unusual position of moving to the role of secretary of state at the same time as the appointment of a new schools minister, Robin Walker, giving them a chance to establish a new set of relationships with all interest groups. The tone of that relationship and how it unfolds will be important influences on the climate in schools themselves. Walker set the tone for that relationship when he told us: 'My political tagline has always been about efficiency with compassion. I think we need to look at both when it comes to the school system.' He added: 'I'm not going to say on day one that I want to change X, Y and Z. I always consider myself very much a pragmatist rather than an ideologue.'

---

5   Department for Education and N. Gibb, Nick Gibb at the Jewish Schools Award [speech] (28 January 2016). Available: https://www.gov.uk/government/speeches/nick-gibb-at-the-jewish-schools-awards.

Special political advisers and their different briefs

While ministers are a vital part of the agenda, the secretary of state and ministerial team seem to rely most closely on advisers who come in two forms: policy advisers, who work for the DfE, and their own SpAds. The SpAd is usually a close confidante of the secretary of state.

Nearly all of our secretaries of state remarked that they could not have achieved what they did without their SpAd. As David Laws, a coalition schools minister under Michael Gove explained, their roles are vital:

> The policy SpAds are really important because if you get serious people, rather than just souped-up press officers, they understand the ministers and where they're coming from. They can feed them policy ideas that they know they're interested in, they can liaise between the civil service and ministers and improve communications. They can also say things to ministers that can't be said to ministers by civil servants: 'You're talking nonsense, minister, and this idea of yours is idiotic.' I think policy advisers are very important and it can be an extremely beneficial and constructive role. But you have to get the right person.

To highlight how vital and how varied they can be, Laws talked of the team around Michael Gove and his ministers:

> There was Dom Cummings and Sam Freedman on the Tory side, both of whom Michael respected and listened to a lot, who influenced his thinking and were also his 'enforcers'. On my side of the coalition, I had two brilliant SpAds but they weren't truly special advisers. They were actually a new breed of policy adviser paid for by the civil service, but where ministers could bring [their own] people in. I had Tim Lloyd who is absolutely fantastic, one of those very, very rare people in government who are very thoughtful about policy, very evidence led and also understand the politics of things.

Sam Freedman, who was senior policy adviser at the beginning of the coalition government, explained the different sorts of policies that secretaries of state develop:

> There are important priorities of principle that are not detailed and need considerable work to develop, such as the pupil premium. Then there are those that prove of little interest to ministers but needing doing, such as funding system restructure.
>
> The policy that drives so much work is the one where there is a coherent ministerial rationale and the minister is personally interested. Examples would be Michael Gove's view on curriculum or Nick Gibb and his views on basics, such as phonics or saying multiplication tables. Lastly, there are what we might call 'pure whim' policies, such as sending a copy of the King James Bible to every school.

Jon Coles talked about the way policy could take shape, explaining how a 'sweet spot' can take hold with ministers: 'The point of policy work is to find the sweet spot where the policy solution isn't just politically desirable for ministers (which, of course, it has to be for them to do it) and deliverable, but also shown by the evidence to be capable of achieving the desired outcomes.'

Robin Alexander described to us the challenge of 'not invented here', when ministers are not well disposed to accommodate ideas, policies and evidence that others have generated, unless they can rebrand them as their own.

If secretaries of state have policies but lack confidence in their department to deliver, then it is natural to turn to their SpAds – people they trust implicitly. Nicky Morgan told us: 'Michael Gove had taken one of his [SpAds] and I was offered the other one. I needed people who were "my people". You are responsible by the ministerial code for what they do. I struck gold by relying on people that I trusted.'

This issue of trust is central. Damian Hinds was convinced too: 'The SpAds make all the difference. This was my first cabinet spell and I had two fantastic advisers. The first six weeks is the hardest when you really need your SpAds but you don't have any. It is a fault in our system.'

For those in schools and elsewhere, these SpAds are shadowy characters on the edge of government. Sam Freedman explained how they might work: 'There is a media SpAd who deals with spin, and a policy SpAd who works with think tanks and the like and on specific agenda. Then there is a chief of staff SpAd who is looking at strategy and making it happen.'

Nick Stuart, a senior civil servant at the DfE with many secretaries of state, talked about how a catalogue of SpAds had had influence:

> Keith Joseph liked to use SpAds to galvanise discussion and thought that things would improve through a sort of shared understanding of the problem. Kenneth Clarke appointed as his SpAd a well-connected conservative called Tessa Keswick, who worked closely with him over several years and in a number of departments. At the DfE, she allied herself firmly with the right-wing critics of education policy and later became executive director of the Centre for Policy Studies.

These SpAds matter. Alan Johnson was clear that 'Any success I managed was due to the SpAds who worked brilliantly with civil servants. I took my advisers with me. It was my one condition when Tony asked me to take on the role.'

Most were described to us as highly capable, energetic and thorough. Jon Coles, from the civil servant's vantage point, said: 'A good special adviser knows the mind of the secretary of state – what they're looking for, how they see the world, what sort of solutions appeal to them. A good SpAd can make a big difference to how department and ministers work. David Blunkett's team [Conor Ryan, Hilary Benn, Nick Pearce and Sophie Linden] was particularly effective.'

This view is echoed by Nick Stuart: 'David Blunkett appointed a trio of exceptionally able and supportive advisers. Between them, Hilary Benn, James Purcell and Conor Ryan were always able to give constructive advice about how to proceed and the direction of the secretary of state's thinking.'

The reliance on SpAds is a significant change in the role of secretary of state. It is a fairly new role, only developed in 1968, and has been influential in policy terms. Stuart explained: 'Oliver Letwin went to Number 10 and he helped Margaret Thatcher with education. She had always been interested. He also worked with Kenneth Baker and it was out of that the Education Reform Act took shape.'

Similarly, Sam Freedman reflects on a SpAd who became notorious under Boris Johnson's premiership and was previously Michael Gove's SpAd: 'Dominic Cummings was extremely unusual. Over time, he developed a more important role of influencing how departments and government work. The DfE had become systematised in the 1990s and Labour systematised the civil service generally, and Dominic set out to challenge so many of the systems.' Of course, Cummings has gone on to become an influential figure in British politics. Sometimes seen as a pantomime villain, he spent considerable time working for Gove in education and honing his approach.

Some secretaries of state seemed not to rely overmuch on SpAds. Stuart reflected that at the time of the Education Reform Act, 'I don't recall Kenneth Baker having SpAds. They didn't feature. I don't recall many confidantes in the unfolding events leading up to the Education Reform Act and its path on to the statute book.'

David Bell voiced a similar view of a later secretary of state: 'When Ed Balls became secretary of state, he was very clear what he wanted to do. He was his own SpAd.' Balls recalled his own way of working with his SpAds: 'I was a very meetings-based, collaborative type of secretary of state. I wanted and needed them to tell me what they thought. We spent a lot of time together on thrashing out the issues, so hopefully they liked it. Once we got to the point where they told me what was going on, it was me that decided where next.'

Some seem to develop this team outlook with ministers and SpAds. David Bell noted:

> I never got a huge sense that Dominic Cummings was a deep and wide-ranging educational thinker. There were one or two things he got interested in, particularly A levels and exams. There was a dynamic tension between Nick Gibb and Michael Gove. Michael wanted to stand back and allow schools greater autonomy but Nick wanted to specify detail – for example, on the teaching of phonics. Dominic Cummings was very focused on particular issues but Sam Freedman oversaw the education brief as a whole.

This reliance on the SpAds and the influence on senior DfE staff seems to have had an impact on the morale and effectiveness of the DfE as a department. Jon Coles' observations were astute here:

> When I started in 1997, the idea that the department was about real-world delivery was very new. When I took the job of implementing the class size pledge, I was told more than once that it was a poisoned chalice – that we couldn't effect that sort of change from the centre.

> Blair made education a salient political issue and raised the status and profile of the education department. That was good for the department, but it came with an expectation of real-world delivery which didn't suit and even alarmed some long-serving colleagues.

> The closeness of Gordon Brown and Ed Balls could be a real advantage – it helped to get things agreed and move things forward at pace. It also meant that the secretary of state was more fully involved in the wider government agenda and Number 10's priorities unrelated to education and children than at any other time – which could be a double-edged sword.

> I notice a huge difference since I left. The civil service as a whole now expects senior staff to move regularly between departments, and so there are few DfE officials with deep experience of education. Decision-making is more centralised in Number 10 than ever and Treasury financial controls are limiting DfE freedom of action. There isn't a strong sense of agency or self-confidence in the department.

Other sources of policy and advice

There is plenty of advice about, and for secretaries of state, the challenge of building a policy framework usually means seeking guidance from the circles we have described so far and from a wider group of what are increasingly called 'stakeholders'.

Government usually knows the direction in which it wants to travel. The challenge then is to find people who will give advice which supports that direction and persuade those who don't to acquiesce without too much protest.

The tension created by the demands coming from Number 10 to the DfE troubled Estelle Morris:

> I remember feeling confused, torn between listening to good friends whose advice I trusted and listening to the advice of people who were paid to advise. Downing Street risks falling prey to small groups of articulate people at any one time having undue influence. You know how that happens because Downing Street is criticised if they don't consult people, but they're not in a position to consult everyone. They make the mistake of gathering to them people who think like them. So what they tend to do is to know in which direction they want to travel and find people to advise them on how to make the journey. They don't find people who challenge their direction of travel. Maybe I did the same.

So, who might be the 'good friends' to whom Morris and others turn? Nicky Morgan, who was trying to push character-building aspects of schooling, said: 'I needed allies to support me and help me shape policy. When I was in office and we were working on character, I involved people like James Arthur[6] and Anthony Seldon.'

Gillian Shephard explained the spheres of advice to which she turned:

> In my first cabinet post, employment, the hugely able and experienced Geoffrey Holland was the permanent secretary, and I was happy to discuss policy with him, and indeed some of the other senior officials. At education, however, I felt I knew a fair amount already, and therefore if I wanted to test out ideas or gauge opinion, I would talk to people I had known for a long time in the field, like chief education officers, university vice chancellors and heads of FE colleges, people in local government and, of course, teachers and head teachers, and also HMI. At the time I worked well with some of the unions. It was only after my time at the DfE that I really found out what the Institute of Education could have offered.

---

6   James Arthur is director of the Jubilee Centre for Character and Virtues at Birmingham University and professor of education and civic engagement.

David Bell told us: 'We didn't know who was advising those around Michael Gove in the run-up to the 2010 election. John McIntosh, previously of the Oratory School in London, was influential and seemed to pop up afterwards when Michael was the secretary of state.'

It was Labour that began the practice of working closely with chosen people from schools. 'Under David Blunkett and Michael Barber, the department brought in head teacher gurus to describe what would happen with policies,' observed Nick Stuart.

And why would secretaries of state not listen to people they respected? Most people ask colleagues, friends and experts. Gove was different, though, famously claiming in connection with the referendum on European Union membership in 2016 that 'people in this country have had enough of experts'.[7] He had displayed a similar view during the review of the national curriculum in 2013 with his restating of Margaret Thatcher's maxim, 'advisers advise; ministers decide'.[8]

Secretaries of state also find some advice discomforting. HMI used to be based within the DfE and were seen by some as part of the problem in shifting the culture of schooling. Stuart believed that 'part of Kenneth Clarke's purpose in creating Ofsted was to remove HMI from the DfE. After 1992, the influence of HMI in policy formation rapidly dwindled.'

This contrasts with David Bell's relationship with the DfE 20 years later: 'When I was HMCI, Charles Clarke and David Miliband were very keen to have me and others round the table when they were debating policy. We had to be careful; we couldn't be seen to be marking our own homework but we had constructive sessions where inspection data was taken very seriously.'

Few secretaries of state talked of working with other departments to support mutual agendas. David Blunkett found 'working with Tessa Jowell in health and developing the early years Sure Start programme was fantastic. It wasn't about buildings but services. We provided 3,000 Children's Centres and affected children's lives and the lives of their parents too.'

---

7   M. Gove, interview with Faisal Islam, *Sky News* [video] (3 June 2016).
8   Quoted in F. Millar, Who Is Really Behind Michael Gove's Big Education Ideas?, *The Guardian* (3 December 2013). Available at: https://www.theguardian.com/education/2013/dec/03/michael-gove-education-dominic-cummings-policies-oxbridge.

Delivering policy

The DfE's remit is to enable the secretary of state's policy intention, to help take it through legislation (if required), to organise its implementation, to support its effectiveness through resource allocation and, if necessary, to evaluate its success. Whether this is done well or not depends on a range of factors, but the concept of delivery has been a growing part of the DfE remit since Kenneth Baker, gathering pace with David Blunkett and since. However, as we show in later chapters, the DfE is not consistently good at delivery.

David Carter, who held the role of national schools commissioner from 2016 to 2018, observed: 'The DfE divides people into two teams: the policy-makers or the delivery teams. The reality of the DfE is that if you're really ambitious and you're highly regarded, you set your sights on being in the policy team, which means that often not enough of the strongest people get to even visit a school, let alone see how the policy works.' He added: 'There is a cultural clash for me with policy when policy is created in a vacuum inside the DfE without the implementation challenge for schools being thoroughly examined.'

We have described the lack of confidence in the DfE to cope effectively, which is a consistent theme in our book, but our view is that few have tried to address the issue of effectiveness. The frustration is apparent.

One technique employed by secretaries of state is to use arm's length bodies or non-departmental public bodies (NDPBs) to deliver and manage their policies. This enables their influence to be centralised and avoids it being interpreted differently by local authorities. Ken Boston, former chief executive of QCA, used to talk about the benefits of an arm's length organisation lying entirely within the minister's purview because they could decide how long the arm was and adjust it. If things were going well it was a short arm – holding the organisation close to them and to the centre. When things were going wrong the arm was very long indeed – shoving it away to stand or fall alone.

It was Thatcher's government that began the push towards NDPBs or quangos to manage delivery. Typically, it is all about initials: TTA, SSAT, MSC, QCA, QCDA, NCSL, NS, NGA, Becta, Ofqual. Each new government creates a novel unit or agency and eventually the field becomes crowded. Every now and then, there is a 'bonfire of the quangos' under the guise of saving money, although it is often to regain control from the agencies they believe have exceeded their power or are distracting from the big agenda of the moment. One example would be the NCSL, established under Labour, which was increasingly valued by the profession but closed within 15 years of its inception. Not only was the entity shut down, but funding for leadership development was also reduced to a fraction of what the system had valued.

The NCC, which was formed in 1988 to generate the first national curriculum, was replaced by the School Curriculum and Assessment Authority (SCAA) in 1993, which became QCA in 1997. In 2008, Ofqual and the Qualifications and Curriculum Development Agency (QCDA) merged, only for QCDA to be dissolved in 2011. At present there is no government organisation beyond the DfE responsible for the curriculum. Is that a bad thing?

Mick recalls:

I remember the excitement when the first national curriculum was published. I also remember wondering why we still needed a national curriculum organisation (NCC) once the curriculum was 'decided'.

Of course, they had employed a lot of people and now they needed to give them something to do. Before long, we were getting non-statutory guidance and ring binders explaining every detail of their own work. It would have been better to send these excellent curriculum thinkers back to schools to teach their curriculum until we needed the next revision.

Many years later, when I found myself as director of curriculum at QCA, I was convinced that the job was to spend time helping the community of learning gather around the curriculum to see its benefit and to make it work for young people.

There was growing interest in how the curriculum could work with pedagogy, and any reviews of key stage requirements always focused on how the learning would meet the learner. There was a lot of professional enthusiasm in schools too, and it was always a worry for the DfE and some ministers that the curriculum might get in the way of education policy.

One problem is that in order to retain central control, managerialism increases at every level as government tries to control its many delivery agencies, now including schools themselves. Steve Munby observed:

> The system gets stuck in bureaucracy so the solution seems to be to create a new delivery chain, and when that doesn't work, create yet another one. The DfE gets dragged into managerial behaviour and drags others in to join it. If you ask DfE officials to make something happen, you are probably asking the wrong people. Their understanding of effectiveness means having meetings. Doing a RAG [red, amber, green] risk analysis is very business-like but does not address the risk – it just monitors it ... But it suits busy people.

Secretaries of state are often given advice, welcome or not, from select committees. These all-party groups, elected by MPs, are a powerful voice, although often irritating for secretaries of state in that they interrogate major policies through their reports, usually the result of taking evidence from numerous relevant witnesses. None of our secretaries of state mentioned education select committees.

Anne Longfield, the outgoing children's commissioner, told us of her concerns about schooling as part of her brief, but she acknowledged that her influence on ministers had to be through their willingness to act on the reports from her office. She was pleased that Parliament was focused on the work of her team and reflected that in her time in the role she had appeared before select committees far more frequently: 'It used to be that I was a part of a meeting once a year, but now they are devoting up to 15 meetings per year to consider our work.' Of course, many of these committees are concerned with aspects of childhood other than schooling and, in any case, the secretary of state is not always influenced by them.

David Carter talked about their work in connection with his role as national schools commissioner: 'The Education Select Committee was an excellent sounding board. I do think that was partly because of the way it was chaired, but it was an excellent opportunity to communicate important messages about the challenges and opportunities of system-wide delivery change.' Often, the select committees produce critical reports with clear advice for government, but whether this produces results is debatable, although there are examples of their reports being used as justification for tweaks of policy.

Other voices come from the all-party parliamentary groups which investigate and report on issues of the day and prompt debate about policy. Damian Hinds reflected: 'I worked on the All-Party Parliamentary Group on Social Mobility. It was one of the most important pieces of work I was ever involved in, but I don't think we made as much impact as we should.'

Advice beyond government

Secretaries of state increasingly look beyond their own department and the NDPBs they have established – and further afield than their invited reviews and commissions – to outsource policy and delivery functions to the private sector.

One problem is that the DfE and many NDPBs hire consultants for specific programmes, who often have even less knowledge of the system than the officials who employ them. The recourse to spreadsheets and strategy papers can become a smokescreen for a lack of progress. Private companies now win contracts for work that previously would have been done at a local authority level or elsewhere in the system.

Ministers use think tanks, especially institutes established by their own supporters, to develop and justify policy. Think tanks provide information on specific political and economic issues, although many are in fact a form of lobby group seeking to build consensus around their own agenda with the aim of influencing government policy. Demos, EDSK, the Institute for Public Policy Research (IPPR) and the Education Policy Institute are examples of think tanks with a leaning towards providing research evidence that is likely to be of benefit to specific political parties. Charities, such as the Esmée Fairbairn Foundation, fund longitudinal research with the aim of improving the quality of life for people and communities, although think tanks bid for work from these sources in order to maximise their agenda.

There are many lobby groups seeking to be a catalyst for change, such as the Big Education Conversation in June 2021[9] and the Foundation for Education Development (FED), which has grown in the recent past and held a summit in 2021. Carl Ward, the chair of FED, explained to us that

---

9   Big Change, the Institute for Public Policy Research and their partners are seeking to build consensus around the transformation of the education system through a five-year project.

the organisation is 'working in a neutral manner to help stakeholders across our system both in a top-down and bottom-up way to have conversations around the benefits of long-term planning in our education system – at least over a ten-year cycle of planning'.

The government is also influenced by publicly funded research organisations. These are non-profit bodies that undertake research with the aim of serving a public policy purpose – for example, the National Foundation for Educational Research (NFER).

Whether these sorts of organisations make an impact in an increasingly centralised system is questionable. While the teaching profession might seek to harness consensus from a broad range of communities of interest, the wheel of government policy is hard to divert as politicians seek the evidence that suits their agenda.

Universities, which in 1976 played a significant role in contributing to educational research, have to a large extent drifted from the picture as far as political influence is concerned. The teacher unions often commission comprehensive research with persuasive conclusions, although for ministers to respond to it is usually a hope too far. What catches the ministerial eye or goes with the flow of the time is influential.

One of the most significant policy developments of the recent past was built on a very small-scale research project looking at the use of synthetic phonics based on a group of schools in Clackmannanshire. The results of this study were published just as the Conservatives were seeking the evidence to justify their preferred approach to teaching children to read; today, the screening check is obligatory in schools – nonsense words and all.[10] While phonetic approaches to the teaching of reading had been used since 1870, they tend to be supplanted by other techniques but occasionally enjoy a rejuvenation. Phonics was part of the approach within the literacy strategy developed under Labour, with Ruth Miskin being a significant advocate. Nick Gibb emphasised the 'new' development in the traditional approach – synthetic phonics.

One growing contributor is the Education Endowment Foundation (EEF), which, in conjunction with the Sutton Trust, produces high-quality evidence on 'live' issues in the schooling landscape. The EEF was established

---

10   R. S. Johnston and J. Watson, *The Effects of Synthetic Phonics Teaching on Reading and Spelling Attainment: A Seven-Year Longitudinal Study* (Edinburgh: Scottish Executive Education Department, 2005).

by Michael Gove in 2011 and is now a widely welcomed part of the educational landscape. Kevan Collins, until recently the chief executive, explained:

> The coalition came up with this one-off capital spend to endow the foundation, which was a good decision. The EEF has become part of the system and still has some money to spend. It has raised additional funds working in partnership with other philanthropic partners. They see that we get a decent return of knowledge and activity. The EEF delivers a legacy of knowledge, not just a legacy of activity, if you invest in education, which is the great prize. The legacy of knowledge is the prize, not the activity in itself.
>
> I wanted to find a way in the EFF of presenting dispassionately to those who make decisions what we know, so they can make better decisions, not to tell them what to do. That's why I got involved in asking whether education is susceptible not only to presenting the evidence in an open way but also to generating new knowledge in a rigorous way.

Other voices

Whatever results from the work of the secretary of state and this complex web of relationships, there is always the challenge of coping with the forces of doubt or opposition – questioning direction, urging caution, proposing alternatives and refusing to cooperate. These come from three main sources: the opposition, the unions and the media, plus occasional public campaigns.

We talked with general secretaries and their deputies from several teacher unions and professional associations. The overriding impression was of a deep commitment to the educational prospects of every child in the nation, a concerned outlook on the educational prosperity of the country, and a wish to help schools be as good as they could be. We were shown documents outlining different unions' positions on issues of leadership, accountability, ethics and the 'forgotten third' of children who struggle to benefit from school. We were pointed to detailed evidence bases, reports by think tanks and surveys of parents, pupils and employers. We explore all of these within the content of later chapters.

It seemed to us that the general secretaries are much misunderstood as a group, living with a past image that is difficult to shed and typecast by politicians and the media in the same way as politicians are often stereotyped themselves. Between them they speak for a large workforce, so they represent a serious challenge for politicians who in the main are used to getting their own way. As Damian Hinds pointed out: 'It's a massive workforce – 450,000 teachers, that is an enormous amount! And 400,000 other adults working in schools … and 450,000 early years staff.'

General secretaries, collectively, also have something that most politicians lack, as well as one thing they are less used to experiencing. First, they have a picture of policy and practice stretching back many years with a close understanding refreshed continuously in schools – an invaluable touchstone. Second, they challenge secretaries of state, their policies and their officials in a more forensic way than most other stakeholders.

Mick recalls:

When I was at QCA, I was invited to a DfE meeting with all the union general secretaries to discuss thinking on the review of Key Stage 3. I was looking forward to it as a chance to get some reaction.

I arrived early and the degree of tension among the DfE officials was palpable. For each agenda item there was an official who was pale with anxiety.

It was like a meeting from a sketch show: unions on one side of a table, DfE on the other, masses of paper, over-talking and little room for discussion, a room with hard surfaces so voices sounded harsh. I remember wondering whether anyone had been on a course.

I enjoyed my bit and things were positive. That didn't help. I felt so sorry for the officials.

For DfE officials, the unions are important. They can make or break policy and also reduce or elevate an official in the eyes of a secretary of state or minister when news of successes or disasters surfaces.

Our politicians referred to the unions in different ways. Nicky Morgan told us: 'I think they welcomed the change at the top. The relationship with union general secretaries was generally good. We had differences of view on occasions but we were always very civil. I talked a lot about reducing workload and the unions couldn't complain about that.'

Charles Clarke had a less positive outlook towards the unions: 'It was important to deal with the unions, though the dialogue was completely deficient. David Miliband negotiated the school workforce agreement, although the NUT refused to be included. I deplore this abstentionist outlook. I refused to go to an NUT annual conference. I didn't think those conferences did well for anyone, in the eyes of parents particularly.'

For Labour in 1997, the relationship with unions generally was a conundrum, but for the education agenda to work it was of particular concern. David Blunkett remarked: 'The NUT had been in charge of Labour Party education policy and we needed a more radical agenda which would rock the boat – and for some on the left it would be a case of going too far.'

Labour's answer was what they dubbed a 'social partnership'. Alan Johnson, a lifelong trade unionist, was clear: 'We wanted the social partnership with unions to work. Co-determination was right and we needed to help unions to avoid being prisoners to the hard left. We wanted the parents' point of view to be appreciated. Having a union background, I knew the danger of "closed shops" and didn't want parents to encounter "closed schools". Their voice needed to be heard and their involvement was, and is, crucial.'

Ed Balls, the last Labour secretary of state before the coalition, saw the benefits: 'I think one of the untold stories was how effective our effort at partnership was in getting the unions to really back sometimes quite difficult things. The stuff we did around the licence to teach, with the rolling professional accreditation alongside master's entitlement, they all signed up to it. Some didn't like it very much but they all signed up to it.'

The coalition entered government with an austerity agenda and cuts to public services in general, which set relationships with the unions back years. This period saw the break-up of much of what teachers and their unions had come to value, and turbulence showed itself in marches and strikes. While it has settled somewhat, the pandemic has shone a light on some of the difficulties for both unions and secretaries of state.

Both are used to talking through the media as much as they are to each other. During the first lockdown, the media would regularly feature union general secretaries commenting on school issues. However, as soon as schools were contactable again, the cameras and reporters were there talking with heads and teachers in more photogenic settings. The media likes the immediate and the relatable rather than the general – and politicians can manage the general with a few sound bites. Off camera, general secretaries typically have more detailed knowledge and specific examples than most politicians and department policy officials. However, officials and ministers pronounce, not always to good effect.

Kenneth Baker spoke with us about his view of the DfE today:

> The actual department has been hollowed out by the reduction of civil servants. Every time there was a call to cut civil servants, the Department for Education volunteered more. The quality of civil servants in the department is now lower than it was 10 years ago, and infinitely lower from what I remember in my day. I had some really high-quality people in the department, and they supported me and I persuaded them to support the policies that I introduced, but it took a lot of time.

Managing the media or 'comms' is vital. The broadcast media, television and press is one area, but the growing social media arena is one both to watch and manipulate. From more formal online communities, such as Mumsnet and Ross McGill's TeacherToolkit, to more spontaneous Twitter communities, politicians generate, respond to and defend standpoints through round-the-clock engagement. Katharine Birbalsingh, the prominent free school head teacher, told us how she emerged from the world of the anonymous blogger to the limelight of school critic by virtue of a political adviser who could see the potential political benefits.

The media is a recurring and dominant theme in the success of a secretary of state. For some of the SpAds it is a key aspect of their work. The SpAds most mentioned by onlookers were those who were savvy with media and adept at spin. The sound bite, the headline and the optics are as important as the policy itself in increasing the credibility of the policy or deflecting attention towards something less awkward.

Sam Freedman was keen to see policies emerge but told us: 'I found politics to be immensely frustrating. Issues such as our GCSE reform agenda were trying to build towards objectives but political briefing ruined it. I thought that there was a desire to maintain, for political and ideological reasons, an image of a fight with the profession. Michael Gove wanted a public fight to be waged in the media.'

And Jon Coles told us:

> Too easily, governments of all stripes find themselves defending the indefensible. It's natural when any policy is new that some people outside the department instinctively resist and criticise – and so, initially, policies need to be defended. But too often that becomes an increasingly entrenched blind defence of the idea the government thought of first. Then you get the horrible 'lines to take' culture, where officials have stopped thinking about how to refine or improve a policy and are just looking for the positive gloss to put on something which isn't working well enough and needs to be changed.

It is a wonder anything improves in schools

At the crux of all the successes or failures of policy sits the relationship between the secretary of state and schools, which is moderated to a large extent by the DfE. The urgency of the great reformers has led to a more centralised approach with the traditional route to schools being by-passed through a direct line of contact. Control has grown to the extent that detailed policy decisions are more likely to be made in Sanctuary Buildings, with the secretary of state having powers that Shirley Williams would not have believed possible in 1976.

Although the system has become centralised and, as a result, more managerial, most of what has been explored in this chapter is about working relationships, trust, communication and purpose. In the next chapter, we explore the changing and declining relationship between the secretary of state and local authorities and the growing and complex relationship with MATs – which, because of the centralised nature of the system, are pivotal points.

So, how do we end this chapter on the relationship between secretaries of state and their working community, and especially their stewardship of the DfE? Let's focus on some good stories. David Blunkett's era helped the department to become more ready to see its role in shaping future success in schooling. It also seems that, since that time, secretaries of state have been able to harness the energy of the organisation to good effect.

Jon Coles observed: 'The civil service tends to like single-minded leadership that knows what it wants but is open and prepared to have straight and honest conversation.' That single-mindedness was a feature of Michael Gove's tenure as it had been with Ed Balls and would be with Justine Greening. Both Balls and Greening explained their efforts to get the department to 'buy into their agenda'.

Balls talked about the challenge of cultural change:

> We launched the Children's Plan in December 2007 and we had this big Children's Plan rainbow hanging in the department. It was everywhere, including the lifts. We came back after Christmas and it had all been taken down. I asked one of the senior staff where it had all gone. He said, 'It's been launched now.' I said, 'That is not how cultural change works. Get it all back up again! It needs to be on every document, every email from the department needs to have a rainbow, we need to be continually asking people whether they are doing everything they could. Are they thinking differently?'

This challenge of developing a culture and involving officials across the department was not new. Kenneth Baker, some 20 years before Balls, told us how he tried to spread understanding and influence:

> I had to persuade the civil servants to support me, so I had several meetings with the three deputy secretaries. I had a very good permanent secretary who very much supported me. But then I said to the three of them, and this was revolutionary, 'At the next meeting I would like to meet your undersecretaries – can you bring them to the next meeting?' That was unheard of; ministers didn't speak to undersecretaries. Then, a bit later, I said that I would like to speak to some assistant secretaries. This seemed to be revolutionary in the Department for Education. It was very, very hierarchical as far as the civil service was concerned.

Justine Greening was someone who seemed to embrace all the current thinking about leadership in her work with her own department:

> I turned up in the department and people were on every floor level looking over balconies to get a look at my arrival. I was so excited

to be finally in the role I'd always wanted and I remember giving them all the thumbs up. I decided to call an all-staff meeting later that afternoon. I had a loose script but I wanted to talk with them about our mission. I explained that the mission we would have was social mobility, and there was an urgency to it and that every single one of them had a role to play in delivering it.

I later wrote to every official in the DfE, at every level, asking them for their ideas on what they felt they and our department could do to enable social mobility. I had a deluge of responses. Across everything we did, I wanted the same clear and enabling objectives: people, processes and systems.

I increased the number of people in delivery teams and was worried that too many officials seemed to like doing policy but were less keen on the gritty but vital work of delivery, so putting more of my focus as secretary of state on it was a way of elevating its importance across the departments. I tried to work out what we could stop doing. We seemed to be trying to do about 130% of our capacity. There was too much on the fringes of policy and I wanted us to focus our efforts where they were needed.

Greening was in office for a short 18 months, yet is remembered fondly by many in schools and across the education community who talked with us. In her description of how she got going in the job, she was more inclusive than some others, seeking to work with people and embrace their ideas rather than impose her own on them or to do her bidding. She had a clear outlook on how the school system would respond:

The department and ministers had previously too often issued edicts and expected schools to do things. This was not going to be acceptable as a sensible way of working. The department had to work effectively with key stakeholders. I wanted things de-cluttered at local levels, so it was clear what the four or five key priorities were and that they were owned by everybody, not just locally. I wanted people to be empowered to take the right decisions. I didn't want people to paper over problems. I wanted them to work out how to solve them and feel they could get on with that.

As Greening describes her influence within the department and on the school system and pupils, so others described political success over time in different terms. Gavin Williamson highlighted the difference between the work in the glare of the media and the hard yards won on the less noticed elements of policy. He told us:

> Invariably, the things that really seem to deliver quite substantial differences to children in an education environment seem to be the things that are quite dry and often quite technical. It's about keeping this whole system grounded. I give credit to Damian [Hinds] for the initial work on the early career framework. I was really driving that forward and building on it with NPQs [national professional qualifications] as well. As I say, no one will ever care about these things, but they'll be far and away the things that outlast myself and several successors. They'll be the things that actually make a real difference on the ground.

The extent to which secretaries of state make a difference or not is debatable and whether any differences are positive and lasting even more so. Yet their actions and policies do influence schooling over time. Estelle Morris was clear about the impact that political change has made to the profession, not simply during her time in office but through the years since 1988 generally:

> One thing I get thrilled about is listening to the professional conversations between teachers. If I look back to my days in teaching, and I only left in 1992, the staffroom conversations were not about pedagogy. They were about behaviour – the child who behaved for one teacher and not for another. Sometimes the conversations were about curriculum content and they might have been about resources. But I rejoice now in the quality of professional conversations that I hear teachers have.

> If there has been a change that we politicians were responsible for, and I played a part in, it is that young professionals now speak like real professionals. They speak about pedagogy, methodology, evaluation and review. I taught for 18 years and I never had that quality of conversation as a half good, decent, committed teacher, and I think that has been a good thing that has come out of those years of reform.

There are examples of how the machinery of government can be very effective, even within education and schooling. The decision facing secretaries of state seems to be where to put their energies during what will probably be a brief spell in office. Some developments have gained traction: the results of evolving centralisation, managerialism and markets have changed the relationship between the secretary of state and the school system. Other aspects seem to remain remarkably stable, perhaps because they are less attractive to a market-driven approach. Would a civil servant from 1976 returning to the DfE notice a different working environment beyond the physical and technological? Yet schools *have* improved. Is it because the relationship with local authorities has changed, and secretaries of state (and their policies) are now connected directly with schools?

Chapter 4

Political involvement in the way our schooling is organised

The decline of local authorities and the rise of MATs – it all ends in tiers

In this country, central government decides on education policy and enacts legislation. Schools are required to work within the framework set down by government. What happens in-between – in the middle tier – has always been the subject of debate and often disagreement.

Our secretaries of state since 1976, along with their predecessors, have grappled with the challenge of ensuring a good experience for children and young people spread across more than 22,000 schools (and previously many more than that) in many different and sometimes unique local environments. The question of how to mediate, manage, interpret, check and amend law so that it meets the needs of all has vexed successive governments. Rather like a celebration cake, a very small top tier (government) and a very large lower tier (schools) is more secure with something stable in-between – hence the middle tier.

It is the middle tier – which, from 1902 was occupied by the LEAs – that is responsible for schooling and other functions in their council area. They have had to share their tier; churches have had degrees of control over some of the schools. In the period of our book from 1976, the middle tier has become more congested with central government using other delivery agencies to bring their policies directly into schools. The questions have always been about the amount of interpretation and the amount of autonomy that is allowable in the middle.

It was always thus. When state education began in 1870, school boards were established to provide schooling where it was needed, rather like the concept of free schools today. Schooling had existed previously for those who could pay for it and through organisations that felt the need to provide it. Forster's Education Act created the school boards as local coordinators and providers of state schooling: 'the most democratic organs of local administration of the century'.[1]

The school boards were dynamic and, in many cases, highly successful, and some were progressive in outlook and beacons of hope for the lower classes. Their impact was also haphazard with variable provision across the country for pupils of different ages and gender, as well as for children who would today be designated as having special needs. There was also the problem that some school boards were misusing the funding, or at least playing fast and loose with the boundaries of regulation, and this left the boards' opponents in a position of strength.

Since 1976, governments have continued with the story of school control but, bit by bit, they have broken the tripartite arrangement that had existed since the 1944 Act, with LEAs as the conduit between central government and schools.

Governments intent on moving forward from the age of doubt and disillusion have tried to avoid their intended improvements being distorted, deflected or diminished on their way to the child. Of all the complexities in the work of the secretary of state, the relationship with the middle tier is the one that has most effect on schools directly.

This shows itself in the decline in the responsibility and impact of local authorities over schools in their areas and the rise of MATs. Many of our witnesses believe that the current arrangement of a middle tier between central government and schools is not only unsustainable but is also failing many children. The mixed economy, with confused responsibilities and suspected motives, represents a return to the late 1800s.

In the rest of this chapter, we will explore first the decline of local authorities and then the rise of MATs. It all ends in tiers.

---

1   See J. Lawson and H. Silver, *A Social History of Education in England* (London: Methuen, 1973), p. 314.

The decline in the relationship between secretaries of state and local authorities

It's 2020 and lots of schools are in a similar situation: huge numbers of teenagers are testing positive for COVID-19 or are isolating. Cases continue to go up across London and the South East. Teachers and unions are increasingly unhappy with the situation and head teachers are reporting that safety is becoming unsustainable. In the last week of term, Greenwich in South-East London tells its schools to close. On 14 December, the move prompts Gavin Williamson to use new emergency coronavirus powers to issue the borough with a 'temporary continuity direction'. In other words, he legally forces the council to keep schools open. But with cases spiking, many begin to question whether schools should now close.

In this embarrassing end-of-term squabble, the tension in the triangular dynamic between the DfE, local authorities and schools was writ large. So much for the rhetoric of the previous years where 'head teachers know best'. An absolutist position at the end of a long period of stress for all concerned played out as a war of words in the media. Just a few working days later, the entire country went into another lockdown.

As we pointed out briefly in Chapter 1, the LEAs had been one of the pillars around which schooling had been organised since they were established in 1902. In 1976, when our book begins, they towered over the schooling landscape, responsible for every aspect of government policy in the local context, including teacher training. Since then, rather like a Jenga tower, the pillar has been dismantled. Secretaries of state, knowingly or inadvertently, have gradually reduced their influence. Various key planks of their function have been removed, building blocks denied and instability brought about by shaking the foundations. What is left of the pillar of local authority influence is a rubble of confusion. There are responsibilities that nobody has yet chosen to remove, possibly because they are unattractive or difficult to define. Other parts of the structure are strong because nobody has attacked them, yet.

In our conversations, few of our secretaries of state expressed a positive view of local authorities, even though many had come into national politics having served in local councils, sometimes prominently. Perhaps that was the reason: they had seen close up behaviours and practices that had been disappointing. Or perhaps the secretaries of state do what Kenneth Clarke accused schools of doing – claiming the credit when things go well but pushing the blame on to others when it is less successful.

What we don't know is whether local council authorities are viewed with such disdain by all departments of government or whether it is only in education that such negativity prevails. If, as we suspect, the same outlook to local authorities is present in housing, social care, policing, leisure and highways, then we should probably be getting that out in the open and sorting it out as a significant issue for a democratic society. As it is, local government is currently a small part of a departmental portfolio (the Ministry of Housing, Communities and Local Government) rather than a separate department of government.

Some of our secretaries of state opted to tolerate local authorities, some to work around them, some to undermine them and some to confront them. Gillian Shephard tried to work with them in a supportive way, citing examples of how she had contacted officials in specific local authorities at times of media interest, such as following particular difficulties or tragedies, to ask whether the DfE could be of help.

Until the end of Keith Joseph's tenure, much government policy has been delegated to authorities to enact at a local level. We deal with the often misunderstood meanings of devolution, decentralisation and delegation and the need to follow the logic of subsidiarity in Chapter 12 on governance and finance. It is sufficient to say here that the confusing process of shifting power to the centre, either overtly or by sleight of hand, began with Joseph and accelerated under his successors.

Did local government ever control except by default?

One constant theme over the last 50 years has been the changing and diminishing role of local authorities and their influence on schooling in their areas. Nowadays, they are used as a conduit to schools for some government actions, almost like distribution agencies – for example, in the attempted delivery of laptops to schools for the use of poorer pupils during the first lockdown. Separately, central government contacts schools directly with revised processes or guidance in which it will often refer to local authorities managing certain aspects in their area. To complicate things even further, many schools now work under the aegis of a MAT and are governed through different arrangements again; many MATs have academies in five or more local authority areas.

In essence, the word 'authority' has very limited meaning for those who attempt to drive the schooling agenda within a local council area. But did local authorities ever lead the schooling agenda? They certainly had a more significant influence than they do today, but for schools that influence was rooted not in statute so much as in an acceptance of local democratic processes and tighter and more directive (or looser and more liberal) relationships between LEAs and schools. In the 1970s, the notion of deference was still prevalent in many aspects of working life. Although schools (particularly primary) were rare examples of a workplace where female workers were in the majority, local authorities were largely led by men.

There was a sense that local authorities were 'in charge' of school staff in their area, but to what extent they chose to exercise that power or influence was very variable. Traditionally, what went on at a school level was decided at a school level through the head teacher. While heads might be constrained by resources allocated from central or local government, there was little to constrain (or energise) their educational vision or practice – or, in some cases, their excesses.

By the 1970s, most LEAs had used their local influence to enhance aspects of learning for pupils through their councils. They were working in the spirit of trust and optimism: if they provided resources, they could rely on schools and teachers to get on with the job, encouraged by advisers and advisory teachers. The provision of library and museum services was extended into schooling through collections of art, archives or music for loan in order to build an appreciation of the arts and to bring teaching alive through the use of artefacts. Many authorities acquired premises for use as outdoor education centres, often in national parks, giving youngsters an experience of fieldwork or adventure.

Through the late 1960s, LEAs had begun to employ advisers who would support head teachers to develop the effectiveness of their teachers. Many local authorities established Teachers' Centres, often with social facilities, where teachers could organise their own in-service courses locally. Some authorities funded premises to act as venues for residential conferences and courses for teachers to consider aspects of their profes-sional work.[2]

These local authority developments were piecemeal. Different local authorities offered different provision and opportunities depending on their political outlook, the level of resource made available to edu-cation and the extent to which it was deployed equitably within their area. Therefore, some authorities had many extras and some had next to nothing, and some schools took advantage of everything within their authority and some took no advantage at all.

As we observed in Chapter 1, while in certain schools there was dynamic and forward-looking thinking, in others there was bizarre practice. The ILEA was seen by most as a driver of innovation and high-quality provi-sion, addressing the needs of its pupils. At the same time, there were schools such as the notorious William Tyndale primary school that under-mined the progress being made.[3]

In the West Riding of Yorkshire, Sir Alec Clegg was a dynamic and charis-matic director of education who built a spirit in that authority based on a clear philosophy for the needs of children, which was met with wide acclaim. At the same time, in the late 1960s, *A Kestrel for a Knave* and the film adaptation, *Kes*, set in the same local authority, resonated with many in its depiction of a largely uncaring school community.[4]

When James Callaghan made his speech at Ruskin College in 1976, the excitement barely resonated with schools. For heads and teachers, this seemed to be just more of the chatter that was a constant noise in the background of schooling. Except that this had a different edge to it. This time it was the prime minister speaking about what should happen in the classroom, what children should learn and how schools should be organised. The speech caused consternation for local authorities which diverged in their responses, especially in respect of galvanising the debate within schools, with some engaging fully and others regarding the debate as a spectator activity.

---

2   West Riding County Council owned Woolley Hall near Wakefield, and it was here that Sir Alec Clegg used to gather together influential people to debate the way forward. He had worked with others to establish Bretton Hall College of Education in 1949, a teacher training college that specialised in the arts. It closed in 2001, although the Bretton Hall estate is now home to the Yorkshire Sculpture Park.
3   See Auld, *The William Tyndale Junior and Infants Schools*.
4   B. Hines, *A Kestrel for a Knave* (London: Michael Joseph, 1968); *Kes*, dir. K. Loach (1969).

Callaghan's call for a Great Debate about education, to be orchestrated by his secretary of state for education, Shirley Williams, could be seen as an attempt to gain control over a discussion that had been underway in any case, perhaps to arrest and harness the growing tide of negative commentary about developments in what was seen as 'progressive' schooling. For many, the prospect of a debate was met with cynicism, but for many others it was the forerunner of what was starting to become commonplace: consultation with the users of a public service.

The culmination of the Great Debate, which was largely limited to regional conferences with a proportionately small overall attendance, was the publication in 1977 of a consultative document called *Education in Schools*, which, for the first time, proposed a common core curriculum of fundamental subjects that would take up about half of the time children spent in school. The wheels turned slowly, although the consultation was probably no more genuine than those of today, and the change of government in the general election in 1979 meant the end of the consultative process anyway.

While Williams had asked local authorities to review their arrangements for the curriculum, there was little to suggest that schools would lose their local autonomy. Indeed, when taking forward the recommendations of the Taylor Report,[5] Williams believed she 'broadened the social base of governing bodies and rooted local schools even more closely into the communities they served'.[6]

While central government seemed to have developed and articulated a degree of frustration about the quality of the education system and brought the period of disillusion to a head, LEAs were still seen as the route to schools. There seemed to be a reluctance on the part of both Labour and Conservative governments to criticise schools themselves and a tendency to talk about schooling more generally. To point the finger of blame at central government would be politically foolish, and so frustration was expressed about a system with local democracy as the lynchpin.

The Conservatives, buoyed by the Falklands War, had secured another victory in the 1983 general election, and Margaret Thatcher's reshuffled cabinet saw Kenneth Baker at education set about tackling their big

---

5   T. Taylor, *A New Partnership for Our Schools* [Taylor Report] (London: HMSO, 1977). Available at: http://www.educationengland.org.uk/documents/taylor/taylor1977.html.
6   Williams, *Climbing the Bookshelves*, p. 236.

agendas with renewed zeal. Over the next few years, the country was to witness the miners' strike, increased IRA activity, denationalisation and public ownership. Turbulence and change. Proposals to change schooling were therefore played out against a background of societal shift.

In 1984, the Conservative government, through Kenneth Baker, published a Green Paper called *Parental Influence at School*, which emphasised the uniqueness of schools and, by implication, the status of head teachers.[7] The subtitle of the paper, 'A New Framework for School Government in England and Wales', was a better description of the content, which asserted that 'every maintained school should have a life of its own within the system of maintained schools in the area'.[8] It also spelled out the powers of all partners to 'secure a firm legal foundation for the role of the head teacher, which clarifies his responsibilities and preserves his authority'. (Note the 'his'; different times.) At this stage, the power of LEAs over what went on in schools was moderated by the governing body, in so far as it could influence the head teacher.

The Education Reform Act 1988 proposed the most far-reaching shake-up of schools since the beginning of state education in 1902.[9] Baker's provisions were extensive and covered almost every aspect of the system. Strikingly, there were some key elements that transferred power towards the centre. These elements would change the power relationship between LEAs and their schools, both individually and collectively. In so doing, there would also be a change in the relationship between central government and schools with the first steps towards a centralisation of the agenda. Headlines included the provision of a national curriculum and arrangements for the local management of schools, as well as the establishment of grant-maintained schools and city technology colleges, and the abolition of the ILEA.

---

7   Department of Education and Science, *Parental Influence at School: A New Framework for School Government in England and Wales* [Green Paper] (London: HMSO, 1984). Available at: http://www.educationengland.org.uk/documents/gp1984/index.html.
8   Department of Education and Science, *Parental Influence at School*, p. 4.
9   See https://www.legislation.gov.uk/ukpga/1988/40/section/1/enacted.

Tim recalls:

It was in October 1987, nine years after I had been appointed Oxfordshire's education officer, when I made one of my most unfortunate mistakes. I wrote an article for *The Observer* criticising 'Gerbil' (the Great Educational Reform Bill) which became Kenneth Baker's Education Act 1988. Headed 'First Steps On a Downward Path', I bemoaned the power grab it endorsed for the minister, comparing it to 'a long-forgotten treatise on pre-war Italy and Germany, the Roman Empire and Napoleonic France – a study in totalitarianism'. I unwisely finished with: 'I cannot rid myself of images of black and brown, of echoing footsteps, of clanging doors – all the chilling paraphernalia which, historically, have followed such tidy measures. Suddenly this autumn after the hurried consultations which didn't quite reach the parents in whose name the proposals are made, I taste panic and fear – not for myself but for our grandchildren.'

Unsurprisingly, although I had written in defence of local government, this did not endear me to the Conservative councillors who had appointed me. At the next county council meeting, I had to listen to a three-hour debate cataloguing my many misdemeanours over the years, which had culminated in this act of lese-majesty, and suggestions about how I should be punished. Hung? Drawn? Quartered? Or all three, and in which order? Fortunately for me, by then they had lost their majority, so apart from the recurring cry of the *Oxford Mail's* paper-seller that evening at Carfax Tower, 'School Boss Must Go', I escaped with only minor wounds.

With the benefit of hindsight, I had been hopelessly wrong in my estimate that the secretary of state was taking 30 new powers, which my councillors had complained was an exaggeration. Far from it: he had paved the way for the most centrally directed schooling system outside North Korea.

To what extent did control move to schools?

There were far-reaching implications for head teachers. Previously, the LEA had taken decisions about staffing levels and premises, including maintenance, and head teachers could control expenditure based on capitation to provide expendable resources. Suddenly, heads were to be in control of their entire budget, devolved by formula from their LEA. Head teachers were concerned about their ability to manage such complex financial administration. To whom did they turn for support and advice? The very LEAs that the government had deemed incapable of managing their budgets. However, even today, the belief persists in many schools that there is very little budget to 'manage', given that the majority is spoken for in respect of premises and staffing. While in theory schools became more autonomous, many simply enacted at a local level the systems that had been pressed on to them collectively by their LEA.

More than 30 years on, there is minimal radical thinking about how staff or premises might be better used to further enhance learning. While the ability to manage funding more strategically at a school level improved the appearance of premises, and successive grants and programmes have seen a better fabric in most schools (or at least the rot hidden), the overall effect has been to make practice formulaic.

The leader of a growing MAT told us:

> Too many schools complain about not having money without ever looking at where their money is really going. We use modern business thinking from the software development industry to develop our budgeting model. Other schools ask how we do it. I suggest they look at their use of what they have and where money is wasted. So much is sitting in stock cupboards and money is spent on cover teachers without thinking of alternatives. Give a maths department a budget and they spend it, whether they need things or not. We use purposeful funding. We buy what we need and we check we haven't already got it. We expect no money from families for any activity that we plan or any visitor to school.

With regard to the national curriculum, about which much concern has been voiced concerning centralisation, there has been a gradual regression to the mean in the way schools organise learning. Little of this, though, is due to the requirements of the curriculum itself or the various modifications and revisions over time. The national curriculum plays second fiddle in the matter of influence to a very tight accountability system: the connected development of tests and examinations, together with league tables and the later developments in inspection.

Did Kenneth Baker intend to centralise or simply to improve the system? Did he want to shift the power from local authorities to the centre? It may be hindsight but it seems not. He told us: 'One thing we have to appreciate is that the Department for Education has no real experience of how to run schools. They have never run schools and they're making a big mess with it at the moment.'

What did occur was growing unrest in schools generally and the view – voiced by teacher unions repeatedly – that central government was meddling in schools and their organisation. The battle over the number of days per year a school should open (with claims of stolen holiday time), the specification of 1,265 directed hours for teachers and the insistence on five in-service training days (known as Baker days[10]) were a source of constant complaint in respect of the diminishing of professional standing.

Too often, though, this came across as carping on the part of the profession, as union conferences, shown on television over Easter and other bank holidays, gave a less than savoury impression of what people associate with professional behaviour. These images of teachers' unions linger and several of our secretaries of state talked about the teaching unions in terms of what they saw as the 'necessary ordeal' of hostile annual conferences.

Nicky Morgan, for instance, a relatively recent incumbent, told us: 'I attended all the conferences I was invited to, but they are strange affairs because you tend to get a certain type of teacher who is prepared to give up their holiday to attend a conference.' The reference to a 'certain type of teacher' is interesting; other types are leading residential activities for pupils at the same time. It is not the giving up of holidays that is notable but the attending of annual union conferences, which is only a small proportion of the membership. Where party conferences have become

---

10 Schools are required to arrange staff training for five days per year. This was originally to support the introduction of the new national curriculum. It was then extended to the introduction of assessment and has since been used to brief staff on new developments including safeguarding and General Data Protection Regulation (GDPR). In fact, there is plenty of new government legislation to use up the time every year.

stage-managed, with one eye on the televisual image, union conferences allow preconceptions to develop among families and the wider public.

Professor Ted Wragg[11] became a much loved and high-profile critic of Baker's reforms, with his regular back-page column in the *TES* mocking government policy and what he saw as the nonsense of the central agenda through the fictitious 'Swineshire'. This satirical column continued for many years beyond Baker's tenure and well into the Labour administration, as central government exerted its growing influence directly on schools, bypassing the LEA.

In effect, central government was shaping the profession through legislation in a way the LEAs had been unable to do previously, partly because they had limited power and partly because they chose not to do so. Baker's reforms placed LEAs in the position of administering new constructs on behalf of the government – a sort of delegated line management function, which had always been implicit, but previously there had been considerable discretion and flexibility for local democracy. Now, very detailed arrangements for schools were coming from the centre at the same time as schools were being encouraged to leave the community of the LEA and become grant maintained.

The failure of grant-maintained schools to take off after the 1988 Act, which made provision for schools to convert, was a puzzle to Conservative ministers. Gillian Shephard thought it was, in part, because the DfE wasn't capable of running them: 'I had to send two of my special advisers to help out when a GM [grant-maintained] school in Cornwall had a tragedy to deal with and where previously the LEA would have helped. But, of course, LEAs – who opposed the reform – were not prepared to help.'

Kenneth Baker makes the same point in his memoirs, similarly regretting the tactics that some LEAs employed to deter parents and governors from supporting heads who were keen to 'escape' LEA control. An alternative explanation is that heads had enough on their plates with the introduction of other provisions in the 1988 Act, such as delegated budgets through LMS and the new and voluminous national curriculum, where the LEA was very helpful to them. They needed little persuasion to pass by, at least for a while, the extra freedoms and responsibilities offered by grant-maintained status. In 1997, one of New Labour's first acts was

---

11   Ted Wragg, professor of education at Exeter University, was known for his advocacy of schooling and objection to political interference. He was a well-respected researcher and much-admired speaker. He used humour well and was a forerunner for the wit of Ken Robinson.

to abolish grant-maintained status, only to bring back something similar later on in the form of academies.

Could the DfE secure control?

The DfE assumed a more significant role, therefore, but on so many accounts it was ill equipped to deliver. Nearly every secretary of state from thereon has criticised the department, with the exception of those in the early 2000s; some more than others. More consistent even than that, though, is their criticism of local authorities.

It would seem that, as Baker prepared for the biggest schooling upheaval in a generation, little consideration was given to preparing the ground and building the infrastructure to make it work. The impatience at slow progress led to continuous criticism of local authorities and frustration with the DfE for not sorting them out.

John MacGregor, who succeeded Baker, reportedly saw problems ahead. Nick Stuart, a deputy permanent secretary at the time, told us: 'John MacGregor is the only secretary of state from Baker onwards whose ruling belief was that things were going too fast and that the reforms had to be entrenched.' However, the imperative for rapid change was driven by electoral considerations: Margaret Thatcher became convinced that the reforms needed to be pushed through at a faster pace. He added: 'I think Kenneth Baker persuaded Margaret Thatcher that things had slowed down and nothing was happening and we needed change.'

It wasn't long before Kenneth Clarke succeeded MacGregor, bringing what he himself calls his 'forthright and traditional outlook'. He saw the problems of educational progress and securing Baker's intentions as resting with the DfE. Of local authorities, Clarke observed: 'Some LEAs were good, of course – and that's irrespective of party, but the quality was very variable and some local authorities were run by some very strange people, in some cases little short of gangsters. It was my decision to take FE colleges out of their control and that was welcomed on the whole.'[12]

The aim of releasing schools from the control of local authorities underpinned Clarke's continuing support for schools gaining grant-maintained

---

12   K. Clarke, *Kind of Blue: A Political Memoir* (London: Macmillan, 2016), p. 271.

status: 'Almost all local education authorities were completely controlled by their large numbers of education officials who sought to impose precisely the anti-academic 1960s culture which government was trying to reverse. I wanted to resume the conversion of as many schools as possible to independent status.'[13] He added: 'Many heads were only too anxious to free themselves from the unwelcome local authority control under which they found themselves.'[14]

However, he was hampered by Baker's concession that parents of current pupils would have a say over grant-maintained status, which 'gave local authorities an important weapon in their bitter fights to retain ideological control of all the schools on their patch'.[15]

Clarke seemed to enjoy the image of battle in much of his politics, and according to his autobiography, he seems to believe that he won most of those in which he took part. His successor, John Patten, was now faced with continuing Baker's reforms some considerable time after the main conflict had taken place and with smaller skirmishes still to be had.

Tim recalls:

I had just finished my first two weeks in Birmingham spent visiting schools, but I wasn't sure if this would compensate for turning up at the wrong venue for an open meeting for school governors. 'Westhill College 7pm' it had said in my diary, but when I arrived the place was locked up and deserted. No mobiles in 1993, so I found the nearest phone box to ring the sender of the letter inviting me, only to be told by his daughter that 'Dad is out at an important meeting of governors who are meeting the new chief education officer'. This much I knew, but sadly his daughter didn't have the vital piece of missing information – the location of the meeting.

With a sinking feeling I realised that her dad was to be disappointed – even angry. On that dreadful night, I never did find out the real venue where 250 people were kept waiting, which was not Westhill but Westbourne College – ironically, close to our terraced house just off the Hagley Road. By the weekend, things had got even worse.

---

13   Clarke, *Kind of Blue*, p. 271.
14   Clarke, *Kind of Blue*, p. 271.
15   Clarke, *Kind of Blue*, p. 271.

When casually watching BBC news, I heard that at a fringe meeting of the Conservative Party conference, the then secretary of state, John Patten, was reported to have said that Birmingham had appointed this 'nutter' as their chief education officer, who, during his time in Oxfordshire (the minister's constituency) had 'run around the streets frightening the children'. I confess that 250 Birmingham school governors might have agreed with him. Apart from trying to repair the damage of my mistake, amid a whirl of unwelcome national publicity, I hoped for a quick ministerial apology, which I would have accepted. Sadly, a drawn-out legal wrangle followed which culminated in it being 'settled' on the steps of the High Court ten months later. I was able to give the settlement proceeds to charitable causes and help the educationally disadvantaged.

What did I learn from these events? Well, first to double-check my diary details. Second, good lawyers are expensive and best left to get on with it (after all, I was preoccupied busily recovering from my bad start). And, third, that however good or bad the situation, there will always be unintended consequences. In this case, they were long term and beneficial.

In those days, secretaries of state were unpopular figures among teachers, so the fact that I had stood up to Patten went down very well among head teachers and school staff. As a result, they were prepared to give me the benefit of the doubt and join in with our school improvement agenda, which I was unveiling at that time, with unusual enthusiasm. The irony was that I always thought the secretary of state, with a stated priority to persuade schools to convert to grant-maintained status, was worried (with good reason, as it happened) that the steady flow of schools from Birmingham becoming grant maintained would stop. He knew very well that, for all my faults, I would be capable of convincing people that such a move would distract them from the vital and urgent task of improving schools, attracting and retaining good teachers, and encouraging all pupils that they could improve on their previous best.

And so it turned out in Birmingham over the next decade or so; in fact, a real sense developed of transforming the prospects of Brummies together. However, there was a longer-term message too – namely, the shifting power (albeit briefly halted in this case) from local to central government.

This episode serves as an illustration of the undermining of local democracy and the strengthening of the central state. My brief and uncomfortable skirmish was just that – no more than a comma, a pause for breath as it were, in the inexorable march towards an over-mighty DfE, as powerful as it is incompetent.

Increasing centralisation

The other area that Kenneth Clarke worked on was the inspection of schools, which is addressed more fully in Chapter 11. When Ofsted was established in 1992, under Clarke, it was run in a low-key way by the vice chancellor of London University, Stewart Sutherland, on a part-time basis. Chris Woodhead took over later when John Patten was secretary of state, and the impact was felt far wider than just schools. The early training sessions leading to accreditation of registered (lead) inspectors were filled with local authority advisers and inspectors seeking 'the badge'. There was a sort of double irony in this in that the very people being used were those who were deemed ineffective in their day job and the training they were undertaking was helping them to do that job better.

In fact, the motive of many individuals who trained was to find out how to do the job of inspecting and to be able to forewarn their local schools of what was to come. In truth, too, many were required to attend because local authorities were now in a more commercial relationship with their schools and needed to have something viable to sell. The establishment of Ofsted did more than diminish local authority influence through inspection itself; it led to a subtle centralisation of the definitions of effective schooling.

As Gillian Shephard took over the role of secretary of state following the short and troubled tenure of John Patten, the Conservative government was in decline, foundering on the unfolding stories of sleaze. The disarray was supposedly mirrored by a fiasco of a false start at the Grand National. Her department began to intervene directly in aspects of the school system until then under local authority jurisdiction. She was instrumental in the closure of Hackney Downs School, which emphasised that a level of underperformance was not acceptable and that central government could override local authority control.

When Labour came to power after the landslide victory of 1997, central government's relationship with local authorities was different from the outset with the DfE communicating directly with schools. Michael Barber recalled: 'The idea was that we would bring not just competence but also be in touch with the system directly.'

In establishing the Standards and Effectiveness Unit under Barber, Labour sought to sidestep the DfE's mechanisms and became a sort of national coordinator of LEAs, taking the government agenda not only to local authorities but also directly to schools, as well as all the other agencies involved in the quest for improved standards. 'Joined up working' was the mantra and the Standards and Effectiveness Unit was intended to achieve just that. What followed was a different sort of central control: delegation of responsibility at a local level approved and checked by central government, rather than devolved responsibility (which it gave the impression of being but wasn't). It should be remembered that communication was becoming much easier than even 10 years previously. The internet and the availability of computers meant that the nation's schools could be contacted swiftly and individually in a way that would have been impossible by letter.

The first White Paper that summer, *Excellence in Schools*, set out a new reform agenda which purported to be about 'standards not structures' and saw a clear local role.[16] However, that local role had to be negotiated between a local authority and its schools under what was called the 'fair funding' agreement. In effect, this put responsibility for many services within the power of head teachers who, through their 'funding forum', would decide on the level of budget to be retained by the local authority to pay for the services they believed they needed. For those schools that were struggling it became logically evident to argue that the local authority had not helped them to improve, and for those deemed successful it was logical to maintain that they were successful in spite of the local authority.

16 Department for Education and Employment, *Excellence in Schools* [White Paper] (London: HMSO, 1997). Available at: http://www.educationengland.org.uk/documents/wp1997/excellence-in-schools.html.

Some local authorities embraced the fair funding concept and included their head teacher community in planning the future landscape. Others shed large sections of the non-statutory aspects of their service which allowed them to sit 'in the market'. This meant that schools could purchase provision locally or from elsewhere. Local authorities began to crumble: already stretched school music services went silent in some places, school library services were shelved and, for some, school improvement became a dramatically reduced function. Certain authorities retained a small cohort of advisory staff and others allowed their staff to form arm's length organisations to offer services to schools.

Fair funding expectations implied that a local authority's support for its schools should be in inverse proportion to their success. It was a concept that was in tune with the Labour government and Barber's data- and target-driven outlook. It meant that support for successful schools would be light touch, while those that were struggling would be at the heart of local authority school improvement measures. This sounded sensible and, for some authorities, created a template for support that had not existed previously.

However, in some places it would take the focus away from schools where problems were emerging without being spotted, leaving over-stretched improvement services lurching from one crisis to the next. This, in turn, led to the impression that local authorities were taking their eye off the ball. When we asked Ben Erskine why his successful school in Peterborough had converted to academy status, his response was that 'The local authority seemed extremely good at supporting poorer schools, but if you were a successful school you were left to get on with it.' This viewpoint was common in LEAs and had been inadvertently planted there by central government.

Labour at least tried to better local authorities and help them to do the job. Barber explained to us: 'We brought in processes for improving local authorities. We brought in education development plans (EDPs) and appointed regional advisers for local authorities, drawn from other successful local authorities' school improvement services. We wanted a sense of a national movement for transformation in the system.'

When it came to the big agenda of improving standards, local authorities were a conduit and a partner, but some of their power was diluted further. EAZs, which had been set up with the backing of business sponsors, were driving the agenda in areas of significant social deprivation across the country and targeting funding where it was most needed. There were 25 EAZs initially and 73 within three years. These were to represent new ways of delivering education – in effect, supporting the notion that local authorities were outdated and unequal to the task.

For the decade straddling the millennium, government resource was available in percentage-specific grants, but it was released only on the premise that it would be used in the way the secretary of state determined. Similarly, a flagship programme, EiC, was to be developed in large urban locations with partnerships of schools and local authorities managing the range of projects with significant extra budgets. Decisions locally were about the best way to access the most resource and where collaboration between schools could be encouraged, but programmes were monitored centrally.

At the same time local authorities were starting to be inspected. Mike Tomlinson recalled that the HMCI he succeeded, Chris Woodhead, 'had a thing about teacher training and another a strong thing about local education authorities, which is interesting having been very involved in both. He wanted to inspect local education authorities. By now we were into a Labour government, Tony Blair's government, and Blair effectively accepted his [Woodhead's] arguments and gave him the powers that he wanted.'

These powers struck at the heart of local authority confidence, which saw their constituencies come under constant attack. As Ofsted moved in on local authorities, the media interest around failure to provide was significant, with Woodhead always providing good copy for newsprint. As the urban metropolis authorities and then the provincial cities were inspected, there was almost a civil war feeling as most weeks produced news of another local authority 'falling' or 'being toppled'.

The government was in a quandary. Here is Michael Barber again: 'There was an ideological outlook from Chris Woodhead that I was trying to manage.' At the same time, though, 'Some local authorities were awful with low expectations, nothing happened, some people were not on the planet we were on.'

The government's reaction was to strengthen central control, including via privatisation. That control was exerted by trying to build capacity and address shortcomings in school improvement as identified by Ofsted. It began with Hackney, Tower Hamlets, Islington, Liverpool and Leicester, and within the space of just over a year, 15 local authorities were the subject of what was called 'intervention'. Barber reflected: 'It was the most difficult thing of all to address. It worked well in places such as Liverpool, Hackney and Islington. Leeds got there eventually.'

The knock-on effect of these privatisations was to sow seeds of doubt about the future of local authorities on a wider scale.

Further seeds of doubt

At the same time as trying to support local authorities, government policy actually undermined it. Collating school league table results and publishing the local authority performance tables implied that the local authority had more control than it did to secure good GCSEs or SAT results. Head teachers, particularly of secondary schools, grappling with the pressure of floor targets, often had little time for the school improvement efforts of their local authority. For local authorities, the salaries of school advisers could not compare with that of head teachers, so status became an issue for some. The accountability screw was tightening all the time – both on schools and, indirectly, local authorities. Those authorities with traditionally strong results were secure and watched from the sidelines as others imploded.

Relatively small acts had a disproportionate impact. In 2002, the government decided that each school should be given direct funding to secure and appoint a school improvement partner (SIP) separate from the local authority. The motive may have been good, but the impact was to further diminish the local authority as an agency of school improvement in the eyes of head teachers, especially those in secondary schools.

Mick recalls:

I remember a conversation with David Miliband, then a minister for schools. He was justifying the new policy for SIPs. I was saying that many heads would simply recruit a partner that they could rely on to write the appropriate reports for their governing body, and the SIP would do that because it was a paid arrangement and future engagement was important. Miliband said, 'Yes, Mick, but who, other than another secondary head teacher, could tell a secondary head teacher what they need to know about their school?' My reply was straight-forward, 'A pupil in Year 9.'

Local authorities tried to respond by entering into power-sharing arrangements with their head teachers, with decisions being made in various proportions by heads on behalf of all schools. They formed partnerships and renamed their advisory teams to try and show a new working relationship. Annual conferences suddenly assumed importance as the heads decided on the agenda and the speakers, although they usually expected the local authority to make the arrangements on their behalf. In some cases, heads determined whether or not to invite local authority staff to join their conferences. This symbolic shift of power was in some ways trivial, but in others it was further evidence of the erosion of local authority influence.

Central government's agenda rolled on through the Blunkett and Morris years with more and more direct DfE contact with schools, particularly in the secondary sector. Where the occasional knighthood might have been awarded previously to a long-serving director of education, it was now head teachers who would be recognised in the Honours Lists. There were high-profile regional conferences, led by the Standards and Effectiveness Unit and attended by ministers, explaining government policy and how it would affect practice. Much of the emphasis was on school performance data, now more freely available and more easily manipulated as computing became more sophisticated.

Almost inadvertently, it seems, the approach was to 'cut out the middle man' of the local authority. Estelle Morris told us about Tony Blair's outlook: 'What I think was immovable was his lack of trust in most local authorities, encouraging the "nanny state", and also that, on the whole, heads knew what they were doing. Those things have an element of truth to a certain degree but life's more complicated than that. I don't think he ever asked us to push it to the nth degree. He never did that.'

While authorities were still central to the work of schools in their local area, the impetus for innovation was coming from the Standards and Effectiveness Unit through the DfE. The government standards fund channelled spending into the school system via the local authority with funding based on local data. This money kept a significant proportion of local authority staff in post and it was clear to all that this was central government policy, locally delivered to a central specification. Michael Barber reflected: 'What got lost in our reforms was the role of the local school improvers. There was nobody local to mobilise the education system and the local community to get behind their schools with a feeling of any loyalty. There were some brilliant examples in places such as Wigan or Blackburn with Darwen or West Sussex, but too often the local school improvement was overshadowed by what we were doing.'

Increased expectations and stretched resources

Labour's agenda was also stretching LEAs by broadening or strengthening their responsibilities. The implications of the Children Act 1989 were taken seriously by Labour. The local authority's responsibility for looked-after children, young carers, children educated otherwise than at school and children with SEND all came to the fore once again, along with a renewed emphasis on children with English as an additional language (EAL) and efforts to build community cohesion. All of these had implications for schools in terms of their responsibilities, but also put them at risk in terms of a growing agenda of high stakes and increasingly punitive accountability centred on examination and test results. While a local authority could exert its influence and direct a school to take a child with a troubled learning history, it was at the same time potentially jeopardising the school's capacity to improve against measures designed to demonstrate school success, which was crucial for Ofsted inspections.

Central government seemed to be losing patience. The 'fresh start' initiative of 1999 saw urban secondary schools with a history of poor performance and identified as requiring special measures being subject to radical intervention. Schools were closed and reopened with a new name, new staff and a 'super head' installed, with the local authority often reduced to the role of a bystander. While most of these schemes had limited and usually short-term success, the principle of radical action was to unfold into the City Academy programme driven by Andrew Adonis from 2002. This removed a school from local authority control and placed it directly under the control of the DfE.

In our conversation with him, Adonis insisted this was not a move to undermine local authorities. He argued: 'My policy was much misunderstood. People thought that what I was doing was "privatising" but it wasn't. It was a new form of state management of the system. All of the academies were set up essentially on a licence from central government because of the need for a school in an area of high deprivation, either as a new school or to replace a school.'

In 2004, the government had announced its Building Schools for the Future programme as a central plank of its improvement and reform agenda, and suddenly local authorities were in a key position. If every secondary school in England was to be rebuilt or refurbished within 15 years, the local authority would have to submit plans for their local schooling estate. Michael Barber expressed the frustration so often felt between central government and local authorities: 'We were asking local authorities to look differently at their school estate but most seemed incapable of doing it with a learning agenda in mind. So many just wanted the new buildings and not to think about the transformative potential.'

The authorities were organised in 'waves' and the Building Schools for the Future programme was centralised through a government delivery agency. One of the first moves was to employ consultants to support the local authority's solution by working with them, and the coupling of centralisation with marketisation became more obvious.

Claire Delaney, former managing director of the Place Group, which was involved in multiple local authorities on the Building Schools for the Future programme, told us:

> We set up our company, Place Group, and tendered to support local authorities. We would work alongside the estates planning team of a local authority and help them think through the educational needs of their community in terms of demography, employment prospects and building stock. Some authorities really knew how to use us and others preferred to go it alone. We became an incredibly successful company. The problem is that a consultancy team is only as strong as their client. If you get a strong client and a strong consultancy team, you can make change happen. If you got a weak link, it would get watered down.

Mick recalls:

I saw the coming together of agendas as a real opportunity for Manchester. We had the children's service agenda and its multi-agency approach, the Every Child Matters agenda, the 14–19 agenda and the link to employment and careers, and Building Schools for the Future. On top of that we had central government promoting academies as a solution to chronic underperformance.

I thought that if we could get secondary schools to work in academy clusters around different business partners and line that up with a multi-agency approach to family and young people's support, we would have a school system to be proud of working on a joined-up agenda to serve the children and young people of the city. We brokered a deal with the DfE that kept the city council's influence over their schools while building partnership with businesses with a local and community interest.

Every school, every community and everybody had something to gain, but everybody also had to compromise. It was one of my best professional moments when I left the meeting of the city-wide Labour group having talked about specifics for two hours and been met with generous approval for the plans.

The magnet of academies and different levels of attraction

Elsewhere, people took a different view of the academy model and resisted the overtures and pressure from Bruce Liddington, the first schools commissioner, and Andrew Adonis. Kevan Collins, at that time director of education in Tower Hamlets, told us:

We came under a huge amount of pressure to put academies into Tower Hamlets. Our outlook was pragmatic. You bring the evidence that this structural change improves schools more quickly than we're improving, and we will respond. They never did.

We actually ended up for a long, long time without any academies, then we had a couple, then it moved on a bit more after that. There were reasons why we resisted it. The councillors were comparatively young on average, a lot of them had children at school. The council was engaged and committed to support the schools. They didn't want to step back. For example, Tower Hamlets received a huge investment from the Building Schools for the Future programme – we were allocated £320 million. The council put in £88 million more of their own reserve because they wanted to build the best schools in London. They wanted them to become community assets and to open them from 8am until 6pm.

I never worked out where the added value was with academies. I used to have a joke – I had a £50 note in my office in Tower Hamlets. I would say to the heads, 'If there is a freedom that you get to exercise in your school by becoming academy, you take the £50.'

The other point I made is that the 'bookends' of learning, particularly for the most vulnerable children, are really important. Early years, speech therapy and all sorts of other support for children comes through public health. That is a council function. If you go to the older end, after school is completed, we would consider access to apprenticeships. We knew, of course, where we had given planning permissions that would yield more jobs in five years' time. We were able to say to the schools that we will need more kids studying tunnelling because we knew Crossrail was coming. These bookends are never going to be managed by schools themselves. They are going to be managed because the local council and governance has access to that knowledge and that resource.

You have to join up at some point, and I think those academy chains that have become semi-detached from place are not doing the best by their children. I'm particularly focused on talking about children who don't go on to university, who for all sorts of good reasons move away and leave the place. I'm thinking about the others [who stay behind]. I'm concerned that schools can become disconnected from the local economy, local opportunities and local resources. Which is exactly what those young people need because they're the ones who are going to stay. I just couldn't work out where the added value was for our most vulnerable children.

The government's agenda had taken another turn in 2003 with the announcement of the publication of a Green Paper called *Every Child Matters*.[17] Interestingly, the bill was introduced by the Treasury, and it set out five key outcomes for children. It was a response to the Laming Inquiry into the circumstances surrounding the tragic death of Victoria Climbié, and proposed that each local authority should appoint a director of children's services (DCS) who would be responsible 'for education and social services and for overseeing services for children delegated to the local authority by other services'.[18] For local authorities and schools, this was both much needed and another challenge.

Schooling is a universal service, but such was the concern about the safeguarding of children and their care that most authorities brought schools within the social care agenda rather than the reverse. Many head teachers now felt their own local authority was drifting away from them, even though there had been a general drift of schools away from their own local authority for some time. This was despite the fact that most schools were experiencing growing levels of concern about their capacity to provide social care, especially in deprived areas.

When Ed Balls became secretary of state with the arrival of Gordon Brown in 2005, the Every Child Matters agenda became paramount. The department was renamed as the Department for Children, Schools and Families, but Balls saw that local authorities had a key role to play. He explained:

> The only way to do this was with the local authorities. I think I was the first secretary of state for years who went to address the local government conference and the local government chief executive's conference. Basically, I wanted to say, 'Nobody is asking you to go back to the 1970s where you are employing all the teachers, choosing the head teachers and running all the schools. I think we've moved from there and we aren't going back to there. On the other hand, if we care about the progress of every child we have control over, lots of the services which would make a real difference to those children's lives – like, for example, Sure Start, family support, early intervention – but also where the school is

---

17 HM Treasury, *Every Child Matters* (Norwich: TSO, 2003). Available at: https://www.gov.uk/government/publications/every-child-matters.

18 H. Laming, *The Victoria Climbié Inquiry: Report of Inquiry by Lord Laming* (Norwich: TSO, 2003), p. 70. Available at: https://www.gov.uk/government/publications/the-victoria-climbie-inquiry-report-of-an-inquiry-by-lord-laming,

going wrong in your area, then as far as I am concerned, in legislation, it is your job to do something about it.'

We asked every local authority area to do a report for us on how all the schools were doing in their area, with a particular focus on those who were below 30%,[19] and we said our view was that it was their job to broker school improvement.

Already diminished local authorities – reorganising their social care and education agendas, grappling with a new 14–19 agenda and trying to address all manner of new requirements for children's safety and welfare – were again under pressure over the performance of all of their schools and were working with a government intent on intervention from the centre.

Here is Balls again:

In the end, it was their job in legislation to step in if something went wrong, so they should do the preventative stuff. We ended up having very tough conversations with Leeds who didn't engage properly initially, Derby who didn't engage properly, and then Gloucestershire and Kent who were very proud of some very high-performing secondary moderns, some really high-performing grammars and some secondary moderns in the middle who were being totally done in. Their attitude was, 'Well, most of our schools are doing really well,' to which we said, 'Well, we are the Every Child Matters department and that means every child in every school. What are you doing?'

Balls was direct: 'We were very tough on some of those authorities. I was trying to re-establish the local authority as our agent for school improvement and intervention.'

A problem for local authorities was that while central government wanted them to intervene and address underperformance, it was often appearing to second-guess central government's next move. In 2008, Balls made a dramatic intervention and published a list of 631 secondary schools achieving below 30% good GCSEs. He called the initiative the National Challenge. This created waves with schools and local authorities, some of which found a quarter of their community 'challenged' and complaints of

---

19   Balls was referring to the percentage of the cohort getting five or more higher grade GCSEs, including maths and English.

naming and shaming. On the one hand, schools were being offered new premises along with flexibility on staffing and pay, but on the other, the squeeze was on them just as it was on the local authorities.

Balls explained to us the thinking behind the National Challenge, which was seen by many as continuing Blunkett's 'name and shame' approach:

> The National Challenge was actually saying, 'What are we all going to do about school performance?' We didn't say, 'You must become an academy.' We said, 'Leeds, that school isn't doing well enough – you need a plan. You can link up with the university. You can get the other secondary schools in the area to link up with it. You have got a range of options. One thing you can't do is shrug your shoulders because we think that is you not taking seriously your responsibility.'

In terms of schooling, a seemingly minor but significant change took place in 2010 with the removal of the word 'education' from its place between 'local' and 'authority'. After over 100 years, the LEA was no more and their traditional duties were passed to a new combined care and education department headed by a director of children's services. That same year, as Labour left office and the coalition under David Cameron took over, local authorities were still reeling from years of being undermined. They were an easy target.

Where Blunkett's reforming policy had been described as 'standards not structures', Gove's reform was to be built around the twin concepts – some would say contradictory, others complementary – of a return to traditional values and revolutionary thinking. In respect of local authorities, Gove wasted little time in enticing schools towards his new academy arrangements and, in effect, potentially breaking up local authorities by default.

Local authorities reacted in different ways. Some threw in the towel almost immediately having seen the writing on the wall. They suggested to their schools that they move towards academisation rather than witness their community of schools offered insufficient services as a result of the savage cuts simultaneously imposed on local authorities as austerity measures started. While they retained their statutory functions, aspects such as school improvement were decommissioned. In other local authorities, the move of schools to academy status was piecemeal. Secondary schools were quicker to take the step for reasons explored in the next section on the development and growth of academies. Gove had dealt local authorities a hammer blow but he had not knocked them out.

Nicky Morgan tried to fix Gove's muddle and brought forward the Education and Adoption Bill in 2015 with the intention of securing full academisation. As the coalition ended, she sought a timetable where local authorities were removed from the education picture. It may have been her ambition but it was never completed. The bill did not pass through Parliament and the confused role of local authorities persists.

Sam Freedman reflected:

> We had 30 years of centralisation and attempted destruction of local authorities. These were two pieces of the mission for which there was no clear direction. Now we are stuck in the current confused status. The role of local authorities should have been strengthened and very different, but they now have no clear function. They should act as the champions of children and young people locally, especially vulnerable children, admissions and work to protect the interests of young people.

Gavin Williamson tried to articulate a renewed function to set alongside his declared intention to encourage schools towards academisation. He told us:

> I do think we're going to move to a fully multi-academy system. Local authorities play an important role. Too often we've had local authorities that have sometimes been a defender of what has been quite poor provision in their areas. Place always plays a role in terms of what we do, what we see and what is driven there, so what you want to be doing is liberating local authorities to be more the advocates for children, as against advocates for a school or head teachers.

What Williamson did not explain was how local authorities might exercise that advocacy role in the context of a fragmented schooling structure where some MATs display little commitment, and sometimes outright defiance, to local arrangements and protocols in pursuit of their own reputations.

Local authorities have a remarkably different role now from that envisaged in Butler's 1944 Education Act. While the period to 1976 may have been one of government optimism and trust in the system, local authorities have been the significant casualty of the period of centrali-sation, markets and managerialism. They have both become agents of central government (when convenient – especially in respect of making requirements on schools in their area) and encouraged to see themselves as standing apart from central government. Many have an uneasy rela-tionship with schools locally: financially stretched, they are often unable to offer the services for which they have responsibility and are there-fore often seen as inefficient, with the upshot that more schools opt to become academies. At the same time, they are faced with the challenge of trying to uphold the rights of children in an arena where a range of incentives and pressures are at play.

One experienced DCS remembered the early signals:

> The statutory role of the director of children's services became really difficult. The fragmentation has made what was compli-cated even more difficult. Any sense of your ability to try and keep the whole show on the road was made hugely more difficult the day Michael Gove went into the Department for Education and took down all the rainbows. It was symbolic. It's led to the dog's breakfast we've got now. You've got a patchwork quilt of all sorts of stuff and the only influence we really have is relationships.

Colin Pettigrew, corporate director for children and families in Nottinghamshire, outlined one of the challenges for local authorities in areas where multiple MAT chains have their own agenda, separate from the ambitions and endeavours of the council: 'We have one academy chain that is the highest performer in terms of GCSE results, while at the same time is also the chain that accounts for the highest number of exclu-sions. They are incentivised to come top of the exams league table while the local authority has to work on behalf of the youngsters they reject.'

More significant, though, is the gradual erosion of democratic influence over schools, many of which are a vital part of a community's social infra-structure and affect the future prospects of families. Nigel Richardson, another experienced DCS, told us:

> Often you find that lots of children are falling between a well-functioning education system and a well-functioning social care system and, because they don't meet specific criteria, get nothing and so families are struggling. Now, before Gove, it wasn't perfect but at least there was a concerted attempt through Every Child

Matters to be true to the aspirations of the Children Act 1989 and set schools and families as the heartbeat of the local community. Children live in families (however defined), families create communities and communities create places. Children spend the majority of their time outside school and what happens outside school massively impacts on what they can achieve in schools, so it has to make sense to keep everything connected: whole child – whole system.

When Gove entered Sanctuary Buildings as secretary of state that whole system idea went at a stroke, as he deliberately dismantled the DCSF and replaced it with the DfE. It was brutal and it had the immediate effect of telling everyone who wasn't directly involved in 'education' that they were less important – a disaster. Well, it almost worked. Thankfully, a number of LAs [local authorities] continued to work in partnership to try and get that back [to the wider agenda] but it takes strong leadership – it was like trying to implement the clear intentions of the Children Act with at least one hand tied behind your back. The key ingredient for success in those LAs was a relentless focus on relationships, and even in the face of great challenges, successful relationships and not losing sight of the whole child were the key.

And don't forget LAs were also hit with the awful impact of austerity, so you fragment the system and then you take the money and resources away and wonder why it doesn't work as well as you want. In that context, all credit to local government and local partnerships for achieving what they have, but how sad to look at that context and wonder about what might have been if we'd been able to keep a coherent whole-child approach that was well resourced.

As one of our DCS witnesses said: 'The middle tier – local authorities – for me are the link between place, history, geography and democracy. In the end, it is essential you live in a place that matters to you. This is your place. These are the children of Derby and it matters, or these are the children of Birmingham or Ipswich or Yorkshire. This does matter.'

If we expect our schools to be part of their community – at the heart of services for children as the universal provider; if we believe in a sense of place – about linking learning to employment prospects locally; and if we believe in responding to the changing demographics caused by housing policy or transport initiatives, an absence of local voice in the coordination of schooling is not the best way forward.

Our secretaries of state and the rise of the MAT

There can be few who have not seen *The Wrong Trousers*, the wonderful animation directed by Nick Park, which reaches its climax with a classic train chase.[20] Gromit, sitting astride the engine from a child's train set, is being pursued by the 'baddy' when he looks up to see the end of the track looming ahead of him. He reaches down and grabs a box labelled 'spare track'. From thereon, at breakneck speed, Gromit leans forward and drops each section of the track in front of the engine as it hurtles into the unknown.

We were reminded of this sequence when the chief executive of a MAT described the development and growth of MATs and their relationship with the DfE as 'being like driving a runaway train. First we are asked to go as fast as we can with no clear direction about where we are trying to get to, and then someone slams on the brake as they feel the power getting away from them.'

The Conservative version of academy policy was introduced by Michael Gove in 2011; the school system has been trying to make sense of it ever since. Ministers and the DfE have attempted to understand their own policy, gain control over it and avoid catastrophes. Gove has moved on, of course, and can reflect on the legacy of a fragmented and often duplicated system of school governance where many, but not all, schools ran away from council control to achieve one of his goals of marginalising local authorities, for whom he, like many others in Whitehall, had no time.

With the Schools Commissioners team tasked with securing as many schools as possible as quickly as possible in order to develop impetus, the tension in the system was palpable. The rush to create autonomous

---

20 *The Wrong Trousers* is a stop-motion animated short film produced by Aardman Animations and featuring the characters Wallace and Gromit. It won an Academy Award in 1994.

academies, along with the allied free school programme, meant that a whole range of school formations developed, giving a new interpretation to diversity in schooling: there were stand-alone academies, academy federations, academy clusters and MATs. Some of the MATs were little more than a cluster of schools in a locality that came together to share professional development opportunities. Other MATs with powerful sponsors were building chains by sweeping up poorly performing schools; to some onlookers it seemed predatory.

New commercial and often flamboyant names for trusts began to appear as groups of schools signed up for a new corporate identity. In many trusts, the sense of place disappeared with the new branding, although some retained the original name of their school. Some academies are stand-alone and called single-academy trusts (SATs – an acronym confusingly the same as tests for children in primary schools) and some are in multi-academy companies (MACs). Some dioceses scooped up all the schools in their district and sponsored the schools they already supported through a more heavenly power. Such was the scramble to gather academies into the fold that scurrilous rumours circulated that Cole Porter's 'Anything Goes' was the background music to the academies team office in the DfE.

Ten years later, we have 9,608 academies and free schools and over half of all schools still under local authority care.[21] Some of those in MATs believe it was the best step that they and their academies have ever taken; others wonder why they took the step; a third group regrets their move. Some academies are now with their second trust having been 're-brokered'. A decade on, those that chose to remain with their local authority are wondering whether now is the moment to leave, while many others have realised that their autonomy – the much promised prize of academisation – is greater where they are in a local authority than anywhere else in the system.

The rate of schools' movement to academy status has slowed: in the year to May 2021 it was below 5%. Just as Labour seems to be deliberating on whether to address the issue of the relatively few grammar schools in a comprehensive system (or whether it is in Charles Clarke's 'too difficult box'), so the Conservatives have to decide whether to allow things to take

---

21   D. Herrington, CST Session (June 2021).

their course or to push for system-wide academy status in some sort of coherent pattern.

Speaking at the FED's National Education Summit in March 2021, Gavin Williamson gave an indication of intent, although without giving much detail:

> We know that schools benefit from being in a strong family of schools, in other words a Multi-Academy Trust.
>
> Multi-Academy Trusts are powerful vehicles for improving schools – by sharing expertise, working collaboratively and driving improvements. It is living proof of the old adage, a problem shared is a problem halved.
>
> This is something we want to see more of, because it shows time and again how the MAT model consistently improves outcomes for pupils.
>
> By 2025 we want to see far more schools residing in strong families than we do today, and are actively looking at how we can make that happen.[22]

While many saw Gove as a man with a plan for academies, few saw a strategy for an academy structure. Jon Coles, a senior adviser at the DfE at the time, told us: 'Michael Gove didn't want to prescribe an "end state" – how the school system would work when the reform programme had been fully implemented. The Nicky Morgan White Paper was an attempt to do that – but the negative reaction and U-turn that followed has made subsequent ministers nervous about trying to do anything similar. Yet it's obvious that the current "mixed economy" isn't a satisfactory end point.'

The academy concept had existed under Labour, of course. The brainchild of Andrew Adonis, who was determined to address the cycle of failure which limited the ambitions of individuals, schools and their communities, academies had first been established in 2001. For Adonis, this was clearly about school transformation:

> I never set up a single academy in opposition to local authorities. It is true that in many cases I was able to persuade local authorities,

---

22 Department for Education and G. Williamson, Education Secretary Speech to FED National Education Summit (1 March 2021). Available at: https://www.gov.uk/government/speeches/education-secretary-speech-to-fed-national-education-summit.

partly by the fact that I was bringing big investment, and money speaks. And I was quite frank, telling some of them, because I didn't think their plans were good enough and they weren't going to produce transformational schools, that we wouldn't provide additional state funding if they didn't go down the academy route.

Before Gove's policy initiative in 2011, there were 203 academies, all in the secondary phase, established in 83 local authorities across the country in areas of historic school failure.[23] Sponsors from beyond the education community had to commit to £2 million worth of investment, head teachers and staff were often new, and premises were either rebuilt or refurbished. Adonis insisted: 'Absolutely central to the academies programme was not just the focus on schools in mixed or deprived areas but also massive capital investment. This was what made them so successful. Take the City of London Academy in Southwark. That was a £25 million new school with state-of-the-art facilities, serving one of the most deprived parts of the country.'

Ed Balls became secretary of state when this programme was underway, and while in favour of any strategy to improve stuck schools, he could see that problems were beginning to emerge. Creating a new academy with new branding, new leadership and investment in buildings was not a panacea. He recalled:

> I actually signed off more academies than any other secretary of state but I abolished the entry fee – the millions of pounds – and I said they had to be behaviour partnerships, they had to teach the core curriculum, and we allowed schools, colleges, universities to come in.

> We had a problem early on with an academy. Because the academies were very new, they only started to get into difficulty during my time. There was this particular school in Carlisle which got into a real mess. I had to get Jim Knight, the schools minister, to sort it out. Jim got on a train, a minister, and went to Carlisle to meet them. We didn't have anybody else to talk to. The local authority didn't really see it as anything to do with them. There was no intermediate tier. We then sent Mike Gibbons[24] up after to

---

23   R. Long, Academies Under the Labour Government. House of Commons Library, Standard Note: SN/
     SP/5544 (20 January 2015), p. 4. Available at: https://dera.ioe.ac.uk/22717/1/SN05544.pdf.
24   Mike Gibbons was the head of the DfE Innovation Unit at the time.

do the turnaround, and we realised quite quickly that we couldn't do that as the group of schools [in difficulty] got bigger.

This approach could be seen as pragmatic by supporters or hand to mouth by detractors. The assumption that academies would be the answer to long-standing and deep-rooted schooling issues, often stretching back decades, was clearly wrong. As Labour attempted to address a range of problems – from negative inspection judgements to community dissatisfaction to matters of funding irregularity – the strategy ran into initial difficulties which multiplied under Gove.

In broad terms, Adonis' programme was beginning to work as the coalition government entered the scene in 2010, and Gove neatly built on the generally positive regard for academies by appearing to mould his own policy to the agenda. He graciously credited Adonis with the foundations and then built something completely different, as Adonis pointed out:

> I fundamentally disagreed with what he did by using the term 'academies' to describe what he was doing. All of the academies I set up were in deprived areas or mixed areas but with schools that were seriously underperforming. What he did, of course, was simply just a great renaming and marginalising of local authorities' exercise, which, by the way, was never my policy. My policy wasn't to marginalise LAs; it was to modernise them. I saw them as playing an absolutely crucial role in education, but not in the direct, day-by-day management of schools. But what Gove, with Cummings, wanted to do was essentially to abolish them entirely, and I didn't agree with that.

Gove's plan was different. In his speech to Parliament supporting the Academies Bill, Gove argued: 'It grants greater autonomy to individual schools, it gives more freedom to teachers and it injects a new level of dynamism into a programme that has been proven to raise standards for all children and for the disadvantaged most of all.'[25]

There was considerable interest from schools which thought they could work out where all this was heading. As well as autonomy, which brought release from the national curriculum, Gove offered inducements in the form of enhanced funding for early adopters and a break from inspection

---

25 M. Gove, Academies Bill [Lords], Volume 514, debated on Monday 19 July 2010, Hansard. Available at: https://hansard.parliament.uk/Commons/2010-07-19/debates/10071915000001/AcademiesBill(Lords).

for nearly three years. The latter was attractive to many schools that found themselves in one of Ofsted's categories of concern. With adroit time management, the adept head teacher could stage the consultations with sponsors and the conversion to academy status to stretch that time to the limit. And for those over the age of 55, there was also the release from the shadow of inspection for the remainder of their career.

Early adopters had a variety of reasons for converting to academy status. Some saw it as the new dawn. As one of our secondary academy head teacher witnesses said: 'It was an obvious decision really. Our local authority was going nowhere and offered us little. Other schools were taking the step and we thought the additional funding wouldn't be there for long.' For others, it was a simple rationalisation, as another head explained: 'We thought we may as well get on with it rather than be pushed into it later with less control over which trust we went with. I wasn't sure about the principle, but it seemed obvious to us that in the end all schools would have to become academies.'

Early adopters

The domino effect started, particularly in the secondary sector, but it slowed more quickly than Gove might have anticipated. Schools judged outstanding by Ofsted were beckoned by the secretary of state, rather like Captain Ahab in *Moby Dick*. Schools deemed to be failures were pushed, rather like the mutineers in old pirate stories who walked the plank to take their chances in the ocean. Gove's intention was that they were thrown a lifeline in the form of a head teacher with a proven track record.

The new MATs developed infrastructure and networks of improvement with an urgency not previously experienced by schools within their local authorities. Other schools wondered what they had signed up to as they suddenly experienced greater scrutiny than they had known for years over anomalies and shortcomings in areas such as performance management, pay, staff appointments, and health and safety. Formerly, the local authority's stretched resources had struggled to get close and some governing bodies had failed to exercise their statutory roles effectively.

Inevitably, some academies struggled, some trusts were ineffective and, worse, a few became cavalier in their practices, prompting charges of empire-building, dubious ethics and malpractice. All became regular stories either in *Schools Week* or through the journalist Warwick Mansell in *The Guardian*. It was clear, as Ofsted visited academies that had previously been failing schools, that while many had been 'turned around', a significant proportion had not improved sufficiently. Simply becoming an academy with a new name and logo, or even new leadership, did not guarantee success.

Setting aside educational success, or otherwise, it became apparent very quickly that some MATs were slipshod in their approach to aspects of school organisation, such as infrastructure and finance, adopting a laissez-faire outlook and leaving their schools to be autonomous units; while others inflicted regimes of control that appeared to onlookers as bizarre. Elsewhere, there were rumours of individuals taking advantage and fleecing the system, with some high-profile cases of misdeeds coming to court.

However, the majority of academies and MATs and their free school counterparts adopted a professional outlook and practices and approached autonomy sensibly and seriously. Many exploited collaborations to the full and developed new leadership models built on trust – a particularly apposite term. For every trust with an unscrupulous leadership, there were many more with ethics beyond question.

Growing problems and what to do next?

What Michael Gove presented as school autonomy leant towards a market approach both in the sense that schools were units to be accumulated and that procedures would be market orientated. Many of the previous regulations were null and void as trusts began to set their own policies and practices, often without reference to long-established national agreements. The problem was that the academy programme would have to be seen to work, but many of the schools that were becoming academies were doing so because they were struggling. The need for rapid improvement meant they had to be managed to some degree but there was no infrastructure in place to do so. This had to be established from the centre.

Political influence and intent had moved schooling towards the market and centralisation, and it wasn't long before that centralisation brought with it increasingly managerial approaches that were very different from the autonomy that had been promised. David Carter summarised the growing problem: 'In 2010, when Michael Gove enabled many more schools to become academies, there were unforeseen challenges in the policy in my personal view. One mistake was that he devolved and delegated autonomy down to the system but didn't put enough checks and balances in to make sure that the people who didn't use that autonomy sensibly or ethically could be held to account.'

The DfE had to get a grip. David Laws told us: 'Michael Gove eventually had to admit that you cannot run 10,000 and more schools from Westminster and performance manage them when things go wrong.' Gove appointed first Lord Hill and then Theodore, later Lord, Agnew to bring order. He also created the concept of the regional schools commissioner (RSC) from September 2014, when eight new RSCs were appointed as directors of the department 'to take decisions in the secretary of state's name on the operation of the academies regime. RSCs, with the help of elected Head Teacher Boards, will approve applications for new academies and free schools, approve and monitor sponsor capacity. They will also take intervention action where either performance [or governance] is poor.'[26] By 2015, the role had moved on to 'help deliver the Department's aim to ensure high educational standards in academies and free schools and to secure sponsorship arrangements for maintained schools moving to academy status'.[27]

We talked with three RSCs, past and present, and were able to trace the development of their role. Our witnesses beyond this group talked about whether the rationale for demarcating the regions was secure. More than once we heard that the justification for having four regions spreading out of central London into the shire counties was a wish on Michael Gove's

26 Department for Education, Accounting Officer: Accountability System Statement for Education and Children's Services. Ref: DFE-00026-2015 (January 2015), p. 6. Available at: https://assets.publishing. service.gov.uk/government/uploads/system/uploads/attachment_data/file/396815/Accountability_ Statement_.pdf.

27 Quoted in B. Durbin, K. Wespieser, D. Bernardinelli and G. Gee, A Guide to Regional School Commissioners (Slough: National Foundation for Educational Research, 2015), p. 4. Available at: https:// www.nfer.ac.uk/publications/rscr01/rscr01.pdf.

part to stop Boris Johnson claiming that success in London was down to him as mayor. RSCs were tasked with commissioning schools from diverse geographical regions that coincided, but did not match, the regions recently established by Ofsted to bring inspectors closer to schools by working in their own regions.

David Carter told us: 'I think the DfE confused itself a little bit about this because I think they would have argued for a degree of devolution when they set up the regional schools commissioners. They created the RSCs for the fairly random regions they put in place. The South West where I started from was pretty logical, but when you've got Cheshire in the West Midlands, for example, you've made the role very difficult to manage.'

Whatever the regions and their logic, the RSCs had twin challenges. First, to secure more schools to become academies, which had now evolved into ensuring that any academy orders were consistent with a thought-through analysis of need and impact. Second, the expectation, born from the realisation that just becoming an academy would not be enough to effect school improvement, that RSCs would work to improve schools across their region.

The RSC concept got off to an uncertain start with a remarkably high turn-over of personnel in the first three years. Pank Patel, who was the first RSC for the West Midlands region, stayed only a year before resigning. He had previously led a highly successful secondary school in Sandwell and decided that the RSC role was not for him, instead deciding that leading another school from special measures to a brighter future would be more rewarding. He told us:

> I was going to build a MAT locally but they approached me and I liked the idea. It was a whole new ball game. Nobody had heard of the role and it was sold to me as an opportunity to really frame education for the future. The RSCs were brought about because the academy network needed greater regionalised development as well as a more organised due diligence-based approach. It seemed to be that existing trusts were well known and given more schools as a result of people who knew people. I remember being shocked at the lack of thorough knowledge of civil servants about how schools work and the accountability measures. This has since changed.

I thought it was a really good move to develop RSCs, but it was just driven by how many schools we could each get and every school becoming an academy by 2020. Why did I do it for such a short span of time? I went from one meeting to another meeting, spoke at one conference and then drove to speak at another conference. I used to leave at 5 in the morning, get home at 9 at night, read my emails and do it all again the next day. Although the role was fulfilling, every time I visited a school, I realised how much I missed the school leader role. I also missed seeing my family.

I felt that I hadn't lived my teaching experience for that, and once the West Midlands region was established, I thought I would leave. As RSC I had developed enormous respect for the heads of schools in special measures and I hadn't had that experience, so that's where I went next, to the headship of a special measures school, and it improved brilliantly.

It was some time before the role settled down. The emphasis on the RSCs to secure new academies has, for the time being, shifted to trying to bring regional coherence and helping to improve quality.

Within academies and MATs, the RSCs have now become yet another of the external agencies they have to accommodate, along with the EFSA and the academies team at the DfE.

David Carter talked about the evolution of the work and his role as national schools commissioner:

The role for me was about not so much growing the system, although that was clearly an element of that, but the levers to encourage good schools to convert weren't there. It was about enacting a policy, when schools went into special measures, to move as quickly as possible to find them a good sponsor. Then, through persuasion, through modelling, through conversation, through your positive experiences from the sector, to go and convince good schools to become academy sponsors in their own right.

I spent a lot of my time trying to talk the language of school leadership, which people in the school sector really welcomed, I think. I also took into my brief oversight of the 12 largest trusts. If you take AET [Academies Enterprise Trust], for example, or E-ACT or United Learning, they would easily have to have had five or six different conversations with regional schools commissioners, and that was just a duplication of everybody's time, so by having one conversation with each of them we were able to streamline the information flow.

Carter continued:

Of course, the accountability mechanisms [which academy leaders now have to follow] drain a lot of time and energy in terms of what you can do with an academy that fails. You often have to wait until it goes seriously wrong before you can do something about it. My argument as an RSC was, in some of those cases, you have to be able to move quicker, because these are children's lives that you're impacting. And, yes, you can re-broker from one trust to another but, fundamentally, if the promise that the original trust made to its community to make things better is not happening, you need a policy that enables you to get it to move faster. I still think that's a significant challenge for the sector.

Unquestionably, there are plentiful examples of schools that are getting better, both individually and collectively. Hannah Woodhouse told us about her work in the South West region as an RSC and the way she is working with academies in sub-regions such as Plymouth to enable improvement built on new forms of collaboration between academies and the involvement of the local authority. She described the work of academies in Plymouth: 'You know what? Three years on, the thinking is almost transformed in terms of politics, education, educational expectations, partnerships and collaboration. There is a story that should be told about this.'

This was echoed by people from those academies in Plymouth and across the border in Cornwall where Kevin Butlin, director of education for Plymouth CAST, told us: 'We've worked productively with the RSC to address school improvement but the challenge of getting close to school improvement where it matters, in teaching and learning, across such a landscape is massive. Collaboration is growing within our trust and beyond.'

As the flow to academy status slowed and the complexity of the local and national picture increased, the parallels with the school boards of the late 1800s became obvious. Getting some sort of order into Michael Gove's initial plan was clearly required, and as he left the stage, the agenda was picked up first by Nicky Morgan and then Justine Greening. David Carter reflected: 'It landed with Nicky Morgan and it landed with Justine Greening. They understood the essentials and had the task of making sense of the academy sector after the launch-pad era when Michael Gove was the education secretary.'

A regional outlook

What seems to have happened is that each RSC (and there have been three in the West Midlands, four in the North East and four in the South West in less than 10 years) has had a different focus for their tenure, while also grappling with the challenges created by the previous one (they must catch this behaviour from secretaries of state). First, there was the visionary period when capturing schools and setting up MATs was the imperative. Next came the time when a concept of 'intentional design' seemed to take hold, with some people being told 'no' because their trust plan needed to fit an evolving map of provision based on certain organisational principles. Next and presently, the focus is on actual performance as many MATs seek to grow.

Hannah Woodhouse explained:

> MATs say to me that they want to grow because they can get more teachers in their organisation, more good practice can be shared and with more capacity there is more potential. They want to grow for good reasons but they can't all grow. For me, a trust is about developing people, and particularly developing leadership at all levels, and giving opportunities for teachers to work in different schools in order to develop their practice as well as having common systems, assessment, curriculum principles and so on.

David Carter talked about having seen quickly the need to move on from the initial model:

> The single-academy trust model is one of the things I tried to influence and to change. If you are good enough to become a single-academy trust, you should be good enough to set up a multi-academy trust. I wanted to see an end, if you like, to good schools just carrying on pulling up the drawbridge and being a

good school, but not taking responsibility for delivering improvement and being accountable for it in other schools. This is more than just sharing best practice and modelling what works in their schools. And, so, while I don't think it was ever enshrined in policy that single-academy trusts could no longer be set up, there was definitely a strong argument for expecting strong single schools to play a wider school improvement role in the system.

But Gove's lack of initial planning remains the problem behind even the ambition to improve schooling. Now that MATs are established as a legal entity, it is not possible to move the pieces around to create systemic coherence. The only way that an RSC, as an agent of government, can relocate a school from one MAT to another or to merge two MATs, is to act on school failure – and that is defined by Ofsted whose inspection cycle is anything but predictable.

After all the turbulence of the past 10 years or so, the schooling system is stirred and very shaken. Academies and free schools make up 79% of secondary schools but just 38% of primary schools. In the special school sector, 41% of schools are academies and 44% in alternative provision. The average MAT has six academies, with 87% of all academies in MATs. Some 1,249 academies are not within a trust and are referred to as 'stand-alone academies'.[28]

There are local authorities that have seen all of their schools become academies, some as a result of their prompting, and there are others where most schools have remained under the aegis of the local authority. Depending on your viewpoint, it is either a rich and varied landscape, Hockney-esque in colour, or an organisational mess and financial drain.

In our view, it is a mess and the government seems at a loss about what to do next. Speaking at the Confederation of School Trusts annual conference in April 2021, Gavin Williamson explained: 'I want to see us break away from our current pick-and-mix structure of the school system and move towards a single model. One that is built on a foundation of strong multi academy trusts. And I am actively looking at how we can make that happen.'[29] His plans included a 'try before you buy' temporary partnership period to experience the benefits.

---

28   The figures come from the office of the national schools commissioner: Herrington, CST Session.
29   Department for Education and G. Williamson, Education Secretary Speech to the Confederation of School Trusts (28 April 2021). Available at: https://www.gov.uk/government/speeches/education-secretary-speech-to-the-confederation-of-school-trusts.

His arguments sounded flimsy. His description of the benefits of trusts would apply to many schools, not simply those that are part of a MAT: 'leaders who know the value of working together for the greater good', 'strong and effective governance', 'a knowledge-rich curriculum' and 'a culture where good behaviour is the norm'. Assertions that academies in trusts had fared better during the pandemic than stand-alone academies or local authority schools seem to be based on scant evidence, and examples of academy initiatives – such as offers of support to and from local communities – might even be insulting to the very schools he would wish to attract.

Just six months after Williamson's urgings for all schools to see the benefits of MATs, and with RSCs actively encouraging conversion in their own regions and some schools looking to form MATs rather than be taken over by what they see as predators, Robin Walker told us:

> I don't come to this with a very hard-line view as to what particular system works best. I'm reasonably comfortable with a mixed system as long as it works for a broad range of people. I've seen great examples of academies and I've seen great examples of maintained schools. Schools need to be encouraged to collaborate and MATs are one very good way of doing that, but equally I think there is good collaboration elsewhere in the system as well. My view is not a fundamentalist one when it comes to whether the system needs academies or not.

Gove's lack of a clear plan when he unveiled the new emphasis on academisation has resulted in stalemate. Those schools that did not join the movement have now existed for a decade without seeing the need to convert. Those schools operating within a chaotic system are for the most part making it work. The system is uneconomic and wasteful. It has not solved and, in some cases, it has created difficulties in certain communities. It has led to a situation where considerable energy and resource is spent in a constant game of cat and mouse. Just as the comprehensive ideal was never secured, so the academies ideal is becoming one of the time and energy traps that have a debilitating effect on the system.

So, is academisation a good thing?

There is no doubt that many have found engagement with a MAT to be exhilarating and pupils in most academies have benefitted. However, some head teachers report that joining a MAT has not turned out to be what they expected in terms of efficiency.

One primary head teacher in a northern region told us how joining a MAT had increased managerial work and leadership burden: 'Not only am I endlessly responding to "cover your back" demands from the CEO of the MAT, but I'm still required to attend meetings relating to social care of children which the MAT leadership does not seem to understand or even care about. It doesn't seem to be on his agenda. He thinks he has the monopoly on my time. Endless demands for trivia do not beat my first priority for children's well-being.'

Another in the south told us: 'I wish I had never said yes. The local authority has been brilliant during COVID and their new strategic director is so organised and clear. Worse than that, I have just realised that I am coming to the end of my Ofsted window. It was the only reason I academised and I have lost that Ofsted-free time being in lockdown.'

David Bell, permanent secretary in the DfE as the academy programme began, reflected: 'The irony is that many schools have less autonomy and freedom as an academy than previously. The control exercised by some MAT CEOs sometimes borders on the draconian.'

Likewise, those who remained with their local authority also offered a range of views. The head teacher of a thriving primary school in London explained that her loyalty to her own local authority remained strong, but 'I'm working with a head nearby to draw up some plans for working together for the benefit of children locally and we are exploring the possibility of building a trust with a couple of struggling schools at the other end of our region on the coast so that we can help them and get some really good different experiences for our own children. I'd be wary, though, if we were pushed towards a big MAT.'

Another northern primary head teacher told us that she was happy with her local authority 'that does the bare minimum and which gives me the opportunity to drive my school forward without looking over my shoulder. I am the one with real autonomy. I contact whom I need, buy what matters, collaborate with people all over the country and beyond, provide great professional learning for the staff and use every wrinkle in the system to bring benefit to our school. I don't have to ask permission, explain or justify ... and I am a very happy professional.'

Richard Kieran spent a good deal of time on the process of applying to become an academy. The main reason was that his local authority services had been outsourced to a private company. Like other head teachers locally, Richard felt that this would be no better than the local authority he knew, whatever its failings, and 'so it turned out as they seemed to behave as though they had achieved their aim in winning the contract. That seemed to be the goal for them; making a difference in schools didn't seem to feature. So, I applied to be an academy and, after considerable time and expenditure, was refused as they changed the policy to say "stand-alone" was not possible. I think we are one of very few who have been denied the chance to take academy status. We feel very special!'

Gavin Williamson's reflection on the introduction and growth of the academy movement was entirely positive: 'Fundamentally, we had a system where everything was preserved in aspic and you didn't have the ability to have insurgents come through and change things.' He continued: 'I would say that most of the leaders of MATs are quite entrepreneurial. It is very much about driving the system forward, being willing to take elements of risk. I think if you look back to 2010, there wasn't a depth of that management experience within the system.' The extent to which those who have so far not taken the step across the academisation threshold believe that the process enables or inhibits entrepreneurial behaviour varies. It seems to us that the much heralded autonomy has proved elusive to many who moved within the managerial embrace of what Williamson describes as entrepreneurial and others as cavalier.

Free schools – another subset

Some academies have grown independently or collectively as part of the other aspect of Michael Gove's agenda – free schools. Gove believed that 'it should also be possible to start a truly autonomous, truly free, school from scratch. So we invited teacher groups, parent groups, charities and others to apply to set up their own schools.'[30]

We talked with four people about the experience of running a free school, all of whom referred to their MATs. They are unusual for a range of reasons – the settings, the buildings, the curriculum and the expectations – yet they all see themselves as responding to the needs of their community.

Gilroy Brown, who had been a founding trustee (and, for a time, head teacher) at King Solomon International Business School in Birmingham described free schools as 'a brilliant model provided the people in charge know what they are doing'. King Solomon School is now rated as good, but had a rocky start with the primary section being very highly regarded while the secondary phase was deemed to require special measures. The school is now seen as good and on an even keel. The school was popular with the community in an area of the city where no Church of England provision was available. It was housed in a former office block and offered considerable after-school hours provision. It was a new concept and, as Brown explained, 'a pragmatic direction of travel at the time with the government seemingly intent in breaking local authorities'.

The same mission to meet the needs of the community was the driving force behind the establishment of Michaela Community School. Founder Katharine Birbalsingh told us:

> I am fine with the marketisation idea from the point of view that it's like a start-up business. I don't own this building. I don't own the school. I don't benefit financially and I'm paid a salary like any other head teacher. I've started from scratch and I really care about it. Some people who argue against free schools might get really offended by that and say, 'Well, what do you mean? You are saying that normal heads don't care about the school.' I'm not saying that. No, of course they care about the school. But it's a different kind of caring. When you've got everything invested in the school, when you've started it from nothing, when you've taken the bins out yourself, when you've helped to paint the walls, when you've been responsible for every tiny detail that's happened at the school, everything from what the carpets look like to what we put on the wall, you just have more invested.

---

30 Department for Education and Gove, Michael Gove's Speech to the Policy Exchange on Free Schools.

The notion of personal influence marks free schools out from trusts, most of which are still led by people who were previously head teachers or who were significant figures in the DfE or local authorities.

The Schools' Buying Club is an example of a commercial business that has entered the world of free schooling. Claire Delaney, in her role as chair of the Bellevue Place Education Trust of primary free schools, explained:

> I work in the private sector and felt that there was something more we could be doing. I think there is always the view that 'they are just taking money out of the system'. What we wanted to do was create a balance where we walked the talk. We got shown an old courthouse in Balham in South London. It was six storeys high and had had squatters living in it, having not been occupied for 15 years. The government basically said, 'Can you write an application and tell us why you should be the people to run a primary school in that building?' We teamed up with another organisation and they brought curriculum expertise. We now have nine schools, all good or outstanding, seven of which were created from scratch.
>
> Imagine: you stick your sign up and say that this is going to be a school. Then it is down to you to sell your vision to your community. We said that we were going to turn this derelict building into an unbelievable school – it takes a certain type of parent to come on that journey with you. There is a real focus on locality and community engagement.

Gove had encouraged free schools to think differently and be different: 'We are not being prescriptive about Free Schools and so they come in all shapes and sizes. Some are housed in existing schools. Others will be based in a range of refurbished and adapted buildings ... The critical point is that we have been thinking creatively about how to secure excellent new schools at a time when budgets are tight.'[31]

Gove's encouragement to be different and his wish to reduce prescription were seized on by doubters and opponents as another step on the road to deregulation and marketisation. Yet, as Gwyn ap Harri, the leader of XP School Trust in Doncaster, pointed out: 'The irony is not lost on me that we could not have existed and done the things we do under a Labour

---

31 Department for Education and Gove, Michael Gove's Speech to the Policy Exchange on Free Schools.

council in a Labour constituency without the influence of Michael Gove and his policy on local determination.'

Many of the free schools have built a MAT around themselves, and others have been absorbed into or constructed by a MAT. As Colin Pettigrew, DCS in Nottinghamshire, remarked:

> Virtually the only way to get a new school built now is to find someone to build a free school. It means the local authority has little control of pupil places beyond identifying where the pressure is. Central government seems to control school building in a very ad hoc way, which is odd considering we used to be called to account for surplus places and this was often a source of tension for local councillors with the prospect of closing schools. It will be interesting to see what happens when the school population downturn starts to bite.

No doubt the market will rule and MATs will tackle the difficulties that local authorities have never found a way of addressing easily. The tensions between MATs and local authorities have existed in different ways in different places, often at school level. Sometimes the relationship is one of mild bewilderment, sometimes resentment, sometimes passing interest. Gwyn ap Harri of XP School Trust talked of the relationship with local schools:

> While we say that we can show you what we do, the other schools tend to ignore us. And then there's local authority and you've got Damian Allen [DCS], who has always been a champion of ours. Then you've got other people lower down who don't particularly like what we stand for. It's a bag of things. What we say about the local authority is sometimes we travel our own route, and sometimes it's the same route as the local authority and sometimes it isn't, dependent on what we intend to do. We have a decent relationship with our local authority.
>
> We are going to do the same thing in Gateshead where we are setting up a secondary school in an existing building, which is interesting, and we want to create a secondary school and then get a few little primaries to join us as well, so we've got a little cluster up there. We'll have to see how that goes down with local schools, but we do want to get on well with them all.

To sit alongside these good experiences of free schools, there are plenty of positive stories in MATs too.

We talked with head teachers from the Elevate MAT in North Yorkshire and they were overwhelmingly positive about the benefits of their trust. Nikkie Beniams explained:

> It's a primary-only trust, so we are not led by secondary colleagues. Also Nigel [Ashley], the CEO, has been a head teacher – which makes a difference. When I was with a local authority, I did not feel that support from advisers made a real impact on school improvement, whereas in a trust you have regular quality assurance visits from your school improvement lead – mine is Narinder. She's challenging, but she's also incredibly supportive, meaning the relationship directly impacts on school improvement.

Such observations, echoed by Alex Hope, another head teacher within the trust, illustrate the potential of collaborative involvement in terms of school improvement: 'One of the benefits of being in a MAT is my school improvement lead. She is invested in me as a leader because she is part of Elevate and wants the trust to do well.'

The collaborative aspect of the work of a MAT is surely the most potent force for good. From Gove's initial plan for the marketisation of schooling through to individual academies improving quality, there seems to be an emerging focus on collaboration within and between MATs. There is a careful line to tread politically, though. As one local authority school head teacher told us:

> One of the problems with the MAT agenda is the political narrative around them. A MAT is a group of schools working together. When you get Gavin Williamson saying at the end of the pandemic that we absolutely know that collaboration works because we saw MATs doing it, that kind of sticks in your throat. It wasn't just MATs. It was local authorities doing it, it was organisations like mine doing it, it was all sorts of organisations, but what got talked about was the MAT rather than the collaboration. The structure doesn't matter if the values are right.

An experienced head teacher from a local authority maintained school told us: 'We mustn't forget that, while collaboration is talked about, the problem is that the MATs are all competing against each other. We have a slightly scaled-up version of individual schools competing. They've got their loyalty to their form of collaboration, if you like, but they need to connect to something bigger than themselves, which is obviously one of the big tasks of leadership. That connection could centre around the notion of locality.'

Julia Cleverdon, who describes herself as 'a campaigner who connects the unconnected', echoed this tension when she reflected on her work supporting communities in Blackpool. She observed:

> Nobody seemed to have questioned the idea that you would have seven different academy trusts working amongst a population of only 140,000 people. The lack of collaboration between the secondary schools in Blackpool meant that the popular schools could exclude any number of kids they liked at the end of July, which led to the sad and tragic situation we had across the community – the sort of deprivation, social and emotional deficit, everything going on in that extraordinary place – was not owned by any of them. Blackpool has the largest pupil referral unit in Western Europe almost entirely because of the selfishness and the alleged market-driven behaviour of those academies.

This issue is not confined to Blackpool. The contest for high performance table results leads to another sort of competition, which leads to a reduction in the time and energy spent on pupils with difficulties – a situation that is exacerbated by political expediency (which we explore further in Chapter 10). Cleverdon was able to point to a way forward: 'The most important single thing we've done is to get a 10-year strategy into Blackpool for collaboration in the future. We have a much greater grip on the behaviour of some of those academies that are now only allowed to exclude three kids before they then carry the entire cost of excluding anybody else. We have slowly begun to understand the unbelievable number of separate silos dealing with young people in Blackpool completely unconnected with each other.'

Rivalry underlies much of the school system today and is one example of the impact of marketisation. School is pitted against school, MAT against MAT, MAT against local authority, usually on the basis of inspection judgements, themselves based largely on SATs and GCSE results. In Chapter 5, we expose the shortcomings in our testing system which unfairly limit the degree of successful outcomes. We would suggest that competitiveness should be focused on improving previous best, preferably collectively, rather than beating all-comers.

David Carter, now working in a different capacity, echoed this collaborative outlook:

> A lot of the work that I'm doing with trusts today is about the principle of saying that in your trust you need to be looking at your maths teachers or your English teachers right across the trust as your 'faculty of education' in maths or English, for example. When you do this, you start to see the 60 English graduates you employ as your talent pool to raise standards in English. How you choose to deploy them and where you want to deploy them then becomes the challenge. Let's stop talking about the group as six discrete English teams and talk about them as one brilliant English team. This approach then enables you to think about how you share the best teachers across the trust, so that as many children as possible get taught as well as possible. This is the basis of ensuring that education opportunity in a trust is equitable.

The Harris Federation is one of the MATs with an image of being very centralised. It is a federation of 50 academies with 36,000 pupils, and was founded by Lord Harris who built the Carpetright chain of stores. Harris first sponsored a school in 1990, and now brings its house style to each academy, almost creating franchises across London and Essex. Dan Moynihan, the CEO, paints a different picture:

> Across the federation our central service runs at about 5% of budget and we provide a comprehensive range of services for that. That 5% is for our secondaries; for our primaries, it's 4% and effectively what we do is subsidise the primaries from the secondary budget.

> We employ consultants. We've got 60 central subject experts whose job it is to go in, convene subject leaders across the group, leading to the production of the best schemes of work. They coach NQTs, all of that stuff, and their allocation to the schools is not based on who's paid what. It's based on need and everyone accepts that.

> We also provide a central team of accountants. Instead of each school having a bursar or paying £40k or whatever it is for a

bursar, we've got a team of 16 accountants, part-qualified or qualified, and they'll do four schools each. So it's much cheaper for the schools.

We have a central IT team and we run a cloud network across the group, so there's much less hardware; it's lower cost, and we have our own data storage centre at one of our schools so they back up into our own cloud. The heads can make it look however they want in their schools – for example, whatever the balance they choose between laptops and PCs is entirely up to them, but the back office bit of the IT we determine centrally, and that's the same everywhere. That doesn't matter because it doesn't affect education, but it sure does affect cost.

We have a central data team – HR, PR, legal – but the main and most important thing of all is the 60 education specialists.

We also have a team of executive heads, who are our turnaround specialists who will have a couple of schools each and will roam around coaching new and inexperienced heads. We've divided our group into four quadrants, so there are four assistant directors, one for each quadrant at secondary and one for each quadrant at primary. We've grown most of our heads, not because we want to, but because there's a shortage of high-quality heads. We have a fast track to headship course, and because we've got this 'executive principal' structure, we can take a risk on younger people with less experience and support them. The executive heads need to be able to do everything: in some schools they might need to do the timetable, in another they might need to walk the corridors and help with discipline or deal with parents.

Generally, that model has led to the production for us of some fantastic head teachers. They just get that incubation for two or three years. And then they fly.

Harris' economy of scale, with its 50 academies, is interpreted by many as a regime imposing its methodology on every aspect of the trust, but Moynihan's explanation counters that with an articulation of the quest for quality and with economy of resource being used to create the most beneficial impact on pupil learning. That, of course, was one of the purposes of local authorities, but, as we have seen, trust in their capacity to do so has diminished over time.

Against this positive picture are the criticisms of Kenneth Baker, who sees considerable problems in the RSC structures and the way the DfE is managing MATs:

> Let me tell you something we should focus upon. The department has decided to hand the responsibility for running schools to eight regional school commissioners, each responsible for over a thousand schools.
>
> The responsibility of the Department for Education is to maintain schools and improve them, but this sits with a junior minister who backs the regional schools commissioners. They have far too much power. They live remotely. They don't go and visit the schools and they don't talk to the local community. The closure of a school in the past was not just a question of judgement about the school itself, it was where it sat in its local community. Whenever a school was up for closure, the local community rose up, but the community now has no influence. Commissioners don't even talk to them. The power of the regional schools commissioners should be challenged. You must write something about it; work it out, it's appalling.

Baker has his reasons for complaining. His UTC development, set up with Lord Dearing, is part of the free school initiative, although it seems to be an unwelcome part. Baker Dearing Educational Trust was developed as an idea in 2007, and David Cameron and George Osborne were supporters when they came to power, earmarking funding for them in the DfE budget.

Gove said during his Policy Exchange speech in 2011: 'We are also encouraging businesses and universities to help tackle the shortage of high-quality technical education by setting up University Technical Colleges.'[32] However, it was mentioned to us more than once that Gove was not wholeheartedly supportive of UTCs and some told us that he actively disliked them. He seems to have tolerated them, supporting them publicly but rarely enthusiastically. Perhaps this is because of the stature of Kenneth Baker in the party and his place in the history of English education.

---

32   Department for Education and Gove, Michael Gove's Speech to the Policy Exchange on Free Schools.

Whether the system can generate a network of MATs that are self-determining, effective and offer consistent quality in schools is still to be proven. How the system will cope with MATs working alongside local authorities is also unclear. Gavin Williamson set out what he wanted to achieve but with little indication of how he would persuade, cajole or force those who had so far not seen the light to move towards it. The view of most people with whom we spoke is that something must be done to address the current complexity, especially around governance but also aspects of finance, school improvement and admissions, and particularly around those youngsters being denied, failed or even rejected by the system, however it is organised.

What does Michael Gove make of the expansion of the academy programme? Has it worked out as he intended or, in retrospect, does he wish he had set about it differently? He told us:

> I remember once being told that in politics it's always later than you think. Or, as Barack Obama put it, those in office must appreciate the fierce urgency of now. So, while we set a determinedly energetic pace for extending academisation, I think we had to in order to move towards a system where school leaders drove change in education. That's what academisation was principally about – empowering great school leaders to spread excellence. Multi-academy trusts have driven school improvement and enabled parents and students to ask, 'If excellence is possible there, why not here?'

> It's sometimes easy to forget that when we proposed extending academy freedoms to primary schools, Labour politicians said it would send a chill down parents' spines. Now, a reversal of academy freedoms is unthinkable. There is still more to do to ensure that great MATs expand in areas of persistent underachievement, but I know that is central to the government's agenda.

Since 2014, when he left education, Gove has worked in ministerial roles in the Treasury, Justice, Environment, Food and Rural Affairs and the Cabinet Office, and he played a key role in the referendum on European Union membership. He has twice stood unsuccessfully for the leadership of his party and the nation. With his new cabinet role as secretary of state for levelling up, housing and communities and minister for intergovernmental relations, he exemplifies the transient nature of political journeys and the fleeting involvement of politicians with their brief.

Many of the people we interviewed for this book hold Gove responsible for some of the fundamental problems with schooling in England today: the mess created by the fractured system of academy and local authority schooling, the worrying rate of exclusions, the curriculum unsuited to a changing world, as well as professional disharmony over salaries, status and working conditions. His legacy has not been a positive one.

So far in our book, we have examined the way the period since 1976 has unfolded and some of the influences on it. We have looked at the complex webs of relationships spreading out from the secretary of state and some of the political reasons why our school system is as it is.

The following chapters consider a series of themes that underpin the system and which have been affected by the era of centralisation, markets and managerialism. We begin with the confused and disputed arenas that shape the ways schools work: curriculum, pedagogy, assessment, teaching, leadership and school improvement. We then consider themes external to the schools themselves but are of significant systemic importance. In our penultimate chapter, we turn to governance and finance and ask at what level decisions should be taken about what happens to, about and in our schools. How should our schooling system be governed?

Part Two

The confused and disputed arenas – the occluded fronts

Chapter 5

Curriculum, pedagogy and assessment: the three-sided wheel driving learning in schools on an unnecessarily bumpy ride

The areas of curriculum, pedagogy and assessment are the lifeblood of schools, and they have been at the root of everything we have done in our careers, whatever the setting and whatever the role. What we decide we want our young people to learn, how we teach it and how we know whether they are learning well is the driving force for the way we organise schools and classrooms and the supporting infrastructure.

Writing about these three areas is difficult because each one is a complex arena with hundreds of publications produced about them. All are subjects for argument, debate and discourse. Teachers can easily get professionally disorientated trying to drive learning on the three-sided wheel: lost in the storms of curriculum, the mists of pedagogy and the fog of assessment. The three-sided wheel is in perpetual motion but it creates a very uneven drive.

One of the biggest problems is that curriculum, pedagogy and assessment are all so complex that they are rarely considered together. First one and then another assumes importance in the national debate – and, in doing so, affects the other two. Central government sometimes considers two at once, but it rarely initiates or orchestrates discussion on all three simultaneously. Very often schools mirror this myopic outlook; as does Ofsted, which is currently asking schools to focus on curriculum as a priority.

When the national curriculum was introduced in 1988, it was shortly followed by new approaches to national testing – referred to as 'assessment'. Pedagogy was seen as the teachers' domain. If teachers knew what was to be taught and tested, the implication was that they were trusted professionals who would teach it well. The 1997 Labour government was the first administration to exert a central influence on pedagogy, and it did so alongside the literacy and numeracy elements of the curriculum. When Labour began to develop the ill-fated diploma programme between 2004 and 2010, it brought together development in both the qualification aspect of assessment and the associated curriculum requirements.

What typically happens is that revision to any one of the three dimensions sends the other two into an unintended spin, along with the teachers who have to cope with the changes. The only exception to this lack of cohesion occurred from 2010, with requirements in the teaching of phonics. Nick Gibb, one of Michael Gove's ministers, made sure that phonics was not only included in the revised national curriculum, but that it was also aligned with a test and prescribed approaches to teaching. Whether this is a good thing or not is widely disputed, but, for once, there was a balance to the three-sided wheel driving curriculum, pedagogy and assessment.

So, why is it so difficult? Why is each dimension so mired in controversy that they cannot be plaited together to form coherence? The answer is that it is impossible to structure a curriculum and assessment with allied pedagogic approaches without having a clear and agreed set of beliefs. In England, the purpose of schooling itself is confused and contested; if the starting point is unclear, what follows is bound to be.

We would suggest that the starting point has to be an agreed set of beliefs. We outlined ours in Chapter 1. What follows from these beliefs and principles are some straightforward questions:

- If this is what we want to achieve for our children, what sort of things do they need to learn about and how to do? This is their *curriculum*.

- If this is what we want to achieve and what we want our children to learn, what are the best ways to teach it? This is the *pedagogy*.

- If we know what we want our children to learn and we think we know how to teach them, how will we know whether we have achieved our ambitions? This is where we can use *assessment*.

While the questions are straightforward, the answers to them are not, because any conversation is influenced by experience, research and prejudice. Very few people will start off from the same place and some will defend their starting point resolutely. Most conversations about curriculum, pedagogy and assessment begin in the present day – the stage we have reached in our evolving development. Lobby groups, interest groups, factions, researchers, practitioners, think tanks and all manner of individuals try to nudge the school system in various directions but the shift that gains most traction is usually government policy.

Yet, in our conversations with our secretaries of state, references to curriculum and assessment were usually tangential or partial rather than explicit. Many talked about things they had tried to do which were about curriculum or assessment and sometimes pedagogy. This is understandable; most were either continuing to some degree the policy of a predecessor and/or reacting to lobbying or other pressures in order to avoid a problem rather than aligning it with an established and articulated set of beliefs. Sometimes their actions could be seen as the result of a personal belief and seizing an opportunity to leave a legacy.

One of the biggest problems is determining what we think we are talking about, especially with the curriculum and to a lesser extent with assessment. Nearly everyone has been to school and has experienced assessment, and that being the case, we tend to assume that we are all considering the same thing. For some, the curriculum is simply subjects – the names on classroom doors; for others, it is the way the timetable is constructed; and for yet more, it is the exam syllabus. For some, the national curriculum is an entitlement; for others, an expectation; and for yet more, it is a requirement. All of these subtly different assumptions are the product of various influences on our outlook on schooling and influence any debate or discussion.

Some believe, as Ben Newmark puts it, that: 'Our curriculum should whisper to our children: "You belong. You did not come from nowhere. You are one of us. All this came before you, and one day you too might add to it."'[1] Many others, reflecting on their own school experience, view the curriculum like a cold shower: we wonder why we ever started it, suffer until it ends and, when it does, shudder and say, 'Never again'.

---

1   B. Newmark, Why Teach? [blog] (10 February 2019). Available at: https://bennewmark.wordpress.com/2019/02/10/why-teach.

This was true of Winston Churchill, whose achievements most British people believe should be included in a national curriculum. However, he wrote:

> I was on the whole considerably discouraged by my school days. This interlude of school makes a sombre grey patch upon the chart of my journey. It was an unending spell of worries that did not seem petty, of toil uncheered by fruition; a time of discomfort, restriction and purposeless monotony. ...
>
> Harrow was a very good school ... Most of the boys were very happy ... I can only record the fact that, no doubt through my own shortcomings, I was an exception. ...
>
> I was on the whole considerably discouraged. ... [My contemporaries] were far better at the games and the lessons. It is not pleasant to feel oneself completely outclassed and left behind at the very beginning of every race.[2]

Our own concept of the curriculum is broad: we see it as the entire learning experience that we plan for our children during their school years. It includes what they should learn in lessons and what they should learn in the rhythm and routine of the rest of their school day, along with those events and opportunities that we provide for them beyond traditional school hours. So, naturally, the curriculum includes planned learning for lessons and also what we plan for children to learn on residential visits, through performance, in assembly, in the library, in an outdoor environment, at after-school clubs or societies, or during charitable events that we help them to organise. There should be planned exposure to a range of cultural experiences, sports and pastimes, and opportunities to learn to play musical instruments, take part in productions and venture abroad. Most people would agree that these are all important elements of a good school. However, most people, when talking about the curriculum, regard it as the part that happens in lessons, with all the rest as add-ons or extras.

Subject disciplines are organised in a structured way because our understanding of how best to address these disciplines has developed over time. We also believe that children should have a range of structured opportunities to apply their learning in different contexts and through the widest possible experiences. We would also like to see a range of

---

2   W. Churchill, *My Early Life: 1874–1904* (New York: Simon & Schuster, 1930).

people beyond teachers sharing their expertise within and beyond schools. Learning could take place in a forest, at a farm, on a beach, by a river, at a station, in a factory or in a city centre, and be brought back to the classroom so children can make sense of it and explore other places and times through the web and texts at their disposal. We believe that seeing the curriculum as incorporating the entire planned learning experience would help us to make sense of learning for some of those pupils who currently come to reject it, as well as giving a firmer foundation to those who currently succeed.

Already, some readers may be seeing a distinction between their own views and our own. A common complaint is that our concept blurs the line between the curriculum and extracurricular provision. Like so much of our education system, this originates in the traditions of public schools, where parents pay for the 'basic' contract (i.e. lessons) and then opt to pay 'extra' for things like music tuition.

In 1979, Mark Carlisle, the secretary of state for education in Margaret Thatcher's incoming Conservative government, asked LEAs to review their arrangements for the curriculum. He and his counterpart in Wales believed 'they should seek to give a lead in the process of reaching a national consensus on a desirable framework for the curriculum and consider the development of such a framework as a priority for the education service'.[3] The following year, HMI provided one of a series of discussion documents to enable that consideration:

> The curriculum in its full sense comprises all the opportunities for learning provided by a school. It includes the formal programme of lessons in the timetable: the so-called 'extracurricular' and 'out of school' activities deliberately promoted or supported by the school; and the climate of relationships, attitudes, styles of behaviour and the general quality of life established in the school community as a whole. Whatever formal programme is adopted, account has to be taken of that other less formal and seemingly less structured programme, and of the interactions between the two. The fact that this short paper concentrates on the formal programme implies no undervaluing of the other educative influences.

---

3 Department of Education and Science, *Local Education Authority Arrangements for the School Curriculum: Report on the Circular 14/77 Review* (London: HMSO, 1979), pp. 6–7. Available at: http://www.educationengland.org.uk/documents/des/circular14-77review.html.

Teaching methods, the way schools manage their time and organise the use of buildings, equipment, books and other materials, and the way in which pupils are grouped and teachers are deployed are not part of the curriculum. They are the means which enable the teaching and learning to take place, although the assumptions they appear to embody may themselves convey attitudes and values to pupils and teachers alike.

'The curriculum' has to satisfy two seemingly contrary requirements. On the one hand it has to reflect the broad aims of education which hold good for all children, whatever their capacities and whatever schools they attend. On the other hand it has to allow for differences in the abilities and other characteristics of children, even of the same age. Within the broadly defined common curriculum individual curricular programmes have to be built up year by year as children progress through school.[4]

This broad HMI view of the curriculum is still largely appreciated by most, but the arrival of Kenneth Baker's defined national curriculum and its allied assessment narrowed the way that we see the offer presented to young people, the core purpose of schooling and what aspects we value. It has shaped an accountability framework and distorted our impressions of school effectiveness. It has meant that a greater proportion of children have seen success in their schooling, but it has also led to frustration for a significant proportion of pupils, some of whom, along with their teachers and parents, see their schooling as pointless.

Our contention is that we have never had a national curriculum that was fit for the purpose of meeting the range of pupil needs in our school system; that we countenance a national assessment system which further exacerbates the problem; and because we put so much store by testing and exams as accountability measures for pupils and schools, the pedagogy we encourage in teachers is bound to be limited, however well it is employed.

The agenda, in terms of curriculum, pedagogy and assessment, suffers from a significant lack of consensus. The issues that Jim Callaghan brought forward in his Ruskin College speech remain today. There is

4   Department of Education and Science, *A View of the Curriculum – HMI Series: Matters for Discussion 11* (London: HMSO, 1980), p. 1. Available at: http://www.educationengland.org.uk/documents/hmi-discussion/viewofthecurric.html.

still widespread disagreement about what should be taught (including superficial arguments about the importance of knowledge and skills) and about teaching methodology. Pedagogy, while essentially considered as a matter for the profession, is also debated publicly – usually in strident terms. However, what has developed since 1976 is a whole new debate about assessment. Many of the disagreements in all three areas tend towards polarity, and politicians – including some of our secretaries of state – have, either by accident or design, stoked that polarity of views through a media hungry for controversy.

Professor E. D. Hirsch, the American educator and literary critic, whose work informed Michael Gove's curriculum reforms, makes a sensible argument for the value of knowledge. Presaging recent developments in the United States and elsewhere, he argues that without a shared body of knowledge, 'Public discourse becomes increasingly uninformed and vitriolic, belief in political leadership dramatically declines and disagreement over policy is translated into demonization of the other.'[5]

Hirsch has spent his career justifying the importance of children being taught core knowledge, for which view he has often been criticised. At the same time, while pleading for people to heed his own words, he rounds on others who promote a different view: 'History, geography, science, civics, and other essential knowledge have been dumbed down by vacuous learning "techniques" and "values based" curricula and "progressive approaches" and "child-centred learning" and "people being indoctrinated".'[6] Lambasting others is unnecessary; it puts people at extremes, exudes a dangerous certainty and leads to the discourse becoming the very 'demonisation' he claims he wishes to avoid.

In England, we have circuitous arguments about skills or knowledge, separate or integrated study of subject disciplines, the basics or a rounded curricular experience, traditional or progressive teaching methods, assessment by examination or coursework and more. Much of it goes over the heads of teachers who tire of the noise and basically just want to do a decent job. Some of the political argument amuses, but much of it is dispiriting, hurtful and counterproductive, as it casts public doubt on the work that teachers and schools do to meet the needs of their pupils. It is

---

5   E. D. Hirsch, *How to Educate a Citizen: The Power of Shared Knowledge to Unify a Nation* (Woodbridge: John Catt Educational, 2020), p. 7.
6   Hirsch, *How to Educate a Citizen*, p. 6.

a peculiarly English disease, not replicated to the same extent in Wales, Scotland or Northern Ireland.

Why is the curriculum difficult?

The national curriculum was introduced as the wrong solution to the right problem. For some secretaries of state, the national curriculum has been the problem they have had forced on them, and for a few it has been a problem of their own creation.

Whereas James Callaghan wondered whether a core curriculum could be one of the solutions to the growing concern about schooling, Kenneth Baker placed the national curriculum at the heart of his reform of the system, believing it would be fundamental in solving the real problem, which was the variability and lack of effectiveness of the state system: 'Children of different abilities were achieving widely different standards depending on what part of the country they lived in. Whether children received good or poor education in the State sector had become a lottery.'[7] A national curriculum was never going to be the answer.

The Great Debate had opened the door and shed light on the 'secret garden' of the curriculum, which only the teaching profession understood and also controlled. LEAs reviewed their arrangements for the curriculum, and most took the time to do so because they had little or nothing coherent in place. Baker pushed on the partly open door to the extent that it came off its hinges. The curriculum would be a matter for the nation, and ever since it has been more a public park than any sort of garden.

While the seed and the germination of the national curriculum were mired in controversy, it proved to be one of those invasive plants that took over the garden. On several occasions, secretaries of state have felt the need to wield the shears to shape their own form of topiary. But the curriculum on its own will never be the solution because it never stands alone. It always influences, or is influenced by, factors such as pedagogy, leadership, qualifications, testing, parental engagement and pupil disposition to learning.

---

7   K. Baker, *The Turbulent Years: My Life in Politics* (London: Faber & Faber, 1993), p. 193.

For all of Baker's insistence that schooling had to perform better, and for all his willingness to face the wrath of the unions, he had missed – or chose to dodge – the fact that some schools and some teachers weren't as good as most at teaching and some heads weren't as good as most at promoting learning. His predecessor, Keith Joseph, had often caused consternation by asking seemingly naive questions about why schools followed certain practices, although he never seemed to dare to set about clearing the brambles in the secret garden. Baker noted that Joseph 'had been concerned about the various extraneous subjects that schools were teaching, calling it the clutter in the curriculum'.[8] Baker seemed to assume, or perhaps he rather hoped, that all teachers would teach well given the pressures of a standard assessment system, although he reflected that his testing proposal was opposed 'because it might reflect badly upon their teaching ability'.[9]

Where Baker tried to curtail debate with a defined national curriculum, what had really set in motion was a public discussion about what schools should teach. This discussion has continued and periodically becomes a battleground of ideas and purposes, with disputes breaking out from time to time with the ever-present likelihood of unpredictable assaults or unwitting victims.

Just as the original national curriculum was met with a range of responses, so too critics reacted by seeking to modify it or negotiate some changes. This process usually leaves the radical reformers disappointed and the traditionalists disheartened, so each goes away to regroup and return at the next possible opportunity to contest their ideas. Such skirmishes reveal people working on unproductive polarities. Some refuse to accept that it is possible to teach traditional subjects and more on future-focused disciplines. Others seem unable to perceive that we can teach knowledge alongside skills and attitudes. They decline to see that scholarly learning works with practical understanding and vice versa. They prefer not to accept that academic and vocational studies can complement each other.

There are others in the battlefield who prefer to see a world of little rigour – of dumbing down, trendy ideas and gimmicks; of giving young people an experience that does not extend them; of failing to open doors to new experiences which leaves them bereft of learning. For example, calls for the decolonisation of the curriculum following the Black Lives

---

8   Baker, *The Turbulent Years*, p. 189.
9   Baker, *The Turbulent Years*, p. 199.

Matter campaign polarised opinion: do we teach historical interpretations or history as a series of headline events? It is reasonable to do both.
Similarly, Gavin Williamson's announcement of a limited programme of
Latin teaching was applauded by those who saw it as promoting traditional values and benefits, but it was criticised by others who saw it as
irrelevant to much wider and more urgent needs.[10] Others question why
Latin rather than Ancient Greek or Mandarin, and many note the irony
of introducing Latin in the same month of proposing a ban on the use of
mobile phones in schools. They are all skirmishing – winning small and
often hollow victories – while the big battle for overall control continues.

Baker had the chance to establish a truly national curriculum, while subsequent secretaries of state have had to make do with revising, reviewing
or reconstructing the one they inherited. His approach was to appoint
Duncan Graham, the director of education for Suffolk, to lead the newly
established National Curriculum Council and manage the process of constructing a new curriculum from scratch.[11] Working parties included all
the usual suspects, but it was in the way they were structured that the
nature of the curriculum was determined. It was to be organised along
traditional lines, reflecting what successful people had experienced in
their own school careers. Many accused the council of being rooted in
the past, evoking an argument that had been brought out in a seminal
work published in 1939, Harold Benjamin's *The Saber-Tooth Curriculum*,
in which he argued that the curriculum will always struggle to keep up
with the times and that some influences will always dominate.[12]

Each of the national curriculum working parties delivered on a 'subject'.
The merit of this was hardly debated, and it was never explained by an
assertive Baker to those, mainly in the primary sector, who had a different
view on how a curriculum might be constructed. The order in which the
working parties set about and concluded their work also signified the relative importance of the core and foundation subjects: English appeared
first, and the last to arrive was physical education. The starting point was
the expectation for the subject by the end of schooling, with key stages
leading to the final destination. The implication of the model was a linear

---

10 Department for Education and G. Williamson, Thousands More Students to Learn Ancient and
    Modern Languages [press release] (31 July 2021). Available at: https://www.gov.uk/government/news/
    thousands-more-students-to-learn-ancient-and-modern-languages.

11 The National Curriculum Council was installed in York and quickly grew into a significant organisation.
    Visitors remarked on the 'NCC' woven into the carpet: whether it was something on which to wipe one's
    feet, deaden the sound or decorate the hallways was never explained.

12 H. Benjamin, The Saber-Tooth Curriculum (New York: McGraw-Hill, 1939).

curriculum, arranged by subject disciplines, and some more important than others.

While Baker stressed that this was the curriculum and that it was for schools and teachers to decide how it should be taught, some professional voices complained about being railroaded, pointing out what was wrong in the assumptions of structure and expectation, what was missing or diminished, as well as where all this might lead. Those who were critical were portrayed as negative to the concept or to the sensibilities of the majority. By and large, though, Baker had the support of parents who, for the first time, were being offered a description of what their children would learn and how they would be assessed. Baker was a skilled communicator and announced his plan for the national curriculum on the television programme *Weekend World*,[13] and on several occasions during party political broadcasts he conducted mini teach-ins aimed directly at parents.

In reality, many teachers – probably a good majority – were fascinated by the curriculum and grateful, if nervous, that there would be clarity about what was expected of them. Head teachers were in the main pragmatic and prepared to accept the certainty of the government deciding the learning agenda in preference to a continuing and sometimes negative debate which risked undermining parent confidence in the system. In practice, therefore, they too were seen as welcoming the concept of central control.

The published curriculum always carries important messages in the way it is presented. The first national curriculum arrived in a series of differently coloured ring binders, one for each subject, with the implicit message that, while subject disciplines were discrete and could be taught separately, sections could be taken from each ring binder and linked through teaching.[14] There were also booklets on cross-curricular themes published by the NCC in 1990, such as 'Education for Economic and Industrial Understanding', 'Health Education', 'Careers Education and Guidance', 'Environmental Education' and 'Education for Citizenship'. While these were advisory rather than statutory, when the binders were all aligned,

---

13 *Weekend World* was a political debate programme, presented by Peter Jay and later by Brian Walden, which aired from 1972 to 1988. It was broadcast on Sundays at midday and was similar in style to today's *The Andrew Marr Show*.
14 Updates could be inserted into each binder but such documents are only current for so long and they quickly became disorganised in many schools. Some ring binders were used to prop up the front of the projector in schools that were lucky enough to have them.

they served to emphasise the daunting size of the national curriculum – a problem that bedevilled it from the outset.

The latest version of the national curriculum, driven by Michael Gove, is by contrast only 200 pages long for the primary phase and just 105 for secondary.[15] This one suffers from complaints about brevity and balance. In the primary phase, 67 pages are devoted to English and 43 to mathematics, with science captured in just 28 pages. No other discipline is described in more than four pages. The subject content for art and design for the four years of Key Stage 2 is set out in 84 words. For computing at Key Stage 4, as pupils prepare to enter a world of employment which is becoming more computer oriented in so many respects, the subject content is defined in just 94 words. These images of the national curriculum and the type of language used are important. For example, it has always had programmes of *study* as opposed to programmes for *learning* or programmes of *experience*. It has always proposed *attainment* targets as opposed to *learning* or *competencies*.

What Baker missed, and what has eluded most of his successors, is that the national curriculum – the source of such heated debate during revisions – is so easily distorted very soon after publication. The curriculum that leaves HMSO, approved by Parliament, is unwittingly modified by schools and teachers when it is taught in the classroom using inconsistent approaches. Commentators, including teachers, remember the headlines, but typically, thereafter, they talk about it with either positive or negative regard based on what they think is included or what they would like to see included.

Lobby groups continue with the refrain that the way to address every social, health, creative, employment, entertainment or sporting concern is 'through the national curriculum'. Whether it is winning the football World Cup, combatting obesity, helping our industries to become more competitive, stopping radicalisation or making Black Lives Matter, 'we have to begin in our schools' and 'this needs to be in the national curriculum' are common refrains, with the implication that it is teachers who should sort it out. (Interestingly, as we applaud the rapid development of vaccines against COVID-19 and the skills and dedication of NHS workers, there seem to be few who comment, 'This all began in our schools' or 'This is thanks to our teachers'.)

---

15   See https://www.gov.uk/government/collections/national-curriculum.

After each round of often fractious debate about another national curriculum revision, everyone settles down to prepare for the next time. Indeed, many in schools are more concerned about the revision process and the prospect of change in their job than the actual curriculum. For example, there was widespread annoyance at Gove's insistence on a knowledge-rich curriculum, yet a few years later there is little mention of it. Perhaps there has been a wholesale change of staff, perhaps it was the upheaval that was less welcome or perhaps people now accept that Gove was right. More likely, as we discuss in Chapters 6 and 11, it is the effect of a profession heavily focused on accountability and compliance. Teachers get on with teaching what has been published, although even then it is subtly changed by their personal imprint and interpretation.

Why does the curriculum become distorted?

At every level in the system we begin with a *planned* curriculum. At a national level, a school level and even at classroom level the curriculum plan is a statement of intent. As teachers adopt the plan and set out to teach it, it becomes the *taught* curriculum. The plan is usually extensive and teachers elect to teach what is tested, what is inspected, what they know about, what they enjoy teaching and what they think children will enjoy learning. The rest tends to be redundant or receive limited attention. For example, the English national curriculum has always included 'speaking and listening' under various headings over time, particularly in primary schooling. Because reading and writing are tested extensively, it is natural that they assume an importance over speaking and listening, even though the impact of good teaching in these areas would make a difference to reading and writing. Similarly, the changing expectations for GCSE have rendered 'practicals' in two science subjects and 'speaking the language' in two modern foreign languages more or less important and affected practice in schools.

As the planned curriculum – already beginning to distort – meets the pupil, it becomes the *experienced* curriculum. At this stage, it is distorted by the routines and rituals of the school – for example, in terms of timetables or textbooks. The disposition of the pupils and their outlook towards learning will influence whether the teacher arranges practical apparatus work or plays safe with clerical activities. Knowing what is likely to be on the test not only distorts the way the curriculum is taught, but also the way it is encountered, with pupils facing practice tests on a narrow range of content rather than carrying out experiments or participating in creative activities within the broadest scope of a discipline.

Until 2019, inspection pushed teachers towards a shrinking pedagogic repertoire. While Ofsted always argue that they don't support a particular approach to teaching – indeed, their inspectors have been quick to highlight effective practical applications and applied learning – the majority of the examples of good or outstanding practice depicted in inspection reports imply that certain features of a lesson should be present. Over time, an orthodoxy of effective teaching has emerged, steered by Ofsted, which has had a greater impact on curriculum and pedagogy than any secretary of state with the fanfare of a national curriculum revision has been able to achieve.

When Ofsted inspections began in 1992, schools began to panic that they would be failed for not meeting the entire curriculum expectation. As the clamour reached fever pitch in 1993, John Patten asked Ron Dearing to review the national curriculum – a move which was welcomed by unions and teachers generally.[16] Dearing started to raise macro issues about pedagogy. For example, he looked at the use of time and proposed that the national curriculum should be limited to four days a week, with the remaining day focused on the school's own agenda. At the same time, he recommended that the national curriculum should be less prescriptive and the content rationalised. An uneasy peace was restored for a time but the distortion continued.

Curriculum is talked about more in primary schools than it is in secondary schools. For secondary schools, the discussion quickly moves on to exam specifications and syllabus content. As such, it is exams that distort the curriculum; the downward pressure from Year 11 is significant. Tim Oates,

16 In April 1993, Patten asked Dearing, chairman of the SCAA, to investigate possibilities for reducing the burden on schools. His report was published the following year: R. Dearing, *The National Curriculum and its Assessment: Final Report* [Dearing Review] (London: School Curriculum and Assessment Authority, 1994). Available at: http://www.educationengland.org.uk/documents/dearing1994/dearing1994.html. Dearing was a career civil servant who went on to become chair of the Post Office. In later life, he joined forces with Kenneth Baker to form the Baker Dearing Educational Trust and to introduce UTCs.

who led Gove's review,[17] explained the logic behind a national curriculum that was detail-heavy at the beginning and content-lite at the end:

> If you look at what I think is the apparently over-general character of the Key Stage 3 and Key Stage 4 national curriculum programmes of study, the reason they are generalised as they are is because secondary school teachers told us they never looked at the national curriculum in Key Stage 3 or Key Stage 4. Their teaching programmes are determined by GCSE. There were the general things they needed to be doing to meet the legal requirements of the national curriculum in terms of spiritual education, physical education and so on, but actually, in terms of the content of learning, it's about GCSE.
>
> With the increasing tendency towards Key Stage 3 being foundation learning for Key Stage 4, we didn't think we should set up a national curriculum which competed with the content of GCSE. We should go with the flow of the set of arrangements that were in place in instruments that actually operate on schools and, in the review, focus principally on the content of the national curriculum in primary, knowing that the general aims of the national curriculum and GCSE were in place for secondary schools.
>
> Secondary schools were increasingly becoming academies and therefore were not required to do the national curriculum. Taking GCSEs together with key policy instruments, we didn't want to make the national curriculum compete in some way with GCSE. There was precedent: GCSEs and the national curriculum were in tension from 1988–1995, and Ron Dearing had to grapple with that serious competition in his review. We did not want to reignite these tensions.

According to Oates, private sector exam boards were now being allowed to determine the quasi-national curriculum as the market nudged into policy control. Since most secondary schools were soon to take the plunge with academisation, it could be argued that this was immaterial, especially since academies were not required to follow the national curriculum, beyond 'having due regard' to it. However, by 2017, HMCI Amanda Spielman was raising concerns about the over-dominance of

---

17   In 2010, Gove established an advisory panel led by Tim Oates and including Mary James, Dylan Wiliam and Andrew Pollard. The panel's work ended in dispute when Gove was seen to override their advice, which led to the resignation of James and Pollard.

GCSEs and the growing tendency of secondary schools to shorten Key Stage 3. Spielman, who had previously led the exams regulator Ofqual, argued: 'The GCSE tests are designed to cover 2 years' worth of content. It is hard to see how taking longer than 2 years could expose pupils to more knowledge and not more test preparation.' She was concerned that 'for most children, the end of Key Stage 3 is the last time they will take art, music, drama or design and technology'.[18]

While the accountability mechanism was no doubt driving the schools towards a narrow curriculum, there was no attempt by Gove or the curriculum review team to challenge this situation. Oates justified it to us like this: 'Michael Gove was saying to me at the time that the English Baccalaureate was de facto the national curriculum at Key Stage 4. The EBacc specification was developed separately from the review and focused on GCSEs. We recognised that it engaged with the stark reality out in schools.'[19]

While the secondary national curriculum was driven by GCSEs, Oates told us: 'We tried to realise genuinely "fewer things in greater depth" in primary. I think Andrew [Pollard] began to get worried that there was a tendency to overspecify from the centre. And Michael Gove did start to intervene in some of the specifications, like in history. The national curriculum is so important and in law is placed with the serving secretary of state; it's inevitable that ministers are going to be interested in what's in it.'

Oates also described the public spat that developed within the advisory panel in respect of the decision to specify content at a year-by-year level, which led to the resignation of members of the group. Whatever the background to the row, what was equally relevant was the work going on elsewhere in the DfE on assessment, which was intended to include 'a new reporting method which would see each pupil compared against their peers nationally. Each pupil would be placed in 10% bands, or

18 Ofsted and A. Spielman, HMCI's Commentary: Recent Primary and Secondary Curriculum Research (11 October 2017). Available at: https://www.gov.uk/government/speeches/hmcis-commentary-october-2017.

19 Michael Gove proposed an English Baccalaureate of eight subject examinations but formally withdrew his proposals on 5 February 2013, telling Parliament that his proposal was 'a bridge too far': M. Gove, Curriculum and Exam Reform, Hansard HC Deb vol. 558 col. 441 (7 February 2013). Available at: https://hansard.parliament.uk/Commons/2013-02-07/debates/13020759000004/CurriculumAndExamReform.

deciles. Pupils' positions [would] only be made available to parents and schools.'[20]

This was part of a raft of coalition proposals for changes to assessment in primary schools which was going to align with the new national curriculum and linked to better pupil premium allocation. It was no doubt well-intentioned, although a bizarre nod to the past. However, this notion of deciles came to nothing, partly due to the negative response to the consultation but probably due to impracticability. To place all Year 6 children on deciles on a national scale by virtue of a test would mean all children doing nothing else in school but answering multiple choice questions at the rate of one every 20 seconds from the beginning of Year 3. At least someone realised.

Robin Alexander had led the independent Cambridge Primary Review from 2004. The final report was published in 2010 under the title *Children, Their World, Their Education*.[21] It was a comprehensive and thorough analysis based on extensive evidence and research, and it was published to recognise, celebrate and renew the work of the Plowden Committee of four decades earlier.[22] The Cambridge Primary Review had examined 10 educational themes and produced interim reports on each over a period of two years. Several of these publications were used by the media to highlight or question aspects of government policy – such as the impact of the national strategies, assessment, early years provision and the curriculum – all of which had been addressed with integrity by the review. However, as the first interim reports appeared during the post-Blunkett and Morris period and through the musical chairs of three secretaries of state in three years, the DfE found the media attention and, as a consequence, the report itself awkward to handle. Rather than seeing it as a review of 40 years of development, it was instead perceived as an attack on their policies.

Worrying that a parallel conversation was developing, the government tried to head off Alexander's work on the curriculum by establishing a

20 Department for Education, N. Clegg and D. Laws, Raising Ambitions and Standards for Primary Schools [press release] (17 July 2013). Available at: https://www.gov.uk/government/news/raising-ambitions-and-standards-for-primary-schools.

21 R. Alexander (ed.), *Children, Their World, Their Education: Final Report and Recommendations of the Cambridge Primary Review*, 1st edn (Abingdon and New York: Routledge, 2010).

22 B. Plowden, *Children and Their Primary Schools: A Report of the Central Advisory Council for Education (England)* [Plowden Report] (London: HMSO, 1967). Available at: http://www.educationengland.org.uk/documents/plowden.

formal review of the primary curriculum to be led by Jim Rose.[23] There followed two years of simultaneous reviewing which led to confusion for the many schools involved in either or both, and for the wider school community in general which thought that either the two reviews were working together or, worse, in opposition. Of course, the Rose Review was the 'official' one and, as we describe in Chapter 2, the proposed new primary curriculum fell at the final hurdle as Gove refused to support it.

Gove had made curriculum reform part of his campaign strategy, arguing that the national curriculum was overly bureaucratic. Whether he thought that election to office was a vindication of his view and this gave him authority to act, whether he misjudged the situation, whether he was simply intent on disruption or whether he wanted to rein in the perceived dumbing down of standards and the curriculum is not clear. His decision to abandon the proposed new primary curriculum review and begin another one was generally not well received, but some saw it as a lifeline or last-minute rearguard action in the battle they had been fighting and losing.

Gove used all the right words, telling the Education Select Committee:

> I want children to be authors of their own life story. The reason I use that phrase is that I think that education is a process of emancipation, of liberation. One of the problems that this country has had historically is that we've been very good at educating a minority – the gifted and talented – quite well, but the majority of children have not been educated as well as they should have been. The days have gone, if they ever existed, when a society could survive by having an elite who were well educated according to a particular set of narrow academic criteria, and others who were simply allowed to become hewers of wood and drawers of water later on. ...

> School should be an enjoyable time. Horizons should be extended. Children should have an opportunity to encounter worlds and ways of thinking that have taken them outside their environment, whatever that is, so at the end of compulsory schooling, yes, children are equipped to work well and yes, children are able to make their own economic choices, but they feel enriched. They're able

---

23 J. Rose, *Independent Review of the Primary Curriculum: Final Report* [Rose Review] (Nottingham: Department for Children, Schools and Families, 2009). Available at: http://www.educationengland.org.uk/documents/pdfs/2009-IRPC-final-report.pdf.

to enjoy music and literature. They're scientifically literate, so they can reject bogus arguments put forward by people who are trying to seduce them into lazy ways of thinking. They can analyse what politicians and people in power say and know what's rubbish and what's sensible. Above all, they can be happy, confident citizens and parents of the future. That is my overall vision.[24]

However, his actions belied his fine words. Gove's promotion of the EBacc in secondary schools did not go down well as it appeared to do the opposite of what he had suggested to the Select Committee and, in fact, narrowed down the curriculum. In setting up the curriculum review under Tim Oates and shredding the work of the Rose Review, Gove alienated many whose views on the curriculum chimed with the Every Child Matters agenda, which had also been symbolically purged. The minimising of citizenship and PSHE emphasised that the wider curriculum would be pared back. As Nick Gibb began to insist on certain approaches to the teaching of reading and subtraction, after years of national literacy and numeracy strategies, teachers resented yet more ministerial intrusion. The reduction of funding for the arts, culture, libraries and youth services – all presented as part of the austerity agenda – added to many teachers' impression that what Gove wanted to do was to get schooling back under tight government control.

In our view, schools have largely come to terms with the revised expectations of the national curriculum. Most of the fuss and fury about interference has died down; a largely compliant profession has got on with it in the face of accountability measures, a relatively vague curriculum and new exam specifications, most of which have now been assimilated. In the majority of schools, the distortion we described earlier in this chapter has already happened: most teachers in most schools are teaching what they think is in the curriculum, what is tested or inspected, what they enjoy teaching and know about, and what the children enjoy. Many primary schools still use what they call the 'Rose curriculum' and a lot still use the Cambridge Primary Review work they developed. Ofsted's recent focus on the curriculum has made schools look again at what they think they are trying to achieve, yet most of them continue with what they were actually doing before they worked on their 'intent'. For our part, the last 10 years has shown us that no amount of central interference can

24 Commons Select Committee, The Responsibilities of the Secretary of State – Education Committee, Examination of Witnesses (28 July 2010). Available at: https://publications.parliament.uk/pa/cm201011/cmselect/cmeduc/395-i/395-i02.htm.

achieve uniformity, and we are reassured by that. At the same time, we recognise the way that centralisation and managerialism can inhibit and restrain the imaginative professional, and like most who have spent a lifetime in and around schools, we are disappointed by that.

The most straightforward analysis of where we are today with respect to the national curriculum came from Kenneth Baker, the politician who started it all. He was scathing in his views:

> It really is appalling that we're working to a 1904 curriculum. Gove's curriculum is simply Progress 8[25] and EBacc. All the schools are now measured on Progress 8. So the heads have cut out a huge number of subjects; they've cut all the cultural subjects, dance, drama and music by over 25%, and the broad and balanced curriculum is disappearing. They've also slashed by 70% design and technology, which I introduced. We're the only country in the world that is not teaching students below 16 some technical skills. The Gove curriculum dominates the Department, and no one is brave enough to say boo to the goose. That's where I stand.

The influence of pedagogy

Curricular distortions are the inevitable outcome of pedagogical judgements: how do we teach, and how do we seek to extend a pedagogic repertoire to best teach what we have decided is important for our young people to learn?

Kenneth Baker knew that something needed to be done about consistency.[26] However, he steered clear of suggesting too loudly that some teachers would need support and help with pedagogy – an area even more closely guarded than the curriculum. It was to be another 10 years before the issue of pedagogy was addressed centrally by David Blunkett with the introduction of the national strategies.

---

25 Progress 8 is a complex calculation of each secondary school's performance based on calculating the average score across eight subjects for each and every pupil and comparing their progress from their attainment at age 11. This reveals a figure that is designed to show progress for all pupils compared with a national average. While the EBacc was dropped by Gove in terms of individual pupils, it remains in place along with the Progress 8 measure and is an 'accountability' factor both in league tables and Ofsted inspections.

26 Baker recognised the need for every teacher to be trained, insisting on five days a year, which were dubbed 'Baker days'. They are now called training days, INSET days, CPD days or closure days.

A few years prior to that, in the mid-1990s, Gillian Shephard had begun to make tentative inroads through the introduction of the Language in the National Curriculum programme, which was provided centrally and delivered locally. She had also initiated the first efforts to address the challenges in those areas of the country with perceived underachievement, using evidence from the increasingly sophisticated performance tables of both schools and local authorities. She established some small-scale school improvement programmes for groups of primary schools in local authorities with poor performance. Initially, the programmes were not well received by those schools invited to take part, many of whom resented the suggestion that they needed improving or felt the attention to be unfair or professionally embarrassing. Instead of grasping the nettle, local authorities renamed the programmes 'challenges' – a term that would resurface under Labour.

Tim recalls:

I remember visiting a Birmingham primary school on one of the city's many estates and met a longstanding male head teacher who had been a silent participant in one of the school improvement sessions I had started in my first term. It was his silence that had brought me to the school. After the polite introductions and a tour of the school (which I had suggested and he had reluctantly agreed to), he brought out a file to show me the error of my 'improving on previous best' ways. 'How can I?' he asked. 'Look at these reading scores over the last 17 years. Every year they have gone down. I have made a study of it. Standards are falling. It's the pupils and their families.' I politely enquired if it might be affected by his attitude and a good debate followed. I got him to visit other schools and slowly he changed his tune. It left me more than ever convinced that the mantra of 'improving on previous' and brooking no denial was the key to changing culture.

Mick recalls:

In 1993, I was invited by Sandwell Council to lead a short pilot pro-gramme to support school improvement. The local authority had come bottom of the national performance table for SATs results and had received funding from the DfE to support the 12 lowest perform-ing schools in the borough. The programme was to last two terms and we devised a course for two classroom teachers from each school on what we would now call pedagogy to be held at the local CPD centre. Teachers were supported through in-school coaching by a couple of seconded teachers. It was a very innovative approach for the time.

I suggested to the local authority that it would be sensible to meet with the head teachers before we began to explain the conditions and how the programme would work. At the meeting, the chief adviser was explaining to the heads how the money had become availa-ble and was challenged by several over the use of the term 'school improvement'. He was asked outright whether he could possibly be suggesting that the schools needed to improve. It took a lengthy dis-cussion to persuade them that they were being offered a resource to support their effort rather than being punished for poor performance.

The programme, the Tipton Challenge, turned out to be successful, not for its immediate impact on results but because it awakened in teachers within and beyond the central course an excitement about teaching and a belief that through *their* teaching they could make a difference to children's life chances. The teachers and head teachers on that pilot programme became advocates for the extended two-year programme for 30 schools that Gillian Shephard approved the following year as a result of the evaluation. The word 'improvement' could have scuppered it all, such were the sensitivities.

Nowadays, schools in Sandwell generally have a highly developed sense of mission, and many of them are driving a positive agenda to link schools with the community through multi-agency approaches.

This focus on pedagogy at the school and teacher level would have been better addressed alongside the introduction of the national curriculum. As it happened, pedagogy was coming under the spotlight some 10 years after the curriculum had arrived. Pouring refined curriculum oil into an old engine was never going to improve acceleration.

A centralised pedagogy

The incoming Labour government of 1997 grasped the nettle of pedagogy that local authorities had avoided. In introducing the national strategies, it focused on pedagogy with the concept of the literacy and numeracy hours. This was prescriptive stuff: primary teachers were trained in how to manage an hour of teaching with specific sections determined by recommended minutes of activity. What only a short time before would have brought howls of protest instead produced little more than a whimper. The government had centralised teaching like never before and most teachers were enthusiastic. The approach was classic cascade delivery: a centralised programme with accompanying standardised resources and taught to trainers who trained classroom teachers in a standardised way. Local authorities employed the trainers and were funded via a grant called the Standards Fund.[27] There was no doubt that although the trainers were employed locally, the intention was that they would deliver a centrally prescribed programme.

The benefits were many and the side effects not long in showing. The programme was successful: some of the most dramatic transformations ever seen in the English system occurred as results rose because of a directly attributable innovation. Christine Gilbert, who at the time was a secondary school head teacher, told us: 'In Tower Hamlets, we loved the literacy and numeracy strategies. They had a huge impact. For the first time, children felt ready and able to learn. Secondary schools began receiving children who could read and write.'

At the same time, there were complaints, in spite of the generally dramatic rise in pupil attainment as measured by SATs. One was about the pressures being exerted on schools, particularly as Ofsted was now checking that the strategies were being followed. There was an impression that professional autonomy was being reduced. As Estelle Morris observed: 'We should probably have produced more than a single model for the

---

27   The Standards Fund was a device used by government to ensure that local authorities addressed the national agenda. Each year, LEAs had to agree targets with central government which relied on the appointment and deployment of key staff for which they would be funded.

strategies and given schools more choice over how they did things. Yes, perhaps we were too prescriptive.'

David Blunkett, however, was very clear that this was an adventure into unknown territory: 'The truth is we were all learning as we went along. People misinterpreted the literacy and numeracy agendas. You were not compelled to follow certain practices.' He added: 'We needed to persuade people that they were innovators and experimenters. I'm not sure we managed that.'

As the national strategies reached secondary schools, there was equal anticipation and excitement, with training focused on the 'three-part lesson' and the 'diamond-shaped lesson'. While an orthodoxy was being promoted, Ofsted was continuing to accrue greater influence in the form of examples of good teaching in their reports. Certain lesson features began to appear in the spotlight with increasing frequency: the starter, the lesson objective, questioning, quality of task, marking, feedback, the plenary and homework. These as well as other features of teaching assumed dramatic importance and swept through schools like waves, with leaders increasingly homing in on a narrow range of elements to convince inspectors that they were focused on the quality of teaching. Ofsted later published good practice guidance but took the web page down as it was creating 'myths'. One example of this was their guidance on 'triple marking', which became questioned on the basis of workload. Ofsted recognised its influence and produced a 'myth busting' document to try to distance itself from the waves.[28]

All of this assumes that pedagogy was getting better. Standards were rising as measured by national tests and exams and schools were improving as measured by inspection, yet, from the start, there was a significant proportion of pupils for whom the system wasn't working. David Blunkett expressed his ongoing frustration, present even today: 'There is something about the nature of teaching in secondary schools. I thought, and still think, that teaching in secondary education is way behind what might be seen as inspiring, especially in science and technology and so on.' He continued: 'Why is teaching stuck in the past in terms of pedagogy? Why do the same thing over and over again when it is patently failing? Why don't we say, "What isn't working, and let's do something about it?"'

---

28 Ofsted, Ofsted Inspections: Myths (28 February 2019) [withdrawn 2 September 2019]. Available at https://www.gov.uk/government/publications/further-education-and-skills-inspection-handbook/ofsted-inspections-myths.

One of the purposes of the proposed introduction of diplomas as a result of the Tomlinson Report in 2004 was to make learning more relevant, bringing academic and applied understanding together in a practical and scholarly way and interwoven with appropriate assessment.[29] Tomlinson had highlighted the cluttered curriculum at Key Stage 3 and the lack of coherence for youngsters aged 14–19, with multiple examinations and courses that were unlikely to prepare them for future life in work. We chart the fated course of the diploma programme later in this chapter, but the work done in preparing for diplomas was built on a clear coherence between curriculum, pedagogy and assessment in its broadest sense. It is a shame that it collapsed.

As the national strategies took hold and Ed Balls brought in the wider children's agenda and Every Child Matters,[30] a revision of the secondary curriculum was underway. Balls' articulation of 'five outcomes' that matter most to children seemed to resonate with teachers generally. They were: being happy and healthy, staying safe, enjoying and achieving, making a positive contribution to society and enjoying economic well-being. It is unlikely that Balls realised that these outcomes implied a curriculum with a wider outlook. The focus at the time was on raising scores each year in SATs and GCSEs, and the consensus was that this priority could only be achieved through dedicated and well-used time on the 'basics', with enjoyment added through wider experiences as treats.

The Tomlinson Report had highlighted pupil engagement as a significant issue, especially at Key Stage 3, which has always been and remains the point in a child's schooling where progress is most likely to stall. The review of the Key Stage 3 curriculum was an opportunity to bring the wider agenda of Every Child Matters into line with the developing diploma programme.

---

29 M. Tomlinson, *14–19 Curriculum and Qualifications Reform: Final Report of the Working Group on 14–19 Reform* [Tomlinson Report] (Nottingham: Department for Education and Skills, 2004). Available at: http://www.educationengland.org.uk/documents/pdfs/2004-tomlinson-report.pdf.
30 Every Child Matters was presented to Parliament by the chief secretary to the Treasury, Paul Boateng, in September 2003.

Mick recalls:

During the QCA review of the Key Stage 3 national curriculum, we worked hard to get teachers involved in the development of content. Over the first year, QCA had done a lot of scoping work and we were due to begin a series of regional conferences for secondary school curriculum leaders. On the evening before the first conference, at which we expected around 100 senior teachers from secondary schools, we were running through the plan for the day.

Some QCA colleagues were expressing concerns about the first hour. The plan was to offer the briefest background introduction and then ask people to work in groups to list the sorts of outcomes that children would need at the end of their secondary schooling. After that, they were to be asked to position sticky notes on the outline of little stick children to show whether the outcomes related to head, hand or heart. In the planning session, some QCA colleagues thought that the teachers wouldn't expect to take part in this type of activity and would instead be expecting to simply hear the new national curriculum requirements and have an opportunity to comment on them. They believed there might be a poor reaction to this activity early in the day.

In the end we went with it, and the reaction was surprising, even for those who wanted it to work. The teachers' enthusiasm for thinking differently about learning and the curriculum was unbounded, and what some feared might be dismissed as a simplistic task was instead perceived as a way of both structuring thinking and explaining the purpose of the curriculum. The stick figure outlines and resultant lists of 'head', 'heart' and 'hand' learning that evolved and provided the basis for ongoing consideration have since been used in sessions to think about curriculum purpose in many parts of the world with groups of politicians, parents, employers, teachers and children. I have never seen it fail to resonate.

What this incident also highlighted in a small but tangible way was the willingness – indeed, thirst – of teachers to be involved in creating a curriculum that matters to the young people in our schools. Ever since, and especially with the review of the primary curriculum led by Jim Rose, the idea of the co-construction of the curriculum has been harnessed and explains why the curriculum proposals coming through were well received by the majority of the teaching community. The word 'majority' is important; as a groundswell of support grows, it is sadly typical in England that a contrasting oppositional view also grows.

By the time the notion of a national strategy had extended into social and emotional aspects of learning (SEAL),[31] such developments were receiving a mixed reception. On the one hand, SEAL was welcomed and applauded, and on the other, it was met with a level of dismay by those who felt that they had been pushing the agenda for years and that what had been produced did not match their message precisely.

One of the perennial problems in the curriculum and pedagogy agenda is the reluctance of people to embrace a new form of the agenda they hold dear. The potential benefit of a number of factions striving for almost the same thing is often diminished by an inability to compromise with someone whose ideology is just fractionally different. For example, there are several organisations that seek to promote environmental and sustainability issues or values and compassion, but they find it difficult to form a coalition with political influence. Instead, they each seek to show schools how *their* approach reflects the national curriculum or fulfils Ofsted's expectations. Schools latch on to these movements, which gather momentum in the system, but they often run in parallel with national requirements.

We have lost count of the number of curriculum and teaching and learning initiatives that have swept through primary schools over the years. In the search for the magic bullet for children's learning, new approaches seemingly spring up everywhere. They usually have their root in theory, but the top line of the practice is what spreads. Things sail through on the wave and create a massive splash in schools and in the system. Depending on their age, teachers will remember de Bono's Six Thinking Hats,[32] Reggio Emilia approaches to early years education,[33] Gardner's

---

31   See N. Humphrey, A. Lendrum and N. Wigelsworth, *Social Emotional Aspects of Learning (SEAL) Programme in Secondary Schools: National Evaluation* (London: Department for Education, 2010).

32   Edward de Bono (1933–2021) promoted ideas on lateral thinking that were used by businesses to improve management communication. The principle was that each participant in a discussion wore a different coloured hat in order to make a specific type of positive contribution. This was translated into the school setting during the 1980s.

33   The Reggio Emilia philosophy emanated from a small town in Italy, following the work of Loris Malaguzzi who opened a pre-school in 1963. Early years practitioners have visited Reggio Emilia and brought back principles and practices that explore the 'hundred languages of children'.

multiple intelligences,[34] Bloom's taxonomy,[35] Dweck's mindsets[36] or Rosenshine's principles of instruction,[37] all of which have a validity based in neuroscience and pedagogy but can become a trend.

Once the wave recedes, rock pools of practice continue. Some teachers carry on using these approaches, often very well, since their reasons for adopting them was well understood at the outset. Stephen Cox of Osiris Education, which has run CPD programmes for 25 years, talked about this tendency to follow the trend. He told us: 'Teachers need to be trained far better in terms of some kind of evaluative model. There's so much stuff out there at the moment that it's actually a bit of a minefield to walk through as a teacher. Our schools are at risk of being over-programmed. Do we have a notion of what the features of good practice are? I think moving towards the evaluative outlook, and doing that on a collective basis, is the way forward.'

There are three significant developments that have become prevalent without a wave. They have grown steadily over a long time from small beginnings, spread throughout the system and become embedded without prescription or even encouragement from central government or the inspection regime.

One is Forest Schools.[38] There has been no government initiative, yet school after school has gradually started to see the benefit of exposing children to learning experiences which make the maximum benefit from being outdoors and near trees, however scant the 'forest' may be. From a couple of trees, to a copse, to a veritable glade, adults are connecting children quite literally with a natural approach to learning. Pupils'

---

34 Howard Gardner's *Frames of Mind: The Theory of Multiple Intelligences* (New York: Basic Books, 1983) advanced a theory of multiple intelligences which gathered pace in English classrooms from the mid-1990s. A valid concept which was misunderstood by some, converting the idea into 'learning styles' with sometimes contrived and questionable pedagogical practices.

35 Benjamin Bloom and David Krathwohl published *A Taxonomy of Educational Objectives: The Classification of Educational Goals, Volume 1* (New York: Longmans, Green, 1956), which offered a classification of questions to denote the complexity of cognitive challenge. Bloom's taxonomy appears in charts used in classrooms today, although is not so evident in the discourse between teachers and pupils.

36 Carol Dweck's work on fixed and growth mindsets became influential in English classrooms from 2010 onwards. See, for example, C. Dweck, *Mindset: The New Psychology of Success* (New York: Ballantine Books, 2016).

37 Barak Rosenshine's principles, first expounded in *Teaching Functions in Instructional Programs* (Washington, DC: National Institute of Education, 1982), have been promoted by the wave of advice following the emphasis on knowledge accumulation and retention since 2010.

38 The Forest Schools movement, which has grown rapidly in recent years, encourages an active, child-centred curriculum focused around outdoor learning: https://forestschoolassociation.org.

excitement at being in the forest is matched only by parents' enthusiasm for their children having some very elemental experiences.

A second development that has sustained itself and grown is Mantle of the Expert, initially developed by the late Dorothy Heathcote.[39] It gives young children a learning impetus by creating a real sense of purpose and audience within the context of a dramatic construct. Over the years, teachers have worked together to shape their understanding of processes and practices, although always without becoming formulaic.

A third example of classroom practice that has gradually extended its reach is Philosophy for Children, or P4C.[40] Here, children come to terms with intellectual constructs, think through really big ideas and questions, and challenge themselves and others within a set of working protocols. P4C began in the early 1960s with exploration and research focusing on children's capacity for profound thought and expression. The example practices of P4C encourage the consideration of logical problems and complex interrelated issues, as well as some perspectives on mature themes that affect us all in a changing world. Some schools use P4C techniques to consider relationships, justice and moral dilemmas.

These three developments have become embedded in a significant number of primary schools and some secondaries. They have lasted the course because the teachers involved have committed to deep understanding rather than being busy spotting the next initiative on the horizon. Teachers have engaged in extended training, well led by the organisations themselves, they have made a meaningful analysis of impact, and they have worked with like-minded colleagues over time to challenge their thinking and approach.

From time to time, lobby groups get to influence politicians and policy directly. Andrew Adonis lent his support to the Manifesto for Learning Outside the Classroom in 2008, promoting the work of nine organisations that were trying to attract schools to their facilities.[41] Pressure from

---

39 Mantle of the Expert has grown since the 1980s under the guidance of the much admired Dorothy Heathcote (1926–2011), a lecturer at Newcastle University. The approach is articulated in D. Heathcote and G. M. Bolton, *Drama for Learning: Dorothy Heathcote's Mantle of the Expert Approach to Education* (London: Pearson Education, 1995).
40 Philosophy for Children emerged from the work of SAPERE, which was founded in 1994. P4C seeks to engage children in discussions about a range of pertinent matters. The aim is for each child to participate in examination, questioning and enquiry before reaching a conclusion.
41 Department for Education and Skills, *Learning Outside the Classroom: Manifesto* (Annersley: DfES, 2006). Available at: https://www.lotc.org.uk/wp-content/uploads/2011/03/G1.-LOtC-Manifesto.pdf.

members of the House of Lords keen to promote the organisations they patronised – from the National Trust and Wildlife Trusts to the RSPB – drew ministerial support. This was a good initiative but exclusive in the sense that there were thousands of other organisations that could have been included in a national programme to support the curriculum. Adonis seemed to treat the issue of fieldwork, as do many others, as a useful addition to proper learning. We think it is integral to proper learning for most pupils.

Many of our secretaries of state argued that they tried to widen the curriculum offer. Estelle Morris explained: 'I think we did really quite well with the sports agenda. We identified a structure for delivery as it wasn't something that government could deliver effectively by itself. We formed a strong partnership with the Youth Sport Trust and worked with them to develop and deliver a programme. We got it right with that relationship. We provided the money and the trust was absolutely respected by the field and had the expertise and experience. People never associated us with the initiative.'

On the other hand, Alan Johnson reflected: 'We struggled – no, failed – to get anywhere with an earlier start to children learning modern foreign languages. I wanted children enjoying languages from an early age, but there is something about the British reserve that means parents don't seek it in schools.'

He had the same experience with music, bemoaning that: 'Music in schools always bothered me. We kept pulling the lever and nothing happened. With sport, when you pulled the lever, it was action, but music – nothing. We tried all sorts of things: musical instrument teaching, specialist teachers, everything – it just never took off.'

Since we have limited consensus about an agreed belief system, the government is always susceptible to lobbying from interest groups. At a school level, there can be a stream of offers to support learning from organisations trying hard to achieve a mission which, for them, is vital. These range from charitable concerns such as the Royal British Legion's annual Poppy Appeal[42] or the local hospice, to those instigated by commercial concerns such as World Book Day which is sponsored by National Book Tokens and the UK's booksellers and publishers.[43] Celebrities launch charitable efforts to raise the stakes of a particular curriculum area, such as Darcey Bussell's DDMIX, which aims to build confidence and well-being in children from deprived backgrounds through dance.[44] Organisations such as the Country Trust seek to excite an understanding of food and farming in children from schools in deprived areas.[45]

All of these initiatives are available to the school system and resonate with most schools, but the take-up and organisation is ad hoc. Whether children who most need wider experiences outside the classroom are able to access them depends on a range of factors: an alert teacher, a willing head teacher, other priorities and the pressure of accountability. Jill Attenborough, CEO of the Country Trust, told us:

> We offer schools in socially disadvantaged areas an opportunity to bring children on a farm visit. We arrange it, host it with the farmer and sometimes we are even able to help with transport costs. The response from schools and children is fantastic. Schools tell us it is a brilliant learning experience and supports personal development, but there is still an underlying need to justify opportunities and experiences. Over the years we have tried to show how our work fits with literacy and numeracy strategies, social and emotional learning, and the sustainability agenda. Then there was the new Ofsted framework and talk of cultural capital. More recently, we have picked up on what Anne Longfield [the then children's commissioner for England] said about childhood and the post-COVID agenda. It is so sad when head teachers say they can't take

---

42 The Royal British Legion organises the Poppy Appeal in the lead-up to Remembrance Day on 11 November. Until the late 1990s, the commemoration was lessening in prominence and was not generally observed in schools on the actual day. Since the millennium, with the involvement of Britain in wars in the Middle East and significant anniversaries of the First and Second World Wars – as well as the expectation that British values would be taught in schools – there has been a greater emphasis on remembrance in schools.

43 World Book Day is held annually, and children and school staff are encouraged to dress up as their favourite literary character. In recent years, there have been some complaints about the pressure on parents and the tendency to resort to shop-bought 'superhero' costumes.

44 Darcey Bussell, former principal dancer at the Royal Ballet and judge on the BBC's *Strictly Come Dancing*, co-directs DDMIX, a social enterprise aimed at encouraging dance in all its forms.

45 The Country Trust was established in 1970 by Lance Coates, an organic farmer and businessman, to promote sustainable organic farming and champion human health. Today, the trust works with farmers and schools to offer children from socially disadvantaged communities the opportunity to learn about farming and food in practical and enjoyable experiences.

part because they are in an inspection category and have to focus on the basics. Learning about food and farming should be a fundamental for children; after all, we all eat, and what we choose to eat shapes our own health and the world around us.

Set against all these efforts, though, is always what schools see as the prevailing wind. Gavin Williamson asserted: 'We know much more now about what works best: evidence-backed, traditional teacher-led lessons with children seated facing the expert at the front of the class are powerful tools for enabling a structured learning environment where everyone flourishes.'[46] It is not hard to see why schools and teachers are restrained and tentative about being seen as out of step.

It is, of course, the high-stakes accountability system that most distorts pedagogy and, in turn, the curriculum. One continuing source of argument about the world of assessment is its effect on the quality and emphasis of the curriculum and pedagogy, and – as we have already seen – they are influenced in themselves by polarities of viewpoint.

And so to assessment

Assessment is perhaps the stickiest swamp in the debate, although many find it an arid desert around which we wander in search of an oasis of common sense.

When Kenneth Baker introduced the national curriculum in 1988, he also introduced a national assessment system. In doing so, he argued that he was helping parents to understand how their children were progressing as compared with expectations for the average child. He had commissioned a report from the Task Group on Assessment and Testing (TGAT), chaired by Paul Black.[47] Baker took forward their recommendations for standard assessment tasks (the origin of the term SATs), which were envisaged as operating in class time and administered by teachers. These

46 Department for Education and G. Williamson, Education Secretary Speech to FED National Education Summit (1 March 2021). Available at: https://www.gov.uk/government/speeches/education-secretary-speech-to-fed-national-education-summit.
47 Department of Education and Science and the Welsh Office, National Curriculum Task Group on Assessment and Testing: A Report (1987). Available at: http://www.educationengland.org.uk/documents/pdfs/1988-TGAT-report.pdf. Paul Black is a highly regarded educationalist, a positive critic of assessment practice and well known for Inside the Black Box: Raising Standards Through Classroom Assessment, written with Dylan Wiliam, of which there have been several iterations.

standard tasks were to be used in a formative and diagnostic way at ages 7, 11 and 14 with summative testing used at aged 16 with GCSEs.

Primary teachers moaned about workload and complexity when the SATs were introduced as tasks in Key Stage 1 from 1991, but it was when they were later implemented at Key Stage 3 that there were legal challenges by teacher unions over workload and pay. The Dearing Review came up with the solution: external pencil-and-paper tests. While the unions celebrated a victory, the centralised testing system would now furnish government with national summative data that they could use to inform development. At the same time, teachers began to see assessment in the limited terms of summative testing rather than the beneficial but complex influence on learning described in the TGAT report and outlined later in this chapter. Centralisation was to deskill many teachers in a fundamental aspect of their work and pupils started to become a control measure of school production.

TGAT had clearly made a link between pedagogy and assessment and warned of the dangers of sharing assessment outcomes more widely than for educational purposes. In other words, they foresaw the dangers of performance tables. It is worth noting here that John Patten had introduced school performance data for the GCSE in 1992 and SATs results were added in 1996 during Gillian Shephard's tenure. The introduction of performance tables was in tune with Prime Minister John Major's Citizen's Charter which sought to improve the quality of public services through openness. Assessment was now part of the growing centralised accountability regime.

Schools respond to central accountability by introducing internal accountability, with 'data drops', often linked to teachers' performance management, now a regular feature of the school year. The pressure for secondary schools and teenagers to succeed at GCSE and the trial-by-ordeal approach to assessment creates a corresponding need for mocks and now pre-mocks, all of which take up valuable teaching time and render gyms and dance studios redundant and unavailable for teaching for weeks on end. For many children in primary schools, Year 6 is a series of practice tests until after the SATs when it becomes a chance for staff to atone for the experience so far with an extended period of enjoyment on the way to secondary school. This is distorted curriculum and pedagogy.

The issue of assessment is a seemingly never-ending source of concern to somebody somewhere on the grounds of morality, child development, accuracy and validity, professional trust, autonomy, accountability and more. Arguments range from the perceived stress on children and adults to 'hot housing' and gaming, so it is difficult to pin down, let alone manage, the discussion or its outcome. Bill Lucas sums up the issues in *Rethinking Assessment in Education: The Case for Change* as 'focus', 'methods', 'consequences' and 'validity'.[48] In the same publication, we were also taken by this image from a former commissioner of education from Colorado:

> To solely use standardised achievement is like casting a net into the sea – a net that is intentionally designed to let the most interesting fish get away. Then, to describe the ones that we caught strictly in terms of their weight and length is to radically reduce what we know about them. To further conclude that all the contents of the sea consist of fish like those in the net compounds the error further. We need more kinds of fish. We need to know more about those we catch. We need new nets.[49]

What we have found is that teachers have become deskilled in assessment largely because the important accountability processes have been carried out centrally and they have not been supported in seeing assessment as part of the learning agenda beyond the managerial and functional activities.

The confused purposes of assessment

One problem is that the purpose of assessment is so rarely considered because it has always been part of schooling and has become too closely tied to accountability. The types of assessment are little understood and the use to which they are put even less so. That said, there seems to be a more determined search for some clarity about what assessment is. Currently, the term is used to include a whole range of activities and, since this is causing some confusion, the terminology we use is important.

---

48 B. Lucas, *Rethinking Assessment in Education: The Case for Change* (East Melbourne, VIC: Centre for Strategic Education Leading Education, 2021), p. 12.
49 W. T. Randolph, a commissioner of education in Colorado, quoted in Lucas, *Rethinking Assessment in Education*, p. 3.

Assessment is applied in all kinds of contexts. In recent years, it has often been used as a sanitised term for 'testing' and often used to imply a 'product control mechanism'. So, by assessing pupils (testing), we can measure the effectiveness of a school, department or teacher (accountability process).

Accountability is a process that can utilise the results of test scores because these are measurable, but it can also make use of all sorts of other evidence. For example, if we measure the accountability of a teacher based on a percentage of their pupils achieving a certain grade in a test, we may assess that the teacher has demonstrated accountability, when in fact the pupils not successful in the test could be deemed to have been let down. A teacher's accountability is for the progress, growth and well-being of *every* pupil, so the narrowing of the measure to a test score can serve simply to make management's job easier, but in truth it reduces accountability.

Accountability necessitates that the leadership team are convinced that the individual has done everything they can to act professionally to achieve the aims and purposes of the organisation. The sources of evidence are multiple.

Types of assessment

Our view is that assessment is much misunderstood because it is considered so lightly by teachers. The centralised political agenda has reduced consideration of assessment to a low base. Politicians oversimplify what is a complex arena, emphasising testing at the expense of other forms of assessment. Teacher training disregards assessment beyond the rudimentary requirements of accountability. For this reason it is worth setting out some principles.

Assessment is put to many uses and comes in many forms, commonly including summative, formative, diagnostic, evaluative and ipsative. These forms of assessment beg the question: what do we moderate against – a criterion-based judgement or the norm? If we use clear *criteria* which can or cannot be achieved, we are referencing our assessment against benchmarks that do not move. Examples would be a driving test: if we can do it, we pass.

If we compare members of a group against each other, or judge them against the average, or from best to worst, we are using a *norm* reference. Our assessments can be informal or formal (usually through tests). In schooling, the model of assessment via controlled tests and exams is administered by central agencies and has been mirrored throughout the system in schools and classrooms as part of the general approach to teaching.

Both normative and criterion-referenced assessment can take place naturally and unofficially. For example, we categorise children within a family as taller than their siblings or as a better reader/runner/swimmer than most of the children we know (normative, i.e. measured against others), or we notice that a child can ride a bike now (criteria, i.e. measured against the expectation), regardless of whether others can or not.

Norm-referenced tests are designed to distribute entrants across a bell curve of performance as compared to the rest of the cohort rather than whether they have achieved specified criteria. On the other hand, criterion-referenced tests which measure performance against a fixed set of standards tend to provide a more precise outcome.

Norm-referenced testing is made worse when, irrespective of the standard achieved, it is predetermined what percentage of pupils will pass a high-stakes test. For example, the best 20% going to the grammar school is a norm reference, as is selecting the best performers (say, 36 individuals), irrespective of the number of entries or the standard they achieve. Selecting all those scoring over the pass mark in the test is criterion referencing, since the actual number selected will be governed by the criteria, regardless of whether there are 37 or 95 entries and regardless of the level of achievement. Norm referencing is often used to restrict the entry to higher education, with numbers receiving grades being controlled by availability of places; hence the problems with two years of COVID-affected exam results, which have led to a move away from norm referencing to looking at what pupils can do.

Criterion referencing sets the criteria: the ticks to be achieved on the MOT test, the length to be swum for the beginner's swimming certificate, the standard set for a musical instrument grade exam. Premium Bond winners are norm referenced as about 1% of entries are drawn each month. Football leagues are also norm referenced. The champion this year may have many more points than last year, and relegation is the fate of the last three teams, irrespective of how many points they secure.

Setting in schools is usually portrayed as criterion referenced – that is, selecting pupils based on their aptitude for each set. The reality is that it is usually norm referenced, in that the acceptable size of the set dictates the criteria. If 37 out of 100 pupils score way higher than others, it is rare to put all of them in the top set, if what is required is four groups of 25 for timetable and staffing convenience.

To summarise, the types of assessment are:

- *Summative* assessment is used to measure the individual's performance as a snapshot to see how well they compare with the average, where they come in a ranked order and whether they have accomplished a particular skill or reached a particular level.

- *Formative* assessment seeks to inform the assessed or the assessor, so they can amend their work. It can operate through informal or formal methods: an anaesthetist will monitor vital signs to vary the levels of drugs to a patient, and a gas boiler check will involve a series of tests which tell the engineer whether to make adjustments and if further tests will be required to verify the outcome.

- *Diagnostic* assessment asks why. Why is this person not keeping up? Why is this boiler not firing up? Why are these children not learning to read? Why is this musician not hitting the high notes? Whether they are the best or worst in a group is not at issue. The question is: what can the assessor do to improve the position? This might involve a diagnostic test and often utilises detailed observation. It goes beyond criterion referencing, which might show that a group cannot do a certain operation successfully, and instead seeks to determine what, beyond needing more practice, can be done to improve things.

- *Evaluative* assessment sets out to measure the provision, not the learner. The testing of pupils is designed to check whether one approach is more successful than another. It usually involves an experimental group and a control group which doesn't receive the approach. Evaluative testing can be used when two parallel classes have covered the same course of study but with different resources or experiences to check which approach is most effective. The problem is being sure that the two groups being tested are equal in all respects. Our concerns about experimenting with children's futures inhibits this sort of evaluative testing, but we see plenty of examples of experiments based on little more than hearsay.

Ipsative assessment is generally overlooked, partly because it is less well known and partly because it is difficult to formalise and record. Ipsative assessment is intensely personal as it is owned by the individual. It is used as a motivator in sport in the context of encouraging individuals to beat their previous best. At its root, ipsative assessment involves the individual rating the assessment offered by others, whether criterion or norm referenced, and making a decision about how valid they think it is. The individual might win a race and be applauded for doing so, but deep down they might know that they expended little effort. Similarly, receiving a certificate of achievement might please onlookers, but the individual might regard it as of little consequence. A wall containing a set of framed certificates (swimming one width, first aid training, PhD and so on) will have different values to the learner in terms of the actual achievement; it is why people are sometimes proudest of the seemingly insignificant achievement.

Schooling makes relatively little use of ipsative assessment and is often unaware of it. We often hear athletes and sports commentators talking about their personal bests or PBs. For pupils this is a much underused approach, particularly in incremental learning. Ipsative assessment does come into play when children become absorbed in building their score on a computer game. The 'feedback' is impersonal – it simply tells them how they compare with other players or with their previous best. It is essentially normative referencing, but the ipsative element is a powerful driver in assessing whether or not to keep going. Eventually, for most people, the addiction goes because the normative referencing feels futile.

The ipsative outlook is vital in schools where teachers put effort into marking and commenting on pupils' work. If the pupils believe in and trust the teacher, they will react by pushing themselves further, whereas a pupil who does not have trust in the teacher will play the game as necessary and sometimes withdraw from the game completely. This is one reason why some pupils seem unconcerned at coming bottom or top of a group, or whether they get things right or wrong. Indeed, many who do well in memory tests of coursework resent their teachers and their comments, and only play the game out of respect for their parents or others.

To try to summarise the complexity of all this, let's look at assessment in the context of a real-time experience: marathon runner Josh Griffiths.

Josh Griffiths' first ever marathon was the 2017 London Marathon. He finished in 2:14:49, which means little until compared with other times. His time was the thirteenth fastest (summative/norm referenced) out of thousands. He was the first Briton to finish (summative/ norm referenced). His time qualified him for the World Athletics Championships (summative/criterion referenced). At the halfway point, he received advice from another British runner about maintaining his pace (formative/criterion referenced). He knew he was doing well when he overtook many of his heroes and this spurred him on (ipsative/criterion referenced). Josh said: 'The goal for me was to try and run the Welsh Commonwealth Games qualifying time of 2:16:00. It never crossed my mind that I would be running in the World Championships in the summer [ipsative].'[50] He vowed to experiment with his training regimes and diet to see whether he could improve his performance (evaluative).[51]

Assessment misunderstood

We have no intention of demeaning teachers by suggesting that assessment is misunderstood. However, what appears to be a straightforward process has become incredibly complex and made more so by the use of statistics and data. The word 'assess' comes from Latin, *assidere*, and means 'to sit beside'. In an ideal world, we would sit beside the learner and support them, but logistics make that impossible. Instead, we create assessment systems, and sometimes those systems – at a classroom or national level – can run out of control, especially when not fully understood.

David Blunkett summed up a significant problem with the use of assessment at a national level: 'I wish I had understood better what norm

---

50 *BBC Sport*, London Marathon 2017: Club Runner Josh Griffiths Finishes As Fastest Briton (23 April 2017). Available at: https://www.bbc.co.uk/sport/wales/39686121.

51 Josh Griffiths did run in the World Athletics Championship that summer, but he ran a slower time (summative/criterion referenced). His personal best is now 24 seconds quicker than his London debut.

referencing is and how that distorts and reduces the opportunities of youngsters.' It is our view that Blunkett would be one among many.

At a school level, Mick Walker, vice-chair of the Chartered Institute of Educational Assessors (CIEA), told us:

> We find that many teachers are interested in assessment and tell us they understand assessment and are confident about it. What we realise is that they understand their school's processes and procedures – things such as how to provide the required data and submission deadlines. What they don't typically understand is how assessment works and some of the benefits and pitfalls of certain approaches.
>
> It is so complex – different sorts of assessment, what recording methods are used, the assumptions that can be made – and then we get into issues such as interpretation and judgements that can fit a formula but not be accurate, valid or reliable. People try to simplify a very complex process.

Mick recalls:

When I was at QCA, one of the select committee hearings I had to attend was about whether the country needed a national curriculum (I think the committee was trying to second-guess the Cambridge Primary Review at the time by looking at several aspects of schooling).

The first question caught me out a bit. It came from a Conservative MP who later defected to UKIP: 'Mr Waters, please can you explain why, after over 20 years of all schools having to follow a national curriculum, 25% of children end up in the bottom quartile?'

I was unsure whether this was an ice-breaking joke, but nobody else was laughing, so I said, 'That's a hard question – it could almost be on a GCSE exam paper.'

This did make the panel smile and the politician came back good-humouredly with: 'Only GCSE? I thought it was much harder – A level standard.'

To which I replied, 'No, standards are rising so that will now be GCSE.'

'Surely it is easier if it is GCSE level – standards would be falling?' he said.

I knew it was going to be a long session – and I had come to discuss curriculum rather than assessment and standards.[52]

The lack of understanding in schools is due in part to the centralisation and the allied marketing of a key part of assessment – the management of GCSE examinations at 16. After the reform of the system under Kenneth Baker, the exam boards subcontracted the marking to serving and retired teachers, but this was purely transactional and was not used profitably to improve learning for pupils in the long term.

Mick Walker explained his experience while teaching:

> To my surprise, when I went to a meeting of the Yorkshire and Humberside board I bumped into two colleagues from my own school, one who marked for English and the other history, but none of us would ever have a conversation in school about it. It was kind of pushed under the surface in my mind. We did pick up quite a bit from marking and working out how standardisation worked and how moderation worked. We did get five days off each year to do this – my head was really supportive. What should have happened was, when we went back into school, somebody should have just said: 'Right now, what are they up to, and can we learn anything from what is happening elsewhere?'

The CIEA was first proposed by Ken Boston, then the CEO at QCA, to try and widen the understanding of assessment in schools.[53] Mick Walker told us:

> Ken Boston set up a taskforce to consider the establishment of an institute. A number of things came out of this, especially support for those who worked in schools on the exams system.

---

52 It did make me realise why politicians get excited about their share of the vote when they have polled 40%. They seem not to realise, or choose not to do so, that it was 40% of a voter turnout of 20%, which is actually 8% support. This often happens at local elections, police and crime commissioner elections and used to happen with elections for members of the European Parliament.
53 Ken Boston (who was made an Officer in the Order of Australia in 2001 for his services to education and training) was recruited by Estelle Morris following the resignation of Bill Stubbs after another exams fiasco. He had a quiet but profound influence on English schooling but resigned after being cruelly treated by Ed Balls after an outsourced contractor failed to deliver on the SATs in 2008.

Chief examiners were largely unsupported and didn't receive the training that the public might expect. They tend to learn on the job. I was a chief examiner for years and I never went on a course on assessment; I picked up the tricks of the trade from being a marker or moderator but there was no formal training. There was an issue that these people don't get recognised. So 60,000-odd teacher markers every year trip out of the schools and colleges, mark GCSEs and A levels, and somebody [the exam board] says thank you – well, they hardly say thank you very much – and they just finish marking and then go back to the day job.

The influence of the CIEA is building within the education community the commitment to enable, understand and secure sufficient expertise in each school to allow assessment practices to support learning and achievement. Progress is slower than hoped, partly because exam boards are invariably reluctant to engage fully. The reasons range from exam boards wanting to offer their own provision for examiners to suspicions that the CIEA is a quasi-union which is seeking to question processes and procedures or argue against the present system under which exam boards make considerable profits from each annual round.

What this lack of understanding fosters, however, are practices born of a managerial approach, which are used by leadership in schools to gain approval from an inspection regime that seeks evidence in the form of managerial efficiency. Baseline testing in secondary schools to predict GCSE grades five years hence, target-setting for pupils, data drops and flight paths (which Walker calls 'the devil's work') are some of the developments that can have a negative impact if not used well, and which we refer to in Chapters 8 and 10 where we discuss pupils who find motivation difficult.

Yet assessment continues to have high profile in schools, dominating the landscape for older pupils in each phase, while simultaneously being narrowed down to the process of testing and calibrating children as units of production.

Where does assessment figure in policy terms?

There was limited talk of assessment in our conversations with politicians. Most of the heads and leaders of MATs that we met spoke of assessment in the context of accountability and implied that it was a way to determine the success of their schools – although, of course, they delighted in the success of individuals. Few questioned the impact of assessment on pedagogy and curriculum; assessment was often discussed in managerial terms as an indicator of school and teaching effectiveness, a support to performance management practices and a means of categorising pupils.

Although results carry so much weight, there is little awareness among many in schools that tests and exams are largely norm referenced and that however well pupils perform, they cannot all reach the highest grade. In effect, schools are in competition, not with the examiner but with all other schools taking the exam; as some succeed on a norm-referenced test, by definition, others will not. GCSEs and SATs do not measure what a child can do against set criteria; they measure how they have performed against others. Worse, the grade boundaries are decided only *after* the results are known. An equal mark in an exam two years running can elicit two different grades. Pupils, parents and the wider public are being duped into believing that exams provide consistent measures of achievement across the years.

When Simon Lebus, interim chief regulator at Ofqual, was asked on BBC Radio 4's *Today* programme about the difference between exams and teacher assessments, his response provoked a storm of criticism.[54] He explained that 'Exams are a bit like a snapshot, a photograph – you capture an instant. It's a form of sampling.' Teacher assessments, he suggested, allowed staff to 'observe student performance over a much longer period and in a rather more complex way, taking into account lots of different pieces of work and arriving at a holistic judgement.' Detractors baulked at the idea of the exams regulator questioning the very standards being protected and Ofqual was quick to assert through a spokesperson that he was talking only in the context of the current year when he said: 'I think from that point of view we can feel satisfied it's likely to give a much more accurate and substantial reflection of what their students are capable of achieving.'

---

54   *Today*, BBC Radio 4 (9 August 2021); see also *BBC News*, A-level Results: Students Have Been Treated Fairly – Watchdog (9 August 2021). Available at: https://www.bbc.co.uk/news/education-58141518.

Our view is that Lebus' comments deserve deeper consideration before the system lurches back to the previous regime of terminal examinations simply because of the need for normality. Ofqual's announcement that in 2022 there will be fewer top grades,[55] alongside Nadhim Zahawi's justification that 'We've put fairness at the heart of our approach',[56] illustrates the extent to which the system is misrepresenting pupil achievement. Variations on the word 'fair' appear 10 times in the Ofqual announcement, but in what way is it fair to imply to pupils that their knowledge, skills and understanding will be recognised if the measure is not applied to the extent to which they meet the criteria but to a comparison with the performance of others? Do the parents, pupils and teachers listening to these announcements realise that pupils are not being challenged to demonstrate their own learning against clear benchmarks, but are, in fact, in a race with their peers to be awarded a predetermined number of top grades?

Robin Walker seemed to believe, like so many, that our 'normal' exams system is based on pupils meeting set criteria when he explained to us the reason for the decision about 2022: 'It's important that, for every student going into exams, they know that they're going to get a fair crack to demonstrate what they have worked to achieve and what they have learned.' Whether he was simply toeing the party line or believed this to be what the exams will do, he is wrong.

Some union leaders raised with us the issue of the impact of assessment. For example, Geoff Barton at ASCL talked of 'the threat to progress and aspiration in the system. We all want youngsters to get as far as we can by age 18. I simply do not understand how we can argue that the best way to achieve that, the best way of all the options we have, is to hit youngsters around the head with really big and difficult qualifications at 16, make them fail and put them into the "forgotten third",[57] having made them hate the subjects.'

---

55 Ofqual and J. Saxton, Ofqual's Approach to Grading Exams and Assessments in Summer 2022 and Autumn 2021 (30 September 2021). Available at: https://www.gov.uk/government/speeches/ofquals-approach-to-grading-exams-and-assessments-in-summer-2022-and-autumn-2021.

56 Department for Education, Ofqual and N. Zahawi, Adaptations in 2022 Summer Exams to Ensure Fairness for Students [press release] (30 September 2021). Available at: https://www.gov.uk/government/news/adaptations-in-2022-summer-examsto-ensure-fairness-for-students.

57 The Newsom Report drew attention to the waste of talent in a school system focused on the best-performing third of pupils: J. H. Newsom, *Half Our Future: A Report of the Central Advisory Council for Education (England)* [Newsom Report] (London: HMSO, 1963). Available at: http://www.educationengland.org.uk/documents/newsom/newsom1963.html.

Of our secretaries of state, David Blunkett was forthright: 'The exam system is shot. A major challenge is the way the exam system operates.' For most politicians, though, the issues of curriculum, pedagogy and assessment seem like running sores that have to be bandaged or soothed occasionally, rather than being treated as the very lifeblood of our system. Now and again a minister sees the need to start again with curriculum or examinations or testing or screening, and calls it assessment, but mostly they seem to want to avoid or discourage general debate as a distraction from more structural activity.

Those that campaigned hard for social justice, such as Justine Greening or Ed Balls, did not focus on the curriculum, pedagogy or assessment as key planks in their effort. It is as though they saw their agenda on behalf of the forgotten third as running in parallel to a school system that supports the other two-thirds. GCSEs are perceived as a fixed marker of success for the school system, and so the challenge is to ensure that more pupils achieve them. No one seems to be thinking about what we really need to reconsider and build consensus about in our school system: our beliefs.

There were two adjacent areas that received considerable attention from our politicians which could be looked at through the lens of curriculum, pedagogy and assessment. First, there was the consideration of what should happen with GCSEs, especially given the shambles of 2020, although for some this was about logistics and public confidence rather than the efficacy of the exams as a form of assessment. Second, and linked to the first, was what we should do about the 14–19 stage generally. It is to these and other issues relating to curriculum, assessment and pedagogy that we will now turn.

Exams at 16

Most adults smile about the fact that exams are the same today as they were in their day: a 'spit out all you can remember' experience so that we can pass and then forget it all. We persist with this rite of passage for young people, archaic in nature, a sort of trial by ordeal. When else in life would we enter a room, sit a metre away from everyone else and work in silence for two hours? In real life, presented with a problem at work, most people would immediately contact others, ask for opinions, test solutions, seek information, pool knowledge and construct solutions that colleagues would critique. Instead, to measure a pupil's capability, we have the annual mass culling of 16-year-olds alongside the spectacle of celebrations on results day as enormous numbers of grade 9s or A stars are celebrated.

Shortly afterwards, youngsters realise that they didn't really need that many passes. Indeed, once we have the ticket to pass through the turnstile to the next stage of education, training or work, we are rarely asked what we got at GCSE as long as it was a nap hand. For other pupils, the exam process is debilitating. Sarah Finch, CEO of the Marches Academy Trust based in Shropshire, expressed the underlying tension of many who work in schools:

> I think the frustration for me in our education system today is seeing teenagers leaving the school system, or maybe even not leaving but just drifting away so that we don't see them again, and simply repeating the same frustrated lives as their own parents. The next generation can't seem to escape the cycle it seems to find itself in ... of poverty or low aspiration fuelling a lack of belief and worth.

> I was talking with a lad who we had managed to get across the line of the exams and he said to me, 'Well, I'm thick.' I said, 'How can you call yourself thick? You have nine GCSEs.' His answer was, 'They are only grade 4s and 5s and not 8s and 9s.' I'm not someone who looks backwards but I saw a real difference back in 2005 when we were getting youngsters to do practical BTEC courses. I saw children from challenging backgrounds achieving and feeling successful and their families feeling proud of them. I want to see schools and education doing that again: helping someone to feel they have achieved something and that the future holds promise.

Qualifications are important as passports that take us across thresholds, but a long while before the examination, many youngsters are working out that exams are unfair and the focus on them achieving is motivated by something outwith themselves. Too many streetwise pupils see through it all and, sadly, perceive their future in a world of realities that we would not want them to experience.

However, an industry has built up around exams, one that has cashed in on the marketisation of schooling with consummate ease. The awarding bodies are in competition to attract custom. Typically, a school spends around £400 per pupil in Year 11 for exam entries, so with around 500,000 pupils in a cohort it is a very big market. To attract the custom in their competitive market of schools, these awarding bodies need to make their product more accessible – for example, by providing course books to guide teachers and pupils through the syllabus. The books are often written by the chief examiner; it is a type of product endorsement but it smacks of insider dealing. On top of that, there are also training sessions led by the awarding bodies to help teachers appreciate the nuances and expectations of the exams. What school wouldn't try to make sure their pupils were able to kick downhill with the wind?

The trouble is that all this risks spoon-feeding pupils rather than helping them to really experience the excitement and breadth of study of the subject discipline. Indeed, for many pupils, so much of their final year is spent studying past papers and practising the bankers for the final exam that the subject can lose its energy and attraction. Beyond that, schools use facilities such as gyms, dance and drama studios so the curriculum narrows down for all year groups.

The current system also displays a lack of trust in the teaching profession. That SATs have to be marked externally – at a great cost to the nation – is an opportunity wasted. Instead, teachers in a triad of schools could mark each other's papers, overseen by an external assessor (to avoid any accusation of collusion), with the savings going into the schools' budgets.[58] At the same time, the teachers would see close-up the common misconceptions and errors that would then inform their future teaching. Obviously, there is the issue of workload, but advances in technology mean that teachers don't have to gather in one place to mark papers or even mark entire papers; questions can be directed to particular markers – as is now done by the awarding bodies. The same technology could include seeded papers – which are already marked by senior markers – to check marking reliability. It isn't foolproof, but it would be a step forward from what we have and would build on the experience of centre assessment grades (CAGs). Schools would make it work if there was funding available through the release of the huge fees charged by exam board companies.

Secretaries of state tinker with this system. A recent tough, and retrograde, stance was to stop pupils taking GCSEs early, either because they

---

58   Schools would not simply exchange papers for marking but three schools would circulate the papers: school A would mark school B, school B would mark school C and school C would mark school A. Moderation by the CIEA would ensure consistency and probity.

were ready or because their teacher thought the practice would help to boost their confidence. To make matters worse, the DfE instituted the requirement for pupils to keep retaking English and mathematics GCSE after age 16 until they receive a grade 9–4, which is now a condition of entry to FE courses. These are moves hardly in tune with the dispositions of underachieving vulnerable adolescents.

And there, of course, is the problem. The high-stakes testing regime is used to measure schools' comparative performances as much as individual pupils' achievements. There are healthy ways for schools to compete: music, drama, debating, young enterprise, mock trials and sport. But pupils have become a currency in the school performance system, which means that diligent, committed and professional educationalists, heads, teachers and examiners all find themselves pushing on the allowable tolerances in the system to deliver results, and in doing so reducing other educational opportunities.

If we must have an element of GCSE-type exams, do they have to take place at the same time every summer? Could pupils take the exams when they are ready? Could the specific areas of content be made available just 50 days before the exam? (This would require that the big ideas of a subject discipline have been taught and understood prior to this point, in order for pupils to focus on revising specific content.) Or maybe we could publish 150 possible questions two years ahead of the exams and then generate the actual paper on the day? Practice of this sort would ensure breadth and depth of study rather than exam practice. We might end up with real scientists, historians, geographers, designers and linguists, rather than people who pass exams so that they can drop the subject immediately. Or how about introducing the Extended Project Qualification (EPQ), which is close to the best and most rigorous extended project work delivered in primary schools, to the 11–16 assessment programme?[59]

Any reform on 14–19 would naturally include a consideration of GCSEs, another of the windmills often tilted at or stoutly defended. The problem for this exam is that we are not sure whether it is a qualification, a measure of school performance or a motivation for teenagers. Michael Gove

---

59   EPQ is a sixth-form qualification that involves pupils choosing a topic, carrying out research, creating a report (or product and report) and delivering a presentation. Various models of this approach have been used, beginning with what were called Mode 3 CSE courses in the 1970s, which gave schools the opportunity to work together locally to devise programmes for pupils that would build motivation as well as examine their ability within subject disciplines. EPQs were also planned as part of the ill-fated diploma programme.

set out to 'make exams harder' and reduce the number of vocational qualifications following the Wolf Report that he commissioned.[60] At the same time, he fought a long battle to introduce the EBacc, seizing (as he did with academies) on a term that seemed to carry credibility but using a different interpretation. While Gove ultimately pulled back, the Progress 8 measure has now gained real traction in secondary school performance tables and inspections.[61]

Mick recalls:

When I was at QCA, as part of the considerations around the diploma, we were asked to propose some ways forward for exams at 16. We worked with some schools and developed some good proposals around curriculum coherence, with youngsters studying themes such as 'risk', 'conflict' or 'health'. The courses would link history, science, geography and so on, and bring together mathematics, technology and art as well as English as vehicles for learning, assessed to some degree through scholarly projects.

The initial proposals were very positively received by ministers, but it was eventually decided to drop the idea because, with the planned introduction of the diplomas, the GCSE was best left to wither on the vine. GCSEs are still here and yet more memory based.

Kenneth Baker's patience with the exam that he relied on for his changes in curriculum and accountability has run out. He told us he would dig up his own plant:

I would remove and replace GCSEs with a well-devised system of teacher assessment. I would try to get to a standard method of teacher assessment, which might involve two teachers: one making the judgement and the other one making a moderation, saying, 'Yes, that's okay.' I think that is the sort of system that is needed. I would certainly abolish sitting in large halls at desks for two hours. Universities have devised methods of assessing

---

60 A. Wolf, *Review of Vocational Education: The Wolf Report* (London: Department for Education and Department for Business and Innovation, 2011). Available at: https://assets.publishing.service.gov.uk/government/uploads/system/uploads/attachment_data/file/180504/DfE-00031-2011.pdf.

61 It is important to emphasise that Progress 8 is a relative measure, calculated each year on the basis of the actual results of all pupils taking exams at the end of Key Stage 4.

students with open-book exams on their own computers instead of sitting down in a hall and writing in longhand for three hours.

The pandemic has brought the issue of qualifications to a head. The summer of 2020 brought the problem of CAGs[62] and the 'mutant algorithm',[63] both of which caused political discomfort and saw the departure of the CEO from Ofqual. The results of the 2021 round, which relied on CAGs at GCSE and A level, have been met with further debate about the fairness of grades, grade inflation and the potential for universities to be overwhelmed by successful candidates. As school closures affecting Year 11 and 10 pupils occurred randomly and for differing lengths of time, Gavin Williamson's pragmatic adjustments to the way grades were decided have been important steps in trying to keep the show on the road. He told us: 'We had to bite the bullet and say children were going to be assessed on what they had been taught as against the whole curriculum because we were facing a situation where the disparities were starting to emerge and only getting wider.'

There has been a sustained call to get back to the 'traditional' or 'normal' exam system as soon as possible. Williamson summed up the simplistic outlook of a politician spotting the smooth water ahead: 'I just think the difficulty is where you move too far away from exams, you then end up in a situation where it becomes too tempting and there is too much of a desire for people to want to start tweaking and influencing the system to a political agenda and rather than being focused on education.' The return to an unsatisfactory normal is more enticing than deep consideration of the effectiveness of the normal system and any potential improvements. Williamson added: 'How we transition back to regular forms of assessment is really important. I do think getting back to exams is so vital.' It is not very visionary; a vision for a more productive system is taking second place to political expedience.

There is no doubt that there is much to improve about the system, but a retreat to the past represents a failure to take the chance to consider the future. If A levels (and by implication GCSEs) really are entrance exams for

---

62 CAGs were used in 2020 and 2021 in the absence of the GCSE exam. Concerns have been expressed about validity, reliability and grade inflation.

63 The term used by Boris Johnson to excuse and gloss over the chaos and resentment about the way CAGs had been moderated by exam boards, under instruction from Ofqual: see H. Stewart, Boris Johnson Blames 'Mutant Algorithm' for Exams Fiasco, *The Guardian* (26 August 2020). Available at: https://www.theguardian.com/politics/2020/aug/26/boris-johnson-blames-mutant-algorithm-for-exams-fiasco. The algorithm was apparently harmful since resignations followed.

the next phase of learning, should we not say so and admit that grades are manipulated each year depending on the availability of higher education places (i.e. norm referencing). If large numbers of pupils deserve high grades because they have met the criteria, should we not award them and celebrate the success of our schools? Why is so much concern expressed about high numbers of pupils doing well? How do we communicate that grades are not given for effort and hard work but for reaching the criteria and demonstrating the required ability or knowledge (criterion referenced)?

There is no doubt that the CAGs system has not been fully effective during the pandemic, but that is no reason to dismiss it as a possibility for part of the examination process. Teachers may have been under undue pressure, but it could have been ameliorated through better planning and preparation. There may have been unconscious bias through their knowledge of their pupils but that too can be overcome through effective moderation.[64] In a normal year, the variable syllabus coverage by pupils would be reduced. We believe that the call to return to the traditional method of examination is misplaced. It is not as trusted or trustworthy as many imagine.

What is not realised by many is that the 'normal' annual GCSE exam cycle is affected by algorithms to the same extent but the inaccuracies and unfairness are buried. Our view is that the COVID-19 pandemic has brought to a head some of the historic failings of exams for 16-year-olds. While we are in this period of uncertainty and change, we should look at what sort of exams we need and when we need them. Our emphasis now should be at 18, which represents the end of compulsory education.

As a first step in the reform, GCSEs could be replaced by a combination of coursework (produced over the duration of the course), projects and exams set nationally – at least twice and preferably more times a year, marked locally by teachers, and moderated and quality assured regionally by a nominated university and the CBI. Each school would have a chartered assessor among its teachers and use a licence to assess; in the

---

64 Mary Curnock Cook, the former head of UCAS, has examined the relative performance of boys versus girls over four years with insight into the effect of CAGs: Systemic Bias Against Boys? Unexplained Differences in Teacher Assessed Grades Between Boys and Girls in This Year's A Level Results, *Higher Education Policy Institute* [blog] (23 August 2021). Available at: https://www.hepi.ac.uk/2021/08/23/systemic-bias-against-boys-unexplained-differences-in-teacher-assessed-grades-between-boys-and-girls-in-this-years-a-level-results.

case of unacceptable reliability, the school could be suspended or school put under the aegis of another school for the period of the suspension.

The chartered assessor model is already developing. Mick Walker explained:

> The idea is that each school has people called chartered assessors who bring challenge about effective assessment into their school, and across a partnership of schools can enable awareness, understanding and skill to grow. It is perfectly feasible to construct a system that would enable pupils' efforts to be assessed and moderated locally and fairly, with sampling used to ensure parity across the system and consistency year on year. The outcomes for pupils over time would be seen through more informed teachers enabling improvement in learning and through more insightful teaching.

Our suggested model (i.e. local marking, regional moderation, quality assurance involving a university and the CBI) could gradually form the basis of assessment at 18, where scholarly, academic and vocational subject disciplines in various combinations would form part of a new and better baccalaureate – the sort that employers have been calling for over time. It would also have a unifying requirement that all candidates should complete both an EPQ – whether an academic treatise, practical or creative project – and a computer-based assessed course, ensuring that citizens are abreast of their responsibilities in relation to the small (e.g. finance, health, family) and larger (e.g. sustainability, macroeconomic) challenges they will face as qualified adults committed to the fulfilment of their fellows. The EPQ would have an oral assessment element because oracy is a vital adult skill which has been relatively neglected in recent years. This would form a much more balanced picture of pupil achievement and attainment.

We are not suggesting that such reforms should start now, but the hard-pressed secretary of state could use the present crisis to take small steps in a direction which we think would be welcomed by universities, employers, parents and teachers.

Revisiting 14–19

Besides the GCSE, the other issue often mentioned to us was disappointment that the diploma programme planned at the end of the Labour government, and resulting from the Tomlinson Report, never came to fruition. For several witnesses, this was one of the biggest missed opportunities of the period we are considering.

The CBI has been pressing for a more relevant secondary school experience for years. In 2011 (as Michael Gove shifted towards the EBacc), the CBI's chief policy director, Katja Hall, called for a broader curriculum with more appropriate qualifications: 'Every school or college leaver needs the right skills, knowledge and attitude for success in today's competitive workplace. But currently employers find that too many young people lack employability skills such as customer awareness, self-management and problem-solving.'[65]

Charles Clarke, the secretary of state who commissioned the Tomlinson Report,[66] told us: 'The biggest failure of the Blair government was not implementing Tomlinson. And then Brown's government pushed up the school leaving age without thinking what to teach. As I moved on to the Home Office, I said that David Miliband should take things forward, but the prime minister appointed Ruth Kelly. If I had stayed in that job, I would have been able to carry it through.'

The plight of the Tomlinson Report proposals illustrates the way in which the secretary of state can be derailed by the political world. Mike Tomlinson told us the story of the reform that could have been:

> I was effectively given two years with an interim report. And much to Charles Clarke and David Miliband's credit, they agreed to my request that I would be able to consult with other political parties during the course of the work. That normally does not happen, but I had said to them, 'Unless there is some sense of political consensus on this matter, you're not going to achieve anything.' They agreed to it so I was able to involve all parties.
>
> We had a group consisting of people from all areas including higher education, further education, the voluntary sector,

---

65 Quoted in *BBC News*, School Leavers 'Need Work Skills and Knowledge' (11 March 2011). Available at: https://www.bbc.co.uk/news/education-12701594.
66 Tomlinson, *14–19 Curriculum and Qualifications Reform*.

independent sector, maintained sector and so on, and it soon began to emerge that there was a considerable consensus about what direction all of this ought to go in.

There were some extensive discussions and certainly not least over the question of where and what is the role of GCSE, because by that time Labour had introduced the concept of 14–19 education into law and set a timetable, by which time students couldn't leave at 16 or 17, unless they were going into education or training, or both.

The question was, how you would assess students' work and achievement at a point when they were leaving the maintained sector, wherever they were going, and, naturally, are they on the right course? I find it ironic that right now we're relying on teacher assessment which we proposed quite a bit of in our final report. Chris Woodhead wrote a scathing little piece about it because, of course, it was challenging the status quo, at least with GCSE.

By the time we came to publish the final report, we had got a broad political consensus for what we were proposing. Higher education was onside. Most of the employer organisations, including the CBI, were onside, apart from one influential person.[67] Well, all his committees, not least the Education and Training Committee, supported it, but he wasn't prepared to put his name to it. But the real issue was when the report would be formally published.

We had a reception for all those who had participated, hosted by Charles Clarke and David Miliband. At that unlucky evening, they said what they said, and I was able to thank everyone for all their hard work and so on. Charles Clarke was adamant that this report would be implemented. He saw no reason why it shouldn't be and David Miliband was of a similar inclination. What we knew was that the prime minister was likely to make a speech that evening; there had been tentative conversations with Number 10 and particularly with Andrew Adonis.

Part of the agreement was to keep the then Conservative leader [Michael Howard] informed, so they had the report 48 hours before it was presented to Parliament. That same evening, Michael

---

67 Interested readers can look up who was the director general of the CBI at the time (2004).

Howard was also giving a speech in a different venue to Prime Minister Tony Blair. During Michael Howard's speech, which was prior to Tony Blair's speech, he referred to my report; not directly, but indirectly, which he should not have done in terms of political protocol as it had neither been published nor presented to Parliament. In that speech, Michael Howard said that whatever the proposals that came forward were, there would be no way that A levels and GCSEs would be abandoned. I hadn't suggested abandoning either of them. That was his interpretation.

The prime minister decided, despite advice to the contrary, to play the statesman and say, 'I have no comment to make on this until we have properly considered this and it has been presented to Parliament.' But in the end, he couldn't resist and in the speech that evening, while we were being told it was going to be implemented, Blair was saying 'no change to A levels at all'.

Timing is crucial, of course, and with an election on the horizon, Blair would have been worried about being compared negatively with the leader of the Conservatives, who had portrayed himself as maintaining standards. It was a tipping point – purely political.

As Ed Balls recalled: 'I inherited the diploma programme. You spend hours trying to think about the post-16 curriculum and trying to build a coalition; the truth was that it had been sold the moment Tony Blair dumped the Tomlinson Report. And there was maybe no way back, so we should have done less and not tried to rescue those kinds of things.'

Clarke's picture of the position was that: 'In late 2004 we were about to implement Tomlinson, but just before the election there was argument about A levels. I think that I could have sorted it out.' Clarke cares deeply about the issue to this day. He added: 'I believe we should work on 14–19 rather than 14–16 and 16–19. We can't get to that without a lot of structural change.'

Ruth Kelly, who succeeded Clarke, told us:

I got such a tough time on the Tomlinson reforms because the headline was that I rejected them. The reality is a lot more subtle than that. I tried to embed existing qualifications in the diplomas, so that the credibility of the reforms to parents and to employers and to universities wouldn't be jeopardised by any radical transition.

I was accused of ditching the diploma. If it had been adopted as it stood, there would have been no A levels and GCSEs for people to take. I think parents would have revolted. It would have posed a huge risk to their success. So, I tried to pull off the trick of embedding existing qualifications in them, so that at least pupils were graduating from school with something in their back pocket that people would recognise.

I have always been a believer in practical work alongside academic work, and the idea of being able to work towards a school certificate, externally validated, which combines academic and vocational work, strikes me as absolutely the right thing to do. I was widely accused of having ditched it entirely, which was an unfair accusation.

Alan Johnson, who in theory was still overseeing the development of diplomas until Labour lost power in 2010, said: 'I'd get rid of GCSEs. They are surely not needed now we have education to age 18.'

Jim Knight, who as a minister with Johnson had tried to guide through the diploma programme, told us: 'If there was one thing that I could do now, it would be a rapid refresh of Tomlinson because I think the appetite among the employer community is there with different leadership at the CBI.' He would be supported by Kenneth Baker, who said: 'It was a huge mistake that Labour didn't implement the Tomlinson Report. Labour has got to rethink its basic policy now on education – they are not leading the field at this moment. They ought to be much more creative and go for 14–18 phase in the curriculum.'

The 14–19 arena remains the one where the searchlights of the curriculum, pedagogy and assessment debate intersect. The assessment issue is dominated by qualifications and, within that, arguments about what is a valid assessment. Whatever the qualification that is in place or sets the specification and the syllabus for the pedagogy, which prepares pupils for their assessment, the backwash from the qualification is significant. Traditional arguments about the regard we have for scholarly approaches, as opposed to practical outlooks, mean that we continue to argue about the merits of practical application, workplace learning, online teaching and assessment, project work, periodic assessment and 'when ready' testing, among other things.

The current government is bringing forward proposals for a new T levels qualification, which is being promoted as equivalent to three A levels. Gavin Williamson announced it as another new dawn: 'T Levels are a game-changer, providing a high-quality technical alternative to A Levels. The new qualifications have been created in collaboration with leading employers so students can get the skills they need to succeed and businesses can access the talent they need to thrive.'[68] From our viewpoint, this potentially good move is beset with the problem of wanting T levels to have parity of esteem with A levels, which carries the implication that the award of the qualification is dependent on paper examinations, which has signalled the demise of so many previous developments.

Parity of esteem is one of the myths of our examination system. The notion that, for instance, an A level in Latin is equivalent to an A level in mathematics has been frequently and reasonably called into question.[69] The value of a qualification is determined by the end users – the worth to candidates and the benefit to employers or organisers of future courses of study. Searching for equivalence is one of those time and energy traps that we think should be avoided. As Mike Tomlinson sums up: 'At the end of the day, most qualifications depend for their value on the end user; not the educational establishment or the political classes but the end user. If you give the end user what they want, they will value that qualification. You don't need to be deflected by parity of esteem; you don't need to go searching for this nonsense.' It is that ipsative assessment issue again.

The politician with one of the most thoughtful outlooks on reshaping curriculum, assessment and pedagogy in the secondary phase was Jim Knight. He told us:

> We need to be more flexible at the skills end of our learning and remix the blend between the role of the teacher and the technology for learning. I saw what some teachers were doing with whiteboards and mobile phone and thought that if we got this

---

68 HSDC, HSDC Welcomes Education Secretary Gavin Williamson to its South Downs Campus (18 September 2020). Available at: https://www.hsdc.ac.uk/news/2020/09/18/hsdc-welcomes-education-secretary-gavin-williamson-to-its-south-downs-campus.

69 See, for example, ARD Data & Analytics Team, Data Bytes: The Most Popular A Level Subjects since 2000, *Cambridge Assessment* (January 2016). Available at: https://www.cambridgeassessment.org.uk/Images/the-most-popular-a-level-subjects-since-2000.pdf; and https://eal.org.uk/support/document-library/7-uk-qualifications-comparison-table/file.

right, we could transform practice. We could use the ability of technology to match learners with teachers and learners with learners to get groups really well aligned and learning together. We could show teachers what the levels of engagement are really like. Artificial intelligence is starting to do that now as it gets more and more sophisticated.

He was also clear about how the 14–19 agenda might be changing in terms of destinations:

We need to get our children to see that change is not something to be scared of but something they can shape. We should encourage entrepreneurship and show them that they can play a part in change. Our current system forces them into straitjackets that does not suit a third of children.

Employer behaviour is changing. Employers are sifting less on the basis of GCSEs and CVs. They know that qualifications are a proxy and so they are devalued. Starbucks is doing deals with ASU [Arizona State University] to offer degrees online, and AT&T are using micro-credentials to grow their own talent. People are gaining qualifications as they are paid rather than facing debt. This will disrupt the university system a lot and they need to partner more with employers. Some universities will find it very difficult to survive.

More and more parents will wonder whether university is right for their children; that traditional rite of passage will be questioned in the face of earn-as-you-learn solutions. It won't be long before the destination point is likely to be work as much as university. This will be exciting and give opportunities to groups not likely to go to university. It is already happening, companies are edging towards it, regardless of the UK government.

The profound change that Knight predicted brings us round again to the link between curriculum, pedagogy and assessment. Anthony Seldon picked up the point about artificial intelligence (AI). Our conversation with him touched on the potential benefits of AI to schooling as well as the concerns:

We have to take AI seriously in education and we have to get ahead of it now before the big tech companies. Whatever high-minded words they might have about the educational benefits of what they're doing, what they want to do is to make money.

The most important point I'd say about AI is that in some ways, it would be better if it hadn't been invented. But we cannot uninvent it. We cannot undo AI. If we use it well, it can liberate young people in a way that conventional education systems often have not done or not done sufficiently well. If we get it wrong, it will infantilise young people and all of us, by taking the challenge, the meaning, the choice and the difficulty out of life. It will render us useful idiots and will be an agency of even further government manipulation of education.

Seldon was keen to point out the potential of AI and why we need to move quickly, especially in terms of more effective pedagogy creating scope for a more profound curriculum ambition:

AI can enormously help in the selection and individualisation of materials, in the delivery of materials, in the assessment and formative assessment of a student's work and in the assessment of the rates of progress, therefore rendering exams unnecessary. It will help with the identification of the students' strengths diagnostically – what they need to do and what might be the appropriate next steps. If we get ahead of it, it can give a top-quality education for all, and if we don't get ahead of it, it will be all over us before we or our education secretaries work out what AI stands for.

There are hundreds of thousands of teachers in England and tens of millions of teachers globally who don't need to spend all that time marking because the technology will be much better. They can spend much more time thoughtfully planning, learning themselves and stimulating their own minds, and we can have far more profound and inclusive schools if we get it right.

AI explodes the notion that school is about bricks and mortar, with the school day having a beginning, middle and end, or a school year. If schools are only about learning academic subjects, this can be done as well with the students at home. As we know, some are better early in the morning, some learn better in the evening, some learn at weekends or they can learn in holidays. A Year 6 child can be at Year 13 level in maths but at Year 2 level in English, and individualisation means that the learning can be done far better. Homeschooling has gone up very considerably during lockdown. It may well not fall. So, this would just be an extension of homeschooling but individuated by tutors and teachers in every subject. If that's all school is and, indeed, all university is, then there isn't much future. But, of course, schools are about much more that, and it therefore means that schools will need to adapt to personalised learning, which works out how the child's mind works.

In a school day, 80% of the child's time in school is in lessons. It could well be that only 50% of the time is now needed to be spent in learning in front of the machine because it's so much more efficient, or even 25%, which frees up the time in schools. This is why I think schools are needed for social learning, for project work, for problem-solving, for team-building, for the development of creative skills, entrepreneurial skills, for speaking in public, for understanding the arts.

Seldon's outlook will be exciting for many and threatening for others. The prospect of a school system that can provide more efficiently the core of what schools have offered traditionally and afford opportunities for a whole range of experiences previously denied to so many should be magnetic. If we want to achieve the beliefs we list in Chapter 1, AI could provide a breakthrough. For those who see an old order crumbling, it will be easier to dismiss thinking such as Seldon's as 'future gazing' and react with the suspicion applied to technology in education generally. An opportunity is unfolding that could take learning to new levels, widen the scope of human understanding and stretch our ingenuity. As the AI revolution unfolds, our schooling system is folding in upon itself with a shrinking range of learning opportunities, narrower teaching repertoires and more pedestrian assessment.

Since curriculum, assessment and pedagogy are at the heart of the teacher's role in the classroom and influence so profoundly the success of pupils in their own eyes, we believe that the shrinking of the three-sided wheel has been regrettable. A constricted curriculum, however much schools try to widen the school experience and make it enjoyable, tested on a limited range of metrics simply to satisfy an accountability regime cannot be the right way to meet the sorts of purposes for schooling we set out in Chapter 1 – purposes with which we think most people would agree. Add this narrow regime to an increasingly formulaic pedagogy channelled towards exams or tests, and we see a school experience that falls short of extending our most talented pupils, and at the same time sees many young people rejected (or feeling rejected) by the school system.

We have developed a national curriculum with a focus on pupils reaching A level. We thread all pupils through the same eye of the needle of progress. The fortunate ones pass through without touching the sides and reach the goal of A levels; others become tangled along the way and reach a level of a different sort, one that frustrates and, in some cases, creates a cost for society in health, legal and judicial terms. As the broadcaster Robert Peston put it:

> One of the things that concerns me is that so much teaching in recent years has been on a sort of 'Memorise this and this is how you pass the exam' basis. A sort of 'This is the marking score, do the following things and you'll get the right kind of grade'. It looks to me from the outside that too much teaching is essentially turning kids into robots. In an age where robots can do the thinking, you will need children who are creative. There needs to be a much greater emphasis on resilience, on creativity, on social skills, on being able to adapt to changing situations, problem-solving and the rest. I just feel that there is far too little of that, because there's still a massive focus in the curriculum on grades.

He added: 'It is important to say that quite a lot of my thinking is conditioned by how I see the world of work and the economy developing and changing, and working back from that. I don't want to overstate things, but we do need more thought about all of this.' Now, Peston's background is in economics, yet so often when ministers introduce their new policies for curriculum, pedagogy or assessment, the rationalisation is economic. However, their economic justification is rarely challenged or even questioned.

We continue with a system that was outdated long ago, tinkering around the edges or bringing in a new vanity project from elsewhere in an off-the-shelf format, shoehorning everything into a set of conditions that constrain the very system we seek to improve. Politicians talk glibly about improvement in schooling, while ignoring the forgotten third and using spurious managerial data to promote success. Are we even aiming at the right things?

As Bob Moon, an experienced head teacher and academic, told us:

> We have a pressure to make sure pupils progress, and too often that is matched to age. We move children on to the metaphorical book two, three and beyond before they have really grasped the metaphorical book one. So we see pupils floundering around trying to hang on when, if they had really got to grips with book one, they might be more confident in the basics. Think about modern foreign languages; wouldn't it be better if we were all much more confident at the metaphoric book one level and enjoying it?

So much of our consideration of curriculum, pedagogy and assessment, especially in respect of older pupils, has reflected back on the purposes of schooling. The various national policies and developments in schools ebb and flow based on our complex and often contentious beliefs about the role of schooling in serving the needs of the economy, helping young people to develop as rounded individuals and the extent to which their views should be heeded. Julia Cleverdon highlighted the importance of the school experience being responsive to maturing young people: 'The sharing of power with young people about how they are going to shape the future seems to me to be a conversation that is really needed.' Perhaps we need to ask pupils themselves how they might like to learn.

In our final chapter, we make some proposals for ensuring that the curriculum remains authentic for pupils as they progress through to Year 9 by undertaking programmes that build on their interests, encourage talent in its widest sense and ensure participation within a wider community. Elsewhere in our book, in our chapters on teaching, accountability and barriers to learning, we highlight ways in which curriculum, pedagogy and assessment need to work to build the beliefs that we seek for every pupil in the school system.

What do we think we should do?

Whatever we aspire to, we need gradual change born of deep consideration and based on large-scale consultation to reach a consensus and leave behind the tendency to polarise. We need a civic conversation about what a curriculum might aspire to achieve in an age of hope, ambition and collaborative partnerships. In her book *A Curriculum of Hope*, Debra Kidd offers a starting point to add to our considerations in this chapter:

> What kind of curriculum holds hope for young people and for the world they will inhabit and shape? What kind of curriculum helps children to appreciate their community? What kind of curriculum looks beyond the national, the immediate, the tyranny of the test and builds this kind of learning experience? Perhaps it is one that resists the notion of learning as a race and instead embraces exploration. What if, instead of running to the end point of the education system, or even to the end of a unit of work, the purpose of the course lay in the journey itself?[70]

In *Rethinking Assessment in Education*, Bill Lucas outlines the developing practice and promising steps being taken around the world to assess dispositions such as creativity.[71] We have mixed feelings about these developments: they have an attraction because they widen the image of assessment, but, as we have pointed out, poorly managed and sometimes abused assessment practices can corrupt the very purposes of schooling. In terms of systematised assessment, we are left wondering whether it has done more harm than good. Furthermore, any developed approach needs to take the teaching profession with it rather than be imposed.

This means that curriculum, pedagogy and assessment need to be seen as an entity, with each strand dependent on the other two. A series of steps might pave the way for a more productive future that best serves the purposes of our beliefs set out in Chapter 1.

First, we believe that the world of curriculum, assessment and pedagogy should be depoliticised and developed on an all-party set of beliefs led by an independent national council called something like Pedagogy, Assessment and Curriculum in Education (PACE) which would work within a national framework for schooling policy. We explore this further in Chapter 13 within the wider context of policy influence.

Second, we should ask that body to consider building on the work of the existing CIEA, removing private companies from the equation and using the school system judiciously. This would improve assessment processes dramatically, as teachers would become more knowledgeable about

---

70 D. Kidd, *A Curriculum of Hope: As Rich in Humanity as in Knowledge* (Carmarthen: Independent Thinking Press, 2020), p. 18.

71 Lucas, *Rethinking Assessment in Education*.

assessment and more proficient, and it would save billions of pounds that could be better spent on learning.

Third, and as part of that work, PACE should consider the 14–19 experience, rethinking qualifications, how we examine and what sort of pedagogy fits the qualification and youngsters' outlooks.

Fourth, we should look at assessment processes for children from the early years that build a recognition of what they can do using criteria-based observations and diagnostic tests in a 'when ready' form. These should make use of practical demonstrations, computer-generated random questions and authentic settings.

Fifth, along with a reconsideration of Ofsted's remit, we should determine how to spread interesting and effective practice in pedagogy, assessment and curriculum to encourage research-based innovation and collaboration. In Chapter 6, we discuss the role that the Chartered College of Teaching and the Education Endowment Foundation could jointly play.

Sixth, we should invest urgently in a rigorous consideration of the use of AI to positively affect the work of schools in terms of curriculum, pedagogy and assessment.

Seventh, we should consider seriously the potential for an Open School (described more fully in Chapter 13), which would develop a pedagogic repertoire for teachers and draw children and young people into a bigger learning world.

Eighth, we should unleash our ambitions for young people from the limits of exam and test success and develop a Seeking Talent and Extending Participation Scheme (STEPS) for all primary and secondary pupils, along with an Extraordinary Learners with Exceptional Creative Talent (ELECT) programme, encouraging children to explore their interests and passions through purposeful and personalised individual coaching. Again, we return to this in our final chapter.

Ninth, and potentially most important, we should develop a Curriculum for Childhood and a Curriculum for Adolescence. Both should seek to respond to the changing pace of maturity in pupils and develop a learning programme which brings together their breadth of need, encourages purposeful and relevant assessment, and supports contributions from other sectors alongside the universal provision of schooling.

In this chapter, we have explored some of the complexities of the turning of the three-sided wheel of curriculum, pedagogy and assessment which, if not considered, addressed and practised in harmony, will leave those we are trying to help with a very bumpy learning experience. Our view is that these matters have become over-centralised and over-managerialised, with the market playing too significant a role. It is surely the teaching profession that should be entrusted to drive development. However, in a democracy, wider debate is important to build consensus about such important matters, which is why we suggest lightening the touch of politics on the wheel. For this to be successful, the teaching profession will need to grasp the opportunity and extend its innovative and creative thought and action in a spirit of ambition, hope and collaborative partnership.

Chapter 6

Securing a sufficient supply of suitably qualified teachers and then keeping them going

Two developments since 2010, when taken together, could represent a step change in the way teachers as professionals are regarded and rewarded in England. Those two events are the founding of the Chartered College of Teaching and the establishment of the Education Endowment Foundation.

We start with the college before rehearsing some of the fashions and influences which have been sprinkled over the teaching profession from time to time and consider how the EEF represents a chance for teachers to work out more accurately what is worthy of their attention. We then examine the way we educate and train teachers now, before ending the chapter with an examination of what it means to be a professional and some proposals for change, which would put expert teaching in our society on a new and better level.

The Chartered College of Teaching

If teachers create the weather in the classroom, then the Chartered College of Teaching affects the schooling ecosystem and, in turn, the way that teachers influence the climate. It is not so much a jet stream gusting through as a gentle breeze warmed by the deep ocean currents of thinking, practice and research, drawing thoughtful professionals into a powerful alliance around learning – the essence of their role. Relatively recently established – the college is less than 10 years old – it represents the nearest we can find to an organisation in England which speaks on behalf of the profession as a whole.[1] Although the teaching unions represent their members not just in matters of salary and conditions of service, but also to instigate dialogue on effectiveness in schooling, the reception they receive rarely recognises the effort they make to support progress for schools.

Alison Peacock, the chief executive of the Chartered College of Teaching, described the role of the organisation and her ambitions for it:

> Essentially, pursuit of fairness and equity has been what has driven me right from my very earliest days as a teacher. It is what drove me to work with researchers from the University of Cambridge to write books about the Learning Without Limits project. Then, as my own school improved, I used it increasingly as a sort of provocation to the system: 'We've bought a double decker bus now, we've built a Celtic roundhouse now, we've got a Forest School going on in the woods now. Why not?' This was all about what it was possible to do as a head teacher with a supportive governing body. I knew I was swimming against the tide and deliberately set about challenging notions about perceived constraints.
>
> Teachers often want to be compliant; we crave the approval of others. In my case, I was more worried about gaining the approval of educational academics than from those in the local advisory service. As a teacher, and latterly as a head teacher, I remember thinking that if only I could meet with the secretary of state for education of the day and just explain to them what the issues are for teachers for half an hour or so, they would understand and act accordingly. The closer I have come over time to witness the workings of government, the more I now understand that actually ministers are not really in control either. The real power lies with the schools – the irony being that in many cases the schools don't realise this.
>
> Over time, working from the position of head teacher and then with many other schools in a local alliance, I began to recognise that when colleagues in schools worked together, inspired by big ideas, it was possible to really start to generate change. Change takes place in the classroom with the way the teacher speaks to

---

1 There is a General Teaching Council (GTC) for Scotland and the Education Workforce Council (EWC) in Wales, which fulfils a more regulatory purpose. The GTC in England, established by the Blair/Brown government, was short-lived and abandoned by Michael Gove.

the child, because the teacher has so much influence. If teachers feel hidebound, monitored, worrying that every minute must be accounted for, this will inevitably affect what could otherwise be a good, high-quality relationship with their class.

So, moving beyond headship to the Chartered College of Teaching was about me asking myself, how can I take forward this restlessness that I've got from the position of being a head teacher? What can I do that might mean we could build the confidence of teachers in classrooms to be able to question things and to be able to ask, isn't there a better way of doing this? Or to hold on to some principles that they came into the profession with and question, what's right for children? And then be able to act accordingly. How could I create that connection and collaboration nationally?

When I first began working as chief executive of the Chartered College of Teaching, I realised very quickly that not everyone agreed with some of the principles that I mistakenly thought were universal. I realised that there are many who don't believe in listening to teachers; they believe in telling people what to do. There are others who don't believe in listening to children; actually, there are a lot of teachers who don't believe in listening to children and a lot of policy-makers who say they do but who never do. I'm not sure our society genuinely values children. Witness the fact that children and young people were invisible during lockdown – there were certainly none in the media.

I realised that in trying to build a new professional body, my opinions and stories of practice were not going to be enough. I needed to engage colleagues at all levels across all kinds of organisations, to try to align with them and to understand their priorities. It was important to see where the points of synergy were, where there were things that the emerging Chartered College could learn from other people and what they might learn from us, so that we could move forward a little.

Reflecting on this, I feel this is perhaps quite a female style of leadership. There has been a lot of growth by stealth at the Chartered College. As our membership began to increase to tens of thousands of members, we naturally started to grow in influence. Some in power started to look and think, is this what we really want? Certainly, the schools minister was very worried about what he described as 'capture'. In 2020, we became financially independent from government funding and, consequently, I have felt liberated to speak out on behalf of teachers. We are not a union, so avoid speaking about working conditions, but the opinions and priorities of our members are important and deserve recognition. We are seeing a groundswell of more and more teachers joining us.

As a professional body, the College of Teaching needs to work with as many teachers as we can to help them see that the power doesn't actually sit with government, nor does it sit with Ofsted, nor does it sit with regional commissioners: it sits with them – the teachers. All of these different places have different elements of power related to how much money they give you, what label they give you and whether they smile on you or not. The reality is that the fundamental difference is made in classrooms – by teachers. This is why I think the work we are doing with teachers and school leaders to help reconnect them with the core purposes of education is so important: what do we actually know about how children learn? What do we actually know about how teachers can learn? There is not that much difference; there are a lot of things that they've got in common, to be fair, and what we can do at the Chartered College of Teaching is to really start to awaken this sleeping beast, which is the whole teaching profession, not in an angry, reactive kind of way, but in a way that says, 'Of course we would like to call ourselves professionals. We would like to be further recognised by wider society. We would like to feel that when we look at a situation in the classroom and decide what to do next, that our judgement is understood and is not called into question but is carefully considered.'

The teaching profession would like to be in that position, and actually we realise that teachers can't just demand this but will need to earn it. So, how can we begin to do this? This is where the Chartered College of Teaching is about building colleagues' knowledge and expertise so they can articulate not only what they are doing but why.

It strikes me that as soon as we start to have those conversations, colleagues within schools feel able to be far more confident about their actions. If teachers know that their methodology is sound, they can move beyond the defence of 'we've always done it this way' or 'the head of department once told me to do this' or 'that's what she does next door'. We need teachers working together within their schools who are increasingly thoughtful about their practice, making the best decisions they can for the children they are working with. The children must be our core priority. We want our children to thrive – this goes way beyond teaching for a good set of results. With the best of our schools, you've only got to walk in the door and you can feel it. A school that is collegiate, where they care about everybody, where there's a sense that regardless of your starting point and regardless of your talents, you're going to be known and understood as an individual. These kinds of schools don't all look the same; they may be at different ends of the spectrum with regard to how they are organised, but there's a heart to them.

Naively, I came into the job at the Chartered College thinking that my experience and values would hold me in good stead. I haven't previously been a CEO. I haven't run loads and loads of schools. I'm leading from the heart. I'm being honest with people, completely honest with people. Most of the time that approach has served me well. There have been times when I felt quite vulnerable because if you're going to lead in that way, then occasionally you open yourself up and sometimes people may imply that you're not good enough. Those instances are far outweighed by the drive and energy that comes from building a sense of optimism that working with our profession is something to celebrate and to be proud of. Colleagues respect a leader who they can identify with, someone who shows they care, someone who is authentic, who gets things done. This is what I tried to do as a head teacher and is still what I'm trying to do today. I truly believe we can raise the status of our profession by supporting each other, and that we should be accountable for the ways that we collectively ensure every child is celebrated.

Michael Gove approved the reinvigoration of its Victorian royal charter and ensured initial seed-corn funding and the Chartered College of Teaching received the imprimatur of the Privy Council in 2016. Current membership is pushing past 40,000 and growing. If it could increase to the extent that the Chartered College of Teaching becomes *the* natural professional community for teachers, we believe that it could transform professional outlooks and behaviours towards the profession. In effect, it would be a guardian of the profession in the way that the General Medical Council is for doctors.

Who are our teachers now?

Over the period that our book covers, teaching has become more professional in some senses and less so in others. The plural noun is always a problem (there are 500,000 teachers currently serving in England) and, just like any other group, teachers vary in personality, work ethic, background, qualifications and experience.

Not all teachers are the same but most commit themselves to their work, spend long hours in planning and preparation, and deliver polished lessons – all followed up with extensive marking and further planning. They attend the required meetings and contribute to the routine of their school. They are diligent and efficient and want to do a good job. In these senses they are business-like. Most are committed to their school and its community, their colleagues and, most of all, the children, especially the ones they work with directly.

Some teachers are professionals in the truest sense. They are all of the above and they have that 'something else'. Professional teachers are deeply interested in their work and fascinated by its intricacies. They know the pupils they teach as maturing young people and form a purposeful working relationship with them, both individually and collectively. They are continuously intrigued by the challenge of teaching – pushing learning below the surface and taking children deeper and higher than they thought they could travel. They constantly hone their skills through practice, purposeful research, working with communities of interest, reading and trying innovative approaches in a disciplined way. It is second nature to them to work with others, lending a hand in their school or striving to be part of a bigger community of professionals. They welcome people who feel themselves to be novices and encourage them to enjoy the challenges, frustrations and successes of the role.

At the same time, they push themselves into challenges of understanding, proficiency and knowledge. They question practices and point out the side effects of accepted routines, while also suggesting alternatives. They worry and seek solutions to seemingly intractable problems. They are confident without being too certain. They share. These highly proficient individuals see themselves as belonging to a bigger global community of educators and commit to a notion of public service in its widest sense. These are the true professionals. It is these teachers that Alison Peacock believes can lift the expectations of our schools to a new level.

When someone becomes a teacher, they are said to join a 'noble profession'. The teachers who sign up help children and young people to make their way from home and community into the big wide world. They try to equip them with the life skills and knowledge that will help them to make the best of their future lives. They work with the young as an investment in the future in the belief that they are helping to make the world a better place. Revisit the list in Chapter 1 and think about how a good teacher helps their school to meet the sorts of beliefs about the purpose of schooling summarised there.

Why teaching has not always been seen as a profession

Teaching has always struggled to be recognised as a profession, even by its own membership. It is a community relied on by so many, as the coronavirus pandemic has shown, yet it is not truly valued, no matter how much difference an individual teacher makes to the life of an individual child. We have all heard people say things like, 'If it hadn't been for ...', 'There was one teacher who ...' or 'I remember a special teacher who ...' The National Teaching Awards were established in 1998 as an annual opportunity to recognise the work of the profession through the acknowledgement and celebration of the exceptional.[2] However, few of our witnesses, and particularly those close to policy-making, referred to teaching as a profession. It might have been that during our conversations we were sharing certain agreed but unexpressed assumptions about the professionalism of teaching, but occasionally we doubted it.

---

2   The National Teaching Awards were established by the film producer Lord Puttnam in 1998 to engage the profession with a wide audience and to promote teaching as a career. The awards are now supported by the educational publisher Pearson and other sponsors.

The subtle imagery which people used to express themselves might illustrate the way that teachers are viewed. Michael Barber's extensive use of the term 'the front line', echoed by Andreas Schleicher and others who work closely with national politicians, to describe teachers in schools implies a group who will receive orders from above and act correctly and without question. When he was prime minister, David Cameron talked of 'going to war on coasting schools',[3] and head teachers were regularly 'parachuted' into struggling schools. Similarly, Gavin Williamson talked to us of 'insurgents' driving forward progress in school improvement.

What sometimes gives the game away is the analysis, first promulgated by Michael Barber 20 years ago, when he defended a national prescription of what teachers and schools should do by coining the phrase 'uninformed professionalism' as the state of schooling and teaching at that time.[4] He went on to say that eventually when they had become 'professionally informed' they would earn the trust to get on with things. Our reaction to that, two decades later, is that despite over 80% of our schools being rated good or better, teachers are still waiting to be trusted. As Tracy Smith, an experienced head teacher and now leader of a schools' partnership in London, told us: 'I find it very surprising that the government tells us how to do our jobs and the profession lets that happen.' Can you imagine a similar approach being taken to doctors, surgeons, lawyers and accountants? We think not.

Andreas Schleicher of the OECD was clear:

> You need to get people at the front line to become owners of their professional practice. You need to establish a good balance between professional autonomy and a collaborative culture. Professional autonomy without a collaborative culture gets you into the kind of very atomistic school operation you have now.

> In England, you have focused on making teaching financially a bit more attractive, but it is intellectually not very attractive. Unless you address that issue, and that largely comes through professional collaboration, you will find it difficult to move forward significantly. If you do not make teaching intellectually attractive,

---

3   See R. Winnett, David Cameron Goes to War on Britain's 'Coasting Schools', *The Telegraph* (13 November 2011).

4   M. Barber, *How to Run a Government So That Citizens Benefit and Taxpayers Don't Go Crazy* (London: Allen Lane, 2015).

you will not get the people you need to work in your schools. I think this is something that deserves a lot more attention.

However, the experience of three lockdowns may have tipped the image of teachers in a positive direction, if the profession is quick to use the goodwill created. Remote online learning has meant that teachers have had to practise their work in public. They have taught in pupils' homes, watched on by parents who, for the most part, have appreciated the work they do, even if their teaching was inhibited by the medium.

Using an evidence base or sprinkling the latest fashion?

Teaching has always been susceptible to trends and fashions. In the primary phase, those professionals who were forward looking grabbed the next wave, while others were reluctant, even resistant, to let go of cherished practice. By the 1980s, teachers were being implored to use 'real books' and 'big books' as opposed to the structured reading schemes that had held sway for years. Until then, the debate had been about whether to use phonic or word recognition approaches, which affected the choice of reading scheme. The national literacy strategy pushed teachers to use preferred approaches at text, sentence and word level, as well as emphasising the importance of quality literature.

In primary schools, the national numeracy strategy settled the argument, at least for the time being, about the application of practical concrete approaches or mechanical rote learning or abstract aspects. Again, in primary schools, there have been variations in the approach to early years education, with an emphasis on play-based strategies in some schools, while others have focused on subject disciplines through discrete or themed study.

Secondary schooling experiences less debate about practice and politicians are more inclined to defer to the expertise of the subject specialist as the driving decision-maker. However, like primary schooling, the influence of inspection has changed the shape of lessons and the teacher's role within them. The question is the extent to which teachers have read the research about the practices they employ and whether they have considered the implications and properly implemented the findings, which is what distinguishes the true professional from the rest. In that respect, the Chartered College of Teaching and the EEF can help teachers to avoid the attractions and temptations of fads in their practice.

Just as fads develop in teaching, so the macro teaching agenda of a school is influenced by the trends and background of the head teacher. It is often possible to tell in which period a head teacher began their career, almost like carbon dating the person from the approaches they use in their school. Indeed, Ofsted is correct in that schools judged in the best categories come in many different guises and offer a range of different approaches; their argument is that it is the impact rather than the approach that counts.

Ben Erskine, principal of a primary academy in Peterborough, told us about his approach to curriculum organisation, which in many ways mirrors the engaging approach to learning promoted by the Plowden Report in 1967. The school has environments that immerse the children in experiences linked to themes of study. The teaching, though, has moved on and adapted to current pedagogical and curriculum thinking and urgencies:

> We've adapted over time, so we don't do the thematic curriculum we used to do, but we do still have thematic areas in schools. So, for example, we've still got the Anderson shelter because in their history lessons they'll study World War Two. We've moved some of the areas in the corridors more towards an environment that they come across within the books they learn and study. Mary Myatt asked us, 'What do you want to be remembered for ... your corridors or the curriculum and the learning?'[5] And I think that hit home; that prompted us to change quite a few things.

The image of teaching in this school is a world away from the approach to learning that runs through the free school led by Katharine Birbalsingh in North London:

> The senior team can have such impact on what goes on in the classroom because we articulate all the time what the school stands for and then create a kind of 'singing from the same hymn sheet' set of practices, which teachers follow and are therefore so well supported by the culture of the school that they are assured in what they do. They are confident in delivering what we believe

---

5   Mary Myatt is a recognised authority on curriculum and a published author.

in. Whereas I would say that, for some teachers elsewhere, the support netting isn't as tight and the words and the tune of the hymn are not as well-known and the harmony isn't as clear. Sometimes, there are so many holes in the support systems that teachers are constantly stumbling, and then in order not to fall over, they just don't follow through on, say, the behaviour policy or they don't follow through on high expectations because they know that there's nothing to support them.

What I'd say is that the power of culture is enormous; Apple, for instance, has a culture. You go into an Apple shop and you don't find the guys who work there telling you about how great PCs are, right? They all love Macs, are obsessed with them, would spend 24 hours a day talking about Macs. I don't think that's wrong. I think that's good. And I think too often in teaching we dislike that about marketisation. I believe in that. I believe in a school having a particular culture which they push forward in the way that, say, Apple does.

But not all classroom practice is thought-through. In classrooms and schools, 'must have' practices spread, often arising from a slick presentation at a conference. Usually, these are based on a reasonable premise and often with a sound research or evidence base, but because of variability of people, classrooms, pupils and other influences, distortion, side effects and misapplication are legion. If an Ofsted report gives an example of what a school does, and the judgement for the school is outstanding, the practice will proliferate widely but it will always be subject to contextual distortion.

Mick recalls:

It was a Sunday morning very early in April 1989 and I was leading the morning session at a weekend residential conference for head teachers in a hotel just off the A1 in the North of England. As everyone came into the room, I was talking with someone I knew who said, 'I hope this will be good.' It was a session about observing learning in classrooms in primary and secondary schools. My friend told me that she thought a lot of the other heads wouldn't enjoy a focus on classrooms because they were into 'managing their schools', although if there was something with initials they could use as 'management-speak', they would be content.

The session began well. We were basically looking at videos of children learning in classrooms and talking in small groups, with me drawing attention to specifics or summarising. Shortly before the break, I introduced them to some new research that had shown how easily classroom learning can be misinterpreted through the incidence of peripheral distortion syndrome (PDS). What the research had shown was that, if classrooms were observed through a PDS visualiser, the acuteness of observation was enhanced because peripheral distortion was reduced. I invited the group to experience the phenomena of PDS and, while we hadn't got the equipment, we could perhaps improvise by rolling some sheets of A3 paper into tubes.

The group watched the next video clip through the rolled-up tubes (portrait, not landscape) and immediately discussed the difference once PDS had been discounted. I summarised and, during the coffee break, could hear people discussing the influence of PDS.

After the break we did various other activities and, with a quarter of an hour to go, I began to review the key points of the session (an early version of plenaries made popular by Ofsted). As I revisited the main ideas, I talked about us experiencing PDS 'on this special day' and how PDS would 'resonate when we reflected on the particular day'. I thought there would be a dawning, and there was for a few, but over lunch, as some were still discussing the PDS phenomena, others smiled that their colleagues had fallen for the April Fool.

Mick recalls:

When I was at QCA, I was in one of my meetings with David Bell, who was then in charge at Ofsted, and I was trying to convince him that one of the biggest influences on practice in schools was inspection. I asked him to let me put a spoof sentence in each of three reports on schools judged to be outstanding. He declined, of course, because the documents are official.

I wanted to add a sentence into each of the three reports about roller skating. In the first, I would insert something saying, 'Attitudes and behaviour have improved since the roller-skating club was formed at lunchtime.' In the second, something such as, 'Attendance has improved dramatically since children were introduced to roller skating as part of PE.' In a third, I would add a sentence saying, 'Children report that the after-school provision, including roller skating and embroidery, is of the highest quality.'

That was all – just three quiet mentions among the vast number of reports produced every month. My prediction was that head teachers would be looking on the web to read reports, spot what was featuring and act accordingly. Many people don't realise that inspectors also scan reports for fear of being found wanting by their own assessors. Before long they too would be asking teachers, 'Do you do roller skating in school?' and 'Have you thought about roller skating as an attendance strategy?' and reporting their answers.

My bet with David was that, within three months, roller skating would feature in the provision of most schools across the country.

In the 1990s, Shirley Clarke's research showed that helping pupils to understand the purpose of their learning in a lesson helped to enhance it.[6] To make this accessible to children of primary age, two characters were created: Walt and Wilf. Pictures of them were used by teachers who wrote out for children the learning intention (we are learning to) and key criteria (what I'm looking for) using the colours Clarke had suggested. With the introduction of the national literacy and numeracy strategies at the end of the 1990s, this practice was woven into the literacy hour. As the strategies reached Key Stage 3, the same sensible practice was adopted within the three-part lesson, although to take account of the growing maturity of pupils, the intentions became 'learning objectives' (quickly shortened to LO) and the children were expected to record them.

As inspection reports started to document that the best judged schools made the learning intention clear at the start of the lesson, so the practice of pupils recording LOs started to spread, and in primary schools,

---

6 S. Clarke, *Enriching Feedback in the Primary Classroom* (London: Hodder Education, 2003). In this and more recent work, Clarke explores the use of formative assessment and feedback. She has been a constant promoter of effective classroom strategies for teachers.

the children (rather than the teacher) began to record their own WALTs. Now, 20 years later, it is almost universal practice for children to start each lesson by writing down a WALT or LO, every day of the year, four or five times a day. This would be fine if they could read it, if they could understand it and if the intention was discussed at the end of the lesson. Too often, though, it is a perfunctory activity, with the children not even knowing what a WALT is except for being something they have to write down. Do they think it is a process, an activity, a period of time or a bodily function? Ask them what they are doing and they will say, 'I'm doing my WALT.' It fills the time: over the course of a year, a conservative estimate is that 50 hours are spent on it. That is the equivalent of two weeks in school every year or half a year over a pupil's school career spent writing what I am going to do if I get this written down. And, of course, inventing LOs and WALTs to keep the evidence flowing in exercise books takes up teachers' time too.

Our schools abound with rituals and acronyms, usually resulting from empirical social science or educational research, which is then interpreted in a pupil- or teacher-friendly way in laminated posters on classroom walls. We have WAGOLL (what a good one looks like), EBI (even better if), WWW (what went well), RUCSAC (read, understand, choose, solve, answer, check), DIRT (directed improvement and reflection time)[7] and DR ICE (deepening thinking, role modelling learning, impact on learning, challenging expectations, engaging in learning).[8] Dweck's work on mindset[9] and Claxton's 5R's[10] implore children to be resilient – a quality they will certainly need in order to cope with the vagaries of this odd world of learning. Done well, all of these techniques have benefit; used in an unthinking or managerial way they can cause problems greater than those they seek to address.

None of this is to denigrate teachers. It is just to point out that some practice mushrooms for a variety of not always fully understood professional reasons, and often those employing them struggle to know why they are doing so. Currently, Ebbinghaus' forgetting curve is much referenced by teachers. Few seem to know that it is a theory first espoused in 1888 – it nearly got forgotten.

---

7   DIRT aims to improve pupils' work via feedback.
8   DR ICE is a template for an outstanding lesson.
9   Dweck, *Mindset*.
10 The 5R's (resourcefulness, remembering, resilience, reflectiveness and responsiveness) were developed by Guy Claxton as part of his work on the Curriculum for Lifelong Learning.

Kevan Collins drew attention to this hearsay and piecemeal-influenced outlook on good practice:

> I think our theory of change in the education system is incredibly weak – the infrastructure in the English education system which tries to make change happen. In fact, I don't think we have a theory of change. There still seems to be a view in Whitehall that if I make a speech or send an email or publish some guidance brief for our sparse regional teams, that will be enough for it to be activated and come to life and emerge as good practice across the land. So, the question now for me is: who is responsible for building the capacity of the system and ensuring that we are the best at getting better?

The real point is that professionalism is not about dogma but about evidence-based practice and the capacity of people to work both as effective individuals and as part of an effective team and profession which are all well led.

Evidence-based practice and the arrival of the Education Endowment Foundation

It is the level of evidence that has traditionally left the profession short. Persuasion has relied on the 'if they can do it, can't everybody?' approach, while resistance has relied on the capacity to find a reason why not – different children, different environment, different families, different anything.

Kevan Collins touched on this when he recounted the work of the EEF:

> I've always thought that we haven't got a broken system, we just haven't got a system that's good for everybody. Variation is our biggest issue. When I look back at the EEF, what drove me on was trying to work out why some schools were better than others. My conclusion was that in the schools that performed well, the leaders and teachers make better decisions.

They make better decisions; they're not better people. And leadership, in the end, is all about making decisions. I was interested in how well you are supported to make better decisions because that would make outcomes better for children.

I wanted to find a way in the EEF to dispassionately present what we know to those who make decisions so they can make better decisions, not to tell them what to do. That's why I got involved in asking the question, is education susceptible not only to presenting the evidence in an open way but also to generating new knowledge in a rigorous way? My feelings after eight or nine years of running it were that there is an appetite to know and to have access. There is a desire to be involved in enquiry and to remember that teaching is an intellectually curious act.

When half the schools in England ended up being in a trial that we funded, when we were told at the beginning that you'd never get people to do RCTs [randomised controlled trials], or according to the independent work of the audit commissioners, that nearly 70% of heads said they used the Toolkit to make decisions, I now reject the idea that education can't be an evidence-informed profession. I'm resentful of the rump of people who have continued to govern or lead others without taking the trouble – from prejudice or ignorance or even laziness – to just go and look at the evidence, which I think is now available.

It was Michael Gove who initiated the setting up of the EEF in late 2010 to research successful practices, emulating the No Child Left Behind programme in the United States. It has proved to be one his better initiatives – perhaps even his finest legacy. Built on a one-off capital spend to which philanthropic partners contributed, it is now part of the fabric of the schooling landscape. The research activity is matched by the value of the knowledge that is accumulating. In this case, Gove was right about the importance of knowledge. Collins explained:

It's actually about halfway through its spend. It was supposed to live until 2026 – it was a 'sunset fund' – but we invested it pretty well and we had lots of match funding coming towards us. It's now moving its ground from the presentation of evidence, which was the Toolkit, to funding studies: those two things are ongoing processes. What's interesting about the Toolkit is that we increasingly build it by taking evidence from across the world. There's a Latin American Toolkit that is running and there is an Australian Toolkit. The top page of the toolkit is the world's evidence, but as you go deeper they then interpret the findings in context for their own communities. There are now 17 partners in the EEF family from around the world.

Kevan Collins' and Alison Peacock's views are on the same agenda but from different perspectives. Peacock wants teachers to assert themselves with more clarity of intention and Collins is seeking to reinforce that assertion with good evidence for innovation and practice. Both see the need for teachers to be a self-respecting and self-determining profession.

How have we trained and developed our teachers in the past, and how do we do it now?

We now turn to the initial training and education of teachers, and, once trained, how we retain and help them to prosper in the profession.

The initial training and education of teachers was one of just three powers bequeathed to the secretary of state following the Butler Act of 1944. It was a duty taken very seriously, not least because after the war there was a serious teacher shortage. Teaching was seen, like many other professions, as a mainly male activity (although not exclusively – primary schools had a greater proportion of female teachers). The first initiative after the war was to offer an emergency six months of teacher training to returning demobilised armed services personnel, provided they had roughly the equivalent of the old Higher School Certificate (although exceptions could be made and graduates could teach without any training).[11]

Apart from these untrained graduates, who mainly taught in grammar or independent schools, there were two routes into teaching. The main source for infant, junior, primary and secondary modern schools was through a network of teacher training colleges, with their intake carefully

---

11   The Higher School Certificate was replaced by the A level in 1951.

planned nationally through an Advisory Committee for the Supply and Education of Teachers (ACSET). This committee included representatives of the teaching unions, local authorities through the powerful AEC, civil service, HMI and other experts invited by the secretary of state. New colleges were planned and built to meet the need for more teachers following the post-war bulge in the birth rate. Information was fed up and down through a network of area training organisations (ATOs) run on behalf of the DfE by LEAs. On completing their training, newly qualified teachers applied for a probationary teacher's post in any LEA 'pool' in order to be allocated a school. Some people would apply in areas close to their family but most sought employment near to the college where they had trained. This informed the regional planning of initial teacher education (ITE) places. The content of the college courses was a mixture of subject knowledge, education history, child psychology, philosophy and pedagogical methods. Certain colleges acquired a reputation for preparing teachers well and their students were sought in preference to others. Other colleges developed specialisms in niche areas, such as Loughborough (although it was known by a different title at the time) for PE and design and technology and Bretton Hall for the arts.

The second route into teaching was via the post-graduate one-year course established in most universities and expanded by new education faculties in the new universities during the 1960s and 1970s.[12] These were created following the Robbins Report to meet the expansion in numbers entering higher education.[13] They too fed information into the ATOs.

Like everything else in the public sector at a time of post-war shortages, it was a very carefully planned process. Unfortunately, the plans began to go wrong in the 1970s when the DfE was slow to react to a dramatic fall in the birth rate. There was a mass closure of colleges and regional planning was largely abandoned.

---

12   Essex, Sussex, Kent, East Anglia (Norwich), Lancaster, Warwick and York were all newly built universities at this time and added to the red-brick universities of the provincial cities in the West Country, the Midlands and the North and the various outposts of the London universities which became independent, such as Keele and Hull.

13   L. Robbins, *Higher Education* [Robbins Report] (London: HMSO, 1963). Available at: http://www.educationengland.org.uk/documents/robbins.

Tim recalls:

I was a very young senior assistant education officer (I confess: I remember with shame the pride I felt at being 'senior') with Buckinghamshire in 1969, and I visited Lady Spencer Churchill College in Oxfordshire to plan their extension. (Unusually, Buckinghamshire serviced this college because after the war it had been rehoused from Bletchley in Buckinghamshire, and Oxfordshire then was a small LEA and it made sense for its larger neighbour, which already had another college, to run it.) But my real excitement lay in planning a new college for Milton Keynes which was created as a new city during my time in Buckinghamshire. It was a hugely impressive design. The college was being built amid great anticipation when the decision was taken not to open it because of the fall in demand for teachers. In vain did we point out the likely regional need. The DfE, faced with the certainty of having to close colleges elsewhere, felt they couldn't justify opening a brand new college. It was handed over first to the Post Office and then became a training facility in the private sector.

At the start of our story, Shirley Williams recalled that the worst aspect of her tenure as secretary of state (1976–1979) has been to take the unpleasant and unpopular decision to close a number of colleges. By then, they had been renamed colleges of education and ran either three-year Certificate of Education courses or four-year Bachelor of Education (BEd) degrees, both of which carried qualified teacher status (QTS). The James Report had signalled, among other things (such as induction and CPD), the need for an all-graduate profession.[14] But not all was bad in teacher education; CPD was to enjoy a brief flourish, at least in some areas.

Tim recalls:

The James Report's suggestion that teachers should enjoy sabbaticals and that every secondary school should have a professional tutor as part of CPD was being taken seriously by the time I arrived in

---

14 Teacher education was given a huge boost by the James Report: E. James, *Teacher Education and Training* (London: HMSO, 1972). Available at: http://www.educationengland.org.uk/documents/james/james1972.html.

Oxfordshire in 1978, mainly because Harry Judge had been a member of the Committee of Inquiry. He was also the founding principal of Banbury School and had become director of Oxford University's Department of Educational Studies which ran a strong PGCE course.

I was faced with a brigadier as chair of the Education Committee, who was committed to cuts in the face of falling school rolls. 'You need to shoot the 200 teachers surplus to our requirements, Brighouse,' he briskly advised. 'But the *Oxford Mail* will make hay – and think of the scoop for the *Daily Mail*,' I replied. 'And we shouldn't sack them anyway – think of the women and children.' (Well, in those days, we were all un-reconstructedly politically incorrect and caught in conscious and unconscious biases. I had to appeal to his better nature in some way which, to my good fortune, was never far from the surface.)

'Well, what do you namby-pamby pinko from the ILEA advise?' he challenged with a smile. And then an angel descended onto my shoulder and from the dim recesses of my memory I recalled the uncapped pool. This meant that if you sent a teacher on a diploma or master's degree course, the LEA had to pay 25% of their salary. The rest would be charged to the national uncapped pool and be shared out among all the LEAs. I had worked out that, even if you paid a quarter of their salary plus the full cost of their lower-paid replacement probationer, it was less than paying the full salary of the senior staff you had seconded. You made a profit at the cost of other LEAs.

The brigadier loved finding gaps in hedges and, after suspiciously asking the county treasurer to confirm my arithmetic, declared, 'You can send the whole blankety-lot away if you like!' We didn't do that, but we had solved our budget problem and arranged courses locally through the polytechnic (now Oxford Brookes University) and Harry Judge's department at Oxford University. But we did more than solve a budgetary problem: we also created sabbaticals for CPD along the lines advocated in the James Report and reinvigorated tranches of teachers who still stop me in the street to recall the excitement they experienced as part of a group of teachers who worked together to find out more about a curriculum issue or pioneer a new method of unlocking the minds and opening the shut chambers of the hearts of their pupils.

However, these CPD opportunities also ran into problems when Margaret Thatcher's government stopped the uncapped pool in the late 1980s.

How has the supply of suitably qualified teachers through the provision of initial training and education and subsequently CPD fared in the age of markets, centralisation and managerialism?

Everything started to change during Keith Joseph's time as secretary of state. The origin of the shift owes something to the doubt and disillusion that the Ruskin College speech epitomised. As we noted in Chapter 1, perhaps the first indications of this disillusion were the student riots of 1968 when an unhappy prime minister summoned embarrassed vice chancellors to Downing Street to explain what was going on. Universities were the institutions where teachers were studying PGCE courses, where educational research was going on and from where there was increasing criticism of the application of neo-liberal economic theory, which Thatcher's government had later adopted.

The suspicion was that perhaps some of the real and imagined criticisms of the schooling system had their roots in the universities and colleges of education which educated and trained the teachers. Joseph had voiced his doubts, but as with the curriculum and so many other schooling matters, it was left to Kenneth Baker to take action. He created CATE to take on the task of accrediting initial teacher education and training. Meanwhile, the professors of education and college principals were summoned to meetings at the DfE where they were grilled to make sure no heresies were being promulgated on their courses.[15] Soon, PGCE courses were required to follow the school-based model, which had been successfully introduced by Harry Judge in Oxford and by the University of Sussex. Lecturers were expected to have 'recent' and 'relevant' experience in schools. Universities protested, but HMI and then Ofsted inspections of university courses soon became mandatory.

A distance learning PGCE was introduced by the Open University and became a vital supplier of maths and other teachers. After the introduction in 1989 of a licensed teacher scheme, whereby a would-be teacher

---

15   Tim experienced such a grilling but it was helped by two factors: he had helped to create the school-based PGCE internship scheme in Oxford, and David Winkley, a primary head on the CATE panel, had prepped him on what to expect.

could be trained on the job, all manner of school-based initial teacher training (ITT) courses were born. Acronyms have abounded as the courses have multiplied: SCITT (school-centred initial teacher training) courses were run by groups of schools where QTS could be gained, alongside optional PGCEs outsourced from the nearby university, which could also validate the QTS element.

School Direct became a variant on SCITT. Teach First, based on Teach for America, was part-funded by a charity and the Labour government to increase the quality and supply of good honours graduates into secondary schools, initially in London as part of the London Challenge. The original idea was that graduates destined for a career in business or industry would opt to teach for two years first in some of the most challenged inner-city schools. (The London Challenge was also helped by two developments which sadly proved to be short-lived: the Chartered London Teacher[16] and the emergence of real career professionals called advanced skills teachers (ASTs) – a concept we shall return to later.)

The Teach First course involved an intensive summer school followed by a school placement with a slightly lower starting salary than an NQT would receive and QTS after a year with close mentoring support. They not only attracted some excellent candidates and the scheme has expanded enormously geographically and in scope, but initially it also had a galvanising effect on recruitment to PGCEs in the prestigious group of older and red-brick universities.

But mistrust of university influence had been growing too. Some leading educational academics and education officers were referred to as 'the real heart of darkness' by HMCI Chris Woodhead[17] and as 'The Blob' and 'enemies of promise' by Michael Gove and others on the right of the traditional/ progressive binary line.[18] It was all good press copy.

---

16 Chartered London Teacher status was a qualification open to any teacher in London. It required them to build a portfolio showing how by inter-school visits they were extending their skill, knowledge and learning about their subject, their pedagogy, barriers to their pupils' learning and how to overcome them, teaching children from different backgrounds and the community in which they taught.

17 Quoted in M. McMahon, Profile: Chris Woodhead – Mr Standards Slips, *The Independent* (23 October 2011). Available at: https://www.independent.co.uk/life-style/profile-chris-woodhead-mr-standards-slips-1069410.html.

18 M. Gove, I Refuse to Surrender to the Marxist Teachers Hell-Bent on Destroying Our Schools: Education Secretary Berates 'the New Enemies of Promise' for Opposing His Plans, *Daily Mail* (23 March 2013). Available at: https://www.dailymail.co.uk/debate/article-2298146/I-refuse-surrender-Marxist-teachers-hell-bent-destroying-schools-Education-Secretary-berates-new-enemies-promise-opposing-plans.html.

Once university fees were introduced and raised the cost of doing an unpaid PGCE, the government found itself offering huge bursaries for subjects facing shortages to avoid those who had graduated but wanted to teach accumulating debt. Having casually given up his duty to secure a sufficient supply of suitably qualified teachers, Gove pursued his 'letting a thousand flowers bloom' policy by creating teaching schools based on more than 100 schools which were judged outstanding by Ofsted.[19] Their role consisted of overseeing local SCITT and providing some CPD, often in conjunction with maths and science centres, some of which were run by selected MATs. Teaching schools also had the remit of helping school improvement (see Chapter 7).

As we write, two other developments regarding the initial training and education of teachers have occurred. First, the Teaching Schools have been replaced by 87 teaching hub schools geographically spread. They have been charged with making sure that there is a sufficient supply of teachers through the various routes and overseeing the new early career framework (ECF) concept which will ensure that NQTs can receive continuing CPD support via a group of approved bidders in their first year after QTS (i.e. their second year in the classroom). The teaching hub schools will also supervise the portfolio of national professional qualifications (NPQs) available for middle senior leaders and would-be head teachers. They will have no role in school improvement. This development of what the DfE calls the 'golden thread'[20] of teacher development is contentious and is considered as part of Chapter 7 on school leadership.

There are now many different providers and routes into teaching, most of which are of short duration and involve on-the-job training. This is relevant because, in supporting trainee teachers, England is departing significantly from the other UK nations. There have been no comparable developments in the three other nations, which have all chosen to retain the traditional college/university routes and rely on master's courses for ambitious and aspiring teachers.

However, in 2008, a new phenomenon emerged in Scotland: TeachMeets. These are voluntary, after-school gatherings of teachers from up to a

19 Department for Education and M. Gove, The Education Secretary's Speech on Academies at Haberdashers' Aske's Hatcham College (11 January 2012). Available at: https://www.gov.uk/government/speeches/michael-gove-speech-on-academies.
20 Department for Education, *National Professional Qualification (NPQ): Leading Teacher Development Framework* (October 2020), p. 5. Available at: https://www.gov.uk/government/publications/national-professional-qualifications-frameworks-from-september-2021.

30-mile radius who come together in a school and share ideas (typically for five minutes each) that have worked for them in the classroom. These are sometimes phase-specific and have been variously facilitated by subject centres or associations, MATs or diocesan groups. During the pandemic, some of them used Teams or Zoom to continue their CPD virtually. TeachMeets and the use of online CPD have become a regular feature of the lives of some of the most committed teachers. There has also been a flowering of web-based groups that share ideas about curriculum and pedagogy.

Defining professionalism and proposing a new route

What does it mean to be a professional, and what are the elements of professionalism? At the time of the guilds, during the Middle Ages, professionals were a class of people, alongside merchants, artisans and labourers, whose services came at a considerable cost. Medicine and law professionals were richly rewarded because they were acknowledged as 'learned'. In those times, education professionals were to be found in universities or as tutors for the children of the rich. As the state began to provide schooling at the end of the Victorian era, teachers were seen as being vocationally driven in the same way as priests or nurses in the other caring professions.

Ever since, teachers have grappled with the tension of wanting to be appreciated, like priests and nurses, while also wanting to be rewarded, like doctors and lawyers. Recently, as the success measures of business have been brought into schooling, a third tension has arisen in terms of teachers wanting to be valued in the same way as other successful business people.

It has not helped that some politicians have seen teacher training as being spoiled by its association with the university sector, where academics are not slow in criticising government actions. As James Noble-Rogers, executive director of the Universities Council for the Education of Teachers (UCET), reminded us: 'Michael Gove insisted on speaking of teaching as a craft and that the best training was to sit at the feet of a successful practitioner who would teach them all they needed to know.' As Noble-Rogers also pointed out, the commitment of university vice chancellors to getting involved in ITE has in many cases been ambivalent.

The first visits by HMI to university departments in the 1980s had been resisted and the prospect of Ofsted inspections were only overcome by shifting the funding arrangements to the Teacher Training Agency (TTA), thereby creating a separate finance stream for teacher education within universities. The TTA's first CEO, Anthea Millett, aimed to reduce the proportion of new teachers being educated and initially trained in universities from more than three-quarters to less than a quarter. Millett succeeded in her first objective of securing inspection of university departments, therefore, but the system continued to depend on the university sector to provide a substantial proportion of ITE places. Noble-Rogers observed: 'It has remained the same and the university sector has been remarkably resilient, providing the bulk of new teachers and cooperating with school-based schemes both in providing expertise and in validating courses.'

In terms of the development of the ECF, the DfE's Initial Teacher Training Market Review, chaired by Ian Bauckham,[21] which reported in summer 2021, caused tension for higher education providers of ITE, who variously see the proposed reorganisation as over-centralised, an affront to their integrity or another step in the assault on universities' involvement in teaching that Keith Joseph and Margaret Thatcher initiated. It is undeniably market driven. Many observers across the system see the Market Review as a dangerous development, giving politicians too much control over the learning agenda of teachers and the pupils they teach through the management of the processes involved without the need for legislation; thereby, centralisation, markets and managerialism are all in focus.

The DfE acknowledges the issue in the report:

> We know there are those who fear that a strong emphasis on evidence in teacher training and professional development will reduce teacher autonomy by dictating a set of narrowly prescribed or mechanistic teaching behaviours which will be expected of all teachers. We do not share this perspective. On the contrary, our view is that while teaching is without doubt a highly skilled activity, training which is based on evidence, including relevant aspects of cognitive science, or the science of learning, will enable

---

21 Ian Bauckham was appointed as the chair of Ofqual in January 2021, replacing Sally Collier who resigned in the aftermath of the problems with GCSEs and A levels in 2020. Bauckham has held significant posts, including being a member of the project board for Oak National Academy.

teachers to be more critically reflective and more, rather than less, professionally autonomous and self-efficacious; it will equip them to understand and evaluate, in light of research, the very many approaches they will encounter in different contexts once they start teaching.[22]

This is reasonable logic. If we know what constitutes good practice, shouldn't all new teachers meet the criteria through carefully controlled programmes? The Core Content Framework is one of the areas that faces most criticism, along with structural proposals over the organisation of school placements. However, the All-Party Parliamentary Group believes that the Market Review itself is flawed and represents an existential threat to teacher supply.[23]

Robin Walker, the incoming schools minister, seemed to offer a placatory outlook when he told us: 'There are different scare stories depending on whom you talk to. Some think it's all about disestablishing SCITTs or it's all about disestablishing higher education institutions and their role in ITT. I think both have a really important role to play. I want to make sure that when we respond to the Market Review, we are very clear about wanting to support good ITT in both the higher education sector and on a school-based basis.'

Wherever the true need for development sits, it seems to us that government has ventured too close to the detail. We don't believe that it is appropriate for politicians or the DfE to prescribe the curriculum for those training to teach whether directly or through the device of a narrow group of selected providers. After all, one of the devices used by totalitarian and authoritarian states to maintain power is the political domination of teaching in schools.

---

22 Department for Education, *Initial Teacher Training (ITT) Market Review Report* (July 2021), p. 12. Available at: https://assets.publishing.service.gov.uk/government/uploads/system/uploads/attachment_ data/file/999621/ITT_market_review_report.pdf.

23 All Party Parliamentary Group for the Teaching Profession, *If It Ain't Broke, Handle with Care: Report by the Special Interest Group on Initial Teacher Training (ITT)* (2021). Available at: https://appgteachingcom. files.wordpress.com/2021/07/21.06.30-report-of-the-ite-sig-to-the-appg-on-the-teaching-profession-jmc4.pdf.

Maintaining ideals in a more centralised and managed world

Typically, the term 'professional' is now applied to someone who is on top of their job, who works efficiently, effectively and with panache – the consummate professional. With schools adopting practices from the world of business, there has been a move towards industry standards to ensure professionalism. The first Teachers' Standards were published in 2005 as part of an effort to professionalise teaching (the latest iteration was published in 2011).[24] This provided a definition but it also had an unhelpful unintended consequence – it standardised the role. Whether the Teachers' Standards are describing the teacher or the teaching has never been resolved. They were intended to act as a barrier over which the successful would-be teacher had to jump, but they have become what Matt Burnage so eloquently describes as 'the heart and soul' of what teaching is meant to be about.[25] Set against other developments over time, this seemingly minor shift would become one more nudge on the road to centralisation and managerialism.

The downside of establishing a set of expectations is that they can become a minimum; measurable standards that are accepted as the norm and exclude imagination. Normal daily life in school is now littered with scripted conversations and announcements which are examples of the pseudo-personal professional impression this can create. The standards do at least reduce the idiosyncratic behaviours that can cause problems, but equally they can risk the possibility of not giving enough scope to professionals to express themselves or exploit their own personal qualities. Securing a teaching job involves making sure that the interviewing panel's boxes are ticked, as well as a series of procedures including an application form and letter of application, teaching a class and meetings with children and staff. All of these are helpful, of course, but the suite of exercises should leave the appointing panel convinced enough not to have to check their decision through a teaching observation so frequently, given that most candidates have met the standard in their regular work.

---

24 Department for Education, *Teachers' Standards: Guidance for School Leaders, School Staff and Governing Bodies* (July 2011; updated July 2021). Available at: https://www.gov.uk/government/publications/teachers-standards.

25 M. Burnage, The Teachers' Standards: A Think Piece Working Paper. In *CollectivED Working Papers, Issue 7* (Leeds: Carnegie School of Education/Leeds Beckett University, 2019), pp. 40–44 at p. 40. Available at: https://www.leedsbeckett.ac.uk/-/media/files/research/collectived/collectived-issue-7-mar-2019.pdf.

The upside is that minimum standards help to avoid amateurism – the polar opposite of professionalism. Whether practices *look* professional matters because shambolic or untidy behaviour risks undermining confidence. (Oddly, the police may recognise a crime scene with grudging respect as a 'professional job'.) Perhaps the best aspect of setting standards is the potential for the profession itself to exclude those who fall below the minimum level.

The Labour government's first Education Act in 1997 brought in provision for a GTC to maintain professional standards with the power to strike off teachers from a central register (similar to the General Medical Council). From the outset, the GTC was fraught with difficulty, not least because all serving teachers were expected to pay to register. Furthermore, it was never expected to enter the territory of self-determination, which the Chartered College of Teaching appears to be making its defining feature.

On top of the basic industry standards of professionalism there is the idea of the professional being prepared to walk the extra mile in the interests of those they serve – their school or the profession itself. The excellent teacher teaches good lessons most of the time (and rarely teaches a poor one); they are poised and composed; they are prepared and adaptive in their teaching. To this they add intuitive contributions to their school. They notice the child on their own in the playground and find a way to start a conversation that leads naturally to the question, 'Is everything alright?' The excellent teacher responds empathetically to their answer. They offer to help with stage design for the Year 9 performance because it is a chance to spend time with pupils they used to teach a couple of years ago and find out how they have developed. They put themselves forward (perhaps as a member of the art department, for example) to join a Year 7 residential history study visit to the First World War battlefields, so they can spend time with their pupils and bring their subject discipline into a different context. In short, the excellent teacher contributes professionally to the wider agenda of the school.

The performance management process brought in after 2002 linked teacher pay to pupil performance in tests and exams. This was highly controversial at the time and harked back to 1862 when the Revised Code of Regulations was introduced. It was 'a view of the nature of elementary education from which it took the system generations to recover'.[26] The

---

26   J. Lawson and H. Silver, *A Social History of Education in England* (London: Methuen, 1973), p. 292.

resulting payment-by-results culture has gone on to become ingrained in teachers.

Have we got time to be professional?

In 1987, Kenneth Baker had stipulated, against considerable opposition, that teachers should work for 1,265 hours per year. These were the hours that could be 'directed' by their head teacher and still applies today, although we find that many teachers are largely unaware of it and even when they are, they have stopped bothering. Directed time had the effect of demanding more of some teachers and proving a cause of resentment to others who felt their wider contribution was going unrecognised. Teachers then, as now but in a greater proportion, committed their school holidays to residential visits, their evenings to clubs and societies, band practice and sports, and their weekends to museum visits, together with countless acts of unprompted thoughtfulness to pupils and colleagues, taking up a few minutes here and a few more there. They also spent their evenings at Teachers' Centres and their weekends at residential conferences. They belonged in greater numbers than now to subject associations. Teachers' belief in the public service element of the job and the commitment to wider professional ideals was strong (and still is) in many individuals. By instigating the process of counting working time in schools, Baker weakened this professional ethic.

Directed time also focused attention on time as a limited resource and how to get the most from the hours available. This has led to the school day gradually becoming more truncated and hurried. This can reduce the need for lunchtime supervision, but it also leaves less time for relationships to grow informally between staff and pupils.

As schools shortened their days, so the rise in concern about teacher workload increased, which has been a recurring theme over the last 20 years. Unions have long argued with government about teachers' work–life balance and the increased pressures resulting from centralising and managerial policy expectations. The issue is complex.

Labour, under Estelle Morris, who had been a teacher and never forgot what a teacher's life was like – a characteristic which was effortlessly evident in her words and behaviour and endeared her to the profession

– had established a group of head teachers in 2001 who met termly at the DfE to consider all initiatives and requests from central government in terms of their workload implications. The unions claimed a breakthrough in 2005 when the government accepted the concept of PPA time, where 10% of the working week would be allocated to each teacher for planning, preparation and assessment. Its impact was felt mainly in primary schools where, until then, teachers had no free time from classroom teaching, whereas their secondary colleagues had some time set aside in their timetables.

Although teachers, like any other workers, need time to plan and prepare, the definitive 10% of their working week is almost demeaning in implying that this is the total amount of time spent on such tasks. Nicky Morgan told us: 'I talked about workload a lot and the teacher unions couldn't really complain about that.' But the issue of work–life balance hasn't been addressed by the 10% allocation. Workload has become a catch-all term to describe the pressure and relentlessness of the machinery of accountability – the lack of training and experience to deal with, for example, the multiplying complexities of SEND or the negative impact of social media on young people. We could add many more examples of workload issues to this list. PPA time simply doesn't solve the problems of a schooling system, which is weighed down by a myriad of accumulated regulatory and accountability imperatives emanating from increasingly centralising and managerial governments.

We asked our head teachers whether PPA was beneficial. Richard Kieran told us: 'We couldn't do without our PPA. It is the chance for teams of teachers to get together on a regular basis to really think through the learning ahead. Time for professionals to come together to anticipate and plan is vital. If we didn't have PPA, the staff would still make the time, but it definitely adds to the quality of what we do.'

While Kieran and others gave examples of the way that the 10% of flexibility had been absorbed and used well in their schools, others talked of PPA as yet one more working complexity. In schools where lesson planning pro formas are scrutinised by leadership, teachers use the time as an added hour on the laptop. Other contributors gave a picture of the resource becoming a strain. 'It is a nuisance,' said one primary head teacher. 'I struggle to get cover, it costs me a lot, it affects pupil behaviour and some of my teachers think nothing of walking out and leaving the class uncovered.'

In terms of professionalism, such developments have ensured that, over time, the role of the teacher has become more standardised, less open to being exploited and has more consistent expectations. However, the same developments have reduced rather than increased professionalism in its widest sense.

Andreas Schleicher of the OECD described teacher professionalism in the context of governments' continuing attempts to reduce class size and with reference to international perspectives:

> One of the trade-offs that you got by reducing class sizes and hiring all of the assistant teachers has been that teachers thought more and did other things less.
>
> Take the extreme: Shanghai in China, top performer on the PISA scale. Teachers teach, say, a maximum 16 hours per week. But they work more than an English teacher and they spent a lot more time with individual students outside the classroom. They spend a lot more time with their colleagues, there's a lot more time on curriculum design, a lot more time on technology, pedagogy, sharing, partnering with other schools. It's a very different model, and that is what drives the attractiveness of the profession – that you are actually a designer of innovative learning environments, rather than just an instructor over a kind of canned curriculum.
>
> If you want to look at a system that is doing really well on that kind of human resource management in schools, it's Singapore. They have an amazing system that builds careers to enhance the mobility of teachers. Most teachers in their working lives work in school, they work in research, they work in policy and so they know all sides of the job. They have 100 hours every year where they go back to the National Institute of Education. They meet their former colleagues. All of that works together to create a very supportive ecosystem.

In 1976, the limit of the demand on teachers' time was the school term, although the implication was that some additional time would be required during the school holidays. The general public joked enviously about teachers' holidays, but there was an implicit acknowledgement that they did things beyond. In any case, most people left school with very limited qualifications and saw teachers in the category of organisers of society – talented people devoted to their specialism, engaged in a pursuit that they enjoyed, dedicating time in an unstinting way to achieve their goals.

The concept of unrestricted time is a double-edged sword. While wage slaves envy the relatively flexible working lives of the salaried professional, they also admire the readiness of the professional to commit to the job in hand. In schooling, the admiration for teachers has decreased in recent years in the light of criticisms of school performance and media perceptions of teacher effectiveness set alongside the perceived perks (such as extended holidays). However, the coronavirus pandemic may have engendered a new respect for teachers and other school staff who have worked hard to support children – and in many cases their families and communities – in the widest possible educational sense during the lockdowns.

Joining a profession involves reflecting and being worthy of its values and making a contribution to the benefit of the cause. Central to professionalism is engaging with research, being driven by the evidence to move practice forward and being willing to adopt new techniques. Medical professionals are expected to record their growing experience and ensure they learn new procedures from more experienced colleagues as part of a career-long process of self-development within an evolving field. Innovation should emerge naturally from a profession steeped in ongoing action research and the mentoring of others.

The teacher's professional career: from training and beyond

Throughout the period our book covers, there has been a series of ongoing and interlocking debates about what sort of people should become teachers, the training and education of teachers and how to get enough of them, entry into the profession and retention, their career pathway and how to make them effective. Each of these issues has the potential to create divisions and distraction.

Michael Barber's much quoted statement that 'the quality of an education system cannot exceed the quality of its teachers' is one of those self-evident truths.[27] The who and the how of training and career development are therefore vital. Proposals to ease the entry route into teaching in order to maintain an adequate supply often bring protests from the unions, who are keen to protect teachers' professional status. Although shortly afterwards, ironically, the selfsame unions recruit the selfsame career entrants into their fold.

As we have explained, the gradual rise in entry expectations to ensure a degree-level profession gave teaching a status that was later undermined for some by the introduction of first shorter courses and then school-based provision. A significant and often critical voice in that debate has been those already in the profession who had entered by a previous route. When the BEd was extended to four years, the three-year trained wondered how another year would help. When the PGCE was introduced, there was scepticism about whether someone could train in a third or a quarter of the time they had taken. When school-based routes emerged, those who had entered through higher education courses questioned the academic rigour. When the concept of Teach First arrived, it was met by some with disdain and rejoinders such as the one offered by one of our witnesses: 'Can we try brain surgery first and then go and pursue a career in banking?'

With each new development, there are those who think there might be something in it, who give it a go and usually find that it works, probably because of their professional investment. Others have reservations that are gradually moderated by experience. Then there are doubters. When SCITTs began, there were questions about the links to research and the depth of the courses. On the other side of the debate, there were questions about the cumbersome nature of higher education institution (HEI) validation processes and their capacity to be as fleet of foot as SCITTs.

Sam Twiselton, professor of education at Sheffield Hallam University, talked about the differences between the various training routes:

> When setting up a SCITT, you're thinking from scratch, only thinking of the best principles. I think you have the potential to be really good if you put enough expertise and resources into it because you can control the variables so much better. SCITTs tend to be quite small. A traditional HEI might have a thousand

---

27 M. Barber and M. Mourshed, *How the World's Best-Performing School Systems Come Out on Top* (London: McKinsey & Company, 2007), p. 19. Available at: https://www.mckinsey.com/industries/public-and-social-sector/our-insights/how-the-worlds-best-performing-school-systems-come-out-on-top.

students on placement in hundreds of schools. We can't possibly control things in the same way, so we are relying on the professional quality of the teachers but less directly than a SCITT can. Whereas if you've got just 50 trainees in 10 of your schools, then you have a lot of influence over shared values, which can create a much more coherent and conducive sort of training environment.

At Sheffield Hallam, we are working in partnership with SCITTs in the region who use us extensively to support their programmes. I think there is real potential in building a more extensive career entry plan, balancing both longer and shorter training experiences.

Mick recalls:

Listening to Sam Twiselton made me think about learning to teach in Sheffield. It was a very long time ago and I did the standard three-year course at the City College, which later morphed into the Hallam University. We did a lot of weeks each year on placement (then called teaching practice); from the first week we visited a local school where the lecturers led teaching sessions with students watching. We also went to a local school for one half day a week for a term to work beside a pupil as lecturers taught, to see up close what they could or couldn't do (mine was called Philip).

Our group of students had to work with a local school to plan and teach a series of lessons with others critiquing. We had to join residential field study programmes for pupils, visit youth centres for 10 evenings, and visit local libraries, museums and galleries to be shown how to use archives in schools. We had to spend a short time on a health education agenda and I had to spend three days helping in a hospital school. On top of all that school-based work, we had the widest of curriculum studies programme and brilliant courses on psychology, sociology and the history of education. We even did a few sessions on comparative education.

The lecturers were a mixed bunch, but many filled me with a fascination about learning that my schooling had failed to ignite and some instilled a sense of purpose that has been career sustaining. They contributed to student-led opportunities for people to take part in arts, drama, music, sport or the outdoors. One of them still visits schools in role as Charles Dickens to bring literature to life![28] They cared about teaching and what sort of teachers they were easing into the noble profession.

When I started work, I met many who said that their training was poor, but I could never agree, although I could concur with the bit about not being taught how to teach a child to read. It was only later that I realised that it remains the unsolved mystery. We have got better at it but there is a way to go – continuous improvement.

The initial training and education of teachers took another turn in the early months of 2021 when Nick Gibb announced the establishment of an Institute of Teaching to be launched in 2022.[29] Reactions have been mixed. One vice chancellor described the proposal to us as 'a solution looking for a problem' and another felt that 'the balance between HEIs and SCITTs has just about settled down. Why is there need to create complication?' The leader of a teaching school alliance told us it was 'an example of a ministerial vanity project; totally unnecessary'. Others saw a more centralised agenda at work.

As the flagship teacher and leader development provider, with at least four regional centres, the Institute of Teaching will deliver ITT and a range of NPQs. No capital funding is being made available, so successful bidders will have to make use of existing buildings. We did think that the old NCSL building in Nottingham might have come in useful had it been available.

Just as the teaching school hubs and the providers of programmes to them are being run by MATs, so the expectation is that the Institute of Teaching will also be driven by an organisation dependent on MATs and, in turn, on the private sector. Many are concerned that this is one more significant step towards centralised control within a market context. For others, it represents centralised control of the curriculum content that teachers will encounter on their professional pathway. Some see the hand of Nick Gibb controlling pedagogy and reducing discourse, while others

---

28 If you ever get to read this, Mike Gardner, it is you. Along with Dr Halliwell, Miss Fyffe, David Turner, Don Mattam and many others, you gave a lot of impressionable students an image of what the job was about, which has affected the life chances of thousands. Thanks.

29 Department for Education and N. Gibb, New Institute of Teaching Set to Be Established [press release] (2 January 2021). Available at: https://www.gov.uk/government/news/new-institute-of-teaching-set-to-be-established.

judge that he is acting on his convictions with tenacity and determination to ensure that teachers learn about what we know works for children.

What is needed is for the EEF, which is independent of government, to continue to take as its model the National Institute for Health and Care Excellence (NICE, which endorses and sanctions approved clinical procedures) or the Medicines and Healthcare Products Regulatory Agency (MRHA, which approves the use of medicines). As we explain elsewhere in this book, schooling suffers from trends in practice.

One of our witnesses, John West-Burnham, was clear that teachers (experienced and inexperienced), inspectors and providers of CPD need to avoid fads and instead use authenticated research evidence:

> We need an authoritative view of the nature of the learning process – how we understand it now. We then need to build on that in terms of implications for practice; saying that, we've got enough evidence now which tells us that some things are just dumb. We need to say that some things are stupid. Unless we implement them properly, they are more dangerous than not using them – for example, learning styles. These alleged cognitive developers can be just rubbish, but they are nurtured and take hold. We need a system where schools use an approach to learning that has at its heart proper evidence-based practice.

Of course, there is research available for schools to use but increasingly the DfE publishes central guidance on aspects of teaching or leadership and decides on the appropriateness of research to support and promote. John Hattie's comprehensive international research on the effect size of strategies and approaches to increased school effectiveness is enthusiastically followed by many schools in pursuit of 'visible learning'.[30] Hattie's work is used in a piecemeal fashion by the school system, with elements positive to government policy being referenced and others ignored. Similarly, the work of organisations such as the British Educational Leadership, Management and Administration Society (BELMAS) or British Educational Research Association receives scant attention from government. Established research organisations, such as the NFER, or research supported by charitable foundations add to the complex picture but the findings rarely achieve prominence or have practice-changing influence as happens in medicine.

---

30   J. Hattie and K. Zierer, *Visible Learning Insights* (Abingdon and New York: Routledge, 2019).

At present, the EEF is the central agency for researching practice. While universities engage with educational research, in general they find it hard to get traction behind their findings unless they happen to catch the breeze of government priorities of the time. There are examples of universities helping research to have direct impact on practice in schools, such as the Bedford Borough Learning Exchange (known as the 'Bubble'). Here, the local authority has supported a collaborative programme linking expertise within the University of Bedfordshire with school-initiated research to support teachers enquiring into their own practice. Too often, though, universities tend to be ponderous and have an inward focus, seeking to sustain their Research Excellence Framework (REF) rating to secure future funding on a circuit of mutually supporting dissemination activities rather than setting out to directly influence the experience of learners.[31]

The EEF has made a very good start: it is widely used and appreciated by the profession, although it also runs the danger of being a sort of 'Which?' guide,[32] comparing one approach with another or one published product with another against a learner's notional linear development. We believe that the EEF should use its undoubted early start to grapple with the issues in teaching that will really affect practice and, with the Chartered College of Teaching, become the accepted agency for the school equivalent of NICE and the MRHA.

Recruiting good teachers

If how we train is one focus of activity, then how we recruit and retain sufficient good teachers is another. The reality is that because the school system has often been at risk of losing more teachers than it gains, quicker and more diverse routes become important.

Teaching is a recruiting rather than a selecting profession – that is, it has to attract entrants rather than pick from those wanting to enter. This

---

31 The REF is a research impact evaluation of British HEIs. It is the successor to the Research Assessment Exercise. It aims to provide accountability for public investment in research, establish a reputational yardstick and thereby achieve an efficient allocation of resources. Critics argue that the REF does more harm than good to higher education – a bit like league tables and inspection in schools.

32 *Which?* was set up in 1957 to promote informed consumer choice based on product comparison.

means that issues of quality on entry and the rigour of the course are always tempered with concerns about there not being enough teachers.

Estelle Morris did much, both as a minister and as secretary of state, to enhance the professionalism of teaching. The 1998 Green Paper that she championed, *Teachers: Meeting the Challenge of Change*, offered a comprehensive approach (as did everything else during Blunkett's tenure) to modernising the profession, addressing everything from training and pay to leadership, career routes and better staff facilities.[33]

At the time, the expectation that teachers would need to demonstrate their professional competence to pass across the threshold sent a jolt through a profession that had seen its membership relatively unchallenged about personal effectiveness through the course of a career. That this was linked with pay added extra urgency. As with so many aspects of schooling in our book, this development and long-term performance management procedures quickly became managerial, with the preparation of internal documentation to satisfy scrutiny from outside that procedures were effectively overtaking the rigour of professional challenge.

Collegiality has always mattered in schools. A head teacher cannot afford to lose the staffroom, so identifying teachers as 'best' or 'worst' has rarely featured. For a profession so focused on giving feedback to learners, we are not very good at shining a spotlight on the very best of the profession or opening the trap door for the worst, although this has improved markedly in the last 20 years.

Of course, how well a teacher does their job and the impact they make throughout their career is very much influenced by their early career experiences. So, for long-term progress, it isn't just a case of recruiting and retaining teachers but providing them with positive experiences early on. Many of Morris' developments have endured for good or ill, and subsequent modification has been piecemeal until the recent government recruitment and retention strategy instituted by Damian Hinds.

Sam Twiselton, who is a member of the government's advisory group developing the new ECF, told us: 'It seemed to me to get to a turning point in terms of the government finally admitting there's a problem with teacher retention, and that therefore leads to a problem with teacher

---

33 Department for Education and Employment, *Teachers: Meeting the Challenge of Change* [Green Paper] (London: HMSO, 1998). Available at: http://www.educationengland.org.uk/documents/gp1998/teachers-change.html.

recruitment, because of the fact that more and more teachers were leaving earlier. It is a circular problem. I felt they were taking it quite seriously in terms of really looking into why it is that teachers are leaving and what they can do about it. This focus on early career support is right, I think.'

As we have seen, the Teachers' Standards were brought in to improve quality and consistency. The problem was that they were introduced into a profession that was becoming highly managerial. This was being influenced by Michael Barber's emphasis on models from other sectors and by an accountability regime that was demanding more and more evidence. Vincent Ashworth, a former HMI for ITT, reflected:

> The minute the teaching standards came out, they were distorted into some sort of progression model that the providers then used for formative assessment, when actually they're a benchmark for going into the profession. The programmes started to become about gathering evidence rather than any sort of deep reflection on what they need to do to improve. When you went to do inspections, you'd be faced with mountains of lever arch files, each containing a mass of paper dealing with policies, observation records, pupil work, meeting notes, timetables and lesson plans, over which we had to clamber to try and find evidence for individual standards.

The dilemma for teaching standards was that there was always a dual purpose: to regulate and validate induction to the profession and to provide a formative agenda for early professional learning. The need for new teachers to evidence the rigour of their work could often outweigh the emphasis on their development. Even Ofsted acknowledged that the Teachers' Standards had driven some providers towards getting lost in regulation and grading as their primary reference point.

We believe that the focus on the 'standard teacher' and the risk of the 'identikit' professional might be one of the reasons for the high departure rate from the teaching in the first five years. Research shows there to be many reasons,[34] but we think that more needs to be done to welcome

---

34 See, for example, J. Worth and G. De Lazzari, *Teacher Retention and Turnover Research. Research Update 1: Teacher Retention by Subject* (Slough: National Foundation for Educational Research, 2017); R. Morris, B. H. See and S. Gorard, Teacher Shortage in England – New Evidence for Understanding and Addressing Current Challenges, *Impact* (February 2021). Available at: https://impact.chartered. college/article/teacher-shortage-in-england-new-evidence-understanding-challenges; and R. Long and S. Danechi, *Teacher Recruitment and Retention in England.* Briefing Paper No. 07222 (14 April 2021). Available at: https://commonslibrary.parliament.uk/research-briefings/cbp-7222.

people into the profession as positive contributors rather than feeling as though they are constantly having to prove themselves until some distant time in the future when they might be fully appreciated.

As Vincent Ashworth explained:

> We have to avoid it being like a sausage factory where we push them through their early career in a year. So, instead of thinking about the ECF as extending the NQT year to two years, it's much more about that professional formation and trying to get providers to think about the professional curriculum at the front end rather than using the Teachers' Standards to grade teachers. What do these new teachers need to know and understand to set them up? They've got the two years for this professional formation and then the Teachers' Standards come into play. I think we're getting the framework right, but we have to get people's hearts and minds closer to what is a good ITE curriculum and career start.

This view was supported by Sam Twiselton, who argued: 'The thinking behind the early career framework is absolutely right. We need to really look after our new teachers with coherent support and development because, after all, the initial teacher training can be so very short. I wouldn't say I'm a massive fan of all the mechanics of what it looks like, but making sure people are properly supported and helped to develop is crucial.'

It is in this area of what 'proper support' looks like that the ECF is attracting attention. For many, its development, coupled with the establishment of teaching school hubs and the identification of a limited number of approved providers for the NPQ and ECF programmes, is a further step towards centralisation, with an ever-shrinking group of influencers exerting disproportionate control over the system, which will have repercussions for a generation.

Twiselton is pragmatic:

> I come in as somebody who has a bit more sympathy with that worry about teacher training than some others, in that I think there was a flaw in the level of teacher training. For most new teachers it is nine months, with most of that time spent in school, but the experience within school is so variable in terms of the quality of support, development and good practice the trainee

teachers see when they're there. That's the bit that's exciting me about review because we're focusing on trying to come up with a better model. How can we craft those field-based experiences?

The curriculum by which we train teachers, whether initially or in an ongoing way, is vital. I think that there is a real danger in the very black-and-white way that we become convinced we know what makes somebody a good teacher. We need to be wary of a very technical, mechanistic view, a new kind of transmitting, where we just need to put it in front of these teachers and assume they'll be better teachers.

David Gumbrell, a lecturer in ITE at Kingston University and former head teacher in Surrey, told us: 'It is essential that we encourage young teachers into a wider professional experience. They need to feel prestige, build their credentials and feel valued as new professionals.'

Our view is that we need to do more in the arena of professional awareness and prestige. Too many of those new to teaching understand little of the structure of their school, let alone the wider system. Too many describe their role in the professional world in terms of being an 'operative', providing a set number of lessons per week with some additional institutional duties.

Retaining good teachers

Even if we can recruit good teachers, another challenge is to keep hold of them. One of the reasons for the development of the ECF was the need to retain teachers beyond the early stage of their career. There is much concern about the growing tendency for teachers to leave the profession after four or five years. Research on the attractiveness of teaching suggests several potential reasons, the main one being workload, along with teaching being similar to other employment sectors and suffering from the 'millennial' outlook.[35]

While we think that the attention to a career pathway, and the ECF in particular, is welcome, more consideration needs to be given to the early phase of a teacher's professional life. Good schools make sure that new

---

35   Morris et al., Teacher Shortage in England.

teachers have a long-term view of their teaching career. However, the induction year, and potentially the ECF, risks giving new teachers an image of themselves as people with limited employment horizons. While it sets out the expectations and the hoops to jump through, there is little about the wider range of experiences that all new teachers should encounter.

Early career teachers need to understand how schools are led and managed and how their department or phase team is structured. Too often, schools are hectic places where experienced colleagues always seem to be looking over their shoulder or feeding a machine of accountability. Therefore, new teachers' interactions with these more experienced colleagues are sometimes restricted to planning and checking. The danger is that in doing so we close down horizons; we push them towards the view that they are more like a technician trying to get a procedure right rather than a contributing and capable professional, and that being business-like is more important than being professionally curious.

Most schools take the induction period seriously, dedicating time and people to enable new teachers to have good experiences across the spectrum of the professional standards. They engage them in the totality of school life in a positive way and build a feeling of contribution and worth. For too many, though, their first year in teaching is spent at the bottom of a tall hierarchy that they don't understand.

Getting out of the foothills of the profession feels a far cry from the enticing posters, websites and cinema adverts that persuaded many people to join. The award of QTS means little beyond permission to pass to the next level of scrutiny. At the end of the NQT experience lies recently qualified teacher (RQT) provision. The image of colleagues with years of experience and obvious expertise being 'observed' periodically exemplifies a system that is bleak rather than enticing. Professional influence, trust and autonomy seem hard to attain.

New teachers' understanding of education beyond their school is often minimal. They recognise the MAT or local authority as an important element, but often without knowing what it is or does. Many have little concept of being part of something bigger than their school and express the view that they should not be involved in something that has not been set up for them. Would the NQT (or trainee teacher for that matter) consider going to an open conference or workshop after school, or would they feel that it's not for them? Too often, teachers introduce themselves, or are introduced to us, as an NQT. The notion that they will be a 'real teacher' one day, but aren't at the moment, is strong.

From the start of their ITE programme and into induction, trainees need to be exposed to the bigger educational arena and included in debate beyond their university course and induction experience. They need to be invited to conferences and exhibitions and helped to meet and speak with a wide community of educators. They are not at university simply to gain a degree; they are there to learn by degrees about teaching. Learning by degrees involves going deeper and wider into their sphere of interest and understanding. Their induction experience is not just about proving themselves; it is a continuing introduction to a vocational and influential profession within which they are invited and expected to exert influence.

The subtlety of this does not often emerge in reports on teacher retention. For too many young teachers, their image of the profession is so limited that they don't know what they are leaving. They have never seen themselves as a professional or felt that they have made a difference or that they are part of something significant. They have felt passive in a job that expects things from them rather than feeling like someone in charge of their own career.

The typical new teacher will have been clearing hurdles since they were learners in Key Stage 2. At each stage, through GCSEs, A levels, degree and ITE, they will have been supported by diligent professionals responding to the prevailing accountability regime by explaining how best to please the examiner. It is unsurprising, therefore, that the new teacher sees the induction period as leading to yet another hurdle, and so seek support from a mentor to tease out what exactly they have to do to 'pass'. Is it any wonder that when they begin the NPQ programme and realise just how many steps to heaven lie ahead that a proportion decide there are other things to do in life?

Even in the classroom, where many believe their professional contribution will be most profound, they can feel stifled. Typically, their short training programme has versed them in the 'standard lesson' and it is this that awaits them in their working life – four or five times a day for the foreseeable future. They become highly competent at the prescribed approach but quickly recognise its limitations.

Peter Hyman of School 21 was clear about the need for teachers to build up a repertoire of pedagogy, and why it matters: 'It's no wonder that so many teachers leave the profession after four or five years. They thought they were entering an intellectual, layered, complex, collaborative profession and end up realising that they are simply cogs in the exam wheel. The beautiful repertoire of teaching is being replaced by a limited version of direct instruction which makes the profession less appealing.'

Mick recalls:

My first year in teaching (then called the probationary year) was a smashing professional experience. I had been allocated the job through the 'pool' system and received a handwritten letter from the head welcoming me to the school community and inviting me to come in a week before term began to get to know the place.

It was the start of the best of mentored experiences, although the term 'mentoring' had not yet emerged and nobody was given the specific task of supporting me. Dave, the deputy head, shepherded me through the early bits of the routine, joining me for yard duty and coming to help me escort youngsters on the half-mile walk to the swimming pool for the first six weeks. In those days, walking a class alone was normal. I learned how to take a class across busy roads safely, and I am still amazed that teachers today often don't know how to do it. Mitch would come along at lunchtime and help me make the classroom an engaging learning environment. Another Dave would ask me to help him with his planning and took the chance to show me how he did his planning without it taking lots of time.

Staff treated me as one of the team, although they all looked out for me. I took assembly after about five weeks and was invited to work with Stuart in his classroom to explore group work techniques as part of some work he was doing on a course. In the second term, the deputy head suggested I join a group of staff on a weekend conference and I mixed with people at all levels in the local authority. The head teacher suggested I might enjoy a short in-service course being held at the Teachers' Centre, where I met teachers from other schools as well as having a change of scene for one afternoon a week.

Towards the end of the year, I was asked to supervise a mature first-year student who was 15 years older than me. I accompanied a residential visit during half-term in the summer term. Shortly before the end of the year, it was suggested that I should think about doing a degree, and a first step might be to register for night school and do another A level to add to the one I had. I was pointed towards a good psychology course being run by the university.

All year long, people on the staff talked with me about teaching in a highly professional as well as a down-to-earth way. They always gave me the impression that I was a key member of staff and never completed a pro forma to show that I had met an expectation or standard, although they were quick to tell me when I was falling short. I had been welcomed into a team and a profession in which I felt I belonged.

Early career experiences are important and the way we use new talent is vital. Vincent Ashworth commented on the link between early career and quality in the school system:

> I spent time with a really good SCITT in one area of Greater Manchester and the trainees were spectacular. The SCITT leaders had done some really deep thinking about an ITE curriculum. They were really getting underneath it and developing excellent teachers.

> But they were all then being sucked in and employed in their own schools. The teaching school was part of the MAT and they were all being employed directly into the MAT. You saw all these fabulous teachers being recycled into what was an outstanding MAT, but this wasn't benefitting any of the surrounding areas. When you think about other parts of Greater Manchester, there's an issue about how to get really well-trained, effective teachers out into schools where their needs are. Maybe that's the link that needs to be rethought: where ITE fits into the school improvement model.

It was Teach First that first made the link between school improvement and new teachers. Today, 20 years on and after several Teach First graduates have become head teachers or even leaders of MATs, the reach has spread beyond the big cities into disadvantaged areas (and some not so disadvantaged). Even at the level of the website, which talks about potential, vision, impact and equality, Teach First imbues its people with belief. In contrast, the websites of many traditional providers, both

HE and SCITT, are full of perfunctory and managerial or administrative information.

While Teach First graduates were always pushed by government towards the most challenged schools, there has been concern for a long while about NQTs being employed in schools requiring special measures. 'I could never quite balance that one with my own perspective,' said Vincent Ashworth, 'because I think what this school actually needs is that lifeblood being brought into it.' But then he countered: 'You can't just drop the NQT into those schools and think they're going to work miracles. There needs to be that infrastructure. That's one of the reasons Teach First worked. They provide an infrastructure.'

The necessity of including all teachers within the school improvement effort is crucial, although it is a problem that has vexed governments throughout the period of this book. Michael Barber's view is that if we got the systems right and well resourced, then improvement would follow: a well-trained, well-deployed and performance-managed workforce would carry the managerialism forward. This means, however, running the risk of creating identikit teachers – technically competent but without the flair and imagination which are the hallmark of the outstanding practitioner and vital to high-performing schools. While this may be attractive to central government for a range of reasons, we believe it is short term and horizon limiting for schools.

It cannot be the case that the limit of our ambition for our children is that they have effective teachers when they could have transformational teachers. Surely, we want our children to encounter inspiration rather than perspiration. Of course, we want proficient, business-like teachers, but our profession – and the future of our children – deserves more. We want our children's education to be touched by the highest levels of professionalism and expertise.

We think that the success of the London Challenge was due, at least in part, to the fact that schools and their teachers knew they were being encouraged to think for themselves. Furthermore, in the first five years, all London teachers were eligible to apply for Chartered London Teacher status, which required teachers to meet a range of standards and demonstrate professional reflection. Over 30,000 teachers took it up.

Concerns about the overbearing influence of the centre on teaching has fuelled doubt and distrust from the profession towards central government. Starting in 1988 with a prescribed national curriculum and accelerating through the national literacy and numeracy strategies, many now see a profession being told what and how to teach – whether that is three- or four-part lessons in the secondary sector or specified phonics approaches for the early years or 110 pages of advice on how to teach reading.[36] At the same time, inspection focuses on aspects of teachers' 'performance' of lessons. All this has occurred during a period of increasingly tight accountability, strengthening performance management regimes and against a backdrop of political rhetoric that fluctuates between thanks, praise and blame for the profession.

Many now see a profession that generally keeps its head down, does as its told and feeds the machine – the ultimate effects of managerial centralisation. One of our witnesses tried to put her finger on the issue:

> I don't know whether there is a lack of imagination, rooted in an ideological position and just maintaining control and having standards, or whether it's market driven. If everybody has the same diet, then you can open up opportunities for selling packages of materials to schools. There is talk about standardised training materials because apparently the reason teachers are leaving the profession is they're not getting the right training [she laughed], so we'll have some government-approved CPD providers and government-approved ITE providers. In that way, we can manage the message that is being given to every single teacher.

This notion of the central message is important. The suite of NPQs provides a career pathway, but who approves that pathway is moving away from the profession. As it develops, and not only the pathway but each cobble and even the cement in-between is decided centrally, who will check on the foundations? As we all tramp along the career route, the risk of unison, uniformity, conformity and control are significant.

Hywel Roberts, widely acclaimed for his insight, enthusiasm and ability to inspire teachers to better classroom practice, was worried about teachers generally:

> There is almost a sense that too many teachers feel they aren't allowed to be professionally curious or professionally imaginative,

---

36 Department for Education, *The Reading Framework: Teaching the Foundations of Literacy* (July 2021). Available at: https://www.gov.uk/government/publications/the-reading-framework-teaching-the-foundations-of-literacy.

unless it's been the government's idea. So, even just in discussions we have around behaviour, we need a behaviour tsar for that. We don't want teachers to ask too many questions. What we seem to want is 22-year-old graduates who are desperate to change the world, and we then knock that out of them, just as long as they can deliver a set of standard lessons – and, by the way, here is how to deliver the lessons. It's almost de-professionalism.

I think the word we need to use is 'creativity', which has fallen out of fashion. I removed it from my Twitter biography because I didn't want to give the wrong impression, but I think it's going to come back in; some of the head teachers I work with are really creative. We need to reclaim the word and start shouting about it again.

I'd love to see teachers with the ability to bend and be flexible to the needs of youngsters, make the learning they are planning creep up on children, pounce on them and not let them escape. We need thoughtful, agile teachers. That's what I really love to see – so do most children.

How teachers are led in their professional pursuit, as opposed to how schools are led, is a justifiable question. Professionals take responsibility for themselves, as Alison Peacock's piece at the beginning of this chapter stressed. If we have a career pathway akin to a hierarchic control process with the aim of running schools effectively and efficiently, then we will reach a point where continuous improvement stalls.

John West-Burnham, after a career spent urging improvement, suggests that schooling needs to be flipped[37] and rethought by focusing on the way teachers conceptualise their role:

We have a focus on getting a language around learning embedded into the school system. We should really talk meaningfully about the learning process so that children can talk about it for themselves and know that parents understand the learning process. Essentially, the purpose of teaching and the curriculum is to serve the ability and capacity of somebody to learn effectively.

---

37 M. Groves and J. West-Burnham, *Flipping Schools! Why It's Time to Turn Your School and Community Inside Out* (Woodbridge: John Catt Educational, 2020).

We need teachers to develop a considered view of the nature of the learning process, what we understand about it now, and then build on that in terms of intelligence for practice. I suppose in the emerging language it's positive enabling leadership, as opposed to hierarchical controlling managerial leadership, using positive psychology. It's all about relationships, and you can't be an effective leader in education unless you're good at human relationships. The result will be transformative.

Teachers also need to be enabled to develop that considered view and to be encouraged to believe in their own professional purpose.

Mick recalls:

I had called in at an exhibition of children's work that was being staged across a group of schools. Talking to a teacher about the pupils' efforts, we were remarking on the quality and how she had developed as a teacher in the three years that I had known her.

I asked her where she thought she might move next in professional terms. She was perplexed: 'I'm just a classroom teacher. I don't have aspiration to lead or be a head teacher or a manager. I just get on with it in my classroom with my class.'

I talked informally with her about having a broader influence, sharing her undoubted skill with others and taking a higher degree course. 'Just think about it,' I said. 'Someone like you should be taking a lead in this profession.'

Twenty minutes later, I met her head teacher in the throng of people enjoying the children's work. He said, 'Thanks for having a chat with Teresa. She's quietly pleased you think she could have influence. She said nobody's ever talked to her about her future before.' I politely told him that it was the sort of conversation that he should be starting regularly at the right moment with the right teachers.

Teresa has since moved on and is making a big impression on learning and teaching in another school.

How we build into the school system the leadership of professionalism, as opposed to settling for the leadership of the institution called the school, is one of the things we highlight as a crucial step in our next age of hope, ambition and collaborative partnerships. Our view is that the schooling system is crying out for opportunities to engage in deep and purposeful consideration of how teaching can transform pupils' lives. However, not everyone is ready to engage.

The profession needs to be mature enough to recognise that there is a spread of enthusiasm for truly transformative engagement. A proportion of the profession is satisfied with being business-like and efficient, committed to the aims of the school and the best interests of the pupils they teach. This group also know that another segment of the teaching profession is deeply interested, intrigued and committed to the pursuit of further understanding and exploring the nature of teaching and the difference it can make. These are the teachers who become a natural focus for their colleagues, who respect their expertise, admire their skills and wonder at their capacity for depth. It is these transformational professionals that we believe can lift the profession and the pupils we serve to greater educational heights in the broadest sense.

The expert consultant teacher

Aided by the Chartered College of Teaching and the EEF, that is exactly what we think teachers who are in the profession for the long term should do. However, we don't think this route is appropriate for two groups. First, those who contribute competently, as we have set out above, but see their role in a limited context. These are the people who either see their job for the short-term (rather as Teach First originally envisaged their graduates teaching for a few years before changing career instead of staying in the profession and becoming an expert teacher). Second, those who are content to remain in teaching but recognise in other colleagues an expertise or professional drive that presently they do not possess.

These two groups often recognise in other colleagues certain aspects of pedagogy and turn to them for advice about assessment, paired teaching, group work, blended lessons and barriers to particular pupils' learning. These are the transformative expert consultants – similar, we believe, to the intention underlying the early tranches of ASTs: they are in it for the long haul and never believe they have 'arrived'. These teachers are restlessly seeking new ways of unlocking children's minds and, in the process, seeking out the next generation of transformative practition-ers. They will be interested in research but not researchers, they will be considering theory in the light of practice, and they will be collaborating and writing the occasional paper for the Chartered College of Teaching about some aspect of the interplay between curriculum, pedagogy, learn-ing and assessment practices. They will be leaders of pedagogy within a discipline or between disciplines. They will also be leaders at the heart of the four activities that mark out the phase, department and school which demonstrates in its activities the proof of Judith Little's observation that you know a good school because it is a place where teachers engage in talking about teaching; teachers observe each other teach; teachers plan, organise and evaluate their teaching together; and teachers teach each other.[38] In short, they will be expert consultant practitioners in schools, members of the Chartered College of Teaching, informed about the EEF's latest findings and honorary members of the local/regional university's education faculty.

These teachers will have a 'mastery of teaching' qualification, which would be earned through a combination of school-based research into an aspect of pedagogy and by demonstrating their understanding and application of the various aspects of being a consultant expert teacher. This will be separate from the encouragement for all teachers to proceed to a master's degree after they have completed their PGCE. This sugges-tion is not intended to cut across the expanding menu of NPQ courses for middle leaders which, ironically, at last give reality to the recommenda-tions of the James Report of 1972. Expert consultant teachers will have followed the ECF during their first and second year, but they will have been impatient because truly great teaching consists of more than the statements in the framework or other teaching standards. They know that their future lies in the classroom, where they take delight in being, but they will move beyond the 'identikit' model – as one of our witnesses described it – which the various frameworks are in danger of creating.

Essentially, they aspire to be a transformative teacher whom their pupils would recognise in the following blog post by Eddie Playfair:

> 'Teaching to Transgress' is as fresh and powerful in 2021 as when it was first published in 1994. Its messages about teaching as discov-ery, resistance and liberation are as vital today as ever.

---

38   J. W. Little, The Power of Organizational Setting. Paper adapted from final report, *School Success and Staff Development* (Washington, DC: National Institute of Education, 1981), pp. 12–13.

Reading bell hooks is like having a fascinating conversation with your best teacher – with the kind of teacher all teachers should aim to be.

This is the teacher who acknowledges you, knows you, loves you, values your experience and your identity, respects you and understands where you're coming from. The teacher who stands alongside you in your struggle and learns as you learn, who gives of themselves, drawing on their own story and hearing yours. The teacher who helps you connect to something wider; something you don't yet know.

A teacher who doesn't have all the answers but gives you the confidence that they are worth searching for. A teacher who expects a lot from you, shows you how to think critically about yourself, your circumstances and the wider world. A teacher who encourages you to question, disagree, argue and resist. A teacher who values intellectual activity, who knows that learning is full of joy and who wants that for everyone.

A teacher who shows you how the 'other', the 'abstract' and the 'theoretical' are connected to your experience, who helps you understand how power operates and how to expose and confront injustices and oppression, whether systemic or individual.

A teacher whose committed and rigorous pedagogy cannot easily be labelled 'progressive' or 'traditional'. A teacher who sees the classroom as a place of possibility and transformation; safe for everyone without being uncommitted or unchallenging. A space where equality, democracy and solidarity can be practised and built.

We often say we are 'passionate' about our work when we really mean 'interested', 'enthusiastic' or 'committed'. This kind of routine hyperbole puts the meaning of the word at risk, and as 'passion' creeps into job adverts and job descriptions it becomes the new baseline term for simply 'doing a good job'.

Reading bell hooks reminds us what it really means to be a 'passionate' teacher, and in 'Teaching to Transgress' we find the case brilliantly made; not for a generalised enthusiasm, but for a thought-through, focused and specific passion for what teaching can be.

This is the description of the 'passionate' teacher we would all want to know or to be.[39]

Such teachers are rare and precious and will be paid accordingly. As an acknowledged authority, they will know (or know someone who knows) where the latest thinking is on teaching and learning strategies which might help to solve issues presenting themselves in the classroom. They are seen as experts by heads of department and senior school leaders. They will each have a team of junior colleagues ambitious to follow in their footsteps. They liaise with colleagues and are available for professional advice.

We have seen and met such teachers frequently on our travels around schools. It is a matter of chance whether all pupils get to meet such teachers. In the interests of equity, we think that is wrong and it is why we are advocating this change.

There should be a target for an expert consultant teacher: a pupil ratio of 1:120 working with a team of four teachers to spread and increase expertise. We have mentioned the part that we believe a combination of the Chartered College of Teaching and the EEF should play in developing and overseeing the new 'mastery of teaching' idea, which should be provided in universities on a part-time basis.

This would create a challenge for the teaching profession and those within it. Many teachers are modest and self-effacing. There will be a need for those who thirst for professional challenge to step forward and for the profession as a whole to accept the different motivations within our schools. We believe that the creation of the role of expert consultant teacher will lift the status and effectiveness of the profession, galvanise schooling and increase immensely the life chances of the children in our schools.

In this chapter on teaching, we have argued that school leadership has been detached from the essence of the profession. It has become more

---

39 E. Playfair, Reading bell hooks (5 April 2021). Available at: https://eddieplayfair.com/2021/04/05/reading-bell-hooks. He was reviewing the book *Teaching to Transgress* by bell hooks (Abingdon and New York: Routledge, 2014).

managerial and oriented towards centralised agendas. Instead, we are proposing that teachers should be led with an essentially professional emphasis by those with expertise who remain close to teaching staff in their classrooms, laboratories, gymnasia, workshops and studios. In the next chapter, we will explore the role of leadership in school improvement – a world that has changed and continues to change dramatically.

Chapter 7

School improvement and leadership – creating a climate where the weather can improve

Until the last 30 years, little or no attention was paid by schools, local authorities or governments to school improvement. The conventional wisdom was that the individual teacher made *all* the difference. While we agree that the individual teacher makes the *most* difference – indeed, in Chapter 1 we used the Ginott and Fried quotations to underline this point – we don't think it is the whole story.

Apart from factors outside school – such as community, parents, poverty, admission practices and specialist resources, all of which affect the teacher's impact on an individual pupil – how the school is organised and led powerfully affects the likelihood of an individual teacher creating a climate in which the children will optimise their learning. We would argue, therefore, that the head of department/phase and the head of the school itself also affects the likelihood of the teacher having the best chance of making good weather for the children. Beyond the school, other interested parties have their say too – not always to good effect.

But it was not always so. In the UK, at least until Michael Rutter published *Fifteen Thousand Hours* in 1979 – a study of 12 secondary schools in Inner London – the overwhelming message from researchers was that housing and other socio-economic factors were important but that the school itself as an organisation was insignificant.[1] The curriculum and resources to help teachers make the best of it were the meat and drink of LEA advisory work and the many Teachers' Centres dotted across the country, but not school improvement.

---

1   M. Rutter, B. Maughan, P. Mortimore and J. Ouston, *Fifteen Thousand Hours: Secondary Schools and Their Effects on Children* (Cambridge, MA: Harvard University Press, 1979).

Tim recalls:

For me, it all started in earnest at a secondary heads' meeting at the Spread Eagle Hotel in Thame, shortly after Rutter's report was published. I can remember vividly the emotional excitement even among the most gnarled of the group about the impact it could have, as I outlined with scribbled transparencies on an overhead projector the main lessons from the research. At every subsequent meeting, somebody volunteered to describe a feature of their school that they thought was going well and a problem about which they were puzzled as to the best solution. I listened attentively, adding all the time to my growing fascination with why some schools with apparently similar intakes were such different places to be and seemed to have widely different outcomes.

I discovered that the more curious members of the group had begun to visit each other's schools to compare notes. And, of course, they were undertaking the first school self-evaluation schemes, so they were motivated to improve. They were also armed with our local authority published results when comparing five or more percentage scores at higher grades in GCE (A–C)/CSE 1 and GCE/CSE and were using the advisers' analysis of schools by performance in different subjects.

I arranged personal visits to different schools to do what we called 'pupil pursuits', which involved spending the day with a couple of pupils as they moved from lesson to lesson, in order to get a feel for what it was like for the pupils in the school. These occasions were highly illuminating in getting a snapshot impression of pupils' views on a whole range of issues in and out of school. Of course, I was careful to treat what I heard with complete discretion and was meticulous in following up with handwritten notes of thanks to every teacher whose lessons I had been in. I gave a purely descriptive account to the head, picking out good points of the day. I learned a great deal and puzzled over how to share it in a non-threatening way.[2]

---

2   Eventually, Oxfordshire published in 1987 – almost a decade before national attention was given to the mechanics of how external agencies could influence school improvement – a paper which we called 'Effective Schools', which divided types of hypothetical schools, soccer-style, into four divisions, with the characteristics of each described in provocative detail. It was the first and only LEA in that decade to start a conversation about school improvement.

There was a different challenge in the primary sector, where there was a long and unusual tradition in Oxfordshire of advisers and advisory teachers working alongside head teachers and their staff and focusing on pedagogy across the whole school without labelling the curriculum with subject definitions. Many primary heads were therefore used to sharing ideas and welcomed the publication of Peter Mortimore's account of research into the subtleties of what went into making a successful primary school in 1988.[3]

Mick recalls:

When I was appointed to my first headship, the senior adviser for the local authority spent time with me telling me why the school had to do better by its pupils. He promised me support from the local authority as far as resources would allow, although there were many limits because this was the era of the Thatcher government's restraint.

He also put me in contact with other heads focused on the challenge of improving their schools. Compared with nowadays the resource was minimal, but his regular visits and appreciative enquiry approach (although it was not called that then) meant that momentum was built and maintained. I always thought that school improvement was on the agenda and it was clear to me as a head that our school should do better.

The conversations were rigorous and challenging. I trusted the evidence of an insightful, experienced colleague as well as the thoughtful and focused advice that emerged.

Our recollections show how one LEA was groping towards, while another was seeing the simmering beginnings, of what we called a whole-school effect on children's learning. It was the start of something very different, which is now labelled school improvement and is seen as one of the purposes of those influencing schools from the outside – a defining rationale of the schooling system, whether through the MAT, local authority, RSC

---

3   P. Mortimore, P. Sammons, L. Stoll, D. Lewis and R. Ecob, *School Matters: The Junior Years* (Somerset: Open Books, 1988).

or the more elusive self-improving schooling system. The metrics of accountability have influenced how we measure schools' relative success in terms of improvement; therefore, the many Ofsted frameworks, together with published data on exams, test scores and attendance, have tended to dominate how we have evaluated school success. It will be clear from Chapter 1 that we think this is far too limiting.

Taking the story forward, we turn again to another cameo from our personal experiences.

Tim recalls:

I left Oxfordshire at the end of 1988 and joined Keele University, where I founded the Centre for Successful Schools. When not acting as tutor to PGCE, MA and PhD students and trying to run a department of very awkward but delightful academics, I put together a group of part-time early-retired school leaders (we had no grant money). We visited secondary and primary schools in Staffordshire, Shropshire, Hampshire, and Hereford and Worcester, and speculated about processes and practices that might reveal a more fine-grained understanding of what heads and their staff were doing which contributed to, or detracted from, schools being 'successful'. As a group we studied avidly the available literature and research. I had already come across the Canadian Michael Fullan, who was to have very significant influence on English thinking about school improvement,[4] and the Americans Roland Barth and Art Powell,[5] both of whom had spent time in Oxfordshire's schools when on sabbaticals at the university.

Four years later, I was lucky enough to become education officer in Birmingham and started an unrelenting push to improve all the city's schools. I was extremely fortunate to work with a selfless team who lived to work rather than worked to live, and for a while we were reasonably good at holding up a mirror to really good practice in schools and speculating about what would come next. The phrase 'improving

---

4   Michael Fullan is a good friend to us both and many will know his excellent writings. His 1991 book with Andy Hargreaves, *What's Worth Fighting For? Working Together For Your School* (New York: Teachers College Press) became an essential text for many people. His website contains volumes of wisdom that continue to influence thinking globally: https://michaelfullan.ca.

5   See R. Barth, *Run School Run* (Cambridge, MA: Harvard University Press, 1980); and A. Powell, E. Farrar and D. Cohen, *The Shopping Mall High School: Winners and Losers in the Educational Marketplace* (Boston, MA: Houghton Mifflin, 1985).

on previous best' became a mantra and we built a culture on the back of it.

All primary heads were invited to attend a day of workshops led by the education officer and the advisers at the Botanical Gardens, which ended with a good dinner. They attended in 11 groups of 30-plus, chosen by the length of time they had been in post. The agenda for the workshops involved extended discussion and debate about the subtleties of seven processes of school improvement. That discussion and debate needed to be as extensive as possible and a prompt for head teachers involved in career-long intrigue about school improvement.

The seven processes of school improvement will be recognised by most school leaders today as their relentless quest:

1   Leading creatively at all levels within the school.

2   Managing effectively (and sometimes creatively) at all levels within the school but especially at the whole-school level.

3   Creating an environment fit for learning – aurally, visually and behaviourally.

4   Teaching, learning and assessing appropriately and with ever-growing confidence.

5   Reviewing regularly with the help of outsiders.

6   Developing all staff within a coaching environment (CPD).

7   Involving parents and the community.

Clearly, each of these processes required elaboration and represented our 'shared map' of how to hold on to what schools get up to every day in one way or another. It wasn't that we knew everything that would have the most impact in every different context, but with a common language and map we could learn more. That was to become the work of the years ahead. It all occurred as Ofsted was being formed and school results were being published for the first time. Nationally, it was easy to see that improving school performance was going to take centre stage. If we weren't driven morally – and we were – we were going to be helped by the political weather.

In pressing for improvement against previous best, our progress was helped by five key interventions or emphases.

First, the city's education department had an extraordinarily talented statistician who was well ahead of his time in how he could cut the data: it was possible, therefore, to compare pupil and school performance by ethnicity, gender and entitlement to free school meals (FSM). Schools were shown in one of four quadrants on a graph with the horizontal axis representing 'points per pupil' and the vertical axis 'rate of improvement'. This became known as the 'family of schools database' because schools were grouped according to the socio-economic profile of their intake. This meant they could see which quadrant they were in among either (a) a 'low points per pupil and low rate of improvement' group, (b) a 'low points per pupil but high rate of improvement' group, (c) a 'high points per pupil and high rate of improvement' group or (d) a 'high points per pupil but low rate of improvement' group. Schools might be in one group overall but in different quadrants for maths, English and science in primary, as well as other subjects for secondary schools.

The aim of the database was to enable inter-school visits in locations that were not in competition in order to learn from each other. This would become a much stronger feature of the London and Greater Manchester Challenges where, because there were many more schools in the database, many more could be identified that might be in a particular quadrant overall but were not in that quadrant for all their outcomes.

The second key development was for schools to organise reciprocal visits with groups of schools from other local authorities which would visit to find out what was happening in Birmingham, while our schools learned from those in other cities.

The third development was for members of the advisory team to write anonymised stories of good practice seen and observed in schools within Birmingham in the termly magazine and to think aloud, as it were, about what would happen next.[6]

---

6   The magazine was produced by the LEA and was sent to schools where it was widely read; it contained updates on all manner of events and resources available to schools.

The fourth factor was to be clear about what values lay behind our approach to school improvement. These were often summarised as:

- Striving for success for all rather than for the many.[7]

- Believing that assessment should be ipsative, not normative.

- Regarding intelligence not as general, inherited and predictable but as multifaceted and without limits.

- Schools should be inclusive rather than exclusive places.

- Education is a lifelong, not a once-and-for-all, activity.

It is perhaps the fifth way in which Birmingham interpreted school improvement that made it acceptable to schools. The Wragg report carried out for the city council in the summer of 1993 had introduced the idea that targets for *outcomes* should be introduced (as well as targets for *input* – represented in terms of extra resources, and targets for *experiences* for children in and out of school).[8] This concept owed much to the evidence Ted Wragg had discussed with teaching union representatives, but unlike the national introduction of targets five years later, these were bottom-up rather than top-down. There is a crucial difference.

The setting of outcome targets was based on the good pedagogical practice of using the words *estimate* (to mean 'what pupils like you have achieved in the past'), *prediction* (to mean 'what, knowing you as a pupil, I would predict you will achieve by the end of your time with us – that is, if you carry on as you are with the same habits') and *target* (to mean 'after our conversation today, what do you really want to achieve?'). The outcome of these discussions would be a school-based prediction of two sets of targets: what could we achieve with a fair wind at our backs, and what might do if the wind is against us? In terms of school improvement, we would make far more progress if this were the way we all used the words estimate, prediction and target.

What we were aiming for – and is at the heart of school improvement – was a *change in culture*. But the culture needed to release energy for

---

7   Tony Blair coined the phrase 'the many, not the few': Tony Blair's Speech [at the Labour Party Conference], *The Guardian* (2 October 2001). Available at: https://www.theguardian.com/politics/2001/oct/02/labourconference.labour6. A schooling system needs to try to bring the taste of success to all pupils.

8   Birmingham Education Commission, *Aiming High* [First Wragg Report] (Birmingham: Education Department, 1993).

improvement, rather than provoke energy-consuming demands and resistance. In Birmingham, Manchester and London, schools needed support and well-judged challenge; the external weather and weather forecast needed to fill people with hope rather than gloom. Real hope for schools and teachers only trumps misty optimism if the climate in which they work is full of speculative 'what if?' and 'how about?' questions, rather than top-down directives and prescription.

Mick recalls:

One of the things I was trying to help develop in Manchester was a culture of 'we're all in it together', and we came up with the idea that advisory staff from the local authority could offer tangible help in schools.

Advisers formed into teams (which we called 'crews'), supplemented by secretarial and other staff from the local authority who had DBS status. Each crew would work in a school for a day, with advisers teaching and supported by admin staff acting as teaching assistants. Each crew was made available to teach a phase, a whole primary school or a department in a secondary school for a day. The stipulation was that the crew could teach its own thing on their days, appropriate to the maturity of pupils but possibly not on the school's plan.

This happened only on the first Monday of each month and schools could bid for a 'Manchester Monday', with allocation depending on demand. The school staff were also able to visit other schools around the city or further afield, sometimes for the morning, and then return to share their observations and perceptions in a session facilitated by another adviser for the rest of the day. The take-up was strong, school staff benefitted, pupils received some very well-prepared and well-staffed teaching sessions, admin staff from 'the office' saw the impact of their work first-hand and the credibility of advisers rose. It supported the feeling of school improvement as a shared enterprise rather than a top-down exercise.

As an aside, after a few months the *TES* got in touch to write a piece about the advisers working in schools. They asked why it was called 'Manchester Mondays', which I thought obvious, but explained that it was alliteration – for example, if we were in Folkestone it would probably be Fridays or in Tottenham in would be Tuesdays. On publication, I got messages from head teachers cruelly suggesting that their experience of school advisers in classrooms was 'Never in Nottingham' or 'Seldom in Sunderland'.

The point here is that school improvement must be a shared responsibility and, while teachers make the most significant direct impact on pupils, a collegiate outlook within and beyond the school is vital for encouraging them to be the best they can be. If teachers are so important among school staff, how can they best be supported?[9] It requires leaders to show that they act and are guided by knowing that teachers need the following:

- *Permitting circumstances*, which means working in a place where they are encouraged to try things out, but when things go wrong or if they take a calculated risk and make the occasional mistake, their leader will take the blame in public.

- *New experiences*, which means working in a school where CPD is an entitlement, where the school is in a partnership in which inter-school visits are part of the warp and weft of their professional fabric, and where intellectual curiosity and growth are part of the school's DNA.

- *Responsibilities*, which means having the chance to lead a team as well as being a key support member of one.

- *Respect and recognition*, which means, like anybody else – and perhaps more so than anybody else, since their time is often taken up in the finely judged and sometimes exhausting task of trying to ensure their pupils are motivated to make best of their opportunities in the classroom, on residential trips and during extracurricular activities – teachers appreciate the occasional acts of unexpected thoughtfulness from school leaders, especially when their efforts are generously given credit.

A culture propitious for school improvement succeeds if the local external environment is seen to add something to their own efforts. Attracting

---

9   Throughout this passage, we trust that readers will be critical but understanding of our emphasis on teachers at the cost of appearing to ignore the many other staff vital to a school's success. Nobody needs to be reminded of the crucial roles played by other support staff. Everything we have written here applies to them too.

the best teachers to work in schools in their area used to be one of the main tasks of local authorities. It was certainly one of the purposes of the London Challenge, which focused on housing, pay and professional development to make London *the* place to be in teaching. Now that task falls to smaller units like MATs, which are too small to make a huge difference other than to the tiny fraction of schools for which they are responsible. Teaching school hubs are also responsible for that herculean task but with scant resources and in groups so small that they find it difficult to bring within their grasp those brilliant practitioners just beyond their reach.

We need to explore the potential of curriculum design, the power of pedagogy, the approach to learning that ignites pupils' interests and what we mean by terms such as success and excellence. Our chapter on curriculum, pedagogy and assessment (Chapter 5) linked with the one on the pressures that build for some pupils (Chapter 10) might prove to be the next arenas for leadership and further school improvement. As we explain in Chapter 12 on governance and finance, we believe that some sort of regional approach to both school improvement and the recruitment and retention of teachers needs to be developed in order to make the best of efforts by MATs, local authorities, individual academies and schools.

We turn now to a consideration at greater length of how the approach to school leadership has changed over the years, before returning at the end of the chapter to explore how school improvement should be taken forward now.

Leadership in schools: how it is today

Paradoxically, while leadership in schools is stronger than it has ever been, many of those leading schools feel (and are) far less secure than in the past. Lots of leaders are confident educationalists, assertive in applying their beliefs to their school setting, offering a picture of the unfolding potential of their school. They bring on their colleagues as professionals, build a community commitment, and make sure that the young people in their care have the best possible life chances. Conversely, other school leaders are tentative, lacking in inner confidence and waiting to be directed.

As we have seen, there is much talk about school-led and self-improving school systems through what might be called 'transformational leadership', yet the reality for many individuals is very different. Leaders in schools are expected to deliver on a template laid down centrally, sometimes interpreted and modified locally, which inclines them towards 'transactional leadership'. They experience a high-stakes national accountability regime which carries severe institutional and personal penalties for falling below expectation. The layers of scrutiny have increased and the managerial and regulatory aspects of leadership are so heavy and so pervasive that they overwhelm those who wish to be the sort of leaders who encourage staff to try out something new (when asked) and who speculate aloud about what collectively the school will achieve next – in short, those who exercise the flair and professional judgement that is the true currency of successful school leaders.

Leaders at every level, in schools and beyond, often lack the autonomy to lead for the want of confident delegation. They spend time looking over their shoulder and feeding the machine of accountability, rather than looking to the horizon and planning where they can travel next. All this personal scrutiny and institutional accountability leads to trails of decision-making, modes of ensuring consistency, records of supervision, scrutiny and analysis, which too often become counterproductive or an end in themselves. Debra Kidd writes about the impact of these outlooks on curriculum and pedagogy in schools where leadership ensures highly developed (or extreme) systems of curriculum planning and the teacher's duty is to:

> pass on this vision as accurately as possible – uninterrupted and unsullied. We see this in some schools in the form of scripted lessons which are written by managers and delivered by technician teachers, often unqualified or in training. The idea is that the lesson, designed by an expert, can be reliably passed through a conduit because the content is reliable and the reaction of the recipient predictable. ...

> The possibility that other factors might influence the design through-line is disruptive to the ideology, and therefore all distractions and outliers must be eliminated. Draw the blinds down if it snows! Remove dissenters from the classroom! Provide not only a script but a cross on the floor for the teacher to stand on to

ensure they don't deviate from the plan! It's a garden of artificial, plastic plants.

It's not clear where the motivation for all this comes from ... an attractive business proposition: sell an off-the-shelf curriculum model with assurances that 'it will work' ... a seductive way to reduce workload and effort around planning ... For some fiscally squeezed senior leaders the prospect of being able to ensure 'quality' ... But it's an illusion. Children are not predictable and neither are the communities in which they live.[10]

In the conversations we have had in preparation for this book, we have heard stories of school systems that are sometimes funny but often have an element of pathos or sympathy for the teachers, leaders, parents and children sucked into the bizarre management behaviour. For example, we heard about a secondary teacher under pressure to give detentions to meet his 'quota', so that all teachers in the school would be consistent in terms of behaviour expectations. We also received this note from one of the people we interviewed, showing how the school's policy on pupils' presentation of work was affecting their perceptions of ability:

In my son's first maths homework at secondary he was given 20 equations to solve; he got them all right and he received 20 ticks. At the bottom of the page it read, 16/20. My son couldn't care less, but my wife was incensed that his maths teacher could not add up and instructed Carl to ask his teacher to correct the error. On presenting the teacher with the issue, this little lad – in his first week telling the head of maths that she couldn't add up – was told that four marks had been removed because he'd put the date of the lesson on the left- rather than the right-hand side of the page and he'd underlined the title of the work and not used block letters. This seemed odd to Carl, as Mr Jones, head of history, had already covered the layout of classwork and it now seemed it was not the universally accepted approach. (I remember Carl commenting: 'Don't these people speak to one another?')

When Carl reported this to his mum that evening, violence was threatened. So, when the first parents' evening came about later that term, Carl asked that only I attend to avoid police action. When I raised this as instructed, the head of maths apologised for

---

10 Kidd, *A Curriculum of Hope*, p. 19.

not making her marking scheme open to her pupils, but quickly added that there was something else I needed to know about the school marking policy. The system stipulated that each pupil must be given a grade at the end of each week. As such, in a class of 30, she could award three A's, four B's, eight C's, eight D's, four E's and three F's. Recognise the bell curve? *But*, what she was also keen to explain was that Carl was part of a group of eight outstanding mathematicians who continually deserved the grade A. As the system didn't allow for the awarding of eight A's, she had come up with a rota system. So, she explained, we should not worry if Carl came home with a B now and again – it was simply his turn to receive a B.

This example shows managerialism in the raw: the leadership keen to ensure consistency, data needing to match norms and children's efforts having to conform to predictions. These are instances of tails wagging dogs and the denial of teacher professionalism.

What struck us from our conversations is that the outlook of many school leaders has been shaped by the very recent past. The contextual influences from the time when they started their careers and the time when they first led schools has had a powerful impact on their approach and values. We talked with serving head teachers whose earliest memories of headship went back to 1995. Most head teachers we spoke to began their teaching career in the period following Blunkett's era of transformation in 1997, and some have known headship or even teaching only since Michael Gove's tenure as secretary of state.

Our schools are led by head teachers from the era of the first national curriculum (a few), the national strategies (a few), Every Child Matters (about a quarter) or Gove's new curriculum (more than half). It is almost geological. There are heads from the performance management era, the safeguarding era, the data era or the three-part lesson era. Some heads fit different Ofsted frameworks, being from the value-added era, the progress era or the recent intent era. Some heads adjust to the requirements of the various periods and hold on to some basic principles while also adapting to the pressure; others carry forward and adapt their proven formula for success to meet changing expectations; a third group folds their first image of successful schooling into the bedrock of their school's beliefs.

Yet, as Andreas Schleicher reminded us: 'In high performing systems, school leaders are really investing themselves in pedagogical leadership, as opposed to just administrative leadership. I do think school leaders play a very important role in framing that organisation in the school. You get school leaders who are great at enhancing collaboration, school leaders who are great in developing the careers of their staff – giving people aspirations.'

The changing expectations of headship

The role of the school leader has evolved and continues to do so. Until the watershed moment of Callaghan's Ruskin College speech in 1976, the role of the head teacher had remained stable for a long while. The head was largely a first among equals, the in-school organiser and the point of contact within the school for the LEA (often referred to as 'the office'). The job was to represent the staff and make sure they were able to do their jobs. Decisions about how to run the school were largely taken by the office (LEA), which dealt with finance, premises, the supply of materials (from exercise books to toilet rolls), approved staffing numbers and changes, including appointments and redeployment from one school to another.

In primary schools, the head was often a class teacher; deputy heads had only been instituted in 1961. In many secondary schools, the head was often seen as the person who dealt out the ultimate disciplinary sanctions and met with awkward parents and other visitors, as well as responding to the local authority. Decision-making was mostly limited to a very flat structure. Head teachers could adjudicate while some ran fiefdoms. They were also faced with vital decisions about such things as whether women teachers should be allowed to wear trousers to work!

Heads of department in secondary schools managed resources for their team of teachers and were mainly autonomous and left to their own devices unless there was some untoward incident. On behalf of the head teacher, one deputy would manage the timetable and curriculum and another would look at pastoral issues, which usually meant aspects of behaviour and what form tutors and heads of year did (this was initially confined to large comprehensive schools[11]). Both deputies used the head teacher as the last resort.

The role of local community figurehead was very much part of the job of the head teacher, particularly in more rural areas. The involvement of parents in schooling had seen some of the new school buildings of the 1960s and 1970s designed with a community focus in mind. This period also saw the growth of parent–teacher associations (PTAs) which raised money to provide additional facilities. Local authorities had begun to appoint advisers to support schools during the early 1960s, and 10 years later, most authorities had an accurate picture of their most effective and least effective schools. This helped them to employ the most appropriate heads in primary schools and support them with resources, but they were sometimes frustrated in their succession plans for promising deputies by the regulations concerning the role of governors (then called local managers) in appointments. They often appointed against the advice from the LEA! Some heads were highly innovative and built schools that pushed at the boundaries of practice, while others stood still and watched from the sidelines, dubbing the new approaches as 'progressive', while they in turn were chided for being 'traditional' in their outlook.

What the Ruskin College speech of 1976 did was to expose the chasms between these two approaches in primary schools, which had the effect of continuing to unsettle much of the previous public trust in schooling. Individual schools that lost the plot were used to point out the excesses of a system at risk of losing its way. William Tyndale Junior School was held up as an example of the consequences of progressivism, with the findings of a subsequent enquiry (the Auld Report) making national headlines. Primary schooling that had previously been largely trusted, or at least left alone, became a focus for public debate. An episode of *Panorama* (a significant weekly event at the time) brought to the small screen images of traditional and progressive primary schools in considering research by Professor Neville Bennett of the University of Lancaster which linked teaching styles with pupil progress.[12] Heads who had overseen the shedding of some traditional approaches in their schools, either by persuasion or benignly watching as their staff responded to the urgings of various

11   The movement to comprehensive schools in the 1970s meant the merger of grammars with secondary modern schools, which usually led to the staff of the former getting the heads of department (curriculum) jobs and the latter the heads of year (pastoral) ones.
12   N. Bennett, *Teaching Styles and Pupil Progress* (London: Open Books, 1976).

national reports, suddenly had to defend their schools and what went on inside them to a wider public. The leadership role was changing.

For the next few years, schools were subject to gradually increased scrutiny and, by implication, so were heads. Mark Carlisle and Keith Joseph implemented the recommendations of the Taylor Report, and a governing body was established for each school with local community representation. Carlisle also approved proposals for local authorities to begin the appraisal of head teachers which, although it would be seen as very tame today, was viewed as intrusive by unions and the beginning of a move towards line management.

Interest in the leadership role was growing and the DfE provided resources for local authorities to develop extended management courses for primary and secondary sectors in partnership with local teacher training colleges. The 30-day programmes were spread over a school year, and LEAs tried to select appropriate people, reaching perhaps 5% of their schools annually.

These developments were overtaken by the Education Reform Act 1988. The tentative shadow boxing of the previous decade was dealt a knock-out blow as Kenneth Baker brought forward a national curriculum (there was now no need for the head to bother about that; it was a given) and LFM and placed new responsibilities on schools and heads. Suddenly, schools were to be in charge of their own budgets, including the management of staffing and premises. Over the next few years, as the national curriculum was introduced, along with allied testing and GCSEs, the use of computers to analyse data began to reveal the differences between schools' performance in measurable pupil outcomes rather than the descriptive ways of the past.

In the space of two or three years, the role of the head teacher moved from being the representative of staff and liaising with the local authority to being held accountable for the quality of what the school provided and achieved. The job of the head was changing to that of a manager.

Local authorities supported nervous head teachers with finance and personnel issues, with teams leading training to demonstrate how systems previously used in the LEA could be continued in individual schools. Ironically, the very practices that had caused concern about the capabilities of local authorities were now taught to individual schools. Formulae were also offered to schools to show them how much money should be spent on staff and premises; in practice, there was little left over for schools to allocate.

It was at this point that the system missed a chance to truly address the opportunity offered by the new national curriculum. Instead of considering the best ways to teach the new requirements, it was assumed that they would be provided using the prevailing model. Kenneth Baker's insistence that teachers would be required to work 1,265 hours per year of directed time meant that, for the first time, heads had to decide how their teachers would work rather than make the most of what time their teachers were prepared to offer. For some heads this was profoundly uncomfortable and many sought to sidestep the issue or took the chance to retire early with added benefits.

The arrival of Ofsted inspection pushed headship to a new level. One of the four areas of the inspection framework related to the quality of leadership.[13] The term itself was relatively new in schools: heads were supposed to be leading their schools, along with governors, but the framework focused on the efficiency of their financial management and its influence on the quality of the teaching. It was the gradual ratcheting up of the intensity of inspection that brought the responsibility of heads for the performance of staff into focus. They were now responsible for a growing definition of the quality of their school, which seems obvious but may not have been fully appreciated previously. John Major's Citizen's Charter to improve public services was beginning to bite: Ofsted was shedding a light on school effectiveness and heads were representatives of the system's effectiveness.

During the 10 years following Baker's seismic proposals, many schools felt under attack and struggled to cope. They did not universally welcome LFM, and as the expectations of the curriculum and public test results grew, along with their perception of Ofsted as an ogre, so disenchantment with local authorities began to grow too. Schools and heads often felt under pressure but local authorities seemed unable to exert enough influence to support them. There were notable exceptions, of course, but most were gradually turning into organisers of DfE-driven programmes.

These centrally provided programmes were yet another twist for school leaders. Gillian Shephard had required the TTA to develop the first

---

13   The first Ofsted common inspection framework was published in a ring binder and 'chalked' on the front cover was the slogan 'Improvement Through Inspection'.

national professional standards for head teachers (NPQH), which were adopted in 1998. The notion that head teachers should be qualified before taking on the role was significant; coupled with the Headteacher Leadership and Management Programme (HeadLAMP), the development of a coherent pathway into leadership had begun. Gillian Shephard also felt that something had to be done about ineffective schools. In discussing support for head teacher development, she was quick to remind us: 'I was certainly the first secretary of state to send what others called "hit squads" of school inspectors into failing schools, and as a result, a number were closed and relaunched, to the great benefit of their pupils.'

From time to the time, while the government tried to offer a structured approach to leadership development, cases of school breakdown came to fore in the media. In Calderdale, the Ridings School hit the national headlines in 1996 as teachers refused to teach some groups due to unacceptable behaviour.[14] The school was closed for a short while and reopened with a new head teacher and a volley of exclusions. The notion of head teachers being parachuted into difficult school situations grew and, with it, the acceptance that some schools were in a dire state and failing their pupils significantly.

Leadership carried the expectation of success for pupils, which ought to be obvious but until that time had been assumed and often excused when it wasn't achieved. When Labour was elected and brought forward the *Excellence in Schools* White Paper in 1997, there were two significant ways in which heads were being encouraged to lead as well as manage. First, Blunkett proposed 'fair funding', where a head teachers' forum would determine with the local authority the proportion of the budget to be spent on services to schools. This potentially put the notion of the authority with the schools and especially those heads who wished to be influential. Second, he proposed a programme, to be driven by Estelle Morris, which would aim to professionalise teaching. This included provision for ASTs who would influence practice and exercise leadership from the classroom. Morris told us: 'We wanted school transformation. Heads were key and we got further in the primary sector where leadership grabbed the agenda. We set about transforming secondary education and made good progress … Among other things, we were relying on the

---

14 The Ridings crisis provoked a stormy debate in Parliament about behaviour in schools generally, as well as the particular situation in Calderdale: Hansard HC Deb col. 285 col. 38 (11 November 1996). Available at: https://publications.parliament.uk/pa/cm199697/cmhansrd/vo961111/debindx/61111-x.htm. The school was 'turned around' but closed in 2009.

AST programme to work. Not everyone wants to move into a management role and we thought ASTs could affect change.'

However, before this worthwhile development and the establishment of the NCSL could get underway, there was a brief period of naming and shaming 'failing' schools, for which we think there should be zero tolerance.

A new phenomenon emerged during these years. As some schools rose from the ashes of a disastrous Ofsted inspection or a history of dreadful results, the spotlight naturally fell on the head teacher. Heads with the Midas touch became hot property and were very quickly dubbed 'super heads' or 'hero heads', often appearing in the media and sometimes generating their own publicity. Local authorities desperate to escape the clutches of Ofsted would broker arrangements, coaxing sought-after individuals to trouble spots. Of course, that involved pay increases, made possible by the Education Act 2002, and began the process of disrupting the pay and conditions framework for teachers.

The 'turnaround' heads were often idiosyncratic and passed across the weather map of a school briefly like an occluded front, often causing stormy turbulence and a trail of havoc and sometimes without any discernible improvement at all. They were mostly what Alex Hill and colleagues would later describe as 'surgeon' heads, although some of them prided themselves in not needing an anaesthetist.[15] The researchers compared five types of secondary school leadership with a focus on good improvement over time and costs across 163 settings. The types suggested the management style: *surgeons* cut things out in order to heal, *soldiers* improved efficiency by attacking weakness and *accountants* remodelled budgets in order to grow. These three types of leader would make a dramatic impression over a short period of time, but their impact would often subside after the first wave and, in many cases, decline. On the other hand, *architects*, who carefully charted an agreed course and built for the long term, and *philosophers*, who actively engaged people in considering many dimensions of development and improvement, both saw slower but greater and more sustained improvement.

---

15 A. Hill, L. Mellon, B. Laker and J. Goddard, The One Type of Leader Who Can Turn Around a Failing School, *Harvard Business Review* (20 October 2016). Available at: https://hbr.org/2016/10/the-one-type-of-leader-who-can-turn-around-a-failing-school.

In terms of recognition, the surgeons were by far the highest paid – on average twice as much as the lowest type in terms of pay, the architects. In the study, all of the knighthoods and damehoods were bestowed on the surgeons, although none of these accepted the role of national leader of education (NLE), whereas the philosophers accounted for 80% of the 59 NLEs among the sample.

The leadership styles show the range of ways in which schools were – and perhaps still are – led and what their leaders thought about the purpose of schooling: a surgeon dealing with a prone subject, a soldier going into battle and trying to beat competitors, an accountant dealing with the back office, an architect building for the future or a philosopher engaging people with ideas. The ideal leader would ensure that all five elements were addressed, but that is hardly likely without training – and that is what the NCSL provided. The question is whether what we do now, after its closure, is sufficient for the longer term.

The National College: school leadership takes centre stage

One of the key developments in the Labour government's school improvement agenda was the establishment of the NCSL in Nottingham in 2000. After an uncertain beginning, Steve Munby took over in 2005 and exercised the sort of leadership that would galvanise school leaders.

The investment by government in leadership development was significant. When Gillian Shephard instigated the first NPQH programme in 1994, she was taking a step that the profession had not taken for itself. Until then, the development of head teachers had been an implicit task of serving head teachers and, as such, one that was of variable quality. Whether the serving deputy had learned well or badly at the knee of an effective or ineffective head teacher was a lottery, and only became clear later when the die had been cast.

David Blunkett, and particularly Estelle Morris, picked up the mantle of leadership development laid down by Gillian Shephard. Morris told us: 'We believed that we had to try to take head teachers with us on our standards agenda, while at the same time trying to help them see school leadership in a more dynamic way; one where they were responsible and accountable for the life chances of their children. But many were not going to do that without good training.'

Munby echoed this: 'The most important thing you can do is develop the next generation of school leadership. If you only work with those already leading schools, you will get a mixed response, but over a 10-year period working with those who wish to step up into headship, you can make a massive, massive difference.'

Morris matched intent with action and oversaw the establishment of the NCSL: 'For me, the NCSL was a sign of worth. I believed that it would show school leaders that they were valued and their job had real prestige.' She took a personal interest in its work well after leaving office.

The building in Nottingham was the headquarters and hosted leadership gatherings, but it was also the focal point for the drive to develop a coherent programme of leadership development that extended from headship through the whole profession. After a slow start, the NCSL – as a concept as well as an entity – began to have significant influence on the profession, particularly under the guidance of Munby as CEO.

As Munby explained to us: 'We needed to get out there and build a sense of "collective". It is doable in England, in spite of its size. Good developments that work have usually developed because people have used the opportunity to shape them. They have been genuinely engaged, not just consulted and asked to respond to something that was going to happen anyway.'

Many of our head teacher witnesses, some now CEOs of MATs, talked of the influence of the NCSL. One told us: 'I changed my thinking a lot as a result of being involved with the leadership college programmes. I built a better theoretical base to put alongside my pragmatic self and I became a better leader because of it.' Rachel Tomlinson remarked: 'The NPQH was the best of times. I learned so much. It lifted my thinking, gave me experience and prepared me for the job of making a difference.'

Munby was clear about its purpose:

> I wanted our team to ensure that all school leaders were valued. Wherever they were from, whatever their school, however successful it was supposed to be, we were there to help them develop and improve their school. We were serious about engagement. I remember we used to hold big conferences where we invited

people to type their comments on a tablet at their table and these used to appear on a big screen behind us. We were being transparent. At the end, they had to vote for how confident they were about the direction of travel and the results were shown in a graph on the screen for all to see. Over time, I think we built genuine belief.

The defining characteristic of the NCSL's influence on schools and the schooling system was to bring research-based non-prescriptive advice to existing and prospective school leaders. Possibilities of style were explored: leadership was seen as starting with the teacher and learning assistant in the classroom, extending to posts of responsibility and, ultimately, to the head teacher. If not described as democratic, then the preferred style was certainly participative. Munby himself was a living example in that he went to enormous lengths to consult widely and thoroughly on strategic decisions, and he influenced the schooling system with his personal concern and evident obligation towards others.

The Labour government invested heavily both in terms of personal commitment and funding. While successive secretaries of state challenged schools – and, by implication, the leadership of head teachers – they also continued to support the development of leaders, particularly those moving towards headship. By 2010, according to Munby, the investment in school leadership development was £140 million per year, about £5,000 per school per year or about £25 per school per day.

Living (or surviving) off the fat: the impact of austerity on school leadership development

According to our sources, at the time of writing, in 2021, the investment in school leadership development is £10 million per year, about £400 per school per year and £2 per school per day. The contrast is telling and shows just how investment in future school leaders has fallen away. But the price has yet to be paid, as the investment during what can be seen as the years of plenty has carried us through the decade of austerity.

Headship qualifications have continued under a range of accredited providers, but many argue that gaining a qualification has now become even more vital than acquiring leadership experience (despite the fact that it is no longer a mandatory requirement). As an example we were told of a recent programme: 'It felt a like bit like jumping through the right hoops, so the organisers would be able to show we had ticked all the boxes.' (Which sounds a bit like what some 16-year-olds say about GCSEs.)

In the main, the real development of future leaders has fallen to partnerships of schools – MATs especially – who enlist trusted providers operating on a national or regional scale, such as the Ambition Partnership or Future Leaders schemes. What has emerged in terms of leadership development over the last 10 years, and the arrival of MATs on the scene, is the concept of 'growing your own' leadership. Michael Gove used the assertion, developed under Labour, that 'head teachers know best' to dispense with the NCSL in 2015, suggesting that in future the development of head teachers and other leadership expertise would lie with providers of NPQH training and teaching school hubs.[16]

His notion was simple and logical: assemble the head teachers of the best schools and ask them to lead education in England. Hence, the NLE became the new role with the potential to make a difference on a wider scale. At the same time, for those who liked status, being listed as an NLE was the cream on the top of outstanding school recognition from Ofsted. As Gove gathered the initial group together and referred to them as 'heroes' who were to 'go out and change the lives of children across the nation', he signalled a step on from SIPs and federations, which were introduced during the Blunkett and Morris years: this was to be a taskforce of expertise.

Like many good ideas, the problem lay in the overlooked complications and assumptions. First, the initial criteria for recognition as an NLE was an outstanding inspection judgement, but as we explain in Chapter 11, inspection judgement is far from reliable. Some schools performing at much lower levels were being led by exceptional leaders who were achieving remarkable improvement, but they did not qualify for the status. Indeed, some leaders in 'struggling' schools were acknowledged as more experienced and secure than their supporting NLE. Every profession

---

16 For example, Department for Education and M. Gove, Teachers, Not Politicians, Know How Best to Run Schools [press release] (26 May 2010). Available at: https://www.gov.uk/government/news/gove-teachers-not-politicians-know-how-best-to-run-schools.

has those who seek and those who shun the limelight, and many head teachers who would have made exceptional supporters of others chose not to become NLEs because of a sense of embarrassment, while others took the step hesitantly.

Many MATs have taken the task of growing future leaders seriously. Dan Moynihan explained the approach to leadership development in the Harris Federation: 'There is possibly a case for a proper leadership college and leader training. Our programme is to get candidates that we fast-track for headship; we get them at assistant head level and they're on a two-year programme. We move them around and we have a programme and experiences for them where they get detailed codes. Surely, that model would work for most people but they don't get a chance to do it.'

One MAT CEO that we interviewed voiced the opinion that the development of MATs was going some way to partially addressing a recruitment crisis in the system. Jonathan Johnson, CEO of the Teaching School Hub in Cumbria, observed:

> I'm not convinced that multi-academy trusts haven't also arisen because of a dwindling population of heads and because we haven't properly addressed the quality of training for leaders. We haven't demonstrated how attractive leadership can be for the benefit of the children we serve and the adults that work with them. Nor do I think we've genuinely made teaching attractive enough to keep teachers in the profession long enough to see them aspire to leadership. So, those existing leaders who are considered successful, according to whatever measure, are invited to take on schools where there may be a gap in leadership and we start to form multi-academy trusts. But what will happen when you start to find out you haven't got enough chief executives?

Tim recalls:

I wrote a paper for what is now *BELMAS* in 1989. I subtitled it 'Can the Headteacher Succeed Where the Education Officer Failed?'[17] It was a *cri de cœur*, regretting the failure of myself and my contemporary

---

17 T. Brighouse, Politicising the Manager or Managing the Politicians? Can the Headteacher Succeed Where the Education Officer Failed?, *British Educational Leadership, Management and Administration Society*, 16 (1988): 97–103.

education officers to persuade national governments that we in LEAs could be trusted to deliver improvements. I was speculating about whether the head teacher, who was inheriting most of the LEA's powers, would be able to succeed in proving to national governments that people locally could be trusted to create conditions in which we would defeat ignorance, and to an extent that we, the education officers, had not. I never imagined the extent to which national governments would centralise decisions over curriculum assessment and pedagogy. Nor did I really believe that they would row back from the idea of school autonomy to the extent they have with MATs.

A fragmented system with many patterns of school leadership

Given national government's distrust of local government, we think that the MAT model – suitably reformed and developed – is the best way to deal with both the looming crisis in the supply of sufficient numbers of suitable and qualified school leaders, and to sustain the sort of school improvement across the board that we will need in the years ahead if we are to achieve real equity for every child. We have also seen enough examples and been persuaded by enough people with whom we have talked to be convinced that MATs can work well, especially when their efforts are coordinated and when they are active in the locality beyond their academies. The challenge now is not to see the current arrangement as the finished product; we need to keep learning and improving the system.

As we have seen, the role of the head teacher is more varied now than it ever has been. Alongside the differing contexts of school settings, which has always existed but has grown as society has changed, there is now an added complexity created by the development of academies and free schools. The role of 'head teacher' can mean working directly with the DfE, collaborating with perhaps six other head teachers while a valued colleague acts in the role of respected coordinator, or being held to account by a CEO as part of a group of upwards of 30 schools with a reduced decision-making role (sometimes scaled down to 'head of school'). Alternatively, the head teacher might simply lead their school on behalf of the local authority as they have always done.

What is clear is that the expectations placed on school leaders have multiplied in the period since 1976: from the role of figurehead, staff and local authority representative and organiser of the previous age, to school manager with accountability for the site, staff and quality of the teaching. With data and computers aiding school-by-school comparisons, the head has also become responsible for a range of outcomes and the performance of their staff. The shifting awareness towards ensuring safeguarding and legal compliance with regulations, along with pupil outcomes, has made the head teacher not simply accountable but answerable to their MAT or local authority. This has led to two problems: first, rather than exchange the range of roles one for the next, head teachers have accumulated responsibilities; and, second, as the role has developed, school leadership has not been reshaped in the eyes of the public.

The duty of the leader to ensure the efficiency of systems on behalf of the school and to enable, represent and care for staff was a significant duty of heads in the 1970s. The pandemic has thrust head teachers and their schools into the centre of their communities, with many schools taking on the responsibility of supporting families and old folk in their neighbourhood. Some schools have become lynchpins and head teachers have become key figures for community togetherness. However, a head teacher in 1976 would find the role of manager, compliance checker, safeguarder, legal enforcer and, ultimately, being personally accountable and answerable for the work of the school – on top of organisational and representative functions – and an important and respected local community leader, to be beyond comprehension.

What essential qualities and skills does the leader of a MAT or a stand-alone school need to bring about school improvement successfully?

School leadership, whether at individual school or MAT level, can be and often is very effective. We have met leaders who are thriving on the challenge of seeking to constantly improve the work of their school or schools. They seem able to sustain an energetic drive towards their vision for the pupils in their charge. They are comfortable in the many roles they take on and are discerning in the developments they pursue. They innovate and collaborate in a measured way, always striving to encourage those who work with them to build their professional expertise. They create opportunities for colleagues, enable the local community and keep a weather eye on possibility. We found such people among our head teacher witnesses both in local authority and MAT settings.

Primarily, they are clear about their values. This fundamental tenet of leadership, which transcends the managerial, is often called 'moral authority', but we have to be sure not to let clichéd phrases become an easily said but poorly enacted feature of leadership. Lisa Williams, head teacher of a Lewisham primary school, spoke about this issue: 'We all have a level of professional accountability. This is not just accountability to our employers. It is our responsibility to the children and to the school community to do better. We are civil servants and we should all be accountable to our communities. In all my jobs this has been a positive driver.'

Narinder Gill, who led a school in challenging circumstances for nine years, recalled:

> Chasing a quick turnaround and an Ofsted grading was not for me. I could leave after three years and think, I've got a good inspection judgement or I could stay and really get beneath the surface, and not just plaster over what was going on within that school. The way I changed it was to go towards coaching. I became a certified coach and that helped me to develop my own resilience and to keep thinking, I can do this. I recruited people that I thought would take the school forward in a sustainable way.

It's really hard: you have to keep your ego at the door and think, it's not about me, especially when people say, 'It's career suicide in this school and you'll never progress to an NLE.'

So, what are the essential habits that help school and MAT leaders to make school improvement happen, and how do they spend their precious time? They carry out six essential tasks:

1   They create energy. The leader's own example – what they say, how they behave, who they are – is one of indomitable will and a passion for success. They ask 'what if' speculative questions. They are fussy about appointments, taking care not to fritter time on 'energy consumers'. Because they are full of hope they look for optimists – those who say 'how we could' rather than 'why we can't'. They show interest in every aspect of school life. They lead assemblies that talk as much to staff as pupils, and convey messages about what matters in 'our' school. They realise they are a role model all the time and express a faith, which brooks no denial, that all pupils 'can do'.

2   They build capacity. Heads set an example. They teach themselves and are observed by staff doing so, or they take over a class to let others observe someone else's practice. They rotate the chairing of meetings to grow the skill of others. They ensure that young staff members are involved in a school improvement group and act on their suggestions. They have a programme for staff development which considers the better future of individuals as well as the school. They know and cherish the interests of all the staff, especially those that people used to do in previous jobs or in the world beyond school. They use the collective first person pronoun 'we' rather than the singular 'I'. They take the blame when it isn't their fault and they are generous with praise to others for collective success. They set an example of learning – for example, by adopting an annual learning plan. They read and share articles, and encourage others to do the same.

3   They meet and minimise crises. At a time of genuine disaster they find cause for optimism and hope, for points of learning. They stay calm. They acknowledge their own mistakes. They are pogo-stick players: they can simultaneously be in the thick of things, yet still see the wider picture. A crisis is a source for vital learning and

future improvement. They show a willingness to be a utility player – one who *in extremis* will turn their hand to any task.

4   They secure and enhance the environment. They ensure that classroom teaching and learning materials are well organised and in plentiful supply, and that resources match the learning beliefs held by the school. They make sure that management arrangements are seen by staff as fit for purpose – right in detail and serving the needs of staff and pupils alike. For example, they often review meetings to ensure that transactional or business procedures are minimised. The staff handbook – so often now in electronic form – is repeatedly updated. The computer system works and provides a useful database for staff, each of whom have laptops. Pupils and parents have access to lesson plans, homework tasks, reports and progress grades, both at school and remotely, via the internet. They make sure there are plants and flowers around the school. They improve the staffroom and the whole environment of school, visually and aurally.

5   They seek and chart improvement. Leaders themselves use comparative benchmarking, comparing data from their own and other MATs and schools. They are keen on benchmarking, but they do it in a climate of encouraging risk and striving for the El Dorado of 'the best it can be'. They ensure there is a proper mix of appreciative enquiry and problem-solving. They seek and put improvement at the heart of what they do, and mark steps in the journey by celebrating success. Of course, they know it must be genuine because the best of genuine is an improvement on past practice, either individual or collective. They celebrate other social events too, creating a climate of energy, capacity and ultimate success. Governing board and staff meetings, awards ceremonies and briefings are crucial to this. They are, above all, good at collective as opposed to individual monitoring.

6   They extend the vision of what is possible. Clearly, this involves being both historian and futurologist. Any leader wishing to extend the vision of what is possible is deeply aware of this double requirement: the present dominates so much of school life. And if, sometimes, that present seems overwhelming and the energy levels drop, telling stories that remind people of past success and keeping respected predecessors present and honoured are things that wise leaders do. They are also forecasters of the weather and

describers of future possibilities: they confidently describe a path from the present to the future. They are good listeners and readers. They ask 'why not' aloud and 'why' silently in their heads.

Tim recalls:

'It's all very well to look at Belbin and Myers–Briggs,' a colleague in the education department leadership team remarked ominously one day, 'but I think the infant teacher could teach us a thing or two about what to look for in a leadership team. After all, she assesses her charges' progress in listening, speaking, reading and writing, and while they are doing it, she looks to see whether they are thinking and learning. If we could get that right in our team,' she concluded with a smile, 'we would be doing alright.'

She was referring to our practice of putting every new member of staff through the Myers–Briggs profile of preferred leadership operational styles and then inviting an external coach to talk to us about the ways in which we could improve our collective efforts. Nothing too unusual in that: most school leadership teams in larger schools do something similar. They use coaches, assess leadership styles and work at the gaps. But we never quite forgot our colleague's remarks. The more we thought about them, the more sense they made; we realised how easy it was to neglect one or more of the four activities of listening, speaking, reading and writing. It certainly provides a very useful compass for looking at how successful head teachers spend that precious commodity – time.

Leaders who are school improvers are experts in the use of time. First, there is the obvious point about the much misunderstood 'time to think'. As a head teacher once told us: 'I do my thinking all the time. It occupies every waking moment. When I want to focus the sum total of my thinking, I spend an evening writing or speak with a group of colleagues. Out of that comes my own, or our collective, refreshed direction of the solution to a problem.'

Second, if we analyse what we do each day, it can be broken down into listening, speaking, reading and writing. Most forms of human activity (apart from sleeping) usually involve one or more of these.

Third, and this is surely the key for the successful head teacher, we can only read and write in isolation, whereas we need people to talk and listen. This is presumably why another successful school leader said to us forcefully: 'The time the school is in session is precious. The whole community is there. And that means it's time for the pupils, staff, governors and other members of the wide community.' She went on to add that if she ever found herself inadvertently backing away from that guiding principle and staying in her office, she knew she was on a very slippery slope.

Time is so precious that some people say that learning to use time wisely and to best effect is *the* key skill for a school leader to master. It is why the listening, speaking, reading and writing overlay on the use of a head's time is so useful; it helps them to guard against wasting time by being alone during the school day. Indeed, it has led more than one head we know of to share an office with their deputies, so that when they are in the same place together, they are also sharing ideas about (or for that matter agreeing) an approach to a difficult immediate issue. They claim there is never a problem about finding a room for a private meeting when necessary. Schools are places where there can never be too much of the senior team being around the place and lending a hand.

We should add two points of caution and a health warning. The first is pretty obvious: namely, that school and MAT leaders, whether they are successful or not, are deeply conscious of the fragmented nature of their days. They flit from one activity to the next, sometimes spending very short time spans on any one task before moving on to another. Successful heads know this to be a tendency but guard against life becoming too ad hoc. They know that over a day they may not achieve the planned allocation of time they would like, but over a week or a term they can and will. Distraction is inevitable but it can be defeated in the long run.

Second, when we total the amount of time spent on the various activities, it will always add up to more than 100% of the notional number of working hours. That is because the key starting point is that successful leaders use time twice or three times over. They have mastered the skill of doing things simultaneously rather than sequentially; not for everything, of course, but for many tasks. While they are doing their regular daily classroom rounds, they may also be doing business with a visitor or reinforcing a singing-from-the-same-song-sheet message with staff. Quantitative surveys of the use of time, of which there are many, may serve solicitors, architects and accountants for cost allocation to charge clients, but they are a dangerously misleading way of measuring school leaders' time.

And that brings us to the health warning: we used the words 'dangerously misleading' because the great problem with successful school leaders and their staff is that they are so committed. They worry that if only they had devoted more time to this or that person or activity, then the outcome (in their private and unvoiced opinion) would have been better. They will also quickly feel guilt over the contested issue of how they use their time. Indeed, as an antidote to guilt, it is probably as well to say that whatever the pattern of their schedule, successful head teachers need time off – not necessarily to think but to draw breath and recharge. That won't be on a daily or weekly basis, but it will be taken in dollops every now and then. And they need to ensure that their staff do the same.

One of the problems with the structure of the school year is that everyone is on the same cycle: the sprint-and-stop mentality of half-terms. This means that everyone is tired at the same point and a sort of institutional fatigue can set in, unless the leadership does something to reinvigorate people now and again. One of the benefits of attending a conference, visiting another school, joining an educational visit with a teaching group or being asked to attend a planning meeting for a local community event is that they provide a variation in routine; not a rest or a break but a different rhythm.

There are four stages to any sort of leadership that involves people, so what follows also applies to senior posts of responsibility. The first stage is *initiation*. It is when all your stakeholders – staff, pupils, parents, governors and the local community (in the case of head teachers) – are trying to match up what you say and what you do with who you are – or not, as the case may be. The better your homework about people before you arrive, the sooner you will form a trusting rapport based on their certainty that you know about and appreciate their individuality. The more you put yourself about, the quicker the initiation phase will be. Until it is over, it is difficult to make energetic progress based on shared commitment. One more thing about the initiation phase: avoid all mention of where you have worked before. Too much of that and colleagues will silently wish you were back where you came from.

The second *developmental* stage is when, after listening to everyone's hopes, you are privileged to steer the school or MAT through the next chapter of the story. You will find yourself using a few key defining phrases over and over again – sometimes, so often you feel self-conscious about repetition. You constantly need to affirm and reinforce the vital essence, purpose and values of the shared enterprise with all members of the community – pupils, staff, parents and governors. You know you are winning when you hear others using the same language. Another important ingredient of this phase is to focus on staff development, so they never run short of intellectual curiosity and energy. Usually, the ambitions set out for the school are realised within seven to nine years, and a new defining chapter needs to be agreed.

The third phase is a dangerous one for leaders because the *plateau* stage can so easily become a stall. Can you summon the imagination and resolve for another sustained period of development? Or do your colleagues know you so well that they can be quietly effective in resisting any more of your ideas? Are you so exhausted by obligations to so many stakeholders that, in the event of this situation, you can no longer lead? Should you leave for another school? Certainly, taking a break after seven or so years is a good idea – ideally, for half a term but even a month-long study visit will recharge your batteries.

This is a common practice in parts of Australia and Canada where salary schemes exist to allow all teachers to take a sabbatical term on full salary every seven years. The schemes were set up in the days of mass settlement in the early 20th century when teachers returning to the UK to see their family would need more than the length of holiday to make the voyage, but the professional benefits were realised and it has remained as a policy. Is this need to recharge your batteries why Peter Mortimore's research showed heads to be at their best between their third and seventh year?[18] Is it also the reason why a good many MAT chief executives are individuals who have completed about seven or eight years of successful headship and feel ready for a bigger challenge, something with a wider scope? There are lots of exceptions to the rule, although we haven't met too many heads who tell us that their second 10 years were better than their first! However, we do know for many that past the 15-year mark, longevity becomes a benefit as the head has more experience than most staff at the school and the wisdom of being able to reflect on the changing system. Past success and experience, and

---

18 P. Sammons, J. Hillman and P. Mortimore, *Key Characteristics of Effective Schools: A Review of School Effectiveness* (London: Institute of Education, 1995).

the implied good judgement which underpin them, mean that heads can assert considerable professional authority.

Most people emerge from the third stage with a new defining chapter, or they leave. But, of course, there is no way of avoiding the fourth stage of leadership – the *decline* or end phase when you have decided to go. The school goes on hold as people pay less attention to you and await your successor. So, don't hang around and allow things to lose momentum. Don't keep saying that you are going to retire or move on and then post-pone it for one more year. In fact, if you are going to leave, decide where you are going before telling your community. There are few positives about working for someone who has indicated that they would rather be elsewhere. Once you have made the decision, stick to it and announce it with the minimal notice consistent with not leaving the school in a mess. A long goodbye after great success can evoke good feelings, but it can also make things very difficult for your successor.

Leaders know when they are in the declining or stalling phase – it is when they are running out of the following five essential qualities which all school leaders need in order to thrive and survive:

1   *Unwarranted optimism.* It will appeal to the experienced hard-pressed leader as they reflect on the number of occasions they have had to appear determinedly upbeat when, at the time, it was hard to see their way through the apparently insurmountable difficulties confronting them – not least during the COVID-19 pandemic.

2   *To regard crisis as the norm and complexity as fun.* As anyone familiar with school life will know, there will be no shortage of opportunities for this to show itself – again, especially during a pandemic.

3   *An endless supply of intellectual curiosity.* If the leader isn't speculating about ideas and possibilities – especially those offered by others – a school starts to stall and teachers lose their creativity.

4   *An absence of paranoia or self-pity.* Leadership can be lonely and difficult decisions are sometimes made when problems arrive thick and fast on the head teacher's desk. The buck has to stop with you and decisions, sometimes unpopular ones, have to be made. There is a real danger that you can start to feel sorry for yourself and this needs to be resisted.

5   *A capacity to spot gaps in hedges.* Leaders can see gaps in
     regulations or spot ways of bringing an apparently unconnected set
     of possibilities together to solve a problem or enable a longed for
     change to happen.[19]

If there were enough of these sorts of people, not just in schools but in
all the mechanisms around them, including politicians, then the system
would know no bounds.

The reality is that, over the years, increasing central control coupled with
a high-stakes accountability agenda and a complexity of expectations
has, for a significant proportion of school leaders, reduced their role to
that of the managing director of their school. In turn, their staff have
become operatives and young people regarded as units of production,
represented in highly calibrated data sets that serve to demonstrate the
effectiveness of the leadership.

Most of our witnesses had an image of leadership that was to a large
extent built on the point at which their awareness began (as, we suspect, do we) and the degree to which they have been able to adapt with
caution or guile to the demands placed on them (as, we hope, we have).
Some have exploited each opportunity, from LFM to accountability, to
deliver ongoing success to their school or schools. Some have become
concerned about meeting the demands of a complex job, so much so
that, in order to serve the accountability regime, they have resorted to
gathering the appropriate evidence and expect their staff to do the same.
The managerial aspects of the role consume their time and they have little energy left for the part of the job that makes the difference – working
with people.

In what was once hailed as the 'paperless workplace', we are now
expected to read more than we interact. The pandemic is a case in point.
Once it had been decided to reopen schools, the DfE issued guidance
which was updated almost daily. This was sent directly to schools, but
most local authorities also sent their own guidance on the guidance to
support their schools and to explain any particular matters relating to
their situation. Many CEOs of MATs also produced guidance that interpreted the DfE guidance for their own schools. It is hard not to conclude

---

19   An example here makes the point: the introduction of the Apprenticeship Levy means that some local
     authorities have a big pot available for employees to use. One primary head told us it was funding CPD
     at Levels 5, 6 and 7 for many of her staff, thereby proving a boon to collective thinking and individual
     growth.

that a lot of what was being produced wasn't for the benefit of schools but to cover the back of each organisation. It was managerialism.

For the first few weeks, each update was a repeat of the whole guidance with amendments made in the light of experience. It is perfectly reasonable to expect changes in a fast-moving situation, but making them easy to grasp would seem obvious – unless, of course, making people read the whole document over and over again was a ploy to make sure it was clearly understood. A regular broadcast via the BBC or even the Oak National Academy platform could have provided a more personal approach. Live online chat facilities could have pointed out key areas of concern and guidance would have been more familiar and less daunting when it landed in schools.

It was not wrong for the government to take control. What disappointed many in schools was the inept handling of the problem and their sense of powerlessness in the face of distant, insensitive and centralised power. For the last 20 years, the managerial drive in schools has seen every level of leadership expected to carry out regular risk analysis, including meticulous RAG ratings and proposed mitigations. The prospect of a global calamity, including a pandemic, will have been on many of those risk assessment charts, but, when it came to it, did we turn to the spreadsheets and charts? For most of us, it felt as though Lance Corporal Jones from *Dad's Army* had been asked to take command. It has made a lot of people wonder whether the time spent in all those meetings pre-planning a crisis would not have been better spent talking with a teacher new to the profession, organising an educational visit or listening to a child read.

Our point is that leadership and school improvement become real at a school level, where people work together with a head teacher who creates the circumstances that enable improvement to happen. These intensely personal efforts should be supported by managerial approaches, not driven by them, and helped by central approaches, not controlled by them.

Where do we go from here?

What we need to do now is to establish a climate and culture at a national level that chimes with the idealism and sense of moral purpose that attracts people into the profession, and which is beautifully encapsulated by Alison Peacock in Chapter 6. We won't achieve this by bending the knee to the long age of markets, centralisation and managerialism of which the system has grown so tired.

The 'golden thread' of a coherent approach to leadership development and training is envisaged in the present government's unfolding provision. This sees the 87 teaching school hubs as commissioners and quality assurers for a suite of incremental, career-long NPQs. The range of qualifications has expanded greatly since Gillian Shephard set up the first one for head teachers. The current suite, which successive governments have extended, includes an NPQ for every aspect of school leadership.

The concept of a golden thread is surely sound, so why should there be growing concern about unfolding developments? The answer is that, as with the development of the ECF, there is unease about the increasing degree of control from the centre. With teaching school hubs acting as brokers for the very limited range of DfE-approved accredited providers, many fear that consistency runs close to conformity.

A presenter of a middle leaders programme told us: 'It is a uniform programme. There is a script and PowerPoints are provided and therefore there is no deviation. There is little opportunity to personalise or relate issues to different settings. All coursework units are done to a template and most of it is comprehension and cloze procedure. Participants are pushed towards seeing getting the accreditation as more important than thinking about leadership.'

We share concerns about the managerial approach and the need to feed the machine of accreditation. We are also concerned about the subtle centralisation through political influence on the complex structure of hubs serving the golden thread. As one of our witnesses put it: 'I could – and probably will – characterise it as a long culture war to take over education. Total control of teacher education will complement the almost total control of the school curriculum.'

The channelling of practices from the various hubs for aspects such as behaviour, mathematics, English, modern foreign languages, music and the like through the teaching school hubs at the appropriate leadership level sounds straightforward and managerially attractive. The concept relies on those in headship seeing a different role for themselves as they gradually become the 'in-school' coordinator of policy and practice that is developed centrally. The notion of the head teacher as a branch manager carrying out government policy is not one that governing bodies have yet to recognise fully, and with the enormous variety of school contexts may not be appropriate anyway.

As we have seen in this chapter, the role of the head teacher in school improvement is key and the task of school improvement is the principal leadership function, always striving to improve on previous best. As the government attempts to roll out its system of hubs across the country and centralise leadership development, another element of its agenda – MATs – offer an additional route to continuously improving schools.

We know that RSCs are interpreting their role within MATs with a clear focus on school improvement, albeit measured in a way that is constrained by what we can measure rather than all that we value and because the government needs academisation to be seen to be effective. As we have stated, we think that the MAT is the right unit and mechanism, provided it has some local democratic input, which we have outlined in the chapters on accountability and governance (Chapters 11 and 12 respectively). Indeed, we have heard persuasive stories of developments in this area. Over the longer term, the NLE role seems to have developed well, except that it is underused because so many NLEs have their own MATs to bring to success. Where RSCs are building a collective belief in school improvement, such as in the South West, NLE work is an integral part of a coordinated and collaborative approach.

From our viewpoint, there is no contradiction in having a system of close support for schools that is coordinated regionally through MATs, while individual academy schools collaborate across their local region to build partnerships for learning. The self-contained and inward-looking MAT, however, with each school an identikit branch or franchise – in effect denying professional judgement – will wither. Professionals collaborate, as the worldwide search for a coronavirus vaccine has shown. It may have been portrayed as a race by the politicians, but the scientists involved were sharing their results, findings, hypotheses and breakthroughs in the search for a solution.

Of course, collaborative approaches are not restricted to local authority schools. Dave Baker described the MAT he leads and his approach:

> You have to decide where to be on a continuum: whether you're going to be at the dictatorial end or whether you're going to be collegial and collaborative in the way you go about getting to the point of consensus, so that you can move forward. If you're dictatorial, you don't get the values and buy-in right. If you believe in consensus, then it's slower. It takes a long time, but actually you probably end up in a better place overall. You could choose between the values and the identity or image. I tend to believe in shared values, and I think our community of academies is growing stronger because of it.

Clare Flintoff of ASSET Education Trust in Suffolk told us:

> There are so many connections between schools now at so many different levels and we're working so collaboratively that it just happens. What we're able to do as a trust is work with head teachers and all of our staff in our individual schools, connecting in so many ways. They're part of connections where there's a subject leader network and curriculum leaders who oversee the curriculum across the whole trust. Our teachers are part of a bigger network where they're sharing their plans for learning, sharing their resources, sharing their ideas. We've got reading advocates who work across all of our schools who are all talking about the best texts that are coming out and widening our children's reading.

Similarly, Rob Carpenter, chief executive of the Inspire Partnership of primary academies based in Greenwich, Medway and Croydon, was clear that:

> The reason our schools are improving and continuously work so well is because we've got a very, very strong ethos and collaborative outlook. Collaboration is the hardest thing, not the easiest thing, to get right. We build the partnership around this ethos of meaningful and deep collaboration, and it has created a culture where people are continuously moving between each other's schools, willing to share, willing to give: capacity-givers and capacity-receivers.

Cosy spaces don't get it right. There's a lot of horizontal account-ability, which makes it uncomfortable because teachers are continuously in a space where they're seen in a very visible way. Our code of excellence is made very visible and you can't escape it; it becomes an artefact for what you believe in as a school. It's everywhere.

Janice Allen was one of several head teachers we talked to who was concerned about the professional role and status of the head as an aspect of their development. 'I do worry that we risk producing identikit head teachers,' she told us, and several others talked of 'clones', 'template heads', 'clockwork heads' and 'mini-me' head teachers. Would that be a problem? Commercial companies do it. The manager of one supermarket in a chain carries out the same procedures as the next, controlled by head office, as do managers of hotels, car dealerships and franchises for all sorts of businesses. Perhaps the difference is that they are template businesses, and chains typically aim at a customer base from the same subsection of society. Users of their services know what to expect. Critics of the (often overstated) highly centralising MATs usually disregard the benefits to the head teacher of much being decided for them centrally.

The approach of CEOs creates a dilemma because the more they control each academy in their trust, the less responsibility there is for the new emerging role of head of school, which could be seen as a proving ground for leadership or a limiting line-management role akin to that of a branch manager for a corporate enterprise. This notion of in-house training and development has an attraction, especially in the world of centralisation and markets. In the private sector, companies invest in and train their best people for leadership, and the notion of a house style builds both in terms of the leadership approach and the quality of service offered.

Mark Grundy, CEO of Shireland Collegiate Academy Trust, was clear about his expectations:

Schools become part of our family. They pick up our curriculum and our assessment processes. We have a standard curriculum template, with a primary model and a secondary model, and that is reviewed annually. All school leaders have an input. There is a core part and then we look to amend it, and people will bring forward change by virtue of different circumstances or because they have someone new on the staff who has got this great attribute we have never had before. The core of it, the heavy lifting, is done for you. All the central processes are done by the central team. For our heads of school, we do as much of the heavy lifting as possible around finance, HR, estate, technology, safeguarding and all those structural things to allow them to have the maximum amount of time and energy to focus on delivery, on relationships and on developing teams.

This notion of a community or family of schools seems to be more palatable to many in the schooling system than a corporate approach or house style, yet in essence they are the same thing, although perhaps explained and managed more sensitively. The argument is often rehearsed, though, that however they operate, they risk removing the individuality, intellectual curiosity and innovation of people in their school.

One of our MAT leaders compared the different styles of leadership in MATs using a range of metaphors:

> I assumed that one particular MAT, which has a head office image, used a cookie-cutter approach, but it doesn't. It is much more of the Wild West with an 'I don't care what you do, just stand and deliver.' It is sort of Murdoch style: 'I want you to jump this high. How you get there is up to you.' Whereas another MAT, which is often lumped in the same centralising category, is much more French style: it is Monday at 2 o'clock and all the schools will be doing the same thing, using the same lesson plans, prepared for them and pre-cooked.

She added that 'Both CEOs [whom she named] are straightforward, committed, focused and driven.'

Just as schools used to be different because of the leadership approach of the head, so, it seems, MATs are different because of the leadership style of the CEO. As before, where that works and delivers the outcomes sought with the support of the staff and community and in the best interests of the pupils, all is well. At other times, and there are examples of dreadful MATs in all respects, the impact is on a larger scale. Local authorities were and are varied too, but while the accountability sat at school level, the possibility of collective success or failure at scale was reduced.

Michael Fullan describes the challenge of balancing the ownership and impact axis as being one of 'creating a culture of purposeful learning that is neither tightly controlled nor too loose, in a culture that is simultaneously bottom-up, top-down and sideways'.[20] From the understanding we derived from our conversations, the place that a MAT (or school) has on a continuum from autonomy to alignment to collaboration is influenced by both the attitude of leadership and the state of play in the community at any one time. A MAT with a school (or schools) in the eye of a storm might be different in outlook from one where the sun is shining.

This chapter is about the leadership of schools. Perhaps one of the challenges for the next phase of development is how to best build leadership strength across the school system, and to do it through a more diverse set of arrangements – although, ironically, in respect of headship, a more collaborative culture than existed under local authorities.

We believe that MATs provide the opportunity for a *concerted* consideration of leadership that needs to be unleashed. The current drive for establishing school improvement processes, exploring new possibilities and building success being experienced by many MATs needs to be seen as a chance to propel schooling and leadership to a new level, and that will be best achieved through cooperation between MATs and recognising that all academies and schools exist as local entities for their parents and their communities. We need a cross-fertilisation of approaches, a positive commitment to collaboration and a robust analysis of what works well, with people at every level feeling that they belong to something bigger than the unit in which they work.

Our call is for a concerted push, so we believe that the secretary of state should instigate opportunities for the CEOs of MATs and local authority leaders to come together with RSCs to release the energy in the system at a regional level, with practices and approaches that can be shared nationwide. This concerted push does not need a new infrastructure or a new agency to manage it. It needs some resources, and we would suggest not too much, along with a good measure of something that is built into the language of academisation – trust.

If we are clear about some of the mechanisms and approaches for encouraging school improvement in the ways we have discussed in this chapter, how should we change the way we assess school improvement? Is it simply the metrics we use at the moment – namely norm-referenced pupil

---

20 M. Fullan, The Elusive Nature of Whole System Improvement in Education, *Journal of Educational Change*, 17(4) (2016): 539–544 at 543.

test/exam results, attendance figures and Ofsted verdicts? If so, we are inviting market principles and failure for some through unhealthy competition rather than ambitious collaborative partnerships. Or could we be more ambitious and look at some of the purposes we set out in Chapter 1. In short, is it possible to create a balanced scorecard of performance indicators by which we can assess a school's progress in improving on previous best?

The concept of a balanced scorecard was considered but not trialled during the tenure of Ed Balls, who wanted to see leadership refocus around the Every Child Matters agenda and the five outcomes for all children. Balls told us:

> The question was, how could you not lose the testing and the comparator but try to find a way in which you could have a communicable context? The problem was that the complex way of contextualising was pretty much incomprehensible to the ministers, let alone anyone else, to get their heads around it. We thought we could call it a report card, which would have had a simplified grading of the contextualised value-added alongside raw attainment plus other measures of progress and satisfaction. So, as a parent, you could look across five metrics at what your school did for all kids – for kids who started behind, kids who needed extra help, satisfaction or well-being and happiness, all those kinds of things.
>
> And we considered it, we consulted on it. Lots of schools that were challenging didn't want it, and lots of schools that knew it was good for them really wanted it. Lots of heads couldn't be bothered and didn't want it at all. One of my regrets would be that we just weren't able to get to the point where that could be nationally agreed.

John Dunford, who was general secretary of ASCL at the time, talked of the effort to achieve a different form of accountability: 'I thought that the concept of the balanced scorecard had real potential. Like a lot of things, though, when the DfE started to work on it, everything became so complicated and mired in complexity. It seemed to end up on the shelf for a long while and then the moment was gone.'

If we could build on the concept of improving on previous best and overhaul the ways we judge the progress of schools, would it be possible to reform inspection and accountability processes? It might also be the right time to ask whether we need to move on the concept of school improvement and have greater ambition. The practice of school improvement has evolved, and most leaders within and outside of schools are aware of the various approaches and principles that are known to lift performance.

Where we might drive the agenda next for schooling is in a collective outlook, where disciplined innovation becomes the lifeblood of the system within a spirit of collaborative partnerships, sharing carefully structured trials, with insights critiqued, evaluated and shared. We will return to the key changes needed to establish the new age of ambition, hope and collaborative partnerships in our final chapter.

Incidentally, every head teacher should guard against shelving too many challenges. While time and energy traps can consume or be left to wither in Charles Clarke's 'too difficult box', the awkward problems can slip down the list all too easily, never rising into the urgent category until it is too late. We need to deal with those 'stone in the shoe' problems rather than hope they will go away. Many of the issues addressed in this book have been left for too long; in some respects, we wish we had been able to do more during our own careers.

Part Three

Overcoming barriers to success: institutional barriers and obstacles to pupil fulfilment – the doldrums

Chapter 8

Admissions, attendance, exclusions and behaviour – a cocktail of unfairness

How to get their child into school and then how to keep them there sounds straightforward enough. For some parents, however, it involves finding a path through a maze too difficult to navigate.

They aren't helped by the mixed messages about the value of learning in schools. For example, it used to be the case in our own schooldays that a visiting dignitary, on a school speech day, would listen attentively to a catalogue of academic, sporting and other achievements delivered by a rose-tinted, bespectacled head teacher and then suggest, 'This deserves a proper reward, headmaster [well, it was a long time ago]. I declare an extra day off school at the next half-term!' The unintended subtext was that one less day of learning was a bonus. And, of course, the old log-books of rural primary schools record a multitude of days off for potato picking and other farming-related activities.

That was yesterday. Today, there is another mixed message when certain children (particularly in their teenage years and from 'difficult' families or with 'difficult' histories of schooling), who are finding it frustratingly impossible to live by classroom rules, act up deliberately in order to get excluded from lessons and sent to an isolation room – sometimes called a reflection or recovery room or, more ominously, a red zone – prior to what is too often a fixed-term exclusion. So prevalent are these practices that over 438,000 fixed-term exclusions occurred in 2018–2019 (the last year for which there is complete data) – that is the equivalent of three secondary schools being shut for the whole year.[1]

And all this in schools which assert that one of their driving ambitions is to be inclusive.

---

1   See https://explore-education-statistics.service.gov.uk/find-statistics/permanent-and-fixed-period-exclusions-in-england#dataDownloads-1.

Admissions

First, there is the question of securing a fair deal for a child's entry to school. What ought to be the simple task of finding a suitable school place can be far from simple for parents, especially if they live in what are euphemistically described as 'challenging circumstances' and particularly for those with children out of school in their teenage years and who find themselves without a school place.

Tim recalls:

'What do you think, Tim?' asked the prime minister. 'As commissioner are you happy with it?' In a crowded room in Downing Street, ministers, DfE officials and Number 10's policy unit were discussing the draft prospectus for the London Challenge.

Should I speak truth to power? After all, I was more than happy with what was in the prospectus, especially its combination of data- and research-driven strategies combined with positive rather than negative language. It was an omission that bothered me – namely, no mention of the chaotic state of secondary school admissions in the capital. I had raised it earlier and Charles Clarke had advised, 'Tony won't want it in but, of course, you can raise it if you really want to.'

I could guess why, having once met John McIntosh, the head of the London Oratory School, who told me that crucial to maintaining a good school was that the head should have some say in who should and should not be admitted. The Oratory School was where Tony Blair, controversially exercising parental choice, had sent his own son.

I screwed my courage to the sticking place and replied to the prime minister's query, 'Yes, it's excellent but it's not what's in it that bothers me, it's what isn't.'

'And what might that be?' he enquired with a quizzical raise of an eyebrow.

'I think we should have something in about admissions. I reckon there are well over a thousand kids roaming the streets south of the river who are unable to gain admission to a secondary school.'

My remarks were greeted by an audible silence in the room. After the pause, I was advised to the effect that the London Challenge wasn't the vehicle for tackling the problem and the time wasn't right. I muttered something about the Damilola Taylor murder case and that when another similar tragedy occurred, and was committed by a kid out of school, we might regret not addressing it.[2] But to my eternal discredit I backed off. The London Challenge is lauded as a great success, but it will always haunt my conscience for what we failed to do.

Mick recalls:

I had been chief education officer in Manchester for just a few weeks when one of our senior staff excused himself from a meeting because he had to be at a Tuesday afternoon school at the Jehovah's Witness Hall in the city centre. When I asked him what that was, he said he had made an arrangement on Tuesday and Thursday afternoons to help newly arrived refugees and asylum seekers who couldn't get into a school place. I felt I had to go and have a look.

The place was full of youngsters aged between 6 and 15 (so they claimed) who were being taught by our advisory teachers. I found this troubling, given that I was aware of bits of space in schools I had visited. I did two things: first, I set three people to report, with a swift deadline, on how many children we could find who had no school place and, second, I asked another adviser to approach and have conversations with selected head teachers to ascertain why this was happening.

I could guess, as well as you can, the answer to the second question. The accountability system was the deterrent. A significant proportion of secondary schools were performing below the floor targets and primary schools were being bitten by league tables. Why would they want to make themselves even more vulnerable by taking in children who would put their annual results at risk? The city was in the league table relegation zone along with Knowsley, Hull and Stoke,

---

2   In 2000, 10-year-old schoolboy Damilola Taylor was stabbed and killed in a stairwell in South London. It took more than six years and three trials for two brothers, aged 12 and 13 at the time of the killing, to be convicted of manslaughter.

so the pressure was on all of us. The answer to the first issue was a shock, though: my three advisers, by asking around and checking up on newly arrived children and those excluded, found 747 children without a school place.

I remember the number because it is an iconic one: when I went to the DfE, I recall telling officials that I had 'a Boeing' of children lost to the system. I explained that the reasons were of their own making and suggested a solution to the 'Boeing problem' that we would pilot (very apt). I proposed that we start a 'village school' (after all, it takes a village to raise child) which would have a DfE reference number. We would register the children to the local authority and then place them in schools across the city. If the children did well in exams and tests, the school could have the result, and if they did badly, the village school would have them. I predicted that the collated village school results would be awful but I would deal with that when it happened.

The rather decent DfE official was taken with this idea and we spent a good deal of time planning how it would work. A few days later he informed me that he thought he could allocate the DfE number of a school that had recently closed. We started to place the children in schools across the city with the support and a deal of goodwill from head teachers. They would take two or three children each and we would save a few quid a week on the hire of the hall in the city centre – and give children the learning they deserved.

About two weeks later, I received a call from the crestfallen DfE official who told me that 'higher ups' had quashed the scheme for fear of 'unintended consequences'. What were they? Everywhere else would want to do it, the school results and the local authority results wouldn't tally and schools might add potential strugglers to the village school roll.

We worked it out locally and did our best for the youngsters. Nobody wanted to do them down. I like to think that what emerged later as 'virtual schools' had its roots in our Boeing conversation – and I would like to think that the current virtual schools could move on from their very limited remit.

These two cameos illustrate one of two problems with admissions which, if left unresolved, can leave a fair schooling system always tantalisingly within reach but out of our grasp. The first issue is fair in-year access (when a parent is seeking a school place after the school year has started because they have moved or their child has left another school). The second is well known to all parents who try to be what Bettelheim calls 'good enough'[3] – a difficult task at the best of times and never more so when their children start primary school and again on transfer to secondary school. Naturally, they want them to attend a good school and encounter teachers who will have a powerful influence on their child's life chances. Deciding how pupils access schools needs to be fair, therefore, if all children are to have an equal chance of attending a suitable school. At present, the admission system is not as fair as it could or should be, especially for those from disadvantaged communities and particularly children from challenged families in those communities.

One third cameo shows how different it can be.

Mick recalls:

We had a secondary school in Birmingham in 1998 which found itself in a sorry state. It was in one of Ofsted's negative categories (rightly) and was leaking children and staff to nearby schools. Because of the empty places, it was now a 'recruiting' school and was trying to attract pupils to keep going.

Tim persuaded an experienced head teacher to take over and see whether he could change its fortunes. With a combination of experience, wisdom and humour, Bob, the new head teacher, managed to kick-start the process. People knew that he cared about them and their school, and so things began to improve.

At the time, there was an influx of new arrivals from overseas: Eastern Europeans, asylum seekers, refugees, economic migrants from Africa, South America and Asia. Many of these new arrivals were seeking a school place and Bob hit on the idea of providing free travel permits to school. Before long, the school was filling with a pupil league of nations, all bringing their cultural contribution to one of the most

---

3   B. Bettelheim, *A Good Enough Parent: A Book on Child-Rearing* (New York: Vintage Books, 1988).

amazingly rich learning environments. EAL was widespread; the number of languages it was additional to was astounding. It was such a dynamic school.

Results began to rise as pupils entered the available qualifications, including a range of language GCSEs. Ofsted duly noted the improvements and the image changed locally to the extent that the school was now secure.

I recall that on one occasion, I was asked to host a visit from a senior DfE official who was enquiring into the impact of one of their programmes. He asked whether he could visit a school and talk with the head teacher, so I decided we should visit Bob. After a brief introduction, Bob led us into a conference room where about 25 pupils sat in a circle ready to join in the conversation with the 'man from the government', as Bob introduced him.

It was a lovely hour. The official asked a question and the pupils who managed English well translated it into an array of languages. Responses came back and were passed from Serbian to Albanian to Greek to Turkish and back into English for the answer, or they circled the Latin quarter or the Asian sub-continent before emerging as a definitive reply. To his credit, after initial bewilderment, the DfE official managed the situation well and gained a lot for his enquiry and report.

Bob managed the school skilfully. His retirement celebration 10 years later was just that: a couple of hundred now adult ex-pupils returning to spend an evening with the head teacher who had opened doors for them, first into school and then into jobs, careers and life opportunities.

In the age of optimism and trust, before the start of our story, where pupils attended school was decided by the LEA. If a county or voluntary controlled (i.e. state funded but not voluntary aided) school ran out of space and exceeded its admission limit, most LEAs would either expand the school with temporarily erected classrooms, extend the school permanently or build a new school and redefine the catchment area. Others would redirect the parents living furthest away from the school. In a world of post-war cash shortages, planning provision was a guiding principle in securing best value for scarce resource.

In the case of access to secondary schools in areas that were selective, the process was complicated by the need to qualify for a grammar school place, but, once again, parents were expected to accept the offer of a place in their designated school, which might vary according to the IQ-based score of the 11+ (although some parents did refuse a grammar school place).

If families lived beyond two miles (or three miles at secondary level) from their designated school, transport to and from school would be paid for by the LEA. If parents requested that their child attend a school that was not their designated school, and there was room available, LEAs usually agreed to their request, provided no unnecessary extra transport costs were involved.

This relatively simple system, in a country where people typically responded to what was arranged for them by the state, enabled LEAs to plan school places with relative accuracy and have a good chance of not having too many costly surplus places within the system. They were held to this goal of economy, efficiency and effectiveness – a vital and difficult task as school rolls fell in the first decade of our second age – by the Audit Commission.[4]

All that changed with the 1981 Education Act when parental preference – always described by national politicians as 'choice' – was first introduced by law. The transformation was dramatic, especially as competition between schools increased, as it did from the late 1980s onwards. Kenneth Baker called his approach to parent choice 'open enrolment' and notes that there was 'considerable opposition within the department because of the view that education was like a see-saw – if one end rose because of improvement, the other end would sink under the weight of failure. This analogy failed to take into account the motivation of those in less popular schools to improve their performance or even change their staff.'[5] This was part of the beginning of the market-driven outlook which, impacted by the economy, saw the start of families moving home to gain access to the 'best' schools, which in turn affected the housing market.

As we have explained, parental choice was one of the guiding ideas – along with autonomy, diversity and accountability – for competition between schools. It was also fuelled by published exam and test results in a marketplace of schooling. As we heard from one of our witnesses,

---

4   The Audit Commission, along with many other quangos, was dissolved in 2015 as part of austerity measures introduced by the coalition government.

5   K. Baker, *The Turbulent Years: My Life in Politics* (London: Faber & Faber, 1993), p. 213.

Michael Barber, choice was given a boost by Tony Blair after the 2001 election following a long session at Chequers to come up with a strategy to promote it across all the publicly provided services: 'Someone, probably knowing in advance that Blair would seize on it, threw choice into the mix. Shouldn't there be a fourth principle that, whenever possible, we would offer the patient, the parent, the citizen, the choice?'[6]

The development of diversity – by design, accident, or poorly received or managed policies; or through different sorts of secondary school, such as city technology colleges, grant-maintained schools, foundation schools, trust schools, academies, UTCs, studio schools and free schools – was accompanied by certain freedoms, such as the right of academies not to follow the national curriculum but instead to devise one of their own design, provided it was broad and balanced, which would be agreed in a separate contract with the secretary of state. After 2010, such schools were allowed to select 10% of their entry according to aptitude or ability, extend their capacity and, like voluntary-aided schools, set their own admission criteria in the case of over-subscription (rather than, as hitherto, be bound by the LEA oversubscription criteria). They could also run their own admission arrangements, although, in practice, most have chosen to let the local authority run the annual secondary application scheme in the autumn term of the year preceding entry.

The abolition of the Audit Commission in 2010 coincided with a spur from Michael Gove towards market competition for existing schools by extending the academy programme from an initiative to convert existing schools with a long history of underachievement in challenging areas, to one which was open to state-maintained secondary schools (which, moreover – at least initially – would gain extra funds just as school budgets were being squeezed). At the same time, free schools could be set up by parents and interested other parties who were dissatisfied with local schools or to meet local demand. Now, over 75% of secondary schools have become academies and therefore have the capacity to set their own criteria admission.

In short, the process of admission to secondary schools – with its often-changing kaleidoscope of criteria – has become more confusing for parents and more open to calculated abuse among a proliferation of admission authorities.

---

6   M. Barber, *How to Run a Government So That Citizens Benefit and Taxpayers Don't Go Crazy* (London: Allen Lane, 2016), p. 60.

Even before the introduction of the complicating factor of academies and free schools, LEAs had been encouraged to support increases in a particular school's admission limit to respond to parental choice for popular schools. AMA and ACC had published the first guidance – in effect a code of good practice – in 1990 and promoted it through the churches and LEAs. This offered advice on policies, how to administer the process and how to set up a fair appeal system for parents.

The incoming Blair government in 1997 decided that school admission needed to be fair to all parents and that some of the existing arrangements were inequitable in practice. To address this concern, the government published a code of practice which admission authorities had to observe and created the Office of the Schools Adjudicator (OSA), which was independent of the secretary of state.

The chief schools adjudicator investigates complaints and makes regular annual reports to the secretary of state pointing out where there have been breaches of the code or where it might be clarified. Some of the offences have been sufficiently serious to hinder the establishment of a system fair to all schools and, most importantly, fair to all pupils. For example, schools have covertly (and even overtly) selected pupils or parents – it is not always obvious which – in order to improve the school's chances of achieving recognised success.[7] In Ed Balls' time as secretary of state, an investigation by barristers exposed a school that was charging an 'entry fee' for pupils to increase the school's budget; as he put it: 'Frankly, some of the abuses would make your hair stand on end.' More than one of our ministerial witnesses commented approvingly on the work of the OSA in gradually eliminating what they recollected as unacceptable practice.

Most ministerial witnesses were also at one in agreeing their commitment to admission arrangements that served the interests of social justice and being what one described as a 'level playing field for all parents and their children'. Unfortunately, in 2012 Michael Gove significantly weakened the powers of the OSA, thus slowing the rate of improvement that had previously been achieved.

---

7   Read John O'Farrell's novel *May Contain Nuts: A Novel of Extreme Parenting* (New York: Open Road and Grove/Atlantic, 2007) to enjoy the most vivid and amusing description of just how bewildering and stressful secondary school admission systems can be in an urban environment. It captures South London with cruel brilliance.

Whatever ministerial hopes may be, the reality in some MATs is very different, as one correspondent described:

> When I arrived at the MAT, one of the MAT-wide responsibilities I had was governance. I was able to appoint an admin lead to support on this. We soon realised that no one had ever really got to grips with admissions – policies generally were in a bit of a mess. We had academies across dozens of authorities and each had inherited a slightly different approach to admissions – some areas had fair banding, aptitude tests, etcetera. No one had ever really supported schools from the centre with this and some got it wrong, so there was a ticking off in relation to one school with the adjudicator. Publishing and changing the PAN [published admission number] wasn't always done properly either. I ended up getting advice from a wonderful woman who worked for the LA – she had supported schools for years in carrying out consultations on PAN/admissions criteria and she was very knowledgeable. We didn't have that level of expertise at head office that LAs traditionally had. When you think about the size of a large MAT (running perhaps 30–40 schools across a huge geographical area) and the traditional medium-sized LA running hundreds of schools, it is no wonder!

Alan Parker, former director of the OSA, has summarised the outstanding problems and some of the solutions for us as follows: 'Too often what is presented as providing opportunities for parents to choose school places actually results in schools choosing the children they will admit. This is wrong. There are small but significant changes that could be made to the Admissions Code which would allow more parents to get what they want, and their children deserve.'

We agree with him, and although between us we share 45 years of experience of being responsible for the oversight of what we hoped were fair admission arrangements (but which, because of national policy, we knew were not working in the interests of the least advantaged pupils), we asked Alan, who unlike us is an expert, to write a report as though to a national policy-maker advocating changes which would make the system more equitable. This is what he wrote.[8]

---

8   A version of Alan Parker's text first appeared in Comprehensive Future, *Decision Time: A Plan for Fairer School Admissions* (2018). Available at: https://comprehensivefuture.org.uk/wp-content/uploads/2018/09/Decision-time-A-plan-for-fair-admissions-FINAL.pdf.

Improving the School Admissions Code

The main purpose of the School Admissions Code is to ensure that school places are 'allocated and offered in an open and fair way' and that the 'criteria used to decide [this] are fair, clear and objective'.[9] This is universally supported. However, these terms are subject to interpretation, and subtle unfairness can go unchallenged. The Code could be strengthened by reviewing the permitted oversubscription criteria to reduce the scope for covert selection.

Problematic school admissions occur because it is often not a particular criterion but the way they are used that cause problems. For example, a school might set a catchment area covering a few local villages but choose to avoid the one village with the most local authority social housing. Most people would feel this was unfair, but in practice subtle admission breaches are rarely scrutinised or challenged. Any complaints must be lodged by parents with the Office of the Schools Adjudicator (OSA), and it is difficult to achieve a successful challenge and to get a decision implemented. Guidance in the Code should be strengthened by emphasising the overall objective of fairness for parents and children over the convenience and institutional advantage of schools.

Over-complex and elaborate religious criteria are sometimes found to have a socially selective effect in faith schools. The Code should provide a stronger role for central religious bodies in providing guidance on appropriate arrangements and advice on their interpretation, in order to ensure that fairness to parents and children is paramount. The 2017 chief adjudicator's annual report indicated that the Catholic Education Service had been working with OSA and DfE to this end.[10] More could be achieved if all religious authorities were required to provide such guidance and advice.

There are many aspects of what Alan told us that point to unfairness and the manipulation of the system – for example, issues relating to different sorts of housing or communities.

---

9   Department for Education, *School Admissions Code: Statutory Guidance for Admission Authorities, Governing Bodies, Local Authorities, Schools Adjudicators and Admission Appeals Panels* (December 2014), p. 7. Available at: https://www.gov.uk/government/publications/school-admissions-code--2.

10 Office of the Schools Adjudicator, *Annual Report: September 2016 to August 2017* (February 2018), p. 5. Available at: https://assets.publishing.service.gov.uk/government/uploads/system/uploads/attachment_data/file/680003/2017_OSA_Annual_Report_-_Final_23_January_2018.pdf.

Tim recalls:

When I arrived in Oxford in 1978, we bought a house on the edge of the city between Rose Hill and Iffley. Our nearest upper school was Peers, which served the parents of car workers on what was, and is, the 'wrong side' of the city.

I had to explain to a disbelieving, headshaking brigadier, who was chair of the Education Committee, that this was the school my eldest would attend. 'But its results are terrible and it has all sorts of children there,' he protested, suggesting that I send him instead to Magdalen College School, an independent day school. 'No,' I replied. 'He'll find his own friends and there are some superb staff at the school and the head is a very good guy.' The brigadier went away as puzzled by my answer as I had been disappointed by his initial reaction.

I soon discovered the reality of Oxford at that time, when I was invited to high table at various colleges. I discovered that the dons had children who were either 'too clever', 'too average' or 'too slow' to be trusted to the state schools! What this seemed to disguise, for me, was an unwillingness to let their children mix with the children of people from all walks of life during their teenage years for fear of undesirable peer group influence. Such concerns (in my view, unfounded) are often at the root of parental choice of school.

These are many subtle matters within the agenda of parental preference. The chair of governors of a primary school near a market town in the countryside explained to us:

> Our school was down to 14 on roll and we thought that closure was a certainty. We had the idea of taking a few leaflets around places in town, like doctors' surgeries, clinics, playgroups and the arts centre – we even put some in car showrooms. Anyway, they started to come from town and, over four years, we are up to 40 children and thriving. It is the same for small schools all around here now. Parents are bringing their children out to our friendly little schools and taking them back to town for second-ary school. What we offer is a friendly school with good results and the parents also know that their children will be mixing with the children of people like them – people who can be bothered to

drive 10 miles morning and afternoon to make sure their children are with the right sort of other children.

Let's continue with what Alan Parker told us.

End schools fixing their own admissions

Admission arrangements for community schools are determined by the local authority and for faith schools by the governing body. For academies (and free schools) the decision rests with the academy trust and is mainly exercised at school level. Where MATs operate schools in different areas of the country, their arrangements can be incompatible with those for other local schools. The chief schools adjudicator has reported concerns that confusion as to who is in control of admissions for which school has meant the rules have not been followed. Even when individual schools are compliant with the Admissions Code they can sometimes interact so as to produce unfair outcomes. For example, feeder primary schools are a common admission criterion which can work well, but there was a trend for academy secondary schools to set the trust's own primary schools as the feeder schools. This invariably benefits the MAT but is not always in the best interests of local families.

Many schools do not manipulate their admissions criteria to their own advantage; however, those that do undermine public confidence in the whole system.

Too often what is presented as providing opportunities for parents to choose school places, actually results in schools choosing the children they will admit. Schools that successfully manipulate their intake to admit the kind of pupils likely to succeed in exams present themselves as better than they are, and they make it more difficult for other local schools to succeed and put pressure on other schools to follow suit to counter unfair competition. It is unethical.

Schools that do not wish to game the system have no need to have direct control of oversubscription criteria or oversee the practical administration of admissions. All schools should be able to develop a distinctive character and propose a set of oversubscription criteria to reflect this. However, no school should be allowed to manage its own admissions or use unclear, obscure or elaborate arrangements to skew their intake by excluding or discouraging 'undesirable' applicants.

Consequently, the system should be simplified and made to work in the interests of parents and children in the following way:

- Every school would have the right to propose an admissions 'policy' that identifies oversubscription criteria (i.e. how places are allocated if there are more applicants than places) which support the character of the school, whether religious or otherwise, within the constraints of a strengthened Admissions Code.

- An independent body, such as an area admissions authority (AAA), should be established in each area and required to translate the wishes of all local schools into a formal set of arrangements for them. The AAA would ensure that the formal arrangements were clear, consistent, coherent and compliant with the code. The authority would make it as easy as possible for applicants to understand their options, and to ensure as far as possible that intakes are balanced and reflective of the local community.

- The AAA would also be responsible for the administration of all admissions within the area, removing the burden from schools, in addition to ensuring as far as possible that the implementation of the policy was fair and transparent for parents. Issues such as faith schools using long and complex forms asking parents to describe religious practice would be challenged by an AAA. They might also creatively combat other local admission problems, such as an oversubscribed school using distance as an admission criterion, encouraging inflated prices in the streets around the school. They could change this to random allocation for all applicants living in a priority area to combat 'house price selection'.

- The OSA would continue to be responsible for policing the system. They would be able to receive, investigate and rule on any objection from interested parties that schools or the AAAs were acting inappropriately, and they should continue to collate information from the areas and report on best practice admissions.

Making change happen

Under these proposals, the role of the OSA as independent arbitrator for all disputes relating to school admissions arrangements would remain broadly the same. However, the OSA's task would become simpler as (a) there would be many fewer admissions authorities to scrutinise and (b) AAAs, being 'disinterested', would have no incentive to avoid implementing OSA decisions.

Two further improvements requiring legislation should be considered:

▪ Decisions of the OSA should alter admissions arrangements directly, rather than placing a duty on admissions authorities to make necessary changes (as was the case pre-2012).

▪ Additional code requirements should be brought within the jurisdiction of the OSA (e.g. the injunction proscribing school uniform policies that discourage applications from poorer families).

There would be other beneficial outcomes if these proposals were implemented:

▪ In respect of admissions appeals, locating responsibility within the AAA would aid efficiency and transparency to the benefit of the appellants.

▪ In respect of exclusions and transfers, the former would remain a school-level issue, while the latter should be managed by the AAA through a more streamlined and efficient process.

▪ In respect of fair access protocols (which can lead to schools being directed to admit hard to place children), compliance would be secured more easily if the powers were located within the AAA.

In summary, these proposals for making the existing admissions framework function more efficiently would help to significantly improve the collaborative relationships between schools, maximise the possibilities of real parental choice, and respond to the urgent need for greater fairness and social cohesion.

We agree with Alan Parker's conclusions and believe it is even more urgent after the COVID-19 pandemic that admission arrangements should reflect a determination to make them more equitable because unfair arrangements usually hit poor families hardest.

One head recalls her experience of her school being regarded as having an excellent SEND resource: 'Some schools became very good at directing parents with children with SEND elsewhere. We had a fantastic SEND department, and I know parents used to arrive to look round having been encouraged by others in the area to send their child to us as we had a "great reputation" for doing well with SEND students.' Other experts, including Alan Parker, provided us with helpful case studies which illustrate the pluses and minuses of various criteria used in admission policies.

Case studies: a brief look at the reality of school admissions

Schools use a wide range of admission criteria to decide which pupils should attend them if there are more applications than places. Research in 2016 showed that 59% of schools received more applications than they could accommodate and used oversubscription rules to determine which pupils were offered places.[11]

Oversubscription criteria vary from school to school, but here we list some of the most common ways used to determine places.

- *Distance from school:* Pupils' home addresses are placed in order of distance and those living closest to the school are offered places. This is also the most common 'tiebreaker' mechanism when more applicants meet a requirement than available places.

---

11 J. Andrews, *School Performance in Multi-Academy Trusts and Local Authorities – 2015* (London: Education Policy Institute, 2016). Available at: https://epi.org.uk/publications-and-research/school-performance-multi-academy-trusts-local-authorities.

- *Priority areas:* A catchment area is defined and pupils in the priority area are offered places ahead of those who live further away.

- *Feeder schools:* Secondary schools prioritise entry for pupils attending specific primary schools.

- *Fair banding tests:* Primary school pupils take an ability test and secondary schools use these test results to create an 'all ability' intake using equal bands of ability (e.g. 25% low attainers, 50% medium attainers, 25% high attainers). This is usually used in conjunction with other criteria (i.e. catchment and distance).

- *Random allocation:* Schools use a computerised lottery system to randomly allocate places to applicants. This is also commonly used as a 'tiebreaker' mechanism, particularly when distance measurements give the same answer for more than one applicant.

- *Ability tests:*[12] England's 163 grammar schools use 11+ tests to admit high-attaining pupils to the school. Some grammar schools offer their places to the pupils with the highest ranked scores while others use a test with a pass mark, which then has to be used in conjunction with other criteria to distinguish between those who have achieved the threshold score. There are also 38 partially selective schools using an 11+ test to select a proportion of pupils based on ability.

- *Aptitude tests:* Schools are allowed to select up to 10% of pupils who demonstrate 'aptitude' for a subject such as sport, music or language. These tests are not allowed to judge proficiency in any subject but must judge potential. This means schools testing for language aptitude would not set a French test but would use a made-up or obscure language to attempt to judge a pupil's potential.

---

12 We both believe that there is no case for selection, whether overt or covert, especially at 11. We should add that we both worked together in Birmingham, which since the 1970s has been 'super-selective', and while we were not impressed by the performance of every one of the few remaining grammar schools, it didn't materially affect the energy, culture and pupil outcomes of most of the other secondary schools. It did, however, diminish the number of middle-class families sending their youngsters to private schools. We would note that we have also lived all our lives in a schooling system that selects at 16, except in those areas that have sixth-form tertiary colleges.

▦ *Proof of faith:* Faith schools can select pupils based on supplementary information showing a child is connected to a specific religion. This might involve proof that parents attend a specific place of worship, that a child has attended Sunday School, been baptised or that the parents have performed duties associated with their place of worship.

▦ *Priority for specific groups of pupils:* Children in care are among the most vulnerable children in society and all schools must give first admission priority to looked-after children and previously looked-after children. An admission policy might offer priority to siblings of current pupils, the children of teachers at the school or children from disadvantaged backgrounds.

▦ *A combination of admission methods:* Many schools combine admission methods, sometimes in unusually complex ways. One London school allocates places according to faith, language specialism, banding, distance and sibling criteria. Its admission policy runs to 11 pages.

Some common problems and best practice with the exercise of these criteria:

▦ *Fair banding: common problems.* Fair banding admissions can cause problems if they are operated in a way that is not actually 'fair'. For example: unless the bands reflect the bell curve of performance, the school may skew its intake to affect favourably its future performance. Or a school might arrange a test at a weekend and fail to promote it widely enough, thereby reaching only keen, middle-class parents who can arrange for their children to take the test while other pupils miss out and do not even apply to the school. One Liverpool school uses an eight-page application form for parents to apply for its fair banding test, with only one Saturday morning session available to sit the test. If a school is 'banding' the children of a small group of motivated and wealthy parents, it can skew the ability profile of the school. The profile of this one Liverpool school shows that 0.8% of pupils are low attainers, 27% medium attainers and 72% high attainers. In effect, the school has a similar profile to a grammar school because it misuses a banding test to skew its intake towards higher-ability applicants.

- *Fair banding: best practice.* Fair banding admissions are used for the majority of secondary schools in Hackney. A common banding test is offered to all primary school pupils as a matter of course, and when applications are determined each secondary school aims to achieve a similar proportion of high, medium and low attainers. All Hackney's secondary schools are rated good or outstanding, and this method helps to avoid potential competition between schools for high-attaining pupils in order to boost league table rankings. A more balanced mix of pupils helps ensure that each school has a similar socio-economic profile and it helps prevent popular schools unduly affecting local housing costs.

- *Faith admissions: common problems.* Some faith schools use complex religious affiliation forms – for example, one London school asked all applicants to fill in a form stating the date a child's parents were married into the faith, whether the children have a TV at home and how often they use the internet. Such questions ensure that only children of this faith attend the school, even if answers to these personal questions cannot officially be used to determine places, while questions about TV/internet use might be used to screen those of lower socio-economic status. When faith schools use admission forms like this it is highly unlikely that any child of an alternative faith, or no faith at all, will ever access the school, and poorer families could be excluded. Other schools have used elaborate systems where 'points' are accumulated through providing proof of a range of activities, such as volunteering to decorate the church with flowers, beyond strictly religious participation. These criteria discriminate against disabled, single or working parents.

- *Faith admissions: best practice.* Nigel Genders, chief education officer of the Church of England, supports the idea that new Church of England schools should have 'open door' admissions with no proof of faith required. According to Genders, 'In practice most of the new schools that the Church of England has provided in recent years have all been entirely open admission policies so that they would serve their local community.'[13] St Luke's Primary School in Kingston upon Thames changed its admissions in 2015 to abandon any need for proof of church attendance. The local vicar said he was uncomfortable recording parents' church attendance and felt that 'cynicism' was motivating some parents to attend church to win a school place. The school now has a Christian ethos but selects pupils by distance; the opportunity to attend the school is open to all local children, regardless of faith. Even where priority is given to members of the faith group, a simple and straightforward way of establishing membership is much fairer than elaborate mechanisms to differentiate between degrees of religious practice (e.g. many Roman Catholic schools require only that applicants have been baptised).

Priority areas: common problems. A heavily oversubscribed secondary school with a proud record of GCSE and A level results uses two admission priority areas, but due to its popularity all its successful applicants live in the first, smaller priority area. This means that the furthest distance any pupil lives from the school is just 1.1 km. This has given rise to much discussion among prospective parents (for example, on social media sites like Mumsnet) about ever-changing priority areas, with claims from some parents that they have paid a premium price for a home only to find that they were suddenly not eligible for the school of their choice. The school's policy is encouraging wealthy parents to buy houses ever closer to the school. There are ways the school could mitigate these effects. At present most pupils live within a 10-minute walk of the school but expanding the priority area might allow a wider range of pupils an opportunity to win a place and discourage the inflated house prices near the school. It is also the case that a more equitable overall approach would allow other local schools to improve – thus reducing the pressure on the currently most popular.

---

13   Quoted in A. Lusher, New Church of England Schools to Adopt 'Open Admissions' Policy, *The Independent* (11 June 2014). Available at: https://www.independent.co.uk/news/education/education-news/new-church-england-schools-adopt-open-admissions-policy-9525134.html.

Priority areas: best practice. One popular London school was keen to represent its community and avoid rising house prices near the school. This school used an 'admission area' comprising the two postcode areas closest to the school with random allocation of places among all applicants living in this zone. The school is also keen to admit a cohort that is representative of pupils from the local community, so ahead of this criterion it prioritises 27% of places to pupils eligible for the pupil premium.

Feeder schools: common problems. As mentioned above, this criterion has been used to prioritise primary schools run by the same MAT. It can also be used to limit secondary faith school admissions to those who attended a similar faith primary. Again, feeder schools could be chosen exclusively from affluent areas. In all these cases the effect is to force parents to consider their preferred secondary school before primary entry – seven years ahead of the normal decision time. This distorts 'parental choice' and excludes anyone who doesn't want, or cannot get, a place in a feeder primary; moves into an area after their children are 5; or is not in position to plan that far ahead. Such people are disproportionately likely to be from disadvantaged communities. It is telling that such arrangements are rarely supported by primary head teachers.

Feeder schools: best practice. There are few valid reasons to justify secondary schools using this criterion. The most common excuse – to promote links and ensure smooth transition from primary to secondary school – does not withstand scrutiny. All secondary schools can, and should, liaise with their de facto feeder schools to do this without any need for admissions priority. It is justified where children at the feeder school might otherwise be left without a suitable option if denied a place at the only school they could reasonably attend – for example, linked infant and junior schools in a locality where the only other option is all-through primaries.

Some summary thoughts

In the mid-18th century, around the time Captain Cook was exploring the Pacific, the early hospitals opening in England were mainly in urban areas. They were called infirmaries, where physicians were to engage in their practice on patients who were ailing. The demand was immediate so people who required treatment were vetted. Only patients with letters of recommendation were admitted. No one with an infectious disease was allowed in, or expectant mothers, the dying or those of unsound mind. What the infirmaries were doing was trying to guarantee their success in terms of patients who were worth treating. To be a successful hospital, it helps if your patients are not too ill.

So it is with schooling. Our early schools took children from those who could pay but, to guarantee their continuing income, needed to recruit those children who would most likely succeed, so they set entrance exams. Where they got it wrong and pupils did poorly, they wrote reports for parents that pointed out that it was the child who was at fault.

Philanthropists opened schools for the poor, but had to persuade parents to allow their children to attend rather than lose the chance to gain meagre amounts of money legally or otherwise.

The tension between the selector schools and recruiters began a very long while ago. Today's grammar schools are the equivalent of a hospital for the very fit and healthy where you are admitted as long as you can prove you are well.

Just like universities, some schools today are 'selecting' schools and some 'recruiting' schools. Schools that select their intake create rules, and the more selective, the more complex, often to ensure that they remain selectors by as far as possible guaranteeing their result.

Schools that are recruiting their intake often try to make an attractive offer – an engaging curriculum experience or modern equipment – while the selectors can hold fast to what has worked for them over time and imply a mild sympathy for those schools which cannot have their standards or expectations. The recruiting schools are a useful outlet if any of their selected pupils struggle to respond to their ways and they often kindly negotiate for the pupil to transfer to the 'much more appropriate school down the road' rather than struggle or cast doubt upon their effectiveness.

There is no one-size-fits-all approach to school admissions because of different philosophies in a market-driven, high-accountability environment: local factors will always have a bearing on the best method to use or the best guarantee of the outcome sought. However, it is clear that many of the admissions criteria currently employed work well in some cases and cause problems in others, and that some form of official and local supervision is necessary to make sure that admissions methods are fair to pupils and schools in what has become a competitive market economy. There is a problematic lack of oversight of school admissions at present, and while schools with the very worst policies are asked to make changes if they breach the code, thousands of schools are able to use policies that cause various forms of more minor unfairness or encourage social selection. Long application forms, expensive school uniforms and the tradition or reputation of a school are all subtle factors which can encourage socio-economic selection.

The proportion of high attainers and disadvantaged pupils attending a school gives clues to social selection caused by poor admissions. Some of the schools, quoted above, in the 'problem' case studies, have more than 60% high attainers, while an average school contains around 30%. Again, these schools each have less than 10% pupil premium pupils, while the average proportion is 28%. It is clear that complex or weakly overseen admission policies often benefit wealthier families and exclude poorer pupils.

Many schools will continue to operate the admission policies that permit them the most favourable intake of pupils, particularly in such a competitive landscape, unless an effective new local body takes charge to oversee school admissions. A new admissions body would look out for the interests of all local pupils and ensure every school serves its community well.

There are three further points that we would add to Alan Parker's rehearsal of the current problems and a way to overcome them.

First, the usual tiebreaker in oversubscription is distance but this too has disadvantages. For example, parent A lives a long way from their closest school – say, in a rundown housing estate on the edge of a large town or city (which may have lost its secondary school at the time of falling school rolls) – while parent B lives on the salubrious side of town closer to where there may be three schools from which to choose. In the case of oversubscription, parent B would be selected ahead of parent A for all three schools. This is not a hypothetical example but one that we have each encountered in our work in LEAs.

Second, we noted that parent A – so often a poor family – had to be allocated a school place for their child which might be far distant from his or her home, often incurring extra travel costs for the local authority and a long journey to school for the pupil. In this example, parent B's *choice* has overridden parent A's *wish* (some would say right) for their child to attend the closest school. That right – to attend the school closest to where you live – should be established as having priority over the usual tiebreakers.

Third, and most important, we think that a national decision is required to:

1   Set up area admission authorities (AAAs) with democratic input into running school admission cycles each year for the start of compulsory schooling and at 11 (or 9 and 13 in middle school systems) and to settle arrangements for in-year transfers between schools, for whatever reason, as well as new arrivals in the area. AAAs could be vested within the existing local authority framework, either singly or in larger combinations of authorities.

2   Determine what, if any, national priorities – such as, in the interests of equity, giving priority to FSM-entitled children as well as the already prioritised children in care and those with an education, health and care plan (EHCP) for SEND – should be preconditions for the AAAs in establishing local school admission policies. Such policies, after consultation with all schools and other interested parties, would be determined to secure equity and equality of opportunity consistent with parental choice of school.

3   Revise the Code of Practice in the light of (1) and (2), to be undertaken by the schools adjudicator, which should be made mandatory for all AAAs and the schools and academies in their area.

Attendance

Once admitted to school most children are fine and take full advantage of what is on offer, certainly socially and often academically. For a minority, however, for a variety of reasons, school is an acquired taste which they either never fully or even partly acquire, or it is something they eventually get after a long period of coming to terms with the habit.

Good schools are conscious of this and make all sorts of adjustments to overcome pupil or family reluctance to attend. There are legions of examples of schools adjusting their own practices to improve timely arrival, ranging from addressing the ethos of the start of the school day, to tolling the ancient school bell in the village primary schools of Tim's childhood to encourage late risers, to offering class and individual incentives, to adjusting the timing of tutor periods in secondary schools when the senior leadership team (SLT) realise that attendance is related to how welcoming the form tutor is.[14] And, to their credit, many schools have made sense of these changes to timing by realising that what really makes the difference is a pupil day with an engaging curriculum and pedagogy, along with purposeful assessment.

That schools have always known that attendance figures mattered is also reflected in the fact that even 150 years ago 'payment by results' depended not just on pupil performance but also on them being in school in the first place. The oldest among us who have kept their school reports will notice that among the sepia-tinted pages there is a numerical record of attendance.

Mick recalls:

When I was a pupil at primary school, each Monday morning assembly saw the head teacher award the three painted plywood shields to the winning classes to hang outside their classroom doors until Friday. One shield was for the class that had added most to the school fund (we were expected to take in a penny per week!), one was for progress (although I have no idea how that was measured, and nor, I suspect, did the school) and the third was for the class with the best

---

14   Of course, we might criticise such actions as avoiding the issue of making sure that all tutors make their tutor or form periods a welcoming and worthwhile time.

attendance. That shield was embellished with the chevrons of the old-fashion register.

I remember watching this weekly ceremony and thinking that this was a strangely unfair competition. A family with chicken pox could take down the results of four classes and potato-picking week spoiled the game entirely. Mind you, my family used to stay with my uncle 'on holiday' for the last week in September each year as the working day on building sites shortened towards the end of summer and my father's earning potential dropped. No wonder the head teacher moaned when I asked for a holiday form, which families were supposed to complete to ask for permission.

Nowadays attendance figures can be a make-or-break feature of a school's Ofsted inspection. But there was a period, in the age of optimism and trust and earlier, when it didn't matter much, and when, as we have seen, potato picking, blanket closures of schools at the first sign of snow and the odd prize day-announced day off combined to provide mixed messages about the importance of learning. In those far-off days, the school bobby would chase the awkward families about attendance. The school bobby gave way to the education welfare officer, who – in one further upward step of professional social mobility – became the education social worker. The latter two postholders were much preoccupied with the social problems of families rather than school attendance per se. Some were even rumoured to complain that if they were still of school age, there were certain schools where they wouldn't want to go. Vexed by this, one or two brave LEAs decided to base their education social workers not in a comfortable office but to disperse them into schools where it was hoped the culture clash would sort itself out.

Eventually (and we think properly), schools themselves became the prime movers on attendance. Someone within the school was given responsibility for chasing non-attenders; someone who was conscious of the distinction between authorised and unauthorised categories of absence and the implications for the school of too high percentages in their returns to either their MAT, local authority or visiting Ofsted inspector.

Any time lost from schooling is potentially a lost opportunity for pupils' learning, both from teachers and each other. We say 'potentially' because if they are fortunate enough to be taught by teachers at the top of their game, as so many are, they may miss moments when they are surprised into mastering the fundamentals of a skill, understanding a concept or internalising the learning of essential knowledge, which previously they had thought out of reach. If no such magic moments occur, the loss of a day's schooling is not so serious. Since we work on the assumption that moments like this do occur, schools have become used to doing their very best to ensure attendance, including providing free breakfasts for either all children or those from the poorest families, so that they have an incentive to come to school and will start the day ready to learn rather than hungry.

The efforts by schools to sustain learning during the pandemic show how vital the routine contact between teacher and pupil can be. Even though the BBC established lockdown learning opportunities, international celebrities 'taught' classes online and the web was deluged with impromptu lessons in everything from keep fit to languages, the contact (even through a screen) with a teacher who knew them and being in virtual proximity to their friends was important to many pupils, although not those on the wrong side of the digital divide.

However, such efforts should not put a rosy glow on an endemic problem for some families and schools. Finding out the reasons for absence or lateness – whether that is caring responsibilities or the family being recent arrivals with a low command of English – is clearly the best route to take, and many schools can and do achieve much through home visits and going the extra mile.

We regret the increasingly ubiquitous use of fines. Some might argue that fines work and that not to levy them is being 'soft'. The problem isn't so much their use as the circumstances that sometimes precede their use and the way they are imposed. Fines are commonly levied for one of two reasons: persistent absence or deliberate avoidance by families who choose to take a holiday during term time. In both cases a fine is usually recommended by the school and imposed by the local authority. On the principle of subsidiarity, there is no reason why schools shouldn't be the body recommending and then imposing fines. (In the case of MATs, the individual school is not a legal entity so this is a duty that the trust would have to shoulder.) It is conceivable that schools could abuse this power or be harassed by an aggressive family; therefore, there should be an appeals process similar to that which exists for permanent exclusions.

There are myriad reasons why sensitivity is required by schools when dealing with absence – for example, difficult cases of school phobia or bullying or the child acting as an unsupported family carer. There are estimated to be 800,000 school-age children across the UK acting as a carer in their family.[15] That is about 30 per school on average. These children often wash, clothe and feed others, as well as administer medicines, before coming to school. A fine for lateness is hardly going to help. Most schools are sympathetic to absences caused by mental health issues, domestic violence and so on and refer families to social care services and other appropriate agencies.

There remains one other cause of absence that usually leads not to a fine but to the more serious outcome of removing the child from the school roll. It arises most often when a first- or second-generation Asian child makes a long visit to the Indian subcontinent for family reasons. The solution to this ought to be an agreement (which many individual schools have pioneered) that the visit, which ideally should not occur at key periods of the pupil's school career, is an opportunity for the completion of an extended personal learning task, which can be accredited on their return to school. If this were adopted as universal practice, it would avoid the danger of unconscious racism in those very few schools who don't blink an eye at taking an Asian pupil off roll, but do turn a blind eye to the child of the local university academic sojourning for a term in the United States or Europe.

The managerial approach to attendance has expanded massively in recent years. While it was, and is, needed in some schools, for the vast majority of pupils it is not a significant issue. Most schools are well attended. However, like the teacher who 'deals with' the whole class because one pupil is out of line, so the system invests in mechanisms to deal with the few and thereby spoiling the climate for the many.

---

15 See https://www.childrenssociety.org.uk/what-we-do/our-work/supporting-young-carers/facts-about-young-carer.

Mick recalls:

In some Black Country schools, we had historic poor attendance from the pupils of parents who themselves had 'wagged off' or couldn't be bothered to turn up in the first place. All the usual tricks had been tried: rewards, punishments, charts, graphs and teddy bears to be cared for by the highest performing class. The figure was hard to shift.

We found that attendance dropped off when children transferred to secondary school. A combination of the new journey and morning routine, an unfamiliar building, requirements for personal possession of equipment and books and so on all became too much for some in the first few weeks. Children who were delayed and feared being 'in bother' decided it was easier to stay at home or hang around in the park, shops or bus shelters rather than go to school.

A few schools decided to develop a transition project about going to school. An example of the learning activity was Year 6 children doing work related to maths and geography, creating their route from bed to desk, measuring it accurately and creating a map. As part of their induction arrangements prior to attending secondary school, they produced another accurate map, including bus routes or parents' cars, as appropriate. Back in primary schools, teachers worked on journey times – mean, median, mode, range, average – and the difference between primary and secondary journeys.

A theme on schools was developed for both phases to use, including learning about why we have schools, how they began, different sorts of schools and the cost of running a school (per year, week or hour). The children studied famous educators (there are some) and famous celebrities who used to be teachers (there are many) and considered whether they would like to be taught by them. Extracts from classic literary texts were used to glimpse schooling in different times and places. Assemblies over several weeks considered the UNICEF images of children across the globe striving to get to school: by canoe, tuk-tuk, sledge or zip wire. Schooling must be worth it was the message.

When Year 7 attendance was analysed after the first eight weeks, the results were a significant improvement on previous years. Was it the theme? Who knows, but teachers thought it was – and, anyway, the project was productive and fascinating.

Another group of schools in the Olympus MAT in South Gloucestershire have developed an 'identity' theme to bridge the transition from primary to secondary. With the children they call it 'People, Places and Me' as it sounds more accessible and immediate. Children do challenges (often with their family) linked to 'The Maths of Me', 'The Art of Me', 'Musical Me' and so on, and arrive at secondary with a suite of products that serve as a resource for further learning. The quality of the children's products has generally been high. This is a massive step forward on the rather perfunctory 'Myself' work that often takes place in tutor or form time in Year 7.

The key point is that attendance tends to get worse in the early months after the transition between each stage of schooling. Rather than trying to mop up afterwards, it might be better to head it off beforehand. Addressing the issue of transition between the primary and secondary phases positively could do much for school success in improving attendance. One of our major recommendations about starting a research project in Year 6 and completing it in Year 7 (see Chapter 13) would improve matters greatly.

Similarly, schools could look closely at the possible negative effect of homework policies, lunch and break times, responses to lost equipment, the impact of 'no excuses' policies and places in school where there are crowds (for example, imagining the impact on an autistic pupil of a flash mob dance, however well intended). All of these, as well as one of the most important – how the exit from school at the end of the day is managed – will affect attendance. Too many of our approaches are about the school maintaining its reputation in the eyes of the majority rather than considering the effect on certain pupils. Usually, considering the impact for some will have a positive impact for all. Humane organisations tend to be more attractive to humans, including young ones.

Finally, we think the damage that absences cause to pupils can be mitigated by the clever use of new technologies and the possibilities which would be opened up by the creation of an 'Open School' (which we outline in Chapter 13).

Behaviour and exclusions

Just as attendance has always been a challenge to the school system, so too has behaviour. Schools are generally disciplined environments; indeed, many represent an oasis of order in pupils' chaotic lives. Yet, politicians often allude to their commitment to good behaviour and discipline as though there is a problem to solve. Head teachers manage the organisation of the school and teachers manage the organisation of the classroom and, in doing so, they seek to contribute to the overall learning of each pupil by teaching them how to conduct themselves in the company of others.

More than 150 years after the beginning of state schooling, the system still grapples with the challenge of how to purposefully accommodate all pupils with their different maturities, personalities and outlooks in a harmonious daily routine, and with what to do when things don't go as we would wish. The school system is burdened by the rites and rituals of tradition; the expectations we have for young people in schools are very often different from those in the world outside. Views on good behaviour are as polarised as they are on pedagogy and curriculum, with schools drawing attention to themselves for supposedly forward- or backward-looking practice.

We are going to explore some of the issues as they have unfolded and suggest that they need to unfold better. Let's start in the period at the beginning of our book.

Tim recalls:

It was 1980. Two years earlier, I had arrived in Oxfordshire from an ILEA that had abolished caning in its schools. Being very young, I was impatient to follow suit but sensible enough to know that a county council with 61 conservatives and eight others – and, as such, committed to making the cuts in budgets demanded at that time – might be likely to greet any policy paper of mine raising the issue of corporal punishment by asking me, 'How many more canes do you need, education officer?'

I knew that wasn't the route to take. Instead, I surveyed the county's 48 secondary schools, establishing in confidence how many times they used the cane, which a few had already abandoned. I sent the resultant league table back to the schools, showing them where they stood individually in an otherwise anonymised list. We then engaged in discussion as a group, reaching no conclusions except that we would repeat the survey in a year's time. By then there were just two schools still using the cane and by the following year, with the retirement of one of the heads and second thoughts on the part of the other, there were none.

Of course, I was quietly pleased with myself, but I have never forgotten one head smiling at me and asking how many exclusions there had been in previous years. The answer was one. 'You might see that figure rise' was his speculative observation.

We need to start by saying that we are not arguing for the return of corporal punishment, but we are concerned about the use of fixed-term exclusion as one of the rungs on the ladder of school sanctions.

The thought of excluding a pupil from a school is invariably the decision that causes the most distress for a school leader. It is the final stated stage of any school's approved discipline policy. Ideally, these policies (often called 'behaviour for learning' policies) are brief; the best are written in positive language and start with a reiteration of the school's values and aims. Too often, however, the policies are both too long (we have been sent many examples and some run to over 30 A4 pages of guidance for all teachers in the MAT group) and too weighted towards a deficit model. They are increasingly based on assertive discipline or offshoots such as the SLANT technique.[16] Behaviour ladders mean that the pupil is moved to the next rung of consequence without the adults addressing the behaviour that is causing difficulty. Similarly, traffic light systems and red and yellow cards focus on the consequence rather than the pupil. Some policies are reinforced by methodologies based on how the teachers will be checked for compliance – in effect, making sure that teachers are behaving themselves.

The best behaviour policies start with advice to teachers on how to win the support of their pupils with time-honoured strategies such as

---

16 Sit up, listen, ask and answer questions, nod your head and track the speaker conveniently spells SLANT, one of the many acronyms to which schools seem attracted.

greeting them at the start of the day and creating a positive atmosphere from the beginning; they are deeply conscious of the Ginott quotation we mentioned in Chapter 1. The best schools recognise that they need to help children learn how to behave appropriately and to exercise self-regulation for the good of the community in which they spend their time. It is more than a case of setting the rules and stating what will happen if they are not obeyed.

Over the years, schools have been offered helpful advice, even if some of it falls into the grandmother sucking eggs variety. In the decades since 1976, it came first through the Elton Report (1989)[17] and the Steer Report (2009),[18] both of which responded to comments we have heard in secondary school staffrooms during the whole of our careers – occurring most often as the February half-term approaches and following the darkest part of the year – that 'pupils' behaviour is getting worse'. These two reports contain messages that are still relevant today and emphasise points about the school climate with a few clear rules, an engaging curriculum, good teaching and assessment, positive relationships and effective school leadership (which we cover in Chapter 7).

Behaviour has vexed politicians for a long time. Andrew Adonis, whose own schooling experience had been hindered by the poor behaviour of others, was quick to acknowledge that government should have done more to address the matter:

> A mistake I made as minister, and from my own experience of school was, because having disruptive kids in the school is a real problem, the thing to do is to get them out. I'm afraid I perpetrated that mistake: I did nothing to change the regime of exclusions. What should have happened was to radically improve the way that schools deal with poor behaviour: better facilities and much better training for teachers. When I look at so much of what is happening, particularly boys who get fixed-term exclusions or permanent exclusions, it leads them straight into the criminal justice system. It is a catastrophic policy.

---

17 R. Elton, *Discipline in Schools* [Elton Report] (London: HMSO, 1989). Available at: http://www. educationengland.org.uk/documents/elton/elton1989.html.
18 A. Steer, *Learning Behaviour: Lessons Learned: A Review of Behaviour Standards and Practices in Our Schools* [Steer Report] (Nottingham: Department for Children, Schools and Families, 2009). Available at: http://www.educationengland.org.uk/documents/pdfs/2009-steer-report-lessons-learned.pdf.

I think if we'd abolished fixed-term exclusion that would have driven dramatic change in the whole way that we manage behaviour in school and in the whole way that we value learning for more disruptive children. It would also have dramatically reduced permanent exclusions as well. The number of fixed-term exclusions is astronomical – it's hundreds of thousands.

Ed Balls saw one way forward in the world beyond school:

I had tensions with Gordon [Brown] and Louise Casey[19] because Gordon didn't want to lose the hard edge of the Anti-Social Behaviour Unit, but actually our focus was much more on youth services – things like identifying learning difficulties in speech or communication which often then led to behavioural problems. I was trying to have with the police a targeted youth support for kids who were at risk and there was a big shift more generally to prevention. It was trying to think about the whole child and every aspect of how their life affected their prospects and how public policy engaged with their prospects, and then a focus more on collaboration and less on the individual school going their own way.

More recently, secretaries of state have appointed 'behaviour tsars'. Charlie Taylor (2011) and then Tom Bennett (2017) gave respectively shorter and lengthier advice to schools,[20] before Edward Timpson (2019) was commissioned to write a report which would face up to the reality of ever rising numbers of fixed-term and permanent exclusions from schools.[21]

Taylor's and Bennett's reports are written in a different tone from the others. In keeping with the political times when they were commissioned, they imply that effective schools keep their pupils under control by doing certain things well and, therefore, that behaviour will be good if we all

19 Dame Louise Casey is highly regarded for her insight, broad experience and campaigning in working to support disadvantaged people. She has led many government reviews and inquiries.
20 C. Taylor, *Getting the Simple Things Right: Charlie Taylor's Behaviour Checklists* (London: Department for Education, 2011). Available at: https://assets.publishing.service.gov.uk/government/uploads/system/uploads/attachment_data/file/571640/Getting_the_simple_things_right_Charlie_Taylor_s_behaviour_checklists.pdf; and T. Bennett, *Creating a Culture: How School Leaders Can Optimise Behaviour* (London: Department for Education, 2017). Available at: https://assets.publishing.service.gov.uk/government/uploads/system/uploads/attachment_data/file/602487/Tom_Bennett_Independent_Review_of_Behaviour_in_Schools.pdf.
21 E. Timpson, *The Timpson Review of School Exclusion*. Ref: DfE-00090-2019 (May 2019). Available at: https://assets.publishing.service.gov.uk/government/uploads/system/uploads/attachment_data/file/807862/Timpson_review.pdf.

do what outstanding schools do, particularly brooking no argument or debate. Both mention the importance of having 'red lines' and the need to be seen to be dealing effectively with transgressions as an example for the majority who do not misbehave. The problem with having red lines and insisting that erring pupils depart 'our school and its values' is that they have to go somewhere and, in practice, that often means travelling on a downward path to a life that is painful to themselves and others.

We interviewed the current tsar, Tom Bennett, who makes no secret of his background and his difficulty in relating to head teachers:

> My management experience was in nightclubs in Soho, so I can't really speak for school leadership too much here, but what we see is this: I find a great number of leaders absolutely paralysed with incapability of how to line manage people. They don't know how to have an assertive but supportive conversation with somebody, and they will do anything rather than say, 'Actually, you need to do this – you need to teach better.'

> To some extent, I do sympathise with a lot of exclusions. There is a lot of dysfunction within the system just now. This is why I'm still broadly an advocate of exclusion as a part of the process that exists within a healthier process, which includes support up to that point.

When it comes to the circumstances that lead to exclusion, Bennett observed:

> One of the things that always animates me is when I go to a good PRU [pupil referral unit] or a good AP [alternative provision], I'll say to them, 'How many children have you got here that need to be here. You know, who really can't cope in a mainstream school?' They usually say to me: 'About two-thirds or four-fifths of the children need to be here because they've been so damaged and brutalised by their circumstances and have been let down so many times before this, so they're broken. They need to be here for people like us to help build them up again.'

This suggests that a lot of children can't cope in some circumstances, unless we radically rethink what mainstream schools are and have some kind of wrap-around social care or something like that, and also that there's a very real need for high-quality exclusion destinations. It also suggests to me that about a third or possibly even a fifth of children who are in these destinations could probably have been retained within a mainstream environment if they'd had higher levels of high-quality support prior to the point that they were excluded.

The government's acceptance of Timpson's recommendations included the announcement at the end of February 2020 of a task force led by – you guessed it – Tom Bennett and Charlie Taylor.[22] Their working group, which was formed a short time before schools began to cope with the consequences of the pandemic, will presumably run over the same ground with a view to implementing Timpson's recommendations.

As one head teacher, Janice Allen, remarked: 'Timpson's report seems sensible and workable: in our school, we have been considering the language we use. We have stopped using the word "challenging", for example, to describe behaviour and use the word "distressed" because the reason a child loses control is usually distress of one sort or another. Although we still use the language of choice and consequences, we have doubts about language which causes the classic fight-or-flight response.'

Another of our witnesses wisely remarked that 'getting behaviour right involves knowing your teachers and your pupils and contacting parents when things go well as well as when they go wrong'. This is how another one put it:

> I have always felt that fixed-term exclusions are often pointless. I much prefer internal exclusion where you can do some work with them, some restorative discussions and so on. We also worked with some schools close to each other where students went to another school to do their exclusion and that worked quite well. The problem you often have is staff – they are often of a mind-set that unless a child has been FT [fixed-term] excluded then it hasn't been dealt with. I do think there has to be some message for children that says, 'If you don't get it right, you can't be part of the pack!' Also, the best part about an FT exclusion is getting the parents in afterwards. For internal exclusions I would do that too – that bit is key.

---

22 Charlie Taylor was appointed as HM Chief Inspector of Prisons in 2020.

One interesting comment about online learning during the pandemic was that those pupils who didn't log on are largely the same pupils who find it difficult to concentrate in class and are therefore the cause of low-level disruption. Consequently, teachers in schools that have really risen to the challenge of online learning are less hassled by poor behaviour, which, of course, highlights ongoing problems in other schools and consequently prompts reports like those from Elton, Steer, Taylor, Bennett and Timpson. While low-level disruption is a theme in the Elton and Steer Reports, the incidence has been reducing for many years according to inspection reports. The government policies launched during the first decade of the millennium, which led to increased numbers of teaching assistants and learning mentors, were seen by many as influential in distinguishing those pupils with significant social and emotional challenges from those for whom curriculum access was challenging in general. We cannot help noticing that the gap between the Elton and Steer reports is 20 years but since then we have had three reports in less than 10 years.

Politically, it has become important to talk about discipline and behaviour – what David Laws called good 'retail politics', something that the electorate buys. Most parents want to know that their child's school insists on good behaviour, until it is their own child who is in trouble and then they prefer more understanding approaches. Tom Bennett reflected: 'I think what is particularly interesting is that a lot of Conservative secretaries of state make a lot of hay with an emphasis on discipline. That appeals to a certain demographic.'

In his opening address to the FED Education Summit in March 2021, Gavin Williamson spent over a third of his 12 minutes emphasising the importance of behaviour – more time than he spent on academies, COVID or his proposed Institute of Teaching.[23] When talking with us, Williamson restated the simple premise: 'Actually, exclusion is difficult and you sometimes have to make difficult choices. You have to show that, where boundaries are crossed, there are consequences. By putting a real drive on strong discipline and behaviour, I think you'll massively reduce the number of exclusions.'

Is it that simple? Are firmly enforced discipline policies the solution or part of the problem? As a solution, Williamson's premise is clearly failing

---

23 Department for Education and G. Williamson, Education Secretary Speech to FED National Education Summit (1 March 2021). Available at: https://www.gov.uk/government/speeches/education-secretary-speech-to-fed-national-education-summit.

because exclusions, both short-term and permanent, are rising year on year. Are societal changes having a deeper impact on pupil behaviour over time, or are other factors proving to be influential? It could be that the narrowing of the curriculum, the competitive focus on measurable academic outcomes in frequent high-stakes tests and exams, and the forcing through of the EBacc (which was introduced without parliamentary approval) have changed the culture and climate in schools. Certainly, Ofsted has been sufficiently concerned to change its framework to assess the breadth of the curriculum that schools offer. Three of the HMCIs we interviewed thought the curriculum was too narrow and the accountability system essential but too blinkered and tight.

Kenneth Baker, speaking about UTCs, has seen the difference that a practical and authentic approach to the curriculum can have with teenagers:

> Very quickly in our UTCs, there's a behavioural change with many of our students. We don't have bloody-mindedness in our schools. There's a mutual respect between the teacher and the student. Sometimes they call the teacher by their first name, they don't mind that at all. They go into the workshop and talk to the people running the machines, and they are learning to make things, handle metal, tools and machinery like a 3D printer. These are skills that will get them a job and that's transformational.

We don't think policy-makers or other people within the schooling system appreciate just what an exception England is in relation to exclusions.

In the course of our research for this book, we came across the figures for permanent exclusion in 2018/2019.[24] These reveal that whereas England (with a total population of c.47 million) had 7,894 permanent exclusions,[25] Wales (with a population of c.3.5 million) had just 165 and Northern Ireland (with the equivalent of half the Welsh population) just 33. What, you may ask, are Northern Ireland and Wales doing differently? Well, it would be worth finding out the answer, but first go to Scotland with a population of c.4.7 million because in that year Scottish schools

---

24 I. Thompson, Poverty and Education in England: A School System in Crisis. In I. Thompson and
    G. Ivinson (eds), *Poverty in Education Across the UK: A Comparative Analysis of Policy and Place*
    (Bristol: Policy Press, 2020), pp. 115–140 at p. 118.
25 Department for Education, Permanent and Fixed-Period Exclusions in England 2018/19 (2020).
    Available at: https://explore-education-statistics.service.gov.uk/find-statistics/permanent-and-fixed-
    period-exclusions-in-england.

permanently excluded just five – yes, five! – pupils (in the following year it was three).

Gavin Williamson's speech to the FED summit also asserted: 'What we cannot do and what we won't do, is write off any child … And this is the morally right thing to do, if we want to level up our country, deliver equality of opportunity and realise the potential of every child.'[26] But how much do his words express a genuine commitment to realising his expressed purpose given ministerial unwillingness to confront the different story of Scotland?

Most of our witnesses were unaware of the Scottish figures and shocked when they heard them. The one witness who did know was Tom Bennett, himself a Scot, but he cast doubts on their relevance:

> Something that comes up time and time again is that in Scotland numbers have gone down enormously in terms of exclusion. What Scotland has done is to stop excluding. What that doesn't necessarily mean is that they've done so in a meaningful way which doesn't harm the system up to that point. But what they've done for the past 10 years is record very little. Teachers are frequently penalised for speaking publicly about circumstances and conditions in their own school, in a way that was similar to England back in 2010 – until the rise of social media which rather short-circuited these kinds of processes. In Scotland, you can still be very heavily penalised by your school for speaking out, with it written into your contract.

We have not been able to confirm this assertion from reliable sources. In Scotland, there is a different and broader curriculum and the teacher unions and Scottish GTC are robust in their exchanges, but there is also broad support for a more humane and thoughtful approach to behaviour issues and broader social justice matters. We believe that the rise in so-called 'zero tolerance' behaviour policies is creating school environments where pupils are punished, and ultimately excluded, for incidents that 'could and should be managed within the mainstream

---

26 Department for Education and Williamson, Education Secretary Speech to FED National Education Summit.

school environment'.[27] In their 'Who's Left' research, Philip Nye and Dave Thomson of FFT Education Datalab showed that between Year 7 and Year 11 some 7,000 pupils 'disappear' from school rolls each year and estimate that in 2017 as many as 22,000 were removed from school rolls.[28]

Debra Kidd talked of the tensions that can occur with the no excuses policy:

> I think we have a culture in England, and I don't know where it's come from, because it actually predates the Gove era, where teachers seem to have been advised that if you focus in on minute details, like the colour of shoes or how many stripes of the tie are showing, then somehow you save yourself from bigger battles. I don't think it's true and I think that's evident in our exclusion figures. If you factor in the fact that those small misdemeanours lead gradually to whole days in isolation rooms or fixed-term exclusions, when they never really interfered with learning in the first place, then you've got this cycle of educational deprivation, where children have missed a week of school, they've missed this key bit of information in maths, they're frustrated, and then behavioural issues escalate.
>
> We don't seem to have the support networks around children, particularly children who've got psychological difficulties or are in poverty or are carers for adults or parents who need it. We don't seem to have the support systems at work to allow them to function at a level where they can cope with some of the strains and stresses in the classroom. It's complicated and we can't treat it as straightforward.

If we really do believe that data might tell a story, the data on permanent exclusions reveal an epic page-turner which is brutal.

---

27 Department for Education, *Government Response to the Education Select Committee's Fifth Report of Session 2017–19 on Alternative Provision* (October 2018), p. 5. Available at: https://assets.publishing.service.gov.uk/government/uploads/system/uploads/attachment_data/file/748723/ESC_Government_response_FINAL.pdf.

28 P. Nye and D. Thomson, Who's Left 2018, Part One: The Main Findings, *FFT Education Datalab* (21 June 2018). Available at: https://ffteducationdatalab.org.uk/2018/06/whos-left-2018-part-one-the-main-findings. L. Menzies and S. Baar (eds), *Young People on the Margins: Priorities for Action in Education and Youth* (Abingdon and New York: Routledge, 2021) reveals similar data, the alarming extent of the problem for young people and their futures, together with some very helpful calls for action.

Louise Blackburn of Raising Attainment for Disadvantaged Youngsters (RADY) was aware of the disparity in exclusions between Scotland and England. Her response was thoughtful:

> When I read about exclusions from school in Scotland and across the UK and saw the impact of their approach to inclusion in Scotland, several things occurred to me. Firstly, why was this not being used as a starting point for work in England and Wales? Secondly, why was it getting virtually no press attention? Finally, how were they doing it? I read the Scottish document *Included, Engaged and Involved*.[29] In stark contrast to the English equivalent, the Scotland document outlines why schools need to be inclusive and even the appendices are all about how to keep children in school. What's also clear is how inclusion fits with all other aspects of education, including integrated services and curriculum. In my opinion it's no wonder they have such low exclusions. The wonder is, why are others not recognising the impact and adopting or at least considering the approach? Especially when, according to 2018–2019 figures, a child was 4.5 times more likely to be excluded if they were in receipt of FSM.[30]
>
> The schools we work with on RADY look at proportional representation of FSM learners in all aspects of school life, including things like exclusions and attendance. What they find most often is their poorest learners are over-represented in these excluded groups. We challenge schools on this, getting them to look deeply at why that might be.

We asked Michael Gove about exclusions and he told us: 'What I would like to see is every child who receives more than one fixed-term exclusion, especially at primary school, referred for a Child in Need assessment or Stronger Families support. We know the path from fixed-term to permanent exclusion is marked by failure to help the pupil or sometimes their family with problems which are often nothing to do with school.'

---

29 Scottish Government, *Included, Engaged and Involved Part 1: Promoting and Managing School Attendance* (14 June 2019). Available at: https://www.gov.scot/publications/included-engaged-involved-part-1-positive-approach-promotion-management-attendance-scottish-schools; and Scottish Government, *Included, Engaged and Involved Part 2: Preventing and Managing School Exclusions* (19 June 2017). Available at: https://www.gov.scot/publications/included-engaged-involved-part-2-positive-approach-preventing-managing-school.

30 Department for Education, Permanent and Fixed Period Exclusions in England: 2016 to 2017 [statistical release] (19 July 2018), p. 6. Available at: https://assets.publishing.service.gov.uk/government/uploads/system/uploads/attachment_data/file/726741/text_exc1617.pdf.

This recognition of the complexity of the issue, albeit with hindsight, and the need for a sensitive and wide-ranging response is a far cry from the public 'get tough' outlook of successive secretaries of state.

Gove also said that he thought permanent exclusions are a 'necessary evil'. Well, we believe they are evil too, but we also believe that much of the school system has convinced itself – falsely in our view – that the evil is necessary because that is easier than getting to the root causes.

Exclusions have become a sad feature of the English education system – one that is at risk of being regarded as acceptable in the search for better national PISA results or, worse, as a perverse indicator that discipline is strong. We think that the figures would change markedly if there were performance tables for schools showing the number of annual exclusions. We are not necessarily proposing this, but we are suggesting that the current accountability regime contributes to a problem that should not be ignored.

Rob Carpenter, the CEO of a MAT who has extensive experience of the school system, gave us a harrowing account of his frustrated efforts to help a child and support his family after he had been excluded, unfairly to his mind, by a secondary school. He described the way in which the system became adversarial and allowed the pupil to slide into the abyss of exclusion rather than admit to any sense of responsibility. Others told us of the way exclusion becomes an expedient or economic way of addressing problems that lie more within the school but which result in the pupil being disadvantaged.

Robin Walker, the incoming schools minister, seemed more aware and troubled than most when he responded to our challenge on the exclusion figures by saying, 'That's the tip of the iceberg, because a very large number also appear to me to be ending up going into a form of elective home education. One of my key concerns is the number of people who seem to be falling out of the system one way or another, which I think needs to be a real focus going forward.'

Schools currently manage exclusions differently: some as a deterrent and seemingly a badge of honour, some as a necessary evil, some to prevent discipline problems for their own staff. Others see the use of fixed-term exclusions as a way to reduce permanent exclusion, although the logic of this escapes us.

John Vickers, chair of trustees at a MAT in the Midlands, put it well: 'Children don't set out to be excluded. Teachers need to have time to work out how to embrace their needs and circumstances. So much of the issue is to do with relationships and who knows whom properly, so that every youngster feels a part of the place.'

Alternative provision is available in some communities of schools. This sort of facility is a move on from what existed in the past; we have progressed through behaviour units to PRUs – new names for old practices. But not *so* old. Tim's recollection of the abolition of caning, with which we started this section, probably represents the beginning of the slither into poor practices. A leading member of the ASCL in Scotland pointed out that abolition there was accompanied by extensive debate about appropriate reactions to misbehaviour to avoid the disaster of a pupil being excluded. This was not replicated in England where the curriculum narrowed more than it did in Scotland, which has a more intelligent accountability system.

Julia Cleverdon added to the points made by our Scottish witnesses by reflecting on her own work in Scotland: 'If you talk to the Scouts, they say that the [school] curriculum in Scotland is producing more resilient, more energetic and more emotionally rounded young people because they could compare and contrast what comes out of Scouting in Scotland with what comes out of Scouting in England. What does that mean for our curriculum?'

One of the difficulties has been the traditional expectation in English schools that the head teacher is the person who deals with discipline problems. The mark of a good head teacher was once the extent to which they could mete out discipline. While a good head teacher shows leadership by standing with their team, one of the best signs of a good head teacher is someone who puts the interests of the pupils above all else. It is very difficult for a head teacher to respond to staff concerns about incidents of poor pupil behaviour or disruption with a conversation about 'how we are going to deal with the underlying problems', but, in effect, this is the only way to reduce incidents.

Tom Bennett was clear that the approach of school leaders is crucial, not in producing and managing of policies but in building the climate: 'A lot of mainstream schools do not teach the behaviour that children need in order to flourish in school. They simply say, "Behave, behave!" as if that word alone will activate any number of complex social skills. I think we need to acknowledge that our children come to school with very frail understandings of what it means to be kind, to collaborate, to share, to be patient, to wait your turn and so on.'

Bennett sees managerial leadership approaches as part of the problem:

> We have created this dreadful climate where the accountability is incredibly infrequent and incredibly high stakes; once a year you get some performance management review, which is just a ridiculous process to manage teachers, and that's not a good way of modifying our teachers' behaviour.

> So many leaders in schools would rather do anything than line manage their staff. If staff aren't trained or supported, and their own behaviour isn't seen as something which needs to be trained, then the inevitable outcome is higher levels of unsatisfactory outcomes for the pupil, the class, the teacher, the whole school and the whole community. It's dysfunctional.

> The academy trusts themselves need to step up and say, 'Okay, so a school within our trust has excluded a child; fine, that child now must be retained within our academy trust in some way.' Whether or not they have some kind of internal provision, which is collectively and collegially produced between the trust or with a special school down the road, or whatever. That's what they should be looking at, so they feel a sense of ownership or responsibility over that child rather than a sense of expulsion.

Andreas Schleicher of the OECD picked up on this sense of collective responsibility when he told us:

> Exclusion is just one symptom in a system that is highly stratified. In my own country, Germany, they do not have exclusions but they have a highly tracked school system. It's very easy for teachers to demote students with lower performance projections in school. If you aren't doing very well, you are put into a vocational school. I think that sets the incentive to exasperate inequality in that society; exclusion is just the last element in the chain.

Some MATs have developed a reputation for excluding pupils whose presence in their academies might be detrimental to their prospects of success, leaving other schools to take on the responsibility for their failings. Colin Pettigrew, DCS of Nottinghamshire local authority, reminded us that the academy group with the highest exam results also had the highest exclusion rate. As advocate for children, the local authority has little clout without resorting to letters of direction, which often do no more than find the pupil a place in the short term until the next crisis arises.

Many MATs make every effort to address pupils' needs. Richard Gill, CEO of a trust in the West Midlands, told us:

> Generally, I'm not a fan of alternative provision, albeit I appreciate that it does have a place if considered as a carefully planned part of the curriculum available to a student or group of students. My preference is more towards managed moves. We will move students from one school to another within the trust as a supportive measure. This has been fairly successful to date, and there are many occasions where that 'mini-break' of going to a different school has actually ended up with that child going to that school permanently and then flourishing.

We have more to say about the exclusion and inclusion dilemma when we discuss SEND in Chapter 9, where we advocate placing more children close to their home in welcoming mainstream primary and secondary schools with appropriate specialist resources.

We were astonished to hear from Kate Brunt that her trust was being supported by Worcestershire Children First (WCF) to build a new alternative provision free school facility to accommodate 10 children from schools across a geographical area. The idea that our school system accepts, as a given, the need to find alternative facilities for children who cannot cope seems to us to demonstrate either the intransigence of the zero-tolerance community or resignation to the failure of the curriculum and pedagogy to engage youngsters. Positively, however, Brunt sees alternative provision as an opportunity to show what can be done. She explained:

> WCF will fund 10 permanent excluded places, but hopefully we will be able to manage this resource creatively to support schools to prevent permanent exclusion as we know this is a last resort.
>
> It's about working with schools to empower them to know how to deal with awkward situations, to be able to train staff up to go out and really do the right things for these youngsters. In the end, it is all about ensuring the right curriculum is in place for these

learners, and teachers receive the CPD necessary to deliver this curriculum. Ofsted's three 'I's begins with intent – what do we want to achieve? For these youngsters our intention has got to differ from the norm.

Too many people are afraid of Ofsted and what Ofsted will say. There is no 'Ofsted curriculum'. We need to take risks and be ballsy leaders and believe that what we put in place meets the needs of our learners, both primary and secondary. I sometimes say, 'We'll just do that,' and they'll say 'We can't.' My argument is that we can because, actually, if it's right for kids, you can do it. There are lots of fantastic heads in schools and we, as a profession, need to know we are able to question the powers that be.

I taught and led in a number of PRUs for over seven years of teaching Key Stages 1–4. During that time, I worked with kids that others said were difficult, and they were if the right curriculum and support weren't in place. I want to give all teachers within our trust the chance to work with the full spectrum of need. Getting it right for those youngsters is as important as any. I love it.

I would advocate that we haven't got things right for all our more disadvantaged/tricky children. I think we've got to do more proactive work – getting out there. One of the things I said to the local authority was, 'Rather than giving money to a school for a teaching assistant when these children are finding it tricky, give the money to me. I will employ the teaching assistant and develop their skills using high-quality CPD/relevant experience in order for them to empower staff within schools.' The rationale behind this is that often when these vulnerable pupils kick off, schools end up employing naive or inexperienced teaching assistants and put them alongside our trickiest children, and then we wonder why things don't improve. It's down to training – it's CPD. We should put our most experienced teachers with these children. So, that's why we're doing it, and it's one of my passions really.

Ministers have made two errors of omission when dealing with exclusions, as advised by Taylor and Bennett. First, HMI input into the working groups has been missing, yet they are the independent observers of practice in schools on a daily basis. The survey reports they produced on school issues in the 1980s had a powerful impact on practice.[31] Modern equivalents to these reports would be even more powerful, since they could be informed by evidence collated from school inspections. Second, the most recent efforts from Taylor and Bennett have lacked feedback from university-based researchers, so there has been a complete absence of quantitative analysis of fixed-term and permanent exclusions data (which are readily available). The irony is that such data are examined meticulously at a school level but seem to be ignored as not sufficiently important to be included in reports by the unfortunately named national tsars, especially given the topic under consideration.

We hope, therefore, that when the task force – set up in response to the thoughtful Timpson review – resumes work after the pandemic, that HMI expertise is added to its team and schools are afforded access to a comparative data set, equivalent to what is available for exams and tests.[32] Schools would then see for themselves which schools in comparable socio-economic circumstances seem to be better at avoiding exclusions (whether fixed-term or permanent) and, consequently, they would resolve to get the culture right, as this cameo sent by one of our witnesses confirms.

Getting the culture right

In a deprived, semi-rural, ex-coal mining community, ensuring that students feel like they belong and everyone is in their corner is critical to good behaviour. A curriculum that taps into the local culture supports this. Our Seed to Feed project was one of many (football being another) that supported this. It involved some of our most challenging Key Stage 3 students running their own market garden. Every couple of months they would invite family members (invariably allotment-owning grandparents) to dine on their home-cooked,

---

31 Her Majesty's Inspectors of Schools, *Primary Education in England* (London: HMSO, 1978). Available at: http://www.educationengland.org.uk/documents/hmi-primary/index.html; Her Majesty's Inspectors of Schools, *Aspects of Secondary Education in England* (London: HMSO, 1979). Available at: http://www.educationengland.org.uk/documents/hmi-secondary/hmi-secondary.html; Her Majesty's Inspectors of Schools, *Education 5 to 9* (London: HMSO, 1982). Available at: http://www.educationengland.org.uk/documents/hmi-5to9; and Her Majesty's Inspectors of Schools, *9–13 Middle Schools* (London: HMSO, 1983). Available at: http://www.educationengland.org.uk/documents/hmi-9to13/hmi-9to13.html.

32 Families of Schools was a database used by the London Challenge and later by the Greater Manchester Challenge to encourage inter-school learning and collaboration (see Chapter 7). The prototype was developed by Birmingham LEA in the 1990s.

home-grown produce. They also became successful entrepreneurs, selling hanging baskets at every school event. Some of the toughest characters turned their behaviour around in other lessons, knowing they had afternoon gardening. It was an area in which they could exceed and be proud of, and led to renewed commitment and loyalty to the school community. They just felt part of it.

This issue of where to start is important. The Elton Report found that schools which began their approach to behaviour by determining the consequences tended to have more problems than those schools which looked at antecedents and what was happening to set the tone for good or poor behaviour: curriculum, teaching, relationships, people, resources, space.

While any organisation needs routines and agreed ways of working, the outlook that says 'on our terms or else' is likely to elicit the 'or else, thanks' from those who would rather not be in a recruiting school anyway. Schools exist in the social climate of the day: Blair's 'tough on crime and tough on the causes of crime' outlook sounded good, but anti-social behaviour orders (ASBOs) became something of a badge of honour for certain individuals, communities and gangs. Nobody thought of what would come next.

Janice Allen told us about her first year in teaching:

> I was in a boys' secondary school with a troubled history in Manchester, and Mel, the new head, said that the government and Ofsted's outlook on behaviour meant we should run the school as a cross between an officers' mess and a rugby club. However, he thought that probably wouldn't work, so should we try using the arts, sport, science and literature and showing the children why we like learning ... and use the national strategies as well. That school just became so good. The lads responded and we all just enjoyed being there. We thought we could achieve anything.

One of the problems is that so many of the approaches used to manage pupils in schools mirror practices from the military, sporting, hospital, justice and prison systems. Schools also apply the same procedures used in adult institutions, even though they are designed for mature individuals, not children who have yet to reach that level of understanding. Michael

Gove's simplistic solution included training ex-soldiers to teach via the Troops to Teachers programme[33] and Gavin Williamson announced government support to re-establish Cadet Forces in schools.[34]

The idea persists in government and elsewhere that if our schools could be stricter then all would be well, that good behaviour can be imposed, that schools with high fixed-term exclusion rates (often for trivial offences such as wearing the wrong uniform) are doing a good job – until this reaches an unspecified unacceptable level when suddenly they are doing a bad job. We have a prime minister who deliberately ruffles his hair and whose shirt is often untucked. In every sphere of official life we have become less deferential and more informal – except for schools where, in recent years, we have gone into sharp reverse gear. Our teenagers are particularly attuned to institutional hypocrisy. If we ask or tell pupils to do or not do certain things, then why don't adults follow the same rules? If teachers can colour their hair, wear jewellery then why can't pupils, especially if they are deemed mature enough to decide for themselves whether or not to have a COVID vaccine?

Mick recalls:

I was talking to a teenager in a Manchester school and was impressed by her maturity, confidence, articulacy and worldliness. She told me how she spent her time before leaving home in the morning, helping her mum who suffered from a long-term illness. She would bathe, dress and feed her mum and then give her the right medication, leaving her midday medication and food ready. She complained that, having done all that, she might be 'in bother' when she arrived at school for having neglected to change her trainers or forgotten her homework and possibly put in detention, which caused her to worry about being late home. All she wanted was somewhere confidential to ring home from in the middle of the day.

---

33 Department for Education, *The Importance of Teaching: The Schools White Paper 2010* (Norwich: TSO), p. 22. Available at: https://assets.publishing.service.gov.uk/government/uploads/system/uploads/attachment_data/file/175429/CM-7980.pdf.

34 Department for Education, B. Wallace and G. Williamson, Thousands More Pupils to Benefit from Cadet Programme [press release] (2 April 2021). Available at: https://www.gov.uk/government/news/thousands-more-pupils-to-benefit-from-cadet-programme.

The simplistic conditioning theory of behaviourism, which is applied to many institutional management processes in schools, begins with the concept of controlling passive participants who react as predicted.[35] However, attachment theory – which was first developed by John Bowlby and is now used extensively by foster carers and adoptive parents – offers the potential for a much deeper understanding of young people's behaviour.[36] It encourages practices that address the antecedents or root causes of misbehaviour, alongside strategies to support the pupil's improved engagement in learning.

We must act, of course, when young people deliberately breach the clear and reasonable expectations of their school community – for example, by bringing drugs or weapons into school or engaging in unwanted sexual activities. The protection of others is a serious and necessary consideration. However, our actions should not make the child more vulnerable or increase the potential harm they might cause. When we cast out a young person, sadly, there often is someone willing to catch them: the drug dealers, groomers and gang leaders who feed off their need for self-esteem and attachment. Schools that actively resist exclusion turn to restorative justice techniques instead.

Schooling is intended to make lives better for all, so if we value the purposes of schooling outlined in Chapter 1, then we must ensure that young people who face poverty and social marginalisation are seen less as a problem to get rid of and more as revealing problems that we need to solve. Permanently excluding a child involved with drugs and leaving them at the mercy of county lines dealers is not making their life better and risks endangering many more. Similarly, a child who is excluded for carrying a knife may become a victim of gang culture and, in turn, present a more serious problem for wider society. Many head teachers express the anguish they feel at a permanent exclusion, while those temporarily excluding a very young pupil know that while it may provide short-term respite, it will often be the first step on a miserable downward trajectory.

In our view, not enough attention is focused on prevention or rehabilitation. We do not seek to minimise the enormous challenge that some children present to their school communities. However, some reasons for

---

35 Many practices in schools emanate from the work of behaviourists, such as Pavlov's classical conditioning of the early 20th century and Skinner's operant conditioning of the 1930s. Typically, they experimented on other animals and applied their findings to humans.

36 John Bowlby developed thinking on attachment theory from the 1960s through to the late 1980s. His work led to many advances in the psychology of children's close relationships.

exclusion are so petty that it is hard to see them as anything other than acts of deterrence or retribution. While the prison system has moved towards rehabilitation in recent years, there is limited evidence of a comparable shift in the school system. To address this growing problem will require significant investment as well as a change in thinking and practice. It will also require the rejection of exclusion as an acceptable practice.

Schools need to be supported more effectively than they are at present by a combination of their MAT, local authority's co-ordination of public health services and the DfE. As Anthony Seldon told us:

> At the moment, mental health services wait for young people to have a breakdown, to have an eating disorder, to cut their wrists, and then rush to help when they hit bottom, but it's much harder to put children together once they've fallen. If we can work to build capacity, to build resilience, to build self-respect, to build self-knowledge and to build self-efficacy, the ability of young people to manage their own lives and negotiate the difficulties they have without catastrophising, without taking amyl nitrate or whatever behaviour it is, their mind will give them something that would be a lesson for life. In schools and universities, far too much effort goes into counselling, therapy and CAMHS [child and adolescent mental health services]. I'm not saying that we don't need therapists or psychiatrists or that we don't need drugs, but we do need more work in the building of capacity.

Working on antecedents is a whole-system challenge. Government must address a curriculum and qualification approach that is debilitating for too many pupils and an accountability system that terrifies too many teachers and results in practices that harm the very children we most need to succeed. Ofsted has to wake up to the way in which its algorithms of consistency are encouraging dreadful consequences. Tom Bennett calls for better training at all levels, but we suspect that his image of training would be little different from the repressive management techniques that are currently espoused as good practice in some learning environments. The challenges of bringing in a new order while still living with the old one are significant.

Some different perspectives on setting a climate with learners

Twenty years ago, the concept of 'pupil voice' was beginning to grow as young people's participation, contribution and influence was welcomed in certain school contexts.[37] Various studies confirmed the benefits of pupil voice: increased pupil engagement, improved relationships between pupils and teachers, better communication between pupils and school, and providing the right conditions for the school community to become a learning community.[38] For a while, many schools were becoming genuinely collaborative places.

The basis for pupil voice is found in Article 12 of the United Nations Convention on the Rights of the Child, which sets out the right of children to express an opinion and to be included in decisions that involve and affect them.[39] Some schools have successfully addressed this issue of what is essentially a lived curriculum. At that time, pupil voice began to appear in the inspection framework and was seen to be informing judgements; it seemed to be gathering momentum. However, when Michael Gove became minister he put an end to SEAL, diminished personal, social, health and economic (PSHE) education and citizenship, and moved the inspection framework towards valuing a type of pedagogy which saw the teacher's role as the dominant conditioner of learning. The general move towards pupil voice quickly fell away.

Pupil participation, which is surely better than exclusion, can happen in a variety of ways – for example:

▓   As part of Assessment for Learning.

▓   By involving pupils in school self-evaluation and assessment.

▓   Groups such as school council, eco-council and healthy schools.

▓   Developing resources and facilities (e.g. sport, IT).

▓   Fundraising, links with charities and the wider community.

---

37   J. MacBeath, K. Myers and H. Demetriou, Supporting Teachers in Consulting Pupils about Aspects of Teaching and Learning, and Evaluating Impact, *Forum*, 43(2) (2021): 78–82. DOI: 10.2304/forum.2001.43.2.11

38   J. Flutter and J. Ruddock, *Consulting Pupils: What's In It for Schools?* (Abingdon and New York: Routledge, 2004).

39   See https://www.unicef.org.uk/what-we-do/un-convention-child-rights.

- Improvements to the school environment (e.g. school buildings, playground, toilets).

- Proposals for aspects of timing of the school day and teaching sessions.

- Development of a whole-school environmental policy.

- Involvement with staff recruitment.

- Involvement with planning activities beyond the school day.

- Involvement with planning, reviewing and implementing school policies.

- Involvement with the school development plan and school budget.

- Consultation mechanisms such as surveys, suggestion boxes and circle time.

- Caring for the school and its grounds.

- Being an advocate for the school and its work.

What we know is that pupils who feel they have a contribution to make tend to have a more positive experience of school. Making a contribution and being generous of self typically helps people to feel like they belong.

Mick recalls:

Over the years, in various roles, I have been asked by schools to help them sort out behaviour or to help them produce a behaviour policy. What they usually mean, often without realising it, is that they want a rewards and punishment policy.

As a short activity, I ask people to sit in pairs and list all of the formal rewards or punishments they can think of (not smiles or frowns or raised eyebrows or hurt looks), anything they know schools do or used to do from their own experience, or what they have seen in films or read in books or someone has explained to them.

After 10 minutes we collate the list; we have to stop then or the list would be too long. As it is, the catalogue of things that have been tried over time is extensive. We have to allow time for laughter, shock and disbelief as people describe the bizarre ways that schools have sought to control children. Some are attractive, even the most bizarre.

Next, I ask people to consider whether there are potential side effects to each of the rewards and punishments on the list. For instance, keeping children in at break for not completing work will mean a potential lack of application to learning on a cold or drizzly day – or a welcome relief for the child who is being bullied. After due time, we consider the examples that do not have side effects. It doesn't take long because there are none. Those that people suggest are soon shot down by others. I explain that pretty well anything works for a week or two but then the novelty wears off.

Teachers create the weather. The best way to encourage children to be positive is to explain regularly the logic behind the organisational decisions being made and to thank them for being accommodating. Few schools have reported children blatantly disregarding COVID precautions, for example. They have put up with new rules about social distancing, mask wearing, hand washing and regular lateral flow testing. This might be because they recognise the need to think about others as well as themselves, because they have seen the evidence and understand why it matters, and because the measures have been explained carefully rather than simply imposed. The expectation is a courtesy or an understanding, rather than a rule.

It is okay to have rules, but *understandings* are better; they can be amended for maturity, for special need and for setting. There are understandings for different sorts of assembly; understandings for the laboratory, art room or PE changing room; understandings for the museum visit or the school bus. Understandings can be built around three key principles: be kind to people, and at the minimum don't hurt them physically, emotionally or socially; don't be lazy and waste resources – the biggest of which is you; and don't be dangerous to yourself or others. Theory has it that negatives are bad but we all have to live within some limitations.

The best approach is to explain to pupils how the ways in which they behave will help us to teach them well, thank them for helping us and enjoy being with them – and, above all, tell pupils we like them.

Tom Bennett picked up on the issue of sanctions, which has become a more acceptable word than punishment, when he told us: 'I think sanctions are an essential part of the school system, but just part of the school system, and people are constantly having to reinvent the systems for themselves. They think that if children misbehave, I'll react to it. That reactive mechanism frequently falls into sanctions and rewards because people can't think of anything else.' It is the managerial clarity of that sanction and reward outlook that has gained traction in schools at the present time.

Over the last 15 years, we have witnessed what we both regard as an alarming trend that started in secondary schools and has also spread to some primary schools: zero tolerance. The influence came from outside but the phrase has become increasingly common in all sorts of managerial contexts. It soon expanded to inform what became known as 'assertive discipline' policies; although the term is not used as much now, the procedures persist. Classroom and school practice began to include 'red' and 'golden' areas/zones, lists of pupils who have misbehaved (and deserve punishment) or been good (and deserve reward), names on the whiteboard with consequences for every sort of action – which was soon followed by isolation rooms, complete with solitary confinement booths – and informal exclusions of one sort or another.

One of our primary head teacher witnesses despaired as she told us:

> Locally in our feeder secondary school, toilets are locked unless it is break or lunchtime – girls can't change their sanitary wear. Detentions are given for children having the wrong colour ruler. One of our ex-Year 6s had a detention this week because his black school shoes had the wrong type of soles. One of our ex-pupils told me that 'their new breaktime bell is like a siren'.

Some of these behaviour policies and the resultant practices become a burden for staff and a routine for some pupils to manipulate. Lisa Williams told us about her experience as a new head teacher in a school with a strong behaviour policy and poor discipline to match:

> I got rid of the charts saying who is in the golden zone or the red zone. One of the little boys who was prone to being excluded or missing his playtimes and lunchtimes came up to me and said, 'What have you done with all the red zones? Where am I going to

go? I'm always supposed to be on red and you've gone and got rid of it.'

I think that's a learned behaviour for a 7-year-old little boy because of the behaviour system that has been ineffective for him within school. A lot of children were, 'Oh, forget it, I'm not doing that work – you can just exclude me' because they'd come to expect that. 'I don't want to do the work or listen to that teacher. Just exclude me, then ring my mum and then send me home.' We said, 'No, if we're going to exclude anybody from anything, it will be from the classroom but not from the learning.'

We struggle to see how sitting a pupil in a solitary confinement cubicle, facing three plywood walls, will help them to build stronger relationships with others. Of course, allowing a distressed child time out in pleasant surroundings where their distressed and distressing behaviour can be the topic of appropriate discussion or an opportunity for in-depth, well-calibrated conversation with a skilled member of staff, or even where they can learn online, does need to be part of our provision.

Secondary schools are beginning to use the common primary school practice of establishing 'nurture rooms' for those youngsters who struggle with social and emotional relationships. The argument is often made that such facilities might be more attractive than classrooms and that pupils enjoy the close attention, but this highlights a failure to appreciate the different needs of an individual. On the contrary, schools that adopt this type of provision don't tend to regret the decision.

For those pupils who deliberately cause difficulty (and there aren't many), schools that claim to help each pupil reach their potential tend to deploy in their sanction ladders appropriate opportunities for reparation, often using the equivalent of 'community service', so the youngster can demonstrate by their actions that they are engaging in activities which help rather than hinder others.[40] In our extensive interview with Tom Bennett, such reparation hardly featured.

Too many approaches to encouraging children to exercise self-discipline seem to be about retribution or setting an example to quell the mob. In the late 1970s, when our book begins, one of the junior education ministers

---

40   The motto of one school is: 'Think for yourself and act for others'.

was Rhodes Boyson.[41] In this capacity, he sought to uphold schools' right to use the cane and was nicknamed the 'Minister for Flogging' by the Society of Teachers Opposed to Physical Punishment. He had been the head teacher of a secondary school, and with his presentation of himself as a traditional disciplinarian, he would explain how he kept order in his schools with regular resort to the cane. Although it obviously made him feel better, it didn't stem what he saw as the rising tide of ill-discipline. It seems to us that systems which serve as examples to others without securing reparation are not good systems.

Dave Whitaker's recent book, *The Kindness Principle*, doesn't carry a title that will attract zero tolerance and no excuses advocates, but it does deserve to be the subject of secondary SLT meetings on a chapter-by-chapter basis. It deals with various aspects of pupil behaviour, including the issue of exclusion. Whitaker asks:

> Should we, as educational professionals, regard schools as successful if they do not do their very best to work with the most challenging and vulnerable children in society? Some children need additional support, guidance and flexibility in their educational journey. Some pupils have specific additional needs that cannot be met in a mainstream environment. Some need to move to specialist settings because it is in their best interests to do so. However, some are excluded because the system is failing them; they are moved from school to school because nobody is repairing the damage and making the adjustments that they need in order to be successful.
>
> Schools too often focus on dealing with the symptoms of challenging behaviour, not the causes. There is a small but seemingly ever-increasing cohort of children – if my experience is anything to go by – who are either excluded from education or trapped in a cycle of punishment, which seems to be considered an acceptable consequence of a widely used and highly regarded behaviour strategy. We must ask ourselves whether this is OK. Behaviour management in schools begins with our choices as adults and our behaviour as professionals.[42]

---

41 Rhodes Boyson was a regular on panel discussions such as *Question Time*. He had the bearing and appearance of a Victorian gentleman and was forthright in portraying his 'tough stance' outlook.

42 D. Whitaker, *The Kindness Principle: Making Relational Behaviour Management Work in Schools*. (Carmarthen: Independent Thinking Press, 2021), pp. 2–3.

Finally, therefore, we turn to a subject that will be contentious. We think the time has come to abolish fixed term-exclusions and reserve permanent exclusions for the most extreme circumstances – that is, where pupils' actions cause irreparable damage to themselves or others in their school. In a system which rightly places emphasis on the value of school attendance, it is a paradox that pupils who misbehave (and are sometimes extremely distressed) should be temporarily excluded from the community they are told is so important to their future. It makes us wonder whether there needs to be a more detailed look, as we have said above, at the ladders of consequences, which often start with the first reproof for minor misbehaviour in class and end with exclusion. Rituals and routines like detention have negative effects in so many schools, spoiling relationships in settings where managerial approaches to school leadership expect an allocated number of detentions per teacher as a measure of consistency. This, in turn, leads to the futility of children playing the detention card as an alternative to applying themselves to a task. For instance, if they fear being exposed as struggling when their work is marked, which they may find embarrassing, it might be easier to avoid the marking by not doing the work and taking the hit of a few minutes sitting with 'people like me' in detention.

Mick recalls:

It was a few minutes after school on a Friday. I met Julie, the deputy head, in the corridor of a big secondary school and we exchanged some pleasantries.

I looked from the corridor through the window of a classroom and saw a group of pupils sitting around and apparently doing nothing. I asked her whether this was an after-school club but she told me it was a detention group. As we talked I counted up and said, 'It's been a busy day – there are 23 in there.'

'You don't know the half of it,' said Julie. 'There are two more detention rooms further along. It is the head teacher's extended detention today for all the ones who ignored their detentions during the week.'

We chuckled wryly at how well this was going as I counted through the windows. 'Seventy-six!' I said. Julie had more ammunition for next week and her ongoing battle to try to get things changed.

I mused that the one-metre tall strapline on the outside of the building would need to change: 'Everybody Successful, Every Day'. Given that today 76 pupils, and presumably the same number of adults, had had a bad day, it might be a trades description issue. Then again, an accurate slogan wouldn't have the same ring to it: 'Quite a Lot of Successful People, Most Days'.

Exclusion is a serious blight on the school system. It has its roots in the harsh Victorian view of childhood which was prevalent when state schools began in 1870. This was affected by all manner of influences, from the public school sector to the recruitment of regiments of ex-military personnel as teachers after the Second World War, with their recent combat experience to add to the pot. Society has changed and is changing. Schools have a stronger moral code than most places in wider society where client groups are managed effectively with a good degree of social psychology, such as shopping centres, motorway service areas and airports.

This is contentious territory. Our view may be seen as a romantic contrast with the reality of the problems caused by the disruption wrought by a few. We believe in pupils learning to exercise self-discipline through a carefully managed and well-explained positive environment. We believe in rules, but only a few. The best self-regulated discipline occurs in communities where relationships are strong, where people know they matter and where systems help the organisation to run smoothly without being overbearing.

Childhood today is more complex than ever and the pressures are significant, not least the influence of social media. However, the way we treat our young people in schools has to move away from binary rhetoric, superficial arguments and simplistic programmes to satisfy our accountability regime. We agreed with Tom Bennett when he told us: 'I think, in general, the public debate we have about behaviour is immature to the point of irrationality.'

When we asked Michael Gove what he would have as priorities were he still the secretary of state, he told us: 'Reducing exclusions and absenteeism. There are hundreds of thousands of children missing out on school because they simply don't show up. Good schools find out why and get them back into school. Bad ones don't. They should. We think COVID may have worsened this problem and it needs to be a priority.' As often with Gove, his outlook is forthright and urgent, tuning in to a concern of the moment. But it is also simplistic and ignores his own part in the situation we have today. Since his symbolic removal of the Every Child Matters agenda in 2010, there has been little more than rhetoric about exclusion from secretaries of state, with the notable exception of Justine Greening who continues to fight for social mobility in her life beyond politics.[43]

Compared with most of the politicians with whom we talked, Andrea Leadsom offered more clarity in her understanding of the issue of exclusion being about more than simply school management and pupil compliance. She saw the long-term implications when she told us: 'The fact of the matter is that we need to get it right in the perinatal period in terms of value for money and effectiveness. I would say, invest antenatally and perinatally and you won't need to invest during puberty, other than in a few small cases and then you could definitely provide intensive support.'

We need to focus on the obvious – namely, learning as the starting point for everything we do in schools. Indigenous North American groups were studied by Larry Brendtro, who found that adolescents were helped through the rite of passage to adulthood by being given a maxim which helped them to visualise a 'circle of courage'.[44] Courage would come from being able to achieve 'mastery' of certain skills.

The more we can do, the more we can contribute to our group, and in doing so, we feel generous. We give of ourselves and we sense that we belong. This circle of courage can be joined at any stage and the important point is that it is virtuous: once we have completed the circle, we want to keep on building courage. Even if our young people cannot do things *yet*, we still want them to belong. If they feel they belong, they might be inclined to try new things. Let's give our children courage: our foundation stones in Chapter 13 signal some ways of achieving this.

---

43 Along with David Harrison, Justine Greening has founded the Social Mobility Pledge, which encourages businesses to address social mobility in terms of outreach, access and recruitment. See www.socialmobilitypledge.org.

44 L. K. Brendtro, M. Brokenleg and S. Van Bockern, The Circle of Courage: Developing Resilience and Capacity in Youth, *International Journal for Talent Development and Creativity*, 1(1) (2013): 67–74. Available at: https://www.academia.edu/7847130/The_Circle_of_Courage_Developing_Resilience_and_Capacity_in_Youth.

Chapter 9
Special educational needs and disabilities – unfulfilled good intentions

We deliver some therapy for children in local mainstream schools. This might involve working with children directly but we also work with mainstream teachers to support them to integrate therapy into their teaching and provision. We see this as being part of our duty as a special school trust – our responsibilities include supporting children in our local area and not just the children in the trust.

Susan Douglas, CEO, Eden Academy Trust

The background

The words of Susan Douglas set the scene for the issues first raised when junior and adult training centres were transferred from the Department of Health and Social Security to local government in 1971, where they became the responsibility of education and social services respectively. Prior to this, mentally handicapped children in JTCs and special care units had been considered ineducable. Now, they were entitled to attend special schools for the severely educationally subnormal (ESN(S)), as compared with ESN(M) (M standing for moderate or mild). This added to the growing number of different sorts of special school that were being created either by LEAs, charities and entrepreneurs in the independent sector.

The nomenclature evolved too. Over the years, we have become much more sensitive about the damaging impact of language. A leader in this, as in so many matters affecting special education, was Professor Ron

Gulliford, who first challenged the use of the term 'educationally sub-normal'. He designated such schools as being for pupils with 'moderate or severe learning difficulties'. Schools for 'the deaf' (which our Victorian ancestors had called Institutes for the Deaf and Dumb) became schools for 'hearing impaired children', and schools for 'the blind' became schools for 'children with visual impairment'.

Developments in the use of language to avoid conveying or reinforcing unconscious prejudice soon informed all educational contexts, not just those in special education.[1] As research advanced, we discovered more about disabilities. We learned about children who experienced specific learning difficulties in reading and called them dyslexic, a condition that educational administrators had denied the existence of for many years as they tried to guard scarce resources. Then there were children who shouted or swore, unprovoked and apparently uncontrollably, who suffered from Tourette's syndrome, as well as a growing number of children with Asperger's, a form of autism spectrum disorder (ASD). Acronyms such as ADHD (attention deficit hyperactivity disorder) and EBD (emotional and behavioural disorder) multiplied and split into more exact descriptions as we extended our knowledge and awareness of the often complex care and education interventions which could make a difference. Children who would never have survived childbirth and infancy even 20 years ago (still less at the start of our own careers), now increasingly live on into adolescence and adulthood.

Advances in medicine have also increased our understanding of more, and more definably different, conditions which are amenable to specialist interventions. All children, even those with the most complex and severe needs – with the right education and care – can take advantage of staff expertise in special schools and special units within primary and secondary schools to make the type of progress that thrills them, the staff and their families.

There is a continuum of life-limiting conditions within which we all exist at different stages and contexts of our lives. Those with the most formidable barriers to their own and others' fulfilment deserve the very best we can offer them. Equity demands nothing less. In our view, it is not a matter of compassion, although compassion helps in every educational

---

1   Work in this area is often criticised as being politically correct, but to make our values plain, we believe that language and its use is crucial in setting the climate and affecting the weather, which the teacher makes in the classroom, the head makes in the school and the minister makes in Westminster and Whitehall.

setting. It is a matter of rights and human dignity. To the relief of the most hard-pressed parents and families, the transfer of those first JTCs heralded a long (and at first slow) period of better quality provision.

Four factors have slowed our progress:

1   There has been an ambivalent approach to the inclusion of both the pupils and the provision within mainstream primary and secondary settings.

2   As with the health service, our understanding of the detailed nature of special needs, and what we can do to meet them, advances faster than the resources that central and local government are able or willing to provide.

3   The first two factors have led to poor strategic and day-to-day administration and management within national and local government. This has been compounded by the statementing system introduced following the Warnock Report[2] and its successor process (EHCPs) following the Families and Children Act 2014, which made cosmetic rather than fundamental changes to a flawed system.

4   Primary and secondary schools have appointed special educational needs coordinators (SENCOs, now renamed SENDCOs to include 'disabilities' in line with the 2015 Code of Practice[3]), plus many schools employed tutors, mentors, coaches and counsellors in the years of plenty. In the 2010–2020 austerity decade, however, these additional staff were the first to be sacrificed, often because they didn't contribute to the accountability measures developed during the same period. The SENDCO role can sometimes – unhelpfully – undermine the fact that all teachers are teachers of children with different learning needs. While the role of the SENDCO brought SEN out of the broom cupboard (where children were being segregated and given individual tuition) initially, it also meant that it was all too easy for the fainthearted or failing classroom teacher to say that the SENDCO should deal with SEND issues. How SENDCOs are deployed in schools is therefore crucial.

---

2   H. M. Warnock, *Special Educational Needs: Report of the Committee of Enquiry into the Education of Handicapped Children and Young People* [Warnock Report] (London: HMSO, 1978). Available at: http://www.educationengland.org.uk/documents/warnock/warnock1978.html.
3   Department for Education and Department of Health, *Special Educational Needs and Disability Code of Practice: 0 to 25 Years* (2015). Available at: https://www.gov.uk/government/publications/send-code-of-practice-0-to-25.

We shall return to these issues, which still loom large, among the problems highlighted later in this chapter by the external inspection of local authorities and school SEND provisions.

In terms of the first of our factors that have held back progress, ambivalence towards inclusion at a central government level has spread through the system. Andrew Adonis was forthright in his views on what the government's stance should be:

> In terms of special educational needs, I think one of our big mistakes was to say that you had to choose between special schools and mainstream schools. It became ideological. What it seemed to me we needed was much better special educational needs provision in mainstream schools but also much better special schools. Most of the areas of special educational needs are on a spectrum, and for much of the spectrum it's perfectly reasonable to expect that mainstream schools – with proper support – can cater for that need. But there are extremes of the spectrum which it isn't possible for mainstream schools to address well. I thought that both extremes were wrong.

> This is a Blairite, third-way person speaking, but it is my view of this, and I felt very strongly about it from engagement with the system and relentlessly visiting special schools. Some local authorities abolished all their special schools, I thought betraying many of their children and parents, because they didn't have the specialist resources to be able to deal with children with very intensive needs.

> I thought for social reasons, as well as educational reasons, it was right to mainstream most special needs provision, but without abolishing special schools catering for extreme needs. I thought we should invest more in them. The really desperate situations which I often had to deal with, when MPs were sending their constituency casework to me, were the parents who thought they were getting a very raw deal. These are cases that ended up in a special educational needs tribunal. Basically, the families weren't offered a choice, and it was children who were on the cusp between what a mainstream school could reasonably be expected to provide and a special school for whom the problem became most acute. What they wanted was choice.

The Warnock Report and its significance

To understand what we need to do now, however, requires a brief detour back to the beginning of our story. Part of Shirley Williams' good fortune as secretary of state was to inherit the publication of one of the last, and arguably most influential, of the major national committee reports – the Warnock Report, which changed our approach to special education.[4]

Before tracing the main continuities in SEND provision and practices from Warnock to the present day, we set out Tim's recollection of its initial impact.

Tim recalls:

In 1978, I was starting out as education officer in Oxfordshire. The Warnock family was well known in Oxford: both were distinguished academics, Mary having also been head of a local prestigious independent girls' schools (Oxford High). Her children were in the county youth orchestra and I knew her through her great support for Harry Judge, the inspirational and creative director of Oxford University's Department of Education. She was a familiar figure to members of Oxfordshire's Education Committee.

As a very young education officer, I saw the Warnock Report as a chance to push through ideas about the schooling system in which I strongly believed. Because of Mary Warnock's local connections, I assumed the county council would react positively to her report – provided it didn't mean spending more money (which, of course, it did) – but I thought we could override that objection given the topic and the local connection. I was also very persuaded by the section in the report which dealt with what she called 'integration' and which we all came to call the 'inclusion' debate. Conceptually, the progression from 'locational' to 'social' to 'functional' inclusion was beautifully simple, easily understood and logical.

---

4 Mrs Thatcher doesn't always get the credit for her earlier role as secretary of state for education, partly because she became known as the 'milk snatcher' after her decision to remove free school milk. However, she was the person who commissioned the Warnock Report.

Why couldn't children with disabilities be accommodated in the same school, wearing the same uniform, eating the same school meals and being in the same pastoral system as all the other children? They might need to be taught in different groups in appropriate facilities and it might be that, for some of them, there wouldn't be much meaningful 'taught' inclusion. But to be on the same site and in the same institution at least increased the opportunities for that to happen. Even if the provision could only be located on a primary or secondary school site, then at least some social interaction could take place; it would be a matter of professional judgement by those in charge as to how far functional inclusion could happen. Ideally, of course, there would be a single management structure which would not leave it to goodwill, but, as it were, give goodwill a more propitious context in which to work.

It had always struck me as odd that you could believe in the comprehensive ideal, but at the same time think that it was acceptable to segregate children with disabilities and hide them away in special schools, where their expert teachers and other specialists sometimes achieved amazing results which nobody noticed. You might think that acceptable in a selective system but not in one that had abolished selection.

The Warnock Report set out the alternative with simple clarity, and I was determined to act on it.

You can imagine my dismay when I discovered that we had just built a new ESN(S) school, Bishopswood, to rehouse pupils from health settings in neglected, isolated buildings which were unfit for their purpose. Furthermore, the new school had been constructed in a beautiful leafy glade close to the Berkshire border, remote from any other school provision.

But that was when I got lucky. The new head of Bishopswood School, Mike Hudson, was so morally driven by the arguments outlined in the Warnock Report that he was prepared to turn his back on the state-of-the-art new school and its gleaming facilities if we could just convert some spare space in Chiltern Edge – a comprehensive school – and in one of its partner primary schools in Sonning Common. He explained that he would send his staff and the children, apart from the most severely disabled and non-ambulant pupils, to the local secondary and primary school where they could socialise with other children and join in some of the school activities. We were fortunate with the staff in the schools involved, who took the lead in enthusiastically welcoming the development and enabling the pupils to become members of both schools' communities.[5]

I became a proselytiser of Warnock-style inclusion, and what happened at Bishopswood proved to be contagious. Soon another new head, Tim Southgate, at the Ormerod School for physically handicapped children, wanted to move his pupils from another rebuilt facility on the edge of Oxford to attend the secondary school in Woodstock. Again, the professionals were the moving force, encouraged by the then assistant director for SEND, Jo Stephens, who became my successor and took things much further, always listening to the special school heads who were instrumental in the whole exercise. They knew their specialist knowledge and skill was being valued and not threatened and they wanted their children to have as normal a school experience as possible.

There seemed to be no limit on what was possible, despite the fact that Oxfordshire County Council appeared determined to show that it could slash local government spending, including education, more radically than other authorities. This created another opportunity, however. We needed to cut our budget, but we were sending children with SEND 'out county' to very expensive residential special schools, some of which were run by organisations driven more by the business model of the school than by ethical standards.

Why couldn't we create more places for the 300-plus children in the schools nearer their homes in Oxfordshire? Our strategy was not to bring back children already in existing out-county placements but to stop sending them. In those far-off days, before the creation of special needs tribunals, we could be confident that would happen, although I confess that when I looked at the first quarter's figures we were so hopelessly off-target that the figures had gone up! Drastic action

---

5   The people who deserve the praise are Mike Hudson, the Bishopswood head teacher; Ken Fitt, the head of Chiltern Edge Comprehensive School; the heads of Sonning Common Primary School and Stuart Pitson; as well as Graham Phillips, the principal of Henley College. Bishopswood's story is set out at: https://www.bishopswoodschool.co.uk/page/?title=HISTORY+OF+OUR+SCHOOL&pid=52.

was required, so I simply said that no child could go out county without my specific approval. A smack of desperation often leads to less delegation (some would say poor management)!

However, this decision taught me a lot about SEND as well as why the numbers are always difficult to control. The complexity of the cases and the heart-rending tales behind the requests were revealed after the files were given to me by staff with grim smiles on their faces. The whole exercise gave me more than a few sleepless nights, but we needed to spend (on new places close to home) to save (the high charges of out-county places). Even though the county treasurer had been convinced by my arguments, the chief executive was not. My committee chair, Brigadier Streatfeild – who was used to getting his own way – spoke to his friend, the leader of the Conservative Group, and we set off on our journey.

One final memory of the impact of Warnock was the introduction of statements, which I, along with many others, deeply regretted. We became one of a few LEAs which, Canute like, tried to hold back what we saw as the approaching tsunami of tribunals, with costly and adversarial lawyers consuming vital resources and creating an expectation of conflict between sympathetic staff and desperate parents. We became a 'non-statementing' authority for as long as we could and tipped some of our resource directly into schools to head off costly form-filling and what we saw as an undermining of mutual trust. Well, at that stage I still believed that some of the few good things from the age of optimism and trust could be salvaged.

The Warnock Report, which ran to 400 pages, changed the way we looked at special education in many important ways, most of which have stood the test of time. The report opened the eyes of mainstream schools to a world that had previously existed behind a curtain of concern, nervousness and fear about children who were beyond their expertise and experience.

We have picked out nine key messages from the report's main findings and 225 recommendations which we believe are as important today as they were then:

1   Regarding parents as partners influenced LEAs' whole attitude towards all parents,[6] as well as offering advice to them on how exactly the parents of children with SEN should be involved at every stage of the assessment and placement process leading to special provision.

2   The advice on teacher education and training is as relevant today – in fact, more so – as it was when it was published. In the late 1970s, there was a coherent system of initial teacher education and training, so the report could confidently specify which bits of the three-year CertEd, four-year BEd or one-year PGCE should be accompanied by specialist SEND advice. Now, there are 37 routes into teacher qualification and the SEND content is minimal. NQTs arrive with very little understanding of the differing needs of some of their pupils.

3   The report offered detailed guidance for LEAs on how they should organise their SEND advisory services, especially their ongoing responsibilities for annual reviews of individual pupils' progress and the suitability of provision, as well as how LEAs should relate to what went on in the independent sector (on which the state relied so heavily) by supervising placements.

4   The importance of early identification and intervention was stressed, including detailed advice on the urgency of expanding pre-school settings, especially well-staffed nursery provision – which was embarrassing at a time when existing nursery provision was being threatened in some places.[7]

5   There was an emphasis on the need to create multidisciplinary teams from specialist health, education and care professionals from different agencies. Herculean efforts would be necessary to secure effective joint working.

6   How to overcome the interaction of educational factors with those that arose from social characteristics.

6   The Education Act 1981, which enabled some of the Warnock Report to be brought into effect, also gave parents the right to express their preference for a school – so-called 'parental choice'.
7   In 1978, protesters threatened Oxfordshire County Council with High Court action to halt proposals to close all nursery schools using evidence from Rab Butler, the author of the 1944 Act.

7   The rich tradition of SEND research in some universities, which has influenced the best provision, should be sustained and expanded. (It was clear that research influenced Warnock's policy advice and, importantly, the language we now use to describe SEND.)

8   The extent to which there was incidence of SEND and the (often misunderstood) statistic that up to 20% of the pupil population may have some sort of special educational need *at some point of their school career*. The need might not be severe but it would require sensitive school staff to notice changes in pupils' behaviour and take appropriate action. The misunderstanding – which has never been properly laid to rest – initially prompted all schools (even those in the most salubrious and well-off communities) to list 20% of their pupils as SEND. This led to the misdirection of resources and the need for LEAs to moderate; what one school listed as a child with SEND, another school regarded as normal.

9   Warnock suggested that LEAs should integrate SEND provision with the delivery of schooling for all pupils. (The report laid out the locational, social and functional continuum highlighted in the account of progress in Oxfordshire described above).

The Warnock Report had a beneficial and salutary impact throughout the UK – not just in England – and internationally.

The unintended consequences of Warnock

Nevertheless, in combination with the later introduction of measures, such as delegated school budgets, the publication of exam and test results, and a narrowly drawn but tough accountability and inspection system (which diminished some schools' interest in and tolerance of children who would not contribute to those measures), Warnock also had some unintentional consequences. These included greater hostility to inclusion and a tendency to be preoccupied with any pupils' differences that would allegedly require extra resource – a development which is not paralleled in some other developed countries.

Moreover, the mechanism of securing statements and later EHCPs exacerbated this consequence for two reasons. First, it is the only part of the school funding process that requires individual pupils and their particular characteristics to be identified.[8] When funding has been constrained – and state-maintained schools (except in the Blair/Brown years) have always experienced squeezed budgets – schools have been anxious to use any device available to increase their income. They can therefore see statements and EHCPs as a means of either securing extra resources or offloading children the school cannot manage. Frequently, the home–school exchanges during the statementing or EHCP process lead to worry and stress for parents; rather than improving matters, it has often done the reverse, as Andrew Adonis' earlier remarks illustrate. The austerity decade (2010–2020) has markedly exacerbated parental distress as their demands for statements and EHCPs have put huge pressure on those running the system.

Second, parental demands for the process to be invoked, and the process itself, have led to additional bureaucratic demands on the local authority, both to complete the EHCP in as timely a fashion as possible (taking up the valuable time of the multidisciplinary teams who are required to contribute) and then to secure (at additional expense) more places in specialist provision, either within the authority or in independent (usually residential) schools outside the authority.

This immediately ran into the problem that independent schools can charge what the market will bear. With an increase in the numbers of children in the 'high needs' category (i.e. severe and profound multiple learning difficulties), such schools, conscious of the problems that local authorities face in controlling and managing the sector, recognised that the market will bear a great deal. Their fees rose accordingly, putting even more pressure on hard-pressed, publicly funded budgets and adding to the costly and slow-moving bureaucratic process that causes anxiety for already distressed parents. Furthermore, some of the schools in the independent sector are based in old country houses and staffed by poorly trained or untrained staff and run for profit.

One further factor demands notice – namely, the home-to-school and school-to-home transport arrangements which some children attending SEND provision require. The costs of these have grown like topsy. Bespoke transport is provided when normal public transport would do, and vice versa, while the health and safety and safeguarding standards

---

8   This was true until 2011 when per pupil premium funding was introduced for children eligible for free school meals.

of providers has been compromised in some areas due to poor manage-ment by a stretched service and/or shoddy contractors.

In recent years, local authorities have been exposed for their faults in a succession of Ofsted and Care Quality Commission (CQC) inspections. However, although local authorities are managing SEND in a local con-text, which affects their policies and processes (for example, it is much more difficult to promote inclusion in a selective secondary system than in a comprehensive one), they are hugely compromised by the national failure to face up to the contradictions between accepting the Warnock recommendations for statements/EHCPs and devolving budg-ets to a school level. Between 1981 and 1988, it was possible for a local authority to be a 'minimum statementing' authority promoting inclusion because budgets could be juggled to promote it to parents and schools (suitably recompensed) could be persuaded to accept the pupils. After the introduction of Kenneth Baker's local financial management (LFM) with delegated school budgets, this became more difficult, especially as simultaneously parental advice teams were created to give impartial information, which often, quite properly, pointed parents in the direction of legal advice. Too often, the choice for a parent has been a secluded special school setting or a place in an under-resourced and sometimes covertly reluctant mainstream primary or secondary school.

SEND services operate locally in a context set nationally, which induces the escalation of expenditure and runs counter to the very inclusion that Warnock set out as her ideal. It *is* possible to rein in the mutually incompatible pressures we have exposed by enormous effort and by understanding the pressures endured by distressed parents and well-intentioned professionals running cash-starved schools.

We have looked at a number of local authorities where adverse Ofsted and CQC inspection reports have been issued. In summarising their responses, we are struck both by their good intentions and the similari-ties among their weaknesses, which suggest a problem with the national framework within which they operate. Ideally we would want:

- Increased confidence, expertise and inclusion within a locality of schools through a more highly trained workforce, enhanced support and additional resources that are equitably distributed, of high quality and value for money.

- A local offer that enables children and young people to have the same offer as each other and to be educated with pupils of their own age in their local community school, which is properly equipped and fit for purpose.

- A system that has the capacity for prevention as well as providing for those young people with the most complex needs and is flexible and responsive to those needs with minimum levels of bureaucracy.

- A system that uses evidence to inform decisions and has robust quality assurance processes and high accountability to children, parents, fellow professionals and councillors.

- Parents and pupils who have better access to information and support and who are included in the decision-making process.

- A system that focuses on maximising independence in preparation for adulthood.

But we don't live in an ideal world and all such good intentions are undermined by systemic faults which can be traced back to the statementing/EHCP process being rendered toxic by schools having devolved budgets where per pupil funding means that on each occasion a child with more than usual extra needs regrettably becomes a bargaining factor with a local authority also strapped for cash.

These issues are experienced differently in different local authority contexts dependent on factors such as the urban or rural spread of the schools, the historic outlook on inclusion, the ongoing impact of inspection by Ofsted or the CQC, and the financial constraints both locally and nationally. Unless these issues are resolved – with coherent and urgent national and local action – the life chances of the children that Warnock tried to improve will continue to founder.

The government launched a review into supporting children with SEND in September 2019.[9] The COVID pandemic has obviously been disruptive to its work and to date there is little evidence of tangible progress.

---

9   Department for Education and G. Williamson, Major Review Into Support for Children with Special Educational Needs [press release] (6 September 2019). Available at: https://www.gov.uk/government/news/major-review-into-support-for-children-with-special-educational-needs.

Are there ways forward?

Six other developments could assist local authorities in their efforts.

First, the DfE and their RSCs have unwittingly put back the chances of inclusion, as well as creating a magnet for separate provisions, by allowing special schools to form MATs as a special schools group. In doing so, the DfE has not encouraged special schools to join or lead MATs of primary and secondary schools, thereby making inclusion less likely. They could and should address this defect and can easily do so as they form and reform MATs.

Few MATs include a special school. The reasons why are complicated but it is hard to see any evidence of a climate of inclusion. Susan Douglas, CEO of the Eden Academy Trust, a nationwide group of special schools, told us:

> If I had a magic wand, I'd put every special school on a campus with a mainstream school. I would always say, place mainstream and a special school together on one site. That was where I started. I was a mainstream head and I shared a site with a special school, which is now one of our academy schools. It was brilliant because we had a vision for a campus where children and staff moved between the two settings seamlessly. You could have one of the children who was registered at the special school being house captain in the mainstream school. We did performances together, we did sports days together, there were opportunities for playing together – all that sort of thing. There was also really specialist provision for those children that needed it.

She added: 'All of our schools have connections with mainstream schools. For some, this means children having opportunities to meet other children for concerts or events, but we also have some children on dual placements. It depends on the needs of the child.'

The second development relates to the way in which local authorities are working together in regional informal partnerships to compare notes on best practice, share information about independent schools in the region and decide how to make the best use of the high needs places available in each other's provision. If central government could provide a high needs grant scheme in return for a regional plan, so much more could be achieved. We also believe that a regional approach to reducing exclusions would pay dividends, especially if collective progress was rewarded by grants.

Andrew Adonis emphasised to us the importance of the social benefits for children and explained that an integration of facilities across MATs would be a positive move: 'A lot of the academy sponsors were very keen to do it because they were passionate about special educational needs. As a matter of national policy, I think that location is key: providing a diverse range of services, some of which will need to be highly specialist, purpose-built facilities, but integrating children in areas where they can cope. I think that is the way to go.'

Some special school MATs are planning to build more new special schools rather than developing new resource units on mainstream sites. This tendency needs to be halted immediately if there is a genuine will to make the system as a whole more inclusive and, therefore, more equitable.

Third is better trained teachers. We deal elsewhere with the need for a sufficient supply of suitably qualified teachers (see Chapter 6), but one area of growing concern is that as programmes to enter teaching shorten, the more chance there is that SEND issues receive less attention. NQTs report anxieties about their capacity to address the needs of children with SEND and the new ECF has but a fleeting reference to this area.[10]

We think we could learn from what is happening in Wales: in Bridgend, there was a pilot scheme for NQTs who spent three terms in either a special school, a PRU (in England it would be alternative provision) or a resource base; in turn, this allowed the specialist providers to release their highly skilled teams to deliver outreach support to local mainstream schools.[11] This way of working enabled newly trained teachers to understand how to support and unlock the potential of learners with different needs and barriers to learning, and at the same time, enabled specialist teams to work with mainstream schools to develop classroom skills to meet the needs of all their learners.

---

10 Department for Education, *Early Career Framework* (January 2019). Available at: https://assets. publishing.service.gov.uk/government/uploads/system/uploads/attachment_data/file/978358/Early-Career_Framework_April_2021.pdf. New reforms to the framework were introduced in September 2021 – see: https://www.gov.uk/government/publications/early-career-framework-reforms-overview/early-career-framework-reforms-overview.

11 The pilot was a preparatory element in the roll-out of the additional learning needs transformation programme, which is part of major education reforms currently underway in Wales. This includes a greater emphasis on the experience and training of new and established teachers.

A related initiative, analogous to Teach First, would be to use higher grade apprenticeships to attract university graduates to take additional SEND-related diplomas while working in the same settings as those in the Bridgend scheme. At the moment, the capacity of mainstream schools to be inclusive is hampered by the lack of experience and training of many of the teachers.

Bart Shaw, in his excellent analysis of what needs to be done about SEND provision, especially in the mainstream, described how he first came to be interested and then fascinated and committed to the cause. He was teaching geography:

> James arrived at our school midway through Year ii. He had autism and appeared to be struggling in GCSE. He wrote well but appeared not to understand the concepts. I was trying to teach. In those days we were encouraged to tier GCSE entries into higher and foundation papers, with the foundation papers limited to grade C at best. My instinct was that James would be out of his depth on the higher paper so, thinking it was for the best, I suggested he take the foundation paper. Of course, I was wrong and James' mother knew that.
>
> Determined to advocate for her son, James' mother persuaded me to enter him for the higher paper. Over the next few months, I provided him with extra work and had the genuine pleasure of sitting with him after school, providing the extra support he was keen to receive. Later that summer, the annual ritual of results day came round, and James clasped the exam board's verdict proudly. He had achieved the A* that he and his mother knew he was capable of. I felt chastened but relieved by the experience.[12]

So many Jameses don't have the good fortune to meet a teacher like Bart or find themselves in a school where unless they fit the pre-set tramlines, they either sit out the duration of schooling or drop out. The issue of better CPD for teachers is urgent.

Fourth, it would help if there was greater clarity in Ofsted's frameworks on the characteristics of excellent primary and secondary practice. This

---

12 B. Shaw, Special Educational Needs and Disabilities, in L. Menzies and S. Baar (eds), *Young People on the Margins: Priorities for Action in Education and Youth* (Abingdon and New York: Routledge, 2021), pp. 32–50 at p. 32.

would show how good intentions are translated into reality, rather than the sham of inclusion.

Fifth, we are moving into a period of falling rolls in some areas of the country. These should be pinpointed so that local authorities/MATs working in regional partnerships could use empty classrooms to repeat the Bishopswood story (recounted earlier), but with the added caveat that no move of this sort should take place without adequate SEND expertise in mainstream schools to set pupils on an accelerating path of social and functional inclusion.

Sixth, the respective roles of local authorities and schools need to be more clearly defined, especially in terms of funding, admissions or transfers, and levels of support. Mary Bousted of the National Education Union (NEU) offered a starter for ten:

> The local authority should be in charge of the CAMHS, the speech and language therapy and so on. It should be in charge of a special needs budget for the local area, and then there should be a national special needs budget, incorporating higher need as well. There are aspects which a local authority should be in charge of and which a MAT or mainstream school should be required to engage with and to be constrained by.

Ironically, the fact that MATs receive all their school budgets and then top-slice it means they could get into a position similar to that of the LEAs before 1988 when individual pupils weren't bargaining pawns for cash as they are now. MATs could powerfully affect the inclusion movement, if central government wished it to happen.

There is one other point that demands attention if this strategy is to be successful, and that is knowing and being confident that mainstream schools are welcoming of children with varying degrees of disability and extra needs. This involves something more than resource bases and expertise; it requires a mainstream school to have truly inclusive practices as part of their DNA. However, the present approach, especially in terms of good practice on differentiation – apparently approved of by Ofsted – encourages setting, often with the 'best' teachers allocated to the top sets.

Internationally, there is support for inclusion as a defining feature of mainstream schools: UNESCO's Salamanca Statement on the principles, policy and practice in special needs education argues that 'regular schools with this inclusive orientation are the most effective means of combating discriminatory attitudes, creating welcoming communities, building an inclusive society and achieving education for all; moreover, they provide an effective education for the majority of children and improve the efficiency and ultimately the cost-effectiveness of the entire education system'.[13]

The Incheon Declaration, agreed at the World Forum on Education in May 2015, led to the publication by UNESCO of the *Education 2030* framework for action.[14] This emphasises that inclusion and equity lay the foundations for quality education. It also stresses the need to address all forms of exclusion, marginalisation, disparities and inequalities in access, participation and learning processes and outcomes. In this way, it is made clear that the international Education for All agenda, first established in 2000, really has to be about *all*.

Lest we think that it is impossible to repeat the Oxfordshire story of co-location from the 1980s, what follows is a brief account of a co-location in Derbyshire in 2012. The two heads developed the plan, which was helped by the same person being the chair of governors at both schools: Shirebrook Academy and Stubbin Wood School.

We have elected to summarise the key reflections of Julie Bloor, the then principal of Shirebrook Academy, as a series of bullet points on the process involved:

- Prior to the new build and being co-located, the head of the special school and I visited some other co-located special/mainstream schools. In all those we visited, they weren't really sharing the curriculum and often didn't share the space either. We wanted to make sure we did.

- We had joint training days and so on to bring the staff together.

---

13 United Nations Educational, Scientific and Cultural Organization, *The Salamanca Statement and Framework for Action on Special Needs Education* (Paris: UNESCO, 1994), p. ix. Available at: https://unesdoc.unesco.org/ark:/48223/pf0000098427.
14 United Nations Educational, Scientific and Cultural Organization, *Education 2030: Incheon Declaration and Framework for Action for the Implementation of Sustainable Development Goal 4* (Paris: UNESCO, 2015). Available at: http://uis.unesco.org/sites/default/files/documents/education-2030-incheon-framework-for-action-implementation-of-sdg4-2016-en_2.pdf.

- When we moved in together, all my departments had something on their action plans to develop curriculum links with Stubbin Wood.

- We shared eating areas and staffrooms.

- Some of the Stubbin Wood children accessed our curriculum – for instance, a young man with autism studied GCSE computing with us, while others did design and technology (DT) with us.

- Shirebrook children got used to seeing the disabled kids and they were very proud and supportive of them – some of our kids did work experience at Stubbin Wood. Often, our most naughty kids were the most understanding of those with disabilities. Going forward, these young people would live together as adults in the community. I always thought it was good that they got to know each other at school, as Shirebrook didn't have a great history of always being kind to people with learning disabilities in the community.

- We had lots of joint trips and events, including foreign trips. Sports day was at an arena in Derby and I will never forget all the Shirebrook kids cheering and clapping a young man in callipers who finished his race. It was amazing – you would have thought the boy had won a gold medal! The crowd went crazy and he lapped it up.

- A good number of staff taught part of their week at Stubbin Wood. They were very reticent to do it at first – no one had training in teaching in a special school. (Does anyone run ITT to teach in special schools? The head there used to say it did not happen and how hard it was to get staff.) However, the Stubbin Wood staff trained our teachers and they observed classes and so on, and they then felt comfortable teaching there. We did lessons in music, Spanish, computing and DT – specialist things that staff there found hard to deliver. They also got to use our specialist areas. I remember our Spanish teacher saying that teaching the Stubbin Wood children was his favourite lesson of the week; the kids adored him (he was a great teacher), he loved teaching them and they had such fun! As our teachers didn't have the constant worry of accountability or GCSE constraints, I think they could be more creative with how and what they taught. I remember how worried staff were about it initially, but once we got over the hurdle they loved it. We also did one-off things like PE events and included the Stubbin Wood kids in anything we were doing with the primary feeder schools.

- They came to all our concerts, staff pantomimes and so on.

- The two schools had a joint governing committee; I was on the Stubbin Wood governing body and the head from there was on mine.

- Some of our most special needs kids joined classes at Stubbin Wood; this was probably the best bit of all. Those kids who perhaps had always felt they were at the bottom of the pile academically went to Stubbin Wood and grew in confidence. They became the brightest in the class and loved being able to support and help Stubbin Wood kids.

- We learned a lot from Stubbin Wood in terms of supporting our SEND kids. Our SENDCO worked with them and gleaned a great deal about how they carried out their annual EHCP reviews. One thing we did implement was to ensure the reviews were led and centred around the child. We developed the process so that the reviews usually started with the child presenting how they thought things had gone. The staff would work with them to support their preparation for this; they often did presentations with pictures of work and so on. If they were too shy or worried to do this, they could do a pre-recording. We learned a lot from Stubbin Wood about student voice.

Julie Bloor's account is built on the facets of good leadership and, most of all, it is built on belief. Consider how many of the actions the two schools took can be traced back to a belief system, such as our own in Chapter 1. As Mel Ainscow, professor of education at the University of Manchester, told us: 'The issue of inclusion and equity, whichever words we use, is not somebody's job. It's everybody's job, and it's not something you do. It's something you believe and live.'

Helping mainstream schools to become more inclusive places

In Chapter 8, we set out the alarming figures on exclusions that have startled those of our witnesses with whom we have shared them, including the outgoing children's commissioner Anne Longfield. She gave us a glimmer of hope, though, by quoting from one of her reports that 90% of permanent exclusions occur in just 10% of schools.[15] What is needed now is to get that 10% to reflect on their practices. Some of them will be in MATs; therefore, encouraging the larger MATs to publish and compare notes publicly on how well they are doing on inclusion would be a welcome first step.

Mick recalls:

I was recently out for an evening in the town where I taught in 1982. A man leaned over my shoulder and said, 'It's Mr Waters, isn't it?'

'Yes, Kevin, it is,' I replied. I had gambled on it being Kevin, some 30-odd years after I had last seen him, on the basis that someone who referred to me as 'Mr' would be someone I had taught and that Kevin was easily memorable because of the bottle-end glasses he wore. Kevin had a significant sight problem, a form a tunnel vision, which meant that he was called 'partially blind' (although Warnock's influence means that he would now be called 'visually impaired'). It had been recommended to his parents that he attend a residential school for blind children, but they pleaded with our school to keep him, and we had agreed.

True enough, it was Kevin and we exchanged some pleasantries. He then said, 'Do you know what I remember about school, Mr Waters?' I was out for a social evening with friends and wondered what might now be brought up, but he was on to the answer anyway: 'I remember seeing the glow-worms.' I remembered it too.

---

15 A. Longfield, Too Many Children in England Are Still Being Excluded from School [statement] (30 July 2020). Available at: https://www.childrenscommissioner.gov.uk/2020/07/30/too-many-children-in-england-are-still-being-excluded-from-school.

Each year at midsummer, I used to take groups of children to the top of a small mountain to watch the dawn rise. I think it is one of the basics that all children should experience, along with observing the opening of a flower or a bird on the wing. I'd add experiences like this to the necessities of phonics and times tables. I did it as a teacher, head teacher and even when I was education officer: plenty of supervisors, set off at 10pm on a Saturday evening, reach the top of the hill before midnight, eat some food, watch dawn begin to break at about 4am, arrive back at 5am and go to bed. Come to school on Monday and talk about it.

There had been much discussion about whether Kevin should join us on a trek up a hill in the dark, but his parents had been content; there were plenty of us and the other children were great with Kevin. Halfway up the hill, we heard a cry from Kevin who had spotted glow-worms. The females were emitting a fluorescent green light to attract their mates.

Kevin might have seen the glow-worms had he been at special school, but he wouldn't have experienced the acclaim, respect or esteem of his sighted friends, which he was able to recall in an instant 35 years later.

Some schools have internal practices that are inclined towards inclusive outcomes. These include:

- Using a school closure CPD day to send staff to a range of special needs provisions and return to compare notes and consider implications.

- Organising a pupil trail for children with different types of need, to be used by staff on a rota basis with the trailers collating their insights and sharing them with colleagues.

- Analysing the extent to which children with SEND are encouraged to take responsibility, do jobs, participate in performances, contribute purposefully to assembly, host visitors to the school and join school clubs.

- Making sure the school council considers special needs as a regular agenda item.

- Inviting volunteer pupils to experience a school day from the viewpoint of a child with special needs and then report to a discussion group or assembly: a day in a wheelchair, with vision reduced or wearing ear baffles, or simply writing with the less natural hand.

- Letting children with SEND 'have first go' by means of subtle management, especially in the early years where the first to get to a resource will often claim it ahead of the child with the physical need.

- Children with SEND often have a parent with the same need, so making parents' evening experiences favourable and using the parent to advise on beneficial practice helps.

- Holding regular 'ask anything you wish' sessions for staff to address misunderstandings, preconceptions and anxieties.

- Including all ancillary staff who have contact with pupils in the experiences offered to teachers, not just the assigned or attached staff.

- Making sure that any student on placement works with SEND children and encouraging them to produce a case study which is considered regularly for its insights.

- Buying a range of readable key texts for staff and using some CPD time to get people to share their growing knowledge.

- Registering the school with the many charities that address SEND issues. This will provide access to all manner of materials, advice and up-to-date research, as well as a contact point for speakers or people to visit and advise.

- Practising circle time.

- Using restorative practices.

- Using inclusive language – no more zero tolerance – and using 'we' rather than 'you' and 'I'.

- Talking to pupils at break and lunchtime.

- Knowing which pupils haven't got a 'worthwhile' relationship with someone on the staff – because, if not, they may be physically present but not really at school in a proper sense – and doing something about it. Who are the invisible children?

- Having an induction system for new pupils which includes 'buddies' and a phone call to parents at the end of the day with a positive message on how they have settled.

- Allocating time in November for teachers who taught children the year before to observe them and check on progress.

- Adopt 'improving on previous best' as the dominant ipsative assessment process and applying it to a wide range of achievements.

- Having a curriculum that reflects diversity.

- Extending the ways in which pupils can be involved as leaders, managers, mentors, tutors and community workers.

- Making sure staff talk about a child for at least three sentences before mentioning their special need. Always see the person first.

- Most parents want their child to be seen as a person and not as a need. Most also want their child's need to be acknowledged and addressed. Having a child with SEND is an emotional challenge, sometimes harrowing, sometimes awe-inspiring. Let's try to talk regularly with parents about how they – as well as their children – are coping with the school's demands.

- Not assuming that inhibited access to learning means an inhibited ability to learn.

Mick recalls:

I have done my share of attending school performances and know most of the staple ones really well.

In *Bugsy Malone* at a Manchester secondary school, the nightclub entertainment before the big fight was a diabolo performer. A teenager took the limelight for three minutes of action tricks that had the audience gasping at his ingenuity and skill. The lad left the stage to riotous applause, having no further part to play as the mayhem of the fight scene erupted.

He had Asperger's syndrome. He had been included and contributed to the performance in his own way. The teacher had made sure he was part of the production and shown his talent without compromising his needs. He could be anything he wanted to be, as they sang at the end of the musical.

Anne Longfield told us that much of the provision at school level is about trust and confidence, particularly with parents:

> I went to visit Passmores Academy in Essex. The guy who runs it is the *Educating Essex* man.[16] Parents want their children to go to his school because they trust in what he's doing. He's built a school on the basis that there will be some children there who need help at any point. They've got breakout rooms, they do assemblies in a certain way, they incorporate a special needs-friendly environment, and staff are trained in that. They celebrate children's differences. Those parents can have confidence in what that means. I think that's what a good school should be – one that has the flexibility, confidence and vision to be able to support all the children that need them within that environment.

The issue of parental confidence is often mentioned but insufficiently explored in depth. Many families love their special school for a range of reasons. They had to fight to get their child a place there or they felt despair at seeing their child rejected, in their eyes, by the mainstream system. For some families, the special school is a place where they, as well as their children, feel safe and cocooned. They just want their children to be happy, and they want to stay happy because their children are happy. For these families, the prospect of inclusion is something that can wait until childhood is over.

---

16   Vic Goddard is one of the head teachers who have become well known through the *Educating Essex* (and other places) fly-on-the-wall television series.

Mick recalls:

When I moved to Manchester as education officer in 2002, I was presented with the new inclusion plan which had just been approved by the city council after extensive consultation with 'all partners'.

If I had known then about Charles Clarke's concept of the 'too difficult box', I would probably have asked to use it. The inclusion plan had all the hallmarks of one of those 'shared visions' about which many people think that someone else will make the first move, so it will be a long while before they have to actually do anything. As it was, I spent a good many evenings in meetings with representatives of special school communities discussing plans for reorganisation or co-location, which were met with anything but enthusiasm when the reality dawned.

Building Schools for the Future gave us the chance to offer something extra. One evening, I was with my seconded special school head teacher colleague at a moderate learning difficulties (MLD) special school housed in a tired 1920s building. We were discussing its potential relocation to a purpose-built special school sharing a site with a new primary school and refurbished secondary school. A consultative group of governors, staff and parents of the current well-regarded MLD school had raised several concerns about moving to a state-of-the-art, facilities-heavy premises less than 400 metres away in just four years' time. Yes, all the staff would be secure, yes, all the children would be entitled to remain on roll, and the rest. But we were still met with, 'We agree that it's an opportunity too good to miss, but ...' and 'We can see the logic, but ... '

Then one of the governors said, 'You've got to realise that what people are most worried about is the boat.' The room burst into a hubbub of agreement. The old fishing boat on the field had been there for 20 years and it was a symbol of the school. The children had played on it, they had been on imaginary journeys in it, they saw it as a safe place and they had been persuaded to come to school when they didn't want to because of that boat. One parent explained that the boat had arrived while she herself was a pupil at the school. 'Well,' I said, 'of course the boat can be taken to the new site. We can install a flotilla if you wish. Is there anything else that needs to be taken along as well?'

The tone of the meeting changed and an agreement in principle was secured in no time – on condition that the boat could be transferred. On the journey home, my colleague and I talked about the intense emotion that makes a school special and how, for families as well as pupils, a good school is so much more than building and location.

What we need urgently are changes to the curriculum, assessment, admissions and accountability system, and the way in which we finance children with SEND through EHCPs in order to remove practices which combine to become inequitable for some pupils. We deal with all of these issues in other chapters of this book. The major review of SEND currently caught in the mechanisms of government would appear to be limited in scope and we doubt that it will be sufficient to address the range of challenges to SEND arrangements.

In the meantime, partnerships of schools need to establish the goal of being collectively inclusive and sharing with one another the ways in which they assess the reality of their good intentions.

Forty years on from the Education Act 1981 which first made Warnock a reality, it is time if not, as Mel Ainscow told us, 'to put Warnock behind us', then at least to bring together a committee with the same range of expertise and thoroughness as the one she chaired. We need to repeat the exercise in order to solve the issues we have drawn attention to here, and which at the end of the period of optimism and trust she could not have anticipated.

It is not that there is any lack of excellent research or researchers to help such a review,[17] and its terms of reference would be the same. In this way, we could perhaps set out on a route towards inclusion with greater clarity and with some of the recurring obstacles removed from our path. As we write, the DfE has three times postponed what is merely an internal review. The sector deserves better.

---

17   Examples of helpful research are easy to find. We have listed some in the bibliography.

Chapter 10

Circumstances, disadvantage, parents, community, early years and adolescence – lives under a cloud

The journey through the period of our book is one that has been touched by the most tragic of times. Terrible events have affected individual children, their families and communities and have shaped the way we look at childhood and youth. These events are often harrowing to recall and we have considered carefully whether or not to include them in our book. We have decided to do so because our beliefs about schooling are informed by the widest of social contexts.

National tragedies such as the Grenfell Tower fire focus attention and social soul-searching on our treatment of communities. Similarly, the growing awareness of the level of child abuse over generations has led to a resolve to bring to book the perpetrators of crimes against innocence and to make sure we do all we can to stop it happening again. This has given rise to one of the more centralised and managerial aspects of schooling of which we wholeheartedly approve: the requirement for all those who work with children to undergo DBS checks and for teachers, other staff and governors to take mandatory assessed training.

Each decade of the period of our book has been affected by a wretched wrong to individual children which has attracted national attention and outrage, followed by a high-profile review and efforts on behalf of government to ensure 'this never happens again'. As part of the inquiry into the tragic death of Victoria Climbié in 2000, Lord Laming's review made recommendations that led to the bringing together of children's services and education, the creation of the role of DCS and, indirectly, to the demise of LEAs.[1]

The gradually tightening grip on child protection creates inconvenience and delays for those trying to manage schooling, but is also gradually – but not entirely – eliminating some of the most dreadful experiences suffered by children which have existed throughout history and continue in other parts of the world. That the work of the United Nations Children's Fund (UNICEF) and the like is so necessary is a stain on humanity.

We could rehearse many examples of horrific events over the years. Instead, we have chosen to reference four cases that show both the context in which schools operate and the challenges they face in keeping children safe and enabling them to flourish.

Our first reference point is the small Scottish town of Dunblane which, in 1996, was visited by a terrible evil:[2] the biggest mass shooting to take place in the UK which claimed the lives of 16 children and a teacher in a primary school. While the public inquiry eventually led to the amendment of firearms legislation, the government's immediate response was to reassure parents and pupils as well as staff by making schools more secure.[3] In the previous 20 years, schools had become much more open and welcoming places (the Plowden Report of 1967 had recommended better engagement with families as a key ingredient of successful schools[4]), but within weeks funding had been provided to install coded entry systems on outside doors. Since Dunblane, schools have become more remote with restricted access to grounds as well as buildings. Ironically, this has had one benefit, a sort of positive unintended consequence: the provision of good quality play equipment in school grounds because there are fewer fears about vandalism. Furthermore, arson attacks on school buildings have reduced dramatically.

---

1   H. Laming, *The Victoria Climbié Inquiry: Report of Inquiry by Lord Laming* (Norwich: TSO, 2003). Available at: https://www.gov.uk/government/publications/the-victoria-climbie-inquiry-report-of-an-inquiry-by-lord-laming.

2   Head teacher Ron Taylor quoted in *The Independent*, Head Tells of Day 'Evil' Visited School: After the Massacre (23 October 2011). Available at: https://www.independent.co.uk/news/head-tells-of-day-evil-visited-school-1342022.html.

3   W. Cullen, *The Public Inquiry into the Shootings at Dunblane Primary School on 13 March 1996* (London: TSO, 1996). Available at: https://assets.publishing.service.gov.uk/government/uploads/system/uploads/attachment_data/file/276631/3386.pdf.

4   B. Plowden, *Children and their Primary Schools: A Report of the Central Advisory Council for Education (England)* [Plowden Report] (London: HMSO, 1967). Available at: http://www.educationengland.org.uk/documents/plowden.

Our second reference point goes back to 1986 when a 13-year-old boy of Muslim background was stabbed in the playground of a Manchester secondary school. His death had a profound effect. It raised questions about attitudes to racism and integration. Five years earlier, Manchester (along with other cities across the UK) had suffered riots due in part to racial tensions, which schools had worked hard to address. The subsequent Macdonald Inquiry commissioned by the council concluded that much had been done to address discrimination in schools but that the outlooks prevalent in wider society also had to be addressed.[5]

We have dwelt on this dreadful event as an example of some of the issues that still affect young people today: that schools exist within the wider attitudes of the time, that race is still a problem in our society and schools, that weaponry is a worry among adolescents and sometimes even younger children. The knife crime epidemic in London was beginning to make its way beyond the capital as the coronavirus pandemic began and many minds are working on how to address it. The Black Lives Matter campaign highlights the need for our school system to be able to properly support children's understanding of issues which raise emotions and tensions in wider adult society and address contentious issues within the curriculum.

Our third reference point takes us to Rotherham in 2010 where a group of British-Pakistani men were convicted of child sexual abuse; a subsequent review by Professor Alexis Jay found that there was historic evidence of abuse stretching back to 1997.[6] Further similar cases were highlighted in Rochdale, Oxford, High Wycombe and elsewhere. Again, such incidents are part of the wider children's agenda and raise questions about the role schools can play in preparing and protecting children. The Everyone's Invited website, and the issues it raises about rape and sexual abuse, pose important questions for schools about how well they know themselves.[7]

Our final reference point focuses on the day in 2015 when three 15-year-old East London schoolgirls walked through Heathrow airport and boarded a plane to Turkey and onwards to the so-called Islamic State. This event,

5   I. Macdonald, *Murder in the Playground: Report of the Macdonald Inquiry into Racism and Racial Violence in Manchester Schools* (London: New Beacon Books, 1990).

6   A. Jay, *The Rotherham Independent Review. Volume One: A Review into Information Passed to the Home Office in Connection with Allegations of Child Sexual Abuse in Rotherham (1998–2005)* (London: HMSO, 2018). Available at: https://assets.publishing.service.gov.uk/government/uploads/system/uploads/attachment_data/file/726022/CCS207_CCS0318259762-1_The_Rotherham_Review_Part1.pdf.

7   See www.everyonesinvited.uk.

along with related incidents, led to a redoubling of the Prevent agenda in schools. Aspects of the radicalisation of the three schoolgirls is now well documented and both this example and the Rotherham case illustrate that adverse adolescent experiences (AAEs) can affect any youngster, regardless of poverty or affluence.

People who knew the three girls reportedly expressed their surprise that they could have been radicalised; they were described as 'model students' who attended an 'outstanding' school. It is this notion of the 'model' pupil that we want to address within the context of threats to a healthy and enjoyable childhood and adolescence. We think that, for most people, a model pupil is one who is well mannered, punctual, smartly dressed, positive in class and does their homework on time – and who would not want to teach pupils like that? However, if young people are going to embrace the enormous opportunities of the age in which they live and at the same time cope with the risks and challenges they are going to face, they will need a whole range of other characteristics too.

They will need to be worldly-wise, aware of current affairs, considerate and tuned into injustice; an organiser, protester, negotiator and compromiser. They will need to be able to cope with failure sometimes and, probably most important, be ready and willing to say 'no' when necessary. These are the well-rounded children and young people who will do well in life. The model pupil described in the previous paragraph, the 'teacher-pleaser', will no doubt do well at school with a fair wind, but all children need to learn to be sceptical about the communities they enter, and all adults, including those in schools, have a role to play in helping them to develop the techniques they will need in order to manage themselves. This is more subtle than setting rules or having a behaviour policy. For many children and young people the need to be accepted by a peer group is more important and more of an influence than rewards and sanctions policies set by their school.

Nowhere is this more evident than the world that opens up through social media. The ways in which ever younger children are affected and influenced through social media was a significant concern to many of our witnesses. The manipulation of individuals creates mental health and well-being issues as well as social tensions for young people that sometimes spill over in schools. Repressive and inflexible disciplinary and behaviour policies and practices risk compounding the difficulties that pupils experience (as we critique in Chapter 8).

Tracy Smith, the executive director of Tower Hamlets Education Partnership, talked about what we should expect from pupils in terms of the way we manage schools and classrooms: 'Consistency is important but I don't think the solution is silent corridors and crushing children into conformity. One of the points of school is for them to explore who they are, make mistakes, be children, laugh, play, chat and talk, but to be taught how to manage emotions, opinions and situations. They need to learn to organise themselves and present themselves and understand why it helps to do as you are told – but not always.' Self-regulation is a vital aspect of growing up, and a crucial one for schools to take seriously as part of their role in securing the beliefs we discuss in Chapter 1.

Since the Second World War, society has made significant steps towards addressing the five central tenets of the Beveridge Report and provide a better life for children. But so much more needs to be done for those children that society is letting slip from its grasp. We might keep them safe inside our schools as the result of Dunblane, but we need to do much more in wider society to enable them to keep themselves safe. Schools can provide lessons on the perils of knife crime or the dangers of grooming, but when youth facilities and staff are scaled back, an important lifeline is cut for some youngsters.

Over the last 10 years, many indicators in the UK have gone in the wrong direction. Children at risk, children in care, calls to social services relating to concerns about children, children's involvement in organised crime, children's mental health, children in gangs, children involved in drugs, even children's dental health. And that is without considering the impact of the pandemic. *Any* child can be at risk in this opportunity-rich country: smoking, poor diet, lack of exercise, alcohol, sex, drugs, gangs, weaponry, radicalisation, grooming. They are at risk because the technology that opens so many doors to opportunity also invites them into the unhealthy and sordid side of life that a decent and civilised society would not wish upon them. This was demonstrated by the terrible case of the murder of an autistic teenage boy in Reading in 2021. Ambushed and stabbed by two 14-year-olds, having been lured to a field by a teenage girl after a dispute on social media, the boy was the victim of the multiple interconnected dangers that young people face.

Successive governments have been right to stress that children are at risk from poor school attendance and from low attainment, especially in reading, writing and numeracy. Ed Balls was the secretary of state who saw it as an imperative to bring together the agendas of different government departments and build a web of agencies around childhood with his Every Child Matters agenda:

> We had this new department to look at the whole child and to break down every barrier to a child's progress, and to look across all policy areas to try and make health and children's services and early years all part of a family policy – a whole approach to breaking down the barriers to a child's progress. And that came from Gordon [Brown] wanting to focus on standards, and closing the attainment gap, and worrying about the 10–15% of children who weren't getting to the right level at Key Stage 2, and asking what this was about. Was it parental background, was it poverty, was it a special need, was it an educational barrier or was something else going on? If you wanted to keep raising standards for all children, you had to focus on every barrier, and lots of those barriers – in our view – were outside the classroom.

Michael Gove's symbolic removal of the rainbows from the DfE, coupled with the austerity agenda that hit public services hard – particularly the wider early years and youth agendas – began a downward spiral that has propelled more children towards risk and more adolescents towards the social, health, judicial and prison systems – at a considerable cost to society.

Nigel Richardson, an experienced DCS, told us:

> As DCS, you can have lots of headaches around schools and a whole range of particular issues that come out of the school environment, but the part of the job that brings councils down is the awful child protection disaster.

> When you look at the characteristics of what local authorities are dealing with around child protection, a massive proportion of everything that comes through in terms of concerns about children is not serious harm or injuries to children. There is a flatline of about 10% of everything that's going on that is really horrible stuff – the sexual exploitation, the broken bones, the battered baby, serious assaults and neglect cases. They are there and they are very, very serious. But 90% of everything knocking on the front door is about people struggling to bring up their children in conditions of adversity: alcohol dependency, drugs, family violence,

mental health, poor housing, poverty. That is the reality and it is a cocktail of complexity, so dismantling the support networks that help people with those issues makes no sense to me at all.

Gove saw things differently though. With us, he was adamant that 'Throughout my time in office our driving mission was improving outcomes for all, but for the disadvantaged most of all.' He cited the steps taken, reminding us that 'Because educational underperformance is so clearly correlated to broader disadvantage, we introduced a pupil premium to provide additional funding for schools serving disadvantaged communities.' He also asserted that 'Funding is only one part of the equation. We know that a content-rich curriculum, objective assessment and improved teacher quality also help the most disadvantaged most of all and they were crucial to our reform programme.'

Many would argue that Gove's curriculum and qualifications reforms have had a detrimental impact on those children most at risk and that his grasp of the circumstances affecting many young people was loose.

Javed Khan, the former CEO of Barnardo's, emphasised the adverse experiences of some children and adolescents and the vital role of the school in counteracting them:

> Of course, educational outcomes determine life chances, but what children often don't get are the essential prerequisites to effective learning, whether that is support for their mental health or, in the COVID world, how a child is being supported to cope with a bereavement, with hardly any opportunity to grieve with their loved ones or their friends or having any other adults to talk to, which they would have done if they had been in school. All of these things are part and parcel of the future challenge for schools. Schools are the oasis in many children's lives. That's where they can feel safe and confident and less vulnerable, and teachers can help make the weather for that child on that day.

There seems to be a lack of real awareness of the true experience of some families. The consequence of a managerial outlook in a centralised system is that data hides the human picture. Here is Javed Khan again:

> The kids that we work with tell us day in, day out: my mum can't afford to pay the rent this month, so, for me, lessons in school and doing my homework on time – although I know it's a good thing

to do – are not important because we're going to be kicked out on to the street. The only way I can help my mum is not to go to school and to join my mates who are doing county lines drug trafficking or some other kind of criminal exploitation that is on offer to them on every street in their local neighbourhood. Those are the pressures that the vulnerable are living with and they have got worse after a decade of severe austerity.

My great fear is that the next decade will be even worse than we have ever seen before. This £2 trillion-plus bill that we have got to pay back is fast coming down the line and local authorities are not going to have the resources to respond to the needs of the most vulnerable. And when that happens, they turn to people like us, the charities, who often plug the gap, but we are dependent on our donors. And now, of course, our donors are also going to be susceptible to all of the risks that the next decade is going to present to them, so their ability to be confident in their own sustainability through their jobs and so on is going to be dented. Therefore, giving money to Barnardo's, or others like us, is not going to be their priority.

We are not going to have the resources to respond to the growing demand and the growing complexity. We are already seeing this in the numbers of children going into care. It is the highest we have ever had. So, the perfect storm begins and, as usual, the most vulnerable will suffer the most.

Anne Longfield, children's commissioner until 2021, expressed her concern about the focus of the DfE and the lack of priority for families:

The coalition made a big change when David Cameron and Michael Gove turned the department away from children, families and schools and back to education on its own. That was deliberate and people make choices. Family policy hasn't had a home in government for the last however many years. It just isn't anywhere. I think Gavin Williamson had responsibility for families but it's not one that is really talked about. Within all of that children's social care is a very small part of a department which is essentially about education. That is now the focus rather than children and families, so I think that needs to move back.

What can schools do?

Many people, including our politicians, say, 'It has to start in our schools.' Well, schools can be part of the solution but they cannot be the whole solution. Javed Khan made this point:

> To state the obvious, when we talk about the huge and growing inequalities of social outcomes, we often look to schools and teachers to fix it. It's an overly simplistic view which politicians and lots of other institutions have, and the challenge has been made far more complicated by COVID.
>
> I think there is a very big question about whether our institutions are fit to cope with the social reality after the pandemic and the forward thinking that is necessary. There has been a call for a new Beveridge Report, and when I was talking to the new children's commissioner [Rachel de Souza] she was talking about it too.
>
> Teachers are, as we all know, the key universal service that wraps around the child, especially as the village surrounding the child has all but disappeared. The stuff that I grew up with, where everyone around you looked after you in some way, that has all gone. As well as that, the services have been defunded over a long period of time, so teachers have to be social workers, counsellors and a whole range of other roles, as well as having to provide breakfast for the children and everything else.
>
> Teachers in schools can't be the answer to all social problems. Alone, they can't fix poverty, they can't fix social mobility or inequality. I talk a lot about something that is even more complicated than traditional poverty and that is the poverty of hope. A lot of our vulnerable or disadvantaged kids, whatever race or creed they come from, wherever they live in the country, are now experiencing the poverty of hope. They can't see a reason to commit to education, they can't sense anything in their life around them that will give them that aspirational thinking of, yes, I can find a way through this. That poverty of hope is much more difficult to fix than traditional notions of poverty which are financially driven. Most teachers try but they can't do it alone.

Anne Longfield spoke about her thoughts throughout her time as the children's commissioner:

> I always thought, what really is school? School for me has always been a real anchor point within the community, a real asset in the community. I think we've seen that over the last year as schools have really taken on that role at the centre of the community. They've been reaching out to vulnerable kids. Schools are more than what goes on in the classroom and the focus on academic progress; it's also the place that so much more support and opportunities can happen.

> An extended school day for me isn't kids just sitting in a classroom doing more schoolwork. It's the place they can go and have breakfast clubs, they can do after-school clubs, holiday clubs, all of those things which would have that broader kind of extension or enrichment of what they do within school. But it would also have broader developmental opportunities: fun and play and, importantly, provide the kind of support that most parents need to be able to get to work as well.

> I've always been an advocate of David Blunkett's extended schools. I was a big supporter of that, but not just for extracurricular activities which were pretty much leaning towards academia in its broadest sense, but also in that wider play and well-being and social skills sense. This is especially important since we've seen all the rebuilds over the last 20 years. They're brilliant buildings, and actually a lot of them have been repurposed around that notion of community use. The Building Schools for the Future programme had as one of its missions to provide much more of a community use, and that featured in the design.

> You've got schools with really precious assets around sports, around arts. I would love this new era to be one where there was much more of a partnership with a community feel about it. I'd love schools to be open seven days a week, although not wanting to get teachers to work seven days a week all year round. We pay for schools. They're designed for kids and they're in every community. If you were going to design something that got to everyone and was about kids, they're there.

Javed Khan put into sharp relief the problem of those who don't fit:

> I did that work on serious youth violence 10 years ago in London, before I went into the voluntary sector. And there's some learning from that which I think is still very relevant today. At one point, we looked at the case histories of 17 teenage homicides in London, and we looked at the killer and the killed. We looked back at their early years, all the way through their schooling and their teenage life, to see what we could find out about them. Every one of them had had adverse childhood experiences, whether it was violence in the home, drugs fuelled by the kind of community they lived in, poor housing and school exclusion. I went to interview all the head teachers of the schools they had been in, both primary and secondary, and without exception – in all 34 cases (killer and killed) – every one of the professionals who knew them and remembered them said they could have predicted this. The signs were there even at primary school with behaviour issues. The local police sergeants who worked with them said, 'Yeah, we could have predicted this.' So, everybody they came into contact with could have predicted it but nobody intervened to stop it.

Of course, the best thing schools can do is to help children from disadvantaged backgrounds to succeed. Andreas Schleicher of the OECD stressed: 'What we have identified through PISA is the importance of what we call Level 2 performance – that is, basically, when you turn from learning to read to reading for learning. We need to get you to a minimum level of competency where you can, maybe later on, develop talents and build something in your life.'

In Chapter 5, we discussed some of the challenges for teachers in making learning come alive. For disadvantaged children, learning needs to be magnetic. Simon Blackburn from RADY talked with us about the way schools inadvertently create difficulties by adopting practices that they think are expected or have become routine:

> We see the well-intentioned banding of learners that puts limits on future choices. Given that disadvantage has an impact on how a child performs in a test, we know that these limits impact most on our disadvantaged learners. However, often it isn't obvious; the school doesn't call it streaming. For example, on transition from primary to secondary, children are put in sets based on a score in a Key Stage 2 test (or sometimes an average score of a series of tests).

Sometimes, schools confirm the outcome with a further standard age score test. Often, schools also use these test results to generate a target for that child in five years' time.

Why is this a problem? Because a disadvantaged learner who underperformed in a Key Stage 2 test – due to being hungry, tired, adverse childhood experiences or toxic stress – goes into a lower set. They get taught the foundation course from day one. They have no opportunity to demonstrate they are better than that because they never get offered learning that gives them that opportunity. In turn, when they choose options, because of their foundation teaching, they have different opportunities. No language option, no separate sciences, one humanities rather than two and so on. It's so frustrating.

If that child had a pushy parent who was confident and had greater knowledge of how school works, this would probably be challenged and the child may be moved up early enough. Who is being the pushy parent for our most disadvantaged pupils? That's what we challenge schools on. We ask them to look at the proportion of disadvantaged learners in areas such as separate sciences, languages or higher tier maths entry papers, and think about a long-term plan that will ensure that all pupils, no matter what their background, have the opportunity to succeed as they should and could.

John Vickers, an experienced head teacher and now chair of trustees of a MAT, told us:

When I was a head teacher of a big school on a challenged estate, I worked closely with local politicians and had the opportunity to sit in on a surgery with the local MP. Listening to these people, one after another for hours on end coming in to talk about the problems they were facing in their daily lives, taught me so much about the importance of working with families. I think every head teacher should have the chance to join an MP's surgery yearly.

This sort of experience is rarely included in NPQH provision, yet would be relatively simple to organise and the benefits could be immense.

How do schools respond in practice?

How do schools cope with these issues? The answer is very differently; it depends where a school is located and whom it serves.

When it comes to school improvement (see Chapter 7), policy-makers often overlook the fact that lots of schools are only too well aware that parental and community involvement can pay huge dividends in terms of pupil outcomes, not just academic attainment figures but also attendance, behaviour, pupil destinations and local perceptions of the school. But schools serve very different communities, some of which are not local to the school itself, making family and community links far more difficult to secure.[8]

Consider a secondary school in an urban area, for example. There is a world of difference between a 'crossroads' school on a convenient bus or train route which draws its pupils from far and wide, and a school serving a salubrious suburb where house prices rocket as parents move ever closer to try to get their child into the school. And what of the school sited in the heart of a notorious estate where drugs, violence and crime are the challenging backdrop against which school staff carry out their mission to change young lives for the better? All these different contexts require carefully tailored approaches to the matter of parental and community involvement, although even the crossroads school will make links with the businesses, shops, places of worship, museums/art galleries and leisure facilities that might be close by.

In this complicated mix, there is also the factor of pre-school experiences and managing the often turbulent years of adolescence, both of which can be compounded by the impact of poverty and ethnicity.

> I was supposed to be a welfare statistic … It is because of a teacher that I sit at this table. I remember her telling us one cold, miserable day that she could not make our clothing better; she could not provide us with food; she could not change the terrible segregated conditions under which we lived. She *could* introduce us to the world of reading, the world of books, and that is what she did.

---

8   Primary schools tend to be much more connected to their local community. Faith-denominated schools provide for different types of communities, which can also be important to the health of the school.

What a world! I visited Asia and Africa. I saw magnificent sunsets: I tasted exotic foods; I fell in love and danced in wonderful halls. I ran away with escaped slaves and stood beside a teenage martyred saint. I visited lakes and streams and composed lines of verse. I knew then I wanted to help children do the same things. I wanted to weave magic.

Evelyn Jenkins Gunn[9]

The passage above, which is taken from the evidence of a teacher to an American National Commission on Teaching, illustrates not just the importance of teachers as inspirers of learning which proves to be life changing, but that they can achieve this with individual pupils in areas where the barriers to a school's main task are formidable. It is an illustration of the Ginott quote from Chapter 1; teachers make the weather and most try to make the best of the weather, regardless of the climate in which they find themselves.

In the years ahead, when we encounter terrorist attacks, pandemics or disasters created by humans or nature or both, it will be teachers who are central to unlocking the minds and touching the hearts of pupils who will grow up to be the adults who have to solve these issues and overcome threats to civilised societies.

As we have stated, we are writing this book during a pandemic when those who survive ride a roller-coaster of emotions as threats loom and then recede. During such a crisis, we realise how much we owe to those who are on the front line of fighting disease, squalor, want, ignorance and enforced idleness. (It's amazing how Beveridge's social enemies have survived.) School staff find themselves engaged in running food banks and delivering computers and connectivity for those in the greatest need, as well as counselling worried families. We recognise what an uphill task they sometimes face.

---

9   Quoted in National Commission on Teaching & America's Future, *What Matters Most: Teaching for America's Future* (New York: NCTAF, 1996), p. iii. Available at: https://files.eric.ed.gov/fulltext/ED395931.pdf.

The National Institute of Economic and Social Research has reported that the number of households in destitution is rising rapidly.[10] Researchers at Heriot-Watt University estimated that 668,000 households in the UK were destitute in 2015,[11] and government statistics for 2019 show a figure of 3.7 million children in the UK living in 'absolute poverty'.[12] It is no use sweeping the correlation between poverty and fewer life chances under the carpet. It needs to be faced honestly and action taken to address it. We are keenly aware, however, that despite the structural and systemic barriers, progress is possible and not just for individual pupils but for the majority in large pupil cohorts.

Tower Hamlets, for example, has the highest child poverty rate in Britain,[13] but it is also a huge educational success story on the usual measurable outcomes. Former head teacher Alasdair Macdonald put the borough's great success down to a number of factors: 'The councillors are young and have their children in state schools, so they are interested and have a stake in the outcomes. We've also always worked collaboratively as a group of schools. We've had staff who continue to learn from each other and from elsewhere and we've had in succession outstanding education leaders of the education department of the LA.' His successor at the school, Jemima Reilly, confirmed this analysis. We include their insights here to show that, like our American witness at the start of this section, the impact of poverty – and worse – is capable of being addressed and overcome. In future, it should be our goal not to make Tower Hamlets schools the exception but the rule of what can be achieved through exceptional effort in challenging areas.

We underline this because we appreciate that contexts will vary enormously as we now turn to consider parental and community involvement.

---

10   National Institute of Economic and Social Research, Destitution Levels Are Rising Across the Country – and Terribly Worrying in Certain Regions, NIESR Research Shows [press release] (22 February 2021). Available at: https://www.niesr.ac.uk/media/niesr-press-release-destitution-levels-are-rising-across-country-%E2%80%93-and-terribly-worrying. This research indicates that the number of UK households living in destitution rose from 0.7% of all households in 2019 to 1.5% in 2020 based on the income components of the widely recognised Joseph Rowntree Foundation definition of destitution.

11   S. Fitzpatrick, G. Bramley, F. Sosenko, J. Blenkinsopp, S. Johnsen, M. Littlewood, G. Netto and B. Watts, Destitution in the UK (York: Heriot-Watt University/Joseph Rowntree Foundation, 2016). Available at: https://pure.hw.ac.uk/ws/portalfiles/portal/10599861/Destitution_FinalReport.pdf.

12   Thompson, Poverty and Education in England: A School System in Crisis, p. 115; and D. Hirsch, The Cost of Child Poverty in 2021 (Loughborough: Centre for Research in Social Policy, 2021).

13   Tower Hamlets Corporate Research Unit, Child Poverty in Tower Hamlets (May 2018). Available at: https://www.towerhamlets.gov.uk/Documents/Borough_statistics/Income_poverty_and_welfare/2015_Child_Poverty_Briefing.pdf.

Just to illustrate how school steps in when parenting collapses, we have a cameo from one of our witnesses highlighting the issues that can arise all too often when home circumstances for children break down.

Emma (not her real name) was a bright, vociferous and often difficult student. She was part of our 'girls' group' which was run by the deputy head teacher for our most vulnerable Key Stage 4 students. They had a strong woman from the local community come in to deliver tips on make-up (while also talking about sexual health), cooking on a budget, trips to the ballet and other cultural events. Emma's mother had died of cancer when she was in Year 9 and within weeks of her death, Dad moved his 'new' girlfriend in to live with them. Emma spent the next couple of years sofa-surfing with friends and neighbours.

I arrived early on the morning of her Spanish exam in Year 11 to find Dad in reception with her and all her possessions in black bin liners. 'You fucking have her,' said Dad and left. Needless to say, she was distraught. We did all the safeguarding that was needed to get her shelter for that night and she managed to sit her exam; she got a C rather than the predicted B. I was always glad she had taken her maths and English early (as you could back then) and already had them in the bag. Just one of endless examples of the lack of a level playing field faced by children in poor communities. Their lives can often be so unpredictable and fraught that an exam system which puts all the emphasis on the final exams will always disadvantage them.

The teaching profession could fill plenty of books with examples like this, where humble teachers have gone the extra marathon, as much as mile, for individual children. We each know teachers who have performed incredibly humane actions, shown amazing kindness and, in doing so, changed the life chances of children. Like all people in the caring professions, the efforts of teachers who join residential visits, organise performances, run after-school clubs, chat with youngsters in the dinner queue, ask how things are going and do something about the answer make more difference than they ever know – a difference that will last long after the relationship has ended.

Central government has tried to address some aspects of poverty. Free school meals have been around since the 1940s, although the need for a footballer, Marcus Rashford, to make the case for children to be fed during the pandemic must have embarrassed many politicians.

From 1997, David Blunkett's commitment to the early years of a child's life had been supported by the then Chancellor of the Exchequer, Gordon Brown. The Sure Start[14] and Children's Centre programmes[15] were established quickly. While the aim was to support needy families, the services were available to all families in an effort to avoid social stigma. What hadn't been anticipated was the way that more affluent families would take advantage while outreach services struggled to reach those who would benefit the most. Blunkett saw the development of Sure Start as one of his disappointments:

> I wish I had been able to embed Sure Start and explain it better. My successors weren't clear what we were trying to do. That embedding is vital for the future. You can't focus on schools alone. The area I didn't do well enough was family. You can't turn around disadvantaged areas without a focus on family. Some minority ethnic communities are testament to the influence of family.

> The same applies to Education Maintenance Allowance.[16] It made a difference in material terms but also in terms of families drawing breath and saying there is money available so you can stay on at school and study.

One example of definitive action was the introduction of the pupil premium in 2011. Initially referred to as the 'fairness premium', and part of the coalition agreement negotiated by the Liberal Democrats, the aim

---

14 The Sure Start programme was established in the most disadvantaged areas to support parents and children under the age of 4. The projects aimed to deliver a range of services to support children's wider development.

15 Children's Centres were opened next to or near to schools, nurseries and health facilities and were perceived by many as a new form of childcare arrangement. See P. Sammons, J. Hall, R. Smees, J. Goff, K. Sylva, T. Smith et al., *The Impact of Children's Centres: Studying the Effects of Children's Centres in Promoting Better Outcomes of Young Children and Their Families. Evaluation of Children's Centres in England (ECCE, Strand 4). Research Report* (London: Department for Education, 2015). Available at: https://www.gov.uk/government/publications/childrens-centres-their-impact-on-children-and-families.

16 The Education Maintenance Allowance (EMA) helped to increase staying-on rates beyond the age of 16 for children from families of unskilled and semi-skilled workers, the groups where the traditional pressure to leave school or to deny the importance of learning was greatest. The coalition government cancelled the programme in England in 2010 as part of a programme of budget cuts. It has been replaced by a bursary scheme focused on pupils from less wealthy households. The bursary is paid to the educational establishment, unlike the EMA which was paid to the pupil. The EMA continues in the other UK nations.

was to directly support schools to help build social mobility. David Laws explained:

> It was Nick Clegg and others who originally came up with the idea. I then spent a lot of time in our period in opposition designing it and ensuring that it was a political priority for the party. Actually, the problem was that basically a policy that targets disadvantaged youngsters isn't a good retail political offer. It isn't a vote winner. But we did what we thought was right. Nick Clegg said on its launch, 'where ability trumps privilege, where effort trumps connections, where sharp elbows don't automatically get you to the front'.[17]

A key aspect of the funding was that money went by formula direct to schools to decide how to use it. According to Nick Clegg: 'This Government's approach is different. We don't want reams of Whitehall diktat to strangle creativity or kill innovation ... we'll give you the cash; we'll give you the freedom; we'll reward and celebrate your success. But in return, we want you to redouble your efforts to close the gap between your poorer pupils and everyone else. We won't be telling you what to do, but we will be watching what you achieve.'[18] However well intentioned, it was the final sentence that quickly dominated. The DfE was concerned about how schools might be using the money and so Ofsted was asked to inspect. Soon schools began to conform to what was validated by the accountability process rather than exercise the freedom that Clegg offered.

John Dunford agreed to take on the role of pupil premium champion for the DfE (some people are champions rather than tsars). He told us:

> I was asked to go and talk with head teachers in their language about how to make your premium a success. After working on it for a little while, I came up with a seven-stage strategy and gave them some tools to do it. Remember, there is no such thing as a typical pupil premium child; every child has a different set of barriers to learning. However, you do need to have strategies in place that will help you to address learning for each individual. You've

---

17 N. Clegg, Delivering Education's Progressive Promise: Using the Pupil Premium to Change Lives [speech] (14 May 2012). Available at: https://www.gov.uk/government/speeches/delivering-educations-progressive-promise-using-the-pupil-premium-to-change-lives.

18 Clegg, Delivering Education's Progressive Promise.

got home barriers, you've got school barriers and you've got social barriers.

One of the problems was that people focused on the gap – on trying to find ways to close the performance gap. I tried to focus always on raising the achievement. It's an important distinction. Importantly, we were trying to raise the life chances of pupil premium children. That included increasing their cultural capital, and schools really responded to that aspect.

This notion of a targeted funding resource applied universally to schools via a formula was a positive attempt to shift one of the barriers to progress for many children. That central government did not have the conviction to allow schools to innovate and collaborate before applying the mechanical and managerial accountability regime was a pity.

Parental involvement

Parents become involved in the schooling system, and in schools themselves, in three ways: as *first and partner educators*, as *consumers* and, in some contexts, as *captive supporters*.

We don't elaborate here on parents as captive supporters because we think that, typically, it is of less importance than the other two types. An example of captive support would be the PTA, which usually involves a mixture of social and fundraising activities. Of course, the PTA is useful to schools – indeed, it is sometimes key to procuring the facilities a school needs but cannot afford – but it tends to be of more use in well-off communities than for those who gain less from the system. So, if we are sticking to our aim of securing equity, at least as we have defined it, then we need to concern ourselves less with this aspect of parental involvement. Nevertheless, we wouldn't want to play down the fact that in any community the PTA can help some parents with important social interaction and foster the informal sharing of ideas about parenting.

As for parents as consumers, the whole thrust of parental choice – in respect of schools, league tables, Ofsted reporting on school inspections (both with published reports and letters to parents) and the collection of parents' views – testifies to the system focusing clearly on this aspect of their input.

There isn't much to learn on the topic of parental involvement from a historical perspective. Parents have been for too long kept at arm's length and there are few giants on whose shoulders we can stand.[19] Until relatively recently, most schools were regarded as islands where parents should fear to tread. Whatever the context – inner city, urban or rural – there were subtle and not-so-subtle messages to deter even the bravest parent. During the post-war years, architectural design in 'new towns' and elsewhere in the country involved situating new school buildings in the middle of playing fields with a long drive for pedestrian or car access to negotiate what was, in effect, a green moat. In the confined inner cities, there were high walls topped by broken glass and warning notices: 'No parents beyond this point'. Even when the signs were eventually taken down, they were replaced by yellow lines at the school gate limiting access for parents. Schools were a part of the community but apart from it.

It was a rare school that actively sought easy access and the involvement of parents. The most access parents enjoyed at secondary schools – primary schools were slightly more approachable places – were parents' evenings, where teachers would sit in a crowded hall, worried about the appearance of their least promising pupils' parents, while the same parents dreaded talking to the teacher because they knew their child hated their lessons. Both sides were relieved when it was all over. Parents could predict that the end-of-school report would contain a low mark and some terse comment such as 'could try harder'.

To some extent, it was the introduction of parental choice that changed schools' attitudes towards parents, although there had been a few places where a more concerted effort was made to involve parents who are, as we have pointed out, children's first educators and then partners in their education. The fact that children spend just 15% of their waking time in school, while the balance of 85% is controlled by the parent or guardian drove the early pioneers to try to influence the educational possibilities in the 85% of a child's waking time not in school.

---

19 Although C. Desforges with A. Abouchaar, *The Impact of Parental Involvement, Parental Support and Family Education on Pupil Achievement and Adjustment: A Literature Review* (Nottingham: Department for Education and Skills, 2003). Available at: https://www.nationalnumeracy.org.uk/sites/default/files/documents/impact_of_parental_involvement/the_impact_of_parental_involvement.pdf is still a useful starting point for English-based practitioners.

Following the Education Act 1986 and introduction of parental choice, parents were encouraged to join school governing bodies. In the early 1990s, John Major pioneered a 'parents' charter', which led to legally required annual meetings of governors and parents. Ofsted began to send letters to parents after a school inspection reporting on the outcome. During the Blair/Brown years, the emphasis on parents as consumers continued, eventually with the creation of different types of school – first specialist schools, then foundation and trust schools, 'fresh start' schools and finally academies, studio schools, UTCs and free schools (theoretically they could be founded by a group of parents as well as through the more usual business sponsor).[20]

Ruth Kelly recalled proudly her encouragement of parents' close involvement and influence within schools, which she regarded as the priority of her tenure as secretary of state. No other ministerial witness made as much of parental involvement as Kelly, with one drawing an unfavourable comparison with teacher influence, which was seen as much more important, especially during the teenage years.

This push was accompanied by a stress on parents as partners, particularly in relation to regularly set and marked homework (based on contentious evidence of its value, at least at primary stage). In the same vein, there was renewed emphasis on the importance of parents reading to their children to complement efforts to raise pupil outcomes through the literacy hour. In some schools serving disadvantaged areas, this was accompanied by literacy and numeracy classes for parents and, even more imaginatively, for families of children and parents together.[21] School reports to parents on pupil performance are now mandatory and must adhere to central government guidance, although whether the time required to write them is productive for teachers and beneficial for pupils is arguable.

Following the Blair/Brown years, there has been less weight on parents as partner educators. On the contrary, they were sidelined when Michael Gove promoted academisation to schools rated good or outstanding by Ofsted (initially with financial inducements); many secondary schools

---

20 A school in South London was successfully taken through from lobbying to reality by a parent group during the London Challenge, but there has been no great appetite for the parental sponsorship of free schools, which were conceived for this purpose. Much more frequently, teachers and other individuals have set up free schools focused on a particular set of beliefs about teaching methods, curriculum or the aims of schooling.
21 There was a long tradition of outreach family work by primary schools in both Manchester and Birmingham, started by a network of home–school workers in those LEAs with initial funding support from the Bernard van Leer Foundation.

took the bait. Parents had no vote on the move and, once accomplished, often lost the right to be on the trust board that was created as part of the academy governance model (as discussed in Chapter 12). Indeed, in some MATs, individual academies have lost their governing body altogether and some have been renamed. Where they do persist, the terms of reference make it clear that they have very limited powers.

Parents as partner educators

We outlined in our exploration of admissions (see Chapter 8) some ways in which parental choice could be made more equitable – or less inequitable – for poorer parents. We examine here how schools and parents in partnership can help those pupils who are getting the least out of the schooling system. What is appropriate in terms of parental involvement will vary, of course, according to a pupil's age and the socio-economic background of the community within which the school operates.

First, therefore, a few words about those differences arising out from the fact that 85% of children's waking time is spent in the community. In the differing stories of what that entails for some individuals lies a powerful explanation of why some succeed in navigating childhood and adolescence safely and go on and live fulfilled lives, and why others don't. So powerful has the hold of socio-economic background been on the schooling system that all too often we have heard the comment in schools, when explaining or excusing poor performance, 'Well, what more can you expect from kids with backgrounds like this?'

We sometimes wonder if, a bit like embedded and invisible racism, remarks like this are no longer made aloud, but instead have gone underground, buried in the backs of minds rather than truly eliminated. Even researchers spend their time – and substantial amounts of public money – on explaining improvements in pupil outcomes on the basis of socio-economic changes rather than changes in the schooling system or in schools and classrooms.[22] Exhausted by their endeavours, and despite their best efforts, schools are sometimes tempted to believe that some

---

22 The improvements in school and pupil performance in London and other cities has been attributed to socio-economic factors, sometimes without even the caveat that it might be due to other factors, such as the quality of teachers or the leadership of the school or a specific intervention such as the London Challenge.

youngsters are unable to take advantage of what they have to offer for environmental reasons that are beyond the school's control.

The 15% of waking time spent in a good school is disproportionately important because the school has a clear focus on learning: scientists would call it time with a higher valency. The school believes it can over-come barriers to pupils' learning whatever the contextual family and community circumstances.

Nevertheless, family and community variables are considerable and get-ting wider. Annette Lareau has graphically illustrated the contrasting and unequal experiences of children according to, in particular, family income and parenting.[23] She vividly captures the very recognisable advantages and disadvantages (there are some of each for both groups) for, on the one hand, poor children playing with friends down the street and, on the other, their richer peers being ferried by a parental taxi service to a whole series of sporting, drama, musical and other enriching and often participative experiences. She shows how class, poverty, ethnicity and cultural background shape parent–child and parent–institution relation-ships. Although her study is from the United States, it is echoed on this side of the Atlantic.

Another US study by Nadine Burke Harris illustrates ways of overcom-ing adverse childhood experiences (ACEs).[24] This too has resonated in England where leaders of primary schools are very familiar with ACEs. The precise experiences themselves are perhaps less important than a primary school having regular discussions about risk factors, reviewing which of their vulnerable pupils match the list, identifying which ones have a high number of risk factors, evaluating their progress and deciding who from the group needs extra support. They should also discuss and agree on the growing resilience interventions they can deploy to help the development of distressed and vulnerable children.

In our work, we have seen primary schools doing this type of work in Birmingham, Manchester, London and the Black Country (as well as, impressively, parts of Wales) with great sensitivity and huge effort. We

23   A. Lareau, *Unequal Childhoods: Class, Race and Family Life* (Berkeley: CA: University of California Press, 2011).
24   N. Burke Harris, *The Deepest Well: Healing the Long-Term Effects of Childhood Adversity* (Los Angeles, CA: Bluebird, 2018) provides a very readable account of her research and findings while working in a paediatric clinic on the West Coast. She makes the point that ACEs that inhibit development are not confined to children in poverty. ACEs can include, among others, sexual abuse, physical abuse, emotional abuse and verbal abuse.

both also saw it in Oxfordshire and Cumbria; areas of high affluence also have pockets of significant risk and rural deprivation is a very real issue. ACEs work happens elsewhere too, and usually represents a whole-school approach that goes beyond the necessary but slightly formulaic 'team around the family' or 'team around the child' schemes, which are now part of the systemic structure of most schools and local authorities as part of their SEND multidisciplinary activities.

Inter-agency working suffers from all sorts of obstacles, but the risk and resilience analysis and actions mentioned above have the advantage of taking place within the compass of the school itself and can help to refresh its determination to reaffirm its unique and positive culture. These two factors – knowledge of differing home experiences (Lareau) and risk factors (Burke Harris) – are important for schools whatever their socio-economic context, and they clearly have greater or lesser relevance for their practice according to the home and community experiences of their pupils.

Up to now we have been thinking about primary schools and the younger years. By secondary school, children have moved into adolescence; they have ceased to be children and don't yet know what sort of adult they will become. Maturation generally comes very much earlier than used to be the case and yet the period between childhood and adulthood gets longer and longer.[25] The members of a pupil's peer group are growing up in differing directions at constantly changing rates but are trapped in the age cohort organisation of schooling. Suddenly adverse childhood experiences are joined by adverse adolescent experiences. These may include involvement in gangs, drug usage, carrying a knife, shoplifting, alcohol abuse, sexual experiences or abuse, eating disorders, parental breakdown, self-harm, mental ill health and social media dependency to name but a few. As with the primary sector, the best secondary schools also match identified risk factors with individual pupils before applying resilience interventions appropriate to the particular distressed and vulnerable pupil. As the following cameo offered by one of our witnesses shows, some head teachers devise very simple ways to mitigate issues as early as they can.

---

25   Z. Williams, Early Puberty: Why Are Kids Growing Up Faster?, *The Guardian* (25 October 2012). Available at: https://www.theguardian.com/society/2012/oct/25/early-puberty-growing-up-faster. Only 150 years ago, children left school at the end of the elementary phase and went straight into employment. Adolescence had not yet been invented!

We had a fairly simple plan. We decided to ask each of our 10 main primary schools the names of two youngsters they were most worried about making transition successfully and why. We found out what, if anything, their hobby or special interest was and agreed that it was our task as a senior team to help them settle. We liaised with their form tutors, and in our walks around school at break and lunchtime we'd casually waylay them for quick chats once a week. They were as right as rain by halfway through the year when we had reduced it to a quick greeting. Mind you, we were so impressed that we have found another 20 pupils we are worried about and intend to make it a regular feature of our practice.

Adolescents are also growing towards independence and, in the process, the parent–child relationship changes – sometimes in a way that distresses either the child, the parents or both. In many cases, a member of the school staff can become the recipient of confidences which remind them just how difficult the easy phrase *in loco parentis* can be in reality.

Interventions and partnerships with parents change, therefore, according to whether the pupil is a child attending primary school or an adolescent attending secondary school.[26] One of our head teacher witnesses sent us a cameo of her experience which illustrates what can be achieved.

Parents are an interesting group. They are so conservative (with a small 'c') about what they expect schooling to be, and if you want to do something different around marking and so on you have to win the parents over first. Middle-class parents on governing bodies often have unrealistic expectations. When I first started at the school parents weren't really involved and the old head told me I would never get them to come to the school, which was a walk from the town.

We had to think creatively – most parents had very bad memories of the 'comp' and avoided coming if they could. Parents' evenings had 40–50% attendance. We had to do things that were not 'school-like', so the Family Fun Day and Winter Wonderland events saw several thousand people attend. I had some sponsorship money to

---

26 Parental involvement at special schools and for children at SEND units in primary or secondary schools is different again; we deal with this in greater detail in Chapter 9.

make them really good events and got lots of community groups involved. We had to change parents' evenings to be more friendly – putting on sample food from the dining room for parents to taste, offering tea and coffee and then making them all-day events (in that way we fitted around shift work which traditional evenings don't). In that way, we got up to 95%-plus attendance.

If parents missed their appointment they got a phone call. We would rearrange to come and pick them up if they had trouble getting in – we had support staff on standby with the school bus to go out into the community and pick people up. Those that didn't make it were contacted and the head of year would visit; word got around that if you didn't come in, they came out! Once parents came in, they realised it wasn't that bad.

I remember one of the teaching assistants, who was also a local councillor and pretty much knew everyone in the town, told me she knew we had cracked parental involvement when there was an argument in the queue at the local Aldi. One woman was moaning that I wouldn't accept black trainers and all the other women in the queue and the till operator told her to get on and buy the shoes and stop moaning about the school/head. One woman said, 'You wouldn't have wanted to bloody send him there two years ago, so get on and do as she says – it's a good school now.' I thought it was brilliant. Once they get behind you in those communities, they stay behind you.

Parental involvement is so important and, as one of our witnesses reminded us, 'we shouldn't use the pandemic to breathe a huge sigh of relief and continue online consultations only. Face-to-face contact of the sort described here is also essential for poorer communities.'

We have seen a range of resilience-growing experiences for vulnerable pupils at primary and secondary schools, some within the school itself and some within the wider community. The latter varies according to the school's (rural or urban) location, with an extra dimension if it is a faith-sponsored school/academy or one with industrial sponsorship. We have listed some of these experiences in the box that follows, without distinguishing for differing contexts or educational phases (i.e. the activities range across both primary and secondary). Many of these activities would benefit from longer-term partnerships with providers, depending on context and frequency of deployment.

Schools can organise and make provision for these experiences but they also can be provided by parents. Being part of organisations such as the Children's University could be a useful vehicle for arranging activities beyond what schools can do themselves.

We have suggested in Chapter 13 that a voucher should be given to parents whose children are entitled to free school meals to spend on activities for their child, such as learning to play a musical instrument or attending one of the arts, drama or crafts clubs provided in easily accessible places by voluntary/privately run clubs after school and at the weekends. Schools themselves often lay on what they call variously lunch hour, after-school or extracurricular clubs, societies and activities. Schools' progress in this area in the last 30 years has been impressive, with teachers and schools trying their utmost to connect individual children with the right experiences to establish and sustain their well-being and development.

Resilience-growing activities

- Visit a place of worship.

- Visit a part of the local community's 'common wealth' – that is, their museums, art galleries, theatres, stately homes, gardens and nature reserves.

- Take part in a public performance of drama, dance or music.

- Attend a voluntary/privately provided club/society in the arts at a convenient location close to school or home.

- Take part in a competitive fixture in a sport of their choosing.

- Attend at least one public sporting or arts event in each key stage.

- Visit and join the local library in Year 7.

- Enjoy a residential learning experience.

- Receive some coaching from an expert in whatever they are keen on in arts and crafts, music or performance.

- Be part of the Children's University or similar national or international community of learners.

- Contribute to a display of art/poetry/prose writing.

- Take part in debates.

- In Year 6, take part in a 'team' which researches and reports on an environmental matter that affects the local community.

- Host a social event for older people from the local community.

- Represent their school in some capacity.

Examples like these abound in primary schools; they are often called 'passports' or 'home/school learning journeys'. For example, the Shireland Collegiate Academy Trust in Smethwick has developed a 'cultural journey' which guides families in helping their children's development from the early years through to Key Stage 4 and a 'passport to success'. These initiatives have been given added impetus by Ofsted's inspection framework which now includes references to the development of 'cultural capital'.[27]

Of course, such activities are not separate from but part of the curriculum that we describe in Chapter 5 as 'the entire planned learning experience'. In the best schools, the wider curriculum takes subject discipline experience beyond the classroom into real application. This means that school magazines, engagement with older generations, visits to civic/religious/ work/sport/cultural/natural venues and clubs, as well as any passing opportunities, are exploited to full as part of a well-rounded learning experience rather than as an add-on or extracurricular activity.

It is why the Olympus MAT in Bristol has developed an 'Unleashed' curriculum where families are encouraged to engage in 20 purposeful and progressive activities per school year to fulfil the trust's pledge to enable children to become activists, global citizens, scholars, adventurers, performers, entrepreneurs and Olympians. Claire Banks, who coordinates the work of the primary schools, explains: 'We have worked to make learning coherent and we want to encourage families to work with us on

---

27   Ofsted, School Inspection Update: Special Edition (January 2019), p. 10. Available at: https://www.gov.uk/ government/publications/school-inspection-update-academic-year-2018-to-2019.

building a growing awareness and sense of purpose into the learning that all children do.'

Dave Claricoates, senior assistant principal at Bosworth Academy in Leicestershire, said of their approach at Key Stage 3: 'We see the local area as a valuable educational resource. We work with local employers and communities to enrich the learning experience for students whenever possible. This includes authentic projects like pre-apprenticeship programmes, saving the local library, preserving nature reserves, mapping historic sites and connecting with local charities and the farming community.'

There are countless examples across the country of schools making the curriculum matter to pupils and employing the widest pedagogic repertoire. Many schools encourage their pupils to engage with the Children's University, which provides a range of beyond-school learning opportunities.[28] CEO Helen O'Donnell told us:

> Two years ago we introduced a new digital platform – Children's University Online (CUO). It was designed to be a tool for learning providers to validate their activities for children and young people in a uniform way, and a place for children to record their participation in activities beyond the classroom. It has since been used by over 22,000 children to record participation in learning beyond the classroom. The activities that children have done (more than 8,000 of them!) have all been categorised and tagged with skills from the Skills Builder framework as well as careers engagement information in line with the Gatsby Benchmarks.[29] The extensive data set we've gathered as a microcosm of the learning landscape beyond the classroom in England today shows a unique picture of children's participation and the opportunities that are available to them.

In all these matters, the successful school is attempting to put things in place early by giving children the widest possible experiences as a natural part of learning. Not only are schools trying to ensure an equity of experience, awareness and opportunity for all, but they are also building in

---

28 See www.childrensuniversity.co.uk.

29 Sir John Holman worked with the University of Derby to study careers guidance in six countries and produced eight benchmarks for good practice. The review was funded by the Gatsby Foundation, hence the Gatsby Benchmarks: https://www.gatsby.org.uk/education/focus-areas/good-career-guidance.

protection against some of the challenges that young people will face in their future lives.

Parents as first educators

'If you stay long enough in education, you'll see the same things come round again and again,' sighed the silver-haired veteran in the staffroom, bemoaning some 'innovation' seen earlier in their career which was now being trumpeted afresh as the answer to a particular problem.

Nowhere is this more evident than in the pre-school years, where successive governments since Heath's in 1971 have blown first hot and then cold on translating good intentions into practical actions.[30] In the first months and years of life, the play, love, attention and pre-language experiences that an infant enjoys has a profound and often lasting effect on their life chances.[31] For too many, the die is cast and the trajectory of life is set.

Our hope that we might be at a point where government commitment is both real and lasting were lifted by our conversation with Andrea Leadsom, the experienced MP who is the early years healthy development adviser for the government, based within the Department of Health and Social Care. The recommendations in her recent report, *The Best Start for Life: A Vision for the 1,001 Critical Days*, if realised, could break through some of the barriers that have held back so many children since schooling began.[32] Leadsom told us:

> My review is all about services, looking from the perspective of the baby who cannot speak for his or herself. What does he or she need in order to get the best start for life, to be able to go on and be school ready, to go on and form friendships, to be able to learn,

---

30 The Education White Paper, *A Framework for Expansion*, represents the most ambitious plan for pre-school expansion up until that time. It proved to be stillborn because of the oil crisis, but its author was Margaret Thatcher: Department of Education and Science, *Education: A Framework for Expansion* (London: HMSO, 1972). Available at: http://www.educationengland.org.uk/documents/wp1972/framework-for-expansion.html.

31 Many schools have found the writings of Dr Margot Sunderland to be helpful in shaping work with parents – for example: *What Every Parent Needs to Know: Love, Nurture and Play with Your Child* (London: Dorling Kindersley, 2016).

32 A. Leadsom, *The Best Start for Life: A Vision for the 1,001 Critical Days. The Early Years Healthy Development Review Report* (London: Department of Health and Social Care, 2021). Available at: https://assets.publishing.service.gov.uk/government/uploads/system/uploads/attachment_data/file/973112/The_best_start_for_life_a_vision_for_the_1_001_critical_days.pdf.

to be able to hold down a job, to be able to make relationships, to find a good partner in life, to be a good parent themselves? That's the sort of trajectory we want to see.

For many, this heralds a return to the Sure Start programme under Labour some 20 years ago, but Leadsom was adamant that her vision is different. She is determined to set up services that work for families rather than focus on the centre itself. She explained the distinction between this new approach and what has happened previously:

> The difference between Sure Start [Centres] and family hubs is that I don't care what sort of building houses the family hub. What I care about is that the joined-up set of start-of-life services are really offered in that family hub. Then, there is open access so that anyone with a child can go there. It isn't just because you're a 'bad parent', or you're a first-time parent, or you're an immigrant or a traveller; it's not restricted in that way. It's open access and it's universal, so every family can use it.

She then went on to give some examples, such as the centre she described in Manchester which offers birth registration:

> I mean, what a laser intervention that is! The purpose, from the point of view of getting children school ready, is that if everybody from princes to paupers to dustman to scientists, if everybody registers their baby's birth in a family hub, everybody gets the chance to see the myriad of services that are available. If you have your antenatal checks in a family hub, then you'll come to think, gosh, nice place – I think I'll come back here when I'm tearing my hair out with this screaming baby.

We were buoyed by Leadsom's report and by our conversation with her. She was absolutely focused on the early years agenda, has the most inclusive of outlooks and is driven by taking the vision to reality, especially for those families which have traditionally found it difficult to engage. We agreed with her as she continued:

> The problem is that so often the hardest to reach families, the ones who desperately need help, are not reached because they don't want to be judged. You can either say, 'Fine, well, we'll come along and take your children away from you' – and we know what happens to those children. Or, you can take people as you find them,

and you find them where they are and where they are willing to get help. Then you try to engage with them. Outreach, particularly where you have volunteers, is incredibly important. We all want to be a good parent and we don't want to be called a bad parent. In terms of confidence and being willing to accept support, what you actually want is for someone to come along who is not judgemental, who will take you as they find you; if you've not done the washing up for three weeks, if you're not dressed, if you're not showered, if you've got empty beer glasses and ashtrays full of cigarettes, you don't want to be judged.

We were convinced that Leadsom is at the beginning of a process of building a support system for families that could, within a generation, begin to overcome some of the terrible conditions that determine the restricted educational trajectories of far too many children. We know, for example, that by 18 months, the word gap between the most favourable and least favourable households is huge and widens still further by the age of 3 or 4.[33]

This gap is not caused by poverty but it correlates with poverty. It leads, among other things, to what Leadsom referred to as an 'absolute tsunami of delayed speech' and a demand for speech and language therapists that far outstrips the available resources or supply. We believe that the time has come to support the work of these therapists by allocating paraprofessionals to them drawn from among 18-year-olds and young graduates at different levels of the apprenticeship scheme. In this way, they could provide quasi-technical support to therapists (rather like TAs do for teachers) and hard-pressed parents facing poverty and other challenges can be helped in a more timely way to develop their children's language skills.

Speech and language assistants could become part of a team along with health visitors and pre-school workers and operate from the local health clinic/surgery or nursery. This is exactly what happened during the 1970s and 1980s when resources from organisations such as the Bernard van Leer Foundation enabled groups of pre-school workers (chosen for their personal qualities rather than their qualifications) to behave like

33 See B. Hart and T. Risley, The Early Catastrophe: The 30 Million Word Gap By Age 3, *American Educator* (spring 2003): 4–9. More recent studies suggest that the word gap is more like 4 million words: J. Gilkerson, J. A. Richards, S. F. Warren, J. K. Montgomery, C. R. Greenwood, D. Kimbrough Oller, J. H. L. Hansen and T. D. Paul, Mapping the Early Language Environment Using All-Day Recordings and Automated Analysis, *American Journal of Speech-Language Pathology*, 26(2) (2017): 248–265.

latter-day Pied Pipers, pedalling nursery rhymes and simple play habits in various parts of the community such as supermarkets.

Similarly, Sure Start Centres were carefully targeted at areas of disadvantage by David Blunkett. This was expanded into a universal service through Children's Centres, with pre-school entitlement and wrap-around care, although these facilities were savaged during the years of austerity. What is left of the mainly privately provided pre-school provision after the pandemic is unlikely to be in the areas of greatest need.

Moreover, the early emphasis on children being narrowly taught and assessed on the basics from the age of 4 is out of line with all international provision and all that we know about child development. While the Personal Child Health Record, often called the 'red book', focuses on general development in the first two years of life (e.g. physical, emotional and social), the emphasis on intellectual development begins to dominate as children move towards early years settings, which in turn have worked with ever younger children during the period of our book.

In 1976, very few children attended nurseries run by local authorities – and private nurseries were uncommon and affordable only by the wealthiest families. Over the last 25 years, there has been a major expansion in the early childcare and pre-school sectors. There are many reasons for this, not least the growing acceptance of women in the workplace and the need for accessible and affordable childcare. Andrea Leadsom saw the pitfalls in the way the system has evolved when she told us:

> In my view, we've treated the early years as the means to get women back into the workplace. We've seen it as an economic policy, not as a policy to get the next generation up and running. That isn't a disaster, but what it needs is a better balance between the economic argument for having both parents back in the workplace and the argument for helping families to nurture the next generation so they are school ready.

In spite of more and more children taking up pre-school provision, many teachers still complain about the readiness of children to learn when they start school. We believe that formalised learning begins too early in this country. The obsession with measuring children's progress, one against another, has led to an unhealthy demand on schools and on the providers of early years experiences, which has led to a distortion in the way children learn. Andrea Leadsom homed in on this issue in our conversation:

> There are the Ages & Stages Questionnaires: what are we measuring at age 2 to 2-and-a-half by way of fine motor skills? Do you know your times table at age 2-and-a-half? Who cares? But can you play nicely? Can you use a knife and fork? Are you going to answer to your name? Do you share toys? Can you sit up? Are you potty trained? Those are the things that matter at 2-and-a-half. It's those social and emotional areas – how are you doing on that scale? That's what's really important. Not whether you can add 2 + 2 and put the red block in the red hole. If you do not have those things, they will come later.

Folklore has it that it was only because Benjamin Disraeli was anxious to escape the House of Commons for a dinner engagement that we have a school starting age of 5[34] and not 6 or 7 as in most other European countries where there is full kindergarten provision that is the envy of our early years professionals. We believe that all primary schools should be charged with developing such provision with clearly agreed advice from an interdisciplinary group of professionals and a date set for the change of the school starting age.

Community involvement

Considering just some of the activities that form part of the curriculum in many of our schools is to realise just how essential schools are in their community. In the 1970s and 1980s, there was a small movement towards community primary and secondary schools. They explicitly sought to be in a location suitable for adult education and made sure that their facilities were seen as open for use by local people. They took their inspiration from a long tradition reaching back to Henry Morris' Cambridgeshire village colleges which were pioneered during the mid-20th century and copied by a few authorities after the 1944 Butler Act. Morris believed

---

34 The parliamentary debate in 1870 had been about the age at which compulsory schooling should end to allow children to leave school and earn a living. If they were going to leave by the age of 10 or 11, at what age should they begin to learn to read, write and manage numbers? The deliberation about whether to start school at age 5 or 6 was cut short by Disraeli, who needed to be elsewhere. Has policy-making improved since then?

that schools should be a base for lifelong education and the strengthening of democracy.[35] As such, his ideas chimed with those prevalent in the post-war period. Among those authorities that copied this model was Monmouthshire in South Wales, where Tim was deputy warden in one of its community colleges – an exact copy of the village college transformed for a semi-urban setting.

Local authorities and smaller MATs still support and promote the connection between schools and their local community; the best schools still want to contribute to its 'social, spiritual and physical well-being'.[36] Unfortunately, the years of austerity coupled with an overly narrow focus on what school outputs can be measured has meant that national priorities have ceased to include a school's contribution to its community. However, the pandemic has illustrated just how much schools add to and depend on their local area. It should mark the occasion of a renewed commitment to strengthening the connections between schools and the wider community.

Included under the umbrella of community involvement there are a whole range of agencies (such as sports clubs, Scouts and Guides, universities, businesses, places of worship, arts centres, libraries, galleries and museums) which the school can draw on to increase pupils' opportunities to learn, while also enriching those agencies in turn. The degree of involvement will differ according to the school's age range, location (there is a vast difference between a school situated in a village or rural location and one in an inner city or urban area) and expressed purpose. For example, a faith school often serves one sector of the population, while a community school focuses on every aspect of their local communities (there may be more than one) which it serves and draws strength from. In listing some possibilities on the pages that follow, therefore, we are not suggesting that they are appropriate for all schools, but we do think that every school will find it worthwhile to explore the rich possibilities available locally, and which, if taken up, will delight their committed staff and governors, parents and, of course, pupils.

---

35 H. Rée, *Educator Extraordinary: The Life and Achievements of Henry Morris, 1889–1961* (London: Longman, 1980) provides a vivid account of Henry Morris' life and achievements,

36 This phrase, taken from successive Education Acts starting in 1944, was regarded by LEAs as their guiding principle in the age of optimism and trust and was often quoted as a reason for establishing adult residential centres in old country mansions or setting up outdoor pursuits centres for children to visit for a week of adventurous educational activities.

Places of worship

The local mosque, temple, church, chapel, synagogue, gurdwara or meeting house can provide rich sources for the curriculum, links to groups in need (e.g. for food bank collections and other community tasks) and potential members for the governing body if it is a community school. A head teacher, particularly one in an urban or multifaith community, might find attending a service or ceremony enormously helpful both in terms of increasing understanding and developing closer links with different community groups.

Universities

Some schools will have easy access to more than one university and may find a member of the academic faculty among their parents. It is often possible to arrange class visits to academic facilities through such links. For example, the University of Wolverhampton's Performance Hub is a state-of-the-art facility which is used by elite musicians, dancers and actors, as well as by schools and the local community. There may also be the chance for school staff to attend seminars or, in the case of secondary schools, for heads of departments to become visiting fellows while simultaneously carrying out their school role.

Most university faculties are usually amenable (through the student union) to outreach tutorial and mentoring work in schools, which may present a way of making progress with individual pupils. The music faculty, for instance, may be willing for students to serve as visiting musicians who can breathe life into the school music department.

Universities have been known to supply not just governors (in the community governor category for community schools, although this is unlikely in MATs unless the university is a designated sponsor) but also visiting research fellows, who can link up with the deputy designated to lead research-based CPD in an individual school or partnership of schools.

Businesses, professionals and other service providers

The Confederation of British Industry (CBI) has long drawn attention to the need for better links between schooling and business: 'Business has a key role to play in getting young people work ready. 72% employers surveyed for our Education and Skills survey said they were engaged with schools or colleges, but they stand ready to do more. Employer engagement with schools is varied and businesses need to step up to improve social justice and opportunities living in harder to reach areas like coastal or rural towns.'[37]

While the proposed T levels and apprenticeships will make an impact, for young people from disadvantaged backgrounds, the world of work can be an alien concept and schools can play their part, along with employers, in opening up an often mysterious world.

Work experience and careers guidance have had troubled histories. After the school leaving age was raised to 16 in 1972 (disappointing many teenagers who saw little point in remaining in school for another year), the Conservative government authorised the arrangement of work experience though local authority careers services. Over the next 30 years the concept developed patchily. For many pupils, their fortnight of work experience in Year 10 (it is now more likely to occur in Year 12) was a turning point in their school career, offering a glimpse of the adult world of work and giving them the enthusiasm they needed to complete their exam courses – some for the first time.

The principle was good but it was difficult to organise in practice. Like so many schooling matters, work experience was coordinated on a whole-cohort basis. However, placing around half a million youngsters all at the same time in June each year is bound to be a challenge, and some employers who were well-disposed were unable to participate because of the time of year or the numbers involved. Evaluation from teenagers was generally very positive, with teachers reporting an increased disposition for study after their work experience. However, because placement was such a challenge, some schools placed the onus on pupils to find a willing employer. This led to some youngsters returning to their previous primary school for a placement, which hardly gave them an opportunity to extend their horizons.

These administrative problems, in combination with a series of other factors – including health and safety concerns from employers, safeguarding responsibilities for schools, changing accountability expectations, an overcrowded exam syllabus and Michael Gove abolishing compulsory

---

37   Confederation of British Industry, *Getting Young People 'Work Ready'* (2 June 2019), p. 43. Available at: https://www.cbi.org.uk/articles/getting-young-people-work-ready.

work experience in 2012 following the Wolf Report on vocational education[38] – has seen the demise of work experience. While some schools still use 'private' providers, it has been rendered largely unmanageable.

We believe that the world of work should be introduced to children from the early years onwards, with pupils applying concepts and knowledge to real-world contexts. The benefits to children are multiple and, for staff, the focus on working life can bring a fresh element into their teaching. There should also be renewed emphasis on a structured work experience for all teenagers, linked to their school curriculum experience, phased over two years of secondary school life and with selected employers who are enabled to provide an appropriate experience.

Mick recalls:

I remember asking a group of secondary head teachers to second-guess a recent report on occupational sectors in our region as a way of introducing a fairly meaty report. They sat in twos and were asked to list what they thought were the top 10 employment sectors by volume of employees. Most pairs could only get five or six and morale was dropping. I started to offer clues: what if we were poorly? There is a long stretch of tarmac where big metal birds come down from the sky … The 10 sectors would represent the job opportunities for most of their pupils, unless they went to small and medium-sized enterprises (SMEs) – and the head teachers knew even less about those.

Over time, this focus on the world of work will help children to see the structural ways in which business and industry operates and the standards demanded of workers. This can be an incidental aspect of school using examples like these:

- *An A–Z of jobs you have never heard of.* An online resource of short video clips showing jobs that pupils are unlikely to know about and what they involve. This can be done in an informal way and backed

---

38 The Wolf Report was carried out by Professor Alison Wolf of King's College, London: A. Wolf, *Review of Vocational Education: The Wolf Report* (London: Department for Education and Department for Business and Innovation, 2011). Available at: https://assets.publishing.service.gov.uk/government/uploads/system/uploads/attachment_data/file/180504/DFE-00031-2011.pdf.

up by details about the job and how to find out more if they are interested.

▓ *A day in the life of ...* Twelve-hour webcam footage of people in different jobs. Pupils log on to a website and see what a plumber/ nurse/chef/barrister/florist/astronaut/national park ranger/sewage worker/politician is doing at the time – all backed up by further resources about the role.

▓ *A year in the life of ...* Groups of pupils 'adopt' a worker who visits four times a year to explain what they have done in the last quarter and what is coming up. Ten workers would provide an opportunity for one per week.

▓ *Industry on show.* Everyday items being made and mended by skilled local tradespeople – for example, mechanics, plumbers, welders, carpenters, chefs and bakers.

▓ *City exchanges.* Schools and colleges twin up online to show pupils from a different area information about their town or city – for example, 'My Portsmouth' and 'My Norwich' as designed by the pupils.

Health services

The presence of a local hospital as well as links with primary healthcare providers, such as doctors' surgeries and pharmacists, is relevant to both work experience opportunities and (again, in community schools as opposed to the MATs) governing body possibilities. They may also be willing to cooperate on project work.

Aspirational events

We talked with the broadcaster Robert Peston who runs an organisation which tries to open up possibilities for children from less affluent areas. He explained:

I was at the BBC and a reasonably successful journalist who then became a very well-known journalist, and I started getting requests to go and talk to students in schools. All the requests bar none came from the expensive fee-paying schools like Eton, Winchester and Westminster. I didn't get a single request from the kind of state school I attended as a teenager. I just thought that this was ridiculous.

I did a bit of research about why it was that schools like mine didn't get in touch, and it was a mixture of things: incredibly busy teachers, teachers obsessed with simply getting through the curriculum, lacking in networks of relevant people or simply lacking in confidence. Essentially, I decided there was obviously an opportunity to do something that could be quite useful and slightly level the playing field.

People went to talk to the kids at Eton: trade unionists, former prime ministers, archbishops of Canterbury and I just thought, 'Wait a minute – why aren't these people going into state schools?' As a journalist you get to know lots of really interesting, inspirational, impressive people. I rang up loads of them and asked whether they would like to speak in state schools. Almost all of them said yes.

Peston's charity, Speakers for Schools, offers pupils an insight into worlds they only have an opportunity to see from a distance. This is one example of the many affordable possibilities available to schools. While this is a national programme with an infrastructure to make it happen, many schools have a list of local people, perhaps former pupils of the school, who can talk about their experience of working life. Pupils will be as interested in the story of the local lad or lass who set up an advertising business as they will in what it is like to work in a local factory or for a holiday company. Once a network of contributors is established, the pupils can help with the organisation, hosting and management of events.

Voluntary clubs in the area

Many sporting and amateur adult interest clubs (choirs, opera, drama, dance, gardening, history, philately, ornithology, etc.), which usually have 'junior' sections, have links with school staff (who are perhaps members) and are always keen on creating the next generation of enthusiasts.

Charitable concerns (you see them collecting outside supermarkets) offer real opportunities. The Wildlife Trusts, National Trust, English Heritage and plenty of others are worth a school subscription to get journals and magazines for teachers to discuss with children.

And don't forget the traditional clubs for children and teenagers: the Cubs and Scouts, Brownies and Guides, Sea Cadets, boys'/girls' clubs and the Duke of Edinburgh's Award scheme. Many youngsters, and particularly those without wide experience within the family, need an introduction to enable them to cross the threshold; it is often making the first step to go somewhere new that is the barrier.

In 2011, prompted by David Cameron's call for a 'Big Society', the National Citizen Service (NCS) was established. This year-round, government-backed programme for 16–17-year-olds sets out to build skills for work and life, supporting young people to take on new challenges and adventures, make new friends and contribute to their community. Participants engage in a part- or full-time four-week programme that culminates in a social action project, benefitting both young people and society. Like so many new developments, this one seemed to plough its own furrow rather than building on what is (or is not) available in communities and working with other voluntary groups to harmonise the offer to youngsters. Thousands of young people have benefitted from NCS programmes and we have met many who found it life affirming, but whether it finds the ones who need it the most still seems to be left to chance.

The Prince's Trust tends to support young people who have left school but many schools build links to try to find the natural next step for their children. It is another example of why transition needs to be thought through properly, at both ends of secondary schooling.

Sarah Sewell talked with us about Yes Futures, an organisation that is all about empowering young people to believe in themselves:

> We work with groups of students who are chosen by schools, often because they are struggling with their self-esteem. With support from a Yes Futures coach, students set personal goals and are given opportunities to work towards them. One feature of the Yes Futures programmes is World of Work: we link with a range of businesses to show students the world of employment, including careers they might not consider. We have some fantastic partners – like Twitter, KPMG, EY, television studios, football stadia – all showing a wide range of different career options. Another key part of our programmes is Play Your Part: through volunteering, students see the value of social action and boost their confidence by realising that their unique skills are really valuable to society and other people.

Robert Peston brought up 'a separate aspect of unfairness' – work experience:

> I talked to schools and they said they were really struggling to get kids from disadvantaged backgrounds into really interesting employment settings. So we went to a bunch of high-profile employers of various sorts, from the Bank of England to IT companies, and said to them that it would be good to see them taking less privileged kids and giving them work experience. They agreed, and so a few years ago we started doing this work experience strand and, again, it's successful on both sides.
>
> We're getting these underprivileged kids into workplaces that they otherwise wouldn't get into, but the other exciting thing about it is that these are kids who don't feel entitled. When they go into these businesses, they make a massive contribution. They are much more committed to the experience of actually learning. Employers themselves say that they massively prefer having kids of the sort that we provide, because these are kids who actually want to be there and want to make a contribution and want to learn. So, from all points of view, it's been tremendously positive.

Julia Cleverdon told us:

> If you look at the Young Scot programme,[39] it's one of the best organised operations. It ties together kids with the equivalent of an Oyster card, who swipe to get on their bus, swipe to pay for their school lunches (and therefore doesn't show that they're on free school meals) and gives them rewards on their card for things they do in the community. Help me understand why that is impossible to run in Manchester, Birmingham, Bradford or anywhere else.
>
> One of the big things I've been running over the last seven years is called the I Will campaign. How do you support and help young people to be leaders of their community, leaders in their school, to find their voice and all the rest of it?

Schools, particularly secondary schools, can help their pupils to make steps in learning by working closely with voluntary organisations in their

---

39 The Young Scot National Entitlement Card is available to young people aged between the ages of 11 and 26 and aims to help them cope with life's challenges and enjoy its opportunities. See https://young.scot.

area – and they will be appreciated for it. For schools so tuned into marketing these days, it is an avenue that many miss.

Old people's homes

The potential of inter-generational work was shown by the winner of the community and collaboration TES Schools Award in 2020, St Colm's High School in Northern Ireland, which is described in the box below. Many schools are now engaging in similar work and are resolved to do more after the pandemic.

Pupils at St Colm's High School and members of the Cornstore Youth Club, Draperstown, had noticed that the garden at Ballinascreen Fold, a retirement and care complex, was in a poor state and thought they could help. They teamed up with residents from Ballinascreen Fold to improve their outside space. Some pupils had gardening skills, trained others and were not afraid of the hard graft required to revamp the Fold's garden and the Men's Shed. Together, they developed an eco-friendly garden including bird boxes, wildflower areas and features made from recycled tyres. They also made birdfeeders and fat balls to encourage birds to visit the garden. Pupils continue to maintain the garden and carry out litter clean-ups.

The pupils have also organised entertainment nights and social activities for the residents, including bingo and karaoke. They have shared their Snapchat filter skills with Fold members too, who, in turn, have enjoyed sending funny snaps to one another and their grandchildren! The pupils have since organised a coffee morning for charities, including Macmillan Cancer, raising funds of £2,100.

The overall benefit was, and continues to be, the interaction between young people and the elderly, time spent outdoors improving the health and well-being of both groups, and acquiring an understanding of sustainable development by caring for the environment. The bridging of the gap between the generations has benefitted both age groups and fostered good community relations that stretch far beyond the timescale of the project. All the pupils felt a sense of community pride in their work with members of the Fold, who praised the actions, humour and kindness of the pupils. Not only do they look forward to their craic, but they also visit their own grandparents more, use their phones less and spend more time outdoors. Pupils said: 'We thought we were helping them but they taught us so much.'

The project matched UN Sustainable Development Community Action Goals 3, 4.7 and 11.7.

Rotary, Round Table and Lions Clubs

The special schools sector can usually make links with these all-male fundraising societies. They will likely have individual members who are parents and may have connections that will extend opportunities for all pupils.

Staff, particularly support staff who live locally, may have connections that can be exploited; we have both known head teachers who, when looking for new staff, include in the person specification that 'those with a full and active out-of-school lifetime interest in the arts or sport are particularly welcome to apply'.[40] Other schools rightly go out of their way in their daily habits to connect with their community by buying from the local parade of shops or commissioning shopkeepers to reinforce good behaviour policies by handing out credits to well-behaved pupils.

There is no doubt in our minds that involvement of and with the community can be so effective that it can be a key route out of difficulties for a school that has fallen on hard times, as our next cameo illustrates. It demonstrates that looking outwards can transform a school's prospects.

> Newmarket Academy was placed in special measures in 2013. Under new leadership, the school has committed to an outward facing and collaborative community engagement strategy, where it has placed itself at the interface between different aspects of the wider community. The school was judged to be good in 2017 and is now 'a school the community can be proud of'. Over the last five years, the number on roll has risen from just over 500 to 759, reflecting the confidence

---

40   One head confessed that she only appointed staff who were still active sportspeople or practising musicians. We are not sure how that fitted HR/personnel/people department requirements but she said that it ensured a superb staff!

the community now has in the school and the bridges it has created across the community.

The Newmarket Academy Godolphin Beacon Project was established in 2015 to harness the assets of the community to provide a comprehensive and cohesive programme of personal development. In Years 7–8 it focuses on stimulating aspiration and ambition, and in Years 9–11 equipping the students with the skills, experiences and confidence to fulfil their potential. The 35 events held each year – ranging from a complete week of learning for Year 8 in the community to personalised work experience programmes – is now embedded throughout the curriculum, from marketing projects in business studies, such as working with chefs from around the world, to a local history unit.

The programme particularly targets disadvantaged students through the Youth Guide Project in collaboration with the National Horse Racing Museum and motivational work with Horses for Heroes. The project has provided extensive support for SEND/EAL students, helping them find and prepare for future employment through the Careers Fair, our 'speed-dating' event and work experience programme. Through the school's work with the community, we are able to provide a full and complete work experience programme, and across the board our Gatsby Benchmarks figures are exceptionally high and significantly above national averages.

A group of students, with the support of the local council, have raised over £100,000 to create a new skate park for the town. The next project is to use the local community assets to design and build a new landscaped area around a welfare housing development. The school also approached the Newmarket Festival to set up the Dragon's Den, which allows students to apply for funding to fulfil their potential outside school, and also the Live your Dreams Programme, which introduces Year 10 students to the world of work.

This year the community set up a COVID-19 Fund which raised over £60,000, and the head teacher was asked to sit on the committee tasked with deciding on how to allocate the funds. The head was also appointed chair of the Community Engagement and Education Across UK Horseracing Steering Group, which will catalogue racing's community and education projects and advise the industry on how to achieve greater community collaboration and engagement across all centres of racing in the UK. The school is at the heart of its community, working with stakeholders representative of the entire community, who are now collaborating to transform the school and the area for its parents and carers, local primary schools and the region.

Government's attempts to tackle the problems of poverty and disadvantage: the need for a new approach

We have described what a school can do to embrace parents and community almost irrespective of disadvantage. We started the chapter with moving testimony from an American teacher and we pointed to Tower Hamlets as an example of a small London borough with young councillors and the good fortune to be well led by a succession of talented education officers who inherited and recruited school leaders who were willing to improve collectively. We interviewed two of their head teachers and two of the borough's education officers (both of whom became chief executives in Tower Hamlets).

In explaining the extraordinary progress of the schools, Alasdair Macdonald added, almost as an afterthought: 'And, of course, there was the City of London on our doorstep, so we never lacked support and the possibility of business partnerships.' Kevan Collins referred to the borough's partnership with business: 'We could show how we could tackle issues which supported the school's efforts whether in housing, work opportunities, or community facilities.'

Efforts by national government to join up services or work effectively across departments to solve the many challenges posed in communities scattered across the country have been less successful. In failing to solve these multifaceted problems, ironically, governments have reflected one of the perennial weaknesses which so often baffles the best of our schools: namely, the difficulty of helping pupils to master the ability to apply skills learned in one subject to a different situation or context either within that discipline or across disciplines. In almost the same way, governments in general appear blinkered and caught in what Ruth Kelly described as the 'departmental silos of Whitehall' when trying to make their approaches coherent across departments. Maybe it is a particular problem in England because of the size, density and diversity of the population, or maybe it is that matrix management is difficult at the best of times and impossibly elusive in large organisations.

Labour, driven first by Michael Barber in the Standards and Effectiveness Unit and then in the Prime Minister's Delivery Unit, promoted the mantra of 'joined-up thinking' – bringing policies together both within education and across government. However, the increasing focus on targets linked to higher-stakes accountability, again within education and across wider government, gradually encouraged silo working as managerialism grew to ensure that responsibility was individualised and culpability personalised.

Whatever the reason, various education initiatives have foundered due to a lack of joined-up thinking. Let us consider some of these plans – all of which would have helped if other departments affecting health, housing, police, local government and employment had been part of the attempt to improve young people's and their families' chances in life – before making some recommendations for the future.

Education priority areas

Education priority areas (EPAs) were the first intervention based on the idea of positive discrimination to compensate for poor environmental conditions. They were introduced in the early 1970s on the back of the Plowden Report's argument that a major factor in a child's educational performance is the attitude of her parents to education. This had been presaged in the Newsom Report's concerns in 1963 for 'education in the slums'.[41]

In areas of social challenge, so the argument went, parents could be indifferent to their children's success and progress in schools. As a result, extra

---

41 J. H. Newsom, *Half Our Future: A Report of the Central Advisory Council for Education (England)* [Newsom Report] (London: HMSO, 1963), ch. 3. Available at: http://www.educationengland.org.uk/documents/newsom/newsom1963.html.

resources were committed in the areas identified. New school buildings, bespoke curriculum materials and an extra EPA allowance in teachers' salaries were just three of the features of the initiative, which was evaluated and supported by a team of sociologists from Oxford University. It took place at the very beginning of our story and was focused famously on South Yorkshire, but also on other disadvantaged urban areas such as Tyneside, Teeside, West Cumbria, Nottingham, Liverpool and Cornwall where unemployment levels were significant. However, EPAs were identified locally and no national criteria were ever established. Some local authorities established EPAs to introduce additional government funding, while others were shy to do so.

Education Action Zones

Introduced by David Blunkett during the Blair government in 1998, the provenance of EAZs can be traced back to the EPA initiative. They were located in areas of disadvantage and were intended to attract business sponsorship and private sector support, which it was hoped would lead to school improvements and would be reflected in measurable pupil outcomes. They were set up by local schools who created a forum with local partners. However, they suffered from over-elaborate management and governance arrangements and were occasionally hampered by some schools within the EAZ just using the initiative to secure much needed resources after many years of cuts but without a commitment to deliver results. A total of 72 EAZs were established, but often in parallel with their local authorities and so, sadly, sometimes with duplication, sometimes with a competitive attitude, sometimes with considerable success and often with frustration. However, measuring the success attributed to EAZs as opposed to other initiatives was difficult and the scheme was discontinued after the initial five years of funding.

Schools were generally favourable towards their EAZ, associating additional funding with the development, but neither the EAZs nor the EPAs had lasting impact on the communities in which they were placed, although doubtless they contributed to some teachers at the time having a lasting impact on individuals.

In some parts of the country, EAZs were part of a wider investment agenda which encouraged collaboration across school communities in selected city regions. Other programmes included specialist schools, beacon schools, gifted and talented, learning mentors and learning support units, all of which were designed to tackle underachievement and social exclusion (as it was then called). The EiC initiative was remarkably successful in some areas where it was integrated with ongoing school improvement provision. In other areas, a separate infrastructure emerged leading to further duplication and isolation, with EAZs becoming a world unto themselves and in effect a parallel or alternative LEA.

Mick recalls:

When I arrived in Manchester as the chief education officer, EiC and EAZs were well established but I felt there was a lack of coherence. I experienced that feeling of 'I wouldn't have started from here', having arrived from Birmingham where we had worked so hard at collaboration and partnership with programmes integrating with each other. Labour and the DfE were in that period of using super heads and a few self-presenters had curried favour to the extent that other heads fell in behind their direction.

We had two EAZs. The one in East Manchester was a model of how joined-up working could make a difference. The EAZ leader was the unassuming Steve Edwards, who knew the schools in their context and worked with the local authority teams to effect school improvement. Steve was part of an urban regeneration company developing East Manchester, owned by the city council and led by Tom Russell. This team was focused on attracting investment and employment, renewing housing stock, improving transport, developing health and social care services, and integrating community and voluntary sectors, traditional and new.

Steve saw his EAZ role as working for the good of the schools and families, harmonising provision and effort in the present, and seeing improvement in the long term, and he was a big part of a new-found confidence in that part of the city.

The other EAZ was in the south of the city and focused on Wythenshawe. Here, there was no guiding infrastructure beyond the schools themselves which had, in their EAZ director, a version of a Teachers' Centre warden of previous times who was responsible for liaising with the DfE and building relationships with key businesses, such as the nearby airport. I always thought that this EAZ could probably have made the steps it did, in terms of improved attainment, by virtue of central government investment and the schools' own collaboration.

The difference between the leadership of the two EAZs was noticeable in ethos, impact and long-term social change.

A third initiative, to which we now turn, is still in existence.

Opportunity areas

In October 2017, Justine Greening announced that Blackpool, Derby, Norwich, Oldham, Scarborough and West Somerset would become opportunity areas, along with the existing designated opportunity areas of Bradford, Doncaster, Fenland and East Cambridgeshire, Hastings, Ipswich and Stoke-on-Trent. The DfE described the initiative thus:

> [Opportunity areas] will see local partnerships formed with early years providers, schools, colleges, universities, businesses, charities and local authorities to ensure all children and young people have the opportunity to reach their full potential. A key aim of opportunity areas is to build young people's knowledge and skills and provide them with the best advice and opportunities, including working with organisations such as the Careers and Enterprise Company, the Confederation of British Industry, the Federation of Small Businesses, and the National Citizen Service. The Department for Education (DfE) will target its programmes to ensure children get the best start in the early years, to build teaching and leadership capacity in schools, to increase access to university, to strengthen technical pathways for young people, and work with employers to improve young people's access to the right advice and experiences. DfE will work with each opportunity area to respond to local priorities and needs – because each area will have its own challenges.[42]

---

42 Department for Education and J. Greening, Education Secretary Announces 6 New Opportunity Areas [press release] (18 January 2017). Available at: https://www.gov.uk/government/news/education-secretary-announces-6-new-opportunity-areas.

Of all our witnesses, Justine Greening was the most single-minded on the issue of social justice. She tried to develop a strategic approach during her all too brief spell as secretary of state:

> I launched the first wave of opportunity areas within months of taking up the role. These were place-based approaches rather than demand-led programmes provided by Whitehall centrally, but generally taken up by schools able to do better rather than those most struggling. I told my team to look at Peter Senge's work on system dynamics because opportunity areas were about system fix – working inside schools but also outside schools. We know that piecemeal projects are unlikely to shift system out-comes. We wanted fast delivery – there was no need for White Papers or consultations. We trialled work in three distinctly differ-ent 'systems': urban deprived communities, rural communities – I was interested in understanding rural social mobility better – and also in more isolated coastal areas. How could they each do school improvement? We set up the first wave of opportunity areas and harvested the best practice that came out of all of them.

> In the end, there was no silver bullet. What came out of the oppor-tunity areas was that if we could get a nucleus of people to work together as one team – including the DfE officials on the ground – with one set of priorities and one plan to achieve them, and we could more widely as the DfE back up the momentum that was there, we had a chance of driving change – and that's what happened.

Greening was determined and in a hurry. We reflected that it was a pity she had not joined forces with Ed Balls. She said:

> Levelling up is not just for the UK. Inequality of opportunity is a challenge for many developed countries whether you're in the UK, United States, France, Germany or elsewhere. We need to think bigger. We need to bolt things together to drive system change; that means agreed levelling-up goals using a common approach for developed countries to mirror what we have learned from the Sustainable Development Goals which are principally aimed at developing countries. We should apply that mentality to the UK. Levelling up transcends party politics, so we need some all-party agreement, a social mobility action plan – and then we need to use it for the long term.

For me, it is about people having the same chance to get on in life, whoever they are. Young people in niche closed-off sectors are not getting any understanding of our social diversity, including those in private schools. Egalitarianism clearly matters if we want families to aspire. The social, economic and political transformations of our country are inter-related. How much we pay a carer or a banker or a driver is linked to that.

After the Second World War, we understood the need for collective action on protecting people against life's downsides – we protected health via establishing the NHS and protected incomes via the welfare state, but we didn't manage to give the same guarantee of delivering the upside of life. We caught people who were falling without launching people upwards. I believe we can get there. We have made real progress on changes such as greater gender equality. We have to educate people towards understanding why stronger social mobility and equality of opportunity is the vital concept that underpins everything.

These three initiatives have attempted to use education, alongside other agencies, to transform outcomes, principally measured by pupil attainment and attendance. There have been others in particular locations (e.g. EiC, London Challenge, Greater Manchester Challenge, Black Country Challenge and City Challenges elsewhere) which have been unashamedly focused on schools and school improvement. We don't think there has ever been a place-based challenge and resources boost from central government to transform housing, employment, primary health and educational outcomes for school pupils and educational opportunities for their parents in socio-economically challenging areas, which are now euphemistically called 'coldspots'.[43]

In short, most of these well-intentioned projects didn't make a lasting difference[44] – nor as much as they might have done at the time – for want of someone taking on parallel initiatives to simultaneously transform the other social variables, especially housing, employment opportunities and

---

43   Social Mobility and Child Poverty Commission, *The Social Mobility Index* (16 June 2016). Available at: https://assets.publishing.service.gov.uk/government/uploads/system/uploads/attachment_data/file/496103/Social_Mobility_Index.pdf.

44   It is arguable that the London Challenge and Greater Manchester Challenge did make a difference in some important respects – namely, an acceptance that area-wide school improvement was possible. In London, at least, attainment levels rose and some of the attainment gaps were reduced, although it may have come at the considerable cost that an above average number of pupils were permanently excluded, as this wasn't monitored and didn't appear among the key performance indicators.

health/well-being. Labour did set up the Neighbourhood Renewal Fund in 88 local authority areas, and there was considerable progress in pockets of social deprivation, especially in the development of approaches to be used in multi-agency partnerships.[45]

The Blair/Brown governments made a concerted effort to tackle educational standards in general, although there were focused interventions to help two vulnerable age groups: the very young with Sure Start, and adolescents with the Education Maintenance Allowance for youngsters from poor families after the age of 16. These are in urgent need of being repeated.

So great are the challenges after the years of austerity and the pandemic that the gaps between children from different socio-economic backgrounds have widened. Other chapters in this book propose the changes that are necessary in the name of equity and social mobility. Arising from this brief consideration of the early years, adolescence, parents, the community and poverty, we would welcome a coherent strategy rather than piecemeal initiatives. For us that means:

- The setting up of a major inquiry – equivalent to those undertaken in the past – into the school starting age, the nature of pre-school provision and entitlements for parents in housing, health and education.[46]

- The funding and creation of speech and language paraprofessionals and pre-school workers, using the apprenticeship scheme, in the opportunity areas and the former EiC areas for a 10-year period, with a clear plan and evaluation of outcomes.

- An approach being made by government to major charitable foundations (e.g. Joseph Rowntree, Paul Hamlyn, Gatsby, Esmée Fairbairn) to match-fund and lead a multidisciplinary/inter-departmental effort to transform a handful of places drawn from the opportunity areas as a pilot scheme. Each effort would use slightly different project/delivery models but with the same

45 Department for Communities and Local Government, *Evaluation of the National Strategy for Neighbourhood Renewal: Final Report* (2010). Available at: https://extra.shu.ac.uk/ndc/downloads/general/Neighbourhood%20Renewal%20Final%20report.pdf.
46 We mean similar to Newsom (1963), Robbins (1963), Crowther (1959), Plowden (1967) and especially Warnock (1978), with its wider-than-education remit.

agreed key performance indicators (KPIs), so that an evaluation of outcomes in terms of health gains and decreases in crime can be made and compared, as well as educational outcomes.

Justine Greening said to us: 'Our education system should be an engine of social mobility, extending opportunity to every young person, ensuring that they reach their potential.' There is an often-stated political will to secure social mobility. In this chapter we have tried to draw attention to the awkward truth that progress remains to be made on behalf of every child and young person so they can benefit fully from schooling.

Chapter 11
Accountability – room for improvement

Tim recalls:

At its July meeting in 1978, Oxfordshire County Council approved my appointment as education officer, fresh from being a deputy in the ILEA. It also passed a resolution that the Education Committee should publish its exam results so that 'parents could make a better choice of school'. This was 15 years before this became national policy under Kenneth Clarke as secretary of state.

My first meeting in the autumn term with the secondary heads as a group, which occurred three weeks after I had arrived, put me on the spot. They were united in their conviction that nothing could be more damaging than league tables of school results. It was not a good start. I couldn't tell them what they wanted to hear, although I had great sympathy with their view: I was shocked that the council had passed the resolution. (Well, perhaps not too shocked, as my own appointment showed they lacked judgement!) I explained to the secondary heads that their request for me not to publish anything wasn't practical politics. 'But, surely, they'll give you a honeymoon present?' one well-respected and long-serving silver-haired head protested. I explained rather lamely that it didn't work like that.

First impressions are important in any job, especially in a large organisation, and I wasn't doing too well. I ended by saying that they needn't worry: I would publish the results in a form that would baffle most readers and certainly the newspapers. They departed the meeting shaking their heads and avoiding eye contact. I knew I had to prove that I was as good as my word. Fortunately, we had a good statistician on the team who was a whizz with data, so the following year (we managed to convince the councillors that we needed extra time to 'get it right'), Oxfordshire 'published' exam results in the way promised to the secondary heads. The education reporter on the *Oxford Mail* was by then a sympathetic friend and the newspaper didn't show much interest on the grounds that the fuss had occurred 12 months earlier. As he said with a wink, 'It's a dead story now.'

In practice, the results were never examined by anybody other than the heads, their staff, our advisory service, some councillors and the odd interested parent. As time went on, the head teachers liked this professional sharing and found that the subject advisers' analysis of the various departments helped them in in-school discussions on the variability of pupil outcomes. However, that appreciation took place over the longer term. Initially, as I have faithfully recorded and never forgotten, the heads were aghast. They and I (although I pretended otherwise and said it would be all right) had imagined the worst at the outset. But it convinced me that, at least in Oxfordshire and with the councillors we had, we would need to head off extreme manifestations of accountability if we could. It was going to involve me being very persuasive with all the schools and councillors.

This cameo confirms that accountability was in the air in some places as long ago as 1978. Before that it was hardly mentioned; afterwards it would become endemic. This example of publishing exam results was an early manifestation of the link between pupil outcomes and school effectiveness. Until then, it was widely believed that a pupil's success was down to them, and the school simply provided an opportunity for them to demonstrate their talent, or not. Typically, most schools did not want this conversation about results to begin because it would create difficulties for most; relatively few would be able to look down from their perch of success.

While Callaghan's Ruskin College speech had asked questions about the merits of the school system generally, the move towards any analysis of individual school outcomes would create a different sort of pressure for all schools.

Mick recalls:

In 1975, following the Houghton Report, teachers were awarded a pay rise averaging 27%.[1] At an early evening lecture at the local Teachers' Centre in the following year, the speaker was exploring the unfolding educational agenda and predicting the next developments. One of his predictions was that the work of the government's Assessment of Performance Unit would raise challenges for the profession which, when the closer scrutiny of pupil results was evaluated against the significantly increasing pay of teachers, would lead to greater public accountability for schools and head teachers in particular.

At the time, I wasn't really sure what accountability was and, in the coffee break, I found that there were several others in the same position. The term became part of the discussion after the break (we didn't have plenaries back then) and the view arose that there were some teachers who weren't very good and did poorly by pupils and they would be exposed. Most people were fine with that, but I don't think anyone anticipated that in order to bring in accountability there would have to be an accountability system or that the system would become the dominant force it has become today.

The move towards an accountability agenda seems to have emerged naturally from the doubt and mistrust that followed Callaghan's speech. Once it was decided that schooling needed to be better and, given the accompanying lack of confidence in local authorities, successive secretaries of state have judged that the way to improvement has been through forms of accountability. We think it was necessary and much needed, although we would question some of the methodology and some of the consequences which have inhibited the life chances of too many pupils. We also believe that the school system, and indeed society, is ready for a different perspective.

Andreas Schleicher noted the need for a new outlook when he told us: 'I think that what you want is to set the incentives in the opposite direction by incentivising improvement. If you're a teacher in Japan, nobody is caring about the average performance of your school. You cannot afford a

---

1   A. Houghton, *Report of the Committee of Inquiry into the Pay of Non-University Teachers* [Houghton Report] (London: HMSO, 1974). Available at: http://www.educationengland.org.uk/documents/houghton1974/index.html.

single underperformance. Basically, inclusion is the number one criterion. It puts lots of pressure on students, and that's the downside of it, but it has the result that basically you have virtually no failure of the system.'

Peter Hyman, from his current viewpoint in a school, summed up the way it has all unfolded: 'What Kenneth Baker and Kenneth Clarke were trying to put in place through Ofsted and GCSEs and league tables was a set of ways of addressing what people rightly called at the time "the long tail of underachievement". Every government, including ours in 1997, then ratcheted up the high-stakes nature of exams and the overbearing nature of Ofsted.'

Those reforms achieved their purpose, at least to a considerable extent. There are many fewer failing schools: 85% of schools are good or outstanding in Ofsted's terms. We now need a long hard look at what is needed in the future because those same measures that were once necessary have now become a stifling burden and stop schools from taking risks, pushing the boundaries or offering a more expansive education. We believe that a new age of hope, ambition and collaborative partnerships could take schooling into a new dimension of achievement, while also changing our outlook on accountability so that it is more intelligent and incentivises the right things.

The story so far

As we have outlined, at the start of the 1980s, the word 'accountability' began to appear (along with choice, autonomy, diversity and excellence) in all the White Papers that preceded the Education Acts which were to change the way schools were treated – to the point where some of our non-ministerial witnesses said that they knew of heads and staff who were sick with dread at the prospective arrival of Ofsted. We even heard tell of heads who fell from grace and shamefully massaged their GCSE results by off-rolling, or others who 'helped' with SATs at Key Stage 2 or held down results at Key Stage 1 in order to show progress at Key Stage 2. Such stories of dishonesty have appeared over the years in the educational press but are thankfully rare. It is not rare, however, for the head teacher of a school with declining test or exam scores and an adverse Ofsted inspection grade to lose their job. Steve Munby, who is in a position to know, reckons that 'internationally our heads face the fiercest accountability system with the direst consequences of any. And the impact of that is felt further throughout the school.'

Tim recalls:

In 1978, near the start of our story, Oxfordshire not merely became the first LEA to publish results, but it also prompted its officers to debate the way the wind was blowing. It was an uncomfortable time. All of us who were administrators in LEAs had grown up and forged our careers in an age of optimism and trust, and the instinct was to trust heads and teachers to do their best. We began to realise that politicians in particular did not share that trust. They knew that outcomes for those who did not do well at school was unacceptable, as the Newsom Report had pointed out.[2]

Oxfordshire decided to introduce a scheme of school self-evaluation whereby the schools would review all their practices on a four-year rolling programme with the help of an external reviewer of their choosing and report through their governors to a panel of elected county councillors. Schools were helped by a document of questions called 'Starting Points in Self-Evaluation',[3] which was put together by a working group of teacher union representatives and education officers and advisers.

The reports from the schools were intended to contain points for improvement and strong points for further development, while trying to avoid being simply descriptive. The councillors were encouraged to be supportive, but if the occasion required it challenging (they were advised by education officers), but always to accompany the challenge with an offer of help if required. It certainly informed councillors and governors and made them more discerning towards schools. This was accompanied by a focus on school improvement and the county became the first one to produce a document on 'Effective Schools'.

Other authorities renamed their advisory services as 'inspectors'. But too often the quality was seen as inconsistent and their

---

2   The Newsom Report addressed the fact that the bottom half of the ability range were not getting what they should from schools to lead successful lives.

3   The discussions were helped initially by an existing document from the ILEA: *Keeping the School Under Review: A Method of Self-Assessment for Schools Devised by the ILEA Inspectorate* (London: ILEA, 1977).

judgements as unreliable by school head teachers, who knew all too well the strengths and weaknesses of their former advisers. (The issue of variability and lack of quality assurance still exists today but is more hidden within Ofsted.) A few established a 'Chinese wall' between their advisory and inspection functions by ensuring that staff acting as advisers to a particular school were not involved in its inspection – a dilemma which persists to this day in discussions about the role of Ofsted. A few other authorities promoted self-review but of the tick-box variety. Most authorities did nothing, however, choosing instead to await national decisions on what form(s) accountability would take.

While these tentative developments were happening in schools and LEAs, national government was trying to exert pressure on schools. The pressure was gentle, although at the time it was described as interference. School governing bodies (which we cover in Chapter 12) were to sit between the school and its LEA. Annual head teacher appraisal – the mildest of reflection processes – was introduced from 1980 by Keith Joseph as a way of helping head teachers to consider the effectiveness of their work. Some authorities began to promote standardised testing, particularly in the final year of the primary phase to aid transition to secondary school (then called transfer), but many heads were reluctant to take part because of the danger of school comparison.

This world of trusting experiments would be broken up completely by the models of accountability introduced by the publishing of exam results in the form of national league tables, and by a change in the school inspection regime with the creation of Ofsted and the regular inspection and ranking of schools. By the early 1990s, secondary school league tables were all over the national press, tabloids and broadsheets alike. This phenomenon, as well as how Ofsted was created and where it should go in the future, its strengths and weaknesses, its frameworks and struggles for reliability, were all topics of interest to our witnesses. It is to those issues of accountability at a national level that we will now turn.

Accountability must be more intelligent

This comment from one of our secondary school head teacher witnesses sums up the general tension relating to accountability:

> It all comes down to that day in August. Everything you work for, children's lives you affect, efforts to open doors for youngsters to new horizons, dragging some of them back onto the path when they could have fallen by the wayside, getting every member of staff to go the extra mile – and it all comes down to a day in August and one number: the percentage getting good GCSEs. It influences everything. Every year we are hanging by a thread.

There were many direct and indirect references to the pressures of accountability during our interviews. One MAT school improvement adviser, for example, recounting the pressures on a school in a disadvantaged area trying to keep going with multiple cases of COVID-19, told us: 'Our double RI [requires improvement] schools are now receiving their third inspections of the year … When this was pointed out to an HMI during an inspection last week, they rather disingenuously said, "You haven't received three inspections: the first one was research, the second one was an additional interim COVID-19 one, this is your first actual inspection."'

For us, the nub of the issue was the markedly different levels of significance that our interviewees attributed to the accountability regime, depending on their viewpoint. The people who talked earnestly about accountability were those who worked in schools or worked closely with schools and teachers. Politicians and those close to policy rarely mentioned accountability without prompting, and even some HMCIs responsible for the inspection process did not seem to recognise the extent of its influence on schooling. From everyone intimately associated with teachers and school leadership there was a sometimes vehement condemnation of the impact of the high-stakes accountability regime. In contrast, politicians and policy-makers seemed to take regulation for granted and accepted accountability measures as an indicator of quality, standards and progress, as well as a motivator for the profession.

In short, for many at the heart of the schooling system, the accountability screw is too tight and restrains their potential for greater success. For others, it is something they have come to live with; they have learned how to manage the tensions it creates, sometimes using it to their advantage. For policy-makers, the accountability screw is a necessary part of an effective system and they seem to think that those feeling the strain will always make habitual complaints, which they can simply ignore as background noise in their busy worlds.

So, Mary Bousted of the NEU's complaint about unwarranted accountability would doubtless be dismissed by policy-makers. She told us: 'Accountability is out of hand. Workload is excessive, caused by too much demand that is not appropriate. Leadership in schools feels under huge pressure to provide evidence. Whenever the accountability system shifts, we just change the metrics. It has gone from data, data, data to writing long tropes about the inspiration behind your curriculum.' Unfortunately, politicians seem to consider criticism from unions in particular as annoying but predictable, a bit like frost on the windscreen: an irritating consequence of cold weather which passes relatively quickly.

Similarly, this observation from Nick Brook of NAHT might be heard as distant but unthreatening thunder: 'High-stakes accountability is doing more harm than good. We've got a system now where the vast majority of schools are good or better, and yet high-stakes accountability is creating all sorts of perverse incentives in the system, including discouraging good teachers from working where they are needed most.'

Brook adds: 'The approach we have at the moment seems to recognise that 85% of schools are already good or outstanding. All schools are treated pretty much the same. This is a hugely inefficient way of identifying schools in difficulty and provides little insight into those that are not. You can feel the negative consequences of this approach and the fear that comes with it, which is driving many people out of the profession.' Secretaries of state might recognise the issue but not its impact. Nicky Morgan, for example, told us: 'I don't think inspection should create the panic stations it does in schools.'

A common way to deal with a political challenge is to polarise the issue, to make out that negative comments come from people who are opposed to accountability, to keep the argument at a binary level: agree or disagree. So, whether they hear, or choose not to hear, the wider arguments of Bousted, Brook and others who express support for proportionate accountability is unclear.

General secretary of the Association of School and College Leaders (ASCL), Geoff Barton, explained that, as a head teacher prior to taking up his present role four years ago, he 'had been Ofsteded three times, and the last time I said that they may as well have stayed at home if all they were going to do was check the data'.

We heard time and again from people close to schools that they welcome professional accountability but that what they experience currently is anything but. Many also wanted us to quote their concerns but asked them not to be attributed for fear of repercussions. To us, that was a clear indication of a struggling system – one in which people fear to speak truth to power. The accountability system, which is built on an inspection regime that uses examination and test results as a starting point, is crude and disproportionate. We agree with them.

In Chapter 5, we explored the inadequacy of the exam system as a measure of pupils' achievement and an indicator of potential. The way the results of summative exams and tests in primary schools are being used to determine the effectiveness of schools, one against another, piles a series of misplaced assumptions about a school's performance on top of an inadequate and unreliable system of testing. The result is potentially career making or career breaking. The consequences of perceived failure within schools are professionally significant for the leadership and staff, but also for the esteem of the community and the pupils themselves. Perceived success, on the other hand, lifts communities and pupils and sets new career horizons for staff and leadership.

The problems with the current system seem to be:

- The unfairness of the measure in terms of the variable circumstances of schools.

- The reliability of the metric used to judge schools.

- The inconsistency of the inspection process.

- The extent to which the system can be and is gamed.

- The degree to which accountability measures become ends in themselves and reduce opportunities for pupils, constrain teachers and create excessive workload.

- The public nature of the process.

- The waste of money in an inspection system that misuses expertise, analysis and wisdom.

All of these doubts combine to create a growing lack of trust in the system of accountability and those who impose it. This lack of trust extends to suspicions about colleagues who succeed and a hindrance to the collaboration that many believe would enable the system to thrive. It was described to us as 'the dead hand of accountability'.

So, where did it all begin nationally?

When Kenneth Baker brought in the Education Reform Act 1988, he seemed to consider accountability to a limited degree: 'I always believed in, and supported very strongly, inspection, all the way through. I didn't establish Ofsted, it was one of those things I would have liked to have got round to, quite frankly. It's done a good job. And I'm a very strong supporter still of inspections in schools but they are very different now.' It was as if the publication of test and examination results, along with parent preference, would be accountability enough because market principles would pertain. Success would come through the market because parents and children would be drawn to the most successful schools and, presumably, the weak would go to the wall.

A significant problem with this view is that success in the competitive market demands a degree of failure. However, parents and their children cannot walk away from all failing schools in search of something better since the number of school places is finite and (as we explain in Chapter 8) access to a school of your choice is more complex than simply turning up. Baker might argue that the poorer schools today are far more successful than the poorer schools of 30 years ago, and so the system has improved as a result of the accountability regime he introduced. But it is a hollow argument if we tolerate the numbers of pupils who have experienced a poor school experience or who have fallen by the wayside through exclusion.

Ironically, Baker himself sees and regrets the impact of the current accountability regime on his own brainchild – UTCs. Local secondary schools are reluctant to recommend them to their Year 9 pupils, even those with particular aptitudes or ambitions linked to the specialism of the UTC, because they want to hold on to promising pupils in order to benefit from their probable good exam results in two years' time.

The exam system, in theory a process of approving and awarding qualifications for youngsters, is also being used to measure the performance of schools. The same is true of SATs and phonics screening tests. Nick Gibb asserts: 'SATs were introduced in 1990 to hold schools to account. That's the purpose of them. It's that holding schools to account that helps drive up standards across the board.'[4] But as one of our MAT CEOs saw it: 'We have got the great weight of the entire education system resting on pinpricks of data. There is the depressing sense in which teaching to the test, particularly at GCSE and also at SATs, is a miserable but necessary consequence.'

Kenneth Clarke, like Baker, wanted to make schools accountable to parents and offer comparative evidence of individual school success. He believed that 'particularly problematic was a tendency to assume that any failure on the part of individual schools was entirely attributable to the make-up of the local area. In the poorer parts of cities, the most appalling outcomes were automatically blamed on the deprivation in the neighbourhood. Conversely, success was always attributed to the school and not to its intake.'

If this need to expose the variability in the system and make schools accountable to their community of parents drove the origins of the system, it was the introduction of large-scale inspection which tightened the accountability screw. That screw now reaches every aspect of the system; teachers, head teachers, governors, MATs, local authorities and their councils are all held to account for performance based largely on comparative annual results. Performance management of teachers and head teachers is directly linked to pupils' outcomes. Inspection judgements are crucial to head teachers; a top grade in an inspection opens doors to NLE status and other opportunities. For MATs, an outstanding rating for a school means the possibility of acquiring more schools, while a negative inspection can threaten their future existence.

The inspection regime emerged during John Patten's tenure as secretary of state and has been used by successive governments ever since as a marker of the success of their policies. The proportion of schools judged to be succeeding has been continually increasing, alongside a commensurate steady decline in the proportion deemed failures. Successive HMCIs

---

4   Quoted in S. Weale and R. Adams, Schools Minister Denies Sats Place Undue Stress on Pupils, *The Guardian* (10 July 2018). Available at: https://www.theguardian.com/education/2018/jul/10/schools-minister-denies-sats-place-undue-stress-on-pupils.

have been able to justify inspection methods on the basis of their annual announcements on inspection outcomes, in a sense holding their own success to account and thereby, in effect, marking their own homework.

Inspection: a necessary evil?

Surprisingly to us, none of the secretaries of state with whom we spoke mentioned inspection before they were prompted by us a long way into our conversations with them. It is as though inspection is a given and, for them, one of the constants in the system. As Nicky Morgan remarked: 'If Ofsted didn't exist, we would have to invent it.'

Yet, since the inception of Ofsted in 1992, inspection has been one of the biggest system influencers and a vital part of centralisation, marketisation and managerialism. In every one of our conversations with individuals directly connected with schools, Ofsted was mentioned early on as a significant influence on practice. For some, Ofsted represents an indicator of quality, for others the possibility of recognition worth aiming for, and for yet more a constant threatening cloud. Just a confident few could see it as a necessary irritation in schooling.

Many believed that the inspection process and Ofsted should be removed, while others saw it in a positive light and used it as a lever for improvement and success. Almost everyone saw both sides of the argument, and many who edged more towards one side voiced their understanding of the other side. There were few who were categorical: to criticise too much would be to undermine the success achieved, but to praise too much would be to fail to recognise the criticisms of those with a different perspective. While nobody offered unqualified positive regard, many had grudging acceptance and plenty of suggestions on how to improve the inspection regime.

So, what do people like about Ofsted? Those who use the Ofsted framework as their marker for school improvement are vindicated by the positive outcome of an inspection, particularly chief executives of MATs who can demonstrate the overall improvement of their trust in terms of Ofsted ratings. The continuing leadership of the CEO and the expansion of the MAT often relies partly on references to inspection, which can be used to motivate head teachers in schools across the MAT. Successful inspection judgements also provide an opportunity for the MAT to attract new schools to their trust. Various interviewees also spoke about the need for an inspection grade of outstanding to be able to gain recognitions such as NLE or teaching school hub status.

What do people not like about Ofsted? The top concern of most people, even those favourably disposed to the principle of inspection, was lack of consistency. Ofsted's vehement denial of the charge over the years was seen by many as the only consistent feature of the organisation! This is connected to the issue of systemic unfairness: the fact that some schools have been sitting for a decade on outdated outstanding grades, the perception that some schools hoodwink inspectors and the lack of an effective complaints procedure. Also criticised were the endlessly shifting frameworks, the summative nature of inspection and the tone and register of reports. Some believed that Ofsted was inspecting the wrong things by focusing on individual schools. Others believed that the system was creating stress, workload pressure and intolerable career threats. The impact of a negative report on the school, its community and its pupils was a constant theme of school witnesses.

Some of our interviewees saw inspection as a charade; they had worked out how to play Ofsted at its own game. Others saw the process of second-guessing Ofsted as a helpful professional agenda for their school community. Most described their school or school communities or improvement trajectory in terms of Ofsted judgements. Even when head teachers were explaining the complex story of their school in terms of the challenges they had inherited or the solutions they had found, they would slide into a sentence mention of Ofsted's perception of the school as evidence or validation.

CEOs of MATs described their school community in terms of the numbers of schools in different Ofsted categories, and how they could devote more attention to less-than-adequate schools with a view to improving them rapidly. Dan Moynihan at the Harris Federation explained:

> Our consultants will not just go in and work with subject people, they'll go into departments and improve them. This is our SAS who will go into a failing school. There will often be a lot of good people working in a failing school whom nobody has ever shown what good looks like. They might just not know. Our people will go in and model for them and bring in schemes of work and coach people for improvement and help assemble the best possible

subject staff teams. The most important thing is that the subject consultants will, if needed, take the classes themselves and be responsible for the results. It means, in a key exam group where life chances are being determined, if a teacher is away because of maternity or something happens, we can put high-quality people in who will teach those classes for as long as necessary to get those kids the results. Consistently, over the last five or six years, we have been the top-performing MAT in terms of pupil performance. And if you ask, 'What is the one thing that made this happen?' I would say, it is the subject consultants, because not only do they upskill teachers, but they also actually take the classes and they could be in a school for a year.

Such fleet-of-foot management improves the accountability odds but not necessarily by creating the best learning experience for all youngsters. It is strong MAT management, but because exams and SATs are comparative measures, a school can succeed only at the expense of failure elsewhere.

Another MAT employee told us how vital inspection outcomes were and how she had the task of managing the process down to a fine art:

A school would get their inspection call and we would rush across and spend the night there getting ready, putting everything in place. All it needs is someone who knows the framework inside out. I'd work with the leadership and get everything lined up, work out who should see whom from the team, how we would manage their impressions and help them to write the report we needed. It was what I was expected to do, and I did it, and we all celebrated every time, but there was something that felt tacky about it. But that's what Ofsted has caused.

For some working in schools, Ofsted is a shadow on the system and on their careers. A primary head told us: 'The inspection when we were put into special measures was the worst moment of my career and was totally undeserved. I always thought Ofsted had pre-judged our school and the complaints process was terribly unfair. The community and parents never lost faith in the school and stood by us, but the impact on us all was negative.' She later reflected: 'The visits of the HMI while we were in special measures were brilliant. They were challenging and supportive and helped us so much. We should all be entitled to that, but we don't need the public humiliation that goes with unfair special measures.'

For others, the outcome of a good inspection brings accolades and useful publicity which can be used to promote the school. Marketing banners on school fences has been a growth industry as schools find some positives in their report to advertise. However, one of our primary head teacher witnesses told us: 'I would never demean myself and my school by putting an "Ofsted likes us" banner on a fence. How can we encourage people to think we approve of them?'

Three decades of Ofsted

In 1992, Kenneth Clarke established Ofsted and appointed Stewart Sutherland as the first HMCI, albeit in a part-time role. Previously, a team of around 400 HMIs had been led by a senior HMI. In his autobiography, Clarke claimed to have appointed Chris Woodhead to the role but that was later.[5] When we asked him about this he chuckled and said he had misremembered that development, but he recalled being irritated by the way that schooling seemed to tolerate mediocrity, which was why he wanted an independent inspectorate.

What Clarke was possibly recalling was his quite dramatic action to bring certainty and urgency to debates about primary schooling through the review which was carried out by three high-profile individuals: Jim Rose, the senior primary HMI; Chris Woodhead, the chief executive of the NCC; and Robin Alexander, an academic who had recently published research evidencing the variable and often poor provision in primary schools in Leeds and the lack of impact made by the local authority advisory services. The review was commissioned and the report produced in short order; because of the time of year it was quickly dubbed the 'Three Wise Men Report'.[6]

It was hard-hitting, more assertive than most previous reports and reinforced Clarke's intolerance of local authorities and schools being constrained by a culture that belonged in the 1960s. It tightened the screw of accountability and many predicted – correctly as it turned out – trouble ahead for primary practitioners.

---

5   K. Clarke, *Kind of Blue: A Political Memoir* (London: Macmillan, 2016), p. 273.
6   R. Alexander, J. Rose and C. Woodhead, *Curriculum Organisation and Classroom Practice in Primary Schools: A Discussion Paper* [Three Wise Men Report] (London: Department of Education and Science, 1992). Available at: http://www.educationengland.org.uk/documents/threewisemen/threewisemen.html.

When Clarke piloted the bill on inspection through Parliament as John Major's government went into the general election of 1992, he didn't bargain on push-back from the House of Lords. Mike Tomlinson recalled a 'sliding doors' moment that changed the course of Clarke's bill and schooling:

> Now, the bill that went before Parliament to create Ofsted went into the House and, just before it got to its final stages, John Major called an election. The secretary of state had a choice of whether to pull the bill or let it go on. He decided to let it go on and the Lords changed two crucial parts of the bill. The first part was to require that the funding for inspection went through Ofsted and contracts were to be awarded, whereas the initial bill stated that schools were to be given money to purchase the inspection. The Lords were having none of it! They expected schools would just appoint their own cronies. So, the Lords insisted that a contracting system was put in place, which had not been in anybody's mind up to that point in time – even the secretary of state's. The other thing that the Lords also insisted upon was that the inspection should include spiritual, moral, social and cultural education.
>
> When it came back to the Commons it was literally in the last 24 hours of the parliament. Parliament, the secretary of state and the prime minister faced a dilemma: do we accept these changes or not? And, if not, then the bill fails. They decided to accept the changes to get the bill through. That was the [1992] Act, of course, which ultimately created Ofsted – it had a very difficult gestation period. The reasons for it were in a sense multilayered. But, equally, the final product was not the product of the government per se but a change made by the Lords. The government of the day decided to accept it. Reluctantly.

So, but for the bishops in the House of Lords, the inspection system and accountability regime might have been very different!

The arrival of John Patten as secretary of state after the general election led to the appointment of Chris Woodhead to the role of HMCI, and this propelled Ofsted – and Woodhead himself – into prominence both within schooling and in the wider public arena.

The majority of those in teaching today cannot recall Woodhead's era, although it sent a jolt through schools. Previous developments on inspection since 1976 had met with an interested but generally low-key response from the profession. Local governing bodies, head teacher appraisal, LFM and even the national curriculum and assessment had all been questioned, moderated and absorbed by most schools without a dramatic improvement in the system. While the teaching unions complained, the vast majority of schools and their head teachers accommodated the emerging policies, supported by their local authorities who helped them to make sense of the new expectations in the context of the old.

What was radical about Woodhead's new inspection regime was the different vocabulary and, in particular, one word, the word that sent that jolt through the system: *judgement*. Schools, and by implication those who worked in them, were going to be judged against a standard which was, by implication, comparative, and that had the effect of centralising decisions about schooling in a way that no other measure had achieved, as well as increasing the managerial aspects of schooling and influencing marketisation. Accountability was getting tougher for English schools than anywhere else in the world.

While Ofsted has worked through countless inspection frameworks during its 30-year history, always trying to modify the process in the light of criticisms, for most schools an inspection today causes as much nervousness – bordering on dread – as it did when it was first introduced.

Richard Kieran, a first school (age 5–9) head teacher, told us of his inspection experience, which had led to a positive judgement and report: 'We had some overseas visitors in school doing longitudinal research. They had spent a lot of time with us over two years and knew us well. They were reflecting on the inspection and said, "It was very strange to see. The school seemed to lose its heart. It lost its beat and didn't move as much." I thought that was telling and very sad – and true.'

How did inspection centralise schooling? By producing a framework that specified how schools were to be judged, a central inspection agency effectively defined what constituted a good school. By establishing the four categories around which judgements would be made (i.e. quality of education, behaviour and attitudes, personal development, leadership and management), it established the key determinants of quality and gave many in local authorities a touchstone that they had not previously considered.

The initial seven levels of outcome for school inspection were met with the same polite interest and debate about validity that had greeted other developments, such as the national curriculum or LMS, but that changed suddenly when, in November 1992, a primary school in County Durham was deemed to require 'special measures'. The resulting national media attention meant that the school system could be in no doubt that distant thunder could lead to lightning strikes. And it did. Since then, the need to dance to the tune of Ofsted has led to an increasing centralised agenda for leadership, pedagogy, curriculum and accountability.

Panopticon theory:
the side effects of inspection

Inspection has seeped into every pore of the body of schooling. In the late 18th century, Jeremy Bentham developed an idea for a circular panopticon prison, a building and system of control by which inmates were led to believe that they were under continuous surveillance.[7] Consequently, they acted as though they were being watched by their jailers at all times. The prisoners' perception of being constantly scrutinised had a self-controlling effect on them and their behaviour, but also on the warders and their behaviour. Eminent philosopher Michel Foucault noted that 'the Panopticon is a marvellous machine which, whatever use one may wish to put it to, produces homogeneous effects of power'. Within the panopticon, 'one is totally seen, without ever seeing', while those observing 'see everything without ever being seen'.[8] It is the idea of the panopticon, rather than its physical existence, that influences behaviour. Over time, this has been applied to schools, hospitals and other institutions by those managing systems in order to secure the sorts of practices they believe would produce the accountability outcomes sought and which would, in turn, justify their own behaviours.

In his searching doctoral thesis, Doug Lowes outlines the way schools have been encouraged by Ofsted and government to self-evaluate their work. He cites David Plowright's paper on school self-evaluation, who points out that the process enables inspectors to observe schools 'at

---

7   J. Bentham, *Panopticon; or The Inspection House, Volume 1* (London: T. Payne, 1791).
8   M. Foucault, *Discipline and Punish: The Birth of the Prison*, tr. A. Sheridan (Harmondsworth: Penguin, 1979), p. 202.

arms' length and out of sight … and being under constant but unseen observation, schools will be forced into moving the inspection criteria to a daily focus, as they comply with and eventually internalise inspection norms and procedures'.[9]

Lowes notes that 'Ofsted has promoted the use of common criteria and language between schools and inspectors as a good thing. In reality, through the process of self-evaluation, schools have adopted the criteria of Ofsted rather than the other way around. In this way, the strength of discourse within the process of school self-evaluation has been defined by Ofsted and not by schools.'[10] According to Plowright, a consequence of schools being in a constant state of readiness for inspection is that 'they have been in their own version of the Panopticon and that, in their eyes, escape now appears impossible'.[11]

In a similar vein, Jane Perryman uses the expression 'panoptic performativity' to describe 'a regime in which the frequency of inspection and the sense of being perpetually under surveillance leads to teachers performing in ways dictated by the discourse of inspection in order to escape the regime'.[12]

The issue of grading is crucial. The Hampton Review[13] and the subsequent Macrory Review[14] brought forward standards and appropriate sanctions for regulators to apply and use,[15] including the prohibition of grades which seems not to apply to Ofsted. Ofqual, which regulates examination providers, does not use grades, and nor does Ofgem or Ofwat. The panopticon impact of Ofsted, reinforced by horror stories of other schools' inspections, has been profound. The high-stakes graded judgement, which can reduce the whole of a school's work to one word, can result in

9   D. Plowright, Using Self-Evaluation for Inspection: How Well Prepared Are Primary School Headteachers?, *School Leadership & Management*, 28(2) (2008): 101–126 at 121; quoted in T. D. Lowes, To What Extent Do Ofsted Inspectors' Values Influence the Inspection Process (2005–2012)? An Examination of Ofsted Inspectors' Perceptions. Unpublished thesis, University of Hull, pp. 38–39. Available at: http://hydra.hull.ac.uk/resources/hull:14579

10   Lowes, To What Extent Do Ofsted Inspectors' Values Influence the Inspection Process, p. 39.

11   Plowright, Using Self-Evaluation for Inspection, 121; quoted in Lowes, To What Extent Do Ofsted Inspectors' Values Influence the Inspection Process, p. 40.

12   J. Perryman, Panoptic Performativity and School Inspection Regimes: Disciplinary Mechanisms and Life Under Special Measures, *Journal of Education Policy*, 21(2) (2006): 147–161 at 154.

13   P. Hampton, *Reducing Administrative Burdens: Effective Inspection and Enforcement* [Hampton Review] (London: HM Treasury, 2005). Available at: http://www.regulation.org.uk/library/2005_hampton_report.pdf.

14   R. B. Macrory, *Regulatory Justice: Making Sanctions Effective* [Macrory Review] (London: Cabinet Office, 2006). Available at: https://www.regulation.org.uk/library/2006_macrory_report.pdf.

15   The Regulatory Enforcement and Sanctions Act 2008 (see https://www.legislation.gov.uk/ukpga/2008/13/contents/enacted) implemented the key recommendations of the Hampton Review and Macrory Review.

accolades and approbation or professional upheaval, destabilised communities and unsettled children.

As Ofsted began to publish its reports, it also started producing marketing information for schools, probably inadvertently. Schools with good gradings quickly learned to broadcast their success in the local media and display posters advertising their success on buildings and fences. As parental preference began to bite, it wasn't long before estate agents saw the benefit of referring to the status of local schools when it suited them. Similarly, as schools began to be judged as requiring 'special measures', having 'serious weaknesses' or 'requiring improvement', so the local press had a story to tell. As time went on, a fresh story could emerge as schools zoomed from a low category to a high one, and the media could be relied on to proclaim it a 'turnaround' or a 'transformation'.

Of course, marketisation has happened in other ways too. With every new framework, there is a ready market for conference venues hosting the first Ofsted briefings and later conferences for head teachers on how to prepare. There was the growth in 'mocksted' inspections where those with an inspection ticket – such as Ofsted-trained local authority or freelance inspectors – could carry out pre-MOTs.

Local authorities and MATs keen to ensure against failure and maximise success began to develop more intrusive recording systems, which their schools, in turn, replicated for their staff – all aimed at second-guessing Ofsted. To show any future inspector that they know their schools, leaders observe teachers who, in turn, play the game to some degree when being observed by, in effect, spoon-feeding the system upwards. As schools feed the machine, the level of managerialism grows at every level and in every respect.

All the secretaries of state who took part in FED's 150th Anniversary of State Education online event expressed the view that they would have liked more power when in post[16] – a view they didn't always repeat when we interviewed them. Perhaps they had temporarily forgotten that their power lay in defining the terms for the inspection framework and then leaving it to the inspectors? Having said that, it seems that some did recognise the influence they had and sometimes overstepped the mark. David Bell told us that during his time as head of Ofsted: 'We were always

---

16   Foundation for Education Development, 150th Anniversary of State Education: Lessons Learned – The Reflections of 12 Former Secretaries of State [webinar] (17 September 2020). Available at https://fed. education/lessons-learned-the-reflection-of-12-former-secretaries-of-state.

fighting off ministers wanting us to inspect X, Y and Z.' Both Michael Wilshaw and Christine Gilbert also had to resist ministerial intrusions.

Over time, modifications to the Ofsted frameworks have addressed the contentious issues associated with diverse school populations. These have included value-added measures, balancing outcomes with indicators of progress, checking the leadership's judgement of effectiveness and addressing urgent matters such as safeguarding and British values. Each time, in a manner that Orwell would have appreciated, schools rush to show the inspectors what they want to see.

Consistency between inspectors is an issue that concerns schools but not Ofsted. The inspection agency believes that their own checks are sufficient to ensure consistency: a framework, training and report-checking. In fact, the consistency of the report seems to be more persuasive than the consistency of the inspection. Readers, sitting apart from schools, check the reports for consistency of judgement against evidence rather than checking whether the evidence itself is accurate. The focus on consistency is everywhere except within the practice of inspection itself. The CEO of a MAT told us: 'Consistency is a massive problem. The moment we know who the lead inspector is, we know whether we have to pull out all the stops or whether we can breathe easily.' Concern about consistency is everywhere, but it is more than a word that can be repeated endlessly: the only consistent aspect of Ofsted is its consistent inconsistency.[17]

Too often, the outcome of an inspection is the result of a negotiation between head teacher and lead inspector based on their personal assertiveness. The leader of a MAT described their experience of a series of inspections that were mired in inconsistency:

> There was one of our schools where things were not great. There were lots of issues in the school, completely hidden from Ofsted. They didn't notice. They didn't see it at all and graded the school good. I think it's arbitrary.
>
> In terms of the experience that we had over the five inspections, they didn't add value to our system and our schools. They actually took value away and made things more difficult for us. If you put them onto the Education Endowment Foundation framework

---

17 Readers will note that we did not secure an interview with Amanda Spielman, the current HMCI. We tried. We wrote to Ofsted and received the standard automated response saying there would be a reply in due course. This happened six times; at least Ofsted was consistent.

and did a plus or minus in terms of adding value, it would be as minus. They're not adding value to our schools in what they're doing.

Ofsted always rejects any claims of inconsistency, citing studies on their processes and claiming as high as a 92% level of agreement between inspectors: 'The imperative is rightly on Ofsted to ensure that our judgements are as reliable as possible. But a medical analogy may be helpful here: many kinds of clinical testing give both false positive results (where someone doesn't actually have the condition, but appears to) and false negatives (where someone has the condition but is not picked up by the test). Perfectly reliable tests are the exception, not the rule.'[18]

Tim recalls:

I arrived at a secondary school in County Durham to do some school improvement work for the local authority to be greeted by a very upset deputy head. Ofsted had arrived unannounced the day before and it was not going well. They were in with the head and I was invited to take a buffet lunch with Ofsted.

Two inspectors emerged who clearly recognised my name. I asked them if they were having a good day. They were horrified and told me it was a question they couldn't answer. I repeated it, explaining that sometimes I had a good day giving a talk or consulting but sometimes I was off my game. So, how was their day going? 'No,' they replied, explaining that inspectors always had good days. I left them with the thought that inspectors must therefore occupy the only form of human activity where that was true. I confess to making mischief but the school enjoyed the exchange!

Arguably, the first wave of inspection showed the school system at its best. Schools were informed of their inspection eight weeks before the date. They were inspected by a team numbered in proportion to the size of the school. A typical secondary school would receive ten inspectors and a large primary five. Inspectors were everywhere: observing many lessons; meeting groups of pupils, teaching and non-teaching staff,

---

18   Ofsted and A. Spielman, HMCI's Commentary: New Research into Short School Inspections (7 March 2017). Available at: https://www.gov.uk/government/speeches/hmcis-monthly-commentary-march-2017.

parents, governors and local authority officers; reviewing documentation; scrutinising planning at every level; and analysing budgets. Reports were lengthy, detailed and extensive. The inspections were thorough and the review of the school was comprehensive.

From the beginning, though, there was tension. Ofsted set out to inspect every school within four years. Inspection agencies – ranging from the conglomerates in the commercial or charity sectors, such as Nord Anglia, Tribal or CfBT to married couple teams – would bid for the published inspection programme, access to which alerted schools to the fact that they were 'on the list'. This was a new marketplace and schools found themselves being auctioned for inspection like fish on the quayside. These developments tend to build an image of a profession that is not in control of itself and beholden to others.

Ofsted inspection was widely criticised by the profession and by the teacher unions. There were two main areas of criticism: first, the process was too stressful and, second, it was unfair, inconsistent and made too many misjudgements or mistakes. The main complaint about the level of stress came from the fact that the inspection team required information beforehand which had to be assembled, and also that the eight weeks' notice of inspection created anxiety and pressure before, during and sometimes after the inspection. Both complaints had some merit, but it could also be argued that prior knowledge and eight weeks' notice gave schools time to get their house in order and show themselves in the best light. The advance preparation of the school community could have led to better internal communication of values and processes than had ever existed previously. And, if eight weeks every four years was to be the cycle of inspection pressure, was this not tolerable? Currently, some schools seem to spend two years or more waiting on tenterhooks for their next inspection.

Of course it wasn't, because too many schools were disappointed with the outcome of their inspection. The seven inspection categories meant that, even within a few weeks, the enormous variability in the school system was being laid bare. Only a small number were placed in the best category, resulting in widespread dissatisfaction; as a caring profession, schools found it difficult to be critical of those judged to be in the lower categories. But what was often driving the outrage was a fear that they might themselves be placed in one of the three categories below satisfactory and that their local stature as a strong school might be called into question, either fairly or mistakenly. As often happens when a group feels under threat, they band together to throw metaphorical stones at the enemy – but this enemy loved the fight.

As the unions raged, Woodhead faced them down. When he was invited to local authority conferences, head teachers would arrive bristling with indignation and listen to him explain early data variables and inspection judgements and then meet their questions with measured responses. Since most of the heads attending were rational and reasonable professionals, and since most had not yet experienced an inspection but had listened to the emerging stories, Woodhead usually left the gathering with a fair degree of grudging respect.

What schools often failed to recognise was that inspectors were themselves subject to scrutiny, and the prospect of not securing contracts was enough to ensure that they conformed. With thousands of inspectors in hundreds of agencies, achieving consistency between inspections was difficult – and so Ofsted resorted to checking compliance with the framework through the summative report. The inspectors worked out the approach and, in turn, fed their own machine. The internal consistency of each report – that is, between the main report and the summary – became key and even more important than the consistency of the judgements within and between schools. By present standards the data were minimal but at the time they seemed immense and revealing. The emergence of Fischer Family Trust (FFT) data was used by inspectors as the reports became more formulaic.[19]

Many argue that Ofsted's formulaic approach distorts practice. As schools lurch to show inspectors what they need to see, so inspectors – concentrating on their inspection template – miss other features, good and bad. A striking recent example is the government review of sexual abuse in schools and colleges in 2021, prompted by the public response to the #MeToo movement and Everyone's Invited website,[20] which reported that: 'This rapid thematic review has revealed how prevalent sexual harassment and online sexual abuse are for children and young people.

---

19 Fischer Family Trust was founded in 2001 by Mike Fischer and Mike Treadway, who began working with a small number of local authorities to explore school performance through the emerging data generated by national exams and test results. Over time, it has become a source of analysis and is used by the majority of schools in England. The charity also provides materials and resources to support schools.

20 See www.everyonesinvited.uk. The #MeToo movement, which has been gathering pace since 2006, aims to empower the survivors of sexual assault and harassment through compassion and strength in numbers.

It is concerning that for some children, incidents are so commonplace that they see no point in reporting them.'[21] Ofsted's statement spotlights several concerns about the inspection process. This commonplace phenomenon was not observed during routine inspections of thousands of schools over many years and yet the matter was so serious that it immediately became part of the inspection framework (quite rightly). This prompt action should not distract us from concerns about the effectiveness and accuracy of inspection reports as a genuine reflection of what is happening in schools.[22] As Kevan Collins told the Education Select Committee, in inspections you see 'the Ofsted school' rather than 'the lived education experience that the children are having'.[23]

The system still lives with the tensions established at that time. Woodhead's eventual departure was met with a sigh of relief. Mike Tomlinson adopted a more responsive approach, introducing a self-evaluation form to be completed by schools: 'I wanted the unions and schools to be in a position where they actually believed that inspection was something that we did *with* them, not *to* them, because at that time it was always being done to them. You wouldn't get the best out of the system by taking that line.'

Tomlinson brought huge personal credibility to the inspection process:

> I wanted desperately to make sure that nobody, least of all me, gave any talk that was not based on real evidence. Nothing, unless there was clear evidence that would support it. My argument was very simple: everybody in the country is an expert in education because they've had some in one form or another. The only thing that differentiates Ofsted from them is that we have a large and secure body of evidence. And that body of evidence has to be at the heart of everything we say.

---

21 Ofsted, Review of Sexual Abuse in Schools and Colleges (10 June 2021). Available at: https://www.gov.uk/government/publications/review-of-sexual-abuse-in-schools-and-colleges/review-of-sexual-abuse-in-schools-and-colleges.

22 Reportedly, for neither of us has experienced it, some speed awareness courses include Christopher Chabris and Daniel Simons' short video of six people passing basketballs (see http://www.theinvisiblegorilla.com/gorilla_experiment.html). Participants are asked to watch and count the number of passes made by the players. At the end, the course leader asks how many people saw the person dressed in a gorilla suit walk into the middle of the action. Half of the viewers do not spot the gorilla. The message is that too great a focus on features we are told to look for can reduce our awareness of the bigger picture.

23 Education Committee, Oral Evidence: Education Recovery, HC 452 (29 June 2021), p. 9. Available at: https://committees.parliament.uk/oralevidence/2466/pdf.

Over time, each new chief inspector has tried to add something to the pot. David Bell drew out the challenge of Ofsted being simultaneously a regulator and an inspector:

> The idea behind the inspection framework was to encapsulate the characteristics of a good school. We were trying to codify that, but unfortunately – and predictably – it constrained behaviours in some schools and made them overly compliant. As soon as you are in a regulated world, people feel the need to stay on the right side of the line. As a result, they think that their autonomy is constrained.
>
> It is the perennial question of regulation or inspection: how do you inspect rigorously without being a brake on innovation, creativity and excellence? Many schools with a clear vision and purpose were able to thrive and, indeed, often used inspection as a tool for further improvement. Others though were too cautious and unwilling to try to do things differently – even if it was going to be in the best interests of their pupils – because they were afraid of the price of failure.

Like the issue of the validity of using exam and test performance in a credible accountability framework, the issue of regulation versus inspection is probably too subtle for policy-makers who see inspection as a useful panopticon that controls behaviour, motivates schools and restrains excess. MAT CEO Jonathan Johnson drew attention to the dilemma: 'Ofsted shifts in focus between being in the regulatory space and the improvement space depending on who is at the helm and depending on the policy of the day.'

In 2006, Christine Gilbert, who succeeded David Bell, found a subtle way to soothe schools that were complaining about Ofsted. In changing (again) the grading system, she brought in the category of outstanding – which had the effect of changing much of the public discourse. There was less complaint from those judged good but not outstanding because it might sound like sour grapes, and there was always the chance to say, 'The inspector said we would have been outstanding but for one small detail.' For those who were deemed outstanding, why complain? They were now immune from inspection for several years as a result of the judgement.

Many of our witnesses told us that Ofsted still needs to change the way it does things. The shifts in practice over time have tinkered with immediate problems but they have created side effects that undermine the benefits the organisation might bring. Several thought that the image of school was portrayed inaccurately through a process that looked only at aspects of its work. Some thought that the grading system was both too refined and, at the same time, too complex. The decision to leave alone schools judged as outstanding (with some schools now not having been inspected for 10 years) was seen to be creating unreliable indicators of effectiveness. There were so many criticisms that it is hard to see how the organisation maintains its credibility.

One of the difficulties is that there are countless different starting points for how it might be put right depending on what people see as the problem: the changing frameworks, the inconsistency, the inspection process, the reporting or the impact on professionalism and practice.

Christine Gilbert explored a recurring proposal:

> School report cards are an interesting idea. They would give a stronger picture of the school. The Ofsted report and exam results would be included, but just as part of fuller and richer information about the school. For instance, a report card could capture both parents' views and children's views about school life. An annual record of achievement, whereby the school describes its ethos, evaluates itself, outlines its many strengths and achievements, as well as its areas for development, would be far better than the current system. But turning all the components of the card into one grade won't work.

This argument about parents needing school gradings is often raised. Clare Flintoff, CEO of ASSET Education Trust, told us:

> I've spoken to Amanda Spielman who said we need graded judgements because that's what parents need, and I fundamentally disagree. I think no parent in the land wants to hear that their school requires improvement or that their school is inadequate, because most of those parents won't move their children. Most parents will keep them there and most parents are invested in the school. The last thing they want to hear is a judgement like that. They actually want to hear that the school needs to do this to get better and the developmental points in order to get better.

Peter Hyman agreed about the issue of parents needing graded judgements: 'It is said that polling shows parents wouldn't be able to cope without the label of outstanding. It is complete nonsense. People often claim that parents support the grading of schools by Ofsted. There is literally no evidence of this and it is deeply patronising. Parents can cope perfectly fine with a one-page summary that says these are the good things about a school and these are the things that need more work.'

Michael Wilshaw believed he faced a significant challenge in terms of bringing about improvement in Ofsted itself when he arrived from headship in 2011. He tried to reshape the way the organisation would do its work:

> The progress I made, I suppose, was that I got rid of the outsourcing altogether and brought all inspection in-house. To do that effectively, I had to restructure Ofsted because it wasn't a structure which could accommodate that. I had to regionalise Ofsted. There were eight regions with regional directors, and the challenge was to get all the HMIs into the region. The registered inspectors were attached to a region and became responsible to an HMI who monitored the quality of their inspection. Once it was regionalised, things became a lot more efficient and effective.

Wilshaw wanted to see inspection making a difference to outcomes for pupils by improving the weakest schools and addressing the issue of the small group of schools that were not improving:

> The next thing I did was change the categories. I said 'satisfactory' is no good – we can't accept mediocrity – so I replaced it with 'requires improvement'. I then did the tough stuff which was, 'You've got two to three years to get out of satisfactory, otherwise there's a danger of going into special measures.' But, of course, when you challenge people they challenge you back, and they were right to say, 'Hold on a minute. You're challenging us but your bloody inspectors are no good.' So, there were a lot of complaints about the inconsistency of inspection. And I knew deep down that they were right.

In raising the stakes for schools, Wilshaw had turned the spotlight on the inspections themselves and the question of consistency. This was because:

> Some providers believed inspectors relied too heavily on data to make their judgements – that it was very unlikely for a school that had bad data and consistently low progress scores to do well in an inspection. The problem with moving away from data – and I think the current framework has probably done that a lot more – is that you are then heavily reliant on the personal judgement of inspectors who may lack the experience or wisdom to come to the right conclusion. The overall effectiveness judgement needs to be a well-balanced combination of personal judgement and data.

Wilshaw sought to move into yet more complex territory by promoting the notion of Ofsted as an aid to improvement. His concept of regional teams saw senior HMIs being based in regions and leading teams of inspectors to get close to schools, particularly those with difficulties and, most vitally, those with a history of difficulty:

> I said to Michael Gove, 'Look, there will be two sorts of requires improvement school. There will be the schools where the head really knows what to do to improve it and there will be others where the head doesn't or there is a lack of capacity. Who is going to support that head teacher with that lack in capacity? Increasing autonomy has meant a sort of fragmentation of the system; local authorities' school improvement services have steadily been eroded, so who is going to do that?'

> I suggested to him that Ofsted play a part in school improvement, and he gave me about £30 million to set up a system of HMIs running workshops and training for head teachers and governors. However, a growing belief at the DfE that Ofsted shouldn't get involved in school improvement meant the funding was withdrawn.

> I just think Ofsted funding would be much better spent if it targeted and stayed with those schools that needed help and support to improve. It also needs to engage in much more survey work, which HMIs did so successfully many years ago. Can routine inspection survive when inspection resources are spread so thinly?

Michael Wilshaw's time with Ofsted was almost as tumultuous as its time under Chris Woodhead. Many of Michael Gove's reforms were gaining traction as the academy programme was announced and changes to the curriculum and qualifications became a professional battleground. Gove had called Wilshaw 'his educational hero', possibly enjoying the reflected glory of association, so Ofsted was seen to be connected with these controversial developments. The threat of special measures for lack of improvement was also regarded as part of the drive to enforce academisation.

In our conversation with him, Wilshaw was open about his period in charge and offered a cogent and rational analysis of the way he had brought his experience to bear to improve the effectiveness of the organisation: 'Having been for so long a head teacher, it took time to fully appreciate the political nature of the post and how that sometimes got in the way of doing what was right. Did I enjoy my five years in Ofsted? Not nearly as much as being a head teacher and getting the best out of teachers and securing a culture and environment where they and the pupils could flourish.'

Amanda Spielman, the current HMCI, has sought to address some of the unintended consequences of the many previous frameworks. She was quick to spot the problem:

> I need to be clear here – if you are leading a school that enters 90% of young people for the European Computer Driving Licence – a qualification that can take only 2 days to study for – then you must ask yourself whether you care more about the school's interests than about making the most of pupils' limited time at school. If you don't encourage EAL (English as an additional language) students to take a taught language at GCSE because they can tick that box with a home language GCSE instead, then you are limiting their education.
>
> Again, if you are putting more resources into providing exam scribes than in teaching your strugglers to read and write, or scrapping most of your curriculum through Year 6 to focus just on English and maths. If you are doing any of those things then you are probably doing most of your students a disservice.
>
> This all reflects a tendency to mistake badges and stickers for learning itself. And it is putting the interests of schools ahead of

the interests of the children in them. We should be ashamed that we have let such behaviour persist for so long.[24]

Spielman intensified Ofsted's agenda by claiming that teachers were being reduced to data managers and stressed that:

> The cumulative impact of performance tables and inspections and the consequences that are hung on them has increased the pressure on school leaders, teachers and indirectly on pupils to deliver perfect data above all else.

> But we know that focusing too narrowly on test and exam results can often leave little time or energy for hard thinking about the curriculum, and in fact can sometimes end up making a casualty of it.

> The bottom line is that we must make sure that we, as an inspectorate, complement rather than intensify performance data.[25]

At least Spielman has had the decency to recognise the problem of focusing on schools at the expense of pupils: 'I acknowledge that inspection may well have helped to tip this balance in the past.'[26]

She has reinvigorated a focus on curriculum that schools have appreciated, although many, including those in leadership, have seen this as a first step towards curriculum by inspection. Their time in the teaching profession has been so concerned with impact that many have never considered an intent beyond satisfying the accountability system. The 2019 Ofsted framework brings a measured touch to Gove and Gibb's insistence on a knowledge-rich curriculum by intimating pedagogic imperatives.[27] However, we would contend that the focus on the three I's (intent, implementation and impact) will necessitate that as professionals teachers and head teachers need to exercise three more I's: *insight* to ensure that the curriculum retains its *integrity* in order to *improve* on previous best.

---

24 Ofsted and A. Spielman, Amanda Spielman's Speech at the Festival of Education (23 June 2017). Available at: https://www.gov.uk/government/speeches/amanda-spielmans-speech-at-the-festival-of-education.

25 Ofsted and A. Spielman, Amanda Spielman Speech to the SCHOOLS North East Summit (11 October 2018). Available at: https://www.gov.uk/government/speeches/amanda-spielman-speech-to-the-schools-northeast-summit.

26 Ofsted and A. Spielman, HMCI's Commentary: Recent Primary and Secondary Curriculum Research (11 October 2017). Available at: https://www.gov.uk/government/speeches/hmcis-commentary-october-2017 .

27 Ofsted, Education Inspection Framework (updated 23 July 2021). Available at: https://www.gov.uk/government/publications/education-inspection-framework/education-inspection-framework.

Spielman has set out her own view on the purpose of schooling and described some of the ideals – her picture of the intent:

> To understand the substance of education we have to understand the objectives. Yes, education does have to prepare young people to succeed in life and make their contribution in the labour market. But to reduce education down to this kind of functionalist level is rather wretched.
>
> Because education should be about broadening minds, enriching communities and advancing civilisation. Ultimately, it is about leaving the world a better place than we found it.[28]

The launch of a new Ofsted framework is a well-trodden path: HMI visit conferences and leave head teachers feeling reassured. There is interest and even excitement from schools in a potential area of development followed by consultation and pilots, typically with good schools asking (by invitation) to be included for all sorts of reasons of their own. It follows the familiar pattern we described earlier. Ofsted needs to ensure consistency between its teams. As it trains its on-the-ground inspectors, the principles used in the pilot inspections are reduced to an algorithm for creating judgements, alongside an accompanying reporting phraseology. As soon as the first inspection reports are published the heat evaporates from the system. Inspectors read each other's reports to make sure they are all looking for the right things. Meanwhile, heads and senior leaders scrutinise other schools' reports and shift their practice in order to show the inspectors what they want to see. In just a few weeks, the process has become sterile and the panopticon kicks in.

Over time, each change has led to a gaming reaction in the system – for example:

- A disproportionate focus on the children on the cusp, either just below or just above the line of concern (grade 4/5 at GCSE [initially the C/D borderline] and working above the expected at Key Stage 2 [initially 3a/4c]).

- The depression of teacher-assessed Key Stage 1 results to inflate progress at Key Stage 2. (Children in separate infant schools still perform better than children at Key Stage 1 in primary schools.)

---

28 Ofsted and Spielman, Amanda Spielman's Speech at the Festival of Education.

This is one of the several issues to which the system has turned a blind eye.

- The off-rolling of the children most in need but least likely to enhance attainment statistics.

- The narrowing of the curriculum to focus on tests and exams and the shrinking of subject breadth, along with the corresponding over-assessment of children.

Beyond gaming, there are also the long-term effects of the attention on data as the prime and almost sole indicator of quality. Michael Wilshaw reminded us: 'We did a report on Key Stage 3 and called it *The Wasted Years?* in 2015,[29] which mirrored the Tomlinson Report's findings of a decade earlier and highlighted the way the youngest children in secondary education get a raw deal because of the intense focus on the examination cohorts.' All of these are unintended consequences and examples of how some schools deemed to be outstanding have allowed this to happen to secure their grading – an issue that vexes Spielman.

Many appreciate Spielman's candour about the new framework that was just beginning to be implemented as the pandemic struck. Jonathan Johnson, a MAT leader, told us:

> I welcome the fact that they want to drill into the purpose of the curriculum – what you are trying to achieve with the children, the quality of implementation and the impact. I have no issue with all of those things being of equal importance to the outcomes because education is more than just a set of grades. The problem with the framework is it was based on Ofsted's research and, as we all know, the moment you put that in print it is time-stamped. But research by its nature keeps evolving, our understanding keeps evolving. Where is the training for the inspectorate to keep their information updated and evolving alongside ours? If an inspector was trained in 2019 for the start of the framework, where is the ongoing development to make sure they keep on top of current thinking to match ours?

A primary head teacher from the North of England was positive about the recent Ofsted development, but reflected the propensity to do what

---

29 Ofsted, *Key Stage 3: The Wasted Years?* (September 2015). Available at: https://www.gov.uk/government/publications/key-stage-3-the-wasted-years.

Ofsted stipulates when she said: 'We have really enjoyed getting into the intent of our work, being sure why we are offering what we do and what we want to achieve. We feel much more confident about the breadth of our curriculum now but the deep dive into a subject is worrying us.'

Some head teachers and CEOs of MATs told us of their concern that the new framework is likely to take attention away from the emphasis on test and exam success. We heard doubts from people who described their success in terms of improvement in data, which they now felt might carry less currency. We also heard from those who worried that a good curriculum experience was no match for a GCSE when the pupil presented themselves to an employer. Sadly, once again, the debate was polarised. It seems that many cannot accept that a good curriculum experience can lead to good qualifications through exam success.

All of the HMCI we talked with had tried to align government policy with their own wish to support and improve schools through inspection. Like all of us, they were constrained by the expectations on them. The limited resources and demands to inspect a high number of schools per year, the complex perceptions of regulation and inspection, and the ability to manage a large workforce and achieve consistency have all slowed Ofsted's progress to change its perceived character after difficult beginnings.

Secretaries of state seem to assume that the regulator is effective but unappreciated, and attribute any criticisms to a lack of tolerance for any accountability process. The reality for others is different: it is viewed with caution by most in the schooling system. Some individual inspectors are highly respected but as an organisation it is not held in high regard.

All our union, MAT and school witnesses expressed a belief in the need for proportionate or intelligent accountability. Nick Brook of the NAHT told us: 'We should be having light touch inspection to identify where failure exists in the system, and then a deep diagnostic to get underneath the skin of what's going on in those schools and determine how to help our schools to improve.'

Geoff Barton of ASCL said: 'We had for years talked about intelligent accountability. If we are not careful, leadership becomes a minority of time doing the job and the majority of time explaining why we do the things we do. I think we have do something about the very word "accountability" and instead emphasise "responsibility", and that should be in terms of what we can achieve with the resources provided. If we look at basic assumptions about what schooling should provide, we are short of funding. We should apply the same accountability expectation to the nation as we do to individual schools.'

Former general secretary of the National Association of Schoolmasters/ Union of Women Teachers (NASUWT), Christine Keates, said, 'Government must set the accountability framework. It is right that schools are held to account, but they need to be held to account for the right things and the accountability system must be fit for purpose and secure public trust and confidence in public education.'

Is inspection necessary and, if so, could we make it better?

We believe that inspection can be a force for good. However, it needs to be managed carefully; if stirred too much it will behave like the magic porridge pot in the children's story by Joan Stimson.

Before Ofsted began its work, too many schools were clearly not doing well by their pupils or their communities. Most LEAs were not picking up on their failings. Robin Alexander's evaluation of primary education in Leeds in 1986 had shone a light on the ineffectiveness of local authority advice, in that advisers were attracted to the schools that appreciated them rather than those that needed them to address their shortcomings.[30]

As Christine Gilbert reflected: 'Let's be clear. The past wasn't a golden haven and schools are universally better today than when I started teaching. But the public accountability system has too strong a hold on the system. It is holding too many schools back. It needs to change so schools and children can really thrive.'

If, quite properly, we cannot go back to an inspection-free world, is there a way of improving the current system? Having experienced many inspections during our careers, we know the behaviours and the consequences that inspection encourages. We also know that the person who knows most about the school being inspected is the one who leads it. If the head of the school doesn't know more about the school than the visiting

---

30   R. Alexander, *Primary Education in Leeds: Twelfth and Final Report from the Primary Needs Independent Evaluation Project* (Leeds: University of Leeds, 1991).

inspector, then by definition it is probably failing: the leader has lost his or her grip. But in a good MAT today (or LEA in the past) that isn't necessarily the case. Most schools are doing well in some respects, improving in others and trying to do something about knotty problems in other areas. Most leaders are endeavouring to sort out the poor parts, improve what they can and hopefully there are a few (or more) successful features that bear comparison with other schools.

Ofsted inspection shines a light in every corner and reports on every feature, using an algorithm to reach a final judgement. Often, those shining the lights know less about how to improve the situation than the leaders trying to do so – and most of them are trying and most of them will sort out the problems they encounter. The report, though, which purports to be comprehensive, simply exposes to the whole community those matters which would have been addressed anyway, while simultaneously creating as many problems as are solved by implying that failings have been externally identified.

Surely, the reason we inspect schools is because we want to find out something useful. Is it useful to engage in a game of cat and mouse with the system? As each tries to outwit the other, we might identify some of the things we seek, but at the same time we will miss those things that are camouflaged or fail to look at things we need to scrutinise. As it stands, inspection is too often neither accurate nor good value for money.

Peter Hyman questioned what inspection does for professionalism in schools:

> The way Ofsted operates, the high-stakes nature of everything it does, means there is never a proper professional conversation when they descend on a school. The head teacher has to play a cat-and-mouse game, hiding the defects of the school, trying to pretend that something that isn't very good at the school is actually better than it is. Head teachers know there is little point in being open and honest about the challenges because they will be crucified.

This implied dishonesty and subterfuge featured in a lot of our conversations – the cat-and-mouse nature of inspection because of the drastic professional and personal consequences of the outcome. One experienced former school improvement adviser in a MAT told us that she could get an academy ready for inspection overnight: 'You simply had to know the framework inside out, sort out who would deal with each aspect of the inspection, get all the ducks in a row. The challenge was to stay one step ahead of the inspectors and help them to write the report that you need written.'

We will revisit what we need to do about the future of accountability at a national level, but before we do so we will return to the local community where there is daily accountability. Real school accountability starts in the classroom, the staffroom, the school office and the local community.

Local accountability

We started our chapter in a local setting – in Oxfordshire, as it happens, because serendipitously that is where accountability first reared its head in our schooling system. Our experience is that the more local accountability can be, the more effective and less damaging the outcome will be.

Consider: in a school, staff are very aware of those occasional colleagues who don't pull their weight and live up to their responsibilities. Some staff become demotivated if a head of department or a head of phase doesn't do anything about it. The sign of a school going wrong and into decline is when a school leader doesn't call out a member of staff who lets everybody down (and by everybody we mean colleagues, pupils, parents and guardians).

Heads have different ways of tackling poor individual teacher performance but, ideally, they do it discreetly and in private. We know that in schools on an upward trajectory and improving on their previous best, the head will take enormous care over appointments, devise first-rate induction arrangements (with newcomers teamed up with just the right coaching buddy) and ensure that staff are 'caught doing good' to increase their energy and commitment. Doubtless, too, in the best-run schools, when a lapse occurs, a quiet word will iron out any issues at an early stage. However, we can all recall times when all that has failed and someone is simply letting down their colleagues and the children over and over again. If we let it go, we are not calling them to account for their actions or inaction, and nor are we discharging our responsibilities fairly. Dismissing someone is a fraught process, and as staff are collegiate, they will often be sympathetic to the staff member. Afterwards, though, they are usually grateful that action was taken.

Our most keenly felt responsibilities and accountabilities are to those closest to us – our pupils and those with whom we work. In those Oxfordshire secondary schools in the 1980s, forensic discussions were led by the heads of every school with each head of department about comparative results between subjects with the same children in the same school, together with some reflection on comparative results in the same subject between schools. The same heads were also comparing the impact of different tutors on attendance and exam outcomes. In short, all the things we take for granted as part of the warp and weft of school improvement. It is just that we had fewer data to use back then than we do now; the process is similar but it is much more rigorous. What remains identical is the mutual professional accountability: members of a school community know how much they depend on each other and how important their efforts are for the future of their pupils and their families.

This effort for all pupils is vital, but instead we have an accountability approach that has tended to move towards evidence based on trends and patterns thrown up by the data. Raising Attainment for Disadvantaged Youngsters (RADY) is a whole-school approach for supporting disadvantaged children to attain in line with their non-disadvantaged peers. The organisation began in the Wirral when an adviser, Dave Hollomby, recognised that target-setting approaches based on previous attainment were building in failure. RADY is a dynamic community of interest involving schools across the country. Trevor Sutcliffe, one of the organisers, told us: 'The starting point is to increase our expectations to negate the national accountability measure that children will make "expected progress", as the best-case scenario for this is accepting that early gaps remain throughout education. We are aiming to make life-changing differences.'

Most of the successful schools we know are eager to challenge themselves and avoid complacency when it comes to pupils who are disadvantaged. However, they work to make their school equitable, taking every opportunity to help children by providing opportunities they lack and smoothing paths whenever possible, especially where the national arrangements are working against them.

We have both always felt much more accountable to the local body that has employed us and their stakeholders in the community whom we serve than to anyone in distant Whitehall. The LEA education officer could speak to the regional HMI as a trusted critical friend, honestly sharing worries about particular areas of weakness or even a school in trouble and what was being done about it locally. With Ofsted no longer based in the DfE, it became a different story.

One of Michael Gove's reforms was to tell Michael Wilshaw (who as we have remarked, to his enormous credit, re-established the local placements of HMIs in regional teams) to discontinue inspections of local authorities' school improvement services. Wilshaw told us: 'I protested that they [local authorities] ran most of the primary schools and a quarter of the secondary schools. But he was having none of it, preferring to let them wither.' It was not just a faulty decision; it also gives us a clue as to how we could get accountability and inspection right.

If local authorities are going to be the champions of children and parents, which all our ministerial witnesses acknowledged should be part of their role, it follows that individual schools and MATs should be accountable to their local authority. That answerability doesn't apply only to the processes of school improvement (unless, of course, they are in that group of schools still run by the local authority) but also for admissions, fair access, attendance and inclusiveness, since the future health of the community the school serves depends on schools playing their part in developing young citizens who can contribute as adults. That means a focus on exclusion, SEND and links with employment and destinations. It also means local authorities having the power to ensure that the rights of children and families have priority over the short-term needs of their schools and MATs. If that isn't part of local democracy, what is?

The local authority should also be interested in how the RSC is holding to account those MATs serving the local area for the improvement of their schools. Local authorities have an existing 'scrutiny committee' function, which many have used to review the effectiveness of MATs and RSCs. This needs to be formalised with clear terms of reference. These committees need open and honest dialogue with education officers, head teachers and governors and to represent local interests without the distraction of game-playing.

Ofsted's main role should be to inspect local authorities and MATs

As we will see in the next chapter on governance and finance, there is a strong case for schools to work together in collaborative partnerships for school improvement, which is the principal rationale for individual schools coming together in the first place. The MATs we have spoken to see their main purpose as improving schools and are keenly aware that their future depends on them being successful in doing so. Each year, they have a rigorous data-rich meeting with the RSC, who is also trying to make sure that each MAT is making progress in improving on their previous best and that each school within the MAT is also improving – and, if it isn't, making sure the MAT knows where to find the necessary support. Local authorities have a similar interest in the schools in their area doing well, even though they will not own or run them in the future we outline.

A national inspection agency (at present it is called Ofsted but to give it a clean sheet it should probably be renamed) should, among its other duties, quality assure those who are running schools. We have suggested these should be local partnerships of primary, secondary and, ideally, special schools, varying in size, but at least 10 and no more than 30 schools. We shall call them MATs. It would be the case that when each partnership is inspected on a five-yearly cycle, two schools would be inspected from each MAT, to be determined by the renamed Ofsted. The inspector's report would give a detailed picture of how the MAT was improving on its previous best performance in terms of school improvement. It would comment on the MATs' chartered assessor arrangements (see Chapter 5) and how well it was doing against a national framework which the agency will have established for all school partnership work. It would have access to the local authority scrutiny committee reports over the five years and annual reviews by the RSC of each MAT.

In exceptional circumstances, it would be possible for a MAT (advised by the RSC) to call in Ofsted to inspect a school causing concern, or for a local authority (again, possibly advised by the RSC) to call in Ofsted to a MAT causing concern. Additionally, as now, Ofsted would inspect local authority and regional SEND provision. Finally, through its inspection processes, Ofsted would collect themed surveys to inform national debate about improvement based on aspects of the balanced scorecards (outlined in Chapter 7) which are published every year for each school.

The stakes are high for a head teacher and their staff, especially if they work in a school where there are higher than average numbers of challenged children who are on the wrong side of the attainment gap. So, if we are testing these proposals based on first principles, what do we want to know?

1. We want to know that each of our schools is fit for purpose and not allowing their educational offer to fall below a stated minimum

MATs and other school partnerships would be inspected every five years, having been kept under data-rich annual review by the RSC. Two schools from the MAT partnership would be inspected as part of the process, which would also draw on the local authority's scrutiny committee papers for the preceding years. Such an arrangement would not require the current level of inspection or the current overly complex machinery. It would be relatively simple for Ofsted to ask local authorities and MATs to determine annually those schools about which they have most concern. Inspections could then be managed to include the wider community of leadership within the trust or authority.

Do we need to inspect all schools as though we were starting from a blank sheet of paper? Alasdair Macdonald wondered whether 'if over 80% of schools are now good or better, the current model can be argued to have served its purpose well. We now need to focus on inspection that supports those schools to improve from their current good position and move on from the obsession with grades.'

Lucy Crehan, a teacher who has spent time in schools abroad to get first-hand experience of different systems,[31] echoed Macdonald's concern about the one-size-fits-all approach. She told us: 'In the high-performing systems, they're not holding schools accountable for outcomes; they're holding schools accountable for the quality of the professional development. If you're offering high-quality CPD and you're setting up structures for professional learning within a school, then they kind of leave you alone.'

---

31   L. Crehan, *Cleverlands: The Secrets Behind the Success of the World's Education Superpowers* (London: Unbound, 2018).

It would be beneficial to have frameworks that described and looked differently at primary and secondary phases, rather than implying the same experience for pupils throughout their career. Better still might be a framework for the secondary phase that focused explicitly on Key Stage 3.

2. We want to know we are helping those MATs and schools that are not good enough

We think it would be better to have two grades of judgement: one would identify unsuccessful schools and the other would credit schools for their performance and improvement. It would be for the school to convince its pupils, parents and community that it is outstanding for them.

One of our head teacher witnesses told us: 'It's not that you shouldn't be inspecting. What I think it is, is that you don't need a grade, and Ofsted just pits schools against each other so they're competing for the highest grades. Without the grades, we'd be working together and helping each other and challenging each other. We don't need grades and the competition.'

3. We want to know where disciplined and effective innovation is taking place and help that to spread

This is crucial. Inspection needs to identify the improvements that a school and its MAT have made and make sure they know how to push against previous best to improve yet further. This is why Wilshaw's idea of regional teams would have been effective over time, putting people in touch through local knowledge and insight and pushing the bar higher. Lucy Crehan again offered an international perspective: 'In Finland, Canada and Japan, the middle-tier performs the function of bringing schools together, referring head teachers to other schools to visit, and getting groups of teachers to come and co-design the curriculum.'

4. We want to know the quality of a range of aspects of schooling across the nation, so we can develop appropriate strategies to build on strengths and improve

Under our proposals, Ofsted would carry out themed inspections across the country looking at effective practice by sampling a subject discipline, an age phase, a small school organisation and so on. Insights gleaned would inform policy considerations in a structured way. If such a process were planned, developed and programmed, then the involvement of teachers and leaders from within schools would be central. Their participation would have a two-way benefit: it would involve a genuine professional dialogue, with teachers fully engaged with the growth of their own and others' professional expertise.

5. We want to know we have a system where those who are inspected feel professionally respected and engaged

We suggest that the reformed Ofsted inspection system is based on clear principles of professional respect in terms of what we are seeking to achieve through inspection, and that the overt aim should be 'doing good as they go'.

Inspection should be more formative than summative. In those cases where the MAT or school is poor and failing, there should be no hesitation in pointing this out. However, 'Is the MAT or school good enough or not?' should be the extent of the summative judgement.

If the MAT or school is not failing its pupils, then the report should enable school improvement by presenting information in a formative way. It should be an evaluation that informs and extends practice. This would mean identifying aspects of practice that are very well developed and could become examples for other MATs/schools. This, in turn, means that inspectors should be unpicking which aspects are helping these schools to be so good, teasing out preconditions and identifying steps to success. What is it about the leadership, pedagogy, organisation, resourcing or professional learning that has developed such excellence in practice? How has the school managed to overcome barriers to learning? What has got the youngsters so involved in learning?

At the same time, the report could dwell on how the MAT or school is trying to improve on its previous best in every respect. What is supporting the drive for success? What is the MAT or school doing that is tipping the odds in favour of a breakthrough for a knotty problem? How is a MAT or school capitalising on a situation where they are sailing with the wind or sustaining them as they go through choppy waters against the wind? What is the MAT or school doing that is helping them to get out of the quicksand of problems that might otherwise consume them?

A report that looked at these sorts of aspects of a school would recognise what the school is achieving and what it is working on in terms of improvement. For other MATs/schools locally and afar, the knowledge that someone somewhere has travelled this way before or could be a fellow traveller is likely to build a community of interest which could drive improvement at a faster rate and build professional collaboration.

6. We want to know how to encourage our schools to continue to improve

A new wave of interest and restrained optimism ripples through the school system whenever a new framework is published for consultation. Ofsted then embarks on a familiarisation exercise and invites schools to put themselves forward to be involved in a pilot for the revised inspection process.

Perhaps, unsurprisingly, those schools that volunteer are the confident ones, the schools that see themselves as secure in their good or better judgement. The deal is that the pilot inspection is an exploratory process and is not reported on. Typically, the pilot inspections are carried out by experienced HMIs. These highly professional processes tend to go well, again unsurprisingly, since the schools are successful and the inspectors are proficient. Schools speak favourably of the process and its usefulness and the inspectors use examples and feedback in their dissemination sessions with groups of schools across the country. Schools looking on know they need to get themselves ready for the new expectations and start to adopt practices to meet the provisions for the new framework. Heads and teachers who have been involved in the pilots spend supportive time with each other.

This approach demonstrates that school improvement is a tangible process. If only the pilot period could simply continue as the default methodology of the inspectorate! We believe that Ofsted should capitalise on this existing feature of their practice by asking MATs to nominate weaker schools to join confident volunteers in the pilot process. In addition, experienced HMIs should be accompanied by their less expert colleagues to help improve the quality and consistency of inspection teams. Recommendations for improvement should list five schools which can be referenced to explore good and improving practice. Inspectors should be able to use their knowledge of such schools to illustrate what they see as good practice and point others towards them at the right time in their development.

Well-managed inspections of this sort could result in the biggest action research programme ever. Ongoing analysis by highly credible HMIs, who visit MATs and schools and engage in structured dialogue with the profession, could gradually help schools to lift their practice, hypothesise about different options for development and build examples of breakthrough practice – and they could still identify those schools letting down the children and communities they serve.

The collaborative proposals we have outlined here would contribute to a new age of hope, ambition and collaborative partnerships.

An international perspective on accountability

As an aside, entire nations have found themselves in an accountability trap. Reflecting on the panopticon effect that we believe has influenced the schooling system significantly over the last 30 years and caused much of the managerial approach we see today in terms of feeding the machine of accountability, we realise that the same is happening at a government level. Over the same period, politicians have almost sleepwalked into their own panopticon by signing up their national system to the OECD's and other international organisations' battery of triennial testing procedures. These tests – notably PISA, TIMSS and PIRLS – compare nations and jurisdictions around the globe, with the high-profile release of comparative results, detailed analysis on many variables and various reports and recommendations.

Countries often enter the testing regime at the start of an election cycle, thereby taking the chance to set a baseline with the hope of showing progress in time for the next election. Data is analysed according to many metrics, which gives the media everywhere the chance to find fault and ministers everywhere the opportunity to point to progress in some aspect of their policy.

The OECD has expanded its service to governments and is available to work with those seeking to make progress through consultation and reports, which ministers are often keen to commission to record the steps being made and to show proof of independent recognition of their success.

International tests have become a global panopticon, and while we do so with hesitance, we would ask whether this is one windmill at which the global schooling system should be tilting. The OECD has a gentle grip on the world-wide system, and it would take a brave minister of education to withdraw from the process, especially if they were not either highly performing or rapidly improving, because to do so would open them up to accusations of hiding from reality.

However, the reality is that the testing regime has, in part, led school systems to design their own curriculum, pedagogy and assessment approaches with PISA outcomes in mind. The PISA test crept up on the system in England. Estelle Morris told us: 'Michael Barber introduced us to the PISA tests and to OECD, and it was good to see us making progress after the first three years. It sort of vindicated our effort.' The OECD is currently working to reshape the focus of its tests and looking to measure personal qualities and learning characteristics as opposed to narrow pro-cess competence. On one hand, it could be trying to correct the emphasis of previous testing rounds, but on the other, it could be trying to profit from the very situation it has created.

As the spotlight has shifted from Ontario to Finland and Singapore, nations have flocked to find *the* transferable solution. Whether these nations have truly examined the validity of the tests, the samples or the analysis of results is doubtful. Once into the scheme, it is politically diffi-cult to leave. No wonder Michael Gove described Andreas Schleicher, the OECD director, as 'the most important man in English education'.[32]

---

32 Department for Education and M. Gove, Michael Gove Article in 'The Independent' on Education Reforms (28 February 2013). Available at: https://www.gov.uk/government/speeches/michael-gove-article-in-the-independent-on-education-reforms.

The politicians may exploit the headlines but Schleicher points out that the real issues lie in the subtext. He told us: 'I'll give you one important reference point which often gets completely lost in the English debate, where performance is always about schools. According to PISA, it's only 25% of the performance variation that lies between schools. The big problem lies in too many students falling through the cracks within the school and that gets unnoticed because your accountability system doesn't look at it.' Chapter 8 on admissions, attendance and exclusion deals with exactly this issue, although it is worth noting here that accountability has now caught up with our unwitting politicians.

Mick recalls:

I was travelling to New Zealand in December 2013. At Heathrow Airport I picked up a newspaper on which the headline announced that UK countries had performed poorly in international education tests. True, England had done badly in some areas, Scotland in others, Wales in others and Northern Ireland in yet others.

I landed at Kuala Lumpur to change planes and, during the two-hour stopover, I bought a paper which had headlines about the under-performance of South East Asian countries: Thailand, Malaysia and Myanmar should all look to their laurels in respect of some comparative worldwide tests.

My next stop was Sydney, where the papers were reporting on the 'shocking' performance of Australia's school system. As I arrived in Auckland, I was met with newspapers commenting on how New Zealand's schools needed to improve if they were to measure up to the best in the world.

I was very tired – tired of reading about teachers across the world being randomly criticised through an anonymous process with so much influence.

This chapter has looked at inspection in some depth because the accountability agenda comes to a head in inspection. The reform of existing arrangements, which fail to quality assure the real situation in schools and poison the climate so essential to children's futures, is urgent. What is needed is a mature debate about accountability to ensure that it is used proportionately and positively to develop the notion of continuous improvement. Sadly, we fear that it has found itself in Charles Clarke's 'too difficult box' as one of those issues that is better left alone. Accountability polarises opinion, raises emotions and carries many political pitfalls. It is surely one for the Schooling Framework Commission, which we describe in the next chapter, and it is also one of our six foundation stones on which we believe an improving system could be built.

Chapter 12

Governance and finance of schooling – too many cooks and pipers

How the schooling system and schools themselves are governed, financed, led and managed powerfully affects the likelihood of teachers and schools being successful and of their pupils living fulfilled lives.

Governance

In schooling systems in western democracies, there are usually three levels of governance: national government, local government and the school (or groups of schools organised under a school board). Within democratic systems, there should be a built-in concern for subsidiarity – that is, in keeping decision-making to the level closest to where the outcome of the decision is most keenly felt. (In contrast, dictatorships centralise decisions.) It is especially important to observe the principle of subsidiarity in large systems to minimise the risk of alienation among participants, since a sense of powerlessness among citizens is the enemy of democracy and thus weakens it.

Governments, public organisations and large FTSE 100 companies often run into trouble when they are unclear about three related and interwoven concepts: *decentralisation* – a word often used by centralising governments (notably at the end of dictatorships) or large organisations giving the impression of *delegation* and *devolution*. As the box below outlines, they do not mean the same thing.

Devolution means the government handing over power, responsibility and significant fundraising powers (which we argue should be called 'equity taxes') to a wholly autonomous lower body to decide

523

policy and practice. (For example, the devolved governments in Wales, Scotland and Northern Ireland can determine their own education strategies and raise their own resources, but they also receive funding from Westminster.)

Decentralisation means maintaining power at the centre but moving managers closer to the action. The government might delegate (see below) but essentially controls what happens.

Delegation means the government handing over decision-making powers (with or without conditions) to a subordinate person or body who is still responsible to the government (see also the box on page 525).

While we have defined devolution, decentralisation and delegation at a government level, they also occur in any organisation where those with the power and the purse decide how to best manage – including schools themselves.

In the present landscape of English schooling, RSCs are an example of decentralisation. Power remains with the DfE and the secretary of state – indeed, academies are advised that to talk to the RSC is to talk to the secretary of state. However, the RSC, advised by a select board of head teachers, has a regional office and carries out a range of duties, principally dealing with brokering and re-brokering of academies and MATs. It was a small operation initially, but each RSC now has a staff of dozens and has extended their remit into monitoring school improvement in MATs, free schools and academies. RSCs take their instructions from the minister, although this is mediated by the national schools commissioner. Certain duties may be delegated to them, in which case delegation should be used effectively to avoid bad management (see the box on page 525). RSCs check with the DfE for guidance and then either decide the case or recommend it for approval further up the line of command.

Nine levels of delegation

1   Look into this problem. Give me all the facts. I will decide what to do.

2   Let me know the alternatives available and the pros and cons of each option. I will decide what to select.

3   Let me know the criteria for your recommendation, which alternatives you have identified and which ones appear best to you, with any risks identified. I will make the decision.

4   Recommend a course of action for my approval.

5   Let me know what you intend to do. Delay action until I approve.

6   Let me know what you intend to do. Do it unless I say not to.

7   Take action. Let me know what you did and how it turns out.

8   Take action. Communicate with me only if your action is unsuccessful.

9   Take action. No further communication with me is necessary.

In our experience, many failures of management – leading to loss of morale and involving small and serious errors of omission and commission within the DfE, LEAs, MATs and schools (and other organisations in the public and private sector) – arise from not being clear about these three concepts. And even when clarity is established about decentralisation and devolution, poor managers sometimes change their minds about which of the nine levels of delegation they had agreed, and a blame game starts when something subsequently goes wrong.

Tim recalls:

It was 1989 and I visited Chile as Pinochet's dictatorship was coming to an end, which had started with the overthrow of Allende. The British Council had asked me to advise the group determining the post-Pinochet arrangements for their education service. They talked about decentralisation, and I protested that their democracy would only be strong if they went for devolution or at least clearly understood delegation. The whole visit helped them – and me! – to clarify the distinction between decentralisation, devolution and delegation.

Tim recalls:

It was early in my career. I had made the mistake of being flattered to be offered a senior job, which I took – forgetting the basic rule that an interview is a two-way decision – only to discover that my new boss was insecure and lacked backbone. He illustrated this when he told me to get on with organising all the detail of an awards event without reference to him ('I have more important things to do than hold your hand'). I thought he was at level 7 on the delegation scale, but knowing him to be insecure and liable to take credit and delegate blame, I sent him a note of the details, which he didn't acknowledge. Then, when the guest speaker gave a lacklustre address, he said he had specifically asked to be consulted on that detail. I was young at the time and knew nothing of the subtleties of good and bad delegation, but I later reflected that my leader on that occasion was effortlessly moving from level 7 to level 5 or even 4.

We provide two examples (one good and one bad) of the shifting power between the middle and school levels. Subsidiarity is illustrated in the examples that follow.

A good example of devolution and delegation

Following the Education Reform Act 1988, the introduction of the local management of schools, whereby school budgets formerly decided (and often micromanaged and controlled) at an LEA level were delegated to schools, was widely welcomed, especially by governors and head teachers. Indeed, even the many LEAs that lost powers as a result of the change welcomed it, not least because some had introduced pilots, which

Kenneth Baker acknowledged had influenced his thinking.[1] It is a good example of national government learning from good practice in local government, and then deciding from the centre that devolved powers to what we might call the middle tier had to go further and be devolved to the school level.

The *size* of the school budget was still decided in the democratic middle tier,[2] but *how* it was spent was a matter for the school's head teacher and governing body, which the Education Act 1986 specified should consist of elected parents and staff, nominated LEA governors and co-opted community representatives, to be decided by the governing body. There was a conscious effort to enhance democratic input at the level of the school itself two years before the change was introduced and only after LEAs had introduced training for governors, who would have an enhanced role.

A bad example of devolution and delegation

This example followed the decision in 2010 to encourage first good and then all schools that academy status was something to aspire towards, either as a stand-alone institution or as a MAT. MAT governance does not require democratic input and very few of the more than 1,500 MATs have parents on their trust board (in effect, their governance), whether elected or otherwise. Nor are they required to include representation from the staff or local authority. Some MATs have removed governing bodies altogether and others have reduced their powers.[3] In short, they have centralised powers formerly exercised at the level of the school. As a consequence, arguably, the autonomy of schools has been seriously compromised and the principle of subsidiarity has been abused. Unlike local authorities, MATs are not subject to Ofsted inspection and are accountable only privately to the secretary of state. The individual schools cease to have a separate legal identity.

---

1   In *The Turbulent Years*, p. 211, Baker cites Cambridgeshire as one of two LEAs which had pioneered a modest scheme. Unsurprisingly – because he was determined to abolish it – he doesn't mention the largest scheme at ILEA, which had an alternative use of resources scheme running for more than 10 years prior to 1988.
2   In 2005/2006, the amount spent on school budgets was centralised.
3   Many MATs have centralised budgets and have removed the duties of individual school advisory committees (the equivalent of a governing board) to comment on them.

We are not suggesting that a different model, such as a MAT composed of groups of schools working together, is wrong. On the contrary, we believe that schools working in isolation do not improve as well as those working with other schools. School partnerships are essential if the needs of *all* children are to be met and to provide a model which ensures that *all* schools can improve. Our point is that, as with so many of Michael Gove's initiatives, it was a case of act first and address the consequences later.

An alternative view, expressed by some of our witnesses, is that Gove, prompted by his SpAd, the arch-disruptor Dominic Cummings, was simply trying to do his bit to bring about the irreversible wounding of local authorities.

Sam Freedman recalled the period when academies first emerged:

> We'd had 30 years of centralisation and attempted destruction of local authorities. The idea that central government can run 20,000 individual schools in a fragmented system meant we needed an alternative. These were two pieces of the mission for which there was no clear direction. Now we are stuck with the current arrangements. The role of local authorities should have been strengthened and be very different but they have no clear function. They should act as the champion of children and young people locally, especially vulnerable children, manage school admissions and protect the interests of young people.

Above all, we need to be clear what the relationship is between the partnership (whether it is a MAT or any other form) and the individual school, both in terms of governance and management responsibilities, as well as how the MAT (or other partnership) is regulated. Many school governing boards that decided to take their school into a MAT did so with assurances of continuing levels of autonomy and responsibility, only to find themselves undermined later.

One of our witnesses, who had worked for two MATs after a long career with local authorities, reflected: 'Many who elected to become academies now think they were sold a pup. They were offered autonomy and have ended up in a straitjacket.' Susan Douglas, CEO of the Eden Academy Trust, told us: 'Although, originally, the academy programme was sold very much on a "greater autonomy" ticket, I'm not sure what the autonomy was "freedom from".'

As we have seen, Chapter 4 covers in some detail the unfolding story of how MATs arose and the continuing confusion that has arisen at middle-tier and school levels. We shall return to this after considering governance at a national level.

National level governance

As we explained in Chapter 1, stripping out the middle tier of educational powers (and resources) has proceeded apace: many powers have gone to the centre and others to the school. Some estimate that the secretary of state now has over 2,000 powers, whereas at the end of the Second World War there were three.[4] We think that centralisation to this extent is dangerous and creates an unhealthy example for schools and MATs to follow.

Ministers arguably need some curb or limitation of their powers beyond the existing combination of Education Select Committee and questions in Parliament. It used to be the case, for example, that the secretary of state would consult with an arm's length statutory body (or bodies) on any matter concerned with curriculum or qualifications, but the last version of these bodies (QCDA) was abolished in 2013 and now there is no brake on ministerial initiatives in such matters. Several head teacher witnesses referred to ministers interfering in their daily practice, either directly or indirectly. Sometimes this was through the channel of the local authority or MAT leadership, which in its turn becomes attuned to the importance of not upsetting the DfE.

Nationally, to limit but not annul the power of the secretary of state, we favour the establishment of a Schooling Framework Commission, along the lines advocated by Professor Brahm Norwich,[5] to advise variously

---

4   The three powers reserved for the minister were (1) the removal of air-raid shelters from school playing fields and playgrounds, (2) securing a sufficient supply of suitably qualified teachers, and (3) approving the opening and closure of schools and capital loan consents for school buildings. See B. Hudson, M. Leask and S. Younie, *Education System Design: Foundations, Policy Options and Consequences* (Abingdon and New York: Routledge, 2020).

5   B. Norwich, From the Warnock Report (1978) to an Education Framework Commission: A Novel Contemporary Approach to Educational Policy Making for Pupils with Special Educational Needs/Disabilities, *Frontiers in Education* (17 July 2019). Available at: https://www.frontiersin.org/articles/10.3389/feduc.2019.00072/full. Brahm Norwich, professor of educational psychology and special educational needs at the University of Exeter, has written extensively on this matter and can be contacted through the university's Graduate School of Education.

on the national aims and values underpinning our state-funded schools. Initially, it would be charged with advising on two matters – (1) the new less-centralised governance arrangements at regional, local and school levels, and (2) the values, aims and purposes of the schooling system and our schools – before considering other matters affecting the curriculum, exams and accountability, as well as school admissions and teacher supply and development. It would comprise representatives of teacher and support staff unions, HMIs, Chartered College of Teaching, universities, CBI, Chambers of Commerce, Trades Union Congress, governors and MAT trust boards, Local Government Association, and bodies representing churches and faiths. Politicians would be nominated from the main political parties plus others with known affiliations. There would be an additional membership by public election.

The commission would be charged with producing an ongoing 10-year plan for education. HMCI and Education Select Committee reports would be considered and advice would be given to the secretary of state, with copies sent to the Select Committee annually. It would use the device of citizens' assemblies, supplemented by online webinars, so its recommendations would take into consideration the views canvassed (which would be recorded in appendices), as well as data and research, of course. Its agenda would include the issues we raise in this book and summarise with possible ways forward in the final chapter.

The commission's findings would not bind the secretary of state, but there could be an agreement that any proposed statutory changes would show how they were consistent with or different from the commission's conclusions. The body would convene for an intensive series of considerations at set intervals, deliberately designed to avoid synchronicity with parliamentary terms.

What is key is to establish a check on what many see as too many unbridled powers vested in the office of secretary of state. Our suggestion has the advantage that it will address this issue and, in doing so, involve representatives of those interests most affected by ministerial decisions and action. Parliament, embodying as it does democracy at a national level, may also wish to strengthen the role of the Education Select Committee so that their thorough investigations are seen as material evidence for changes in policy.

Devolution to regions: an alternative and complementary approach

It could be argued that if Scotland (population *c*.5 million), Wales (*c*.3 million) and Northern Ireland (*c*.1.8 million) deserve devolved powers over education, then so do Yorkshire and Humberside, Greater Manchester, Greater Merseyside, West Midlands, East Midlands and London. We appreciate that this doesn't cover all the areas where the *c*.47–50 million people in England live. However, as now, there could continue to be different local government structures for rural areas and the large conurbations.

The Redcliffe-Maud Report, which preceded the last major review of English local government in 1974, recommended regional provinces, but this idea was quietly dropped as the new two-tier system in rural and metropolitan areas (after a quickly abandoned trial of overarching metropolitan county councils) and, in some areas, unitary councils were introduced.[6] The whole new edifice (which has been tinkered with and modified in a piecemeal way from the early 1990s onwards as more unitary authorities were created in the two-tier part of the system) has also been hobbled by a succession of unsuitable local taxation systems. However, any attempt to reform local government finance, such as the Lyons Review in 2007,[7] has always been postponed because it is too difficult. Outside London, with a few exceptions, we now have a set of unitary local authorities which are, in the main, too small and in too tightly defined an area to make coherent sense of some service provisions.

Governments use the term 'local authority' to denote councils, whether they are metropolitan district, unitary district, non-unitary district or shire counties. Local authority is considered to be synonymous with the old LEA as education was once part of the council's remit. The minister for local government (a post that has only existed since 2001, with a brief appearance in 1969–1970) devolves or delegates certain powers to local

---

6   The Redcliffe-Maud committee sat between 1966 and 1969 and considered local government arrangements in all of England except Greater London, which had been reformed slightly earlier.

7   The Lyons Review, the inquiry under the chairmanship of Michael Lyons which sat between 2004 and 2007, was commissioned by the deputy prime minister and Chancellor of the Exchequer to make recommendations on the role, function and funding of local government. Among its findings, none of which have been acted upon, was the vital role of place-shaping: M. Lyons, *Place-Shaping: A Shared Ambition for the Future of Local Government. Lyons Inquiry into Local Government* (Norwich: HMSO, 2007). Available at: https://assets.publishing.service.gov.uk/government/uploads/system/uploads/attachment_data/file/243601/9780119898545.pdf.

authorities – for instance, housing or environment. Each of these areas has a corresponding secretary of state who determines policy direction in that sphere.

In education, the local authority is required by government to implement certain national practices, while others are determined locally according to need. The disparities that result often lead to more cries for nation-wide decisions, unless, of course, real powers are overtly devolved (as in Wales and Northern Ireland). It is hard to escape the conclusion that as our memories of pre-war European dictatorships have faded, successive generations of national politicians born and brought up after the war have felt the need for strong local government less keenly. We have observed elsewhere the disregard – in some cases bordering on contempt – for local government that we have witnessed in the civil service and among ministers.

The attempt at the turn of the millennium to 'modernise' how local authorities worked seemed to be a misnomer. It copied the older tra-ditional parliamentary mode; it was imposed by national government, which is itself regularly criticised for allowing the executive to become too powerful; and it replaced the committee system (which involved all councillors) with cabinets comprising fewer than 12. People talk about the relative merits of 'representative' and 'participative' democratic models, but we seem to have representative local democracy in which most of the elected representatives hardly participate. And it's not that different at a national level, except that Parliament sits many more days than a unitary, district or county local authority, albeit with an ordinary MP not having much power to influence the executive.

That has happened in a context where, regrettably, in all the localities in England, whatever their local government pattern, fewer responsibilities are devolved or delegated to local government. This has resulted in a democratic deficit locally, which has resulted from the gradual hoovering up of powers, responsibilities and duties by national government, which, as it centralises, claims that it is addressing the 'postcode lottery' (i.e. when a council chooses to prioritise particular services either more or less generously than a comparable council).

Within the world of schooling, there has been an unrelenting shift to the centre since 1976. As Education Acts pass through Parliament, they have increasingly pushed real control to the centre and responsibility or com-plexity away. The schematic diagram on page 534 gives an indication of the impact of selected Education Acts on schools and governing boards (or more recently trusts) in terms of power. The judgements are subjective, inevitably, although the trend towards ever more centralisation has been fairly consistent under different administrations.

An opportunity to think coherently and sensibly about local government always founders on the reluctance of successive national governments to relinquish control. Their instinct to hold on to power and management within their department, particularly so in the DfE – with popular policies attributed to themselves and less popular to the ineffective agencies they need to rein in – leads more to compliance and subservience than subsidiarity.

This book is not primarily about the balance of power and responsibilities between national government and local or regional governments. However, the failure to address this issue has had a deleterious impact on schools and the schooling system, if only in contributing to a sense of powerlessness, which not only undermines democracy but also depresses professional creativity and the morale of teachers, whose duties include preparing their pupils to live and participate in a secure, vibrant, healthy, productive, caring and innovative democracy.

This is important and disconcerting at every level: parents and families are unsure where to turn when they are uncomfortable with decisions made by their children's schools; the teaching profession becomes more compliant and docile, with the DfE viewed as 'central office' and head teachers acting as branch managers; and local politicians, both council and parliamentary, are factored out of decision-making. As centralisation has expanded, so too has the move to marketisation, along with a greater level of managerial behaviour, distracting all who should be partners from the essential role of providing every pupil with the best school experience possible.

Until the question of devolution within England is addressed, the measure we have recommended here for a Schooling Framework Commission (and for the various issues in each chapter) will be second best. However, it will at least serve to restrain the worst excesses of centralisation and help to unleash the professional energy, creativity and commitment which are essential in what needs to be an age of hope, ambition and collaborative partnerships.

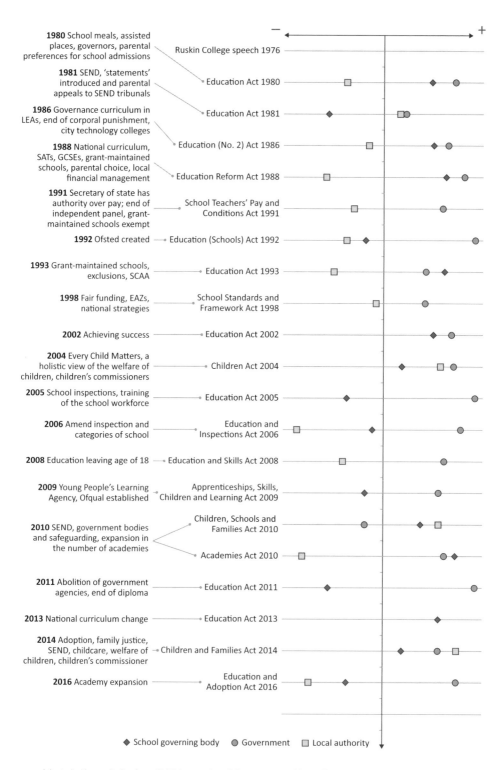

1980 School meals, assisted places, governors, parental preferences for school admissions

1981 SEND, 'statements' introduced and parental appeals to SEND tribunals

1986 Governance curriculum in LEAs, end of corporal punishment, city technology colleges

1988 National curriculum, SATs, GCSEs, grant-maintained schools, parental choice, local financial management

1991 Secretary of state has authority over pay; end of independent panel, grant-maintained schools exempt

1992 Ofsted created

1993 Grant-maintained schools, exclusions, SCAA

1998 Fair funding, EAZs, national strategies

2002 Achieving success

2004 Every Child Matters, a holistic view of the welfare of children, children's commissioners

2005 School inspections, training of the school workforce

2006 Amend inspection and categories of school

2008 Education leaving age of 18

2009 Young People's Learning Agency, Ofqual established

2010 SEND, government bodies and safeguarding, expansion in the number of academies

2011 Abolition of government agencies, end of diploma

2013 National curriculum change

2014 Adoption, family justice, SEND, childcare, welfare of children, children's commissioner

2016 Academy expansion

Ruskin College speech 1976

Education Act 1980

Education Act 1981

Education (No. 2) Act 1986

Education Reform Act 1988

School Teachers' Pay and Conditions Act 1991

Education (Schools) Act 1992

Education Act 1993

School Standards and Framework Act 1998

Education Act 2002

Children Act 2004

Education Act 2005

Education and Inspections Act 2006

Education and Skills Act 2008

Apprenticeships, Skills, Children and Learning Act 2009

Children, Schools and Families Act 2010

Academies Act 2010

Education Act 2011

Education Act 2013

Children and Families Act 2014

Education and Adoption Act 2016

◆ School governing body   ● Government   ▢ Local authority

Adapted with permission from: C. Waterman, Local Government and Local Governance: 1944–2011, *Local Government Studies*, 40(6) (2014): 938–953 at 942. DOI: 10.1080/03003930.2012.719101

Values, aims and purposes
– a national task

Having criticised both the increase and exercise of powers at a national level, it may seem perverse that we should argue for much clearer exposition of values, aims and purpose by ministers at the centre – suitably advised, of course, by a Schooling Framework Commission. We do so, however, because we think that the professionals involved in schooling, especially teachers, will respond to being part of a great enterprise with a clearly articulated moral belief and purpose. In heavily urbanised and rural areas, what unites teachers and school leaders is a passion to change the world for the better through unlocking the talents of their pupils, and the ability to convey this with a clarity which their pupils recognise and which brooks no denial.

This is different from claiming a moral purpose based on rising exam or test results as the only indicator of success. Teachers want to help the children they teach to develop the tools they will need in order to manage their own lives, to help them take confident steps away from home and into the big wide world, to contribute fully to their community and to make the world a better place. Some consensus, debate and an evolving agreement about how this will be achieved would galvanise the profession and those who support it.

No agreed national statement of values, aims and purposes for schooling exists currently. The moral authority resides with the party in power (and too often with an individual prime minister or secretary of state) which tries to make as much headway as possible before an inescapable loss of power and a new government with a new set of values is installed, leading to an inevitable change of direction. Whether this deficiency can be addressed at a UK level is doubtful. Substantial change happened in 1997/1998 when Wales, Scotland and Northern Ireland were afforded full devolution to pursue their own distinctively different educational paths. As we noted above, they still get a share of UK government money, but they also have tax-raising powers of their own and have begun to establish very different schooling systems.

It seems odd, therefore, that – even at a very general level – there is no UK-wide agreement on aims for the schooling system of the sort we explored in Chapter 1. How committed can we be to keeping a United

Kingdom if we cannot even agree among the four nations what we want of our future citizens?[8] Even if some of the statements of purpose that unite us cannot be agreed at a UK level, it should be possible to do so in each nation so that all schools have a similar agenda.

In England, the aims of the national curriculum, as laid down in the School Standards and Framework Act 1998, stipulated that:

> Every state-funded school must offer a curriculum which is balanced and broadly based and which:
>
> - promotes the spiritual, moral, cultural, mental and physical development of pupils at the school and of society and
>
> - prepares pupils at the school for the opportunities, responsibilities and experiences of later life.[9]

In 2013, Michael Gove, in introducing the aims of the revised national curriculum, declared: 'The national curriculum provides pupils with an introduction to the essential knowledge they need to be educated citizens. It introduces pupils to the best that has been thought and said and helps engender an appreciation of human creativity and achievement.'[10]

Each of these declarations contains fewer than 50 words. It could be fairly argued that our schools operate within a vacuum so far as clarity on aims, values and attitudes are concerned. This vacuum does not apply to faith schools, either within or outside the state-funded system. These schools are clear on their values, which derive from religious beliefs and

---

8   When Whitehall attempted a description of 'British values' in 2011, it was in connection with the Prevent strategy, which itself was a response to fears of terrorism. It was updated in 2014 in the following statement by Lord Nash: 'A key part of our plan for education is to ensure that children become valuable and fully rounded members of society who treat others with respect and tolerance regardless of background. We want every school to promote the basic British values of democracy, the rule of law, individual liberty and mutual respect and tolerance for those of different faiths and beliefs. This ensures young people understand the importance of respect and leave school fully prepared for life in modern Britain' (Department for Education and Lord Nash, Guidance on Promoting British Values in Schools Published [press release] (27 November 2014). Available at: https://www.gov.uk/government/news/guidance-on-promoting-british-values-in-schools-published). This announcement, which was accompanied by examples of actions that schools could take, appears at first glance unexceptional, if incomplete. But its origins in Islamophobia are easy to divine and its imprecise thinking about Britain – as opposed to the UK or its four constituent nations – is evident to any thoughtful reader.

9   Department for Education, *The National Curriculum in England: Key Stages 1 and 2 Framework Document* (September 2013), p. 5. Available at: https://assets.publishing.service.gov.uk/government/uploads/system/uploads/attachment_data/file/425601/PRIMARY_national_curriculum.pdf.

10   Department for Education, National Curriculum in England: Framework for Key Stages 1 to 4. Statutory Guidance (updated 2 December 2014). Available at: https://www.gov.uk/government/publications/national-curriculum-in-england-framework-for-key-stages-1-to-4/the-national-curriculum-in-england-framework-for-key-stages-1-to-4.

contribute to youngsters' future behaviour as responsible citizens. Other state-funded schools, however, are operating within disputed territory so far as principles, attitudes and behaviour are concerned, as we saw all too clearly in 2019 when fundamentalist protests about national policy on relationships education occurred outside two Birmingham primary schools.[11]

Connected to this is an absence of any national descriptive elaboration of what or who our children are expected to become as adults. How young people turn out as citizens when they have left school is of concern of most teachers, yet such outcomes are not part of our school accountability system. Schools within the independent sector are more forthcoming. Haileybury in Hertfordshire, for example, was founded by the East India Company and for most of its first 100 years saw its explicit purpose as producing school leavers who would go on to serve the British Empire. All such schools for the privileged few, who are tacitly – sometimes overtly – expected to become the leaders of society, have value-laden school mottos. In contrast, schools funded by the state tend to have mission statements, which are analogous to the slogans found in the business and commercial world.

We are not arguing that all schools should adopt the mottos and other trappings of the private school sector, nor that state schools should lose their identity. We believe that all state schools should mirror the best and 'live the logo'. For too many, such matters run parallel (or at times counter) to the issues of inclusion, admissions, pupil discipline and learning. Many schools produce policies that contradict the sign at the entrance or the images and values in their prospectus. Pupils are often the first to spot the double standards.

We have offered a statement of guiding principles in Chapter 1, but it is for national politicians to agree on a cross-party basis what the underpinning values, aims and purpose of schools should be – advised by our Schooling Framework Commission. Once agreed, it should be binding on the private sector as well as state-funded schools. As part of their task (perhaps the subject of another Great Debate?), we hope they will be able to agree on a list of goals and aims which will make more explicit

---

11 Anderton Park Primary and Parkfield Primary attracted local protests from fundamentalist religious groups, which objected to them following relationships and sex education provisions which Justine Greening saw, rightly in our view, as a long overdue updating of what governments could expect of schools.

what we mean by equity, equality of opportunity and social mobility – terms which can all too readily conceal significantly different meanings.

School-level governance

It is logical, if we follow the principle of subsidiarity, that what cannot be either devolved or delegated to schools might need to occupy a level between central government and schools. This means that first of all we need to determine what is best for each school or group of schools to decide. There is recent general agreement, which supports the subsidiarity argument and is shared by professionals and politicians alike, that a 'self-improving school system' – through school partnerships and collaboration – is the best way to achieve school improvement (see Chapter 7). This has emanated from the influence of OECD and central government, which some believe is a sleight of hand and a distraction from the reality of a more centrally controlled school system.

Governing bodies, from their inception, were variable in the contribution they made to their individual schools. This was in part because not enough thought had been given to how they would operate, so many governors picked up practices from previous arrangements, whereby councillors and other local worthies would meet with the head teacher each term to hear about the school's woes (which usually related to building deficiencies) and pupils' successes. Local authorities were charged with supporting the development of governing bodies and were funded to set up a governor service team. Many began by reassuring head teachers, nervous of what the unions had called a 'busybody's charter', and helping them to work out how to handle governors' meetings. However, the variability that the reform was intended to address continued unchanged. Some head teachers were open and welcomed input from fresh eyes, while others suspiciously feared unwelcome interference.

Those who put themselves forward to act as governors (or were coerced into it) saw their role differently. A governing body was, and still is, comprised in varying proportions of 'sleeping partners' (just let me know when it's time to vote and I'll agree with the majority), 'uncritical lovers' (our school is wonderful and I will defend it against all comers), 'hostile witnesses' (I don't agree with what is happening) and 'critical friends' (let's have a measured debate and select the right course). Obviously, the last of these stereotypes is the most valuable, but the others can make a useful contribution too (apart from the first). What matters is finding the right balance.

For several years, governing bodies were expected to be critical friends, representing their community and supporting the head teacher. At times it was too cosy, sometimes a clique, sometimes pedestrian, sometimes decisive. Many governors simply tried to help, either with time or if they had a business, by providing some of their products at cost or free of charge for school use. Kenneth Baker's 1988 reforms lifted expectations: curriculum and assessment were now being defined and schools were assuming responsibility for premises, budget and staffing. Many governors, especially parents, recognised the direction of travel and, fearful of the responsibility, bailed out, often leaving schools without a full complement of governors.

We have outlined as a positive example of change management the 1986 reforms to school governance that were first advocated by the Taylor Report and Shirley Williams a decade earlier, prior to schools taking on extra responsibilities for the majority of their budgets. Not only were governors a representative body, with staff and parents elected in a democratic way, but LEAs had a non-dominant presence and organised continuing programmes of governor training and induction.[12] Although this model has persisted for the minority of secondary and the majority of primary schools, which remain in the orbit of their local authority as a community school, it has not been applied to the new state independent school status, embodied in city technology colleges, grant-maintained schools, free schools, UTCs, studio schools and academies. Their governing bodies consist of sponsors and self-selected trustees, often with no democratically elected staff or parents and no connection with the local community.

Since 2010, the academy movement, originally intended to give a fresh start to schools or communities with a long history of educational disadvantage, has gathered pace to become a desirable ambition for all schools. Ever since Baker's city technology colleges and grant-maintained initiatives, the idea of the autonomous school – self-standing and unshackled

---

12   Among the requirements was that when a new head teacher was appointed, the process should involve a final decision made by a joint panel of three governors and three councillors from the local authority. In both our experiences, this was the best period for appointing head teachers who proved suitable. When it went wrong, it was usually because the governors had outvoted the councillors who, because they did the task so often, had very good judgement.

from local authorities – has been a driving force for the educational policies of successive governments. As we explain in Chapter 4, since Michael Gove's appointment as secretary of state in 2010 it has accelerated at such a rate that the system has fragmented and lost coherence.

Two generic types of governance now exist at the school level, both driven by the need for school autonomy: academies and local authority maintained schools. They have many common features but also some important differences. The government is perplexed about what to do next; Gavin Williamson suggested a 'try before you buy scheme' to encourage the more tentative. Without an incentive, the trickle of schools becoming academies is unlikely to become a flow when some schools have managed for 10 years without seeing the need to convert. There is an occasional spurt in the rate of conversion when local authority schools sense they are going to be pushed. One primary head teacher told us: 'We are forming a MAT with a local primary school and have big hopes for the future, but the main reason we are doing it is to avoid the risk of being swallowed by one of the predatory large MATs that are hunting in our area.'

After all this time, there is still variability. But what else should we expect with so many governors involved? Although local governing boards and trust boards are typically far more professional than they were in the past, they continue to display the same shortcomings of previous years (as outlined earlier). Emma Knights from the National Governance Association (NGA) was clear that quality matters more than structures: 'It is absolutely not true, despite what some folks say, that MAT governance is always better than maintained school governance. We see good governance in both sectors and bad governance in both sectors.'

Similarly, those involved in MAT governance build loyalty and protect their organisation against perceived external foes, from Ofsted inspectors and RSCs to the DfE. Many head teachers and CEOs even treat their own governors and trustees defensively and their reports and presentations to governing boards often fall short of being fully transparent. It is probably little different in most enterprises.

Tim and Mick both recall:

We both serve on governing bodies and as trustees or members of MATs. We manage our commitment carefully to avoid conflicts of interest, deal with our workloads so that we do it properly and generally commit to just three years of service in any setting to avoid outstaying our welcome.

We often reflect on how different the boards on which we serve are, and with all our experience of the school system, we still find it difficult occasionally to pierce the cling-film surrounding the issues in a meeting about a school or academy. We do the shadow-boxing and we tentatively break the skin on the custard of debate, but often we know that there is a deeper agenda that we will follow up later.

We frequently wonder how governors with no experience of the school system, beyond that as a pupil or parent, cope. Perhaps their comparative innocence is an advantage and benefit. And then we reflect that it was for those fresh eyes that governing bodies were proposed in the first place.

Our witnesses painted a vivid picture, both in favour of and against different models of governance. The Elevate Trust in North Yorkshire is built on collaborative enterprise among seven primary schools. Rebecca Maiden, one of the heads of school, told us: 'I think the value of collaboration with other colleagues and the professional discussion around pedagogy, the curriculum and assessment – and what that brings in terms of skill and depth and listening to other people – can grow your influence. It also brings consistencies and the autonomy to be able to discuss it with other people as well as build a collective view.'

What united our witnesses, whether they were in a MAT or a local authority school, was a common wish to work collaboratively, which we think is one of the strengths that has emerged in recent years, and which in our last chapter forms an essential and permanent feature of the future of English schooling.

The uncomfortable relationship between the original (local authority community schools) and the new (academies, free schools, UTCs) system is complex and costly. Nicky Morgan observed: 'We were heading towards compulsory academisation. If we want a full academy system to work, you have to take the local authorities out of the picture. They would have some roles, such as safeguarding, ensuring every child has a school place, looked-after children and so on, but a parallel system is very uneconomic. It must be costing a fortune, running two systems in parallel.'

With the expansion in the number and size of MATs and the need to deal with schools that are failing, the two main types of school governance have evolved into four distinctly different models for the individual school:

1   Governing bodies within community (local authority) schools that follow the requirements of the various Acts of Parliament, starting with the 1981 and 1986 Acts, and are based on the Taylor Report in 1977 which enshrined the autonomy of the school.

2   Interim executive boards (IEBs), which were introduced in 2001 and consist of a small group of experienced experts who are imposed on a failing school for a set period by the LEA to bring about improvements.[13]

3   Governing bodies which are by law transformed into academy trusts (charities and companies limited by guarantee). They may include parent and staff representatives but not by right or election.

4   Trust boards, where the individual school has lost its legal identity and enjoys more or less autonomy at the discretion of the MAT. These individual academies often have their own governing/advisory committee but the real power lies with the trust.

From our own experience,[14] we note that the DfE and RSCs are impressed by those MATs that insist on common practices in their schools. Some MATs brush aside the awkward question, 'But doesn't that threaten school autonomy?' even though it is presumably a question that has deterred many schools from taking the step and has led to some MATs, which are less well-regarded by DfE, talking of leaving things to individual schools to decide.

---

13   The creation of forced academisation has led to the dropping of what was a highly effective means of transforming a school's performance.

14   Mick accompanied a University of Wolverhampton delegation, which had established a very non-interventionist arm's length MAT, to the DfE only to be met with advice that breached the ideal of the autonomous school.

As David Bell, who has experience as HMCI and running an LEA, remarked: 'Some of them [MATs] behave in a way which even the most controlling LEA would have hesitated to contemplate.' MATs vary in quality and their willingness to delegate. The most directive include Harris Federation[15] and Outwood Grange Academies Trust.[16] There is another group of MATs represented by Ark, United Learning, Oasis, Reach and AET, which are far from hands-off but allow schools more room to do their own thing. More than one MAT in this group talks of constituent academies having 'earned autonomy', which conveys the idea that they recognise different levels of delegation and that an individual school's position will vary according to function and performance. At the other extreme from Harris and Outwood is yet another type among the approximately 2,000 MATs. In these, the parent trust exercises very little influence over its autonomous schools.

Julia Cleverdon was scathing about MATs that impose centralised practices and have an outlook that implies: 'We are the trust that knows. We are the champions. We command and control. This is what you'll do, whether you're in Hastings or Doncaster – when, actually, Hastings and Doncaster are very different places, very different landscapes and have very different histories, very different people, very different aspirations and need a very different recipe. I mean, the basics maybe, but different recipes for each academy, surely.'

Emma Knights discussed the issue of the size of MATs: 'One of the things we argued in our NGA publication *Moving MATs Forward*, in summer of 2019, was that MATs are operating and being governed within frameworks and language rooted in a system designed for single schools.[17] The system is confused as to whether schools still are and should be the key unit in the sector. There are other questions that – as a system – we've never looked at; one of them is size. We've never looked at how big we should let these trusts go. At NGA we're not convinced yet by huge MATs.'

---

15 We interviewed Dan Moynihan, CEO of Harris Federation, and he disputes this categorisation of Harris academies. He explained that collective decisions, such as a recent revision to the curriculum approach, involved all schools and that one school initially decided to 'do their own thing' before changing their mind to adopt an approach agreed across the whole group.

16 Until recently, Outwood Grange, for example, had 30 pages of behaviour guidance for all teachers in every one of its secondary schools.

17 T. Fellows, S. Henson and E. Knights, *Moving MATs Forward: The Power of Governance* (London: National Governance Association, 2019). Available at: https://www.nga.org.uk/getmedia/88e9fcaa-0b91-4639-bba8-61847f77b7c1/MATs-40pp-Report-June-2019-(WEB)-AW-(1)-FINAL-27-06-2019.pdf.

She continued: 'When Lord Agnew said, seemingly off the top of his head, that he didn't think MATs should grow bigger than the number of head teachers you could get around a table and have a sensible discussion, around 15 or 16 heads, I thought, there is some sense in that. It is about human scale as opposed to a giant bureaucracy that is difficult to engage with and truly understand.'

MATs come under increasing pressure from RSCs to be more directive if individual schools in their trust cause concern. Free schools, many of which are independent and, by their nature, start-ups, have their own governance arrangements which mirror those of the MATs, but some free schools are 'stand-alone' and report directly to central government.

Maybe those critical of school autonomy are right and that trying to find competent and inspiring leaders and governors for around 22,000 primary schools and 3,000 secondary schools *is* an impossible task, and that having a system of 25,000 autonomous schools, with the many regulatory duties now imposed on them, is not a sound way of securing equity for all children.

When introducing Michael Barber to speak at head teacher conferences about the national literacy and numeracy strategies, Estelle Morris used to talk about the challenge facing the DfE of managing 20,000-odd outlets. She acknowledged the important role played by LEAs in this process – for example, the government used the national strategies, through literacy and numeracy advisers who reported both to LEAs and the DfE, as the more directly controlled but also more supportive element of Labour's drive for 'education, education, education'.

Some leaders of the teacher unions also pointed out the high turnover of heads in some schools in challenging areas. Steve Munby thought that the supply of school leaders, especially since the demise of the NCSL, might not be enough to guarantee leaders of sufficient quality to lead so many schools successfully: 'The supply of school leaders is a role for the state and we can't just rely on individual schools or on the market to do it.' Emma Knights agreed that it remains difficult to keep up a supply of 250,000 volunteers, all of whom are suitable to carry out the formidable governance duties and responsibilities now required of an autonomous school of trusts, which were not remotely imagined in the 1980s when the model of school governance was created.

Former director general for schools at the DfE Peter Housden reminded us that, for many, the process of becoming a school governor has been the first step in becoming a more active citizen and contributing in numerous ways, either through local government or the third (voluntary) sector, to the health and well-being of our society. There is a strong case to be made for the civic purpose of becoming a school governor. However, it is our experience,[18] from a purely educational standpoint, that very rarely has a school governing body made a significant contribution to school improvement, and some, sadly, have done the reverse. There is a regrettable lack of research on this issue.[19] We certainly think that some form of oversight by a board that is representative of the parents, local community and staff (and, arguably, pupils as they become more mature) at the level of each school is necessary, but that it will vary according to the different forms of partnership which schools now see as essential. Aspects such as the professional development of staff, peer review, sharing scarce skilled human resources (e.g. music teachers, educational psychologists), making provision for distressed children and sharing back office and premises-related services should all benefit from being shared among a group of cooperating schools. The remit of the oversight board of the individual school needs to be well defined, and in the case of groups of schools that have formed a hard federation or MAT, in effect, it will be a subcommittee of the overarching entity. Nonetheless, it could still act as Housden's incubator for volunteers to play a larger part in our society.

At the level of the individual school or academy, governance is increasingly complex, with local governing boards less clear about their remit and role than previously. However, Emma Knights was relatively unperturbed and told us:

> At the NGA, we are fairly relaxed about the school sector being messy. I think that's partly because it has been for a very long time. England has never been absolutely identical everywhere, so we're not one of these organisations that says it all has to be terribly neat and tidy and we've all got to be exactly the same, reporting in

---

18 Lest people dismiss our assertions as simply anecdote based on a few schools: since 1986, we have been responsible between us for close observation of over 3,000 schools in Oxfordshire, Manchester, Birmingham, the Black Country and London, and, of course, we have visited hundreds more in the course of our work in many other parts of the country.

19 S. Ranson, M. Arnott, P. McKeown, J. Martin and P. Smith, The Participation of Volunteer Citizens in School Governance, *Educational Review* 57(3) (2006): 357–371 argues for stronger representation by parents and others, but we could find no study which showed governors to be key to school improvement, except in the case of IEBs installed for a fixed period exactly for that purpose.

exactly the same scenario. I might be proved wrong in five years' time! Because, despite the fact NGA is a governance organisation, we're much more at the end of the spectrum that what makes the difference is good people. You can spend masses of time tinkering around with structure, and it's quite energy sapping and draining, and you spend a lot of time reorganising, which just feels like another distraction. The art is to be able to judge when structures are an impediment to success and absolutely need to change, why and to what end.

In short, the present system of school governance is muddled. While that has always been the case to some extent, in the past it was underpinned by some common principles, especially autonomy. That is no longer the situation.

Next, we will explore the middle tier of governance in the schooling system.

Middle-tier governance

Do we need a middle tier, and if so, how should it be formed and what should it do? Some of the roles and functions that cannot be devolved or delegated, either for reasons of equity or practical management, directly to the individual school (either in whole or in part) include the following:

1   The policies and practice of admission of pupils to schools (see Chapter 8).

2   The planning of school places in the light of housing developments and changes in local birth rates.

3   The provision of necessary school transport for pupils.

4   The planning and provision of services for and placement of pupils with SEND (see Chapter 9).

5   Accountability for the contribution schools make to creating and sustaining a healthy local community.

6   Support to schools for school improvement (see Chapter 7).[20]

---

20   H. Brighouse, M. Levinson and T. Geron, Conceptions of Equity, unpublished paper for Harvard Business School. It is available from the philosophy department at University of Wisconsin–Madison.

In short, services that are focused on the needs of families and children, as opposed to the efficient and effective provision of education, need to be responsibly managed to ensure that the rights of individuals are balanced with equity of provision.

Until the vexed question of devolution is grasped within England, the first five of these functions are the responsibility of existing local authorities. The impractical alternative is for central government to determine every aspect of schooling at the local level for every village, town and city, based on data, evidence or lobbying, and deal with every anomaly as well as every problem or crisis at a local and national scale.

The sixth point in the list, school improvement, is a major concern for local democracy. As a result, the provision of services to secure school improvement has led to all sorts of different models across the country. Arm's length bodies, commissioned by local authorities and offering a range of services that schools choose for themselves, mingle in a marketplace alongside private (for-profit and not-for-profit) providers.

Throughout this book, we have given various examples of programmes designed to improve schooling prospects for pupils which were imposed on local authorities by central government. One such instance occurred in 1991: a decade after riots in Brixton, St Paul's and Toxteth, riots occurred again in estates around England – this time in Meadow Well in North Tyneside and in Dudley.[21] The subsequent urban renewal programmes in these areas sought to improve the environment of schools and establish community hubs that would act as multi-agency centres. In these examples, school improvement comes – if it comes at all – through other government departments, often managed by specially formed social enterprise companies that work through local authorities.

Since 1997, central government has been more direct about the impetus to improve schools. The self-improving school system promoted by the DfE has invariably involved a bidding process. First, there were beacon schools, then research schools, teaching schools, maths hubs, literacy hubs, music hubs and behaviour hubs, and more recently teaching school hubs, which were all intended to do outreach work and lead school-based ITT and CPD activity. These hubs have been promoted as schools themselves leading the improvements in the system. Whether all

---

21 Riots seem to be a feature of years ending in the number 1 while Tory governments are in office. They happen at other times too.

of the best schools or the best improvers have been involved is debatable because the eligibility criteria exclude so many. Other potential improver schools prefer not to bid at all because the ever-present threat of inspection makes them worry about the distractions involved in helping others. Some schools, of course, believe that their designations are an insurance when it comes to inspection.

The government, which as we have seen is not reticent about intervening in school matters that it considers to be important, is unusually unclear about who beyond the school is responsible for school improvement. Action on school leadership lay with the NCSL before it was closed by Michael Gove. Inevitably, its work was tied in with school improvement; indeed, the NCSL's input into the London Challenge was a powerful contributory factor in its success. After its closure in 2013, responsibility for improvement was transferred to the teaching schools initiative, presumably following the logic of promoting a self-improving school system. In 2021, this was followed by the teaching school hubs programme, although school improvement is not included in the remit for the 87 regionally distributed hubs.

Most of the school improvement efforts we have mentioned so far have been generic developments. They start with a national stimulus of some sort and are then infused into the school system. However, there has to be a focus on continuous improvement within each and every school, and it is this emphasis on the success of individual schools, particularly those that are deemed to be less than satisfactory, that has bedevilled the school system since the early 1990s. It was Gillian Shephard who instigated some pilot school improvement programmes specifically targeted at those schools performing most poorly in the then emerging league tables. By identifying the poorest local authority aggregates, funding was provided to target appropriate training to improve teaching in the worst-performing schools. The programmes were devised and managed by local authorities, typically using the outsourced provision that was now becoming available as a result of the Baker day requirement, which brought new in-service providers on to the scene.

Stephen Cox, who set up Osiris Education in 1996, told us: 'The world of CPD was opening up and we took a few tentative steps. At the time, the big organisations, such as Tribal, were bidding for everything and we basically tested the water starting with our background in PSHE. It was clear that people wanted high-quality experiences in CPD so we gradually met the market coming towards us.'

Increasingly, over the last 20 years, there has been a greater focus on the weakest schools and the challenge of improving them. Central government has intervened, Ofsted has tried, local authorities have pressed constantly and MATs have had a go, all of which has led to some success and some frustration, as well as the experience of being blindsided by another school unexpectedly deteriorating. Schools are living organisms and things sometimes go wrong. The Challenge programmes in London, Greater Manchester and the Black Country secured sustainable successful recovery for many schools by providing improvement support and encouraging collaboration.[22] For all the monitoring procedures and managerial processes, spotting the early warning signs remains an art.

Tim and Mick recall:

We spent an inordinate amount of time on struggling schools in Birmingham, some of which had been desperate for years. There were two secondary schools next to each other, separated by a chicken wire fence, both failing. One was the former grammar school and one the former secondary modern, and the negative rivalry of the early 1950s when they were both built lived on. We brought them together as one school under one head teacher and constructed a new Year 7 unit to try and keep the new intake sanitised while we sorted out the rest.

The new school was too big, but the status quo was awful so we had to do something. We stacked it out with experienced teachers under good leadership and it stabilised gradually. Eventually, children began to arrive from primary schools with better literacy and numeracy as a result of the national strategies and employers began to help us give purpose to the older pupils. We would have been much better with smaller schools; we had considered an upper and lower school model on the campus but the logistics kept defeating us.

---

22 With the evident success of the London Challenge, the Labour government set up similar enterprises in Greater Manchester and the Black Country. These were to be followed by Challenges in Tyneside and other conurbations, with each Challenge learning the lessons from the experience of others. The closure of the programmes began with the arrival of Michael Gove and austerity measures.

Some schools are just hard to improve, some are hard to stop disintegrating and some seem to recover without us being able to put our finger on the moment it changed. Schools are living organisms. That is one of the reasons why leadership has to be agile and adept. While a formula can work, leadership usually has to adapt it.

Just as shops, service stations and pubs suffer poor fortune, so too do schools. The difficulty is that the pupils don't all have the option to take their learning elsewhere. Some communities have been blighted by inadequate schooling for decades, despite the best efforts of many. There are examples of spectacular success and terrible failures. There are also examples of schools that were previously flying high that have come crashing down to earth because either the turnaround was too dependent on the leader who then moved on, or the outside-school support structures were too weak, or the way the schools were held accountable and assessed changed, or some combination of all three. While we think that MAT development is the way forward for school improvement, we need to be careful. There are instances of schools that have blossomed within a MAT, while others have imploded in the same MAT. Matching the right schools to the right MATs might be the skill that denotes the best RSCs.

We think there needs to be some authority locally figuring out how to orchestrate support for the schools in its area that need support but are either in denial or don't know where to access the precise help they need. Sometimes the MAT and/or the local authority won't know either, even though they are responsible for the schools. We are therefore attracted to the proposal in Susan Cousin and Jonathan Crossley-Holland's *Developing a New Locality Model for English Schools* which suggests:

> Unify[ing] the governance of the system by bringing together LA and RSC responsibilities for school improvement into a single locality governance structure. The DfE should support each locality to establish a School Partnership Board (sub-regional or local, depending on the area). The Board to be responsible and accountable jointly to the LA and RSC and be held to account for performance. The locality could be based on AEPs [area-based education partnerships], Combined Authorities, LAs or

Opportunity Areas but need to include all types of schools in the area.[23]

As we explain in Chapter 7, improving schools is properly the concern of many players. As we have also explained, national government has shown interest but less coherently and consistently than the situation demands. Various of its own officers and agencies have from time to time been less reticent. At one point, Ofsted showed enormous interest; indeed, in our interview with Michael Wilshaw, he told us of one of his disappointments in his role as HMCI:

> When I resumed the inspections of local authorities, Michael Gove told me to stop doing that. It's one of those conversations which isn't well known. One of the arguments I had with him was that he wanted me to stop inspecting local authorities. I said, 'Well, I'm not going to because 90% of primary schools are still run by local authorities [they were at that time]. My job is to make sure that they're high quality.' He said, 'Well, all you're doing is giving them support and succour and putting fat into the arteries of a dead institution (a phrase that he would like to use).' He wanted me to stop inspecting local authorities because he didn't like them. He thought they should wither on the vine, which is actually what happened, of course, but at that time I refused to do it.

If the local authority used to be the middle tier, the situation is now much more complicated and varies in different parts of the country. Therefore, there is no uniform picture for schools. In effect, either one or two (or more) bodies exist between the individual school and the DfE:

- For the community school, it is the local authority and through them the DfE.

- For the stand-alone academy, it is the local authority for some purposes and the RSC as the local manifestation of the DfE for other purposes, and the DfE itself for yet others.

---

23 S. Cousin and J. Crossley-Holland, *Developing a New Locality Model for English Schools: Summary Report* (Sheffield: British Educational Leadership, Management and Administration Society, March 2021), p. 9. Available at: http://www.belmas.org.uk/write/MediaUploads/Locality_Model_Summary_Report_PROOF_6-1.pdf.

- For faith schools and academies, there is the further influence of the church, mosque, temple or synagogue, according to the faith of the school's sponsor.

- For the academy within a MAT, there is an added layer of control in the form of the trust board.

Unlike local authorities and schools, MATs are not inspected by Ofsted. It could be argued that it is too early for them to be inspected since they have been in existence for such a short length of time. However, given that some academies have now existed for over 20 years and some trusts for 10 years, and that schools within some of these trusts have not been inspected at all during that time, a systematic process of inspection is now important. Currently, individual schools are inspected, with attention drawn to the MAT if too many are causing concern. Ofsted does visit schools across MATs but it does not inspect processes or procedures applied by the MAT in respect of finances or human resources – indeed, all the functions formerly exercised by the local authority. One suspects that Gove would not have wanted to inspect MATs for different reasons than the 'withering on the vine' explanation he gave to Wilshaw for not inspecting LEAs.

David Carter believes that the corruption and excesses that have been regularly exposed over the years by *Schools Week* have now been almost completely eliminated,[24] and that rigorous checks are in place to deter RSCs from brokering stand-alone academies to MATs with a dubious record. His view is that the future pattern of schools should involve a network of around 1,200 MATs or voluntary partnerships, with around 20 schools in each MAT, and that such partnerships would operate to agreed national rules. He agreed with our suggestion that to make the democratic link explicit, the model could involve each MAT having one or two local authority trustees and the local authority could be one of the sponsors. Each constituent school would have a local schools board/council which would report to the MAT on the reality and quality of pupil, parent and staff experiences, as explained above.

---

24 Other witnesses, especially leaders of the teaching unions, are less convinced than David Carter that the ideal of what he calls 'ethical leadership' has been sufficiently realised. As we write, *Schools Week* has revealed another MAT scandal concerning the extent to which trusts take away large sums to cover central staffing costs before distributing shares of the general annual grant received from ESFA to individual schools. The reality is that scarcely a week goes by without some MAT appearing in news reports for all the wrong reasons: J. Carr, Safeguarding Failure Exposed at Trust That 'Cut Cash', *Schools Week*, 24 (12 February 2021): 9. Available at: https://schoolsweek.co.uk/wp-content/uploads/2021/02/SW-240-digi.pdf.

Emma Knights pursued a similar theme in terms of a local element of governance:

> That's why our members volunteer; that's one of their motivations. They care about their community and they care about their local schools. So, for us at NGA, 'place' is really important and, in a way, the governing boards are the guardians of that school in that place. Heads move on and teachers move on, but the board as an entity stays, continuing to safeguard the school. We think that context is really important, and if you have a MAT that straddles two counties or even straddles two or more regions of the country, you might lose that connection. The people with the power at the top, whether they're executive or non-executive, lose that connection with the place; can they and do they listen to each community and each set of governors and understand their place?

Other sorts of partnership

The middle-tier picture is further complicated by three other sorts of partnerships to which individual schools (whether in MATs or not) belong.

The first occurs when schools in an area, often including academies discharging local obligations, form themselves into tight or loose partnerships for all sorts of purposes, including better meeting the needs of the most vulnerable pupils and their families and sharing the commissioning of scarce resources, such as psychologist services or careers advice. These tend to be locally based and serve a definable set of related communities, with participating professionals in the area very conscious of their obligations towards the people living in their market town, rural community or similar set of connected populations within a large city. Such partnerships are usually critical friends to the local authority and other public agencies and strive – not always successfully – to meet the needs of the families in that area.

The other sort of partnership, referred to earlier, occurs when the local authority, conscious of the squeeze on their resources and encouraged to outsource the provision of services, acts as a 'commissioner'. Some local authorities faced with this dilemma, but anxious to retain a local democratic umbilical link to the provider, form an arm's length body – usually a not-for-profit company limited by guarantee or a voluntary sector charity. Examples include Brent Schools Partnership, Worcestershire Children First and Herts for Learning.

These organisations, now collaborating formally within a national network, are led largely by the schools themselves, which determine what their provision needs to be. The leader of one of these organisations told us: 'It's a very messy landscape but a very busy playing field with so many different collaborations. You've got your maths hubs, other hubs, teaching schools, lots of things that came out of the old Education Action Zones. Then you've got schools in various organisations, like PiXL, SSAT [Schools, Students and Teachers Network] and what have you, and that's what makes them a collective. We talk about ourselves as being a kind of glue that brings it all together.'

The third type of partnership is a hybrid model of the first two, often with a more overt remit to enhance outcomes through school improvement. There are around 60 partnerships of the second and third models and thousands of the first, usually serviced through DCS staff in local authorities.[25]

In trying to determine what needs to happen in the middle tier, one more complication at the national level needs to be acknowledged. Most ministerial witnesses testified to mistrust of local government, or at least to a level of frustration. More than one singled out Tony Blair as being overtly antipathetic to local government generally, while others pointed to local authorities' poor delivery of education and more recently children's services. This mistrust of existing structures by national politicians, traced by Peter Housden back to its roots in the 1940s, is one of the reasons why we favour full-blown devolution to a reformed local/regional government framework.

We assume this antipathy is fuelled by two factors. First, even among the generation of politicians who have shaped the age of markets, centralisation and managerialism, Gillian Shephard was one of the few who thought that local authorities were and should be a vital cog in the system. She was also one of many who thought the DfE was not used to running anything effectively and showed little appetite for doing so. There had clearly been one exceptional period to this management deficit in the DfE, which

---

25 C. Gilbert, *Optimism of the Will: The Development of Local Area-Based Education Partnerships. A Think-Piece* (London: Centre for Leadership in Learning, 2017). Available at: http://www.lcll.org.uk/uploads/2/1/4/7/21470046/christine_gilbert_-_thinkpiece.pdf.

coincided with the years when David Blunkett and his successors were secretaries of state: 'I was lucky in having Michael Bichard as permanent secretary, and we set up the Standards and Effectiveness Unit under Michael Barber so we could get things done.' Another witness, Mike Tomlinson, cited the London Challenge as one of 'the examples of DfE managing something successfully'. But running the London Challenge or overseeing the literacy and numeracy hours (and then the national strategies) through advisers based in local authorities is much less daunting than intervening when things go wrong on a daily basis in schools or MATs, particularly alongside the whole machinery of routine management.

The resulting confusion, repetitions, omissions and fragmentation are costly. The running costs of MATs are high compared with local authorities prior to their establishment. Similarly, the running costs of a collective of schools under LFM vastly outstrip that of the local authority for the services they replaced.

One particular issue arises from the creation of academies, free schools and MATs – namely, remuneration. The salaries paid to senior staff are hard to justify if we are committed to reducing inequality. Part of social mobility must involve some sort of agreement about salaries for different occupations, not according to a market that is largely unregulated but to the outcome of a long overdue review of public sector jobs. The 2011 Hutton Review into fair pay recommended that no FTSE chief executive should get more than 20 times the salary of the lowest-paid employee.[26] In a more equitable society, which surely public sector jobs should represent, a figure of six or seven times the average should be the limit for the head of an organisation.

A CEO manager who is running, say, 70 schools and their support services, who is earning almost £500,000 per year (or another earning half that figure to run one school) is an affront to any pretence of a commitment to equality or equity.[27] Now, the highly paid would point to their success and increased operational responsibility, but with that often comes delegated staff who are also paid significant sums. The cost of teaching

---

26 W. Hutton, *Hutton Review of Fair Pay in the Public Sector: Final Report* (London: HM Treasury, 2011), p. 10. Available at: https://dera.ioe.ac.uk/2562/1/hutton_fairpay_review.pdf.

27 These salaries have been reported for MAT CEOs and the head teacher of Holland Park School in Kensington, respectively, in: T. Belger, The Emerging 'Super League' of Best-Paid CEOs, *Schools Week*, 247 (23 April 2021): 13–16. Available at: https://schoolsweek.co.uk/wp-content/uploads/2021/04/SW-247-digi.pdf; and J. Roberts, Headteacher Responsible for One School is Paid £280k, *TES* (23 December 2020). Available at: https://www.tes.com/news/headteacher-responsible-one-school-paid-ps280k.

staff employed not to teach, but to oversee the teaching of others, is disproportionate in most individual schools and unjustifiable in terms of expertise not used for teaching and learning. But there have been other examples of a lack of financial propriety.

The issue of pay creates all manner of reactions within the profession – from envy and ridicule to embarrassment and indignation. Some would argue that the self-levelling of salaries, with the market dictating pay, was an example of a step into the commercial world – the outlook of the private sector. But this is public money and those taking advantage are enjoying private sector advantaged pay with public sector advantages in conditions, including final salary pensions.

There is a trust of primary schools in Nottinghamshire, built on a previous collaboration, which employs one of their former head teachers as a coordinator CEO who has his pay pegged at 60% of the average of the head teacher salaries. This meets the purposes of their democratic organisation. It would not work in an organisation where leadership and working practices operated on a line management or seniority-driven basis.

In a trust in Suffolk, the CEO was open about how their salary was determined: 'My salary is based on a number of factors that trustees go through to set it fairly, using a design tool based on the leadership pay spine as a basis. I refused pay rises and I think my pay is fair. It's more than I could have ever earned as a teacher. It's a big job and I know I'm paid less than most of the secondary heads locally. I think fixing pay scales in proportion to a teacher's salary is more transparent.'

The plethora of governance models creates anomalies in many facets of schooling, and the extent to which the system can or cannot tolerate them is a product of political belief or neglect. The teaching profession is being split philosophically by the market outlook.

With a prospective decline in the pupil population in different parts of the country, we will experience a repeat of the falling rolls period of the late 1970s and 1980s when planned contraction had to be undertaken locally. It could be argued that the existence of MATs will make this easier as individual schools have no legal being and no governing body to obstruct any closures. Equally, a MAT deciding that an academy is uneconomic and shutting up shop is a prospect that cannot be ignored; the consequences for communities can be sudden and devastating.

But MATs are expensive. The DfE expects them to levy at least 5% of each school's budget to pay for overheads, but some charge much more and some do it opaquely by manipulating the general annual grant received from the ESFA.[28] Even 5% represents about twice the amount of comparable overheads in a local authority, where in any case schools increasingly decide whether to 'buy back' services or purchase them elsewhere. Schools within a MAT have no such choice.

The NGA's 2021 Insights paper offers inconclusive analysis on the effectiveness of centralised services in MATs.[29] While leadership teams have emerged as powerful drivers for realising the benefits of trust-wide collaboration, this power and influence has contributed to tensions in respect of individual academy expression. In addition, governance in trusts is variable in terms of its impact on the way central leadership teams operate, further reducing the potential for collaboration. Effective governance at the middle tier and school level requires the resolution of an interwoven tangle of issues including governance itself, local finance, SEND services, admission arrangements, school improvement and democratic accountability.

Javed Khan, the former CEO of Barnardo's, expressed his sadness at the confused organisational structure which contributes to thousands of children having reduced life chances: 'My take on this government is that they're very much in the camp of allowing a thousand flowers to bloom and they don't care too much about the weeds that might grow too.' He used imagery very similar to that in Cousin and Crossley-Holland's report, which stresses the need for the development of a new locality model for schooling rather than depending on remote management from Whitehall.[30]

The key to finding a secure long-term answer to these issues is to know what stance will be taken on devolution in England. Until that is clear, we have suggested some short-term answers (for example, on admissions, SEND and school accountability) which assume there will be no change to our very centralised system but that local democratic accountability will remain essential. An emphasis on structures is less important than standards, but the existing structures are confusing, ill-thought through,

---

28 See, for example, Carr, Safeguarding Failure Exposed at Trust That 'Cut Cash'.
29 National Governance Association, *NGA Insights: Central Leadership Teams in Multi Academy Trusts* (July 2021). Available at: https://www.nga.org.uk/getmedia/1e0655f5-cbbd-44bc-b891-33bab441ee03/nga-central-leadership-20210701.pdf.
30 Cousin and Crossley-Holland, *Developing a New Locality Model for English Schools*.

expensive, inequitable and come to a variety of different answers on the question of autonomy for schools. Most importantly, they damage the prospects of the least advantaged children.

Since MATs now discharge some of the roles formerly carried out by both individual schools and the local authority, legislation is urgently needed to ensure that:

- Their proceedings are recorded and open to public scrutiny.

- There is a specified limit on top-slicing for central functions.

- The upper pay limit for CEO salaries is a nationally specified multiple of the average salary of all staff.

- Top-slicing for some high needs SEND children (matched by local authority contributions from the high needs element of the dedicated school grant) is used as part of a clear agreement to reduce exclusions and make each MAT inclusive in all its constituent academies. With annual progress reports.

- They are regularly inspected by Ofsted.

- They are accountable for their impact on the communities they serve through the scrutiny function of local authorities.

Finance: whoever pays the piper ...

Nationally, the state of the economy and the priority of the government – and especially the prime minister – affects the size of school budgets. The graph that follows, which we discussed with Andrew Adonis, illustrates how between 1997 and 2010 the Blair/Brown governments followed through on the 'education, education, education' slogan of 1997.

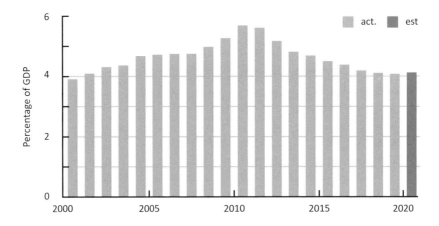

**Recent UK education spending as a percentage of GDP
from financial year 2000–2020**

All our ministerial witnesses mentioned finance, the 'spending round' and the Treasury. For example, Gillian Shephard's view was that the Chancellor of the Exchequer – ironically, at the time, one of her predecessors in education, Kenneth Clarke – had damaged the Major government's general election prospects for 1997 by refusing to boost schools' finances in the previous November's public spending review, especially against the backdrop of Blair's 'education, education, education' priority.

In the main, education ministers' views of the Treasury were less than warm, although the early Blair government ministers felt the prime minister's lead on education was crucial. As Andrew Adonis put it:

> Nothing speaks the language of priorities more than money in government. To those who say that the 'centre should keep out of education', they need to understand that resource decisions are *only* taken by the centre – the prime minister and the chancellor – so saying that the centre should 'keep out' simply means that education should be a lesser priority and have its funding cut or not increased much. Every week that I worked for Tony Blair, I gave him a detailed update on the state of the education scene to keep his interest and engagement in it as a key priority, and he used to write comments and agree to do all kinds of things – speeches to head teachers' conferences, interventions in budget disputes with the Treasury, the prioritisation of education concerns – in consequence. That hasn't happened with any other prime minister ever ...

A crucial part of this is that Tony's children all went to state schools. He had first-hand experience of what was going on, and he used to refer to it a lot. He was the first prime minister *ever* to send his own children to state secondary schools, and he influenced Cameron's decision to do the same for his daughter while he was PM – although his son was sent straight to Eton after he had left Number 10! Attlee, Wilson and Callaghan all sent their children to private schools.

The graph, which is of overall educational expenditure as a percentage of GDP (we are assuming that it also reflects schools spending in those years), shows that spending on schools has fallen back to pre-1997 levels, which Shephard had argued was so low that it contributed to the Major government's downfall. The precise picture is difficult to determine because one of the habits developed by governments in this second age has been to ignore inflation when describing spending plans for public services, which makes informed debate difficult. This was not too serious in the period from 2000 to 2010 because, as the graph shows, schools were being funded in real terms on a rising escalator, either through per pupil funding or through direct specific grants of which there were many. Funding has become a chronic and sometimes acute problem in the years of government austerity since 2010.

This became evident immediately, not merely through the cancellation of the Building Schools for the Future programme in 2010, but also through the little remarked clause in the Education Act 2011, which allowed schools for the first time to charge parents for optional 'extras'. Such a blatant move against the principle of equity was not made even in 1976, when resources were as short as they are now due to the post-oil price crisis squeeze on public expenditure and the problem was compounded by falling rolls due to a decline in the birth rate. A body called the expenditure steering group (education) (ESG(E)) was created, consisting of civil servants from the Treasury and DfE plus local government treasurers and chief education officers. Each year, they considered true costs (including annual estimates of inflation) so there was agreement about what was a cut or a real increase in spending.

Now, there is no longer an ESG(E) and since school budgets were nationalised in 2005/2006, there has been no local voice to raise issues about spending on schools, especially as it has coincided with directors of education being replaced by DCSs who have, in almost all cases, a social work rather than an education background. Whereas most directors of education have worked in schools earlier in their careers and therefore spent much time arguing about education budgets, DCSs have mostly had their work cut out solving the growing number of child abuse crises which have surfaced from time to time (and which have risen on every metric since 2010). This has proved difficult for schools during a period of austerity, as at both a national and local level there are no dogs to bark in the night about the diminishing level of school spending. Head teachers are conflicted because they are in a competitive market with neighbouring schools in seeking pupil per capita funding. If they publicise the damage that diminishing resources might do to their school, they risk losing pupils and therefore more funds.

The only groups that might and do raise the issue are the teacher unions. When they were asked by the DfE at a meeting in 2020 to estimate the extent of the funding gap, they spoke with different voices. As Geoff Barton said: 'When we were asked how much would cure the size of the accumulating problem, we all named widely varying figures.' He and the other teacher union representatives agreed that a standing group similar to ESG(E) needs to be set up involving the Treasury, DfE officials and representative experts from MATs, local authorities and teaching unions to protect schools from exaggerations – even 'fake news' – about the real funding position in schools. But as one teacher union leader put it, 'government will never agree to it' – resigned as it were to their inevitable impotence.

During our interview with Andrew Adonis, he was at pains to emphasise that since money comes predominantly from nationally set taxes, decision-making about the volume and priority of spending for schools should be national too, rather as it was in the days of the percentage grant prior to the introduction of the block grant in 1958. The other side of the argument is that there has only been one Blair/Brown administration, and that governments before and since have been content to place education lower down on the spending agenda.

How did we get to the existing arrangements for funding schools?

The history of spending on schools reveals how changes in national and local funding have influenced ministerial and civil service views of local government.

From the 1970s to 1990s, civil servants and ministers, as Nick Stuart confirmed, were prepared to lend support to the efforts by chief education officers and chairs to win arguments for the education cause, because the power to instigate change lay with the LEA rather than the ministry:

> Against sustained opposition from the Department of Local Government, we had tried and failed more than once to get approval for specific grants over the decade to 1986 when Keith Joseph secured legislation for education support grants to encourage innovation. It took another decade or more for school funding to be ring-fenced and direct grants to schools to become the norm. Historically, Conservative governments had always supported local decision-making, but by the 1980s they were increasingly dismayed by the wide disparities in local government performance. This growing distrust of local government was a central driver of educational reform.

But the worry for Stuart and his DfE colleagues was that too many LEA officers didn't win their local battles for money. Gradually, the DfE began to interfere with specific grants, which some chief executives in the newly reorganised (post-1974) corporate local government opposed, perceiving it as interfering with the priorities established by locally elected councillors.

The next key date was 2005/2006 when all school funding was nationalised and expenditure on schools no longer came through taxes raised locally. This followed the annual spending round the year previously when the DfE had miscalculated school budgets, leading to large-scale dissent. The problem did not go into Charles Clarke's 'too difficult box'. This one was easy: cut out the middle tier and send the money straight to schools. There has been hardly a murmur since from schools, whereas before this they always railed against local decisions. Centralisation can quench discourse and debate.

Post-pandemic, the economic situation means that expenditure on schools and the schooling system is unlikely to be a priority at a national level. This is a bad situation for schools, especially for those in challenging circumstances. This therefore raises the question of whether there are other forms of revenue for the schooling system, especially as local government finance has been left unreformed for a lifetime. Council tax is not quite as regressive as the notorious poll tax but it still hits poor people disproportionately, so what are the options?

A new set of equity taxes at a local level

Pending the reform of council tax, we suggest that a new 'equity tax' is established. Kate Raworth, in her book *Doughnut Economics*, is right to point to the importance of language and that it is essential to change the negative way we look at paying tax.[31] This is encouraged, she observes, by the phrase 'tax relief', which implies that paying tax is a bad thing rather than how we pay for the welfare state's assault on those five horses of civilised society's apocalypse: want, ignorance, idleness, squalor and disease. Equity, along with *absolute* as opposed to *relative* social mobility, will remain utterly out of reach until every area of local governance has shown through its actions its contribution to social justice. Each local authority should have a plan for how it intends to achieve this, which will complement the efforts of national government. We are neither economists nor experts in local government finance, but we think sources for an equity tax might include:

1   A hotel/B&B overnight tax on visitors of £5 per night – a tax that is common in many other countries and could be collected locally.

2   A 2% graduate tax on those in receipt of occupational pensions and with total incomes which mean they pay higher rates of tax.

3   A private school tax to be levied at half the difference by which the school's fee exceeds the average per-capita unit cost of the age group in the local state school system.

---

31   K. Raworth, *Doughnut Economics: Seven Ways to Think Like a 21st-Century Economist* (London: Random House Business, 2018).

4   A one-off 1% wealth tax levied by Her Majesty's Revenue and Customs (HMRC) on those with wealth over £1 million, paid either now or (with interest based on the retail price index (RPI)) at death.

The third tax on our list needs some explanation. We are not among those who would seek to abolish private schooling, although we do share the view that social mobility – whether relative or absolute – is not compatible with a set of privileged schools which dominate the access to leading and disproportionately well-paid careers.[32] We are in favour of allowing those who do use private schools to be reminded of the impact their actions have on the schooling of the other 93% by letting them join the voices calling for state school funding to rise, and thereby reducing the difference between the amount spent on pupils in private schools and that spent in state-funded schools. After all, if the difference was reduced, they would need to pay less equity tax.

We rarely confess to envy because we have been privileged to work in jobs intended to make society a better place, especially for those less fortunately placed than we have been. We have enjoyed ourselves in doing so and been well-rewarded. However, when we have visited independent public schools during our careers, we have experienced unwonted envy and anger on behalf of many youngsters in our state schools. The contrast is vivid and unwelcome.

We are not talking here of the myriad second- and third-rate private schools, which emerge and disappear rather like unregistered pop-up shops in the backstreets of big cities and pose threats to pupils' physical and mental safety, or the commercial chains, like Cognita (founded by the late Chris Woodhead), which appeal to parents with more money than sense. Our concern is with those conveyor belts of privilege conjured up by names such as Eton, Harrow, Westminster, Winchester, Marlborough, Roedean and Cheltenham Ladies' College, not to mention Manchester Grammar, Oxford High, Magdalen College, King Edward's in Birmingham or the nearby Solihull School and Warwick School. In short, the hundreds of privileged day schools where the fees are three, four or five times that spent in local state-funded schools.

Anthony Seldon, with previous successful experience as the master of Wellington College, acknowledged the tension: 'Clearly, the public school

---

32   See, for example, F. Green and D. Kynaston, *Engines of Privilege: Britain's Private School Problem* (London: Bloomsbury, 2019); or R. Verkaik, *Posh Boys: How English Public Schools Ruin Britain* (London: Simon & Schuster, 2018).

problem is a huge British problem. It is wrong that the already most privileged have the most privileged education. In a just world, it should be the other way round. The least privileged should be going to Harrow and Eton. What can we do about it in a way that doesn't create excessive state power or intrusion into individual choice? The hope is that the state sector will improve so much that people don't want to use the independent sector. That is beginning to happen and that will be accelerated enormously by new technology.' Seldon believes that 'AI [artificial intelligence] will actually ensure that every single child, wherever they are born, whatever school they're attending, will have a far better chance to optimise the talents they were born with. At the moment that is not happening, and it's not right, but it will happen. One of the fresh challenges will make certain that if you're really privileged, you will have to find new ways of ensuring that you keep your privileged position.'

Seldon also argued that public schooling is not all about privilege but about parents having the very aspirations they are urged to promote in their children. He told us that relationships with parents in many private independent schools are 'transactional': 'Parents are choosing independent schooling and making sacrifices not for snobbish reasons but because they want their children to have better lives than they did. AI technology will allow every child to get the best grades they can possibly get, not necessarily A*s. Technology will take away a significant reason why many people are paying for private education.'

Although we recognise the argument that Seldon is promoting, we do not share his optimism. The vast resources of private schools have enabled them to steal a march in terms of remote online learning and there is every probability that they will be in the vanguard of AI in schools. One of the drivers for attending a private school is the networking opportunities; the old school tie is still an important social benefit. The advantages enjoyed by the privately educated are not slight, so we need to balance the equation better.

Compared with truly 'public' state-funded schools, their buildings and sports facilities are incomparably better, and their staff – because the pupil–teacher ratio is so much more favourable – stay longer and since 1944 they have received pensions from the state. Children attending these schools are advantaged through richer educational experiences and better prospects in life – all at the expense of the 93% of children who do not attend fee-paying schools. This does not serve the interests of social justice.

Therefore, in addition to the national income raised through an equity tax mentioned above (1 and 3 to be collected locally and 2 and 4 through HMRC and allocated to local councils according to indices of deprivation) would be the proceeds of whatever emerges from a long overdue review of the council tax system, which was introduced in the hurry of abandoning the poll tax. The departments of state could then add matching specific equity grants to local governments in any of the five Beveridge-defined areas of need.

The yield from the first equity tax should be spent on a programme to tackle squalor, since housing is one of the needs that has worsened over recent years and impacts adversely on many distressed children's learning. The other three should be spent on schemes designed to overcome inequity in children's life chances. One of these would involve parental vouchers for families with children eligible for free school meals. Parents could cash them in for musical instrument or singing lessons, drama and arts experiences or related cultural enhancing opportunities – all approved locally and provided outside school hours and at times and locations that do not disadvantage poorer families.

We have set out the need for a review of school governance for MATs in particular, following on from Michael Gove's whimsical expansion programme and later efforts to bring shape to the system described in Chapter 4. A review would also clarify the nature and duties of the middle tier.

As for funding, local government finance has for far too long been in Charles Clarke's 'too difficult box'. Whenever there is a half-hearted attempt to find a solution, nothing is done. If we are ever to have a healthy local democracy – and in a population of over 50 million we need one – local government finance needs to be reformed and local government itself given devolved responsibilities from an over-mighty national government. We think that local democracy is well placed to solve the issue of equity which will vary across the country. Ideally, therefore, any equity tax should be deployed within the regions, which should have substantial devolved powers, including that of raising taxes.

This chapter has explored the question of who should run what in our schools, with finance being a key lever within the system. The age of a centralised and market-driven outlook, which encourages a managerial approach at all levels, is not conducive to good democratic governance. Our proposals to address this and build more effective engagement in governance are one of the foundation stones that we explore in our final chapter.

Part Four

An age of hope, ambition and collaborative partnerships – brighter spells ahead

Chapter 13
Building forward together
Our six foundation stones and 39 steps to success

If we are serious about what some politicians call 'building back better' after the pandemic, we will need to agree on some recognisable characteristics of what we want to build and how it will be better than what exists presently. We also need to build forward *together*.

Do we want a richer society or a fairer one? Or both? Do we want a society where each citizen is more thoughtful of and generous towards others, and where there is therefore less selfishness and corruption? Do we want to see innovative solutions to the challenges of our changing society and global relationships? Do we want to meet the climate challenge and find ways to overcome the next pandemic more efficiently and equitably than we have managed with this one? Do we have the confidence that we will have sufficient future writers to produce plays, poems and novels that will delight us, or good journalists to inform us, or sufficient artists and musicians to inspire us? Will we have enough doctors, engineers, bakers, designers, bankers, butchers, nurses, inventors, teachers, builders, carpenters, scientists, researchers, carers, publishers, drivers, opticians, chefs, pharmacists and IT specialists in an ever-changing kaleidoscope of occupations that will emerge and sustain our society? Do we want to see a more manageable level of demand on our health and social services, courts and prisons, caused mainly by people with unfortunate need as well as those unable to cope with their lives or fit into their society? Do we want to live our lives to the full, supporting those who meet with difficulty, valuing our old and treasuring our young?

It will be the young people in our schools and how we educate them which will materially affect the answers to these questions. We must maximise their talent for so great are the challenges we face that we cannot afford the human waste we have tolerated in the past. Unlocking the talent in our schools will affect the future of our society and, through those who regard the world as their oyster, many others too.

While writing this book we have examined some difficult issues and faced up to the mistakes that both of us and others have made in the schooling system. We are deeply conscious of the personal and collective consequences that follow errors of policy and practice. In making the recommendations set out later in this chapter, therefore, we do so from a belief that there are past mistakes which could be avoided in the future and institutional prejudices which have made it less likely that we have unlocked as much of some children's talents as we could and should have done. We also believe that there is a pent-up desire to see our school system aim for different achievements and more ambitious horizons than is currently the case. Accordingly, we have made suggestions for change with the anticipation that they will prompt fresh thinking and concerted action through collaborative partnerships towards new ambitions. Indeed, we believe that our school system is on the threshold of a new age – one of hope, ambition and collaborative partnerships.

After the Second World War, Beveridge's five priorities served as a defining set of common shared aims for our society; the nation, whatever its political affiliations, rolled up its metaphorical sleeves and got on with the job of attacking want, squalor, disease, idleness and ignorance. In Chapter 1, we explained how this affected educational priorities and how the means of achieving it – optimism and trust – ran out of steam in the 1970s and was eventually replaced by markets, centralisation and managerialism as the defining modus operandi. So far, our book has tried to underline fairly what has worked well, what hasn't worked so well and how to make the best of it.

Javed Khan, the former CEO of Barnardo's, talked of the danger of what he identified as a 'poverty of hope' from which many young people are suffering. The need for hope cropped up strongly among our witnesses. Of course, we know that without hope (and vision, as the Book of Proverbs has it) people perish. Young people deserve to have hope and to see a vision and the beginning of a plan which justifies that hope. We would argue that this is desperately needed in England and across the UK.

Seamus Heaney famously and beautifully encapsulated what we are getting at in the following lines:

> History says, *Don't hope*
> *On this side of the grave.*
> But then, once in a lifetime

The longed-for tidal wave

Of justice can rise up,

And hope and history rhyme.[1]

Hope, therefore, just as it is in a successful school, is an essential characteristic of our new educational age. But so too is ambition – the ambition that every child can grow up to be the best they can become, that we will always encourage them to improve on their previous best in demonstrations of their learning and capability in whatever field, and that in doing so they will contribute to the fulfilment of others. There should be no limit on our ambition for improvement in our learning: it is, after all, essential to the journey towards becoming an ever more sustainably civilised and just society.

We think there is now widespread agreement among educationalists that partnerships of schools working collaboratively are better than a series of nearly 25,000 autonomous schools competing with one another. We will need to adjust our system to encourage, recognise and hold partnerships to account for their collective endeavours.

We are advocating a new educational age of hope, ambition and collaborative partnerships. So, what do we need to do to make it happen?

There are two common threads running throughout our analysis of the period since 1976 and in the chapters of our book that address the themes of schooling: first, there is no national consensus on the purpose of schooling in England and, second, the power of the secretary of state has grown during the age of centralisation, markets and managerialism. The first of these threads creates uncertainty and the potential for confused debates and practice. The second has allowed, and will continue to allow, successive education ministers to focus on the urgent or the convenient rather than the important in a rapidly changing world, emphasising first one priority and then another, while doubling down on what is easily measured and can be presented in the form of data.[2]

The French educationalist Philippe Meirieu, in his 1996 book *Frankenstein Pédagogue*, argues that there has been a tendency to try to manufacture

---

1   S. Heaney, *The Cure at Troy: A Version of Sophocles' Philoctetes* (London: Faber & Faber, 1990), p. 77.

2   Our experience is that understanding statistics is not one of the strengths of officials and politicians at the DfE. For example, the practice of norm-referencing at SAT tests at age 11 and at GCSE at age 16 means that any talk of closing the attainment gap can only be achieved at the expense of other pupils' failure.

children into a predetermined product in recent years.[3] Yet, there is no consensus on what the product should be, which takes us back to the lack of agreement about what schooling is for: if we have no agreed purpose, the whole enterprise is vulnerable to the whims of individuals, whether in schools, MATs or government.

Let us first tackle those two dangerous threads.

Establishing agreed purposes for schooling and restraining the power of the secretary of state

The school system in England needs consensus about its purpose. We think that our list on pages 6–8 would be broadly acceptable to most and would go some way to achieving that agreement. Of course, pupils being test- and exam-ready is important; they are passports to opportunities and are used in various facets of our working life to open doors. But tests are not everything and school should be about more than exams and tests. In 30 years' time, the risk is that pupils in our schools look back on their time in school and reflect only that it did or did not help them to prepare for *terminal* examinations, rather than being an experience that helped them to develop the skills and knowledge they would need to manage their own lives or introduced them to local, national and global perspectives.

We would want them to reflect that their schooling experience, which from a young age was focused on the real world, has been a good preparation for the world of work and adult responsibilities, as well as inspiring them to take seriously healthy and fulfilling activities. We would want them to think that they had been able to enjoy a range of experiences that extended and challenged them, where they felt they had a voice and where they believed they could make a positive difference. In short, we would want them to believe that their schooling had contributed to a joyous and purposeful childhood and adolescence.

---

3   P. Meirieu, *Frankenstein Pédagogue* (Issy-les-Moulineaux, France: ESF, 1996); see also G. Biesta, *The Beautiful Risk of Education* (Abingdon and New York: Routledge, 2014).

In Chapter 12, we sketched out a way to address what could be described as the phenomenon of centralised power which has increased, is increasing and ought to be diminished. We believe that devolution to the English regions will take place, mirroring what has happened in Scotland, Wales and Northern Ireland, but not soon enough; the need to curtail the excessive power of the DfE is urgent. Does it matter if our schooling system is becoming ever more centralised? All democracies understand that, however uncomfortable it may be, decision-making is best when citizens broadly consent. Centralisation can restrict debate, reduce involvement and limit participation, while also allowing governments to exert unwonted and unwarranted control.

Our considerations have led us to develop a literarily convenient 39 steps, which we believe are necessary to create a more equitable schooling system and which will unlock more of our young people's talents. These are built on six essential changes, or foundation stones, which will improve the climate in our schools.

Finally, in deciding to recommend these foundation stones and steps for the future of schooling, we faced a dilemma. Like some of our witnesses, especially Anthony Seldon and Kenneth Baker, we believe that schooling in the future will be almost unrecognisable to those of us who have been through it; we are only too aware that, technology apart, it has changed so little to date that a time traveller from the late Victorian era would find its rites and rituals very familiar.

As Seldon pointed out both to us and in his book, *The Fourth Educational Revolution Reconsidered*, artificial intelligence (AI), enhanced and virtual reality (AR and VR), together with robotics and nanotechnology on the one hand and our expanding knowledge of neurodiversity (especially our increased understanding of how the brain and mind work) on the other, mean it is likely that we are in the foothills of huge change in schooling.[4] But if we had speculated here about the likely long-term implications and revolutionary changes in schooling, we would have been accused of being away with the fairies. So, we have chosen to be practical and suggest changes which would at least move us forward to more readily embrace the future, rather than reinforce the reverse gear that schools' ministers of the last decade have all too often, ostrich-like, seemed determined to preserve.

---

4   A. Seldon with T. Metcalf, T and O. Abidoye, *The Fourth Education Revolution Reconsidered: Will Artificial Intelligence Enrich or Diminish Humanity?* (Buckingham: University of Buckingham Press, 2020).

Six foundation stones for a better schooling system

1. A Schooling Framework Commission

The first of our foundation stones overcomes the twin dangers of a lack of clarity about the purpose of schooling and over-centralised power: a national Schooling Framework Commission which would have a membership that included representatives of teacher and support staff unions, HMI, Chartered College of Teaching, universities, CBI, Chambers of Commerce, Trades Union Congress, governors and MAT trust boards, Local Government Association and bodies representing churches, faiths and charities, together with politicians nominated from the main political parties and an additional membership by public election.

This commission would be charged with producing an initial and evolving 10-year-plan for education. It would utilise citizens' assemblies, supplemented by online webinars, so that the recommendations included in the final report would be based on wide consultation, data, research and reasoned arguments. Its findings would not bind any secretary of state but there could be an agreement that any proposed statutory changes would show how they were consistent with or different from the commission's conclusions. The body would convene frequently for an intensive set of sessions and report at seven-yearly intervals, deliberately designed to avoid synchronicity with parliamentary terms. Its chair would be the chair of the Education Select Committee.

The task of the Schooling Framework Commission would include dealing with all the issues detailed in this book and making appropriate suggestions in their first 10-year plan. Its first undertaking, however, would be to agree – for the first time in England – a set of purposes similar to those set out in Chapter 1.

2. The Open School

Teachers and schools could be helped in their efforts to unlock the minds and open the hearts of their pupils through something that the pandemic has brought to the forefront of their and our attention – namely, the potential of virtual learning to enhance young people's grasp of new knowledge and skills. There can scarcely be a teacher who has not extended their repertoire of pedagogical techniques during the various UK lockdowns; some have transformed their approach to teaching. Pupils everywhere have been encouraged to use digital technologies as part of their learning.

Now is the time to harness the best of the possibilities created by these developments. We think it is time to create an Open School, the outline of which was included in an article for *The Guardian* in May 2020.[5]

> Two developments make us optimistic. First, many teachers and schools have displayed great ingenuity in the way they have provided home support and online learning. The best models are highly relevant to the post-shutdown period. Second, in this emergency, government and local authorities have turned to the BBC for help. Only the Beeb has the reach, competence and infrastructure to rise to this challenge. Go online. From April onwards they have had a magnificent offer.
>
> But we feel these conditions can be pushed even further with long-lasting benefits to the whole-school system. The time is ripe to create an Open School. Fifty years ago, despite formidable detractors, Harold Wilson and Jenny Lee pushed through the creation of an Open University. Look at the success that has been. We should do the same in creating an Open School. Such an institution might be born out of a crisis, but it could play a major role in raising educational standards for decades to come. Other Open Schools, of great repute, exist around the world. In Canada, the Open School of British Columbia has existed since the end of the 19th century. It now offers a rich range of resources and courses for all school grades. In Australia there are other examples – the state of Victoria Virtual School goes back a century or more.
>
> These Open Schools were created to serve isolated communities and learners. But given the revolution in digital possibilities they can now provide a service to the whole school sector. If England,

---

5   The article from which this passage has been adapted was written by Tim Brighouse and Bob Moon, Emeritus Professor of Education at the Open University: Like the Open University, We Now Need an Open School for the Whole Country, *The Guardian* (12 May 2020). Available at: https://www.theguardian.com/education/2020/may/12/like-the-open-university-we-now-need-an-open-school-for-the-whole-country.

perhaps the UK, had an Open School what would it look like? We believe it could:

- Offer high-quality self-learning courses and resources in every subject discipline.

- Provide models of how teachers online and in school could incorporate these resources into their teaching.

- Provide a virtual focus for new ideas in all aspects of teaching and learning.

- Act as a guide and evaluator of the myriad of commercial resources and services being offered to teachers.

- Provide the forum for networking possibilities for learners of all ages, learner to learner, school to school, across districts, regions, nationally and internationally.

- Sponsor innovatory projects in curriculum teaching in mainstream schools and in response to the challenges of creating genuinely inclusive learning modes of practice.

- Act as a staging point for new ideas and research findings.

- Build a network of tutors, inside and outside schools, skilled at offering enrichment activities to the many, but also expert at helping youngsters who have fallen behind to catch up.

The article provoked an enthusiastic responding article from the director general of the BBC.[6] For a brief period, people from the Open University, National Endowment for Science, Technology and the Arts (Nesta) and the BBC met to take the idea further, but it happened at the wrong time as there was a change at the top of the BBC and Nesta altered its priorities. There was no response from the DfE, which had supported Oak National Academy. Although it was a step in the right direction and a decent attempt to respond to the challenge of the moment, Oak is quite different from the Open School concept we have outlined.

The Open School for the 21st century would have learners of all ages at its core, but especially those in childhood and adolescence. The digital

---

6   T. Hall, The Idea of a National Open School Is an Excellent One. The BBC Is Ready to Make It Happen, *The Guardian* (30 May 2020). Available at: https://www.theguardian.com/education/2020/may/30/the-idea-of-a-national-open-school-is-an-excellent-one-the-bbc-is-ready-to-make-it-happen.

environment would be built around this premise. It would offer a parallel but interlinked school programme for everyone to draw on. It would create different working habits. It would link directly with businesses of all types and take children directly into museums and galleries in the UK and across the globe. It could be available at different times on catch-up, repeat or box-set formats. The preoccupations with crowd control, behaviour and even exclusion that have dogged our school system for 150 years could become part of history in a move towards individual timetables. What better way to address the motivational challenge of the adolescent years?

This concept is more subtle than transferring classroom experiences to the screen; instead, it offers an opportunity to provide a blend of learning experiences that will involve and engage pupils rather than simply ensuring delivery, in the way we have known for so long. It offers a chance to manage AI and genuinely offer individualised learning. Pupils could belong to a cohort with their teacher and be part of wider large-scale learning sessions exploring big ideas and joining group discussions with pupils from elsewhere; where interest groups form, develop, sustain and dissolve; and where the knowing teacher points the right individual pupil in the right direction on a personalised learning agenda.

Of course, there are some youngsters who are fortunate to be in a MAT, such as the one Mark Grundy runs in the West Midlands, where an online platform of learning, developed with Hodder and others, offers an ever-widening set of opportunities on the path to such a vision.[7] The platform harnesses new technologies both in school and at home, as Grundy and his team have been sensitive to the digital poverty trap into which the poorest families can fall and must survive as best they can. These children survive and thrive in their learning at MATs like Grundy's and others, but equity, equality of opportunity and social mobility demand that all children should enjoy these and the other advantages offered by the Open School.

Each secondary school in the country would have a stake in the Open School, using their relationships with their own pupils to take what is available online and support, guide and develop thinking, experiences and production as well as subtly opening doors to different areas of the Open School. Teachers in schools become the equivalent of local tutors

---

7   Shireland Collegiate Academy is working with Hodder, a tech company called Gluu and Chris Lloyd's What on Earth Books to produce eduu.school.

at the Open University, and pupils meet other teachers from different schools either locally or further afield, online or at residential courses. Pupils would be invited to exploit a learning community without edges.

There would be a cost, of course. An obvious way of meeting it would be to copy the method used by Michael Gove when he founded the EEF or David Blunkett when he set up Nesta – by providing a capital sum of, say, £100 million and fund it through the interest on the sum invested, with no recurrent demand on the Exchequer. It would become an institution and a resource for all time – and, importantly, independent of direct government interference. Alternatively, it could exist under the aegis of the Open University, which would have the advantage of exploiting their existing expertise and reputation and offer seamless continuity for a student journey into higher education.

We believe that this move is the single most important step to be taken to transform educational opportunities and schooling itself as we attempt to build back better. It would extend the horizons of all pupils and, if developed in harness with the Chartered College of Teaching and the EEF, bring within the grasp of all teachers and pupils the very best resources and materials available. We often hear of the UK's ambition to be world class; the Open School of the sort we have outlined would be the means of ensuring that our schooling system becomes the benchmark against which other societies measure their progress.

3. The Seeking Talent and Extending Participation Scheme

We propose two programmes to capture the interest and build on the talent of all pupils in the school system. The first is a universal provision for children in Year 6 and Year 9, and the second would be offered to a different 20% of pupils in every secondary school annually, with all pupils included over five years.

We propose that each pupil should be able to demonstrate their learning through their participation in a Seeking Talent and Extending Participation Scheme (STEPS) at two points in their school career. The first point would be in Year 6, as First STEPS, and the second, by Year 9, as Next STEPS. Each pupil would, with support, design and manage an extended individual project for a day a week over at least 20 weeks. The project would be expected to focus on the world of work, the function of democracy, the structure of communities or the natural world. The idea is to identify talent wherever it may lay. Each pupil would have to manage a budget as part of the project, of up to £250 in the Year 6 version and £750 in the Year 9 version.

The outcome would be a multimedia presentation by the pupil to an audience, including an assessor. The wider audience for the pupil presentation would need to be authentic and would rely on local businesses and employers, councils and public sector agencies to provide opportunities for people to take part and contribute positively. Year 7 pupils and teachers at secondary schools would be another potential audience, providing a useful positive contribution to transition. The Year 6 outcome could be a starting point for ensuring that pupils show something they are genuinely proud of in Year 7 in their new secondary school, conscious that they will embark on something similar and more advanced in Year 9.

4. Extraordinary Learners with Exceptional Creative Talent

We believe that schools try their hardest to provide pupils with rich experiences across a broad spectrum of activities and consider this to be an important aspect of learning. However, a centralised agenda has meant that the implied dominant purpose of schooling is the test or exam at the end of the primary and secondary phases, while a centralised accountability regime means that all other aspects of school life take second place to the levels or the grades that pupils achieve.

This means that not only are those activities that take place *beyond* the school day regarded as 'extra', so too are many activities that take place *during* the school day. It is as though the sport, performance and representative opportunities, which are part of the rich tapestry that makes up the life of a successful school, are the spoonful of sugar that makes the real medicine go down. If we recognise this to be true, so do many of the young people we teach, some of whom give up too early on the learning that is offered and some of whom cope so poorly that they are rejected by the system itself.

We have devoted considerable thought and time in this book to those who suffer from the consequences of inequality, but we mustn't forget or underestimate those with exceptional talents. Peter Hyman, with experience close to government and with pupils though School 21, sees the emerging challenge:

> For the pupils in Years 9, 10 and 11, every waking moment which might be free, they're crammed with extra exam classes to make sure they've gone through the hoops – so if that means removing them from PE or art or drama, that's the story. I think that's one story that needs to change.
>
> The other thing, which is utterly fundamental it seems to me, is that the old bargain, the old deal, no longer holds. It used to be that if you keep your head down, you get your GCSE and A levels, however boring the diet of school. The ultimate achievement, we were told, is to go to a Russell Group university and possibly get a 2:1. When you pop out the other end, employers will snap you up. Now, that is fundamentally breaking down.
>
> The number of organisations that have now gone qualifications blind, where the 2:1 from universities is no longer a proxy for you being a decent bet, is happening at a rate that schools have no inkling about.
>
> Ten years ago, when I said to parents, 'Look, I can't stand these GCSEs and the way they're done,' I knew what they'd say: 'Well, I know my children come home bored. I know they're not enjoying school but, you know, they've got to swallow the medicine.' If swallowing this medicine isn't even doing what that deal was and getting you to the right place to get a good job, then the whole edifice starts to come down.
>
> We've got to say, let's rethink everything that schools are about because if employers say at your first job interview, 'Give me examples of where you showed initiative, or where you've been a problem-solver, or where you've used great oral communication, or where you've collaborated in the team,' and you look back on your schooling of 14 years and say, 'I remember that once in Year 3 ...' Well, we haven't given people even a half-decent education.

We are always on the look-out for exceptional talent. Pablo Casals once put it beautifully in *Joys and Sorrows*:

> Sometimes I look around me with a feeling of complete dismay. In the confusion that afflicts the world today, I see disrespect for

the very values of life. Beauty is all around us, but how many are blind to it! They look at the wonder of this earth – and seem to see nothing. Each second we live is a new and unique moment of the universe; a moment that will never be again. And what do we teach our children? We teach them that 2+2 makes 4, and that Paris is the capital of France. When will we also teach them what they are?

We should say to each of them: do you know what you are? You are a marvel. You are unique. In the entire world there is no other child exactly like you ... You may become a Shakespeare, a Michelangelo, a Beethoven. You have the capacity for anything. And when you grow up, can you then harm another who is, like you, a marvel? You must cherish one another. You must work – we must all work – to make the world worthy of its children.[8]

We need to look for the likes of those Shakespeares, Michelangelos and Beethovens, not to mention the Berners-Lees or Mandelas, or the pool of often untapped female geniuses – people like Barbara Hepworth, Marie Curie, Ellen MacArthur, Jane Austen, Ella Fitzgerald, Jacqueline du Pré, Sarah Gilbert, or Helen Sharman. All will delight us and make our world a better place. Often, these talented individuals are autodidacts with astonishing resilience, self-motivation and single-mindedness, but they often combine that with an enviable determination (learned through ipsative progress in their chosen field) which they then transfer confidently to acquiring competence in fields where they are more like the rest of us in facing obstacles to their learning. But we need to find them and not allow so many to slip through our fingers.

Our Extraordinary Learners with Exceptional Creative Talent (ELECT) proposal builds on this belief. We also acknowledge the influence of Matthew Syed's persuasive book *Bounce* and his theory that every child has a talent and that if it is encouraged by finding the right coach in the right context, with assiduous practice a young person can walk more than a few steps with genius.[9]

We suggest, therefore, that each school has one member of staff who works closely with their Open School tutor and the appropriate form tutor, who will have a one-to-one with each youngster twice a year to

---

8   P. Casals, *Joys and Sorrows: Reflections by Pablo Casals* (New York: Simon & Schuster, 1970), p. 295.
9   M. Syed, *Bounce: The Myth of Talent and the Power of Practice* (London: Fourth Estate, 2011).

review how they are developing their special talent(s). We recall well the Gifted and Talented programme which was introduced in the years following the millennium. It was a little blinkered and one-dimensional in how it defined talent, but it contained the seeds of a good idea and served as an antidote to the dangers which so many of our witnesses drew to our attention and which Peter Hyman's words express so eloquently.

The programme is called ELECT rather than SELECT. We propose that, each year, schools guide a different 20% of all pupils in Years 5 to 9 towards their 'elective' pursuit. This means spotting when talents and interests are beginning to emerge and trying to sustain them by putting the right people and opportunities in the way of the pupil. This will require effort to organise and manage but it will help those pupils to take the precious first steps towards the personalisation of their learning. Over the five-year period, every pupil will be included as their maturity and interests unfold, including those with SEND and in special provision, with an equal and defined allocation of funding. All pupils will have an opportunity to fulfil more of their potential, wherever it lies; it is one of the familiar goals of many schools, educationalists and politicians.

We are aware that the word 'talent' has become contentious, sometimes implying that only a few people should aspire to be talented. Indeed, Matthew Syed's book carries the subtitle 'The Myth of Talent and the Power of Practice'. We have both enjoyed listening to Olympians explaining that none of us knows our limits and that hard work and good coaching, along with commitment, will bring success. All of these Olympians also explained how they first became captivated by their sport: the role model, the fascination with an event on screen, an influential person giving them a chance or spotting their aptitude and giving them belief in themselves. In short, they believed they had a talent. We also know that when we listen to gold medal-winning Olympians, we are celebrating those who have managed to reach peak performance at just the right moment to win a norm-referenced competition. There were other excellent athletes in the same competition whose equal work ethic and coaching resulted in a less than golden outcome on that occasion but represented a never-to-be-forgotten experience.

We want every child to believe they have a talent and to find someone who can help them to exploit their interests and growing aptitude. We must eradicate the view that still prevails in so many people and communities that only a few will succeed. We want our children to build on their enthusiasms, develop the commitment to persevere and become the best they can be. We wouldn't want to put a limit on the learning and horizons of any youngster; we believe instead that all can find their own talent and have much to contribute, if we can spot their interests and ignite their passion.

> Mick recalls:
>
> I was chatting with some youngsters in a secondary school dining hall and asked what they would be doing at the weekend. One was showing her terrier at a regional dog show, one was chilling out and one was helping his father (a mechanic) to service a car (for payment). The last one was going to the National Windsurfing Championships to defend his under 14's title.
>
> Later, in the staffroom, I was talking with senior leaders and mentioned the windsurfer and was met with blank looks. Nobody seemed to know they had a national champion in their midst. The rationalisation was that teenagers tend to keep things in compartments and don't want everyone to know. That may be true for some but this pupil had told me within 10 minutes of meeting him.
>
> By validating his out-of-school activity, the school might see a greater commitment to other aspects of behaviour in school. That goes for the mechanic and the terrier shower too. And, if they elected to do so, wouldn't extended engagement with their enthusiasm, talent or fascination teach them about the joy of deep involvement and the value of study?

5. The expert consultant teacher

We propose reform of the teaching profession through the establishment, recognition and influence of expert consultant teachers whose finely tuned expertise will benefit all teachers.

A developing role for the Chartered College of Teaching and the EEF, working together with the CIEA, would see them create expert consultant teachers, who would gain their status after five or seven years by obtaining a part-time master's degree awarded by a university. This would be separate from the career framework route from entry into teaching through to senior levels of leadership. It would recognise the makings of the outstanding teacher who remains close to learners within schools, acts as the 'go to' consultant on matters such as support for NQTs and the ECF, offers guidance to lead assessors and advises on professional learning issues or the learning needs of particular groups of pupils.

The expert consultant teacher is the equivalent to the consultant in a hospital trust (obviously, with a different range of expertise, including in the vital area of interpersonal skills) who works on the most challenging agendas, pushing the boundaries of practice and with whom other colleagues are desperate to work and grow professionally. An expert consultant teacher will develop a specialism in a specific aspect of pedagogy, assessment or curriculum, build teams of expertise, work closely with colleagues nationally and beyond, and influence the ways that school are organised through their innovative ideas.

6. A Curriculum for Childhood and a Curriculum for Adolescence

Our society is at a tipping point in respect of how young people navigate childhood and adolescence. The concern about the effect of the COVID-19 pandemic on children's and young people's development is widespread both in terms of the numbers affected and the ways in which they are impacted. This comes against a backdrop of growing concerns about the pervasive impact of social media, well-being, mental health issues, social withdrawal, aspects of poor physical health, learning delays and difficult family circumstances. Kevan Collins has argued in his proposals for the education recovery plan that the investment in schooling needs to be wide-ranging.[10]

We believe that the necessity for services around childhood to work together coherently and effectively is as great now as it was after the Second World War or when Ed Balls set out his Every Child Matters agenda nearly 20 years ago. We are at a critical point.

Schooling is a universal provision and channels access to services for learning, physical, social and emotional health and well-being, as well as introductions to the world of work. These services – as well as those for social care, employment and civic contribution – are coordinated,

---

10 Education Committee, Oral Evidence: Education Recovery, HC 452 (29 June 2021), p. 11. Available at: https://committees.parliament.uk/oralevidence/2466/pdf.

resourced and managed locally and regionally. It is at this level that effective links with housing, transport and family facilities can work alongside local employers and businesses, entrepreneurs and charities to harness opportunities for young people and avert threats to their future well-being.

What would emerge is a Curriculum for Childhood and a Curriculum for Adolescence. This would be more than a school curriculum, with the intention that additions could be offered depending on individual schools or the serendipity of opportunity. The curriculum entitlements for childhood and adolescence would represent entitlements in terms of the broadest learning offer within school and with wider experiences. Our earlier proposals for the STEPS and ELECT programmes both see broad involvement with pupils in their learning, as does the Open School development.

Curriculums for Childhood and Adolescence would supplement and enrich our consideration of what children and young people need to complement the traditional design approach of working backwards from qualifications and a limiting national curriculum. It would also enable more relevant and purposeful assessment which, in turn, would lead to a more balanced outlook on accountability, which would judge the quality of the entire experience being provided for each individual rather than measuring the providing institutions.

The Curriculums for Childhood and Adolescence should be harmonised at a local level, with commissioners for childhood and adolescence assigned to take on this task and with every school, business, hospital, council, voluntary and charitable entity required to commit to the endeavour (depending on their size and other factors). Engaging in continuing regional conversations with all partners – and essentially families – would ensure that the curriculum is responsive and relevant to local circumstances within a national context. This would help us to make sure that pupils make a successful transition from primary to secondary school, that traditional Achilles heel of the school system.

As schooling is but one element in the growth of the pupil, we should not be wedded to the idea that all children are confined to prearranged age cohorts. The link to the Open School, with well-managed tutoring and assessment that looks towards next steps as well as checks on progress, along with peer-to peer learning, all imagine a different approach to schooling. The pupil's school will coordinate their learning rather than delivering it within a narrow, nationally prescribed agenda.

In Chapter 10, we argued that formal approaches to schooling should begin at the age of 6, with excellent childcare in a rich social and educative setting beforehand. Evidence from many other nations shows that a later start to formalised learning accelerates progress, especially in reading and particularly where spoken language is a strong focus in the early years. Indeed, some children have learned to read naturally by the age of 6.

Through universities and our network of expert consultant teachers and the infrastructure of the Chartered College of Teaching and the EEF, we should be able to establish the agreed processes for helping children to learn to read and the alternatives for those children who struggle initially. This development would establish practices that take us away from the centralisation and competitive market of schooling and towards professional system-wide collaboration. Our ambition should be to ensure that all children are natural and fluent readers by the time they are 8 years old, as if their life depended on it, because the future quality of their lives really does depend on their ability to read.

If only someone could develop a potion, vaccine or tablet that would mean every child could read! Since schooling began in 1870, the ability to read has enabled – or restricted – children's success at school. Rates of illiteracy are now far lower than they were in 1976,[11] but almost every non-reader still faces a life of reduced opportunities and society faces the burden of helping them to cope with an inhibited life. Only when children have learned to read can they read to learn. As AI becomes a bigger driver of the cognitive, academic and practical aspects of learning and schools become a place where relationships, contributions, worth and spirit are nurtured to enable our young people to grow into our changing world, the ability to read and understand will be even more vital.

We believe that the Curriculum for Childhood and the Curriculum for Adolescence have the potential to focus attention on building forward in a new image rather than working to return to a pre-pandemic position.

---

11   M. Roser and E. Ortiz-Ospina, Literacy, *Our World in Data* (2013, updated 2018). Available at: https://ourworldindata.org/literacy.

At the start of this chapter, we quoted a passage from Seamus Heaney's version of *Philoctetes* about the need for a 'tidal wave of justice'. Inspiring and transformative though the Schooling Framework Commission, Open School, STEPS programme, ELECT, expert consultant teachers and Curriculums for Childhood and Adolescence will be, they alone they do not represent a tidal wave. An essential part of the wave, yes, but sufficient to make it tidal, no. They provide six new building blocks for modernising the pupil experience and the way the teaching profession organises itself and connects with learning and pupils. For these building blocks to be effective, other systemic steps are also needed.

From the various suggestions we have made in this book, we have devised 39 steps which would constitute, if adopted in schools and the schooling system alongside the aforementioned six reforms, Heaney's tidal wave of justice.

All 39 steps will make the schooling system fairer – in the sense of securing greater equity – and provide a stimulus to equalise opportunity and create schools where many more will succeed as citizens and fewer fail. Some steps, of course, are more important than others. A few are urgent in that they will remove influences in schools that are akin to poisons and which at present lead to more pupils having a miserable adult life than needs to be the case. Two examples will explain better what we mean.

In Chapter 8, we expose what we think is a sobering and even shameful feature of the English schooling system – namely, that whereas 7,894 pupils were permanently excluded in 2018/2019, only five were excluded in the whole of Scotland. The subsequent cost to the individuals and to society during childhood and adulthood (sometimes years wasted in prison) is enormous both financially and in terms of human suffering. It would be easy – but mistaken – to blame schools, and we are sceptical of behaviour policies based on zero tolerance (sometimes called assertive discipline). However, this approach has been peddled to schools by government, and is rarely called out by Ofsted.

Our second example identifies the cause of these permanent exclusions, which are the tip of an iceberg of children lost to the system through off-rolling, temporary exclusions and detention. We believe that the blame lies in an accountability system that focuses on a managerial and perfunctory belief in norm-referenced testing and inspection rather than a commitment to astute analysis, nuanced assessment and incisive inspection based on clearly understood and shared criteria.

We hope you will see the connecting logic behind the 39 steps and share our belief that, if accepted along with the six new reforms set out above, our schools will come closer to creating a truly civilised society. Here they are, divided into sections and with a brief description to set the scene.

Create more rigorous external tests and examinations within a fairer qualifications system at primary and secondary stages

One of the weakest links in our system is the way we set, administer, mark and validate summative tests and exams. One of our ministerial witnesses described the system as 'shot'. Certainly, the exam controversy of 2020 caused by the pandemic revealed some of the flaws which until then had been concealed from the general public. Principal among these are the restricted scope and flawed methodology of examinations and testing, built-in error factors, a reliance on algorithms and the use of norm rather than criterion referencing. What follows is based on Chapter 5.

1   All externally validated tests and exams should be criterion referenced. We have made the case for replacing a variable and unreliable norm-referenced test and exam system, which requires a given percentage of pupils to succeed and fail, with criterion-referenced assessment with clear and rigorous standards.

2   Internal assessment in all schools should be led by a qualified chartered assessor licensed through the CIEA. The chartered assessor will be skilled in diagnostic, formative, summative, evaluative and ipsative assessment and advise on the judicious and sparing use of norm-referenced assessment. In secondary schools, they will ensure that each department is competent in assessment.

3   Primary assessment should start with low-stakes diagnostic tests as a baseline at age 6, carried out internally and assessed and moderated externally. The purpose of this assessment should be to

determine whether individual children have departed significantly from the 'average' expected development, and, if so, to refer them to appropriately qualified expert consultant teachers to advise and oversee their learning. These assessments should build on and contribute to the evolving picture of each child's health and social development.

4   Introduce Young Experts Awards at the end of the primary stage at three specified levels – apprentice, established and experienced – and across a range of activities, including dance, art, science, music, sport, history, constructing, collecting, growing things, oracy, mathematics, writing and reading, with a focus on aspects such as the environment, the community, the working world and health. This should be developed by interested primary practitioners and other specialist bodies (e.g. English-Speaking Union, Associated Board of the Royal Schools of Music, Scouts and Guides) and led by the Chartered College of Teaching. It will require the completion of an Extended Personal Junior Project (analogous to the EPQ at A level) during Years 6 and 7. All of this can link with our proposals for the ELECT and STEPS programmes and the work of the Open School.

5   Introduce a baccalaureate at age 18 which would consist of the Tomlinson recommendations plus no more than seven accumulated criterion-referenced Level 2 (GCSE or equivalent) qualifications, taken at the point when pupils are ready and present themselves for assessment.

6   In order to track national standards over time (at present there is no effort to do this), introduce random sampling of pupils from each school partnership every three years at ages 9, 12 and 14 in areas of knowledge or skills to be determined by the Schooling Framework Commission (see Chapter 12).

Incentivise the right things: replace our backward-looking and distorting school accountability system with one that is more rigorous and fit for purpose

Until the establishment of Ofsted and the publication of school exami-nation and test results in league table form in the early 1990s, national accountability was virtually non-existent. It is now so all-embracing and narrowly focused that most of our witnesses – including some former leaders of Ofsted – believe that reform of the accountability system is urgent but that a rehabilitated Ofsted should play its part. What follows is based mainly on Chapters 11 and 12

7   Individual school or academy inspections should be replaced by a focus on partnerships – in the form of inspections of representative schools or academies to be selected by a reformed Ofsted (see Chapter 12 and below) – and carried out by teams selected by Ofsted. All reports will highlight where school partnerships are in their journey of improvement. If a school is found to be not fit for purpose on the inspection of a partnership, the MAT will be given six months to put things right before a second inspection of the school, with the clear implication that the whole partnership is being judged on whether it is up to standard in terms of school improvement.

8   Ofsted should be reviewed with a view to reducing its enormous scope and function. The system deserves better. As far as the schooling system is concerned, there needs to be an HMCI who is clearly focused on commissioning and supervising school partnership inspections and survey work, collected through partnership inspections and other focused enquiry visits to schools. The HMCI's function should be to give expert advice to ministers and the DfE about schools and the schooling system, and continue the practice of annual reports which would be considered as evidence by the Schooling Framework Commission. Aspects such as regulatory safeguarding, financial audits, health and safety and GDPR inspections should not be part of Ofsted's duties,

but inspected and regulated (as some already are) by separate agencies.

9   Each school or academy should have a published balanced scorecard, available to parents and the media, which should reflect its improvements in terms of pupils' academic progress, inclusion, attendance, personal well-being and development. The scorecard should be officially updated biannually and show four-year trends in these five areas. It will be developed by a group led by the EEF. The scorecard should evolve to include the extent to which the Curriculum for Childhood or Curriculum for Adolescence is being harmonised effectively for pupils within the school. It should be transparent about those elements that are strong and where improvement is needed.

10 Each partnership and its schools should be accountable for its contribution to their community through the local authority's scrutiny committee, and each of these should be answerable to a regional arrangement.

Overhaul governance at a national, local and school level to make it more democratically accountable

Our schooling system is the most centralised of any in the western developed world; some would argue it is so centralised that it would be a model for a totalitarian state or dictatorship. Almost all our school leaders were dismayed by the extent of central direction but, almost without exception, they were unwilling to allow these remarks to be attributed to them directly for fear of repercussions (which appears to prove the point). Almost all our chapters contain material pertinent to our recommendations, although Chapters 4 and 12 have the clearest focus. We have dealt with the national level through the establishment of the Schooling Framework Commission in our first foundation stone. It needs to be complemented by action regionally and at the level of the local authority as well as schools themselves.

11 All schools and academies (with the exception of some stand-alone free schools) should, over a seven-year period, be required to

move into local partnerships of between 15 and 30 schools. There are many different types of free school, although most are new schools that are responding to rising populations and sponsored by existing MATs. We see these as being part of the local partnerships. There are others, however, such as free schools and UTCs, which were encouraged because they offered something different, often in places where there was no basic need. We think they should be left as they are since they represent adventures in schooling which will either flourish or fall according to the quality of the provision. It should be the responsibility of the RSC to oversee these free schools and UTCs. When the learning from these new ventures has been researched and assimilated, these free schools and UTCs could be absorbed into the system of partnerships, either to influence other communities or to embrace additional schools into their orbit.

12   Each academy within a MAT should have a committee with specified powers to hear the views of the staff, parents, pupils and community on the quality of the school experience and the school's development plan. Each of the constituents should elect representatives to the committee, whose reports should be submitted and responded to by the MAT board. (This would also apply to diocesan MACs.)

13   Governance at the level between the school/academy/MAT and Whitehall should rest with the local authority. Its scrutiny committee will oversee school improvement in its area and hold the RSC to account, with whom it will also agree a regional plan for high-needs SEND provision. This will strengthen local community influence and at the same time ensure that government gives the RSC sufficient responsibility to take decisive action where necessary.

14   Partnerships of schools should follow the MAT model, but the trust or company should have democratic local membership that is nominated by the local authority and required through their contract with the secretary of state.

15   The local authority should retain responsibility for policies and practices relating to admission (see Chapter 8), the planning of school places in the light of housing development and changes in local birth rates, the provision of school transport, and the planning and provision of services for and placement of SEND pupils (see Chapter 9).

In the interests of securing a schooling system based on equality of opportunity for all pupils, and therefore an equitable system that will bring social inclusion closer, we need six changes to the funding system for state-funded schools

Our state-funded schools are starved of resources. When compared with independent school fees for day pupils, the state to independent school ratio is 1:3 and ever widening.[12] That is, independent school pupils' fees are three times the level at which state school pupils are funded. In the interests of equity, we propose a mechanism for closing the gap and levelling up. We also suggest other ways in which additional local investment can be made in schools so that all children have a more equal chance of succeeding in adult life.

16   Close the gap between the funding levels in state schools and those at leading independent day schools from the present ratio of 1:3 to 2:3 over a 20-year period. This would be achieved by index linking the age-weighted pupil unit (AWPU) either to the RPI and adding 3% annually or linking the AWPU to the annual index of fees at the schools attended by members of the Cabinet at the time, also adding 3%. (This would also remove the need for the costly monitoring committee outlined in Chapter 12.) This would have the effect of closing the gap between state and independent schools by half of its current level within 20 years. A government with the commitment to so could increase the percentages to speed up the process but the principle is an important one.

17   A private school equity tax to be levied at half the difference by which the average local independent schools' fees exceed the average per-capita unit cost of the age group in the local state school system. The proceeds, pooled nationally and then redistributed according to need, should pay for 'education max'

---

12   We looked up the fees for 20 independent schools across the country, excluding those generally seen as 'prestigious', which advertise in their local communities to recruit pupils.

vouchers for the parents of children aged 9–13 who are eligible for free school meals to pay for enhanced experiences for their children (see Chapter 10).

18 Keep the pupil premium and super premium and continue research into how best to use it on the basis of age and vulnerability.

19 Introduce tighter rules for the remuneration of MAT leaders (e.g. capping salaries at no higher than five times that of an NQT) as an example of social inclusion. There also need to be tighter controls to eliminate any possibility of nepotism.

20 Create regional vehicles for rare high-needs school places and adjust capital funding accordingly.

21 As part of our proposals for reforming the finance of schools and local government, there should be a 2% graduate tax on those in receipt of occupational pensions and with total incomes (pension or otherwise) that make them eligible to pay higher rates of tax, with the funds raised nationally to be redistributed on the basis of local education need.

Secure fair admission arrangements for children to schools and make it more likely that they will enjoy their schooling experience

When parental preference was first introduced in 1980 it was to avoid LEAs determining exactly which school a child should attend. Now, we have the opposite situation where individual schools can choose which children to accept. The recommendations for change are explained in greater detail in Chapter 8.

22 Set up area admission authorities (AAA) with democratic input into running school admission cycles each year for the start of compulsory schooling and at age 11 (or 9 and 13 in middle school systems) and to settle arrangements for in-year transfers between schools, for whatever reason, as well as new arrivals in the area. AAAs could be structured around the existing local authority or

regional framework, either singly or in larger combinations of authorities.

23 Any national priorities – such as in the interests of equity, giving priority to FSM-entitled children as well as the already prioritised children in care and those with an EHCP for SEND – should be subject to preconditions for the AAAs when establishing local school admission policies. Such policies, after consultation with all schools and other interested parties, would be determined to secure equity and equality of opportunity consistent with parental choice of school.

24 A revision of the Code of Practice in the light of steps 22 and 23 above should be undertaken by the schools adjudicator, which should be made mandatory for all AAAs and the schools and academies in their area.

Redefine what makes a good school and ensure that all children enjoy an appropriate curriculum both in and beyond the normal school day and premises

Various of our chapters (in particular, those on influences beyond the school in early childhood and adolescence, such as poverty; the curriculum, pedagogy and assessment; school improvement and leadership; teachers and teaching; and SEND) rehearse the ways in which we believe pupils' experience of school could be much more successful, worthwhile and enjoyable within an inclusive school environment that is committed organisationally to improving on previous best both for the pupils and staff. We think that a more clearly defined and broader curriculum, which genuinely includes the whole of the planned learning experience, is essential. It is here – in the schools themselves – that we need teachers who ask themselves not 'Why?' but 'Why not?' System-wide change will require action on a myriad of fronts, but if just some of the following recommendations are implemented, we are sure there will be more schools where the following will be happening.

Tim recalls:

It was an 11–16 school in Havering at the beginning of the London Challenge. Two Year 11 pupils had been given the task of showing me round. So enthusiastic and natural were they as they greeted fellow pupils or exchanged ideas with staff to whom they introduced me that, after yet another perfectly casual, 'Oh, you must see the science department and you must meet Mr So and So,' I confess I asked a question that I shouldn't have done: 'Tell me, is there anything bad about this school?' And after a brief pause came the reply: 'Well, yes there is. We only have 135 days left. We have to leave next summer.'

We need the pupils in our schools to want to be there, to value the experience, to see school as something to enjoy and consume rather than tolerate. We need all our pupils to value schooling. To do so, we have to address the irreconcilable expectations and images which date from Victorian times that schooling is something to survive and suffer; we still reward pupils and punish them with a 'release' from the burden of schooling. We need to create a school experience that is irresistible, with learning that pupils don't want to turn away from because it is intrinsically absorbing and valuable in the widest possible sense, however challenging and demanding it may be. To miss a day of schooling should be a disappointment, not a bonus, and the belief that all adults in your life value learning should be an entitlement for all pupils.

25 Each partnership of schools, once formed, should establish appropriate short-term in-school alternative provision, examine the effectiveness of their sanction ladder and ensure that within five years no child is permanently excluded from the partnership of schools. Fixed-term exclusions should be abolished earlier and certainly within three years, which will provide a period of preparation and transition. They are currently too convenient and often represent the beginning of an irreversible downward pathway for too many young people.

26 There should be a repeat of an inquiry like the Warnock Report, with similarly expert committee members, to address the many

issues that have arisen that impede the likelihood of unlocking the many talents of children with SEND, including the urgent need to:

- Initially train specialist SEND teachers as well as paraprofessionals in a much more planned way.

- Reform the resourcing system which leads to children with SEND and their parents being used as bargaining pawns.

- Change the systemic factors which make the culture and capacity of some mainstream primary and secondary schools less likely to be inclusive settings for all children, including those with SEND.

- Establish regional collaboration to make best use of the high-needs block funding and to reduce exclusions.

The government review currently underway has been so protracted that the concerns about SEND have become even greater since it began. The problems are so significant that an inquiry, rather than a review, is needed to build confidence in the process, outcomes and commitment to the resultant agenda for change.

27 The funding and creation of speech and language paraprofessionals and pre-school workers, using the apprenticeship scheme, in the current opportunity areas and the former EiC areas for a 10-year period, with a clear plan and evaluation of outcomes.

28 Establish a commission to support the effectiveness of parenting. Chapter 8 highlights the need to mitigate the adverse experiences that can affect childhood and adolescence, and while these are more likely to occur with disadvantage, no family is immune. Most parents will recognise the nagging feeling of not living up to their own expectations of the role. We want all of our children to enjoy the 'enchanted' lives that Bettelheim envisaged,[13] and yet many suffer the hardships that Anne Longfield and Louise Casey have outlined in their numerous roles championing the causes of children and the disadvantaged.

A commission should examine how we enable the most disadvantaged and underprivileged in our society to build the self-image, resources and competence to support their children

---

13   B. Bettelheim, *A Good Enough Parent: A Book on Child-Rearing* (New York: Vintage Books, 1988).

sufficiently to break the cycle of generational struggle that affects so many. At the same time, an examination of the pressures on all parents created by the modern world would provide guidelines and a safety net to enable all to be the 'good enough' parent – and grandparent – they aspire to be. If it takes a village to raise a child, how can we help the village to do it well?

29 Andrea Leadsom's report, *The Best Start for Life* – which was welcomed by the First 1001 Days Movement – underlined the crucial importance of the early years, especially for challenged families.[14] It must not be allowed to suffer the fate of so many government reports, especially with respect to the pre-school years – namely, that the vessel is soon lost at sea. That is especially so with the pre-school years where governments have so often squandered their inheritance. Leadsom's proposals require new and substantial resource and a coherent action plan, which should include frequent access to a first-time parent health visitor/early educator based in every GP's practice, who will also have links with the local nursery class and day-care providers. Recruited for their qualities rather than their qualifications, these new additions to the caring professions should ensure, at last, that every child enjoys 'good enough' parenting and valuable developmental and play experiences during their first 1,001 days, and also that the number of adverse childhood experiences diminishes.

30 A major inquiry into the starting age for school and the make-up of reformed pre-school provisions and entitlements for parents in housing, health and education is essential. The development of pre-school provision has never been fully coordinated with the range of services available to support families. This is a vital element within the context of a 10-year plan.

31 The Open School should create new materials and make available existing materials for parents which will show them how they can help their own children with their learning. An important way to enable consistently effective practice and encourage support for disciplined innovation is to show parents and the wider public the

---

14 A. Leadsom, *The Best Start for Life: A Vision for the 1,001 Critical Days. The Early Years Healthy Development Review Report* (London: Department of Health and Social Care, 2021). Available at: https://assets.publishing.service.gov.uk/government/uploads/system/uploads/attachment_data/file/973112/The_best_start_for_life_a_vision_for_the_1_001_critical_days.pdf. For more on the First 1001 Days Movement, visit: https://parentinfantfoundation.org.uk/1001-days.

developments that are underway in curriculum, pedagogy and assessment in terms of how they affect their children and to elicit their support.

32 Every year, 100 expert consultant teachers paired with 100 trainee teachers should be randomly selected to visit two or three schools from a list of 25 countries, as well as Scotland, Wales and Northern Ireland, to study learning and schooling with the expectation that they will contribute to the Open School programme and the Chartered College of Teaching to disseminate and inspire practice.

33 A professional learning and CPD entitlement for all school staff, with details to be recommended by the Schooling Framework Commission after consultation with the teacher unions, Chartered College of Teaching and the EEF.

34 The Schooling Framework Commission should consider and consult on an alternative model for the school year. For example, schools could open all through the year with children and staff attending for 40 weeks in a cohort, which would give them a five-weeks on and one-week off/five-weeks on and two-weeks off pattern four times a year (with days off for the holy days of all religions). This would reduce the number of individuals in schools by 20%, and free up resources because only 80% of school pupils would be present at any one time (there would be no 'high seasons' for holiday firms either). It would also mean that 20% of people in school – both children and adults – were always fresh, and we would not get that end-of-term feeling when everyone is tired at the same time or the corresponding start-up weeks when the school gets underway again. Some would suggest that such proposals are unworkable, citing families with children in different cohorts, for example. Good schools could manage such matters. Our point, as we suggest in Chapter 8, is that a forward-looking outlook to technology and a questioning look at archaic practices could see schooling reimagined.

Tackling the cold spots in school provision and outcomes

In more than one chapter we have described the spasmodic attempts that different generations have made to tackle poor schooling outcomes on a place-based basis. The latest manifestation has been opportunity areas. We think that nothing less than a whole-community approach is going to enable schools and families in deprived areas to turn around expectations and outcomes, which is why the final five of our 39 steps are focused on supporting this line of action.

35 The government should approach major charitable foundations (such as Joseph Rowntree, Paul Hamlyn and Esmée Fairbairn) to match-fund and lead a multidisciplinary/inter-departmental effort to transform a handful of places drawn from the opportunity areas. Each of the pilots would use slightly different project/delivery models but with the same agreed KPIs, so that an evaluation of outcomes in terms of health gains, employment prospects and decreases in crime can be made and compared, as well as educational outcomes.

36 The programmes should be planned for a minimum of seven years, followed by a review and recommendations on how to amend the scheme in the light of experience and how to extend it to other areas.

37 The Schooling Framework Commission should examine the appropriateness of some schools becoming community hubs, with on-site housing, clinics, libraries, benefit offices, post offices, libraries and other facilities that support families. Such developments have been shown to be successful in parts of England and Wales and evidence should be drawn from their experiences. The hubs should be prioritised in communities within the opportunity areas.

38 As a test case for what is possible, schools in one area should be immediately funded at a level directly comparable to the nearest independent prep or public day schools.

39 Our final step helps us to address a central point in Chapter 1 and one that has been a recurring theme throughout our book: we think that teachers, head teachers, MAT CEOs, civil servants at

the DfE, RSCs and, of course, minsters should all, on taking up a new or promoted post, undertake an induction programme that articulates and reminds them of the differences between terms such as equality, equity and social mobility. It is vital in a country where such words (and others, like social justice, social inclusion and levelling up) are used all too easily without a commonly shared definition. We wish we had experienced something similar because it would have reduced the number of mistakes we have made when helping to make policies and when carrying out the practices that flowed from them.

There is abundant talent in our school system and among those who support it. Politicians from all parties share a wish for schooling to set out young people on a path to a positive and productive adulthood. Public backing for the work that schools do is strong and the pandemic has only reinforced the essential role that schools play within the fabric of local communities. There needs to be renewed commitment to childhood and adolescence by all concerned and a recognition that our children need to see a bright future ahead of them. There also needs to be a shared purpose for schooling's role in that process.

This final chapter has tried to draw out the ways these ambitions could be realised; the reasons behind our recommendations in the six foundation stones and 39 steps lie in previous chapters and in the analysis of our conversations, wider reading and experiences. The contributions from our witnesses have reinforced our view that the marketisation, centralisation and managerialism of the last age has served its purpose but it has now run its course. It is time to move on to a new age of hope, ambition and collaborative partnerships.

Bibliography

Abbott, J. and MacTaggart, H. (2009) *Overschooled but Undereducated: How the Crisis in Education Is Jeopardizing Our Adolescents*. London and New York: Network Continuum Education.

Adonis, A. (2012) *Education, Education, Education: Reforming England's Schools*. Hull: Biteback Publishing.

Ainscow, M. (n.d.) The Warnock Report: A Catalyst for Global Change? Available at: https://onlinelibrary.wiley.com/pb-assets/assets/14679604/13.%20Ainscow%20-1540391987517.pdf.

Ainscow, M. (2015) *Struggles for Equity in Education: The Selected Works of Mel Ainscow*. Abingdon and New York: Routledge.

Ainscow, M. (2019) The British Government Is Failing Pupils with Special Needs – Here's How to Change That, *The Conversation* (16 July). Available at: https://theconversation.com/the-british-government-is-failing-pupils-with-special-needs-heres-how-to-change-that-118143.

Ajegbo, K., Diwan, D. and Sharma, S. (2007) *Diversity & Citizenship Curriculum Review* [Ajegbo Review]. Nottingham: Department for Education and Skills. Available at: http://www.educationengland.org.uk/documents/pdfs/2007-ajegbo-report-citizenship.pdf.

Alexander, R. (1991) *Primary Education in Leeds: Twelfth and Final Report from the Primary Needs Independent Evaluation Project*. Leeds: University of Leeds.

Alexander, R. (ed.) (2010) *Children, Their World, Their Education: Final Report and Recommendations of the Cambridge Primary Review*, 1st edn. Abingdon and New York: Routledge.

Alexander, R., Rose, J. and Woodhead, C. (1992) *Curriculum Organisation and Classroom Practice in Primary Schools: A Discussion Paper* [Three Wise Men Report]. London: Department of Education and Science. Available at: http://www.educationengland.org.uk/documents/threewisemen/threewisemen.html.

All Party Parliamentary Group for the Teaching Profession (2021) *If It Ain't Broke, Handle with Care: Report by the Special Interest Group on Initial Teacher Training (ITT)*. Available at: https://appgteachingcom.files.wordpress.com/2021/07/21.06.30-report-of-the-ite-sig-to-the-appg-on-the-teaching-profession-jmc4.pdf.

Andrews, J. (2016) *School Performance in Multi-Academy Trusts and Local Authorities – 2015*. London: Education Policy Institute. Available at: https://epi.org.uk/publications-and-research/school-performance-multi-academy-trusts-local-authorities.

ARD Data & Analytics Team (2016) Data Bytes: The Most Popular A Level Subjects since 2000, *Cambridge Assessment* (January). Available at: https://www.cambridgeassessment.org.uk/Images/the-most-popular-a-level-subjects-since-2000.pdf.

Association of School and College Leaders (2019a) *The Forgotten Third: Final Report of the Commission of Inquiry*. Oxford: Oxford University Press. Available at: https://www.ascl.org.uk/ASCL/media/ASCL/Our%20view/Campaigns/The-Forgotten-Third_full-report.pdf.

Association of School and College Leaders (2019b) Framework for Ethical Leadership in Education. Available at: https://www.ascl.org.uk/Help-and-Advice/Leadership-and-governance/Strategic-planning/Framework-for-ethical-leadership-in-education.

Auld, R. (1976) *The William Tyndale Junior and Infants Schools. Report of the Public Inquiry* [Auld Report]. London: Inner London Education Authority.

Baker, K. (1993) *The Turbulent Years: My Life in Politics*. London: Faber & Faber.

Ball, E. (2016) *Speaking Out: Lessons in Life and Politics*. London: Penguin Random House.

Ball, S. (1990) *Politics and Policy Making in Education: Explorations in Policy Sociology*. Abingdon and New York: Routledge.

Ball, S. (2017) *The Education Debate: Policy and Politics in the Twenty-First Century*. Bristol: Policy Press.

Bangs, J., MacBeath, J. and Galton, M. (2011) *Reinventing Schools, Reforming Teaching: From Political Visions to Classroom Reality*. Abingdon and New York: Routledge.

Barber, M. (2016) *How to Run a Government So That Citizens Benefit and Taxpayers Don't Go Crazy*. London: Allen Lane.

Barber, M. and Mourshed, M. (2007) *How the World's Best-Performing School Systems Come Out on Top*. London: McKinsey & Company. Available at: https://www.mckinsey.com/industries/public-and-social-sector/our-insights/how-the-worlds-best-performing-school-systems-come-out-on-top.

Barth, R. (1980) *Run School Run*. Cambridge, MA: Harvard University Press.

BBC News (2007) Cameron Steps Up Grammars Attack (22 May). Available at: http://news.bbc.co.uk/1/hi/uk_politics/6679005.stm.

BBC News (2011) School Leavers 'Need Work Skills and Knowledge' (11 March). Available at: https://www.bbc.co.uk/news/education-12701594.

BBC News (2021) A-Level Results: Students Have Been Treated Fairly – Watchdog (9 August). Available at: https://www.bbc.co.uk/news/education-58141518.

BBC Sport (2017) London Marathon 2017: Club Runner Josh Griffiths Finishes As Fastest Briton (23 April). Available at: https://www.bbc.co.uk/sport/wales/39686121.

Belger, T. (2021) The Emerging 'Super League' of Best-Paid CEOs, *Schools Week*, 247 (23 April): 13–16. Available at: https://schoolsweek.co.uk/wp-content/uploads/2021/04/SW-247-digi.pdf.

Benjamin, H. (1939) *The Saber-Tooth Curriculum*. New York: McGraw-Hill.

Bennett, N. (1976) *Teaching Styles and Pupil Progress*. London: Open Books.

Bennett, O. (2019) *Michael Gove: A Man in a Hurry*. Hull: Biteback Publishing.

Bennett, T. (2017) *Creating a Culture: How School Leaders Can Optimise Behaviour*. London: Department for Education. Available at: https://assets.publishing.service. gov.uk/government/uploads/system/uploads/attachment_data/file/602487/Tom_ Bennett_Independent_Review_of_Behaviour_in_Schools.pdf.

Bentham, J. (1791) *Panopticon; or The Inspection House, Volume 1*. London: T. Payne.

Bettelheim, B. (1988) *A Good Enough Parent: A Book on Child-Rearing*. New York: Vintage Books.

Beveridge, W. (1942) *Social Insurance and Allied Services*, Cmnd 6404 [Beveridge Report]. London: HMSO.

Bew, J. (2016) *Citizen Clem: A Biography of Attlee*. London: Riverrun.

Biesta, G. (2014) *The Beautiful Risk of Education*. Abingdon and New York: Routledge.

Birmingham Education Commission (1993) *Aiming High* [First Wragg Report]. Birmingham: Education Department.

Black, P., Harrison, C., Hodgen, J., Marshall, B. and Serret, N. (2013) *Inside the Black Box of Assessment*. London: GL Assessment.

Blair, T. (2001) Tony Blair's Speech [at the Labour Party Conference], *The Guardian* (2 October). Available at: https://www.theguardian.com/politics/2001/oct/02/ labourconference.labour6.

Bloom, A. (2017) Spielman: 'Cutting Teacher Workload Is My Top Priority and Ofsted Is Part of the Problem', *TES* (6 September). Available at: https://www.tes.com/news/ spielman-cutting-teacher-workload-my-top-priority-and-ofsted-part-problem.

Bloom, B. S. and Krathwohl, D. R. (1956) *A Taxonomy of Educational Objectives: The Classification of Educational Goals, Volume 1*. New York: Longmans, Green.

Blunkett, D. (2006) *The Blunkett Tapes: My Life in the Bear Pit*. London: Bloomsbury.

Blunkett, D. with MacCormick, A. (1995) *On a Clear Day*. London: Michael O'Mara Books.

Brendtro, L. K., Brokenleg, M. and Van Bockern, S. (2013) The Circle of Courage: Developing Resilience and Capacity in Youth, *International Journal for Talent Development and Creativity*, 1(1): 67–74. Available at: https://www.academia. edu/7847130/The_Circle_of_Courage_Developing_Resilience_and_Capacity_in_ Youth.

Brighouse, H. (2000) *School Choice and Social Justice*. Oxford: Oxford University Press.

Brighouse, T. (1988) Politicising the Manager or Managing the Politicians? Can the Headteacher Succeed Where the Education Officer Failed?, *British Educational Leadership, Management and Administration Society*, 16: 97–103.

Brighouse, T. and Moon, B. (2020) Like the Open University, We Now Need an Open School for the Whole Country, *The Guardian* (12 May). Available at: https://www. theguardian.com/education/2020/may/12/like-the-open-university-we-now-need- an-open-school-for-the-whole-country.

Brighouse, T. and Woods, D. (2013) *The A–Z of School Improvement: Principles and Practice*. London: Bloomsbury.

Bullock, A. (1975) *A Language for Life* [Bullock Report]. London: HMSO. Available at: http://www.educationengland.org.uk/documents/bullock/bullock1975.html.

Burke, C., Cunningham, P. and Hoare, L. (2021) *Education Through the Arts for Well-Being and Community: The Vision and Legacy of Sir Alec Clegg*. Abingdon and New York: Routledge.

Burke Harris, N. (2018) *The Deepest Well: Healing the Long-Term Effects of Childhood Adversity*. Los Angeles, CA: Bluebird.

Burnage, M. (2019) The Teachers' Standards: A Think Piece Working Paper. In *CollectivED Working Papers*, Issue 7. Leeds: Leeds Beckett University/Carnegie School of Education, pp. 40–44. Available at: https://www.leedsbeckett.ac.uk/-/media/files/research/collectived/collectived-issue-7-mar-2019.pdf.

Butler, P. (2013) Ed Balls: No Regrets About Sacking Sharon Shoesmith Over Baby P Affair, *The Guardian* (29 October). Available at: https://www.theguardian.com/society/2013/oct/29/ed-balls-sharon-shoesmith-baby-p-sacking-payout.

Butler, S. (2021) Gavin Williamson Interview: 'I've Got the Hide of a Rhino – You Need to in This Job', *Evening Standard* (8 September). Available at: https://www.standard.co.uk/news/politics/gavin-williamson-interview-education-b954132.html.

Callaghan, J. (1976) A Rational Debate Based on the Facts. Speech delivered at Ruskin College, Oxford (18 October). Available at: http://www.educationengland.org.uk/documents/speeches/1976ruskin.html.

Carr, J. (2021) Safeguarding Failure Exposed at Trust That 'Cut Cash', *Schools Week*, 24 (12 February): 9. Available at: https://schoolsweek.co.uk/wp-content/uploads/2021/02/SW-240-digi.pdf.

Carr, J. L. (1972) *The Harpole Report*. London: Secker and Warburg.

Casals, P. (1970) *Joys and Sorrows: Reflections by Pablo Casals*. New York: Simon & Schuster.

Children's Commissioner for England (2018) *Annual Report and Accounts 2017–18*. Available at: https://www.childrenscommissioner.gov.uk/wp-content/uploads/2018/07/CCO-Annual-Report-and-Accounts-2018.pdf.

Christodoulou, D. (2014) *Seven Myths About Education*, 1st edn. Abingdon and New York: Routledge.

Churchill, W. (1930) *My Early Life: 1874–1904* (New York: Simon & Schuster).

Clarke, C. (2014) *The Too Difficult Box: The Big Issues Politicians Can't Crack*. Hull: Biteback Publishing.

Clarke, K. (2016) *Kind of Blue: A Political Memoir*. London: Macmillan.

Clarke, S. (2003) *Enriching Feedback in the Primary Classroom*. London: Hodder Education.

Clarke, S. (2021) *Unlocking Learning Intentions and Success Criteria: Shifting from Product to Process Across the Disciplines*. Thousand Oaks, CA: Corwin.

Claxton, G. (2021) *The Future of Teaching: And the Myths That Hold It Back*. Abingdon and New York: Routledge.

Clegg, N. (2012) Delivering Education's Progressive Promise: Using the Pupil Premium to Change Lives [speech] (14 May). Available at: https://www.gov.uk/government/speeches/delivering-educations-progressive-promise-using-the-pupil-premium-to-change-lives.

Coates, M. (2021) Editorial, *Buckingham Journal of Education*, 2(1): 1–8. DOI: https://doi.org/10.5750/tbje.v2i1

Cockcroft, W. H. (1982) *Mathematics Counts* [Cockcroft Report]. London: HMSO. Available at: http://www.educationengland.org.uk/documents/cockcroft/cockcroft1982.html.

Coles, M. (2015) *Towards the Compassionate School: From Golden Rule to Golden Thread*. London: Trentham Books.

Coles, M. with Gent, B. (2020) *Education for Survival: The Pedagogy of Compassion*. London: Trentham Books.

Commons Select Committee (2010) The Responsibilities of the Secretary of State – Education Committee, Examination of Witnesses (28 July). Available at: https://publications.parliament.uk/pa/cm201011/cmselect/cmeduc/395-i/395-i02.htm.

Comprehensive Future (2018) *Decision Time: A Plan for Fairer School Admissions*. Available at: https://comprehensivefuture.org.uk/wp-content/uploads/2018/09/Decision-time-A-plan-for-fair-admissions-FINAL.pdf.

Confederation of British Industry (2019) Getting Young People 'Work Ready' (2 June). Available at: https://www.cbi.org.uk/articles/getting-young-people-work-ready.

Cook, M. C. (2021) Systemic Bias Against Boys? Unexplained Differences in Teacher Assessed Grades Between Boys and Girls in This Year's A Level Results, *Higher Education Policy Institute* [blog] (23 August). Available at: https://www.hepi.ac.uk/2021/08/23/systemic-bias-against-boys-unexplained-differences-in-teacher-assessed-grades-between-boys-and-girls-in-this-years-a-level-results.

Coughlan, S. and Sellgren, K. (2021) School Catch-Up Tsar Resigns Over Lack of Funding, *BBC News* (2 June). Available at: https://www.bbc.co.uk/news/education-57335558.

Cousins, S. and Crossley-Holland, J. (2021) *Developing a New Locality Model for English Schools: Summary Report* (March). Sheffield: British Educational Leadership, Management and Administration Society. Available at: http://www.belmas.org.uk/write/MediaUploads/Locality_Model_Summary_Report_PROOF_6-1.pdf.

Cox, B. and Dyson, A. E. (1969) *Fight for Education: A Black Paper*. London: Critical Quarterly Society.

Crehan, L. (2018) *Cleverlands: The Secrets Behind the Success of the World's Education Superpowers*. London: Unbound.

Crick, B. (1998) *Education for Citizenship and the Teaching of Democracy in School* [Crick Review]. London: Qualifications and Curriculum Authority.

Crowther, G. (1959) *15 to 18: A Report of the Central Advisory Council for Education (England)* [Crowther Report]. London: HMSO. Available at: http://www.educationengland.org.uk/documents/crowther/crowther1959-1.html.

Cullen, W. (1996) *The Public Inquiry into the Shootings at Dunblane Primary School on 13 March 1996*. London: TSO. Available at: https://assets.publishing.service.gov.uk/government/uploads/system/uploads/attachment_data/file/276631/3386.pdf.

Curtis, P. (2003) Estelle Morris's Road to Resignation, *The Guardian* (9 January). Available at: https://www.theguardian.com/education/2003/jan/09/schools.uk.

Davies, B. and Brighouse, T. (2008) *Passionate Leadership in Education*. London: SAGE.

Dearing, R. (1994) *The National Curriculum and its Assessment: Final Report* [Dearing Review]. London: School Curriculum and Assessment Authority. Available at: http://www.educationengland.org.uk/documents/dearing1994/dearing1994.html.

Department for Communities and Local Government (2010) *Evaluation of the National Strategy for Neighbourhood Renewal: Final Report*. Available at: https://extra.shu.ac.uk/ndc/downloads/general/Neighbourhood%20Renewal%20Final%20report.pdf.

Department for Education (2010) *The Importance of Teaching: The Schools White Paper 2010.* Norwich: TSO. Available at: https://assets.publishing.service.gov.uk/government/uploads/system/uploads/attachment_data/file/175429/CM-7980.pdf.

Department for Education (2011) *Teachers' Standards: Guidance for School Leaders, School Staff and Governing Bodies* (July; updated July 2021). Available at: https://www.gov.uk/government/publications/teachers-standards.

Department for Education (2013) *The National Curriculum in England: Key Stages 1 and 2 Framework Document* (September). Available at: https://assets.publishing.service.gov.uk/government/uploads/system/uploads/attachment_data/file/425601/PRIMARY_national_curriculum.pdf.

Department for Education (2014a) *The National Curriculum in England: Framework Document* (December). Available at: https://assets.publishing.service.gov.uk/government/uploads/system/uploads/attachment_data/file/381344/Master_final_national_curriculum_28_Nov.pdf.

Department for Education (2014b) National Curriculum in England: Framework for Key Stages 1 to 4. Statutory Guidance (updated 2 December). Available at: https://www.gov.uk/government/publications/national-curriculum-in-england-framework-for-key-stages-1-to-4/the-national-curriculum-in-england-framework-for-key-stages-1-to-4.

Department for Education (2014c) *School Admissions Code: Statutory Guidance for Admission Authorities, Governing Bodies, Local Authorities, Schools Adjudicators and Admission Appeals Panels* (December). Available at: https://www.gov.uk/government/publications/school-admissions-code--2.

Department for Education (2015) Accounting Officer: Accountability System Statement for Education and Children's Services. Ref: DFE-00026-2015 (January). Available at: https://assets.publishing.service.gov.uk/government/uploads/system/uploads/attachment_data/file/396815/Accountability_Statement_.pdf.

Department for Education (2018a) *Government Response to the Education Select Committee's Fifth Report of Session 2017–19 on Alternative Provision* (October). Available at: https://assets.publishing.service.gov.uk/government/uploads/system/uploads/attachment_data/file/748723/ESC_Government_response_FINAL.pdf.

Department for Education (2018b) Permanent and Fixed Period Exclusions in England: 2016 to 2017 [statistical release] (19 July). Available at: https://assets.publishing. service.gov.uk/government/uploads/system/uploads/attachment_data/file/726741/ text_exc1617.pdf.

Department for Education (2019) *Early Career Framework* (January). Available at: https://assets.publishing.service.gov.uk/government/uploads/system/uploads/ attachment_data/file/978358/Early-Career_Framework_April_2021.pdf.

Department for Education (2020a) *National Professional Qualification (NPQ): Leading Teacher Development Framework* (October). Available at: https://www.gov.uk/ government/publications/national-professional-qualifications-frameworks-from-september-2021.

Department for Education (2020b) Permanent and Fixed-Period Exclusions in England 2018/19. Available at: https://explore-education-statistics.service.gov.uk/ find-statistics/permanent-and-fixed-period-exclusions-in-england.

Department for Education (2021a) *Initial Teacher Training (ITT) Market Review Report* (July). Available at: https://assets.publishing.service.gov.uk/government/uploads/ system/uploads/attachment_data/file/999621/ITT_market_review_report.pdf.

Department for Education (2021b) *The Reading Framework: Teaching the Foundations of Literacy* (July). Available at: https://www.gov.uk/government/publications/ the-reading-framework-teaching-the-foundations-of-literacy.

Department for Education, Clegg, N. and Laws, D. (2013) Raising Ambitions and Standards for Primary Schools [press release] (17 July). Available at: https://www.gov. uk/government/news/raising-ambitions-and-standards-for-primary-schools.

Department for Education and Department of Health (2015) *Special Educational Needs and Disability Code of Practice: 0 to 25 Years*. Available at: https://www.gov.uk/ government/publications/send-code-of-practice-0-to-25.

Department for Education and Gibb, N. (2016) Nick Gibb at the Jewish Schools Award [speech] (28 January). Available at: https://www.gov.uk/government/speeches/ nick-gibb-at-the-jewish-schools-awards.

Department for Education and Gibb, N. (2021) New Institute of Teaching Set to Be Established [press release] (2 January). Available at: https://www.gov.uk/government/ news/new-institute-of-teaching-set-to-be-established.

Department for Education and Gove, M. (2010) Teachers, Not Politicians, Know How Best to Run Schools [press release] (26 May). Available at: https://www.gov.uk/ government/news/gove-teachers-not-politicians-know-how-best-to-run-schools.

Department for Education and Gove, M. (2011) Michael Gove's Speech to the Policy Exchange on Free Schools (20 June). Available at: https://www.gov.uk/government/ speeches/michael-goves-speech-to-the-policy-exchange-on-free-schools.

Department for Education and Gove, M. (2012) The Education Secretary's Speech on Academies at Haberdashers' Aske's Hatcham College (11 January). Available at: https://www.gov.uk/government/speeches/michael-gove-speech-on-academies.

Department for Education and Gove, M. (2013) Michael Gove Article in 'The Independent' on Education Reforms (28 February). Available at: https://www.gov.uk/

government/speeches/michael-gove-article-in-the-independent-on-education-reforms.

Department for Education and Greening, J. (2017) Education Secretary Announces 6 New Opportunity Areas [press release] (18 January). Available at: https://www.gov.uk/government/news/education-secretary-announces-6-new-opportunity-areas.

Department for Education and Lord Nash (2014) Guidance on Promoting British Values in Schools Published [press release] (27 November). Available at: https://www.gov.uk/government/news/guidance-on-promoting-british-values-in-schools-published.

Department for Education, Ofqual and Zahawi, N. (2021) Adaptations in 2022 Summer Exams to Ensure Fairness for Students [press release] (30 September). Available at: https://www.gov.uk/government/news/adaptations-in-2022-summer-examsto-ensure-fairness-for-students.

Department for Education, Wallace, B. and Williamson, G. (2021) Thousands More Pupils to Benefit from Cadet Programme [press release] (2 April). Available at: https://www.gov.uk/government/news/thousands-more-pupils-to-benefit-from-cadet-programme.

Department for Education and Williamson, G. (2019) Major Review Into Support for Children with Special Educational Needs [press release] (6 September). Available at: https://www.gov.uk/government/news/major-review-into-support-for-children-with-special-educational-needs.

Department for Education and Williamson, G. (2021a) Education Secretary Speech to FED National Education Summit (1 March). Available at: https://www.gov.uk/government/speeches/education-secretary-speech-to-fed-national-education-summit.

Department for Education and Williamson, G. (2021b) Education Secretary Speech to the Confederation of School Trusts (28 April). Available at: https://www.gov.uk/government/speeches/education-secretary-speech-to-the-confederation-of-school-trusts.

Department for Education and Williamson, G. (2021c) Thousands More Students to Learn Ancient and Modern Languages [press release] (31 July). Available at: https://www.gov.uk/government/news/thousands-more-students-to-learn-ancient-and-modern-languages.

Department for Education and Employment (1997) *Excellence in Schools* [White Paper]. London: HMSO. Available at: http://www.educationengland.org.uk/documents/wp1997/excellence-in-schools.html.

Department for Education and Employment (1998) *Teachers: Meeting the Challenge of Change* [Green Paper]. London: HMSO. Available at: http://www.educationengland.org.uk/documents/gp1998/teachers-change.html.

Department for Education and Employment and Department of Social Security (1998) *Meeting the Childcare Challenge: A Framework and Consultation Document* [Green Paper]. Available at: https://webarchive.nationalarchives.gov.uk/20100217201306/http://www.dcsf.gov.uk/everychildmatters/research/publications/surestartpublications/523.

Department of Education and Science (1965) Circular 10/65: The Organisation of Secondary Education. Available at: http://www.educationengland.org.uk/documents/des/circular10-65.html.

Department of Education and Science (1972) *Education: A Framework for Expansion* [White Paper]. London: HMSO. Available at: http://www.educationengland.org.uk/documents/wp1972/framework-for-expansion.html.

Department of Education and Science (1976) *School Education in England: Problems and Initiatives* [The Yellow Book]. London: HMSO. Available at: http://www.educationengland.org.uk/documents/yellowbook1976/yellowbook.html.

Department of Education and Science (1977) *Education in Schools: A Consultative Document* [Green Paper]. London: HMSO. Available at: http://www.educationengland.org.uk/documents/gp1977/educinschools.html.

Department of Education and Science (1979) *Local Education Authority Arrangements for the School Curriculum: Report on the Circular 14/77 Review*. London: HMSO. Available at: http://www.educationengland.org.uk/documents/des/circular14-77review.html.

Department of Education and Science (1980) *A View of the Curriculum – HMI Series: Matters for Discussion 11*. London: HMSO. Available at: http://www.educationengland.org.uk/documents/hmi-discussion/viewofthecurric.html.

Department of Education and Science (1984) *Parental Influence at School: A New Framework for School Government in England and Wales* [Green Paper]. London: HMSO. Available at: http://www.educationengland.org.uk/documents/gp1984/index.html.

Department of Education and Science and the Welsh Office (1987) *National Curriculum Task Group on Assessment and Testing: A Report*. Available at: http://www.educationengland.org.uk/documents/pdfs/1988-TGAT-report.pdf.

Department for Education and Skills (2006) *Learning Outside the Classroom: Manifesto*. Annersley: DfES. Available at: https://www.lotc.org.uk/wp-content/uploads/2011/03/G1.-LOtC-Manifesto.pdf.

Desforges, C. with Abouchaar, A. (2003) *The Impact of Parental Involvement, Parental Support and Family Education on Pupil Achievement and Adjustment: A Literature Review*. Nottingham: Department for Education and Skills. Available at: https://www.nationalnumeracy.org.uk/sites/default/files/documents/impact_of_parental_involvement/the_impact_of_parental_involvement.pdf.

Dondi, M., Klier, J., Panier, F. and Schubert, J. (2021) Defining the Skills Citizens Will Need in the Future World of Work, McKinsey & Company (25 June). Available at: https://www.mckinsey.com/industries/public-and-social-sector/our-insights/defining-the-skills-citizens-will-need-in-the-future-world-of-work.

Dorling, D. (2018) *Peak Inequality: Britain's Ticking Time Bomb*. Bristol: Policy Press.

Durbin, B., Wespieser, K., Bernardinelli, D. and Gee, G. (2015) *A Guide to Regional School Commissioners*. Slough: National Foundation for Educational Research. Available at: https://www.nfer.ac.uk/publications/rscr01/rscr01.pdf.

Dweck, C. (2016) *Mindset: The New Psychology of Success*. New York: Ballantine Books.

Education Committee (2021) Oral Evidence: Education Recovery, HC 452 (29 June). Available at: https://committees.parliament.uk/oralevidence/2466/pdf.

Elton, R. (1989) *Discipline in Schools* [Elton Report]. London: HMSO. Available at: http://www.educationengland.org.uk/documents/elton/elton1989.html.

Evans, G. (2006) *Educational Failure and Working Class White Children in Britain*. Basingstoke: Palgrave Macmillan.

Fellows, T., Henson, S. and Knights, E. (2019) *Moving MATs Forward: The Power of Governance*. London: National Governance Association. Available at: https://www.nga.org.uk/getmedia/88e9fcaa-0b91-4639-bba8-61847f77b7c1/MATs-40pp-Report-June-2019-(WEB)-AW-(1)-FINAL-27-06-2019.pdf.

Ferguson, R., Coughlan, T., Egelandsdal, K., Gaved, M., Herodotou, C., Hillaire, G., et al. (2019) *Innovating Pedagogy 2019*. Open University Innovation Report 7. Available at: https://ou-iet.cdn.prismic.io/ou-iet/b0fbe67d-3cb3-45d6-946c-4b34330fb9f9_innovating-pedagogy-2019.pdf.

Finn, M. (2015) *The Gove Legacy: Education in Britain After the Coalition*. London: Palgrave Macmillan.

Fisher, R. (2003) *Teaching Thinking*, 2nd edn. London and New York: Bloomsbury Academic.

Fitzpatrick, S., Bramley, G., Sosenko, F., Blenkinsopp, J., Johnsen, S., Littlewood, M., Netto, G. and Watts, B. (2016) *Destitution in the UK*. York: Heriot-Watt University/Joseph Rowntree Foundation. Available at: https://pure.hw.ac.uk/ws/portalfiles/portal/10599861/Destitution_FinalReport.pdf.

Flutter, J. and Ruddock, J. (2004) *Consulting Pupils: What's In It for Schools?* Abingdon and New York: Routledge.

Foucault, M. (1979) *Discipline and Punish: The Birth of the Prison*, tr. A. Sheridan. Harmondsworth: Penguin.

Foundation for Education Development (2020) 150th Anniversary of State Education: Lessons Learned – The Reflections of 12 Former Secretaries of State [webinar] (17 September). Available at https://fed.education/lessons-learned-the-reflection-of-12-former-secretaries-of-state.

Foundation for Education Development (FED) (2021) National Education Consultation Report 2021. Available at: https://fed.education/wp-content/uploads/2021/07/FED-Consultation-Report-2021-June-Amends.pdf.

Fried, R. L. (2001) *The Passionate Teacher: A Practical Guide*. Boston, MA: Beacon Press.

Froehle, C. (2016) The Evolution of an Accidental Meme, *Medium* (14 April). Available at: https://medium.com/@CRA1G/the-evolution-of-an-accidental-meme-ddc4e139e0e4#.pqiclk8pl.

Fullan, M. (2000) *Leading in a Culture of Change*, 2nd edn. San Francisco, CA: Jossey-Bass.

Fullan, M. (2008) *What's Worth Fighting for in Headship?*, 2nd edn. Maidenhead: Open University Press.

Fullan, M. (2015) *The New Meaning of Educational Change*. Abingdon and New York: Routledge.

Fullan, M. (2016) The Elusive Nature of Whole System Improvement in Education, *Journal of Educational Change*, 17(4): 539–544.

Fullan, M. (2021) *The Right Drivers for Whole System Success*. East Melbourne, VIC: Centre for Strategic Education. Available at: https://michaelfullan.ca/wp-content/uploads/2021/03/Fullan-CSE-Leading-Education-Series-01-2021R2-compressed.pdf.

Fullan, M. and Hargreaves, A. (1991) *What's Worth Fighting For? Working Together For Your School*. New York: Teachers College Press.

Gardner, H. (1983) *Frames of Mind: The Theory of Multiple Intelligences*. New York: Basic Books.

Gardner, H. (2000) *Intelligence Reframed: Multiple Intelligences for the 21st Century*. London: Hachette UK.

Gilbert, C. (2017) *Optimism of the Will: The Development of Local Area-Based Education Partnerships. A Think-Piece*. London: Centre for Leadership in Learning. Available at: http://www.lcll.org.uk/uploads/2/1/4/7/21470046/christine_gilbert_-_thinkpiece.pdf.

Gilbert, C. (2021) Place-Based Leadership in Autonomous School Systems. In P. Earley and T. Greany (eds), *School Leadership and Education System Reform*. London: Bloomsbury, pp. 219–230.

Gilbert, I. (2018) *The Working Class: Poverty, Education and Alternative Voices*. Carmarthen: Independent Thinking Press.

Gilkerson, J., Richards, J. A., Warren, S. F., Montgomery, J. K., Greenwood, C. R., Kimbrough Oller, D., Hansen, J. H. L. and Paul, T. D. (2017) Mapping the Early Language Environment Using All-Day Recordings and Automated Analysis, *American Journal of Speech-Language Pathology*, 26(2): 248–265.

Gill, N. and Darley, H. (2018) *Creating Change in Urban Settings*. Norwich: Singular Publishing.

Gillard, D. (2002) The Plowden Report, *The Encyclopedia of Pedagogy and Informal Education*. Available at: https://infed.org/mobi/the-plowden-report.

Ginott, H. G. (1972) *Teacher and Child: A Book for Parents and Teachers*. New York: Macmillan.

Gomendio, M. (2017) *Empowering and Enabling Teachers to Improve Equity and Outcomes for All: International Summit on the Teaching Profession*. Paris: OECD Publishing. https://doi.org/10.1787/9789264273238-en

Gove, M. (2013a) Curriculum and Exam Reform, *Hansard* HC Deb vol. 558 col. 441 (7 February). Available at: https://hansard.parliament.uk/Commons/2013-02-07/debates/13020759000004/CurriculumAndExamReform.

Gove, M. (2013b) I Refuse to Surrender to the Marxist Teachers Hell-Bent on Destroying Our Schools: Education Secretary Berates 'the New Enemies of Promise' for Opposing His Plans, *Daily Mail* (23 March). Available at: https://www.dailymail.co.uk/debate/article-2298146/I-refuse-surrender-Marxist-teachers-hell-bent-destroying-schools-Education-Secretary-berates-new-enemies-promise-opposing-plans.html.

Gove, M. (2016) Interview with Faisal Islam, *Sky News* [video] (3 June).

Green, F. and Kynaston, D. (2019) *Engines of Privilege: Britain's Private School Problem*. London: Bloomsbury.

Groves, M. and West-Burnham, J. (2020) *Flipping Schools! Why It's Time to Turn Your School and Community Inside Out*. Woodbridge: John Catt Educational.

Hall, T. (2020) The Idea of a National Open School Is an Excellent One. The BBC Is Ready to Make It Happen, *The Guardian* (30 May). Available at: https://www.theguardian.com/education/2020/may/30/the-idea-of-a-national-open-school-is-an-excellent-one-the-bbc-is-ready-to-make-it-happen.

Hannon, V. and Peterson, A. (2021) *Thrive: The Purpose of Schooling in a Changing World*. Cambridge: Cambridge University Press.

Hardman, I. (2019) *Why We Get the Wrong Politicians*. London: Atlantic.

Hart, B. and Risley, T. (2003) The Early Catastrophe: The 30 Million Word Gap By Age 3, *American Educator* (spring): 4–9.

Hattie, J. and Zierer, K. (2019) *Visible Learning Insights*. Abingdon and New York: Routledge.

Haviland, J. (1988) *Take Care, Mr Baker*. London: Fourth Estate

Heaney, S. (1990) *The Cure at Troy: A Version of Sophocles' Philoctetes*. London: Faber & Faber.

Heathcote, D. and Bolton, G. M. (1995) *Drama for Learning: Dorothy Heathcote's Mantle of the Expert Approach to Education*. London: Pearson Education.

Henley, D. (2011) *Music Education in England* [Henley Review]. London: Department for Culture, Media and Sport/Department for Education. Available at: https://assets.publishing.service.gov.uk/government/uploads/system/uploads/attachment_data/file/175432/DFE-00011-2011.pdf.

Her Majesty's Inspectors of Schools (1978) *Primary Education in England*. London: HMSO. Available at: http://www.educationengland.org.uk/documents/hmi-primary/index.html.

Her Majesty's Inspectors of Schools (1979) *Aspects of Secondary Education in England*. London: HMSO. Available at: http://www.educationengland.org.uk/documents/hmi-secondary/hmi-secondary.html.

Her Majesty's Inspectors of Schools (1982) *Education 5 to 9*. London: HMSO. Available at: http://www.educationengland.org.uk/documents/hmi-5to9.

Her Majesty's Inspectors of Schools (1983) *9–13 Middle Schools* (London: HMSO). Available at: http://www.educationengland.org.uk/documents/hmi-9to13/hmi-9to13.html.

Herrington, D. (2021) CST Session (June).

Hill, A., Mellon, L., Laker, B. and Goddard, J. (2016) The One Type of Leader Who Can Turn Around a Failing School, *Harvard Business Review* (20 October). Available at: https://hbr.org/2016/10/the-one-type-of-leader-who-can-turn-around-a-failing-school.

Hines, B. (1968) *A Kestrel for a Knave*. London: Michael Joseph.

Hirsch, D. (2021) *The Cost of Child Poverty in 2021*. Loughborough: Centre for Research in Social Policy.

Hirsch, E. D. (2020) *How to Educate a Citizen: The Power of Shared Knowledge to Unify a Nation*. Woodbridge: John Catt Educational.

HM Treasury (2003) *Every Child Matters*. Norwich: TSO. Available at: https://www.gov.uk/government/publications/every-child-matters.

hooks, b. (2014) *Teaching to Transgress*. Abingdon and New York: Routledge.

Houghton, A. (1974) *Report of the Committee of Inquiry into the Pay of Non-University Teachers* [Houghton Report]. London: HMSO. Available at: http://www.educationengland.org.uk/documents/houghton1974/index.html.

Housden, P. (2000) *Local Statesmen: The Story of Politics in Nottinghamshire County Council*. London: Local Government Centre.

Howard, K. and Hill, C. (2020) *Symbiosis: The Curriculum and the Classroom*. Woodbridge: John Catt Educational.

HSDC (2020) HSDC Welcomes Education Secretary Gavin Williamson to its South Downs Campus (18 September). Available at: https://www.hsdc.ac.uk/news/2020/09/18/hsdc-welcomes-education-secretary-gavin-williamson-to-its-south-downs-campus.

Hudson, B., Leask, M. and Younie, S. (2020) *Education System Design: Foundations, Policy Options and Consequences*. Abingdon and New York: Routledge.

Hughes, M. (2014) *The Magenta Principles: Engagement, Depth and Challenge in the Classroom*. N.p.: Mike Hughes.

Humphrey, N., Lendrum A. and Wigelsworth, N. (2010) *Social Emotional Aspects of Learning (SEAL) Programme in Secondary Schools: National Evaluation*. London: Department for Education.

Hustler, D., Brighouse, T. and Ruddock, J. (1995) *Heading Heads*. London: David Fulton.

Hutton, W. (2011) *Hutton Review of Fair Pay in the Public Sector: Final Report*. London: HM Treasury. Available at: https://dera.ioe.ac.uk/2562/1/hutton_fairpay_review.pdf.

Independent, The (2011) Head Tells of Day 'Evil' Visited School: After the Massacre, *The Independent* (23 October). Available at: https://www.independent.co.uk/news/head-tells-of-day-evil-visited-school-1342022.html.

Inner London Education Authority (1977) *Keeping the School Under Review: A Method of Self-Assessment for Schools Devised by the ILEA Inspectorate*. London: ILEA.

James, E. (1972) *Teacher Education and Training* [James Report]. London: HMSO. Available at: http://www.educationengland.org.uk/documents/james/james1972.html.

Jay, A. (2018) *The Rotherham Independent Review. Volume One: A Review into Information Passed to the Home Office in Connection with Allegations of Child Sexual Abuse in Rotherham (1998–2005)*. London: HMSO. Available at: https://assets.publishing.service.gov.uk/government/uploads/system/uploads/attachment_data/file/726022/CCS207_CCS0318259762-1_The_Rotherham_Review_Part1.pdf.

Johnson, A. (2016) *The Long and Winding Road*. London: Penguin.

Johnston, R. S. and Watson, J. (2005) *The Effects of Synthetic Phonics Teaching on Reading and Spelling Attainment: A Seven-Year Longitudinal Study*. Edinburgh: Scottish Executive Education Department.

Jones, K. (2021) *Leading Professional Learning*. Insight Series. Swansea: National Academy for Educational Leadership in Wales.

Judge, H. (1984) *A Generation of Schooling: English Secondary Schools Since 1944*. Oxford and New York: Oxford Paperbacks.

Keay, D. (1987) Aids, Education and the Year 2000! [interview with M. Thatcher], *Woman's Own* (31 October). Available at: https://www.margaretthatcher.org/document/106689.

Kemp, K. (2021) *A for Achievement. A for Attitude. A for Attendance. The Life-Changing Endeavour of Newlands Junior College – A Glasgow Success Story*. Edinburgh: Mereworth Publishing.

Kidd, D. (2020) *A Curriculum of Hope: As Rich in Humanity as in Knowledge*. Carmarthen: Independent Thinking Press.

Kogan, M. (1975) *Educational Policy-Making: A Study of Interest Groups and Parliament*. Abingdon and New York: Routledge.

Laming, H. (2003) *The Victoria Climbié Inquiry: Report of Inquiry by Lord Laming*. Norwich: TSO. Available at: https://www.gov.uk/government/publications/the-victoria-climbie-inquiry-report-of-an-inquiry-by-lord-laming.

Lareau, A. (2000) *Home Advantage: Social Class and Parental Intervention in Elementary Education*. Lanham, MD: Rowman & Littlefield.

Lareau, A. (2011) *Unequal Childhoods: Class, Race, and Family Life*. Berkeley, CA: University of California Press.

Lawson, J. and Silver, H. (1973) *A Social History of Education in England*. London: Methuen.

Leadsom, A. (2021) *The Best Start for Life: A Vision for the 1,001 Critical Days. The Early Years Healthy Development Review Report*. London: Department of Health and Social Care. Available at: https://assets.publishing.service.gov.uk/government/uploads/system/uploads/attachment_data/file/973112/The_best_start_for_life_a_vision_for_the_1_001_critical_days.pdf.

Lees-Marshment, J. (2021) *Political Management: The Dance of Government and Politics*. Abingdon and New York: Routledge.

Leese, J. (1950) *Personalities and Power in English Education*. Leeds: E.J. Arnold & Son.

Levinson, M., Geron, T. and Brighouse, H. (in press) *Conceptions of Educational Equity*.

Little, J. W. (1981) The Power of Organizational Setting. Paper adapted from final report, *School Success and Staff Development*. Washington, DC: National Institute of Education.

Long, R. (2015) Academies Under the Labour Government. House of Commons Library, Standard Note: SN/SP/5544 (20 January). Available at: https://dera.ioe.ac.uk/22717/1/SN05544.pdf.

Long, R. and Danechi, S. (2021) *Teacher Recruitment and Retention in England*. Briefing Paper No. 07222 (14 April). Available at: https://commonslibrary.parliament.uk/research-briefings/cbp-7222.

Longfield, A. (2020) Too Many Children in England Are Still Being Excluded from School [statement] (30 July). Available at: https://www.childrenscommissioner.gov.uk/2020/07/30/too-many-children-in-england-are-still-being-excluded-from-school.

Lough, C. (2020) Third of Teachers Leaving the Profession Within 5 Years, *TES* (25 June). Available at: https://www.tes.com/news/recruitment-third-teachers-leaving-profession-within-5-years.

Louis, K. S. and Miles, M. (1992) *Improving the Urban High School*. London: Cassell.

Lowes, T. D. (2016) To What Extent Do Ofsted Inspectors' Values Influence the Inspection Process (2005–2012)? An Examination of Ofsted Inspectors' Perceptions. Unpublished thesis, University of Hull. Available at: http://hydra.hull.ac.uk/resources/hull:14579.

Lucas, B. (2021) *Rethinking Assessment in Education: The Case for Change*. East Melbourne, VIC: Centre for Strategic Education.

Lupton, R. and Hayes, D. (2021) *Great Mistakes in Education Policy – and How to Avoid Them in the Future*. London: Policy Press.

Lusher, A. (2014) New Church of England Schools to Adopt 'Open Admissions' Policy, *The Independent* (11 June). Available at: https://www.independent.co.uk/news/education/education-news/new-church-england-schools-adopt-open-admissions-policy-9525134.html.

Lyons, M. (2007) *Place-Shaping: A Shared Ambition for the Future of Local Government. Lyons Inquiry into Local Government*. Norwich: HMSO. Available at: https://assets.publishing.service.gov.uk/government/uploads/system/uploads/attachment_data/file/243601/9780119898545.pdf.

MacBeath, J., Myers, K. and Demetriou, H. (2001) Supporting Teachers in Consulting Pupils about Aspects of Teaching and Learning, and Evaluating Impact, *Forum*, 43(2): 78–82. DOI: 10.2304/forum.2001.43.2.11

Macdonald, A. (2009) *Independent Review of the Proposal to Make Personal, Social, Health and Economic (PSHE) Education Statutory* [Macdonald Review]. London: Department for Children, Schools and Families. Available at: http://www.educationengland.org.uk/documents/pdfs/2009-macdonald-pshe.pdf.

Macdonald, I. (1990) *Murder in the Playground: Report of the Macdonald Inquiry into Racism and Racial Violence in Manchester Schools*. London: New Beacon Books.

Macfarlane, E. (2016) *Who Cares about Education? Going in the Wrong Direction*. Milton Keynes: New Generation Publishing.

Macfarlane, R. (2021) *Obstetrics for Schools: A Guide to Eliminating Failure and Ensuring the Safe Delivery of All Learners*. Carmarthen: Crown House Publishing.

McMahon, M. (2011) Profile: Chris Woodhead – Mr Standards Slips, *The Independent* (23 October). Available at: https://www.independent.co.uk/life-style/profile-chris-woodhead-mr-standards-slips-1069410.html.

Male, B. and Waters, M. (2012) *The Secondary Curriculum Design Handbook*. London and New York: Network Continuum Education.

Mandler, P. (2020) *The Crisis of the Meritocracy: Britain's Transition to Mass Education since the Second World War*. Oxford: Oxford University Press.

Meirieu, P. (1996) *Frankenstein Pédagogue*. Issy-les-Moulineaux, France: ESF.

Menzies, L. and Baar, S. (2021) *Young People on the Margins: Priorities for Action in Education and Youth*. Abingdon and New York: Routledge.

Millar, F. (2013) Who Is Really Behind Michael Gove's Big Education Ideas?, *The Guardian* (3 December). Available at: https://www.theguardian.com/education/2013/dec/03/michael-gove-education-dominic-cummings-policies-oxbridge.

Ministry of Education (1949) *Story of a School*. Pamphlet No. 14. London: HMSO.

Morris, R., See, B. H. and Gorard, S. (2021) Teacher Shortage in England – New Evidence for Understanding and Addressing Current Challenges, *Impact* (February). Available at: https://impact.chartered.college/article/teacher-shortage-in-england-new-evidence-understanding-challenges.

Mortimore, P., Sammons, P., Stoll, L., Lewis, D. and Ecob, R. (1988) *School Matters: The Junior Years*. Somerset: Open Books.

Munby, S. (2019) *Imperfect Leadership: A Book for Leaders Who Know They Don't Know It All*. Carmarthen: Crown House Publishing.

Myatt, M. (2016) *Hopeful Schools: Building Humane Communities*. Worthing: Mary Myatt Learning.

Myatt, M. (2018) *The Curriculum: Gallimaufry to Coherence*. Woodbridge: John Catt Educational.

National Association of Head Teachers (2018) *Improving School Accountability: Report of the NAHT Accountability Commission*. Available at: https://www.naht.org.uk/Portals/0/PDF's/Improving%20school%20accountability.pdf?ver=2021-04-27-121950-093.

National Association of Head Teachers (2020) *Improving Schools: A Report of the School Improvement Commission*. Available at: https://www.naht.org.uk/Portals/0/PDF's/NAHT%20Improving%20schools%20final.pdf?ver=2021-05-31-090628-853.

National Commission on Teaching & America's Future (1996) *What Matters Most: Teaching for America's Future*. New York: NCTAF. Available at: https://files.eric.ed.gov/fulltext/ED395931.pdf.

National Education Union (2021) *Turning the Page on Poverty: A Practical Guide for Education Staff to Help Tackle Poverty and the Cost of the School Day*. Available at: https://neu.org.uk/turning-page.

National Governance Association (2021) *NGA Insights: Central Leadership Teams in Multi Academy Trust*s (July). Available at: https://www.nga.org.uk/getmedia/1e0655f5-cbbd-44bc-b891-33bab441ee03/nga-central-leadership-20210701.pdf.

National Institute of Economic and Social Research (2021) Destitution Levels Are Rising Across the Country – and Terribly Worrying in Certain Regions, NIESR Research Shows [press release] (22 February). Available at: https://www.niesr.ac.uk/media/

niesr-press-release-destitution-levels-are-rising-across-country-%E2%80%93-and-terribly-worrying.

Newmark, B. (2019) Why Teach? [blog] (10 February). Available at: https://bennewmark.wordpress.com/2019/02/10/why-teach.

Newsom, J. H. (1963) *Half Our Future: A Report of the Central Advisory Council for Education (England)* [Newsom Report]. London: HMSO. Available at: http://www.educationengland.org.uk/documents/newsom/newsom1963.html.

Nolan, L., Howard, C. and O'Donnell, E. (2021) *The State of the Nation: Evidence and Impact of the Importance of Learning Beyond the Classroom in 2021 Children's University*. Manchester: Children's University. Available at: https://childrensuniversity.co.uk/media/1377/watermarked-state-of-the-nation-learning-beyond-the-classroom-in-2021.pdf.

Norwich, B. (2019) From the Warnock Report (1978) to an Education Framework Commission: A Novel Contemporary Approach to Educational Policy Making for Pupils with Special Educational Needs/Disabilities, *Frontiers in Education* (17 July). Available at: https://www.frontiersin.org/articles/10.3389/feduc.2019.00072/full.

Nye, P. (2018) Who's Left? Are Schools Gaming the League Tables Through 'Off-Rolling'?, *UK Data Service Data Impact Blog* (30 July). Available at: https://blog.ukdataservice.ac.uk/whos-left-off-rolling.

Nye, P. and Thomson, D. (2018) Who's Left 2018, Part One: The Main Findings, *FFT Education Datalab* (21 June). Available at: https://ffteducationdatalab.org.uk/2018/06/whos-left-2018-part-one-the-main-findings.

O'Brien, J. (2020) *How Not to Be Wrong: The Art of Changing Your Mind*. London: Penguin.

O'Farrell, J. (2007) *May Contain Nuts: A Novel of Extreme Parenting*. New York: Open Road and Grove/Atlantic.

Office of the Schools Adjudicator (2018) *Annual Report: September 2016 to August 2017* (February). Available at: https://assets.publishing.service.gov.uk/government/uploads/system/uploads/attachment_data/file/680003/2017_OSA_Annual_Report_-_Final_23_January_2018.pdf.

Ofqual and Saxton, J. (2021) Ofqual's Approach to Grading Exams and Assessments in Summer 2022 and Autumn 2021 (30 September). Available at: https://www.gov.uk/government/speeches/ofquals-approach-to-grading-exams-and-assessments-in-summer-2022-and-autumn-2021.

Ofsted (2015) *Key Stage 3: The Wasted Years?* (September). Available at: https://www.gov.uk/government/publications/key-stage-3-the-wasted-years.

Ofsted (2017) *Do Two Inspectors Inspecting the Same School Make Consistent Decisions? A Study of the Reliability of Ofsted's New Short Inspections*. Available at: https://assets.publishing.service.gov.uk/government/uploads/system/uploads/attachment_data/file/596708/Reliability_study_-_final.pdf.

Ofsted (2019a) Ofsted Inspections: Myths (28 February) [withdrawn 2 September 2019]. Available at https://www.gov.uk/government/publications/further-education-and-skills-inspection-handbook/ofsted-inspections-myths.

Ofsted (2019b) School Inspection Update: Special Edition (January). Available at: https://www.gov.uk/government/publications/school-inspection-update-academic-year-2018-to-2019.

Ofsted (2021a) Education Inspection Framework (updated 23 July). Available at: https://www.gov.uk/government/publications/education-inspection-framework/education-inspection-framework.

Ofsted (2021b) Review of Sexual Abuse in Schools and Colleges (10 June). Available at: https://www.gov.uk/government/publications/review-of-sexual-abuse-in-schools-and-colleges/review-of-sexual-abuse-in-schools-and-colleges.

Ofsted and Spielman, A. (2017a) Amanda Spielman's Speech at the Festival of Education (23 June). Available at: https://www.gov.uk/government/speeches/amanda-spielmans-speech-at-the-wellington-festival-of-education.

Ofsted and Spielman, A. (2017b) HMCI's Commentary: New Research into Short School Inspections (7 March). Available at: https://www.gov.uk/government/speeches/hmcis-monthly-commentary-march-2017.

Ofsted and Spielman, A. (2017c) HMCI's Commentary: Recent Primary and Secondary Curriculum Research (11 October). Available at: https://www.gov.uk/government/speeches/hmcis-commentary-october-2017.

Ofsted and Spielman, A. (2018) Amanda Spielman Speech to the SCHOOLS North East Summit (11 October). Available at: https://www.gov.uk/government/speeches/amanda-spielman-speech-to-the-schools-northeast-summit.

Organisation for Economic Co-operation and Development (2020) *Education at a Glance 2020: OECD Indicators*. Paris: OECD Publishing. https://doi.org/10.1787/69096873-en

Ovenden-Hope, T. (2021) Teacher As Commodity versus Teacher As Professional: An International Status-Based Crisis in Teacher Supply, *Impact* (February). Available at: https://impact.chartered.college/article/teacher-as-commodity-versus-professional-international-crisis-supply.

Peacock, A. and Swift, D. (2021) Teacher Expertise and Professionalism: A Review of the Initial Teacher Training (ITT) Market Review. London: Chartered College of Teaching. Available at: https://chartered.college/wp-content/uploads/2021/07/ITT-market-review-position-paper.pdf.

Perryman, J. (2006) Panoptic Performativity and School Inspection Regimes: Disciplinary Mechanisms and Life Under Special Measures, *Journal of Education Policy*, 21(2): 147–161.

Playfair, E. (2021) Reading bell hooks (5 April). Available at: https://eddieplayfair.com/2021/04/05/reading-bell-hooks.

Plowden, B. (1967) *Children and their Primary Schools: A Report of the Central Advisory Council for Education (England)* [Plowden Report]. London: HMSO. Available at: http://www.educationengland.org.uk/documents/plowden.

Plowright, D. (2008) Using Self-Evaluation for Inspection: How Well Prepared Are Primary School Headteachers?, *School Leadership & Management*, 28(2): 101–126.

Powell, A., Farrar, E. and Cohen, D. (1985) *The Shopping Mall High School: Winners and Losers in the Educational Marketplace*. Boston, MA: Houghton Mifflin.

Ranson, S., Arnott, M., McKeown, P., Martin, J. and Smith, P. (2006) The Participation of Volunteer Citizens in School Governance, *Educational Review*, 57(3): 357–371.

Ravitch, D. (2010) *The Death and Life of the Great American School System: How Testing and Choice Are Undermining Education*. New York: Basic Books.

Raworth, K. (2018) *Doughnut Economics: Seven Ways to Think Like a 21st-Century Economist*. London: Random House Business.

Rée, H. (1973) *Educator Extraordinary: The Life and Achievements of Henry Morris, 1889–1961*. London: Longman.

Ribbins, P. and Sherratt, B. (1997) *Radical Educational Policies and Conservative Secretaries of State.* London and New York: Network Continuum.

Richmond, T. (2021) *Re-assessing the Future. Part 1: How to Move Beyond GCSEs*. London: EDSK. Available at: https://www.edsk.org/wp-content/uploads/2021/01/EDSK-Re-assessing-the-future-part-1.pdf.

Rickards, F., Hattie, J. and Reid, C. (2021) *The Turning Point for the Teaching Profession: Growing Expertise and Evaluative Thinking*. Abingdon and New York: Routledge.

Riley, K. (2013) *Leadership of Place: Stories from Schools in the US, UK and South Africa*. London: Bloomsbury.

Roberts, J. (2020) Headteacher Responsible for One School is Paid £280k, *TES* (23 December). Available at: https://www.tes.com/news/headteacher-responsible-one-school-paid-ps280k.

Robbins, L. (1963) *Higher Education* [Robbins Report]. London: HMSO. Available at: http://www.educationengland.org.uk/documents/robbins.

Robinson, K. (1999) *All Our Futures: Creativity, Culture and Education. Report of the National Advisory Committee on Creative and Cultural Education*. London: Department for Education and Employment/Department for Digital, Culture, Media and Sport. Available at: http://sirkenrobinson.com/pdf/allourfutures.pdf.

Rose, J. (2009) *Independent Review of the Primary Curriculum: Final Report* [Rose Review] (Nottingham: Department for Children, Schools and Families). Available at: http://www.educationengland.org.uk/documents/pdfs/2009-IRPC-final-report.pdf.

Rosenshine, B. (1982) *Teaching Functions in Instructional Programs*. Washington, DC: National Institute of Education.

Roser, M. and Ortiz-Ospina, E. (2013) Literacy, *Our World in Data* (updated 2018). Available at: https://ourworldindata.org/literacy.

Rutter, M., Maughan, B., Mortimore, P. and Ouston, J. (1979) *Fifteen Thousand Hours: Secondary Schools and Their Effects on Children*. Cambridge, MA: Harvard University Press.

Sammons, P., Hall, J., Smees, R., Goff, J., Sylva, K., Smith, T. et al. (2015) *The Impact of Children's Centres: Studying the Effects of Children's Centres in Promoting Better Outcomes of Young Children and Their Families. Evaluation of Children's Centres in England (ECCE, Strand 4). Research Report*. London: Department for Education. Available at: https://www.gov.uk/government/publications/childrens-centres-their-impact-on-children-and-families.

Sammons, P., Hillman, J. and Mortimore, P. (1995) *Key Characteristics of Effective Schools: A Review of School Effectiveness Research.* London: Institute of Education.

Scottish Government (2017) *Included, Engaged and Involved Part 2: Preventing and Managing School Exclusions* (19 June). Available at: https://www.gov.scot/publications/included-engaged-involved-part-2-positive-approach-preventing-managing-school.

Scottish Government (2019) *Included, Engaged and Involved Part 1: Promoting and Managing School Attendance* (14 June). Available at: https://www.gov.scot/publications/included-engaged-involved-part-1-positive-approach-promotion-management-attendance-scottish-schools.

Sealy, C. and Bennett, T. (2020) *The ResearchED Guide to the Curriculum: An Evidence-Informed Guide for Teachers.* Woodbridge: John Catt Educational.

Seldon, A. (2015) *Beyond Happiness: How to Find Lasting Meaning and Joy in All That You Have.* London: Hachette UK.

Seldon, A. with Metcalf, T. and Abidoye, O. (2020) *The Fourth Education Revolution Reconsidered: Will Artificial Intelligence Enrich or Diminish Humanity?* Buckingham: University of Buckingham Press.

Shaw, B. (2021) Special Educational Needs and Disabilities. In L. Menzies and S. Baar (eds), *Young People on the Margins: Priorities for Action in Education and Youth.* Abingdon and New York: Routledge, pp. 32–50.

Shephard, G. (2000) *Shephard's Watch: Illusions of Power in British Politics.* London: Politico's Publishing.

Sida-Nicholls, K. (2021) How Do Trainee Teachers Perceive Their Future Selves As Teachers, And How Can We Support Them in Their Careers?, *Impact* (February). Available at: https://impact.chartered.college/article/how-do-trainee-teachers-perceive-support-careers.

Siraj, T. and Taggart, B. with Melhuish, E., Sammons, P. and Sylva, K. (2014) *Exploring Effective Pedagogy in Primary Schools: Evidence from Research.* London: Pearson. Available at: https://www.pearson.com/content/dam/one-dot-com/one-dot-com/global/Files/about-pearson/innovation/open-ideas/ExploringEffectivePedagogy.pdf.

Smithers, R., White, M. and Ward, L. (2004) Blair Insists A-Levels Will Stay in Shakeup, *The Guardian* (19 October). Available at: https://www.theguardian.com/uk/2004/oct/19/politics.schools.

Social Mobility and Child Poverty Commission (2016) *The Social Mobility Index* (16 June). Available at: https://assets.publishing.service.gov.uk/government/uploads/system/uploads/attachment_data/file/496103/Social_Mobility_Index.pdf.

Steer, A. (2009) *Learning Behaviour: Lessons Learned: A Review of Behaviour Standards and Practices in Our Schools* [Steer Report]. Nottingham: Department for Children, Schools and Families. Available at: http://www.educationengland.org.uk/documents/pdfs/2009-steer-report-lessons-learned.pdf.

Stephens, H. (2021) An Alternative to GCSEs: Reuniting Curriculum, Pedagogy and Assessment, *Impact* (May). Available at: https://impact.chartered.college/article/alternative-to-gcses-reuniting-curriculum-pedagogy-assessment.

Stewart, H. (2020) Boris Johnson Blames 'Mutant Algorithm' for Exams Fiasco, *The Guardian* (26 August). Available at: https://www.theguardian.com/politics/2020/aug/26/boris-johnson-blames-mutant-algorithm-for-exams-fiasco.

Sunderland, M. (2016) *What Every Parent Needs to Know: Love, Nurture and Play with Your Child*. London: Dorling Kindersley.

Swann, M. (1985) *Education for All* [Swann Report]. London: HMSO. Available at: http://www.educationengland.org.uk/documents/swann.

Syed, M. (2011) *Bounce: The Myth of Talent and the Power of Practice*. London: Fourth Estate.

Taylor, C. (2011) *Getting the Simple Things Right: Charlie Taylor's Behaviour Checklists*. London: Department for Education. Available at: https://assets.publishing.service.gov.uk/government/uploads/system/uploads/attachment_data/file/571640/Getting_the_simple_things_right_Charlie_Taylor_s_behaviour_checklists.pdf.

Taylor, T. (1977) *A New Partnership for Our Schools* [Taylor Report]. London: HMSO. Available at: http://www.educationengland.org.uk/documents/taylor/taylor1977.html.

Thatcher, M. (2013) *Margaret Thatcher: The Autobiography*. London: Harper Perennial.

Thompson, I. (2020) Poverty and Education in England: A School System in Crisis. In I. Thompson and G. Ivinson (eds), *Poverty in Education Across the UK: A Comparative Analysis of Policy and Place* (Bristol: Policy Press), pp. 155–140.

Thompson, I. and Ivinson, G. (eds) (2020) *Poverty in Education Across the UK: A Comparative Analysis of Policy and Place*. Bristol: Policy Press.

Timpson, E. (2019) *The Timpson Review of School Exclusion*. Ref: DfE-00090-2019 (May). Available at: https://assets.publishing.service.gov.uk/government/uploads/system/uploads/attachment_data/file/807862/Timpson_review.pdf.

Tomlinson, M. (2004) *14–19 Curriculum and Qualifications Reform: Final Report of the Working Group on 14–19 Reform* [Tomlinson Report]. Nottingham: Department for Education and Skills. Available at: http://www.educationengland.org.uk/documents/pdfs/2004-tomlinson-report.pdf.

Tower Hamlets Corporate Research Unit (2018) *Child Poverty in Tower Hamlets* (May). Available at: https://www.towerhamlets.gov.uk/Documents/Borough_statistics/Income_poverty_and_welfare/2015_Child_Poverty_Briefing.pdf.

United Nations Educational, Scientific and Cultural Organization (1994) *The Salamanca Statement and Framework for Action on Special Needs Education*. Paris: UNESCO. Available at: https://unesdoc.unesco.org/ark:/48223/pf0000098427.

United Nations Educational, Scientific and Cultural Organization (2015) *Education 2030: Incheon Declaration and Framework for Action for the Implementation of Sustainable Development Goal 4*. Paris: UNESCO. Available at: http://uis.unesco.org/sites/default/files/documents/education-2030-incheon-framework-for-action-implementation-of-sdg4-2016-en_2.pdf.

Universities' Council for the Education of Teachers (2021) DfE Consultation on the Review of the ITE Market: UCET Response. Available at: https://www.ucet.ac.uk/downloads/13250-UCET-Market-Review-Response-%28July-2021%29.pdf.

Van der Eyken, W. and Turner, B. (1969) *Adventures in Education*. London: Allen Lane.

Verkaik, R. (2018) *Posh Boys: How English Public Schools Ruin Britain*. London: Simon & Schuster.

Walker, M. (2021) Issues of Trust on Teachers' Assessment: Can the Profession Move Forward?, *Impact* (May). Available at: https://impact.chartered.college/article/issues-of-trust-teachers-assessments.

Walton. L. (n.d.) Les Walton Speaks About His Life in Education. Available at: http://northerneducation.com/media/display/Les_Walton_speaks_about_his_life_in_.pdf.

Warnock, H. M. (1978) *Special Educational Needs: Report of the Committee of Enquiry into the Education of Handicapped Children and Young People* [Warnock Report]. London: HMSO. Available at: http://www.educationengland.org.uk/documents/warnock/warnock1978.html.

Waterman, C. (2014) Local Government and Local Governance: 1944–2011, *Local Government Studies*, 40(6): 938–953. DOI: 10.1080/03003930.2012.719101

Waters, M. (2013) *Thinking Allowed on Schooling*. Carmarthen: Independent Thinking Press.

Weale, S. and Adams, R. (2018) Schools Minister Denies Sats Place Undue Stress on Pupils, *The Guardian* (10 July). Available at: https://www.theguardian.com/education/2018/jul/10/schools-minister-denies-sats-place-undue-stress-on-pupils.

West, A. and Pennell, H. (2003) *Underachievement in Schools*. Abingdon: RoutledgeFalmer.

Whitaker, D. (2021) *The Kindness Principle: Making Relational Behaviour Management Work in Schools*. Carmarthen: Independent Thinking Press.

Wiliam, D. and Black, P. (2006) *Inside the Black Box. V.1: Raising Standards Through Classroom Assessment*. London: GL Assessment.

Wilkinson, R. and Pickett, K. (2009) *The Spirit Level: Why Equality is Better for Everyone*. London: Penguin.

Williams, S. (2009) *Climbing the Bookshelves: The Autobiography of Shirley Williams*. London: Virago.

Williams, Z. (2012) Early Puberty: Why Are Kids Growing Up Faster?, *The Guardian* (25 October). Available at: https://www.theguardian.com/society/2012/oct/25/early-puberty-growing-up-faster.

Willingham, D. (2021) *Why Don't Students Like School? A Cognitive Scientist Answers Questions About How the Mind Works and What It Means for the Classroom*, 2nd edn. San Francisco, CA: Jossey-Bass.

Winnett, R. (2011) David Cameron Goes to War on Britain's 'Coasting Schools', *The Telegraph* (13 November).

Wolf, A. (2011) *Review of Vocational Education: The Wolf Report*. London: Department for Education and Department for Business and Innovation. Available at: https://

assets.publishing.service.gov.uk/government/uploads/system/uploads/attachment_data/file/180504/DFE-00031-2011.pdf.

Wooldridge, A. (2021) *The Aristocracy of Talent: How Meritocracy Made the Modern World*. London: Penguin Random House.

Worth, J. and De Lazzari, G. (2017) *Teacher Retention and Turnover Research. Research Update 1: Teacher Retention by Subject*. Slough: National Foundation for Educational Research.

XP School (2015) *What Makes a Successful Community?* Doncaster: XP School.

Websites

Birmingham Education Partnership: https://bep.education

Camden Learning: https://camdenlearning.org.uk

Education: The Rock and Roll Years (Les Walton): https://www.education-the-rock-and-roll-years.com

Education in England: A History (Derek Gillard): www.educationengland.org.uk/history

Herts for Learning: www.hertsforlearning.co.uk

Learn Sheffield: www.learnsheffield.co.uk

Leicestershire Primary Partnership: www.lpp-leicester.org.uk

Lincolnshire Learning Partnership: www.lincolnshirelearningpartnership.org

Schools Alliance for Excellence (Surrey): https://schoolsallianceforexcellence.co.uk

Schools North East: https://schoolsnortheast.org

Acts of Parliament

1870 Elementary Education Act (Forster's Education Act): http://www.educationengland.org.uk/documents/acts/1870-elementary-education-act.html

1944 Education Act (Butler Act): https://www.legislation.gov.uk/ukpga/Geo6/7-8/31/contents/enacted

1970 Education (Handicapped Children) Act: https://www.legislation.gov.uk/ukpga/1970/52/contents/enacted

1976 Education Act: https://www.legislation.gov.uk/ukpga/1976/81/contents/enacted

1980 Education Act: https://www.legislation.gov.uk/ukpga/1980/20/contents/enacted

1981 Education Act: https://www.legislation.gov.uk/ukpga/1981/60/contents/enacted

1986 Education Act: https://www.legislation.gov.uk/ukpga/1986/40/contents/enacted

1986 Education (No. 2) Act: https://www.legislation.gov.uk/ukpga/1986/61/contents/enacted

1988 Education Reform Act: https://www.legislation.gov.uk/ukpga/1988/40/contents/enacted

1989 Children Act: https://www.legislation.gov.uk/ukpga/1989/41/contents/enacted

1991 School Teachers' Pay and Conditions Act: https://www.legislation.gov.uk/ukpga/1991/49/contents/enacted

1992 Education (Schools) Act: https://www.legislation.gov.uk/ukpga/1992/38/contents/enacted

1993 Education Act: https://www.legislation.gov.uk/ukpga/1993/35/contents/enacted

1997 Education Act: https://www.legislation.gov.uk/ukpga/1997/44/contents/enacted

1998 School Standards and Framework Act: https://www.legislation.gov.uk/ukpga/1998/31/contents/enacted

2002 Education Act: https://www.legislation.gov.uk/ukpga/2002/32/contents/enacted

2004 Children Act: https://www.legislation.gov.uk/ukpga/2004/31/contents/enacted

2005 Education Act: https://www.legislation.gov.uk/ukpga/2005/18/contents/enacted

2006 Education and Inspections Act: https://www.legislation.gov.uk/ukpga/2006/40/contents/enacted

2008 Education and Skills Act: https://www.legislation.gov.uk/ukpga/2008/25/contents/enacted

2009 Apprenticeships, Skills, Children and Learning Act: https://www.legislation.gov.uk/ukpga/2008/25/contents/enacted

2010 Children, Schools and Families Act: https://www.legislation.gov.uk/ukpga/2010/26/contents/enacted

2010 Academies Act: https://www.legislation.gov.uk/ukpga/2010/32/contents/enacted

2011 Education Act: https://www.legislation.gov.uk/ukpga/2011/21/contents/enacted

2014 Families and Children Act: https://www.legislation.gov.uk/ukpga/2014/6/contents/enacted

2016 Education and Adoption Act: https://www.legislation.gov.uk/ukpga/2016/6/contents/enacted

Index

About the authors

Tim Brighouse and Mick Waters share a wealth of experience of the school system. Both have worked in schools and universities, both have been chief education officers for large local education authorities, and both have worked close to central government in key school improvement and curriculum development roles.

During their careers, they have both been asked to work at policy level with national governments and they have always worked in and around schools; they are often found in classrooms with pupils. In the course of their work and through invitation they have visited thousands of schools. They remain in demand as conference speakers to share their experiences and offer advice to groups of schools and organisations.

Above all, they both count themselves lucky to have met so many people along the way who have shown them what to do and what not to do, as well as the precious ones who have encouraged them to think and think again about what might work better.